An Estimate of the Manners and Principles of the Times
and Other Writings

THE THOMAS HOLLIS LIBRARY
David Womersley, General Editor

An Estimate of the Manners and Principles of the Times and Other Writings

John Brown

Edited and with an Introduction
by David Womersley

LIBERTY FUND

Introduction, editorial additions, and index
© 2019 by Liberty Fund, Inc.

Printed in the United States of America

19 20 21 22 23 C 5 4 3 2 1
19 20 21 22 23 P 5 4 3 2 1

Library of Congress Cataloging-in-Publication Data can be found on the Library of Congress website: catalog.loc.gov.

LCCN: 2019016301

ISBN 9780865979093 (hardcover)
ISBN 9780865979109 (paperback)

LIBERTY FUND, INC.
11301 North Meridian Street
Carmel, Indiana 46032

CONTENTS

THE THOMAS HOLLIS LIBRARY

Thomas Hollis (1720–74) was an eighteenth-century Englishman who devoted his energies, his fortune, and his life to the cause of liberty. Hollis was trained to a business career, but a series of inheritances allowed him to pursue instead a career of public service. He believed that citizenship demanded activity, and that it was incumbent on citizens to put themselves in a position, by reflection and reading, where they could hold their governments to account. To that end for many years he distributed books which he believed explained the nature of liberty, and revealed how liberty might best be defended and promoted.

A particular beneficiary of Hollis's generosity was Harvard College. In the years preceding the Declaration of Independence, Hollis was assiduous in sending over to America boxes of books, many of which he had had specially printed and bound, to encourage the colonists in their struggle against Great Britain. At the same time he took pains to explain the colonists' grievances and concerns to his fellow Englishmen.

The Thomas Hollis Library makes freshly available a selection of titles which, because of their intellectual power, or the influence they exerted on the public life of their own time, or the distinctiveness of their approach to the topic of liberty, comprise the cream of the books distributed by Hollis. Many of these works have been either out of print since the eighteenth century, or available only in very expensive and scarce editions. The highest standards of scholarship and production ensure that these classic texts can be as salutary and influential today as they were two hundred and fifty years ago.

David Womersley

INTRODUCTION

John Brown was born at Rothbury in Northumberland on the auspiciously Whiggish day of 5 November, 1715.[1] His father was a clergyman, initially in Northumberland but latterly at Wigton in Cumberland. Brown attended the local grammar school at Wigton before progressing to St. John's College, Cambridge as a sizar on 8 May 1732. He graduated from Cambridge in 1735 with high honors, and then followed his father into the Church of England, for a number of years quietly occupying minor clerical posts associated with the cathedral of Carlisle.

During the Jacobite rebellion of 1745 Brown saw action during the siege of Carlisle, where according to Kippis he behaved "with great intrepidity."[2] When the Jacobites had been defeated Brown preached two sermons in the cathedral explaining "the mutual connection between

---

1. For the fullest extant account of Brown's life, see Roberts, *Imaginative Feeling*, pp. 3–83. The article by Andrew Kippis in *Biographia Britannica* (1780), vol. II, pp. 653–74 nevertheless has enduring points of interest. James Crimmin's article in the *ODNB* adds useful detail. Both the discovery of the Gunpowder Plot in 1605 and the landing of William of Orange at Torbay in 1688 were commemorated on 5 November.

2. Kippis, p. 653. For Brown's own ebullient account of his duties and behavior during the siege of Carlisle by the Jacobite army, see his letter to William Gilpin of 5 January 1746 (Bodl. MS Eng. Misc. c. 389, fols. 85^{r-v}). Brown's conduct in this emergency would have appealed to Thomas Hollis: cf. Blackburne, *Memoirs*, vol. I, p. 6.

religious truth and civil freedom; and between superstition, tyranny, irreligion, and licentiousness."[3] These Whiggish disquisitions attracted the
attention of the bishop of Carlisle, Richard Osbaldeston, who happened
also to be a graduate of St. John's, and who was himself a zealous Whig.[4]
Brown quickly received preferment, being appointed one of Osbaldeston's
chaplains and receiving from the Dean and Chapter of Carlisle the living
of Morland, in Westmorland. Nevertheless, Brown's personal faith may
have been of a heterodox, Arian or Socinian, cast; he was censured by the
Dean of Carlisle for omitting the Athanasian creed from a service.[5]

Brown's ambitions were not confined to clerical advancement. In 1745
he had published a verse tribute to the recently deceased Alexander Pope,
An Essay on Satire: Occasion'd by the Death of Mr. Pope. This effort had
caught the attention of William Warburton, Pope's friend and literary
executor, who did not hesitate to pronounce it "a masterpiece."[6] So began an association which Thomas Hollis would identify as the tragic
hinge of Brown's existence.[7] Warburton described the earliest stages of
his self-appointed role as impresario to Brown's literary career in a letter
of 30 January 1750 to Richard Hurd:

> Mr. Browne has fine parts: he has a genius for poetry, and has ac-
> quired a force of versification very uncommon. Poor Mr. Pope had a

---

3. Kippis, pp. 653–54. On 27 October 1746 he offered these to Robert Dodsley, the
publisher, remarking that "I know it hath been objected to me, that I should publish
Verses, rather than things that belong to my own Profession" (Bodl. MS Toynbee
d. 19, fol. 16ʳ).

4. Richard Osbaldeston (1691–1764); clergyman in the Church of England: matr.
St. John's College, Cambridge, 2 June 1707; BA, 1711; MA, 1714; DD, 1726; chaplain
to George I and later George II, 23 February 1725; bishop of Carlisle, 4 October
1747; bishop of London, 1762; *d.* 15 May 1764.

5. Kippis insists however that the "omission . . . did not proceed from any scruples upon the subject [and] was merely accidental" (Kippis, p. 654). For a different
view, see Roberts, *Imaginative Feeling*, p. 25.

6. William Warburton (1698–1779), bishop of Gloucester; theological polemicist
and man of letters. For his response to *An Essay on Satire*, see his letter to Brown of
24 December 1746 (Bodl. MS Eng. Misc. c. 390, fol. 398ʳ).

7. For Hollis's view of Warburton's role in Brown's life, see Appendix A below,
pp. 575–80. Once the rupture with Warburton had occurred, Brown would deny that
he had ever been "submissive" to him (Brown, *Letter*, p. 5).

little before his death planned out an epic poem, which he began to be very intent upon. The subject was Brute. I gave this plan to Mr. Browne. He has wrote the first book, and in a surprising way, though an unfinished essay. I told him this was to be the work of years, and mature age, if ever it was done: that, in the mean time, he should think of something in prose that might be useful to his character in his own profession. I recommended to him a thing I once thought of myself. It had been recommended to me by Mr. Pope. An examination of all Lord Shaftesbury says against Religion. Mr. Pope told me, that, to his knowledge, the Characteristics had done more harm to Revealed Religion in England than all the works of Infidelity put together. Mr. Browne is now busy upon this work.[8]

An Essay on Satire had included criticism of the doctrine expressed in Shaftesbury's *Characteristicks*, that ridicule should be the test of truth.[9] Encouraged and guided by Warburton's hints, Brown decided to amplify this criticism, and to reinforce it with two further essays: one attacking Shaftesbury's concept of virtue, and the other his stance towards Christianity. It seems that Warburton and Charles Yorke exerted a powerful influence over the form of the publication, as Warburton revealed to Richard Hurd in late December 1750:

> Mr. Browne is printing his remarks on the *Characteristics*. It will be much better than you could conceive from the specimen you saw of it. Mr. Yorke and I advised him to give it a different form. We said, that if we were to answer a grave, formal, methodical work, we should choose to do it in the loose way of dialogue and raillery: as, on the other hand, if we wrote against a rambling *discourse of wit and humour*, the best way of exposing it would be by logical argumentation. The truth is (*inter nos*) his talents do not seem so much to lie towards fine

---

8. [Warburton], *Letters*, p. 36. On Pope's project of writing an epic poem on the subject of Brutus, the mythical founder of Britain, see Miriam Leranbaum, *Alexander Pope's "Opus Magnum," 1729–1744* (Oxford: Clarendon Press, 1977), pp. 155–74.

9. Brown, *Satire*, pp. 15–16. It had particularly caught the eye of Warburton: "The long note on Ridicule is admirable," he wrote to Brown on Christmas Eve 1746 (Bodl. MS Eng. Misc. c. 390, fol. 398ʳ).

and easy raillery, as to a vivacity, an elegance, and a correctness of observation in the reasoning way.[10]

However, it may be that Warburton influenced the content, as well as the
mode, of these essays. The second, in which Brown deploys the concept
of utility to challenge Shaftesbury's "moral sense" philosophy, may be informed by Warburton's wrestlings with Hume's moral philosophy, as well
as by the work of the clergyman and moral philosopher John Gay, whom
Brown could have met in Cambridge, and whose prefatory essay to his
1731 translation of William King's *An Essay on the Origin of Evil* is an important early statement of a utilitarian approach to morals.[11] In the third,
when Brown chides Shaftesbury's freethinking treatment of Christianity
it is easy to detect the omnivorous but undigested historical and textual
scholarship of the author of *The Divine Legation of Moses*.

The *Essays on the Characteristics of the Earl of Shaftesbury* were published in 1751, and Kippis records that they received "a high degree of applause," while also calling into the field some adversaries who took issue
with Brown and defended Shaftesbury.[12] The *Essays* had to wait until 1838,
however, to receive their most precious accolade, from the hand of J. S.
Mill in his essay on "Bentham": "We never saw an abler defense of the
doctrine of utility than in a book written in refutation of Shaftesbury, and
now little read—Brown's 'Essays on the Characteristics'; . . ."[13] Certainly
Brown's arguments that "the great End of public Happiness" is the criterion of moral rectitude, that "whatever tends to the Good of all, is by the

10. [Warburton], *Letters*, p. 71. "Mr. Yorke" is probably Charles Yorke (1722–1770),
lawyer and briefly lord chancellor; cf. [Warburton], *Letters*, p. 118. Charles was
brother of Philip Yorke (1720–1790), later Lord Royston and second earl of Hardwicke, and Brown's patron at Great Horkesley; politician and writer. Note Brown's
praise of their father, Philip Yorke (1690–1764), first earl of Hardwicke, in the *Estimate* (below, p. 210 and n. 90).

11. See, e.g., [Warburton], *Letters*, p. 14. John Gay (1699–1745); "Preliminary Dissertation Concerning the Fundamental Principle of Virtue or Morality," in William
King, *An Essay on the Origin of Evil* (1731), pp. xi–xxxiii. Cf. Crimmins, *Utilitarianism*, p. 71.

12. Kippis, p. 655.

13. *Mill on Bentham and Coleridge*, introduction by F. R. Leavis (London: Chatto
and Windus, 1950), p. 54.

consent of all, denominated *Virtue*," and that consequently virtue can be defined as "the voluntary Production of the greatest public Happiness," rather than as merely an affective impulse directed in the first instance towards only private and ineffable satisfactions, are the most intellectually powerful parts of the *Essays*.[14]

Encouraged by this success, Brown slipped away from Warburton's supervision and went off hunting in another part of the literary wood. As early as 1744 he had confessed to William Gilpin that he nursed ambitions to become a "Tragick Poet," ambitions he had pursued by beginning to compose a drama on the death of Socrates.[15] Two months later he acknowledged that he had been discouraged by the difficulty of this particular subject, but nevertheless declared that he was "determined to try my Strength & Fortune in this dangerous Warfare" of writing for the stage.[16] Emboldened by the reception of the *Essays*, in the mid-1750s Brown turned again to the theater. His tragedy *Barbarossa* was given its first performance at Drury Lane on 17 December 1754, with Garrick (to whom Brown had been recommended by Warburton)[17] in the part of Achmet. The plot takes great freedoms with the actual life of the Barbary pirate, Khayr ad-Din or Redbeard (*d.* 1546), on which it is nominally based.[18] As with *Athelstan*, the less successful tragedy very loosely located in Saxon history, which was premiered at Covent Garden a little over

14. Below, pp. 105, 107, and 115.

15. Brown to Gilpin, 20 August 1744 (Bodl. MS Eng. Misc. c. 389, fol. 70^{r-v}). For Brown's enthusiastic account of the première of Hoadly's *The Suspicious Husband* in 1747, see Bodl. MS Eng. Misc. c. 389, fol. 87^{r}.

16. Brown to Gilpin, 8 October 1744 (Bodl. MS Eng. Misc. c. 389, fol. 71^{r}).

17. Garrick, *Correspondence*, vol. I, p. 65. For Warburton's warm feelings for Brown at the outset of their relationship, see ibid., p. 77: "I love and esteem Dr. Brown: he vexed me; but I find he must be treated like a mistress as well as a friend

'Be to his faults a little blind,'

and I make no doubt of his always approving himself a man of honour and virtue, and a warm and grateful friend."

18. For Brown's own account of the historical materials on which he drew for his tragedy, see his puffing "tease" ahead of the premiere, *An Account of Barbarossa* (London, 1755).

a year later on 27 February 1756, in these plays Brown drapes would-be Shakespearean language over a dramatic framework adopted from the heroic drama and tragedy of the previous century. The plots of *Barbarossa* and *Athelstan* are little more than a series of contrivances to bring about situations in which inward passion conflicts as poignantly as possible with outward duty. In *Barbarossa*, however, Brown manufactured an outcome in which erotic passion and public duty are eventually reconciled, or at least aligned. The rightful heir to the throne, Selim, survives Barbarossa's malice, and marries the usurper's daughter, Irene, with whom he has been from the first in love. The play ends on a note of providential reassurance:

> Now let us thank th'eternal Pow'r: convinc'd,
> That Heav'n but tries our Virtue by Affliction:
> That oft the Cloud which wraps the present Hour,
> Serves but to brighten all our future Days![19]

But in *Athelstan* Brown experimented with a more complicated final chord. The heroine, Thyra, is unluckily killed by her long-lost father, Athelstan, who then himself expires over the corpse of his daughter, in an obvious *rifacimento* of the final scene of *King Lear*. The concluding lines of the play attempt to enforce the severe moral that such private calamities are only to be expected when men neglect their public duty, for in the play's opening scenes Athelstan has been a Saxon Coriolanus, and has aided an invading Danish army:

> Yet may the Woes
> Which Heav'n's avenging Hand hath heap'd upon thee
> Recorded stand, a Monument of Justice!
> That when in future Times a King shall reign,
> Brave, good, and just, the Father of his People,
> Th' abhorr'd Example may avert those Ills
> Thy traitrous Arm hath wrought—That black Rebellion
> May never rear her Standard; nor unsheath
> Her guilty Sword, to aid the fell Invader!
> That Faction's Sons in thee their Fate may read;

19. Brown, *Barbarossa*, p. 80.

> That by the Father's Crime the Child shall bleed,
> And private Woe to publick Guilt succeed.[20]

A number of influences are detectable here, some biographical, others intellectual. Behind Brown's strictures on rebellion surely lie the events of 1745, where (as we have seen) he observed at first-hand the turmoil brought about when an invader is assisted by guilty swords. But the final insistence that private woe is the child of public guilt evokes and inverts the notorious and paradoxical thesis of Mandeville's *Fable of the Bees*: "*Private Vices, Publick Benefits.*" Mandeville had been one of Brown's targets in *Essays on the Characteristics*, and in his next publication he would once more attempt to discredit Mandeville's mischievous suggestion that modern commercial societies construct passages between the private and public realms in ways that are far from straightforward.

This next publication was the extraordinary *succès fou* of Brown's career, *An Estimate of the Manners and Principles of the Times*, first published in 1757. Its impact was well described by Kippis:

> The reception which this work met with from the public was highly flattering to the vanity of the writer, seven editions of it having been printed in little more than a year. It was, indeed, almost universally read, and made an uncommon impression on the minds of great numbers of persons. To this, besides its own merit, it was, in part, indebted to its being well-timed. It came out when the minds of the people had been extremely depressed by some unprosperous events; and when, consequently, they were the more ready to listen to the melancholy, and, perhaps, too just representation that was given of the manners and principles of the nation.[21]

The unprosperous events to which Kippis alludes were the series of British military and naval reverses which marked the opening of the Seven Years' War, particularly the loss of Minorca to the French. In the words of Macaulay: "The Duke of Richelieu, an old fop who had passed his

---

20. Brown, *Athelstan*, p. 77.
21. Kippis, p. 656.

life from sixteen to sixty in seducing women for whom he cared not one straw, landed on that island, and succeeded in reducing it."[22] The result was public uproar at an insult to national dignity—uproar which it is entirely possible that Brown, whose emotions seem always to have lain close to the surface, sincerely shared. On 5 January 1746, in the aftermath of the Jacobite invasion of the previous year, he had expostulated to William Gilpin on the national shame of allowing a hostile army to penetrate as far south as Derby: "I am almost mad with Rage and Indignation when I consider the present State of our Country."[23]

In the "Prologue" to *Athelstan* of the previous year Brown had warned his countrymen of the peril of their position, placed as they were on the threshold of a global conflict with France:

> *To warn the Sons of Freedom to be wise,*
> *Lo,* Britain's *guardian Genius quits the Skies.*
> *With Pity, Heav'n hath seen thro' many an Age,*
> *The bold Invader lur'd by Faction's Rage;*
> *Seen the dark Workings of Rebellion's Train,*
> *While Patriots plann'd, and Heroes bled in vain.*
> *Behold, your Country's faithless Foe, once more*
> *With threatning Squadrons crown yon hostile Shore.*
> *Behold Oppression's bloody Flag unfurl'd:*
> *See Bolts prepar'd, to chain the Western World.*
> *Rise,* Britons, *rise! to Heav'n and Virtue true:*
> *Expiring Liberty looks up to* You!
> *Pour on the common Foe your Rage combin'd,*
> *And be the Friends of Freedom and Mankind!*[24]

But this warning delivered from the stage had been unavailing. And so, in the midst of the tempest of reproach and despondency which was stirred up by early British setbacks in the war, Brown published his jeremiad on the causes of the miserable condition and parlous prospects of the British nation.

---

22. Macaulay, *Essays*, vol. II, p. 34.
23. Bodl. MS Eng. Misc. c. 389, fol. 85^{v}.
24. Brown, *Athelstan*, sig. A5^{r}.

Kippis gives an accurate summary of Brown's "chief design" in the *Estimate*, which was "to shew that a vain, luxurious, and selfish effeminacy, in the higher ranks of life, marked the character of the age; and to point out the effects and sources of this effeminacy."[25] It is a project with evident roots in the *Essays* of six years earlier, for in Section X of the second essay Brown had read the runes of modern British corruption in very much the language to which he would return in the *Estimate*:

> . . . no People ever fell a Sacrifice to themselves, till *lulled* and infatuated by their own Passions. *Blind Security* is an essential Characteristic of a People devoted to Destruction. . . . One Age is *falsely* polite, *irreligious*, and *vile*; the next is sunk in *Servitude* and *Wretchedness*. . . . Here and there a happy Nation *emerges*; breathes for a while in the enlightened Region of Knowledge, Religion, Virtue, Freedom: Till in their appointed Time, Irreligion and Licentiousness appear; *mine* the Foundations of the *Fabric*, and sink it in the general Abyss of Ignorance and Oppression.[26]

Where the *Estimate* moves beyond the *Essays*, however, is in the light it shines on Brown's intellectual life. The two thinkers to whom Brown pays most lavish tribute in the *Estimate* are Montesquieu and Machiavelli.[27] To both writers it is possible that Brown had been directed by Warburton, who nursed perhaps surprising enthusiasms for the authors

---

25. Kippis, p. 656. This would have chimed with the diagnosis of Thomas Hollis, who on 9 December 1757 following the unsuccessful British assault on Rochfort wrote to a friend:

> It is no wonder if the British nation is hated in France; but it is of late only that we are despised thus. This opinion of us, however, is just; for what can be produced by us that is truly honourable and great, or even considerably successful, when all appearances of private or public virtue are hated, ridiculed, and crushed, and when selfism, steril, exterminating selfism, has got possession every where, and reigns despotic over every rank and order.

(Blackburne, *Memoirs*, vol. I, p. 66; see also the letter of 7 May 1755 to L'Anglois quoted on p. 207.)

26. See below, pp. 157–58.

27. For Brown's comparison of "these two Authors [who] possess the highest Station in the political Scale," see volume II of the *Estimate* (below, p. 429).

of the *Esprit des Loix* and *Il Principe*.[28] Be that as it may, we can see that the content of Brown's critique of Hanoverian Britain has affinities with the republican ideology of Machiavelli's *Discorsi*. The *Estimate* decanted that political content into an essay where the focus on the "Manners and Principles of the Times" betrays a slightly elementary understanding of Montesquieu's concept of "esprit." Intellectually speaking, the result is more an amalgam than an alloy. Nevertheless, Brown's gloomy analysis hit the mood of the time, even if, in the tumult of praise by which the *Estimate* was at first surrounded, some voices were raised in criticism of the preening self-importance with which the author delivered his salutary medicines.[29] William Cowper, in his *Table Talk* (1782), tried to balance the transience of the *Estimate*'s popularity with an acknowledgement of the probability of its analysis:

> *A.* Th' inestimable estimate of Brown,
> Rose like a paper-kite, and charm'd the town;
> But measures plann'd and executed well,
> Shifted the wind that rais'd it, and it fell.
> He trod the very self-same ground you tread,
> And victory refused all he said.
>   *B.* And yet his judgment was not fram'd amiss,
> Its error, if it err'd, was merely this—
> He thought the dying hour already come,
> And a complete recov'ry struck him dumb.

28. [Warburton], *Letters*, p. 83. Still more surprising, perhaps, is the fact that Montesquieu admired Warburton: see the transcription of Montesquieu's letter to Charles Yorke of 6 June 1763 ([Warburton], *Letters*, p. 507). Warburton had sent a parcel of his books to Montesquieu in 1754 (Warburton, *Works*, vol. VII, p. 554). For the limits of Warburton's admiration of Montesquieu, see Warburton, *Alliance*, p. 285, n. d. In *The Divine Legation of Moses* Warburton praised Machiavelli as, with Aristotle, one of the "two great masters in politics" (Warburton, *Works*, vol. I, p. 408).

29. Cf. "his merit as a writer is very considerable, and would be still more so, did not he himself appear so extremely conscious of it"; "a certain air of arrogance and superiority prevails through the whole" (Kippis, p. 657, n. E).

> But that effeminacy, folly, lust,
> Enervate and enfeeble, and needs must,
> And that a nation shamefully debas'd,
> Will be despis'd and trampl'd on at last,
> Unless sweet penitence her pow'rs renew,
> Is truth, if history itself be true.[30]

Cowper's lines reveal how neatly the leading themes of Brown's analysis were matched to widely held assumptions of the time about how and why nations rose and declined.

Perhaps predictably, given that he had not himself supplied the hint for this particular publication, Warburton was dismissive of this latest effort by his sometime *protégé*. He had deplored Brown's theatrical adventures, sometimes referring to him with mocking condescension as the "maker of Athelstan."[31] From Warburton's point of view the *Estimate* must have looked like another descent from the heights (such as they are) of polemical theology to the boggy morass of vulgar opinion-mongering. On 19 September 1757 he wrote to Hurd from Weymouth, where he had been joined by Brown:

> Browne is here; I think rather perter than ordinary, but no wiser. You cannot imagine the tenderness they all have of his tender places: and with how unfeeling a hand I probe them.—It seems he said something to them of *another Estimate*. My wife told him, he must take care of carrying the joke too far. To me he has mentioned nothing of it, nor have I given him an opportunity.[32]

---

30. Cowper, *Poems*, vol. I, pp. 251–52, ll. 384–99.

31. [Warburton], *Letters*, p. 244. "Browne has told me the *grand secret;* and I wish it had been a secret still to me, when it was none to every body else. I am grieved that either these *unrewarding times*, or his *love of poetry*, or his *love of money*, should have made him overlook the duty of a Clergyman in these times, and the dignity of a Clergyman in all times, to make connexions with Players" (ibid., p. 182). A "*grand secret*," because Brown did not publicly acknowledge his authorship of either *Barbarossa* or *Athelstan*.

32. [Warburton], *Letters*, pp. 256–57. Note also the letter to Dodsley of 28 March 1758 from "C. H. H." which advises the publisher to dissuade Brown from "his second Volume" (Bodl. MS Toynbee d. 19, fol. 19ʳ).

But the stupendous sales of the *Estimate* had armored Brown against both the witticisms of Mrs. Warburton and the aloofness of her husband.[33] He went on to publish a second volume, and also an *Explanatory Defence* in which he engaged, to some modest extent, with his critics.

From his youth Brown's mind had given a warm welcome to fantasies of preferment. When the Duke of Cumberland had entered Carlisle on his way to harry the Jacobite rebels in their Highland glens, Brown had presented him with a plan of Carlisle during the siege. It had been graciously received, whereupon he wrote excitedly to William Gilpin confessing that "the Night after I dreamt I was in Lawn sleeves."[34] In the *Estimate* Brown had taken upon himself the role of "Preacher to the Nation," a role he seems to have coveted since at least 1746 when he had attempted to launch a political periodical modeled on Addison's *Freeholder*.[35] Furthermore, in the *Estimate* he had been careful to pay lavish compliments to those possible patrons whose stars were in the ascendant, particularly William Pitt, who was readily recognizable as the "GREAT MINISTER" upon whom in his final page Brown calls to save the nation.[36] What more did a man have to do to become a bishop? However, no overtures were made. As Kippis ruefully noted, "While Dr. Brown was thus distinguishing himself as a political writer, he seems to have gained no ground in the way of preferment."[37]

The only tangible benefit to flow from the *Estimate* came when Brown's old patron, Bishop Osbaldeston, offered him the living of St. Nicholas,

---

33. Brown announced his eventual rupture with Warburton—"all friendship and correspondence are at an end"—in a letter to Garrick of 19 January 1766 (Garrick, *Correspondence*, vol. I, p. 220).

34. Letter to William Gilpin of 5 January 1746; Bodl. MS Eng. Misc. c. 389, fol. 85$^\mathrm{v}$.

35. See Brown's defense of his assumption of this role in the *Explanatory Defence* and vol. II of the *Estimate* (below, pp. 353–55 and pp. 465–68). The periodical was to be called *The Protestant Freeholder* and it was intended to counter "the present Attempts" against the "civil and religious Constitution" of the country; see the description and specimen essay in the letter to William Gilpin of 2 October 1745 (Bodl. MS Eng. Misc. c. 389, fols. 80$^\mathrm{r}$ and 81$^\mathrm{r}$–82$^\mathrm{v}$).

36. Below, p. 344.

37. Kippis, p. 660.

Newcastle upon Tyne in 1760, which was apparently a modest improvement over his present living of Great Horkesley.[38] Brown hesitated before accepting, apparently trying to combine it with retaining his current living and its tithes *in absentia*. But eventually he moved north, and this initiated a busy and productive phase of his life, in which he seems to have mingled happily in the intellectual and musical circles of Newcastle. For a while he left questions of national politics alone. But he was unable entirely to forsake them.

Brown re-assumed the role of national preacher in 1765 with his *Thoughts on Civil Liberty, Licentiousness and Faction*. Much of the analytic substance of this pamphlet is compatible with—indeed, echoes—that of the *Estimate*. Once again Brown inveighs against effeminacy and luxury, once again he extols the "boy scout" virtues of the ancient republics, particularly Sparta.[39] But that surface continuity disguises an extraordinary change of underlying allegiance. As we have seen, the *Estimate* had concluded by implicitly praising Pitt as the only possible savior of the nation. In 1760 Brown had again allied himself with Pitt when he defended him against the criticisms of Lyttelton by publishing *An Additional Dialogue of the Dead* (1760). But the death of George II, the accession of George III, and the consequent rise of Bute in 1760 had altered the complexion of politics; and with Pitt's move into opposition in 1761, the levers of patronage had been transferred to new hands. Brown responded to these changes with a whole-heartedness which does him little credit. For in a series of unmistakable references to the current political and social scene in the final pages of the *Thoughts* Brown associated himself with Bute,

38. For the resentment which Brown stirred up amongst his patrons over the move from his current living of Great Horkesley to that of St. Nicholas, see the correspondence preserved in BL Add. MSS 35606 and 35635. Philip Yorke's rebuke, that Brown had employed expressions "very improper" to be used towards "one from whom you acknowledge you have received a great obligation," is noteworthy (BL Add. MSS 35606, fol. 342ʳ); for in 1756 Yorke had presented Brown with the living of Great Horkesley, on the recommendation of Warburton. Noteworthy, too, is the extract of a letter said to have been written by his new parishioners, and transcribed by Brown himself, in which he is said to be "too much refined for us . . . a weak man . . . a proud Man" (BL Add. MSS 35606, fol. 331ʳ).

39. I owe the phrase "boy scout" to John Burrow.

and branded Pitt with the charge of faction.[40] Thomas Hollis was particularly dismayed by this phase of Brown's career:

> . . . the changes in the upper regions were frequent, sudden, and unforeseen. To these he accommodated himself without hesitation, and it was impossible that so immediate and so nimble transitions in so conspicuous a character should not give the cue to the public to mark *him*, rather than an hundred others who really *temporized* no less than he, but who had the discretion not to notify it upon paper, . . . [41]

Nor was this the end of Brown's political apostasies, if Hollis was correct in his belief that, in his final days and with one last fling of preferment's dice, Brown had turned his hand to drafting a eulogy of Pitt.[42]

Thoughts on Civil Liberty was the inadvertent trigger for the final act in the drama of Brown's life, in which pathos and the macabre would jointly command the stage. *Thoughts on Civil Liberty* concludes by advocating a "general and prescribed Improvement of the Laws of Education," on the premise that:

> . . . for Want of a prescribed Code of Education, to which all the Members of the Community should legally submit, the Manners and Principles on which alone the State can rest, are ineffectually instilled, are vague, fluctuating, and self-contradictory.[43]

According to Andrew Kippis, this coda caught the attention of "a lady of most excellent character and understanding," who on 29 May 1765 wrote to Daniel Dumaresq (then acting as an informal adviser to Catherine the Great) recommending Brown to him as an appropriate person from whom to seek advice on the matter of reforming the Russian education system—a project

---

40. See the annotation below, pp. 552–54. This change of allegiance must have displeased Thomas Hollis, who despised "the Butean arts," and saw Bute himself as "surely a Stuart, [who] odiates liberty, and the abettors of it" (Blackburne, *Memoirs*, vol. I, pp. 340–42 and 445).

41. Below, p. 578. Kippis concurs: "Dr. Brown hath been charged with shifting about too speedily, with a view to preferment; and it must be acknowledged, that his *Thoughts on Civil Liberty, Licentiousness, and Faction,* seemed to have something of this appearance" (Kippis, p. 673).

42. See below, p. 578.

43. Below, p. 569.

which was then under active consideration.[44] Dumaresq wrote to Brown on 8 July and invited his assistance in this important work, without however concealing from him the grave difficulties by which it was surrounded. For Brown it must have seemed that, at last, and after all his disappointments over clerical preferment, one of the fantasies of his youth was about to be realized. On 2 October 1745 he had revealed to William Gilpin that:

> . . . the Attitude in which I chiefly delight to view myself, is that of a potent Magician, who in the Retirement of his Closet, and by the single Virtue of his Wand, controuls the Operations of distant Bodies, forms Councils, assembles Multitudes, and puts mighty Fleets and Armies into Motion.[45]

Elated by the imminent translation of youthful reverie into present reality, Brown replied to Dumaresq on 1 October, accepting the commission and spelling out in great detail the broad principles he recommended (including, interestingly, a stipulation that "a proper and effectual education of the *female sex* is one of the very first steps to be taken for the effectual improvement and civilization of the whole empire").[46]

All seemed set fair. Brown's plans had aroused misgivings in Dumaresq, but had found favor with the empress. Brown was invited to St. Petersburg, and in June 1766 he was advanced £1,000 (of which he drew only £200) to meet the costs of travel.[47] At this period Brown's imagination placed before him almost limitless prospects of benign influence, to which he gave rhapsodic expression in language which recalls the euphoria of his letter to Gilpin quoted above:

> I can fancy that I see civilization and a rational system of Christianity extending themselves quite across the immense continent, from Petersburg to Kamschatska.—I can fancy that I see them striking farther into

---

44. Kippis, p. 663. Daniel Dumaresq, F.R.S., honorary member of the Imperial Academy of Sciences at St. Petersburg; formerly fellow of Exeter College, Oxford; 1747, appointed Chaplain to the English Factory at St. Petersburg; adviser to Catherine the Great, September 1764–January 1766; subsequently prebendary of Salisbury and rector of Yeovilton. Dumaresq was known to Thomas Hollis in the context of educational reform in Russia (Blackburne, *Memoirs*, vol. I, pp. 295 and 444–45).

45. Bodl. MS Eng. Misc. c. 389, fol. 82[r].

46. Kippis, p. 664.

47. Kippis, p. 668, n. [R].

the more southern regions of Tartary and China, and spreading their influence even over the nations of Europe; which, though now polished, are far from being truly Christian, or truly happy. Nay, I am sometimes fantastic enough to say with Pitt, that as America was conquered in Germany, so Great Britain may be reformed in Russia. However chimerical this imagination may be, or seems to be, this I am persuaded you will allow, that it is a great and important object which I have now before me. If in any degree I succeed, it will be well. If I fail, or die in the attempt, I only desire some kind friend to write my apology upon my tombstone,

— *Magnis tamen excidit ausis.*[48]

But in July, his former curate struck a warning note, and advised him that his health (Brown suffered from gout and rheumatism) would not be equal to the hardships of the journey.[49] In August, Brown acknowledged the truth of this, and wrote to the Russian empress and her ambassador in Britain, Pouschkin, excusing himself and accounting for the expenses he had already incurred.[50]

The disappointment, together with the mortification of the public ridicule which followed (for Brown had made no secret of the fact that he had been summoned "to assist in the civilization of a great empire") unhinged a mind which had for long been precarious.[51] Lapsing into a "dejection of spirits," Brown cut his throat with a razor in his London apartment on the morning of 23 September 1766.[52]

---

48. Kippis, p. 667, n. [O]. The Latin phrase comes from Ovid's epitaph for Phaëthon. The whole line reads: "QUEM SI NON TENVIT MAGNIS TAMEN EXCIDIT AVSIS" (who, if he did not succeed, however dared great things; *Metamorphoses*, II.328). Pitt's remark alludes to the grand strategy he pursued in the Seven Years' War. Great Britain funded the campaigns of Frederick the Great in central Europe, thus obliging France to divide her forces between the European and American theaters of conflict. On 13 November 1761, when that strategy was bearing rich fruit, Pitt claimed in the House of Commons that "America had been conquered in Germany."

49. Kippis quotes the letter in full, p. 668, n. [Q].

50. Kippis, p. 668, n. [R].

51. Garrick, *Correspondence*, vol. I, p. 220. In the words of Mrs. Gilpin on the news of Brown's suicide: "His distemper was a frenzy to which he had by fits been long subject; to my own knowledge, above thirty years. Had it not been for Mr. Farish [a fellow clergyman] frequently, and once for myself, the same event would have happened to him long ago" (Kippis, p. 673).

52. Kippis, p. 673.

Thomas Hollis had given a copy of the seventh edition of Brown's *Estimate* to Harvard in October 1764.[53] It is not difficult to see why he would have done so. Brown's warnings concerning luxury, his recommendation of austere and republican virtues, his preference for militias over professional armies, his anxieties about the moral toxins which extensive empire might release into society, his enthusiasm (in that work at least) for Pitt, and his troubled contrast of a newly-energized Roman Catholic Church with what he saw as the somnolent state of Protestantism, would all have appealed to Hollis.[54] Hence the strain of sober elegy in Hollis's character sketch of Brown, whom he depicts as a weak man who nevertheless possessed a measure of virtue and talent, and who fell among thieves in the feral literary and political circles of Hanoverian England.[55]

As an overall verdict, it is surely almost worthy of Aeacus himself.[56] The passage of time has made us less tolerant of Brown's occasional wordiness, and more aware of the derivative character of much of his thought. But, for all that, he remains a notable figure whose writings exerted a powerful influence over one of the protagonists in a great global conflict, and who in consequence was not entirely unworthy to be recommended to the American colonists, as they stood on the threshold of their own momentous struggle with imperial power.

David Womersley
Oxford
May, 2011

53. Houghton Library, press mark *EC75 B8136 757 *el*. Hollis's own copy of the second edition, containing annotations which reveal his broad sympathy with Brown's diagnosis of Britain's ills, is also in the Houghton, press mark *EC75 H7267 Zz 7576. For a transcription of the annotations, see Appendix B below.

54. For this last point, see volume II of the *Estimate*, Part II, sect. iv (below, pp. 407–17). Hollis was alarmed by the resurgent vigor of the Roman Catholic church, and sought to oppose it by making a collection of everything that had been written against the Jesuits (Blackburne, *Memoirs*, vol. I, p. 112; cf. pp. 166, 225–26, 297–98, 360–61, 382–83, 394–95, 429). For Hollis's esteem of William Pitt, cf. Blackburne, *Memoirs*, vol. I, pp. 80, 89, 122–23, 186, 223, 298, 457–58.

55. For Hollis's character sketch of Brown, see Appendix A below. William Roberts misreads Hollis's article as an attack on Brown (Roberts, *Imaginative Feeling*, p. 73). He was apparently unaware of Hollis's gift of the *Estimate* to Harvard, and of Brown's consequential place in Hollis's pantheon of Whiggism.

56. Hollis wrote his character sketch of Brown under the pseudonym of Aeacus, who in Greek mythology was one of the judges of the dead.

FURTHER READING

A: Manuscripts

17 letters from Brown to William Gilpin: Bodl. MS Eng. Misc. c. 389, fols. 58–88

9 letters from Brown to Robert Dodsley, and one letter from "C.H.H." to Dodsley describing Brown after the publication of the *Estimate*: Bodl. MS Toynbee d. 19

3 letters from Brown to Lord Royston (the third apparently a first draft of the second): Hardwicke Papers, BL Add. MSS 35606, fols. 329–32

2 letters from Brown to the Rev. Dr. Birch: Hardwicke Papers, BL Add. MSS 35635, fol. 430 and Add. MSS 4234, fol. 84

Letter from Philip Yorke to Brown: BL Add. MSS 35606, fols. 341–42

Letter from William Warburton to Brown: Bodl. MS Eng. Misc. c. 390, fol. 398

B: Brown's Publications
(for full bibliographic details see Eddy, in Section C below)

Honour. A Poem (London, 1743)

An Essay on Satire (London, 1745)

"Machinae Gesticulantes: The Puppet Show," in *The Museum*, vol. I, no. 3 (26 April 1746)

"Cursus Glacialis: Scating," in *The Museum*, vol. I, no. 8 (5 July 1746)

The Mutual Connexion between Religious Truth and Civil Freedom (London, 1747)
On Liberty: A Poem (Cambridge, 1748)
On the Pursuit of False Pleasure (Bath, 1750)
Essays on the Characteristics (London, 1751)
On the Use and Abuse of Externals in Religion (London, 1753)
An Account of Barbarossa (London, 1755)
Barbarossa. A Tragedy (London, 1755)
Athelstan. A Tragedy (London, 1756)
An Estimate of the Manners and Principles of the Times (London, 1757)
An Estimate of the Manners and Principles of the Times, vol. II (London, 1758)
Prefatory Address (London, 1758)
An Explanatory Defence of the Estimate of the Manners and Principles of the Times (London, 1758)
An Additional Dialogue of the Dead (London, 1760)
On the Natural Duty of a Personal Service (Newcastle, 1761)
The Cure of Saul. A Sacred Ode (London, 1763)
A Dissertation on the Rise, Union, and Power . . . of Poetry and Music (London, 1763)
On Religious Liberty (London, 1763)
Sermons on Various Subjects (London, 1764)
The History of the Rise and Progress of Poetry (Newcastle, 1764)
Remarks on Some Observations on Dr. Brown's Dissertation on Poetry and Music (London, 1764)
Thoughts on Civil Liberty (Newcastle, 1765)
On the Female Character and Education (London, 1765)
A Letter to the Rev. Dr. Lowth (Newcastle, 1765)
A Description of the Lake at Keswick (Kendal, 1770)
"Now sunk the Sun . . . ," in Richard Cumberland, *Odes* (London, 1776)

C: Secondary Material Published after 1900

Crimmins, James, *Secular Utilitarianism* (Oxford: Oxford University Press, 1990)
Eddy, D. D., *A Bibliography of John Brown* (New York: The Bibliographical Society of America, 1971)
Evans, A. W., *Warburton and the Warburtonians* (London: Oxford University Press, 1932)

Roberts, S. C., "Some Uncollected Authors XXIV: 'Estimate' Brown, 1715–1776 [sic]," *The Book Collector*, IX (1960), pp. 180–87

———, "Bibliography of 'Estimate' Brown," *The Book Collector*, X (1961), p. 198

Roberts, W., *A Dawn of Imaginative Feeling: The Contribution of John Brown (1715–66) to Eighteenth–Century Thought and Literature* (Carlisle: Northern Academic Press, 1996)

NOTE ON THE TEXTS

The copy texts for all works included in this volume are the first edition of the work in question, with the exception of *An Estimate of the Manners and Principles of the Times*, where it is the second edition, in which some errors in the first edition are corrected.

The editorial stance is conservative, in keeping with the general policy of the Thomas Hollis Library. Evident slips have been corrected, and the corrections recorded in the list of "Corrections to Copy Texts." Otherwise usage and orthography have been left as in the copy texts, except that "long s" has been changed to "s."

In this edition, numerically-cued footnotes are editorial. All other footnotes are authorial.

Numbers in square brackets in the text indicate the beginning of the specified page in the copy text.

ABBREVIATIONS

Bayle, *Dictionary*	*The Dictionary Historical and Critical of Mr. Peter Bayle*, 5 vols (1734)
BL	British Library
Blackburne, *Memoirs*	Francis Blackburne, *Memoirs of Thomas Hollis*, 2 vols (1780)
Blackstone, *Commentaries*	Sir William Blackstone, *Commentaries on the Laws of England*, 4 vols (Oxford, 1765–69)
Bodl.	Bodleian Library, Oxford
Bolingbroke, *History*	Bolingbroke, *Remarks on the History of England* (1743)
Bolingbroke, *Political Writings*	Bolingbroke, *Political Writings*, ed. David Armitage (Cambridge: Cambridge University Press, 1997)
Boswell, *Life of Johnson*	James Boswell, *The Life of Samuel Johnson*, ed. David Womersley (London: Penguin Books, 2008)
Brown, *Athelstan*	John Brown, *Athelstan. A Tragedy* (1756)
Brown, *Barbarossa*	John Brown, *Barbarossa. A Tragedy* (1755)
Brown, *Letter*	John Brown, *A Letter to the Rev. Dr. Lowth* (1766)

Brown, *Satire*	John Brown, *An Essay on Satire: Occasion'd by the Death of Mr. Pope* (1745)
Burke, *Writings and Speeches*	*The Writings and Speeches of Edmund Burke*, ed. P. Langford *et al.*, 12 vols (Oxford: Clarendon Press, 1981)
Cato's Letters	John Trenchard and Thomas Gordon, *Cato's Letters, Or, Essays on Liberty, Civil and Religious, and Other Important Subjects*, ed. Ronald Hamowy (Indianapolis: Liberty Fund, 1995)
Cowper, *Poems*	*The Poems of William Cowper*, ed. John D. Baird and Charles Ryskamp, 3 vols (Oxford: Clarendon Press, 1980–95)
Crimmins, *Utilitarianism*	James E. Crimmins, *Secular Utilitarianism: Social Science and the Critique of Religion in the Thought of Jeremy Bentham* (Oxford: Clarendon Press, 1990)
Davenant, *Works*	Charles Davenant, *Political and Commercial Works*, 5 vols (1771)
Filmer, *Patriarcha*	Sir Robert Filmer, *Patriarcha and Other Writings*, ed. Johann P. Sommerville (Cambridge: Cambridge University Press, 1991)
Garrick, *Correspondence*	*The Private Correspondence of David Garrick*, 2 vols (1831–32)
Gibbon, *Autobiographies*	*The Autobiographies of Edward Gibbon*, ed. John Murray, second edition (1897)
Gibbon, *Decline and Fall*	Edward Gibbon, *The History of the Decline and Fall of the Roman Empire*, ed. David Womersley (London: Allen Lane, 1994)
Harrington, *Oceana*	James Harrington, *The Commonwealth of Oceana*, ed. J. G. A. Pocock (Cambridge: Cambridge University Press, 1992)
Harris, *Hume*	James A. Harris, *Hume: An Intellectual Biography* (Cambridge: Cambridge University Press, 2015)

Harris, *Treatises* — James Harris, *Three Treatises* (1744)

Hume, *Essays* — David Hume, *Essays Moral, Political, and Literary*, ed. Eugene F. Miller, revised edition (Indianapolis: Liberty Fund, 1987)

Jenyns, *Free Inquiry* — Soame Jenyns, *A Free Inquiry into the Nature and Origin of Evil* (1757)

JHI — *Journal of the History of Ideas*

Kippis — Andrew Kippis, "Brown (John)," *Biographia Britannica*, second edition, 7 vols (1780), vol. II, pp. 653–74

Locke, *Two Treatises* — John Locke, *Two Treatises on Government*, ed. P. Laslett, "Cambridge Texts in the History of Political Thought" (Cambridge: Cambridge University Press, 1960)

Macaulay, *Essays* — Thomas Babington Macaulay, *Critical and Historical Essays*, ed. F. C. Montague, 3 vols (1903)

Mandeville, *Fable* — Bernard Mandeville, *The Fable of the Bees: or, Private Vices, Publick Benefits*, ed. F. B. Kaye (Indianapolis: Liberty Classics, 1988)

Milton, *Areopagitica* — *Areopagitica and Other Political Writings of John Milton*, ed. John Alvis (Indianapolis: Liberty Fund, 1999)

Molesworth, *Denmark* — Molesworth, *An Account of Denmark*, ed. J. A. I. Champion (Indianapolis: Liberty Fund, 2011)

Montesquieu, *Considérations* — Charles-Louis de Secondat, baron de Montesquieu, *Considérations sur les causes de la grandeur des Romains et de leur décadence*, ed. F. Weil, C. Courtney, P. Andrivet, and C. Volpilhac-Auger, "Oeuvres Complètes de Montesquieu," vol. 2 (Oxford: Voltaire Foundation, 2000)

ODNB — *Oxford Dictionary of National Biography*

Pocock, *Harrington* — *The Political Works of James Harrington*, ed. J. G. A. Pocock (Cambridge: Cambridge University Press, 1977)

Roberts, *Imaginative Feeling*   William Roberts, *A Dawn of Imaginative Feeling: The Contribution of John Brown (1715–66) to Eighteenth-Century Thought and Literature* (Carlisle: Northern Academic Press, 1996)

Robertson, *Enlightenment*   John Robertson, *The Case for the Enlightenment: Scotland and Naples 1680–1760* (Cambridge: Cambridge University Press, 2005)

Shaftesbury, *Characteristicks*   Anthony Ashley Cooper, third earl of Shaftesbury, *Characteristicks of Men, Manners, Opinions, Times*, ed. Douglas Den Uyl, 3 vols (Indianapolis: Liberty Fund, 2001)

Smith, *Wealth of Nations*   Adam Smith, *The Theory of Moral Sentiments*, ed. D. D. Raphael and A. L. Macfie (Oxford: Clarendon Press, 1976)

Spectator   *The Spectator*, ed. Donald F. Bond, 5 vols (Oxford: Clarendon Press, 1965)

Swift, *Prose Works*   Jonathan Swift, *Prose Works*, ed. Herbert Davis *et al.*, 16 vols (Oxford: Basil Blackwell, 1939–74)

Temple, *Works*   Sir William Temple, *Works*, 2 vols (1720)

[Warburton], *Letters*   [William Warburton], *Letters from a Late Eminent Prelate to One of His Friends*, second edition (1809)

Warburton, *Alliance*   William Warburton, *The Alliance Between Church and State*, fourth edition (1766)

Warburton, *Divine Legation*   William Warburton, *The Divine Legation of Moses*, fourth edition, 2 vols (1755)

Warburton, *Works*   *The Works of the Right Reverend William Warburton, Lord Bishop of Gloucester*, 7 vols (1788)

Wollaston, *Religion*   William Wollaston, *The Religion of Nature Delineated* (1722)

CHRONOLOGY OF THE LIFE
OF JOHN BROWN

1715   5 November: John Brown born in Rothbury, Northumberland, son of the Revd John Brown (1677–1763) and his wife Eleanor; educated at Wigton Grammar School.

1732   8 May: admitted as a sizar (an impoverished scholar) at St. John's College, Cambridge; 18 December: matriculated.

1735   BA; reportedly as Senior Wrangler (top of the class list in Mathematics).

1738   28 April: takes oaths as minor canon at Carlisle Cathedral.

1739   23 June: nominated to a lectureship in Carlisle Cathedral (relinquished 14 November 1757); 23 December: ordained priest; MA.

1743   6 June: inducted as vicar of Morland, Westmoreland (resigned 1756); "Honour," dedicated to Lord Lonsdale.

1745   *Aide-de-camp* to the Hanoverian militia commander during the siege of Carlisle by Jacobite rebels; *An Essay on Satire Occasion'd by the Death of Mr. Pope*.

1747   Appointed chaplain to the bishop of Carlisle.

1749   *On Liberty: A Poem*.

1750   Preaches at Bath while the guest of Ralph Allen of Prior Park.

1751   *Essays on the Characteristics*; dedicated to Allen.

1752   Appointed vicar of Lazonby, Cumberland (resigned 1756).

1754   "On the Use and Abuse of Externals in Religion"; 17 December: *Barbarossa* premiered at Drury Lane; Brown becomes acquainted with David Garrick.

1755   DD.

1756   27 February: *Athelstan* premiered at Covent Garden; presented with the living of Great Horkesley, near Colchester, Essex, by the earl of Hardwicke, on the recommendation of William Warburton (resigned 1760).

1757   *An Estimate of the Manners and Principles of the Times*; seven reprintings.

1758   *An Estimate of the Manners and Principles of the Times*, vol. II; *An Explanatory Defence of the Estimate*.

1760   Presented to the living of St. Nicholas, Newcastle upon Tyne, by the bishop of London; "An Additional Dialogue of the Dead, Between Pericles and Aristides."

1763   "The Cure of Saul: A Sacred Ode"; *A Dissertation on the Rise, Union, and Power, the Progressions, Separations and Corruptions of Poetry and Music*.

1764   *A History of the Rise and Progress of Poetry*; *Sermons on Various Subjects*.

1765   *Thoughts on Civil Liberty*; 16 May: preaches "On the Female Character and Education"; July: approached by Daniel Dumaresq to guide the process of educational reform in Russia.

1766   *Letter to the Rev. Dr. Lowth*; 31 January: invited to St. Petersburg; April: "A Description of the Lake at Keswick," *London Chronicle*; 3 June: receives £1,000 in travel expenses from the Russian ambassador to the Court of St. James's, M. de Moussin Pouschkin; 30 July: dissuaded from making the journey on the grounds of his "critical state of health" by his former curate, William Stevens; 23 September: commits suicide by cutting his throat; 1 October: interred in St. James's Church.

ACKNOWLEDGMENTS

I am very grateful to Eric Nelson, of Harvard University, for his kindness in inspecting various volumes in the Houghton Library and reporting his findings.

On Liberty: A Poem
(1749)

* Thomas Pelham-Holles (1693–1768), duke of Newcastle-upon-Tyne and first duke of Newcastle-under-Lyme, had become Chancellor of the University of Cambridge in 1748. He succeeded Charles Seymour (1662–1748), sixth duke of Somerset, who remarkably had been Chancellor since 1689.

† In the previous year the Treaty of Aix-la-Chapelle had concluded the War of the Austrian Succession (1740–48). The Duke of Newcastle, who served as a minister responsible for defense from 1739 to 1748, had been instrumental in the negotiations leading up to the treaty, the signing of which had (as he expressed it to his brother) given him "the joy of an honest man."

‡ "As it should be in the case of a sister" (Ovid, *Metamorphoses*, II.14). Modern editions print the genitive plural "sororum," rather than the accusative singular. Brown was evidently fond of this Ovidian tag, and had used it in a letter to William Gilpin of 14 February 1743 (Bodl. MS Eng. Misc. c. 389, fol. 62$^\mathrm{v}$).

ON

LIBERTY

A

POEM,

Inscribed to his Grace the

CHANCELLOR*

And to the

University of Cambridge,

On occasion of the

PEACE.†

By *JOHN BROWN*, M. A.

Qualem decet esse Sororem.‡

LONDON,

Printed for C. Davis against *Grey's-Inn* Gate *Holbourn.*

and sold by M. Cooper in *Pater-noster-Row.*

MDCCXLIX.

ON
LIBERTY

CONTENTS

> At length the hostile Din of War is o'er;
> The Battle's Thunder shakes the Field no more.
> At length with Love and Joy, in Smiles combin'd,
> Fair Peace descends from Heav'n to bless Mankind.
> Where bleeding Earth late groan'd with Warriors slain,
> *She* bids the Harvest wave along the Plain: [6]
> Where Cities sunk beneath the fiery Storm,
> Lo, at her Voice, Confusion leaps to Form!
> The Village Dance, and courtly Pomp confess
> *Her* the sole Source of social Happiness.
> No more the Cannon's Rage shall blot the Flood,
> The guilty Wave no more be stain'd with Blood;
> But the glad Sail shall waft the Vessel o'er,
> And ev'ry Nation visit ev'ry Shore:
> The Blessings of each Clime, each Clime shall gain;
> Nor Ocean spread his mighty Floods in vain.

10

15

But chief, the Pride of Peace, shall FREEDOM smile,
And show'r her Glories o'er BRITANNIA's Isle:
There, clad in Heav'n's own Lustre, TRUTH shall shine,
20   And call forth VIRTUE's awful[1] Form divine.
Congenial Pow'rs! by native Union sway'd!
I sing your kind, reciprocated Aid. [7]

O PELHAM,[2] Thou, to whom the Fates dispense
The godlike Pow'r of wide Beneficence;
25   Deign to the faithful Muse thine Ear to bend:
The Muse is thine, for she is Freedom's Friend.
And Ye, the GUARDIANS of celestial Truth,[3]
Who form the Thought, and strike the Fate of Youth,
With candid Eye the Poet's Labour view,
30   Who paints those Precepts which he learnt from You.

First to my Song, majestic *Freedom,* rise;
And call thy twin-born Sister from the Skies,
Unspotted *Truth:* For Truth from thee alone,
While she augments thy Pow'r, receives her own.
35   Lo, the young Mind, while Things unknown surround,
In the fond Gaze of ardent Wonder drown'd,
With native Joy each hidden Cause explores;
And wakes to Action all her free-born Pow'rs. [8]
On bold, tho' artless Pinion, proud to *know,*
40   She tempts the Heights above and Depths below;
And glad thro' wide Creation's Maze to stray, ·
Soars to the Founts of intellectual Day.

Hence Knowledge springs: Then swells th' unbidden Heart
With gen'rous Pride, that Knowledge to impart:
45   The burthen'd Mind impatient burns to pour,
On each congenial Mind, her gather'd Store:
New Plans of Thought, united Thoughts inspire;
And full Collision wakes a brighter Fire.
The fair progressive Lustre spreading round,

---

1. I.e., proper to inspire awe. Cf. Milton, *Paradise Lost*, IV.847.
2. Cf. above, p. 2.
3. I.e. the academics of the University of Cambridge.

50 The kindled Soul disdains each narrow Bound;
   Her destin'd Height still eager to possess,
   Labours for Action, Truth, and Happiness.
   What tho' she *rear* the mighty *Pile* with Pain,
   Tho' Reason sometimes urge her *Toil* in vain, [9]
55 Oft tho' she lose her fair Reward of Praise,
   Oft *sink* beneath the *Weight* she strove to *raise,*
   Another Age shall see, with glad Surprize,
   On Error's *Ruin* Truth's fair *Structure rise:*
   Freedom shall join t' explore Heav'n's mighty Plan,[4]
60 And vanquish'd Nature yield the Palm to Man.

   Nor less fair *Truth* and *Liberty* combine
   To warm the Heart with *Virtue's* Flame divine.
   Truth bids the Soul to Scenes of Wonder rise,
   And read her Maker's Image in the Skies:
65 Points out, thro' Earth below, and Heav'n above,
   Wisdom and Pow'r the Ministers of Love.
   With native Sympathy the Soul elate,
   Sees to admire, admires to imitate.
   Thence Freedom aids the Heart, by Truth refin'd,
70 To spread her equal Gifts on all Mankind: [10]
   Whom Heav'n thought worthy *Being* to possess,
   She greatly thinks is worthy Happiness;
   Instructs the Heart with boundless Love to glow,
   The gentle Eye to melt at human Woe.
75 Bliss opens round, obedient to her Call:
   And what is *Virtue,* but *what blesses all?*

   Far other Fate attends the free-born Mind,
   In the fell Chain of ruffian Pow'r confin'd:
   Where *Tyrant-Rage,* and *Bigot-Frowns* controul
80 The native Efforts of the struggling Soul.
   Thro' fair Creation's Round tho' Beauty reign;
   For her, Creation's Beauty smiles in vain:
   In vain yon Orbs refulgent roll on high:
   Shut is each Sense, fast-clos'd her ideot Eye.

4. Cf. Pope, *An Essay on Man,* I.6.

85   No more intent to view, or fond to hear,
        Her Wonder sinks to Ign'rance; *that,* to Fear: [11]
        Appal'd she starts at ev'ry Pow'r unknown,
        Nor dares to search God's Nature, or her own.

        Hence *Tyranny* and *Falshood* urge their Art,
90   And blast each *Virtue* op'ning in the Heart:
        While their vain Terrors ev'ry Pow'r controul,
        Bind Thought in Shackles, and subdue the Soul.
        Thus by the Damps of coward *Fear* oppress'd,
        The Beam of Love expires within the Breast:
95   Or if rekindled, *Superstition's* Call
        Contracts the Ray that Heav'n ordain'd for all:
        Impells blind Virtue, in her abject State,
        To love that Pow'r alone she ought to hate:
        To court Oppression, and with mean Disdain
100   To stab kind *Freedom* that wou'd break her Chain.
        Hence, in the Breast what Serpent-Monsters rise!
        (Perverted Virtue is the blackest Vice) [12]
        Hence Nature mourns her gentle Whisper scorn'd,
        And weeps the Graces into Furies turn'd.
105   Hence Justice drags fair Freedom to her Fate;
        And Love destroys beyond the Rage of Hate.
        Hence Heav'n-born Charity herself inspires
        The ling'ring Rack, and slow-consuming Fires;
        Hence teaches in the Breast humane to dwell
110   Remorseless Vengeance, and the Spite of Hell.

        O GRANTA,[5] warm for Truth, in Virtue wise,
        To Freedom's Aid with gen'rous Ardor rise!
        To thy committed Youth the Flame impart,
        And shoot the fair Infection through the Heart:
115   To Heav'n obedient, urge the mild Decree,
        Which warn'd Mankind, "*that Truth shall make them free.*"[6]
        And prove, by pointing Heav'n's extended Plan,

5. The name of the river which runs through Cambridge; metonymically therefore a reference to the University itself.
    6. Cf. John 8:32.

The Foes of Freedom are the Foes of Man. [13]
Bid *Britain's* Sons with pitying Scorn behold
120   Her treach'rous Foes in lurking Treason bold;
Who wish'd,—yet dar'd not lift the coward Hand,
When late Rebellion[7] shook th' astonish'd Land;
Who glad wou'd fix their Idol[8] on the Throne,
That his unbridled Rage might shield their own;
125   Who veil th' Oppressor in the Slave's Disguise;
Willing to fawn, that they may tyrannize:
Who spurn the Gifts of Peace with vile Disdain,
Tho' FREEDOM and a PATRIOT-MONARCH[9] reign.
O bid thy kindling Youth with ravish'd Eyes
130   See thy bright Train of Bards and Sages rise;
Thy Patriots, Heroes, who, inspir'd by Thee,
Or liv'd or dy'd for *Truth* and *Liberty*.
Thy Pledge of rising Day, see BACON shine;
And awful NEWTON, Nature's Boast, and *thine!*
135   Thine moral SPENSER's Heav'n-enkindled Flame:
And thine the great, long-injur'd MILTON's Name;[10] [14]

7. A reference to the Jacobite rebellion of 1745. For Brown's part in this, see the "Introduction," pp. ix–xxv.

8. I.e., the Old Pretender, James Francis Edward Stuart (1688–1766), the Jacobite claimant to the thrones of England, Scotland, and Ireland, who since February 1717 had been resident in the Papal States. The Treaty of Aix-la-Chapelle had resulted in the expulsion of the Young Pretender, Charles Edward Stuart, from France.

9. A resonant phrase in the context of mid-eighteenth-century English political theory. In 1738 Bolingbroke had published *The Idea of a Patriot King*, in which he had explored and extolled how a monarch devoted to "the common welfare, [and] protective of the rights of property and liberty" would become a "Patriot King"—what in his *Dissertation upon Parties* (1733–34) he had referred to with a paradoxical flourish as "the absolute monarch of a free people" (Bolingbroke, *Political Writings*, p. xxi).

10. Francis Bacon (1561–1626), first baron Verulam and viscount St. Albans; statesman, lawyer, philosopher, historian, and essayist. Sir Isaac Newton (1642–1727); mathematician, natural philosopher, theologian, and alchemist. Edmund Spenser (c. 1552–99); poet and courtier. John Milton (1608–74); poet and public servant. All were Cambridge graduates (Bacon and Newton, Trinity; Spenser, Pembroke; Milton, Christ's), and all were prominent in the Whig pantheon of great Englishmen. Milton was "long-injur'd" because his connection with the regicide and the republican administration of the Interregnum had, in the years following the Restoration, damaged his public reputation and suppressed the standing of his poetry.

With Scorn he saw destroying License rise,
Saw impious Wit caress'd in Wisdom's Guise;
And firm to Virtue in degen'rate Days,
140   Prefer'd a World's Reproach to guilty Praise:
O grateful, twine around his honour'd Brow
The *Poet's* Laurel, and the *Sage's* too!
How did thine Eye the gen'rous Sorrow shed,
When Truth and Freedom in thy Russel[11] bled!
145   How flow'd thy Joy, when at the destin'd Hour,
Thy *mitred* Patriots[12] stem'd the Tyrant's Pow'r!
Nor shalt thou less in virtuous Ardor shine,
Still fond to call emerging Wisdom thine:
The first to chase the Gloom, thro' ev'ry Age
150   Of cloyster'd Ignorance, and monkish Rage;
From bigot Pow'r can'st boast Erasmus[13] won,
And mighty Locke[14] thy glad adopted Son. [15]

    Rise, Granta, rise! augment thine awful Train;
Nor let the great Examples shine in vain.
155   With thee fair Praise, or black Reproach must dwell,
The Friend of Heav'n, or Instrument of Hell.
Shouldst Thou—should Isis[15]—by your Foes betray'd,

11. A reference to William, Lord Russell (1639–83), who had been arrested in the aftermath of the Rye House Plot, found guilty of high treason, and executed on 21 July 1683. After the Glorious Revolution of 1688 he was widely viewed as a martyr for the cause of Whiggism. Russell was a member of Trinity College, Cambridge.

12. An allusion to the resistance of the seven bishops to the second Declaration of Indulgence issued by James II on 25 April 1688, which was a prelude to the Glorious Revolution of the same year. The seven bishops were Sancroft (archbishop of Canterbury), Ken (Bath and Wells), Turner (Ely), White (Peterborough), Lake (Chichester), Lloyd (St. Asaph), and Trelawny (Bristol). They presented James with a petition in which they declared the indulgence to be illegal. Put on trial for seditious libel later in the year, they were all acquitted.

13. Desiderius Erasmus (*c.* 1467–1536); Dutch humanist, scholar, and theologian; lectured on Greek at Cambridge from 1511 to 1514.

14. John Locke (1632–1704); philosopher and political theorist. Locke had been educated at Christ Church, Oxford. Locke's philosophical doctrines were influential in both Oxford and Cambridge during the eighteenth century; hence he might be said to have been "adopted" by Cambridge.

15. I.e., the Thames, and therefore a metonym for the University of Oxford.

With foul Defection start from Freedom's Aid;
Should your polluted Streams (which erst refin'd,
160   Pour'd Truth and Wisdom on the thirsty Mind)
O should they, poison'd by fell *Treason's* Hand,
Diffuse Infection thro' the tainted Land;
How would expiring *Freedom* curse the Bane,
And Angels weep their Cares for *Britain* vain!
165   But if the Muse prophetic may divine,
A nobler Lot, my GRANTA, shall be thine.
E'en now her raptur'd Eye, with glad Surprize
Beholds thy long successive Glories rise:
Thy Stream, where Heav'n's reflected Image shines,
170   Brightens by Age, *"and as it runs refines."*[16] [16]
From thee the Sage shall catch the piercing Ray,
And o'er the Depths of Nature spread the Day.
At thy Command, in deep Attention hung,
Shall list'ning Senates bless the Patriot's Tongue:[17]
175   From thee the Patriot's Breast shall catch the Fire,
Fond for his Country's Freedom to expire.
Thy future Bards shall rise the Tyrant's Dread,
And pour the Muse's Thunder on his Head:
Thy glowing Warriors feel the Wish refin'd,

---

16. Cf. Joseph Addison, *Cato* (1713), I.vi.84. This famous image was much quoted (not always reverently) throughout the eighteenth century on both sides of the Atlantic: cf. Nicholas Amhurst, *A Congratulatory Epistle* (1717), p. 13; Anthony Blackwall, *An Introduction to the Classics* (1718), p. 254; Edward Bysshe, *The Art of English Poetry* (1718), p. 17; Friedrich Dedekind, *Grobianus* (1739), p. 222; Patrick Delany, *Observations* (1754), p. 82; John Gilbert Cooper, *Letters Concerning Taste* (1755), p. 36; Thomas Gibbons, *Rhetoric* (1767), p. 422; Hugh Kelly, *The Babler*, no. 122, 28 May 1767; Noah Webster, *Dissertations on the English Language* (Boston, 1789), p. 65; John Hassell, *Tour of the Isle of Wight* (1790), p. 197; Samuel Austin, *An Oration* (Worcester, 1798), p. 36.

17. "Patriot" here is used not simply in the general sense of one who loves his homeland, but in the more specific and technical mid-eighteenth-century British sense of (in the first place) those disaffected Whigs who had opposed Walpole in the 1730s, and subsequently the political groupings of the middle years of the century in which Pitt the Elder (who had also been part of the earlier group of "Patriots") was the dominant figure.

180   And teach the deathful Sword to save Mankind:
Thy Priests, in Hope and Love humanely wise,
Shall raise fall'n Man, and guide him to the Skies.
Whilst thou, high-rais'd on *Freedom's* awful Throne,
Shall justly boast each glorious Toil thine own;
185   O'er ev'ry Pow'r with sov'reign Eye preside,
And be THY GRATEFUL COUNTRY'S JUSTEST PRIDE.

FINIS

Essays on the Characteristics
of the Earl of Shaftesbury
(1751)

ESSAYS

ON THE

CHARACTERISTICS

BY

JOHN BROWN, M.A.

LONDON,
Printed for C. DAVIS against *Gray's-Inn-Gate, Holborn.*
MDCCLI.

ESSAYS

ON THE

CHARACTERISTICS

OF THE

Earl of Shaftesbury

I. On RIDICULE considered as a Test of Truth.

II. On the Obligations of Man to Virtue, and the Necessity of *religious Principle*.

III. On *revealed* Religion, and Christianity.

Ralph Allen,[1] Esq.

SIR,

Did this Address aim no farther than at the common End of Dedicators, I should have been proud enough to have declined the Trouble, and *You* too wise to have approved this public Manner of offering it.

To praise You, were *impertinent*; and to tell others of my Obligations to You, would have the Appearance rather of *Vanity* than *Gratitude*. [ii]

The Truth is; I make free with Your Name on this Occasion, not so much to *protect* my *Book*, as to *complete* my *Argument*.

I have ventured to criticize the Works of a very celebrated Writer, who took it into his Head to oppose the solid Wisdom of the *Gospel*, by the Visions of *false Philosophy*. As His, at best, is but the Cause of *Wit* and *Eloquence*, all the Support he could give it was only to tell us *how* PLATO *wrote:* Mine being that of *Truth*, and *Christianity*, I have the Advantage of *realizing* all I say, in bidding the World take Notice *how* YOU *live*. [iii]

In a Word; I was willing to bring the Question to a short Issue; and shew, by a *known* EXAMPLE, to what an Elevation true *Christianity* can exalt human Nature. Till therefore philosophic *Taste* can produce a parallel Effect, *Religion* must bear the *Palm*; and CHRISTIANITY, like her *Parent* WISDOM, *will be justified of her Children*.[2]

> *I am, SIR,*
> > *Your most obliged,*
> > > *humble Servant,*
> > > > JOHN BROWN.

1. Ralph Allen (1693–1764); postal entrepreneur and philanthropist. Friend of men of letters such as Alexander Pope, Henry Fielding, and William Warburton.
2. Matthew 11:19; Luke 7:35.

Contents

ESSAY II
On the Obligations of Man to Virtue, and the Necessity
of religious Principle.

ESSAY III
On revealed RELIGION, *and* CHRISTIANITY

ESSAYS

ON THE
Characteristics, etc.

ESSAY I
On Ridicule, considered as a Test of Truth

SECTION I

It hath been the Fate of Lord SHAFTESBURY's *Characteristics*,[3] beyond that of most other Books, to be idolized by one Party, and detested by another. While the first regard it as a Work of *perfect Excellence,* as containing every Thing that can render Mankind wise and happy; the latter are disposed to rank it among the most pernicious of Writings, and brand it as one [2] continued Heap of *Fustian,*[4] *Scurrility,* and *Falsehood.*

3. Shaftesbury's *Characteristicks of Men, Manners, Opinions, Times* was first published in three volumes in 1711, although some elements of this collection of essays and treatises had been previously published. A second revised edition, enriched with emblematic engravings, was published in 1714, and was frequently reprinted throughout the eighteenth century (1723, 1727, 1732, 1733, 1737, 1743, 1758). Deliberately miscellaneous in subject matter (embracing ethics, aesthetics, history, the arts, and religion) and oblique in manner, *Characteristicks* was devoted to describing and promoting a de-Christianized idea of virtue. It exerted a strong influence over English moral philosophy during the eighteenth century, not least among those (such as Brown) who opposed its arguments, and reviled Shaftesbury as an enemy of religion and virtue. See most recently Isabel Rivers, *Reason, Grace, and Sentiment: A Study of the Language of Religion and Ethics in England 1660–1780,* vol. II, Shaftesbury to Hume (Cambridge: Cambridge University Press, 2000) and Lawrence E. Klein, *Shaftesbury and the Culture of Politeness: Moral discourse and cultural politics in early eighteenth-century England* (Cambridge: Cambridge University Press, 1994).
    4. Inflated, turgid, or inappropriately lofty language (*OED*, 2).

This Circumstance hath always appeared to me a Demonstration, that Passion and Prejudice have had a greater Share than Reason, in deciding upon the Merits of this Work; which many read with Displeasure, more with Admiration, but few with impartial Judgment. 'Tis probable, the Truth lies between the two Extremes of these discordant Opinions: and that the noble Writer hath mingled Beauties and Blots, Faults and Excellencies, with a liberal and unsparing Hand.

These, so far as they relate to *Religion* and *Morals,* it is my present Intention to point out, without Regard to the bigoted Censures of his Friends or Enemies: While I foresee, that some will *frown* upon me for allowing him any Thing, and others treat me with a *contemptuous Smile* for presuming to differ with him at all.

The first Thing that occurs to an unprejudiced Mind, in the Perusal of the *Characteristics,* is that generous Spirit of *Freedom* which shines throughout the whole. The noble Author every where asserts that natural Privilege of Man, which hath been [3] so often denied him, of seeing with his own Eyes, and judging by his own Reason. It may possibly appear strange to some, why he should so extremely labour a Point so plain. But in Justice to his Lordship these Gentlemen must remember, or be informed, that in former Times, some well-designing Men[5] among ourselves, from a groundless Dread of an unlimited Freedom of the Press, attempted to make a most unnatural and cruel Separation between *Truth* and *Liberty.*

5. A reference to developments in the control and licensing of the press during the later seventeenth century. In 1662 a Licensing Act was passed for two years (subsequently extended to 1679), forbidding the publication of any book or pamphlet contrary to the doctrine and discipline of the Church of England or scandalous to government. Under this act Roger L'Estrange was appointed surveyor of printing presses and licenser of publications. In 1685 the Licensing Act was revived. However, in 1694 Parliament refused to renew it, the case against renewal having been prepared by John Locke (cf. above, p. 10, n. 14). Thereafter the freedom of the press was restrained in a variety of less formal ways, including the issuing of warrants for the arrest of those suspected of printing libellous matter as well as the issuing of general warrants, and differences of political party might play a role in this. So, for instance, Defoe was arrested and pilloried in 1703 for his pamphlets on ecclesiastical matters. More gravely, in 1719 John Matthews was hanged for his Jacobite pamphlet *Vox Populi Vox Dei.* Periodicals such as the *Freeholder's Journal* and *The True Briton* were suppressed in 1723 and 1724.

Having shaken off the Corruptions of *Popery*, and established what they thought a pure and perfect System, they unhappily stopped short in their full Carrier of Glory; preposterously attempting to deprive others of that common Privilege which they had so nobly exercised themselves. This mistaken Spirit seemed entirely subdued by the excellent LOCKE, and others, about the Time of the Revolution:[6] But at the Period when our noble Author wrote, it not only revived, but was heightened[7] by a terrible Accession of Bitterness and Rancour. Hence those frequent Sallies of Invective, which he throws out against this intolerant Principle, which he justly stigmatizeth as equally impolitic, irrational, and unchristian. [4]

'Tis the Glory of our Days, that this accursed Spirit of Persecution is at least dying away. What Pity that we cannot add, it is wholly extinguished! It is true, we most of us profess ourselves Friends to a Freedom of Inquiry, *in the Main*. But why, *in the Main?* Why that needless Circumstance of Hesitation? Would we embrace Error? Or do we think that Truth can suffer by the most rigid Scrutiny? On the contrary, not only the Perfection, but the very Being of Knowledge depends on the Exercise of Freedom. For whatever some may fear from an open and unlimited Enquiry, it seems evidently the only Means vouchsafed us for the Attainment of Truth. The *Abuse* of it may be *hurtful*, but the *Want* of it is *fatal*. Such, indeed, are the clear and undoubted Principles of our Religion: Neither sure can these Declarations surprize us. For if human and political Establishments had been sacred or unviolable, where had been our *Protestantism*; nay, where our *Christianity?* Dare we then to desert or discountenance a Principle, on which not only the Purity, but the very Existence of our Religion depends? Nor is this Principle less consonant with the strictest Reason. It [5] is Falsehood only that loves and retires into Darkness. Truth delights in the Day; and demands no more than a just Light, to appear in perfect Beauty. A rigid Examination is its only Test: For Experience hath taught us, that even *Obstinacy* and *Error* can endure the *Fires* of Persecution: But it is genuine Truth,

6. I.e., 1688.
7. A reference to the "War of Party" between Whigs and Tories during the reign of Queen Anne; cf. *The Spectator*, nos. 81 (2 June 1711) and 125 (24 July 1711).

and that alone, which comes out pure and *unchanged* from the *severer Tortures* of Debate.

It will ever be our truest Praise therefore, to join the noble Apologist in his Encomiums on *Freedom*; the only permanent Basis on which *Religion* or *Virtue* can be established. Nor can we less approve his frequent Recommendations of *Politeness, Chearfulness,* and *Good-humour,* in the Prosecution of our most important Enquiries. The morose, contemptuous, and surly Species of Composition is generally an Appendage to Bigotry, as appears in Instances innumerable, both among the mistaken Friends and Enemies of Religion. On the contrary, the amiable Qualities of Chearfulness and Good-humour, cast a Kind of Sunshine over a Composition, and naturally engage us in Favour of the Writer. They resemble that gentle Smile that often lights [6] up the human Countenance, the never-failing Indication of a humane Temper. How naturally then must we be disposed to listen; how open our Minds to receive Conviction, when we perceive our Opponent's Intention is benevolent: When we perceive that his Aim is not *Victory,* but *Information:* that he means not to *insult,* but to *instruct* us.

So far, out of an unfeigned Regard to Truth, it should be my Boast to take Party with the noble Writer: On the same Principle it will now be necessary to depart from him. For, not content with establishing the free Exercise of Reason, and the Way of Chearfulness, in treating the Subjects of Religion and Morals; he revolts from the Principle on which the rational Advocates for Religion were willing to have joined him, and appeals to a new Test, *the Test of Ridicule.*[8] This, in his two first Treatises, he attempts to establish as a surer Method of Conviction: And *that* Ridicule, which had hitherto been employed in *disgracing known Falsehood,* he informs us, may be successfully applied to the *Investigation* of *unknown Truth.* [7]

He hath gained a numerous Train of Followers in this new Opinion: It may be therefore necessary to examine its Foundations.

---

8. The second treatise in *Characteristicks,* "On the Freedom of Wit and Humour," defends the proposition that (as Shaftesbury puts it in Part IV, sect. 1) "nothing is ridiculous except what is deform'd: Nor is any thing proof against *Raillery,* except what is handsome and just" (Shaftesbury, *Characteristicks,* vol. I, p. 80).

SECTION II

'Tis great Pity the noble Author hath not condescended to a little more *Precision* in treating the Question now before us. He indulges the Gaiety of Spirit, the Freedom of *Wit* and *Humour* so far, that a Reader, who seeks Information rather than Amusement, is often at a Loss to know where his Argument, or even his Opinion, lies. This, no doubt, was in Part owing to a generous Abhorrence of *Pedantry,* which he takes all Occasions of exposing to Contempt. Yet a better Reason may possibly be alledged: For in recommending and enforcing the *Use of Ridicule,* what could be more natural and proper than the *Power of Ridicule* itself? To draw a striking Picture of demure Folly and solemn Imposture, was a Masterpiece of Prudence: But to have argued *seriously,* would have destroyed his Argument: It would have been a tacit Confession, that there is a deeper Foundation, on which [8] Ridicule itself must rest, he must therefore have overturned, even while he intended to establish this new Pillar, and *Ground of Truth.*

Here then we discover why the noble Author is so witty in Defence of Wit, and chuses to maintain the Cause of Raillery by Raillery itself. He smiles at his Adversary, who had attempted to find Coherence in his first Letter.[a] He glories in being an Adventurer in the Way of *Miscellany;* where "Cuttings and Shreds of Learning, with various Fragments and Points of Wit, are drawn together and tacked in any fantastic Form. Where the Wild and Whimsical, under the Name of the Odd and Pretty, succeed in the Room of the Graceful and Beautiful: Where Justness and Accuracy of Thought are set aside, as too constraining, and of too painful an Aspect, to be endured in the agreeable and more easy Commerce of Gallantry and modern Wit."[b] Hence with Reason he proceeds to his Conclusion, that "Grounds and Foundations are of no Moment, in a Kind of Work, which, ac[9]cording to modern Establishment, has properly neither *Top* nor *Bottom, Beginning* nor *End.*"[c]

a. Vol. iii. p. 18, 20.[9]
b. Ibid. p. 5, &c.[10]
c. Vol. iii. p. 8.
9. Shaftesbury, *Characteristicks,* vol. III, pp. 13–14.
10. Ibid., pp. 5–6.

It must be confessed, that in the Conduct of the literary Warfare, they who depend on the Regularity and Force of *Arguments,* have but a sorry Chance against these nimble Adventurers in the *Sallies* of Wit and Ridicule; these *Hussars*[11] in Disputation, who confide more in their Agility, than Strength or Discipline; and by sudden *Evolutions* and timely *Skulking,* can do great Mischiefs, without receiving any. Ill qualified, indeed, is the *saturnine* Complexion of the dry *Reasoner,* to cope with this *mercurial* Spirit of modern *Wit:* The Formalist is under a double Difficulty; not only to *conquer* his Enemy, but to *find* him. Though it must be owned, the Search is a harder Task than the *Victory*; and more mortifying, as it ends in shewing us that this redoubted Figure of *Ridicule,* armed at all Points like *Reason,* is no other than an airy Phantom, tricked up by the Goddess of Folly, to confound formal Wisdom; as that other in the Poet, to mislead his Hero: [10]

> Tum dea nube cava *tenuem sine viribus umbram*
> In faciem Aeneae (visu mirabile monstrum)
> *Dardaniis ornat telis:* clypeumque, jubasque
> *Divini* assimilat *capitis*; dat *inania verba,*
> Dat *sine mente sonum,* gressusque effingit euntis.
> Illum autem absentem Aeneas in praelia poscit.
> Tunc levis haud ultra *latebras* jam *quaerit* imago,
> Sed sublime volans, *nubi* se *immiscuit* atrae.[d]

d. Virg. Aen. x. ℣636, &c.[12]

11. Originally a body of light horsemen in the Hungarian army with a reputation for mobility and ferocity; thereafter, cavalry regiments in other European armies formed in imitation of these Hungarian troops; by metaphorical extension, a skirmisher or freelancer in literary polemic (*OED*, 1a and 2).

12. "Then the goddess fashions out of hollow mist a thin, strengthless phantom in the likeness of Aeneas, a monstrous marvel to behold, decks it with Dardan weapons, and counterfeits the shield and plumes on his godlike head, gives it unreal words, gives it a voice without thought, and mimics his gait as he moves; . . . Meanwhile Aeneas is challenging his vanished foe to battle, and sends down to death many bodies of warriors who cross his path. Then the airy phantom seeks shelter no longer, but soaring aloft mingles itself in a dark cloud" (Virgil, *Aeneid,* X.636–40 and 661–64).

Since, therefore, the noble Writer declines treating this Subject in the Way of close Argument; we must take our Chance with him upon the Terms he hath been pleased to prescribe. We must be content to go a *Gleaning* for his Opinions, and *pick them up* as they lie thinly scattered through a wide Extent of Pages.

But, however, his Lordship's high Quality may exempt him from the established Forms of Argument, it were the Height of Imprudence in Writers of inferior Rank, to attempt an Imitation of his peculiar Manner. His delicate Raillery, therefore, will best be repayed by sober Reasoning. This, sure, his most zealous Admirers cannot take amiss: It is the noble Author's allowed Maxim, that "a Jest which will not bear a serious Examination is certainly false Wit."e Neither was he a Stranger to [11] the methodical Species of Composition: As appears from that fine Chain of moral Reasoning which connects his Enquiry concerning Virtue: Where he proceeds through the Work with a Pace equally regular and majestic. Indeed should we form our Idea of him from the Attitudes in which his sorry Mimics present him to our View, we should see him labouring through a confused Mass of Words and random Half-meanings, entangled in his own Argument, and throwing himself into every unnatural and awkward Posture, to make his Way, though in vain, into common Sense. But this is a very bad Picture of our noble Author: Though it be all his affected Admirers can exhibit of him in their own Productions. Deformities are easily copied: True Features and graceful Attitudes are caught by the Hand of a *Master* only. For in Reality, none ever knew the Value of Order and Proportion better than Lord SHAFTESBURY. He knew that Confusion can only tend to *disgrace* Truth, or *disguise* Falsehood. Method, indeed, may degenerate into Stiffness, but to despise Order, is the silliest *Affectation.* Especially when the slovenly and confused Form of the Com[12]position (if it may be properly said to have any) pretends to the Character of *Elegance,* it becomes of all others the grossest and most *contemptible Pedantry.*

e. Vol. i. p. 74.[13]
13. Shaftesbury, *Characteristicks,* vol. I, p. 48.

SECTION III

The divine Author of our Being having given us several different Powers, *Sense, Imagination, Memory,* and *Reason,* as the Inlets, Preservers, and Improvers of Knowledge; it may be proper here briefly to remark their respective Provinces. As the *Senses* are the Fountains whence we derive all our Ideas; so these are infinitely combined and associated by the *Imagination: Memory* preserves these Assemblages of Things: *Reason* compares, distinguishes, and separates them: By this Means determining their Differences, and pointing out which are *real,* and which *fictitious.*

The *Passions* are no more than the several Modes of Pleasure and Pain, to which the Author of Nature hath wisely subjected us, for our own and each others Preservation.

> Love, Hope, and Joy, fair Pleasure's smiling Train;
> Hate, Fear, and Grief, the Family of Pain.[14] [13]

To these we may add two more of a mixed Kind, *Pity* and *Contempt,* which seem to partake of both Pain and Pleasure.

As the *Senses* and *Imagination* are the Sources of all our Ideas, it follows that they are the Sources of all our Modes of Pleasure and Pain: That is, of all our *Passions.* Nor is any Passion *strongly excited* in the Soul by mere Knowledge only, till the *Imagination* hath formed to itself some Kind of *Picture* or *Representation* of the Good or Evil apprehended. Thus ARISTOTLE justly defines Fear to be a Kind of Pain arising from the *Phantasy* or *Appearance* of future Evil.[f] Consistently with this, he again truly observes, that though all Men know they must die, yet, while *Death* is at a Distance, they never think of it.[g] The same may be observed

---

f. Ἔστω δὴ φόβος, λύπη τις ἢ ταραχὴ ἐκ ΦΑΝΤΑΣΙΑΣ μέλλοντος κακοῦ. Arist. Rhet. l. ii. c. 5.[15]

g. Ἴσασι γὰρ πάντες, ὅτι ἀποθανοῦνται, ἀλλ᾽ ὅτι οὐκ ἐγγύς, οὐδὲν φροντίζουσιν. Ib. l. ii. c. 5.[16]

14. Pope, *An Essay on Man,* II.117–18.

15. "Fear may be defined as a pain or disturbance due to imagining some destructive or painful evil in the future" (Aristotle, *Rhetoric,* II.v).

16. "For instance, we all know we shall die, but we are not troubled thereby, because death is not close at hand" (Aristotle, *Rhetoric,* II.v).

concerning the Belief of *future Existence*; which never sways the Conduct of Mankind, till the *Imagination* is strongly *impressed* by steady and repeated Contemplation. [14]

As therefore it appears to be the Province of *Sense* and *Imagination* to present and associate Ideas, but not to mark their real Differences; and as the Passions are always excited according to the Suggestions of these two powers; it follows, that *apparent,* not *real* Good and Evil are universally the Objects of all our Passions. Thus the respective Objects of Joy, Fear, Anger, are apparent Good, apparent Danger, apparent Injury. Universally, whether the Object be real or fictitious, while it is *apparent* (that is, while the Imagination represents it as *real*) it will produce its relative Passion.

It is the Province of *Reason* alone, to *correct* the Passions. Imagination and Passion can never correct themselves. Every Assemblage of Ideas, every Impression made upon them, hath an Object *apparently real:* Therefore without the Aids of *Reason,* the *active* and *separating* Power, the Mind can never distinguish *real* from *fictitious* Objects. And as it is the Province of Reason only, thus to regulate the Senses and Imagination, and to determine when they impress a Truth, or suggest a Falsehood: so it is no less the Province of the same corrective Power, to [15] determine concerning the Modes of *apparent* Good and Evil, and thus to fix both our *Opinions* and *Passions* on their proper Objects.[h]

Upon this just Dependance of Imagination and Passion on the superior and leading Faculty of Reason, the whole Weight of this Question

---

h. Some of these Truths are both finely and philosophically expressed by our great Poet in the following Passage:

> But know, that in the Soul
> Are many lesser Faculties, that serve
> Reason as chief: Among these, Fancy next
> Her Office holds: Of all external Things
> Which the five watchful Senses represent,
> She forms Imaginations, aery Shapes,
> Which Reason joining or dis-joining, frames
> All what we affirm, or what deny, and call
> Our Knowledge, or Opinion.[17]
>   *Parad. Lost,* B. v. ℣100, &c.

17. Milton, *Paradise Lost*, V.100–8.

concerning the Application and Use of *Ridicule* depends. But that we may obtain as wide a View as possible of our Subject, it may be proper to ascertain the Nature, Limits, and Ends of the different Kinds of literary Composition, which take their Rise from these three different Powers, as they subsist in Man. Thus we shall discover, to which of them *the Way of Ridicule* is to be referred, and determine how far [16] it *may,* or *may not,* with Propriety be regarded as a *Test of Truth.*

Perhaps there is no Species of Writing (except only that of mere *Narration*) but what will fall under the Denomination of *Poetry, Eloquence,* or *Argument.* The first lays hold of the Imagination; the second, through the Imagination, seizes the Passions; the last addresseth itself to the Reason of Mankind. The immediate, *essential* End therefore of Poetry is to *please,* of Eloquence to *persuade,* of Argument to *instruct.* To this End, the Poet dwells on such Images as are *beautiful*; the Orator selects every Circumstance that is *affecting*; the Philosopher only admits what is *true.* But as all these, in their several Kinds of Writing, address themselves to *Man,* who is compounded of *Imagination, Passion,* and *Reason*; so they seldom confine themselves to their respective Provinces, but lay hold of each other's Art, the more effectually to gain Admission and Success to their own. Yet still, the *Masters* in these various Kinds of Composition, know how to keep their several Boundaries *distinct*; not to make unwarrantable Inroads into each other's Provinces, nor remove those Lines which Na[17]ture hath prescribed: But so to limit their Excursions, that the Intelligent may always know what is designed, a *Poem,* an *Oration,* or an *Argument.*[i]

Thus the judicious Poet, though his immediate and universal Aim is beautiful Imitation, yet in order to become more *pleasing,* endeavours often to be *interesting,* always to be *rational.* His Application being made to *Man,* should he let loose Imagination to its random Flights, he must shock the *Reason* of every penetrating Observer. Hence appears the Necessity of cultivating that Maxim in poetical Composition, which the two

i. Would it not carry us too far from our Subject, it might perhaps be both a new and pleasing Speculation, to point out the Writers in these several Kinds, who have been most remarkably *excellent* or *defective,* with Regard to *this just Union of these three Species of Composition.* At present it must suffice, to have hinted such a Criticism, which the Reader may easily prosecute.

best of *French* Critics,[18] *Boileau* and *Bouhours* have so much insisted on; "that all poetical Beauty must be founded in Truth."[k] Because in the unlimited Excursions of Fancy, though one Faculty should approve, yet another is disgusted: [18] Though Imagination *acquiesce* in false Beauty, Reason will *reject* it with Disdain. Thus, although the primary and essential End of Poetry is to *please* by Imitation; yet as it is addressed to Man, *Instruction* makes a necessary, though an *adventitious* Part of its Character.[l]

From this View of Things we may, in passing, further see the *Nature, Limits,* and *comparative Excellence* of the various Kinds of Poetry. The *Descriptive* holds entirely [19] of the Imagination, and may be termed *pure Poetry* or Imitation: Yet, with regard to the *secondary* End of Instruction, it seems to merit only the lowest Place, because it is then perfect when

---

k. Que si on me demande ce que c'est que cet agrément et ce sel—à mon avis, il consiste principalement à ne jamais presenter au lecteur que des *pensées vrais,* et des *expressions justes. Oeuvres de Boileau,* tom. i. *Pref.* p. 29.

Car enfin, pour vous dire un peu par ordre ce que je pense la dessu, *la verité* est la premiere qualité, et comme le fondement des pensées: les plus belles sont vitieuses; ou plutot celles qui passent pour belles, et qui semblent l'etre, ne le sont pas en effet, si ce fonds leur manque. *Bouhours, Man. de bien pens.* p. 11.

l. Hence the Debate mentioned by *Strabo* (l. i.) between *Eratosthenes,* and some of the *Ancients,* may easily be decided. The first insisting that *Pleasure,* the other that *Instruction,* was the only End of *Poetry.* They were both wrong: as it appears that these two Ends must always be united in some Degree. However, *Eratosthenes*[19] was nearer the Truth, as he alledged the *essential* End. 'Tis no bad Description, given by Mr. *Dryden* and others, of the End of Poetry, that it is "to *instruct* by *pleasing."* Though upon the whole, it throws more Weight on the Circumstance of *Instruction,* than the Thing will bear. The Admirers of Lord *S.* who love pompous Declamation, may see a great deal said on this Subject, and with little Precision, in *Strada's* Third Prolusion.

18. Nicolas Boileau (1636–1711); poet, satirist, and critic of a neo-classical bent. Dominique Bouhours (1628–1702); critic, writer, and clergyman. "If I am asked to say in what this charm and piquancy consist—in my opinion, it principally consists in never presenting to the reader anything but true thoughts and just expressions"; "For finally, to say a little of what I think on this score in an orderly way, truth is the first quality, and the foundation of thoughts: the most beautiful are vicious; or rather, those thoughts which pass for beautiful, and which seem to be so, in fact are not, if they lack this basis of truth."

19. Eratosthenes of Cyrene (*fl.* 3rd c. B.C.); mathematician, geographer, poet, philosopher, and literary critic; successor to Zenodotus as head of the Alexandrian Library; the first man accurately to calculate the circumference of the earth.

it satisfies the Imagination; and while it offends not Reason, or the Affections, nothing further with regard to these Faculties is expected from it. The *Tragic, Comic, Satiric,* and the *Elegy,* as they chiefly regard the *Passions* and the Heart of Man, so they draw much of their Force from the Sources of *Eloquence.* On the other hand, the *Didactic,* as it makes its chief Application to Reason, though it retains so much of the Graces of Imagination, as to merit the Name of Poetry, is principally of the *logical* Species. The *Epic,* by its great Extent, includes all these Kinds by turns, and is therefore the *noblest,* both in its *primary* and *secondary* Intention. Much indeed hath been occasionally asserted by several Writers, concerning the superior Dignity of the *tragic* Species[m]: But this hath been more in the Way of Affirmation than Proof. Their Opinion seems to have [20] been founded on a mistaken Interpretation of ARISTOTLE, whose supposed Authority on this Subject hath generally passed unquestioned. But whoever shall thoroughly examine the Sentiments of the *grand Master,* will find he only meant to assert, that the *Mode of Imitation* in *Tragedy* is more forcible, and therefore superior to that of the *epic* Kind; because in the *last,* the Action is only *told,* in the former, it is *visibly represented.* This is the Truth. But if we consider, not the *Mode* of Imitation, but the *Subjects* imitated; if we consider the comparative *Greatness* of the Action which these two Kinds of Poetry can comprehend; and the moral Ends of *Instruction,* no less than the Variety and Beauty of *Description,* which constitutes the very Essence of Poetry; we shall find the Epic greatly superior, on account of the Extent and Importance of those *Actions,* and the Variety of *Characters* which it is capable of involving. Thus for Instance, such an Action as the Death of OEDIPUS or CATO[21] may be more perfectly imitated (because *visibly* represented) in Tragedy, than in the Epos: But a much greater and more extensive Action, such as the *Establishment of an Empire,* with [21] all its subordinate Episodes, religious, political, and

---

m. Thus the excellent Mr. *Addison:* "A perfect Tragedy is the noblest Production of humane Nature."[20] *Spectator,* N° 39.

20. The opening sentence of *The Spectator,* no. 39 (14 April 1711).

21. See, respectively, the conclusions of Sophocles's *Oedipus at Colonus* and Joseph Addison's *Cato: A Tragedy* (1713).

moral, cannot be comprehended or exhibited in *Tragedy,* while yet they may be perfectly described in the *Epopée.*[22]

So much concerning *Poetry* will be found to have Relation to our Subject. But as the Question concerning *Ridicule* will turn chiefly on the proper Subordination of *Eloquence,* it will be necessary to consider this Kind of Composition in a more particular Manner.

Eloquence then is no other than a Species of Poetry applied to the particular End of Persuasion. For Persuasion can only be effected by rowzing the Passions of the Soul; and these, we have seen, are only to be moved by a Force impressed on the Imagination, assuming the Appearance of Truth; which is the essential Nature of poetical Composition. Thus the Lord VERULAM:[23] "In all Persuasions that are wrought by Eloquence, and other Impression of like Nature, which paint and disguise the true Appearance of Things, the chief Recommendation unto *Reason,* is from the *Imagination.*"[n] And the judicious *Strabo,* consistently with this Theory, tells us, that [22] in Fact "the oratorial Elocution was but an Imitation of the poetical: This appeared first, and was approved: They who imitated it, took off the Measures, but still preserved all the other Parts of Poetry in their Writings: Such were CADMUS the Milesian, PHERECYDES, and HECATAEUS. Their Followers then took something more from what was left, and at length Elocution descended into the Prose which is now among us."[o]

Thus as the Passions must have an *apparent Object* of Good or Evil offered by the Imagination in order to excite them; so Eloquence must offer *apparent Evidence* ere it can be received and acquiesced in: For the

---

n. De Aug. Scient. l. ii.

o. Πρώτιστα γὰρ ἡ ποιητικὴ κατασκευὴ παρῆλθεν εἰς τὸ μέσον, καὶ εὐδοκίμησεν. εἶτα ἐκείνην μιμούμενοι, λύσαντες τὸ μέτρον, τἆλλα δὲ φυλάξαντες τὰ ποιητικὰ, συνέγραψαν οἱ περὶ Κάδμον, καὶ Φερεκύδη, καὶ Ἑκαταῖον. εἶτα οἱ ὕστερον, ἀφαιροῦντες ἀεί τι τῶν τοιούτων, εἰς τὸ νῦν εἶδος κατήγαγον, ὡς ἂν ἀπὸ ὕψους τινός. Strabo, lib. i.[24]

22. The genre of the epic poem.

23. Cf. above, p. 9, n. 10.

24. Strabo, I.ii.6. Brown slightly re-orders Strabo's Greek, but in other respects provides an accurate translation.

Mind cannot embrace known Falsehood. So that every Opinion which Eloquence instills, though it be the pure Result of certain fictitious Images impressed on the Fancy, is always regarded as the Result of rational Conviction, and received by the Mind as Truth. [23]

Hence we may perceive the just Foundation of the well-known Maxim in rhetorical Composition, *Artis est celare artem*.[25] In every other Art, where the End is Pleasure, Instruction, or Admiration, the greater Art the Master displays, the more effectually he gains his Purpose. But where the End is Persuasion, the Discovery of his Art must defeat its Force and Design. For ere he can persuade, he must seem to apply to his Hearer's *Reason*, while, in Fact, he is working on his Imagination and Affections: Now this, once known, must defeat his Purpose; because nothing can persuade but what has the *Appearance of Truth*.

Hence too we may see where the true Medium lies between the too frequent *Use*, and delicate *Avoidance* of poetical Images, in Eloquence. Metaphors, Similies, bold Figures, and glowing Expressions are proper, so far as they point the Imagination to the main Subject on which the Passion is to be excited: When they begin to *amuse*, they grow absurd. And here, by the way, lies the essential Difference between the *Epic* and *Tragic* Composition. For the *Epic*, tending chiefly to Admiration and Instruction, allows a full Display of Art: But [24] the *Tragic*, being of the persuasive Kind, must only regard and touch upon poetical Images in this single View, *as they tend to rowze the Passions of the Soul*. MACROBIUS[P] hath collected[26] many elegant Examples of this *poetic Elocution* from the

p. Saturnal. l. iv. passim.

25. "The essence of art is the concealment of art"; a proverbial Latin tag, not to be found in exactly this form in classical literature, although the notion that artifice should be dissimulated is a commonplace; cf., e.g., Ovid, *Ars Amatoria*, II.313. See Samuel Holt Monk, "A Grace Beyond the Reach of Art," *JHI*, 5 (1944), 131–50.

26. Macrobius Ambrosius Theodosius was a Roman official of the late fourth and early fifth centuries A.D., who held high office in Spain and Africa. The *Saturnalia* takes the form of an imaginary dialogue divided between a large number of speakers, and under this pretext gathers together a great deal of miscellaneous literary information and criticism. Book IV has come down to us in a mutilated form, but from what has survived it is clear that its subject was Virgil's use of *habitus*, or outward appearance, to evoke emotion.

Eneid: He hath ranged them in Classes, and pointed out the Fountains whence the great Poet drew his *Pathos:* And sure, it may with Truth be affirmed, that "the Masterstrokes of that divine Work are rather of the *Tragic,* than the *Epic* Species."

These Remarks will enable us to discover the Impropriety of an Opinion commonly held;[q] "that the Reason why Eloquence had such Power, and wrought such Wonders in *Athens* and *Rome,* was, because it had become the general Taste and Study of the Times: That conse-quently these Cities were more sensible to its Charms, and therefore more warmly affected by it." Now, though with regard to pure *Poetry* or strict *Argument,* where either Pleasure or Truth are the purposed Ends, this Reasoning might hold; yet, when applied to *Eloquence,* it seems to [25] be without Foundation. For where *Ignorance* is predominant, *there* any Application to the Fancy or the Passions is most likely to wear the Appearance of Reason, and therefore the most likely to persuade. As Men improve in Knowledge, such Application must proportionably lose its Force, and true Reasoning prevail. Hence it should seem, that they who make the constituent Principles of Eloquence familiar to their Imagination, must of all others be best enabled to separate *Truth* from its *Appearances,* and distinguish between *Argument* and *Colouring.* An artful Oration will indeed afford great Pleasure to one who hath applied himself to the Study of Rhetoric: Yet, not so as that he shall be *persuaded* by it: On the contrary, his Pleasure consists in a reflex Act of the Under-standing; and arises from the very Circumstance which prevents Persua-sion, a *Discovery of the Master's Art.*

The true Reason therefore, why Eloquence gained such mighty Power in these famed Republics was, "because the Orators addressed themselves to the *People* as their *Judges.*" Here the Art triumphed: for it had not *Rea-son* to instruct, but *Imagination* and *Passion* to controul. According[26]ly we find, that no sooner was the popular Government destroy'd, and the

q. See Mr. Hume's Essay on Eloquence.[27]

27. Not in fact a quotation from Hume's essay "Of Eloquence," but a summary of his thoughts concerning why modern Europeans "are still, notwithstanding all our refinements, much inferior in eloquence" to the ancient Greeks and Romans (Hume, *Essays,* p. 98).

supreme Power lodged in a single Hand, than Eloquence began sensibly
to languish and decay: The mighty Orators, who could sway the Passions
of a mixed Multitude, found their Art baffled and overthrown when opposed to the cool Determinations of cunning Ministers, or the determined
Will of arbitrary Masters. Thus with great Judgment, though not much
Honesty, the *Roman* Poet exhorts his Countrymen to disdain the low Accomplishments of Eloquence: He knew they belonged to a Republic:

> Excudent alii spirantia mollius aera—
> *Orabunt causas melius—*
> Tu regere imperio populos, Romane, memento:
> Hae tibi erunt artes.[r]—

With the same Penetration he lays the Scene in a *popular Assembly*, when
he gives us a Picture of Eloquence triumphant. I mean in that fine Passage where he compares NEPTUNE *stilling the Noise of the Waves*, to an
Orator appeasing the Madness of the People: [27]

> Ac veluti *magno in populo* cum saepe coorta est
> Seditio, saevitque animis *ignobile vulgus;*
> Jamque faces et saxa volant; furor arma ministrat;
> Tum pietate gravem ac meritis si forte virum quem
> Conspexere, silent, *arrectisque auribus astant:*
> Ille *regit dictis animos,* et pectora mulcet:
> Sic cunctus pelagi cecidit fragor.[s]—

'Tis true, we have a supposed Instance on Record, of the Power of TUL-
LY's Eloquence, after Liberty was destroy'd, even on the great *Destroyer*

---

r. Eneïd. l. vi.[28]
s. En. l. i.[29]

28. "Others will beat out the breathing bronze more smoothly—others will plead
their causes better—you, O Roman, remember to rule nations with your power:
these will be your arts" (Virgil, *Aeneid*, VI.847–52).

29. "And as, when often in a great nation tumult has risen, the base rabble rage
angrily, and now flaming brands and stones fly (madness provides their weapons);
then if by chance they catch sight of a man respected for his nobility and service
to the state, they fall silent, and stand still with attentive ears: he governs their
minds and soothes their emotions with speech: even so, the whole roar of the ocean
ceased" (Virgil, *Aeneid*, I.148–54).

himself. When we read the Oration,[t] we stand amazed at its Effects:[30] For sure there is nothing *equal* to them in the Composition itself: And it appears an Event almost unaccountable, that CESAR, who was himself an accomplished Orator, who knew all the Windings of the Art, and was at the same Time of the most determined Spirit, should be so shaken on this Occasion as to tremble, drop his Papers, and acquit the Prisoner. Though many have attributed this to the Force of TULLY's *Elocution*;[v] it seems rather to have been the Effect of CESAR's *Art*. We [28] know with what unwearied Application he courted CICERO's Friendship; he saw where his Vanity and his Weakness lay: With perfect Address therefore he play'd back the Orator's Art upon himself: His concern was *feigned*, and his Mercy *artificial*; as he knew that nothing could so effectually win TULLY to his Party, as giving him the Pride of having *conquered* CESAR.

But whatever of Truth there may be in this Conjecture; so much is evident, that the Scene where alone Eloquence can work its mighty

---

t. Pro Ligario.

v. Casaubon, Sir W. Temple, Mr. Hume, &c.[31]

30. Quintus Ligarius had been prominent on the Republican side in the Civil War with Caesar, by whom he was defeated at the battle of Thapsus in Africa (46 B.C.). Ligarius was spared, but not permitted to return to Rome. Later that year a formal charge (on what precise grounds remains unclear) was laid against Ligarius by his former comrade and fellow-Pompeian, Quintus Tubero; and Ligarius retained Cicero for his defense. Caesar himself heard the case in the forum, remarking beforehand: "Why may we not give ourselves a pleasure which we have now not enjoyed for so long a time, that of hearing Cicero speak; since I have already taken my resolution as to Ligarius, who is clearly a bad man, as well as my enemy?" However, the power of Cicero's oratory instead moved Caesar to acquit Ligarius. The source of the anecdote is Plutarch ("Cicero," XXXIX.5–6). Brown's attention may have been drawn to this speech of Cicero by Warburton, who had published a translation of it ([William Warburton], *Miscellaneous Translations, in Prose and Verse* [1724], pp. 10–33; reprinted in [Samuel Parr], *Tracts, by Warburton, and a Warburtonian* [1789], pp. 6–18).

31. Sir William Temple relates the anecdote in his essay "Of Poetry" (where however he makes the accused Labienus, not Ligarius) (Temple, *Works*, vol. I, p. 235); and Hume refers to it in his essay "Of Eloquence" (Hume, *Essays*, p. 105; note the error in n. 15 of that edition). I have been unable to trace the reference in the work of Isaac Casaubon.

Effects, is that of a *popular Assembly*. An absolute Monarchy quencheth it at once.[32] Nor can public Freedom itself give it any considerable Play, where the public Freedom hath any firmer Basis, than that of a mere Democracy. For where the Councils of a Nation depend on the united Reason of elected Representatives, or wise and cunning Statesmen, though the laboured Essays of Eloquence may often *amuse,* they will seldom *determine.* This seems to be the Case of our own Age and Country: And were it necessary to enlarge on this Subject, it might be made appear, that they who complain of the Decay of public Eloquence among us, assign a Cause which hath [29] no real Existence, when they attribute that Decay to a Neglect of the Art,[w] while, in Fact, it necessarily arises from the ruling Principles of the Times, and the Nature of our Constitution.

Thus Eloquence gains its End of Persuasion by offering *apparent* Truth to the Imagination; as Argument gains its proper End of Conviction by offering *real* Truth to the Understanding. Mr. HOBBES seems to have been well aware of this Distinction. "This, says he, *viz.* laying Evidence before the Mind, is called *teaching*; the Hearer is therefore said to *learn:* But if there be not such Evidence, then such teaching is called *Persuasion,* and begetteth no more in the Hearer, than what is in the Speaker's *bare Opinion.*"[x]

Here then we perceive, that the Consequences of Eloquence, with regard to speculative *Instruction* and *Inquiry,* are of a very different Nature from those which relate to *Morals* and *Action.* To Instruction or Inquiry, every Species of Eloquence must for ever be an Enemy: For though it may lead the Mind to acquiesce in a just Opinion, yet [30] it leads it to acquiesce upon a false Foundation: It puts the Hearer or Reader in the Speaker's or Writer's Power: And though he be so honest as to lead him in the Path of Truth, yet still he leads him *blind-fold.* In this Sense, and

w. See Mr. Hume's Essay on Eloquence.[33]

x. Hobbes on Hum. Nature.[34]

32. For a classical text exploring the notion that oratory flourishes only in times of civil disturbance and languishes under stable governments or tyrannies, cf. Tacitus, *Dialogus de Oratoribus,* especially XL–XLI.

33. Cf., e.g., Hume, *Essays,* pp. 99–100.

34. Hobbes, *Human Nature,* XIII.2.

under this Limitation, Mr. LOCKE's Remark is true: "We must allow that all the Art of Rhetoric, besides Order and Clearness, all the artificial and figurative Application of Words Eloquence hath invented, are for nothing else but to *insinuate wrong* Ideas, *move the Passions,* and *thereby mislead* the Judgment, and so indeed are perfect Cheats."[y]

But if we regard what is of more Importance to Man, than mere speculative Truth, I mean the *practical Ends* of human Life and moral Action; then Eloquence assumes a higher Nature: Nor is there, in this practical Sense, any necessary Connexion between *moving* the Passions, and *misleading* the Judgment. For though the Ends of Truth and Persuasion are then essentially different when the Orator strikes the Imagination with fictitious Images, in which case Falsehood becomes apparent Truth, and Eloquence the Instru[31]ment of Deceit; yet the Ends of Persuasion and Conviction, Opinion and Knowledge *concur,* when such Impressions are made on the Imagination and Passions, as consist with the Dictates of right Reason. In this case, Eloquence comes in to the Aid of Argument, and *impresses* the Truths which Logic teaches, in a warmer and more effectual Manner. It paints real Good and Evil in all the glowing Colours of Imagination, and thus inflames the Heart with double Ardor to embrace the one, and reject the other.

Nay, so far is Eloquence from being the universal Instrument of practical Deceit; that on the contrary, it should seem, the *moral* is more natural than the *immoral* Application of it. Because, ere the dishonest Application can take place, Circumstances must be wrested, and Misrepresentations imposed on the Fancy, in Opposition to Truth and Reason: Whereas in the proper Application, nothing further is necessary, than to draw out and impress those Images and Analogies of Things, which really exist in Nature.

It may be further observed, that as Eloquence is of a vague, unsteady Nature, [32] merely relative to the Imaginations and Passions of Mankind; so there must be several Orders or Degrees of it, subordinate to each other in Dignity, yet each perfect in their Kind. The common *End* of each is

---

y. Locke on Hum. Und.[35]
35. Locke, *Essay Concerning Human Understanding,* III.x.34.

Persuasion: The *Means* are different according to the various Capacities, Fancies, and Affections of those whom the Artist attempts to persuade. The pathetic Orator, who throws a *Congregation* of *Enthusiasts* into Tears and Groanings, would raise Affections of a very different Nature, should he attempt to proselyte an *English Parliament:* As on the other hand, the finest Speaker that ever commanded *the House,* would in vain point the Thunder of his Eloquence on a *Quaker-meeting.* So again, with regard to the Oratory (if it may be called so) of the *Bar,* at a *Country Assize* (for the higher Courts of Justice admit not Eloquence) it is easy to observe, what a different Tour the learned Council takes, in addressing himself to the *Judge* or *Jury:* He is well aware, that what passes with the *one* for *Argument* of Proof, would be derided by the *other* as pastboard *Declamation.* This Difference in the Kind, with respect to the Eloquence of the *Pulpit,* is no less remark[33]able in different Countries. Thus the very agreeable and sensible VOLTAIRE observes, that "in *France (where Reasoning hath little Connexion with Religion)* a Sermon is a long Declamation, spoken with Rapture and Enthusiasm: That in *Italy (where Taste and Vertú give a Tincture to Superstition itself)* a Sermon is a Kind of devotional Comedy: That in *England (where Religion submits to Reason)* it is a solid Dissertation, *sometimes a dry one,* which is read to the Congregation without Action or Elocution."[z] And he justly concludes, that the Discourse which raiseth a French Audience to the highest Pitch of Devotion, would throw an *English* one into a Fit of Laughter.

Hence too, and hence alone, we may account for a Fact, which, however, seemingly improbable, is too well-known to be doubted of: "That although in *France,* the applauded Pulpit Eloquence is of the [34] *Enthusiastic,* in *England* of the severe and *rational* Species; yet the Taste of these

---

z. The Passage in the Original is thus: "Un sermon en France est une longue declamation scrupuleusement divisée en trois points, et recitée avec enthousiasme. En Angleterre un sermon est une dissertation solide, *et quelquefois seche,* qu'un homme lit au peuple sans geste, et sans aucune eclat de voix. En Italie c'est une comedie spirituelle."[36]

36. The quotation comes from chapter 1, "Des différents gouts des Peuples," of Voltaire's *Essay sur la poesie epique,* a text commonly printed as an appendix to his *La henriade*; e.g., *La henriade* ("Londres," 1734), *Essay sur la poesie epique,* p. 16.

two Nations in Tragedy or *Theatrical Eloquence,* is mutually *reversed:* The *English* are Enthusiastic; the *French* severe and rational." Now, though this Fact may carry the Appearance of Self-contradiction, yet on the Principle here laid down, the known Circumstances of the two Kingdoms will explain it sufficiently. In *England,* a general Spirit of *Reasoning* and Enquiry hath extinguished the natural Enthusiasms of the human Mind in *religious Subjects;* while our unrestrained Warmth of Imagination, and habitual Reverence for the noble Irregularities of SHAKESPEAR,[37] concur to make us despise the rigid Laws of the Stage: On the contrary, in *France,* the Severities of the *Academy*[38] have utterly quenched the high Tragic Spirit; while, as yet, *religious Criticism* hath made but little Progress among the Subjects of the *most Christian King.*[39]

In further Proof of this Principle, we may appeal to ancient Fact: To the Progress of Eloquence in *Greece.* There we find, it first appeared, decked in all the glowing Colours of Poetry: afterwards, in an [35] Age of more polished Manners and extensive Knowledge, when the Rhetors attempted to carry this Kind of Eloquence to a still higher Degree, they found the Times would not bear it: They were baffled in their Attempt. As succeeding Ages grew more knowing, they grew more fastidious and refined: The Orators were obliged gradually to lower and bring down Eloquence from its high Standard: Till at length it gained a Form and Character entirely new, as we find it in XENOPHON's chastised Manner of *Attic* Elegance.[a]

---

a. See the Passage quoted above from Strabo, p. 22. § 3.[40]

37. Brown is writing at a moment of transition in Shakespeare's reputation, when censure of his disregard for the dramatic rules derived from Aristotle by neo-classical critics ("the rigid Laws of the Stage") was yielding to admiration for his powers as a poet of human nature and character. Nevertheless, English writers later in the century whose taste had been formed by French literature still found the irregularity of Shakespeare, and the English veneration for it, hard to digest. So when writing his autobiography Gibbon would explain that "the habits of pleasure fortified my taste for the French theatre, and that taste has perhaps abated my idolatry for the Gigantic Genius of Shakespeare, which is inculcated from our infancy as the first duty of an Englishman" (Gibbon, *Autobiographies,* p. 149).

38. A reference to the Académie française, established by Richelieu in 1634 to police the French language and its literature.

39. The regal style of the king of France.

40. Cf. above, p. 39, and n. 27.

To conclude with one Proof more in Favour of this Principle. It appears that these different Kinds were acknowledged sufficiently in ancient *Rome*; though the true Distinction between them seems not to have been thoroughly perceived, unless by TULLY himself. The correct and *Attic* Species having gained a Number of Admirers under the Patronage of SALLUST, who first encouraged it in *Rome*,[b] many [36] were the Debates concerning the superior Force and Propriety of *this* or the more *elevated Manner*. The Patrons of the *Attic* Style derided CICERO, as being *loose, tumid,* and *exuberant*:[c] On the contrary, he too had his Partizans, who despised the calm and correct Species, as void of Energy and Power.[d] Thus by overlooking the *relative* Nature of Eloquence, they mutually fell into an Extreme; both forgetting, that either of these Kinds might be of superior Propriety and Force, according to the Imaginations, Passions, and Capacities of those to whom they should be applied. But TULLY,[42] with a superior Sagacity, saw clearly where the true Distinction lay: For, speaking of CALVUS,[43] a Patronizer of the *Attic* Manner, he says, "HENCE his

---

b. Sic *Sallustio* vigente, amputatae sententiae, et verba ante expectatum cadentia, et obscura brevitas, fuere pro cultu. Senec. Epist.[41]

c. Constat, nec Ciceroni quidem obtrectatores defuisse, quibus inflatus et tumens, nec satis pressus, supra modum exultans, et superfluens, et *parum Atticus* videretur. Dialog. apud Tacit.[44]

d. Mihi falli multum videntur, qui solos esse Atticos credunt, tenues et lucidos et significantes, sed quadam eloquentiae frugalitate contentos, ac manum semper intra pallium continentes. Quintil.[45]

41. "Thus when Sallust was in his pomp, phrases were abbreviated, words came to a close unexpectedly, and obscure conciseness was held to be elegance" (Seneca, *Epistulae Morales*, CXIV.xvii).

42. I.e., Cicero.

43. Gaius Licinius Calvus (82–47 B.C.); poet and barrister famous for his rhetoric; friend of the poet Catullus.

44. "It is agreed that Cicero himself had his critics, for whom he was turgid and puffy, insufficiently concise, inordinately exuberant, and redundant—in short, not Attic enough" (Tacitus, *Dialogus de Oratoribus*, XVIII).

45. "I regard those critics as seriously in error who regard only those authors as Attic who, while they are simple, lucid, and expressive, are nonetheless content with a certain frugality of eloquence, and keep their hands modestly within the folds of their cloaks" (Quintilian, *Institutio Oratoria*, XII.x.21).

Eloquence gained a high Reputation among *the Learned and Attentive*; but among [37] *the Vulgar,* for whom Eloquence was chiefly formed, it was of no Esteem."[e]

Now among these several Kinds of Eloquence, Justness of Thought and Expression, striking Figures, Argument adorned with every pathetic Grace, are the Characters of the *highest:* Sophistry and Buffoonry, ambiguous and dishonest Hints, coarse Language, false and indecent Images, are the Characters of the *lowest*. Between these two Extremes, there lies a Variety of intermediate Kinds, each ascending towards the highest, in Proportion as they abound with its proper Characters. For as the Imagination and Passions are then most refined and just, when they bear to the same Point with Reason; so, that Species of Eloquence is the noblest which tends to conduct them thither.[f] On this Principle, and on this [38] alone, we may with Propriety and Precision determine the comparative Excellence and Dignity of those who aspire to the Palm of Eloquence. On this Principle it seems to be, that a severe, but able, Judge

e. Sed ad *Calvum* revertamur—ejus oratio, nimia religione attenuata, doctis et attente audientibus erat illustris; a multitudine autem à foro, cui nata eloquentia est, devorabatur. In Brut.[46]

f Les Egyptiens comparoient ceux qui preferent le coloris au dessein dans la peinture, à ceux qui en matiere d'eloquence et de poesie preferent les pensées brillantes aux pensées justes. Ciceron, le maitre et le modele de l'eloquence latine, a dit en appliquant sa reflexion à l'orateur, que nous laissons bientôt des Tableaux qui nous attirent d'abord par la force du coloris; au lieu que nous revenons toujours à ceux qui excellent par la beauté du dessein, qui est le vrai caractere de l'antique. Sethos, l. ii. p. 80.[47]

46. "But to return to Calvus . . . through overscrupulousness his speech seemed thin, and although scholars and careful listeners recognised its quality, the multitude and the inhabitants of the forum, for whom eloquence exists, consumed it indiscriminately" (Cicero, *Brutus*, LXXXII.283).

47. "The Egyptians compar'd those who preferr'd colours to design in painting, to those who in eloquence and poetry preferr'd bright thoughts to those which are just. Cicero, the master and pattern of Latin eloquence, applying his reflection to oratory, says, That we soon grow weary of those pictures which at first sight attract us by force of colours; whereas we are constant in our admiration of those that excel in the beauty of design, which is the true character of antiquity" (Jean Terrasson, *The Life of Sethos,* tr. "Mr. Lediard," 2 vols [1732], vol. I, p. 97).

prefers DEMOSTHENES to TULLY:^g and on this Principle he deserves the Preference.

Thus we are at length arrived at the Point where Eloquence and Argument, Persuasion and Conviction unite; where the Orator's Art becomes subservient to the Interests of *Truth,* and only labours to adorn and recommend Her.

We come now to the third Species of Composition, that of *Argument:* Which applying solely to the Reason of Man, and to the Proof or Investigation of Truth, is of a more simple and uncompounded Nature in its Principles, and therefore needs not to be so particularly explained. For Pleasure being the primary End of Poetry, and Persuasion that of Eloquence, the real Nature of Things is often in Part disguised, and compelled to bend to the Imagination [39] and the Passions: But *Truth* being the End of Argument, the varying Colours of Imagination and Passion must be drawn off; and human Reason itself bend to the real, uniform Nature of Things.

Yet on this Occasion it may be proper to remark, that the *rational Faculty* in Man cannot be comprehensive or perfect in its Operations, without a Union with a *strong Imagination.* And this, not only in the Arts of Poetry or Eloquence, but in the *severest Investigations* of Truth. For Reason alone cannot search out new Ideas, but only compare and distinguish those which Sense and Imagination present to her, and the Senses being of small Extent, Imagination is therefore the great universal Instrument of human Knowledge and human Action. Without the Aids of Imagination therefore, Reason works in a contracted Sphere; being destitute of Materials; unable to make the necessary Excursions into the Immensity

g. See Dr. Swift's Letter to a Young Clergyman.⁴⁸

48. In his *A Letter to a Young Gentleman, Lately enter'd into Holy Orders* (1721), Swift praised Demosthenes ("who by many Degrees, excelled the other, at least as an Orator") above Cicero on the grounds that the Greek, "who had to deal with a People of much more Politeness, Learning, and Wit, laid the greatest Weight of his Oratory upon the Strength of his Arguments offered to their Understanding and Reason: Whereas, *Tully* considered the Dispositions of a fiercer, more ignorant, and less mercurial Nation, by dwelling almost entirely on the pathetick Part" (Swift, *Prose Works,* vol. IX, p. 69).

of Nature; and wanting that Power which alone can range through the whole Extent of created Being, and bring Home all the possible and apparent Analogies of Things, setting them before her discerning Eye, and submitting them to her sovereign Appro[40]bation or Dislike. From this noble Union arises that *boundless Penetration*, which so far surpasseth *mere Judgment:* and which, according as it is exerted in Poetry, Eloquence, Philosophy, Morals, or Religion, strikes into the various and untrodden Paths of Nature and Truth; forms the distinguished Names[49] of HOMER, SHAKESPEAR, MILTON, DEMOSTHENES, TULLY, ARISTOTLE, BACON, LOCKE, BAYLE, PASCAL, NEWTON, HOOKER, BERKLEY, WARBURTON, giving that essential Superiority and Preheminence, which hath ever been, first the *Envy*, and then the *Admiration* of Mankind.

Thus as it appeared above, how necessary the Restraints of Reason are, to the Perfection of Works of Imagination; so here it is evident, that a full Union of Imagination is necessary to the perfect Operations of Reason. Taken singly, they are each *defective:* When their Powers are joined, they constitute TRUE GENIUS.

But, however requisite the Force of Imagination may be, to the Perfection of Reason, and the Production of *true Genius*, yet still Reason remains the superior and corrective Power: Therefore every Representation of Poetry or Eloquence, which [41] only apply to the Fancy and Affections, must finally be examined and decided upon, must be *tried, rejected*, or *received*, as the *reasoning Faculty* shall *determine*.

And thus REASON alone is the *Detecter of Falsehood*, and the TEST OF TRUTH.

49. Homer (fl. *c.* 9th c. B.C.); ancient Greek epic poet. William Shakespeare (1564–1616); English poet and dramatist. John Milton (1608–74); English poet and man of letters. Demosthenes (383–322 B.C.); Athenian orator and statesman. Tully (i.e., Marcus Tullius Cicero) (106–43 B.C.); Roman orator and statesman. Aristotle (384–322 B.C.); ancient Greek philosopher. Francis Bacon (1561–1626), first baron Verulam and viscount St. Albans; English statesman, philosopher, and essayist. John Locke (1632–1704); English philosopher. Pierre Bayle (1647–1706); French Protestant scholar, philosopher, and man of letters. Blaise Pascal (1632–62); French mathematician, physicist, and moralist. Sir Isaac Newton (1642–1727); English mathematician, alchemist, and natural philosopher. Richard Hooker (?1554–1600); English theologian. George Berkeley (1685–1753); Irish philosopher. William Warburton (1698–1779), bishop of Gloucester; theological polemicist and man of letters.

SECTION IV

He who would judge aright of the Proportions of a spacious Dome,[50] must not creep from one Corner to another by the Help of a glimmering Taper, but rather light up a central Branch, which may illuminate the whole at once. By doing something like this in our Remarks on the three different Kinds of Composition, we have enabled the intelligent Reader to see with ease: "That Wit, Raillery, and Ridicule, in every Shape they can possibly assume, are no other than so many Species of *Poetry* or *Eloquence*."[51]

Pure *Wit*, when not applied to the Characters of Men, is properly a Species of Poetry. It amuses and delights the Imagination by those sudden Assemblages and pleasing Pictures of Things which it creates: and from every common Occasion can raise [42] such striking Appearances, as throw the most phlegmatic Tempers into a Convulsion of good-humoured Mirth, and *undesigning Laughter*.

But *Ridicule* or *Raillery*, which is the Subject of our Inquiry, hath a further Scope and Intention. It solely regards the Opinions, Passions, Actions, and Characters of Men: and may properly be denominated "that Species of Writing which excites Contempt with Laughter."

Still more particularly we may observe, that as Eloquence in general is but the Application of Poetry to the End of Persuasion, so Ridicule in particular is no more than the Application of that particular Species of Poetry called Wit, to the same End of Persuasion. It tends to excite *Contempt*, in the same Manner as the other Modes of Eloquence raise Love, Pity, Terror, Rage, or Hatred, in the *Heart* of Man.

---

50. The image of the "spacious Dome" was popular in eighteenth-century English literature as a symbol of triumphant human artifice: cf., e.g., Pope, *An Essay on Criticism*, ll. 247–52; Thomson, *Summer*, ll. 285–95; and Gibbon, *Decline and Fall*, vol. II, pp. 594–98.

51. Brown here seems to be drawing on thoughts he had first framed in 1745, when writing to William Gilpin on 20 February about *An Essay on Satire*, which also considers the proper use and power of ridicule. In the course of the letter Brown refers to ridicule as "a particular Species of Eloquence" (Bodl. MS Eng. Misc. c. 389, fol. 78ᵛ). This was eventually worked up into the note on ridicule in *An Essay on Satire* which was praised by Warburton as "admirable" (*An Essay on Satire* [1745], pp. 15–16, n. *; Bodl. MS Eng. Misc. c. 390, fol. 398ʳ).

Now, that *Contempt* which certain Objects raise in the Mind, is a particular *Mode of Passion*. The Objects of this Passion are apparent *Falsehood, Incongruity, Impropriety,* or *Turpitude*[52] of certain Kinds. But as the Object of every excited Passion must be examined by Reason ere we can determine [43] whether it be proper or improper, real or fictitious; so, every Object that excites Contempt must fall under this general Rule. Thus, before it can be determined whether our Contempt be *just,* Reason alone must *examine* Circumstances, separate Ideas, distinguish Truth from its Appearances, decide upon, restrain, and *correct the Passion.*

Thus *Ridicule* is no other than a *Species of Eloquence:* and accordingly we find it mentioned and expresly treated as such, by the best Writers of Antiquity. ARISTOTLE, as in every Subject, leads the Way. "As Ridicule seems to be of some Use in *pleading,* it was the Opinion of GORGIAS, that you ought to confound your Adversary's *serious Argument* by *Raillery,* and his *Raillery* by *serious Argument.* And he judged well."[h] Here he first gives the Sentiments of a *Sage;* and then confirms them by his own Authority.

To offer all that TULLY hath said upon the Subject of Ridicule, would be to transcribe a considerable Part of his second Book [44] *De Oratore.* After having gone through several Topics of Rhetoric, he comes at length to this of *Ridicule:* and assigns to the elder CESAR[54] the Task of explaining the Force and Application of this Art. In the Course of his Reasonings on this Subject, he affirms First, That Ridicule is a Branch of Eloquence.[i] 2*dly,* That certain Kinds of Turpitude or Incongruity are its proper Object.[k] 3*dly,* That the Orator must be temperate in the Application of

h. περὶ δὲ τῶν γελοίων, ἐπειδή τινα δοκεῖ χρῆσιν ἔχειν ἐν τοῖς ἀγῶσι, καὶ δεῖν ἔφη Γοργίας τὴν μὲν σπουδὴν διαφθείρειν τῶν ἐναντίων γέλωτι, τὸν δὲ γέλωτα σπουδῇ, ὀρθῶς λέγων. Arist. Rhet. l. iii. c. 18.[53]

i. Est autem plane oratoris movere risum.—Res saepe, quas argumentis dilui non facile est, joco, risuque dissolvit.

k. Locus autem et regio quasi ridiculi, turpitudine quadam et deformitate continetur.—Nec insignis improbitas et scelere juncta, nec rursus miseria insignis agitata ridetur.—Quamobrem materies omnis ridiculorum est in istis vitiis,—quae neque odio magno, nec misericordia maxima digna sunt.

52. Depravity or wickedness (*OED*, 1).

53. Aristotle, *Rhetoric,* III.xviii. Brown's translation is accurate.

54. I.e., Caius Julius Caesar Strabo Vopiscus (*d.* 87 B.C.); Roman barrister; aedile; victim of Marius (Cicero, *Brutus,* LXXXIX.307).

it.[1] *4thly,* That its Force may consist either in Thought or Expression, but that its Perfection lies in a Union of both.[m] And lastly, That af[45]ter all, it is but the lowest Kind of Eloquence.[n]

QUINTILIAN builds chiefly on TULLY, when he treats of Ridicule in the sixth Book of his Institutions. He too considers it as a Branch of Eloquence, and gives Rules for its Efficacy and Restraint.[o]

l. In quo, non modo illud praecipitur, ne quid insulse; sed etiam, si quid perridicule possis: vitandum est oratori utrumque, ne aut scurrilis jocus sit, aut mimicus.

m. Duo sunt genera facetiarum, quorum alterum re tractatur, alterum dicto.— Nam quod quibuscunque verbis dixeris, facetum tamen est, *re* continetur: quod, mutatis verbis, salem amittit, in verbis habet leporem omnem.—maxime autem homines delectari, si quando risus conjuncte, *re, verboque* moveatur.[55]

n. Est, mea sententia, vel tenuissimus ingenii fructus. *De Oratore,* l. ii. *passim.*[56]

o. Risum judicis movendo, et illos tristes solvit affectus, et animum ab intentione rerum frequenter avertit: et aliquando etiam reficit, et à satietate vel à fatigatione renovat.—Habet enim, ut *Cicero* dicit, sedem in deformitate aliqua et turpitudine.— Rerum autem saepe, ut dixi, maximarum momenta vertit, cum odium iramque frequentissime frangat.—Ea quae dicit vir bonus, omnia salva dignitate ac verecundia dicet: nimium enim risus pretium est, si probitatis impendio constat. *Quint. Inst.* l. vi.[57]

55. "And again, it is clearly appropriate for an orator to raise a laugh . . . often matters which are not easily dispelled by arguments can be dispelled by a joke or a laugh" (*De Oratore,* II.lviii); "The field or province of the ridiculous, so to speak, is defined by unseemliness or ugliness . . . Neither outstanding wickedness, such as involves crime, nor outstanding wretchedness is assailed by ridicule. . . . This is why all the subjects of laughter are to be found in those vices . . . which excite neither great hatred nor great pity" (*De Oratore,* II.lviii–lix); "As to this, not only is there a rule excluding remarks made in bad taste, but also, even though you could say something to highly comic effect, an orator must avoid each of two dangers: he must not allow his jesting to decline into buffoonery or mere mimicry" (*De Oratore,* II.lix); "For there are two types of wit, one employed upon facts, the other upon words. . . . For the joke of enduring wit, in whatever words it is expressed, has its roots in fact; that which loses its pungency owes all its humour to its expression . . . men are most pleased when they are moved to laughter by the joint force of matter and manner" (*De Oratore,* II.lix, lxii and lxi).

56. "It is to my mind the poorest return for intelligence" (*De Oratore,* II.lx).

57. "[The talent] of dispelling the graver emotions of the judge by exciting his laughter, frequently diverts his attention from the facts of the case, and sometimes even refreshes him and revives him when he has begun to be bored or weary. . . . For, as Cicero says, laughter has its basis in some kind of deformity or ugliness. . . . Again, it frequently turns the scale in matters of great importance, as I have already observed, as when it often dispels hatred or anger. . . . A good man will see that everything he says is consistent with his dignity and the respectability of his character; for we pay too dearly for a laugh if we raise it at the cost of our own integrity" (Quintilian, *Institutio Oratoria,* VI.iii.i, 8, 9 and 35).

Now, in Consequence of these Proofs, a few Observations will naturally arise with regard to *Ridicule in particular,* similar to those which were made in the last Section, upon *Eloquence in general.*

As first: Ridicule must render every Proposition it supports *apparently true,* ere it can be received and acquiesced it. Thus every Opinion which Ridicule instills, tho' it be the pure Result of certain Images impressed on the Imagination, by which the Passion of Contempt is excited, is always [46] regarded as the Conviction of Reason, and received by the Mind as Truth. And thus by offering apparent Truth, Ridicule gains its End of Persuasion.

Again, it may be observed, that the Consequences of Ridicule with regard to *speculative* Instruction or Inquiry, are of a very different Nature from those which relate to Morals and Action. To the first it must ever be an *Enemy:* But to the latter it may be an Enemy or Friend according as it is fairly or dishonestly applied. It comes in to the Aid of Argument, when its Impressions on the Imagination and Passions are consistent with the real Nature of Things: When it strikes the Fancy and Affections with fictitious Images, it becomes the Instrument of Deceit.

Thus Ridicule may befriend either Truth or Falsehood: and as it is morally or immorally applied, may illustrate the one, or disguise the other. Yet it should seem, that the moral is more natural, than the immoral Application of Ridicule; inasmuch as Truth is more congenial to the Mind than Falsehood, and so, the *real* more easily made *apparent,* than the *fictitious* Images of Things. [47]

Ridicule, therefore, being of a vague, unsteady Nature, merely relative to the Imaginations and Passions of Mankind, there must be several Orders or Degrees of it, suited to the Fancies and Capacities of those whom the Artist attempts to influence. Among these several Kinds of Ridicule, Justness of Thought and Expression, adorned with striking Figures, is the *highest:* Coarse Language, Buffoonry, false and indecent Images, are the Characters of the *lowest.* For as the Imagination and Passions are then most refined and just, when they bear to the same Point with Reason; so, that Species of Ridicule is most genuine which tends to conduct them thither.

But, however Ridicule may *impress* the Idea of apparent Turpitude or Falsehood on the Imagination; yet still Reason remains the superior and corrective Power. Therefore, every Representation of Ridicule, which only applies to the Fancy and Affections, must *finally* be *examined* and *decided* upon, must be *tried, rejected,* or *received,* as the *reasoning Faculty* shall *determine.*

And thus *Ridicule* can never be a *Detector of Falsehood,* or a *Test of Truth.* [48]

SECTION V

In further Confirmation of these Truths, the direct Proofs of which may possibly lie somewhat remote from common Apprehension, let us appeal to Experience; to the general Sense and Practice of Mankind. And here we shall find, that Contempt and Ridicule are always founded on *preconceived Opinion,* whatever be the Foundation of it, whether *Reason* or *Imagination, Truth* or *Falsehood.*

For in Fact, do not we see every different Party and Association of Men despising and deriding each other according to their various Manner of Thought, Speech, and Action? Does not the Courtier deride the Foxhunter, and the Foxhunter the Courtier? What is more ridiculous to a Beau, than a Philosopher; to a Philosopher, than a Beau? Drunkards are the Jest of sober Men, and sober Men of Drunkards. Physicians, Lawyers, Soldiers, Priests, and Freethinkers, are the standing Subjects of Ridicule to one another. Wisdom and Folly, the Virtuous and the Vile, the Learned and Ignorant, the Temperate and Debauched, [49] all give and return the Jest. According to the various Impressions of Fancy and Affection, the Aspects of Things are varied; and consequently the same Object, seen under these different Lights and Attitudes, must in one Mind produce *Approbation,* in another *Contempt.*

If we examine the Conduct of *political* Bodies or *religious* Sects, we shall find it of a similar Nature. Each of these *railly*[58] every other, according to the Prejudices they have imbibed in Favour of their own System. How contemptible and ridiculous are the *European* Forms of

58. To tease, joke, or mock (*OED,* 1).

Government, in the Eyes of an *Asiatic?*ᵖ And do not we on this Side the *Hellespont* repay them in their own Kind? Are we a whit more united among ourselves in our Ideas of the *Ridiculous,* when applied to Modes of Empire? What is more contemptible to an *Englishman,* than that slavish Submission to arbitrary Will and lawless Power, which prevails almost universally on the Continent? And they are little acquainted with the State [50] of Affairs *abroad,* who know not that, within the Precincts of Tyranny, *English Freedom* is one of the commonest Topics of Raillery and Ridicule: Every Man's judging for himself, is the Subject of the *Frenchman's* Drollery: One Man's judging *for all,* is the Subject of ours. The Case is parallel with regard to religious Tenets, where People are at Liberty to speak their Thoughts. Is there any Species of Invective which the Church of *Rome* hath not exercised upon all who have dissented from its Measures? And have not the Divines of the *reformed* Churches been as arrant *Droles,* in Vindication of their respective Systems? What Ribaldry and coarse Banter hath been thrown (nay rather, what hath *not* been thrown) by the *Freethinkers,* on Religion and *Christianity?* And how basely have some of our Divines prostituted their Pens in former Days, by descending to the same dirty Level? Even the Soureness of Puritanism, nay, the Sullenness of *Quakerism* have sometimes relaxed and yielded themselves up to the Love of *Joking:* And sly Hints, in demure Phrase and sober Countenance, have as plainly spoken their Contempt of those they pitied, as the loud Laughter and Grimace [51] of worldly Men, the Disdain of those they profess to hate.

But what need we wonder that a Difference of Opinion in such weighty Affairs as those of Government and Religion should inspire a mutual Contempt, when we see that any considerable Variation of Manners in the most ordinary Circumstances of Life has the same Effect? The Customs of ancient Times have been held so ridiculous by many Moderns, that honest HOMER hath been branded as a Dunce, only

---

p. A *Venetian* was introduced to the King of *Pegu:* When this Prince was informed by him, that the *Venetians* had *no King,* he *laughed* so excessively, that he lost his Breath, and could not speak for a good while. *Recueil des Voyages, &c.*⁵⁹

59. Untraced.

because he hath recorded them. What Raillery hath been thrown on the venerable Bard, as well as the Hero he describes, only because he hath told us, that PATROCLUS acted in the Capacity of *Cook* for himself, and his Friend *Achilles:*[q] And that the Princess *Nausicaa* followed by all her Maids, went down to wash the King's and Queen's Cloaths along with her own?[r] *Rebecca* and her *Historian*[s] have fallen under the same ignorant Censure, because she went down *to draw Water:*[62] And so have the Daughters of AUGUSTUS, for spinning their Father's Cloaths, [52] when he was Master of the World.[63] Thus the undebauched Simplicity of ancient Times, becomes the Jest of modern Luxury and Folly. From the same Principle, any new Mode of Speech or Action, seen in our own Times, appears ridiculous to those who give Way to the Sallies of *uninformed* Contempt and Laughter. What superior Airs of Mirth and Gayety may be seen in a Club of Citizens, passing Judgment on the *Scotch,* the *Western,* or any other *remote provincial Dialect?* while at *the other End of the Town,*[64] the Stream of *Ridicule* runs as strong on the Manners and Dialect of the *Exchange.* The least unusual Circumstance of Habit, beyond what the Fashion prescribes, is by turns so sensibly ridiculous, that one half of the Expence of Dress seems to consist in accommodating it to the Dictates and Caprice of the current Opinion. And it is a just Complaint of the greatest Tragic Poet of the Age, that this indulged Spirit of Ridicule is a fundamental Obstruction to the Improvement of the *French* Theatre. "We dare not, says he, hazard any thing new upon the Stage, in

q. *Il.*[60]

r. *Odyss.*[61]

s. *Genesis.*

60. Patroclus was the son of Menoetius, and the favorite companion of Achilles. For the reference to his cooking, see *Iliad*, XIX.315–18.

61. Nausicaa was the daughter of the Phaeacian king Alcinous; she was approached by the shipwrecked Odysseus after she had finished washing the household linen: cf. *Odyssey*, VI.20–148.

62. Cf. Genesis 24:10–28.

63. Cf. Suetonius, "Divus Augustus," LXXIII.

64. A reference to the social geography of London. In the eighteenth century (and since) the City of London in the east of the conurbation has been the site of finance and trade, while the west end, comprising Westminster, Kensington, and Chelsea, has been the home of fashion and leisure.

the Presence of a People whose constant [53] Practice is, *to ridicule every thing that is not fashionable."*ᵗ

Neither is the Taste of Mankind less capricious with regard to the Methods of Ridicule,ᵛ than the Objects of it. How many *Sayings* and *Repartées* are recorded from Antiquity as the Quintessence of Raillery, which among *us* only raise a Laugh, because they are *insipid?* TULLY himself often attempts in vain to extort a Smile from his modern Reader. Even the *sales Plautini*⁶⁶ have in great Measure lost their *Poignancy.* There is a certain *Mode* of Ridicule peculiar to every Age and Country. What a curious Contrast to each other are an *Italian* and a *Dutch* Buffoon? And I suppose the Raillery of a *French* and a *Russian* Drole are as different as the nimble Pranks of a *Monkey,* from the rude Gambols of a *Bear.* Even the same Country hath numerous Subdivisions and *under* [54] *Species* of Ridicule. What is high Humour at *Wapping,* is rejected as nauseous in the *City:* What is delicate Raillery in *the City,* grows *coarse* and *intolerable* as you approach *St. James's:*⁶⁸ And many a well meant Joke, that passes

t. Nous craignons de hazarder sur la scene de spectacles nouveaux devant une nation accoutumée à tourner en ridicule tout ce qui n'est pas *d'Usage.* Voltaire, *Disc. sur la trag.*⁶⁵

v. Quaenam tandem in loquendo, aut in scribendo, quasi titillatione risum lacessunt? dictum unum, aut alterum: brevicula narratio: nonnihil repentinum, et fortuitum, et recens, et novitate sua primum. Vavassor, *De ludicra dictione.*⁶⁷

65. "We fear to run the risk of staging novelties before a nation given to mocking everything which is not familiar"; Voltaire, "Discours sur la tragedie," in *Le Brutus, de Monsieur de Voltaire, avec un discours sur la tragedie* ("Paris" [London], 1731), pp. vii–viii.

66. "The wit of Plautus." Cf. Horace, *Ars Poetica,* ll. 270–71: "at vestri proavi Plautinos et numeros et | laudavere sales"; "Yet your forefathers praised both the prosody and the wit of Plautus."

67. François Vavasseur (1605–81); Jesuit priest; poet and scholar. "For, finally, what raises a laugh, as it were by titillation, either in speaking or writing? Opinions vary: a somewhat short relation; something slightly unexpected, and casual, and fresh, and eminent in its newness" (François Vavasseur, *De ludicra dictione liber in quo tota iocandi ratio ex veterum scriptis aestimatur* [Paris, 1658], pp. 429–30).

68. Wapping is a working class district in the East End of London. The City is the financial and trade district slightly further west. St. James's, further west again, is the center of political power, noble birth, and high fashion. Brown is perhaps recalling Swift's hyperbole about the geographical specificity of modern humor in the "Preface" to *A Tale of a Tub* (1704): "Such a jest there is, that will not pass out of *Covent-Garden*; and such a one, that is no where intelligible but at Hide-Park Corner" (Swift, *Prose Works,* vol. I, p. 26).

unheeded in all these various Districts, would set an innocent Country Village in an Uproar of Laughter.

This Subject might be much enlarged on: For the Modes and Objects of Ridicule are as indefinite as the imagined Combinations of Things. But from these Examples drawn from the Conduct of particulars, it appears no less than from the general Nature and Faculties of Man, that Ridicule hath no other Source than Imagination, Passion, Prejudice, and preconceived Opinion: And therefore can never be *the Detecter of Falsehood,* or *Test of Truth.*

SECTION VI

The Cause might be safely rested here. Yet, to throw a still clearer Light on the Subject of our Enquiry, let us now examine what his Lordship hath advanced in Support of his new Method of Investigation. [55] And as the noble Writer hath not thought it expedient to descend often to the argumentative Way; we must make the most of what we find in him that looks like a Reason.

He tells his Friend, that "nothing is ridiculous except what is deformed; nor is any thing Proof against Raillery, except what is handsome and just:—one may defy the World to turn real Bravery and Generosity into Ridicule. A Man must be soundly ridiculous, who, with all the Wit imaginable, would go about to ridicule Wisdom, or laugh at Honesty or good Manners."ʷ

Here we have a Mixture of equivocal Language and pompous Declamation. If he means to assert, that "nothing is ridiculous, except what is *apparently* deformed," the Proposition is true, but foreign to the Purpose: Because, through the Error of Imagination, Things *apparently deformed* may be *really beautiful.* If he means to assert, that "nothing can be made to appear ridiculous, but what is *really* deformed," I should be glad to know where the noble Author had conversed: In the [56] *Platonic Republic,* it

---

w. Vol. i. p. 128, 129.[69]

69. Shaftesbury, *Characteristicks,* vol. I, pp. 80–81.

may be so: But, in our *Gothic* Systems,[70] Matters go quite otherwise: So far as common Observation reaches, it is easiest of all Things to make that *appear* ridiculous, which is not *really* deformed: And how should it be otherwise, while the human Imagination is liable to be imposed on, and capable of receiving *fictitious* for *real* Representations?

The noble Author tells us next, that "nothing is Proof against Raillery, except what is handsome and just."—Perhaps, nor *that* neither. Though it be true, that nothing of the opposite Kind is proof against Raillery; yet sure it is a strange Mistake to imagine, that what is really handsome and just is always Proof against it. For, by fictitious Images impressed on the Fancy, what is *really* handsome and just, is often rendered *apparently* false and deformed; and thus becomes *actually* contemptible and ridiculous.

But "one may defy the World to turn real Bravery and Generosity into Ridicule." Safely, my Lord; while they retain their *native Appearance*, and Beauty of Proportion. But alas, how easy is it to *disguise* them! It is but concealing, varying, [57] or adding a Circumstance that may strike the Fancy, and they at once assume new Shapes, new Names, and Natures. Thus the *Virtues* which, seen in a direct Light, attract our Admiration by their *Beauty*; when beheld through the oblique Mediums of Ridicule start up in the Forms of *Ideots, Hags,* and *Monsters.*

But the noble Writer enforces these general Appeals to Fact, by one extraordinary Instance. He tells us, "The divinest Man who had ever appeared in the Heathen World, was in the Height of witty Times, and by the wittiest of all Poets, most abominably ridiculed, in a whole Comedy writ and acted on Purpose: But so far was this from sinking his Reputation, or suppressing his Philosophy, that they each increased the more for it."[x] It must be owned, this is an extraordinary Assertion, unless he means

x. Vol. i. p. 31.[71]

70. Respectively, the utopian political regime described in Plato's *Republic,* and the irregular but liberal political constitutions of the nations of Western Europe which were supposed to derive ultimately from the barbaric political arrangements of the Goths and Saxons. Blackstone would extol the British political inheritance from "our Saxon ancestors" as the "most important guardian both of public and private liberty" (Blackstone, *Commentaries,* vol. IV, p. 407).

71. Shaftesbury, *Characteristicks,* vol. I, p. 20.

to affirm, that the Reputation and Philosophy of SOCRATES[72] arose from his Blood, as "the *Christian* Sects sprung from the Blood of Martyrs."[y] For it appears from all the Records of Antiquity, that the Wit of ARIS-TOPHANES was the most formidable Enemy that ever attacked [58] the divine Philosopher: This whetted the Rage of a *misled* Multitude, and dragged to Death that Virtue which hath ever since been the Admiration of Mankind. In this Opinion, we have the Concurrence of the first Writer of the present Age:[z] And the Confession of another,[75] who, although of a Turn conceited and fantastical enough, is yet of unquestioned Credit for his Ingenuity and Learning. This Writer, speaking of the wild Wit of an ARISTOPHANES, tells us, that "the Comedy inscribed *The Clouds*, is an execrable Attempt to expose one of the wisest and best of Men to the Fury and Contempt of a *lewd Multitude*, in which it had but *too much Success*."[a]

'Tis true, PALMERIUS,[76] a learned *French* Critic of the last Age, had, from the Number of Years between the acting *The Clouds* of ARIS-

y. Vol. i.[73]

z. Ded. to the *Div. Leg. of Moses*, p. 20.[74]

a. *Letters on Mythology*, p. 262.

72. The New Learning associated with the philosopher Socrates (469–399 B.C.) was satirized by the playwright Aristophanes (*c*. 448–*c*. 380 B.C.) in *The Clouds* (423 B.C.). Socrates had made enemies among the Athenians for his independence of mind and his unwillingness to accept at face value the reputations of those considered to be wise. In 399 B.C. he was tried and sentenced to death on a charge of introducing new deities and corrupting youth. His self-possession in the face of death is memorably described by Plato in the *Phaedo*, and had provided the subject for Brown's first attempt at writing for the stage; cf. Brown to Gilpin, 20 August 1744 (Bodl. MS Eng. Misc. c. 389, fol. 70^{r-v}) and the "Introduction," pp. ix–xxv.

73. Shaftesbury, *Characteristicks*, vol. I, p. 17.

74. Cf. above, p. 48, n. 48. Warburton, *Divine Legation*, vol. I, pp. xix–xx (and note the polite reference to Brown in the footnote).

75. Thomas Blackwell, *Letters Concerning Mythology* (1746), p. 262, n. "k."

76. Jacques le Paulmier de Grentemesnil (1587–1670); classical scholar and geographer. In his *Exercitationes in Optimos Fere Auctores Graecos* (Lugduni Batavorum, 1668), le Paulmier offers the following argument for why Aristophanes did not write *The Clouds* in order to procure the arrest, condemnation, and execution of Socrates: "Nunc autem antequam natalia sua ei assignemus, refutanda est quorundam antiquorum sententia, qui eam comoediam volunt ab Aristophane compositam suasu Anyti & Meliti accusationem Socratis praemeditantium, ut ex ea judicii Atheniensium experimentum facerent. Eorum familiam ducit Aelianus lib. 2 cap. 13, qui quidem asserit Anytum & Melitum data pecunia subornasse Aristophanem, ut Socratem ad

TOPHANES, and the Death of SOCRATES, pretended that AELIAN[77] was mistaken in assigning this Play as one of the principal Causes of his Destruction. P. BRUMOY,[78] who has wrote so excellently of the *Greek Theatre*, after having examined [59] the Affair with the utmost Candour,

---

populum traduceret: eum sequutus est Eunapius in Aedesio, quibus astipulatur etiam Thomas magister in hujus fabulae argumento, & alii Scholiastae; & sic videntur innuere eam comoediam prodiisse paulo ante Socratis accusationem & condemnationem. Nam si ea fuit praeparatio ac veluti prolusis accusationis, ex ratione consequens erat, ut recentibus odiis, quae illud drama excitaverat, vorsis armis accusationem instituerent. Sed eorum sententiae ipsa fabula valide repugnat. Nam ex ejus quibusdam locis (ut infra notabimus) patet eam compositam fuisse Cleone adhuc vivente. At Cleon occisus est anno 10 belli Pelopponesiaci teste Thucydide, quo tempore Aminias erat Archon secundum Diodorum anno 2 Olymp. 89. Socratis vero accusatio & condemnatio facta est Archonte Lachete anno 1 Olymp. 95, annis post Cloenis mortem 23. Itaque annis 24 vel 25 praecessisset parasceve haec accusationem Socratis, quod omnino absurdum est. . . . Ergo Aristophanis in Socratem maledicentia causa non fuit corruptela & pecuniarum acceptio ad Anyto & Melito" (pp. 729–30); "Now, however, before we describe his [Aristophanes's] genealogy, we must refute the opinion of certain of the ancients, who will have it that this comedy [*The Clouds*] was composed by Aristophanes at the instigation of Anytus and Melitus, who were planning the indictment of Socrates, in order to manipulate the judgement of the Athenians. Aelian (II.13) is at the head of this troop, who asserts that Anytus and Melitus bribed Aristophanes to betray Socrates to the people. He is followed by Eunapius in Aedesius, and joined in the argument of this fabulous stipulation by master Thomas and other scholiasts. Thus they seem to hint that this comedy was produced shortly before the trial and sentencing of Socrates. For if it were composed to prepare the ground for the trial, it should by reason follow that it would lead the trial toward a violent outcome by means of the fresh resentments stirred up by the play. But the story itself strongly undermines the opinions of these men. For on the basis of certain passages in the play (which we will cite below), it is clear that it was composed while Cleon was still alive. Now Cleon was killed in the tenth year of the Peloponnesian War, as Thucydides attests; when Aminias was Archon, following Diodorus, in the second year of the 89th Olympiad. Now it is a fact that the trial and execution of Socrates occurred when Lachetes was Archon, in the first year of the 95th Olympiad, 23 years after the death of Cleon. Therefore the play was composed some 24 or 25 years before the trial of Socrates; which is wholly absurd. . . . Therefore, Aristophanes was not suborned to blacken Socrates, and he did not take money from Anytus and Melitus." In 1744 Brown had begun composition of a tragedy on the subject of the death of Socrates, and transcribed passages from the work in progress in his letters to William Gilpin (Bodl. MS Eng. Misc. c. 389, fol. 70ʳ⁻ᵛ).

77. Claudius Aelianus (fl. *c.* 200 A.D.); the author of fourteen books of "Historical Miscellanies" containing many anecdotes relating to political and literary celebrities.

78. Pierre Brumoy (1688–1742); Jesuit priest; historian, poet, and literary scholar. Cf. *The Greek Theatre of Father Brumoy*, tr. Charlotte Lennox, 3 vols (1759), vol. III, p. 222.

concludes thus: "His Account (AELIAN's) seems only defective, in that he hath not remarked the long interval that passed between the Representation of *The Clouds,* and the Condemnation of SOCRATES. But although the Comedy did not give the finishing Stroke to SOCRATES; yet it might have indisposed the Minds of the People, since these *comic Accusations* became *very serious ones,* which at length destroyed the wisest of the *Greeks.*"[b] But since the noble Author seems to have adopted the other Opinion, and, as I am told, some shallow Mimics of modern Platonism have lately stollen PALMERIUS's Criticism, and revived this stale Pretence, of the Number of Years between the Representation of *The Clouds,* and the Death of SOCRATES; it may be necessary to transcribe the following Passage from PLATO's *Apology,* which puts the Matter beyond all Doubt:

> But it [60] is just, O *Athenians,* that I should first reply to the false Charge of my FIRST ACCUSERS. Because several laid their groundless Accusations against me, MANY YEARS AGO: *whom* I DREAD MORE *than the Adherents of* ANYTUS; though these too be very powerful in Persuasion: But those are still *more powerful,* who have possessed and sway'd you FROM YOUR VERY INFANCY, in laying false Accusations against me. Many, indeed, have been these my Accusers, and LONG HAVE THEY CONTINUED thus to accuse me, and *persuaded* and *misled* you at that EARLY AGE, when you were MOST EASY OF BELIEF: While I, in the mean Time, was without one Defender. And what is worst of all, I know not so much as their very Names, *except only that of* THE COMEDIAN.—What then do my Accusers say?—SOCRATES is criminal, in that he enquires too curiously concerning what is under the Earth, and in the Heavens, and in that he can make the worse appear the better Reason; and that he teaches these Things to others. Such then is the Accusation: *For such Things you saw in* [61] ARISTOPHANES's COMEDY, where a fictitious SOCRATES *is carried about,*

---

b. Son recit ne semble defectueux que pour n'avoir pas marqué le long intervalle qui se passa entre la representation des Nuees, et la condemnation de Socrate. Concluons que, bien que sa comedie n'ait pas porté le dernier coup à Socrate, elle a pu indisposer les esprits, puisque les accusations comiques devinrent des accusations tres serieuses, qui perdirent enfin le plus sage des Grecs. Tom. v. p. 360.

affirming, that he takes Journeys through the Air, and talking much more idle Stuff of the same Nature."[c]

Here we see, the Philosopher refers their Accusation to its *original Cause:* And this he positively affirms, was no other than the *old Impressions* made against him on the [62] Minds of the *Athenians, by the Comedy of* THE CLOUDS.[d]

So much for the Silencing, which is the only Conviction, of Obstinacy and Ignorance. But in Reality, it is a Matter of small Consequence, in the present Question, Whether the Ridicule of the comic Poet was in Fact

c. Πρῶτον μὲν οὖν δίκαιός εἰμι ἀπολογήσασθαι, ὦ ἄνδρες Ἀθηναῖοι, πρὸς τὰ πρῶτά μου ψευδῆ κατηγορημένα, καὶ τοὺς πρώτους κατηγόρους,—ἐμοῦ γὰρ πολλοὶ κατήγοροι γεγόνασι πρὸς ὑμᾶς, καὶ πάλαι πολλὰ ἤδη ἔτη, καὶ οὐδὲν ἀληθὲς λέγοντες οὓς ἐγὼ μᾶλλον φοβοῦμαι ἢ τοὺς ἀμφὶ Ἄνυτον, καίπερ ὄντας καὶ τούτους δεινούς· ἀλλ᾽ ἐκεῖνοι δεινότεροι, ὦ ἄνδρες, οἳ ὑμῶν τοὺς πολλοὺς ἐκ παίδων παραλαμβάνοντες, ἔπειθόν τε καὶ κατηγόρουν ἐμοῦ μᾶλλον οὐδὲν ἀληθές, ἔπειτά εἰσιν οὗτοι οἱ κατήγοροι πολλοὶ καὶ πολὺν χρόνον ἤδη κατηγορηκότες, ἔτι δὲ καὶ ἐν ταύτῃ τῇ ἡλικίᾳ λέγοντες πρὸς ὑμᾶς, ἐν ᾗ ἂν μάλιστα ἐπιστεύσατε, παῖδες ὄντες ἔνιοι ὑμῶν καὶ μειράκια ἀτεχνῶς, ἐρήμην κατηγοροῦντες, ἀπολογουμένου οὐδενός. ὃ δὲ πάντων ἀλογώτατον, ὅτι οὐδὲ τὰ ὀνόματα οἷόν τε αὐτῶν εἰδέναι καὶ εἰπεῖν, πλὴν εἴ τις κωμῳδοποιὸς τυγχάνει ὤν.—τί δὴ λέγοντες διέβαλλον οἱ διαβάλλοντες;—Σωκράτης ἀδικεῖ, καὶ περιεργάζεται ζητῶν τά τε ὑπὸ γῆς καὶ οὐράνια καὶ τὸν ἥττω λόγον κρείττω ποιῶν καὶ ἄλλοις ταὐτὰ ταῦτα διδάσκων. τοιαύτη τίς ἐστιν· ταῦτα γὰρ ἑωρᾶτε καὶ αὐτοὶ ἐν τῇ Ἀριστοφάνους κωμῳδίᾳ, Σωκράτη τινὰ ἐκεῖ περιφερόμενον, φάσκοντά τε ἀεροβατεῖν, καὶ ἄλλην πολλὴν φλυαρίαν φλυαροῦντα. Plat. *Apol. Soc.*[79]

d. As so much stir hath been made about the Case of *Socrates* with regard to Ridicule, it may not be amiss to shew what *his* Opinion of it was in general, when considered as a *Test of Truth*. In the fifth Book of *Plato's* Republic, *Socrates* proposes that Women should engage in all the public Affairs of Life, along with Men. This, to *Glauco*, appears *ridiculous* in some of its Circumstances. *Socrates* replies, "That may be: But let us go to *the Merits* of the Question, *setting aside all Raillery*, advising the Railleurs *to be serious*, and putting them in Mind, that the very Practice now approved in *Greece* (of Men appearing naked) was, not long ago, treated there with the highest Ridicule: as it is to this Day among many Barbarians."— πορευτέον πρὸς τὸ τραχὺ τοῦ νόμου, δεηθεῖσίν τε τούτων, μὴ τὰ αὑτῶν πράττειν, ἀλλὰ σπουδάζειν, καὶ ὑπομνήσασιν ὅτι οὐ πολὺς χρόνος ἐξ οὗ τοῖς Ἕλλησιν ἐδόκει αἰσχρὰ εἶναι καὶ γελοῖα ἅπερ νῦν τοῖς πολλοῖς τῶν βαρβάρων, γυμνοὺς ἄνδρας ὁρᾶσθαι. The following Part of this Passage I would recommend to the modern Patronizers of the *Way of Ridicule*.[80]

79. Plato, *Apology*, 2–3.
80. Plato, *Republic*, V.iii.

destructive to the divine Philosopher or not. But as it demonstrably was, it is therefore a Case in Point. However, suppose it was not; what is the Consequence? Why, only this: That dishonest [63] Ridicule failed of its desired Success, *in one Instance.* And how does this affect the Question, so long as Ten thousand other Instances may be alledged to the contrary, which no Man, that is not void of common Sense or common Honesty, can possibly deny?

From the Appeals to Fact, already made,[e] may be drawn innumerable Instances of this Nature. There we see Truth, Wisdom, Virtue, Liberty, successfully disguised and derided; by this very means the Cause of Falsehood, Folly, Vice, Tyranny maintained: If to these it were necessary to add more; we cannot perhaps in History find a more flagrant Proof of the Power of Ridicule against *Virtue herself,* than in that Heap of *execrable Comedies,*[81] which have been the Bane and Reproach of this Kingdom thro' a Series of ninety Years. During this Period, the Generality of our comic Poets have been the unwearied *Ministers of Vice:* And have done her Work with so thorough an Industry, that it would be hard to find one Virtue, which they have not *sacrificed* at her Shrine. As Effects once established are not easily removed, so not only this, but the [64] succeeding Generation will probably retain the Impressions made in the two preceding ones; when Innocence was the Sport of abandoned Villany; and the *successful Adulterer decked out* with all the *Poet's Art,* at the Expence of the *ridiculed* and *injured Husband:* When moral Virtue and Religion were made the Jest of the *licentious*; and female *Modesty* was banished, to make Way for shameless *Effrontery:*

> The Fair sat panting at a *Courtier's* Play,
> And not a Mask went unimprov'd away:
> The *modest* Fan was lifted up no more,
> And Virgins *smil'd* at what they *blush'd* before.[f]

e. See above § 5.

f. Essay on Criticism.[82]

81. An allusion to Restoration comedies such as Wycherley's *The Country Wife* (1675), Etherege's *The Man of Mode* (1676), and later works such as Congreve's *The Way of the World* (1700). The sexual license of the Restoration stage had been attacked by Jeremy Collier in his *Short View of the Profaneness and Immorality of the English Stage* (1698), and by Steele in *The Spectator* no. 65 (15 May 1711).

82. Pope, *An Essay on Criticism* (1711), ll. 540–43.

SECTION VII

Here then we have accumulated Proofs of the fatal Influences of Ridicule, when let loose from the Restraints of Reason.

Yet still his Lordship insists, that "Truth, 'tis supposed, may bear all Lights."[g] To which it is replied, that "Truth will indeed bear every Light, *but a false one.*" He adds, that "one of those principal Lights or natural Mediums by which [65] Things are to be viewed, in order to a thorow Recognition, is Ridicule itself."[h] This is full as wise a Method to manifest the Rectitude of Truth, as it would be to shew the Rectitude of a ruling Staff,[85] to immerge one part of it in clear Water. The Staff indeed would still continue strait, but the two *Mediums,* in which it lies, though both *natural* ones, would concur to make it appear crooked. Just so it is with Truth, when half shewn by the *Medium of Reason,* and the other half, by the *Medium of Ridicule.*

But the noble Writer asks us, "How can any one of the least Justness of Thought endure a Ridicule wrong placed?"[i]—I answer, by being *mis-led* or *mistaken*; and then Men are ready to *bear* any thing. Shew me him whose Imagination never received or retained a false Impression, and I shall readily allow he can never *endure a Ridicule wrong placed.* But of this *infallible* Race I know none, except the Inhabitants of *Utopia.* 'Tis true, he candidly acknowledges, that "the *Vulgar* may swallow any *sordid Jest,* any *mere Drollery* and *Buffoonry.*"[k] Indeed! How [66] then can he *defy the World to turn real Bravery or Generosity into Ridicule, or laugh successfully at Honesty or Good-manners?* And where was the Wonder or Improbability,

g. Vol. i. p. 61.[83]
h. Vol. i. p. 61.[84]
i. Ibid. p. 11.[86]
k. Ibid.[87]
83. Shaftesbury, *Characteristicks*, vol. I, p. 40.
84. Ibid.
85. A badge of office in the royal household (*OED*, 7).
86. Shaftesbury, *Characteristicks*, vol. I, p. 8.
87. Ibid.

that the Wit of Aristophanes should incite a *lewd Multitude* to destroy the *divine Philosopher?*[1]

But then he tells us, "It must be a finer and truer Wit that takes with the men of *Sense* and *Breeding*."[m] This Sentence it must be owned is artful enough: Because it obliges one to make a Separation that may look like *ill-natured*, before one can expose its Weakness. A truer Wit indeed may be necessary to take with the *Men of Sense*; but these, I apprehend, may sometimes be distinguished from the *Men of Breeding:* For it is certain, that in most Countries the Vulgar are a much more *considerable* Body, than is generally imagined. Yet, although neither *Reason* nor the *Passions* gain any Advantages from *high Life*, [67] it must be owned, the Imagination acquires a certain *Delicacy,* which the *low Vulgar* are generally Strangers to. The coarse Pranks of a *merry Andrew*[90] that engage the Attention of a *Country Fair,* would make but a poor Figure at *St. James's.*[91] But still it is only in the *Modes,* not the Objects of Ridicule, with regard to which the *Courtier* differs from the *Clown.* The *Peasant* and his *Lord* are equally susceptible of false Impressions; equally liable to have Falsehood obtruded on them for Truth, Folly for Wisdom, Vice for Virtue: The Methods only of Ridicule, the Engines of Deceit must vary; must be accommodated to the different Views of Things and Circumstances of Life, among which they have respectively been conversant. Thus it must indeed be a *finer*, but by no means a *truer* Kind of Wit, that takes with the *Men of Breeding*.

l. L'Impudence qu'il avoit de tourner en ridicule la religion, devoit être reprimée: car une refutation serieuse ne fait pas à beaucoup près tant de mal, que les railleries d'un homme d'esprit. Les *jeunes gens* se laissent gater par ces sortes de moqueurs plus que l'on ne sçauroit dire. Bayle, art. Bion.[88]

m. Vol. i. p. II.[89]

88. "His Impudence in turning Religion into Ridicule ought to have been restrained; for a serious Refutation does not near so much harm as the Jests of a witty Man. Young Persons suffer themselves to be led away by these kind of Mockers, more than can be imagined" (Bayle, *Dictionary*, vol. II, p. 12, n. *C*).

89. Shaftesbury, *Characteristicks*, vol. I, p. 8.

90. A person who entertains people with antics and buffoonery; a clown; a mountebank's assistant (*OED*).

91. Cf. above, p. 57, n. 68.

The noble Writer proceeds to ask, "What Rule or Measure is there in the World, except in the considering the real Temper of Things, to find which are truly serious, and which ridiculous? And how can this be done, unless by applying [68] the Ridicule, to see whether it will bear?"ⁿ— Yes sure, there is another Rule: The Rule of Reason: Which alone can distinguish Appearances from Realities, and fix the true Nature of Things: From whose Determinations alone, we ever can distinguish true from pretended Gravity, just from groundless Raillery. But the Way of Investigation here proposed by his Lordship, inverts the very Order and Constitution of Things: By this means Appearances take the Place of Realities; Imagination usurps the Sovereignty which belongs to Reason; and Ridicule is made the Test of what is rational, instead of Reason being made the Test of what is ridiculous.

Yet still the noble Author suspects ill Consequences: That Subjects "may be very grave and weighty *in our Imagination,* but very ridiculous and impertinent in their own Nature."º True: and on the other hand, Things may appear ridiculous and impertinent *in our Imagination,* which are very grave and weighty in their own Nature. What then is the Consequence in either Case? Why, only this: That *Ima*[69]*gination,* and therefore *Ridicule* which depends upon it, can never be a *Test* of Truth.

But his Lordship insists, that "Gravity is of the very Essence of Imposture."ᴾ Yet this will do little for his Purpose, unless he can prove too, that "Imposture is of the Essence of Gravity." And if so, what will become of the *Enquiry concerning Virtue?* Gravity, it is true, is commonly an Attendant of Imposture: And so is Laughter, generally speaking, of Folly. With as much Reason therefore as the noble Writer infers from hence, that Gravity is Imposture, we may infer that Laughter is Folly in Disguise. In Truth, the Inference is groundless, in both Cases. Though every Knave should affect Gravity, yet every grave Man is not a Knave: Though

n. Vol. i. p. 12.[92]
o. Ibid p. 11.[93]
p. Vol. i. p. 11.[94]
92. Shaftesbury, *Characteristicks,* vol. I, p. 8.
93. Ibid.
94. Ibid.

every Fool will be Laughing, yet every Man that laughs is not a Fool: We may be serious and honest, as well as merry and wise. Mirth and Gravity are both harmless Things, provided they be properly applied: And we have seen that it is the Province of Reason alone, to determine when they are so.

But after all, the Proposition, that *Gravity is of the Essence of Imposture*, is false: [70] It is only an occasional, though, indeed, a pretty close, attendant, since this other Maxim was taken for granted, that *Reason was the Test of Truth*. Let once his Lordship's be generally embraced, that *Ridicule* is so, and we should soon see *Buffoonry* as close an Attendant on Imposture as now *Gravity*. The Tryal has been made; and successfully enough too, by him who has kept the Multitude in Opinion for twenty Years together; and by this Time, perhaps, himself, that Learning and Religion are better taught in his Conventicle, than in all the Universities and Churches of *Christendom* put together. And sure if any thing be the *Essence* of his *Imposture*, it is *Buffoonry*.

And here let us not forget to observe, that the noble Writer often (as in the Passage last cited) confounds *Mirth, Urbanity,* or *Good-humour,* with *Raillery* or *Ridicule:* Than which, no two Things in Nature are more diametrically opposite. The first, as it ariseth solely from *sudden* and *pleasing Resemblances* impressed on the Imagination, is justly regarded by all, as the best *Mediator* in every Debate. The last, as it ariseth solely from *Contempt,* is therefore no less justly regarded by most, as an *Embroiler* and [71] *Incendiary*. He sets out with a formal Profession of proving the Efficacy of Humour and Ridicule in the Investigation of Truth: Yet, by shifting and mixing his Terms, he generally slides insensibly into mere Encomiums on *Good-breeding, Chearfulness, Urbanity,* and *free Enquiry*; and then, from these Premises, often draws Consequences in Favour of *Ridicule,* as if it were an *equivalent Term*. This indeed keeps something like an Argument on Foot, and misleads the superficial Reader.

But the noble Author triumphs in another Observation: When speaking of *modern Zealots,* he tells us, that "whatever they think grave and solemn, they suppose must never be treated out of a grave and solemn Way. Though what another thinks so, they can be contented to treat otherwise: And are forward to try the Edge of Ridicule against any Opinions besides their own."[q] Now, if this be so; how is *Gravity of the Essence of Imposture*, as he had before affirmed? But whatever becomes of that Proposition, the Remark is just. And whomsoever he means to Compliment with the Name of *Zealots*, whe[72]ther in Religion or Freethinking, I shall not compliment as Exceptions to the Truth of it. There is scarce a Topic of Religion, either for its Dishonour or Support, that hath not been exposed to the illiberal Jokes of some Bungler in Controversy. And a much coarser Advocate in the Cause of Ridicule,[r] hath wrote an elaborate and most tedious Dissertation, to prove that the Way of Raillery hath been success-fully applied by every Sect of Religionists and Infidels, to the Destruc-tion of each other's Tenets, and the Establishment of their own. How he gains his Conclusion, that an Engine which tends to fix Mankind in their preconceived Opinions, and establish so many Species of Error, is of Im-portance and Efficacy in the Search of Truth, may not be so easy to deter-mine. In the mean time, in Reply to his whole Treatise, as well as to the last mentioned Remark of our noble Author, it may be sufficient to ob-serve, that Mankind often retain their own, and oppose others' Opinions, from an imperfect View of the Nature of Things: Their peculiar Tenets in Religion, as in other Subjects, are often founded in Imagination only: Their Ob[73]jections to those of others are often as groundless and fanci-ful. How natural then is it for them to communicate their Opinions on that Foundation on which they received them? How natural, that they should throw the Colours of Imagination on the Tenets they oppose? That they should obtrude the like fictitious Images on others, which themselves have embraced as Truth? That they should hold forth Appearances for

q. Vol. i. p. 60.[95]
r. Supposed to be Mr. Collins.[96]
95. Ibid., p. 40.
96. The deist and freethinker Anthony Collins (1676–1729), whose *A Discourse Concerning Ridicule and Irony in Writing* was published in 1729 to defend the view that "the solemn and grave can bear a solemn and grave Attack: That gives them a sort of Credit in the World, and makes them appear considerable to themselves, as worthy of a serious Regard. But *Contempt* is what they, who commonly are the most contemptible and worthless of Men, cannot bear or withstand, as setting them in their true Light, and being the most effectual Method to drive Imposture, the sole Foundation of their Credit, out of the World" (p. 7).

Realities; employ Eloquence instead of Logick; and endeavour to *persuade* whom they should, but cannot, *convince?*

It seems therefore that his Lordship's Observation (which contains the Quintessence of his Associate's Work, and which probably was the *Leaven* that *leavened* the whole *Lump* of Malice and Dulness) instead of being favourable to Ridicule as a Test of Truth, can only tend to disgrace it. For since every religious and unbelieving Sect hath *alike successfully* employed it in supporting their respective Tenets, and in rendering those of their Adversaries contemptible; it follows, inasmuch as Doctrines which are essentially repugnant cannot all be true, that RIDICULE IS ONE OF THE MOST POWER[74]FUL ENGINES, BY WHICH ERROR CAN BE MAINTAINED AND ESTABLISHED.

SECTION VIII

We shall only mention one more of the noble Writer's Arguments in Favour of his new *Test:* But it is, indeed, the very *Key-Stone* of this visionary Arch, which he hath with such fantastic Labour thrown over the Depths of Error, in order to invite Mankind over it as a short and secure Passage to the Abode of Truth and Wisdom.

He tells us, that a new Species of Enthusiasts *(French Prophets)* having lately risen up among us, "We have delivered them over to the cruellest Contempt in the World. I am told for certain, that they are at this very Time the Subject of a choice Droll or Puppet-show at Bart'lmy-Fair.—And while Bart'lmy-Fair is in Possession of this Privilege, I dare stand Security to our national Church, that no Sect of Enthusiasts, no new Venders of Prophecy or Miracles, shall ever get the Start, or put her to the Trouble of trying her Strength with them, in any Case."s [75]

---

s. Vol. i. p. 27, 28.[97]

97. Shaftesbury, *Characteristicks*, vol. I, p. 18. The "French Prophets" were refugees who caused a stir in London for a few months during 1706–7, as Abel Boyer reported: "Towards the latter end of the Year 1706, three *French Cevenois*, vulgarly call'd *Camisars*, came over into *England*, and by their *formal Cant*, which was but an ill Imitation of the *true Prophetick Stile*, we find in the Holy Scripture, and their *feign'd Extatick Fits*, stir'd up at first the Curiosity of several of their Country-men

So far, for Peace sake, we venture to agree with the noble Writer: But now comes a finishing Stroke indeed.

For he proceeds to congratulate the present Age, that in the Beginnings of the Reformation, when Popery had got Possession, *Smithfield* was used in a more *tragical Way*. And that "had not the Priests, as is usual, preferred the Love of Blood to all other Passions, they might in a *merrier Way*, perhaps, have *evaded the greatest Force of our reforming Spirit*."[t]

And now, for Form's sake, let us suppose the noble Author to be what he assumes, a Friend to Religion and Reformation: Under this Character, he recommends *Ridicule* to us, as of sovereign Use to investigate Truth, try Honesty, and unmask formal Hypocrisy and Error. To prove this Use, he tells us, what we should least have expected, that if, instead of the tragical Way of *Smithfield*, the *Romish* Priests had preferred the comic Drollery of Bart'lmy-Fair,[99] they had perhaps gained their Point, and *evaded the greatest Force of our reforming Spirit*. Here the noble Writer forgets his Part, which is that of a *Believer* and a *Pro*[76]*testant*. But, in his Scarcity of Proofs for the *Use* of Ridicule, he has put the Change upon us, and perhaps upon himself, and offered at one to shew its *Force:* Which, without doubt, must wonderfully recommend it to the Favour of all sober Men. Here then lies the Dilemma: Let his Followers then get him off as they can. If their Master be a Believer, he has reasoned ill; if a Freethinker, he has managed worse. Had he been a little more knowing in the Times he

---

in *Soho*; and a few *crazy Persons* of both Sexes amongst them, were so far deluded, as to become their Followers; which gave just Offence to the *soberer Part*, and Generality of the *French* Refugees, and occasion'd dangerous Disputes in private Families" (*The History of the Reign of Queen Anne*, 11 vols [1703–13], vol. VI, p. 368). The supposed prophets were prosecuted and punished by being exposed on a scaffold at Charing Cross on 1 and 2 December 1707, wearing denunciations of their falsehood fixed to their hats.

t. Vol. i. p. 28.[98]

98. Shaftesbury, *Characteristicks*, vol. I, p. 18. Smithfield was a site on the northern edge of the City of London where heretics had been burned to death during the reign of Mary (1553–58).

99. Bartholomew Fair took place in Smithfield on St. Bartholomew's Day (24 August). It was noted for its burlesque dramatic shows and carnivalesque energy, both of which were satirized by Ben Jonson in his *Bartholomew Fair* (1614).

speaks of, he might have found an Instance more pertinent to his Argument, and more conformable to his Character; an Instance which shews, not what *Ridicule* might be supposed capable of doing, but what it actually effected. And this not to stop *Reformation,* but to discredit *Popery.* Bishop BURNET tells us, that in the Year 1542, "Plays and Interludes were a great Abuse: In them, Mock-Representations were made, both of the Clergy and of the Pageantry of their Worship. The Clergy complained much of these as an Introduction to Atheism, when Things sacred were thus laughed at: And said, they that begun to laugh at Abuses, would not cease till they had re[77]*presented* all the Mysteries of Religion as *ridiculous:* The graver Sort of Reformers did not approve of it: But political Men encouraged it; and thought nothing could more *effectually pull down* the Abuses that yet remained, than the exposing them to the *Scorn* of the Nation."[v]

This curious Piece of History is remarkable; and tends no less to support our general Argument, than to recommend, what the noble Writer is pleased to snear at, the Sobriety *of our reforming Spirit. Political* men, says the Historian, whose Business, and therefore whose aim, was to *persuade,* encouraged the Way of Ridicule: But the *graver Sort of Reformers,* whose nobler Ministry, and consequently whose purpose, was to *convince,* did not *approve* of it.

But his Lordship is so fond of his Reflection, that he pushes it still further. "I never heard (says he) that the ancient Heathens were so well advised in their *ill Purpose* of suppressing the *Christian* Religion in its first Rise, as to make use at any Time of this Bart'lmy-Fair Method. [78] But this I am persuaded of, that, had *the Truth of the Gospel* been any way *surmountable,* they would have bid much fairer for the silencing it, if they had chosen to bring our primitive Founders upon the Stage in a pleasanter Way, than that of Bear-Skins and Pitch-Barrels."[w] And as to the *Jews,* he says, that "with all their Malice and Inveteracy to our Saviour

v. *History of the Reformation,* A. D. 1542.[100]
w. Vol. i. p. 29.
100. Gilbert Burnet, *The History of the Reformation of the Church of England* (1737), p. 97.

and his Apostles after him, had they but taken the Fancy to act such Puppet-Shows in his *Contempt,* as at this Hour the Papists are acting in his Honour; I am apt to think they might possibly have done our Religion more harm, than by all their other Ways of Severity."[x]

What a Favourite is that *facetious Droll of Wood and Wire, the Bart'lmy Fair Hero,* with these modern Advocates for Mirth and Raillery! And indeed, not without cause, for of him they seem to have learnt their very wittiest Practices. Who taught them to turn their Backs upon their Betters; to disturb the most serious Scenes with an unsavoury Joke; and make a Jest of the Devil? Indeed they have so well taken off his Manners, that one Description will serve [79] them both. And whether you suppose the fine one which follows to be meant of the *original,* or one of the *Copies* you are equally sure you have a good Likeness.

> Sed praeter reliquos incedit *Homuncio, rauca*
> *Voce strepens;*—*Pygmaeum* territat agmen
> Major, et immanem *miratur turba gigantem.*
> Hic magna fretus mole, imparibusque lacertis
> Confisus, gracili *jactat convitia vulgo,*
> Et crebro solvit (*lepidum caput!*) ora *cachinno.*
> Quanquam res agitur solenni *seria* pompa,
> *Spernit* sollicitum intractabilis ille tumultum,
> Et *risu* importunus adest, atque *omnia turbat.*[y]

x. Ibid.[101]

y. *Musae Angl.* MACH. GEST. by Mr. *Addison.*[102]

101. Shaftesbury, *Characteristicks*, vol. I, pp. 18–19.

102. "But surpassing the rest there advances a little man shouting in a hoarse voice; . . . in his larger size he terrifies the Pygmy troop, and that throng marvels at the huge giant. Relying on his mighty mass, and trusting in his arms that outmatch theirs, he hurls abuse at the puny populace and, amusing fellow that he is, opens his mouth in frequent laughter. Even though serious business is being conducted with solemn ceremony, that unmanageable creature scorns the restless commotion, marks his untimely presence with laughter, and throws everything into confusion" (Joseph Addison, "Machinae Gesticulantes, Anglice: A Puppet Show," ll. 19–30). On Addison's Latin poetry, see Estelle Haan, *Vergilius Redivivus: Studies in Joseph Addison's Latin Poetry* (American Philosophical Society: Philadelphia, 2005). Brown had published a translation of this poem in the periodical *The Museum,* I.3 (26 April 1746), pp. 96–99.

But to return to our Argument. Be you well assured of this, kind Reader, that whatever Impressions are made upon a Populace in the Way of *Scenery* and *dramatic* Representation, are no more than so many Kinds of *silent Eloquence* and *Persuasion:* That Facts which ought to be proved, are always *taken for granted,* and Things and Persons often rendered *apparently* absurd, which *really* are not so. That *the Vulgar* (both *high* and *low*) *are apt to swallow any sordid Jest or Buffoonry,* so it be but accommodated to their *preconceived Opinions:* That this Way of Ridicule, like every other, [80] as it is fairly or dishonestly applied, will sweep away Truth or Falsehood without Distinction: That it will confound *French Prophets* with *English Reformers,* and on the same false Foundation establish the Truths of Protestantism, or the Absurdities of Popery. That as *Virtue* herself cannot bear up against a Torrent of Ridicule, so neither can *Religion:* That therefore *Christianity* had indeed more to fear from the *contemptuous Misrepresentations,* than the *bitterest Rage* of its Enemies: That *Christianity* did in Fact endure this more than fiery Trial: That its divine Founder was *derided*[z] as well as *crucified:* That they who in succeeding Times suffered for the Faith, endured *cruel Mockings* no less than *Scourgings, Bonds,* and *Imprisonment:* That many a brave Martyr offered up his Prayers to Heaven, that he might be released by Death from the *Contempt* of his Enemies: And after being *baited* in the *Bear-Skin,* found a *Refuge* in the *Faggot,* or the *Pitch-Barrel.*[104]

SECTION IX

However, the noble Writer's Modesty must not be forgotten. For while he [81] might have arrogated to himself the Glory of this wondrous Discovery, he hath informed us of an *ancient Sage,* whose Idea of Ridicule coincided with his own. "'Twas the Saying of an ancient Sage, that Humour was the only Test of Gravity."[a]

z. *Prophesy unto us, who it was that smote thee!*[103]

a. Vol. i. p. 74.[105]

103. Matthew 27:68; Luke 22:64.

104. Early Christians were tormented in bear-skins (*OED,* 1b); faggots and pitch-barrels were used to burn martyrs.

105. Shaftesbury, *Characteristicks,* vol. I, p. 48.

The Reader will probably be surprised to find that the Passage here referred to by the noble Writer, is no other than what hath been already quoted from ARISTOTLE[b] as a Direction to the Conduct of an Orator. 'Tis likewise remarkable, that his Lordship, in quoting the original Passage in his *Margin,* has, by the *prudent* Omission of an emphatical Expression, converted it from a particular Rule of Rhetoric into a general Maxim of Philosophy.[c] But 'tis of all most remarkable, that in his pretended Translation, he hath entirely perverted the Sense of the Author, whose Authority he attempts to build upon.

"As Ridicule (says the great Philosopher) seems to be of some Use in Pleading; it was the Opinion of GORGIAS,[107] [82] that you ought to confound your Adversary's serious Argument by Raillery, and his Raillery by serious Argument." This is almost a literal Translation of the Passage. But how the noble Author could so far impose upon himself or others, as to strip it of its native Dress, and disguise it under the fantastical Appearance of a Maxim, "that Humour is the only Test of Gravity, and Gravity of Humour,"—this is not so easy to account for.

However this came to pass, 'tis certain, that the Observation, as it lies in ARISTOTLE, is a just and a fine one: as it lies in the noble Writer's maimed Translation, it is *false,* if not *unmeaning.*

That an Orator should *confound his Adversary's Raillery by serious Argument,* is rational and just. By this means he tears off the false Disguises of Eloquence, and distinguisheth real from apparent Truth. That he should *confound his Adversary's serious Argument by Raillery,* is, if not a just, yet a legal Practice. The Aim and End of the Advocate or Orator is Persuasion only; to Truth or Falsehood as it happens. If he hath Truth on his Side, it is likely what he will have then to do, will be *to confound his* [83] *Adversary's Raillery by serious Argument.* If Truth be against him, he will be forced to change Weapons with his Adversary, *whose serious Argument he must try to confound by Raillery.* This is all the Mystery there is in the Matter? By

b. See above, p. 43.[106]

c. The Words, τῶν ἐναντίων—*Adversariorum*—are omitted.

106. Cf. above, p. 51 and n. 53.

107. Gorgias of Leontini (*c.* 485–375 B.C.), a celebrated sophist and teacher of rhetoric. He figures in the Platonic dialogue of the same name.

which we see, that whenever in this case Ridicule is opposed to Reasoning, it is so far from being the *Test* or Support, that it is the *Destruction of Truth*. And the judicious Quintilian fairly confesses it, where he assigns the Cause why Ridicule is of such mighty Force in Oratory—"Quia animum ab intentione rerum frequenter avertit"[108]—*Because it draws off the Mind from attending to the real Nature of Things*. Thus you see the Propriety and Beauty of the *Saying of our ancient Sage,* when fairly represented.

But as the noble Writer hath translated the Passage, it is a Curiosity indeed. "Humour is the only Test of Gravity, and Gravity of Humour." He applies it not to Eloquence, but Philosophy; not to Persuasion, but Conviction. And so, by the strangest Conversion in Nature, makes the Trier, and the Thing tried, each in their turns, become Agent and Patient to one another. But what Artist ever attempted to [84] *try* the Justness of his *Square* or *Level,* by the Work which he has formed by the Assistance of those Instruments? Or was ever the Gold which hath been put to the Test, reciprocally applied to *try* the Touch-Stone?[109] If therefore *Gravity,* or Reasoning, be the Test of *Humour*; Humour never can be the Test of Gravity: As on the other hand, if Humour be the Test of Gravity, then Gravity can never be the Test of Humour.

Since therefore this *see-saw* Kind of Proof returns into itself, and consequently ends in an Absurdity; 'tis plain, that one half of the noble Writer's Proposition must effectually destroy the other: Let us see then, which Moiety deserves to be supported. His own Comment on the Passage will help us to determine. Which however, he seems desirous his Reader should receive as a Part of the *Saying of his ancient Sage:* But whoever will turn to the Passage, as it lies in Aristotle, will find that Gorgias is entirely innocent of the whole Affair.

"Gravity, says his Lordship, is the Test of *Humour:* Because a Jest that will not bear a serious Examination, is certainly false Wit."[110] True: here

108. Quintilian, *Institutio Oratoria,* VI.iii.1.

109. Literally, a fine variety of quartz or jasper used for testing the quality of gold and silver alloys; metaphorically, that which serves to test or try the genuineness or value of anything (*OED,* 1a and b).

110. Shaftesbury, *Characteristicks,* vol. I, p. 48.

we have a [85] rational Test established. Next he inverts the Proposition, sets it with its Head downwards, like a Traytor's Scutcheon,[111] and now, says he, behold "Humour is the Test of Gravity." To prove this, Reason requires he should have added, "Because an Argument, which can be successfully ridiculed, is certainly false Logic." But this was too hardy a Proposition to be directly advanced: He therefore contents himself with hinting, that "a Subject which will not bear Raillery *is suspicious!*" Now we know, that *Suspicion* is often groundless: That what is suspected to be false, may yet be true. So that the noble Writer again suffers this new Test to slip through his Fingers, even while he is holding it up to your Admiration. But if any thing further be necessary to clear up this Point, it may be observed in short, that Gravity or Argument is the Test of Humour, because Reason marks the real Differences of Things: That Humour can never be the Test of Gravity, because Imagination can only suggest their apparent Analogies.

Thus the Sentiment of GORGIAS is grosly mistaken or designedly misrepresented by the noble Writer: as it lies in [86] ARISTOTLE, it is rational and consistent; as it is taken up by his Lordship, it is chimerical and groundless.

It might have been difficult to assign a Reason, why the noble Writer should have attempted to establish this *two-fold* Method of Proof, had not he explained his Intention in another Place.[112] He there[d] wisely recommends the old *scholastic Manner*[113] to the *Clergy*, as being most suitable to their Abilities and Character: The *Way of Ridicule* he appropriates to the Men of Taste and Breeding; declaring it ought to be kept sacred from the impure Touch of an Ecclesiastic. For as Clubs and *Cudgels* have long been appropriated to Porters and Footmen, while every Gentleman is ambitious to understand a *Sword*; so the clumsy Way of *Argumentation* is only fit for Priests and Pedants, but *pointed* Wit is the Weapon for the

---

d. Vol. iii. Misc. v. c. 2. § 65, &c.

111. An eschutcheon is a shield bearing a coat of arms, which in the case of a traitor was inverted.

112. Shaftesbury, *Characteristicks*, vol. III, pp. 166–82.

113. Literally, characteristic of scholastic philosophy; by extension, pedantic or needlessly subtle (Johnson).

Man of Fashion: This decides a Quarrel *handsomely*. The *pretty Fellow* is at your Vitals in a Moment; while the Pedant keeps labouring at it for an Hour together, and neither gets nor gives so much as a broken Bone. [87]

But still higher is the noble Writer's Idea of Wit and Ridicule: While he applies it not only to *Conquest*, but *Investigation:* And we must own, it was an Attempt worthy of his Genius, to establish this new and *expeditious* Method of Search and Conviction. In which, by the sole Application of so cheap and *portable an Instrument* as that of *Raillery*, a Gentleman might obtain the certain Knowledge of the *true Proportion* of Things, without the tedious and vulgar Methods of *Mensuration*.[114] In the mean Time, we, whom the noble Author hath so often condescended to distinguish by the honourable Title of Formalists and Pedants, finding ourselves incapable of this *sublime* Way of Proof, must be content to drudge on in the old and beaten Track of *Reasoning*. And after all, 'tis probable this new Attempt will succeed no better than the curious Conceit of the *learned Taylor* in *Laputa:* Who being employed in making a *Suit* for the facetious GULLIVER; disdained the *vulgar Measures* of his Profession, and took that Gentleman's *Altitude* by the Help of a *Quadrant*.[115] This, it must be acknowledged, was a Theory no less sublime than our noble Author's: Yet it [88] failed miserably when applied to Practice: For the sagacious Traveller informs us, that notwithstanding the Acuteness and Penetration of the Artist, his cloaths were *wretchedly ill made*.

SECTION X

We have now obviated every thing material, that the noble Writer hath advanced in Support of his new System. But as one of his most zealous Followers[116] hath undertaken *in Form* to explain and defend his Notions on this Subject,[e] it may be proper to examine how far this Gentleman's Argument is consistent with Truth.

---

e. See a Note on the *Pleasures of Imagination*, a Poem. Book iii.
114. The action of measuring (*OED*, 1).
115. Cf. *Gulliver's Travels*, Part III, chapter 2 (Swift, *Prose Works*, vol. XI, p. 162).
116. Mark Akenside, *The Pleasures of Imagination* (1744), pp. 105–6; note to III.259.

He tells us, that "to ask whether Ridicule be a Test of Truth, is in other Words to ask, whether that which is ridiculous can be morally true, can be just and becoming; or whether that which is just and becoming, can be ridiculous."

Here, as the Foundation of all, we see the same Kind of Ambiguity lurking, as was observed in the noble Writer, in the Passage already re-marked on.[f] For if by "that [89] which is ridiculous," he means that which is *really* ridiculous, it is allowed this can never be morally true: But this is so far from proving Ridicule to be a Test of Truth, that it implies the contrary: It implies some further Power, which may be able to distin-guish what is *really* ridiculous, from what is only *apparently* so. On the contrary, if by "that which is ridiculous," he means that which is *appar-ently* ridiculous, it may be affirmed, this may be morally true: Because Imagination and Passion often take up with Fictions instead of Realities, and can never of themselves distinguish them from each other. He tells us his Question "does not deserve a serious Answer." At least it wanted an Explanation.

The Gentleman proceeds: "For it is most evident, that as in a meta-physical Proposition offered to the Understanding for its Assent, *the Fac-ulty of Reason* examines the Terms of the Proposition, and finding one Idea which was supposed equal to another, to be in Fact unequal, of Con-sequence rejects the Proposition as a Falsehood: So in Objects offered to the Mind for its Esteem or Applause, the *Faculty of Ridicule* feeling an Incongruity [90] in the Claim, urges the Mind to reject it with Laughter and Contempt."

Here the *Faculty of Reason* is excluded from the Examination of moral Truths, and a *new* Faculty, never before heard of, *the Faculty of Ridicule*, is substituted in its Place. Now, when a *Stranger* is introduced into good Company, and sure these can be no better than the *Public*, it is usual not only to tell his Name, but *what he is*, and what his *Character:* This, the Gentleman hath not condescended to do: 'Tis true, in a preceding Page he tells us, that "the Sensation of Ridicule is not a bare Perception of the Agreement or Disagreement of Ideas; but a *Passion or Emotion of the*

f. See above, p. 58.

Mind, consequential to that Perception."[117] In another Place he expresly calls it "a gay Contempt."[118] Now, if the *Faculty of Ridicule* be the same as the *Sensation of Ridicule,* or *a gay Contempt,* then by substituting the plain old Term of *Contempt,* instead of the *Faculty of Ridicule,* we shall clearly see what the above cited Passage contains. "As in a metaphysical Proposition, the *Faculty of Reason* examines the Terms, and rejects the Falsehood; so in Objects offered to the Mind for its Esteem and Ap[91]plause, *the Passion of Contempt* feeling an Incongruity in the Claim, urges the Mind to reject it *with Laughter and* CONTEMPT!"[119]—Why was not honest *Reason* admitted of the Council, and set on the *Seat of Judgment,* which of right belongs to her? The Affair would then have stood thus: "As in a metaphysical Proposition, the Faculty of Reason examines the Terms, and rejects the Falsehood; so in Objects offered to the Mind for its Esteem or Applause, *the same Faculty of Reason* finding an Incongruity in the Claim, urges the Mind to reject it with *Contempt* and *Laughter.*" This would have been Sense and Argument; but then it had not been *Characteristical.*

We shall now clearly discover the Distinction that is to be made on the following Passage:[120] "And thus a double Advantage is gained: For we both *detect* the moral Falsehood *sooner* than in the Way of speculative Enquiry, and impress the Minds of Men with a stronger Sense of the Vanity and Error of its Authors."[g]—Here 'tis evident, that the Design "of *detecting* the moral Falsehood *sooner* than in the [92] Way of speculative Enquiry" is an absurd Attempt: But that "to impress the Minds of Men with a stronger Sense of the Vanity and Error of its Authors," when Reason hath made the proper Search, is both a practicable and a rational Intention.

"But it is said, continues he, that the Practice is dangerous, and may be inconsistent with the Regard we owe to Objects of real Dignity and Excellence."[h] Yet this is but a secondary Objection: The principal one is,

g. Ibid. p. 106.
h. Ibid. p. 106.
117. Mark Akenside, *The Pleasures of Imagination* (1744), pp. 103–4; note to III.248.
118. Ibid., p. 105, III.260.
119. Ibid., pp. 105–6; note to III.259.
120. Ibid.

that the Attempt is absurd. However, the Circumstance of Danger is not without its Weight: Nor is the Gentleman's reply at all sufficient—"that the Practice fairly managed can never be dangerous."[121] For though Men are not dishonest in obtruding false Circumstances upon us, we may be so *weak* as to *obtrude* them upon ourselves. Nay, it can hardly be otherwise, if, instead of exerting our Reason to correct the Suggestions of Fancy and Passion, we give them an unlimited Range, and acquiesce in their partial or groundless Representations, without calling in Reason to decide upon their Truth or Falsehood. [93] By this means we shall often "view Objects of real Dignity and Excellence," in such Shapes and Colours as are foreign to their Nature; and then sit down and laugh most profoundly at the Phantoms of our own creating.

But still he insists,[122] that though false Circumstances be imposed upon us, yet "the Sense of Ridicule always *judges right*," or in more vulgar Terms, "The Passion of Contempt always judges right." Whereas, in Truth, it never *judges* at all; being equally excited by Objects real or imaginary that present themselves.

Observe therefore what a Number of *new* Phrases and *blind* Guides this of Ridicule, if once admitted, would bring in upon us, and all on equal Authority. For with the same Reason, as the Passion of Contempt is styled the *Sense of Ridicule*, the Passion of *Fear* may be called the *Sense of Danger*, and *Anger* the *Sense of Injury*. But who hath ever dreamt of exalting these Passions into so many Tests of the Reality of their respective Objects? The Design must have been rejected as absurd, because it is the Province of Reason alone, to correct the blind Sallies of every Passion, and fix it on its proper [94] Object. Now, the Scheme of Ridicule is of the same Nature. It proposes the Passion of Contempt as the Test of moral Falsehood, which, from the very Terms, appears to be a Project full as wise, as to make Fear the Test of Danger, or Anger the Test of Injury.

The Gentleman proceeds next[123] to the Case of SOCRATES. He owns "the SOCRATES of ARISTOPHANES is as truly ridiculous a Character as

121. Ibid.
122. Ibid.
123. Ibid.

ever was drawn: But it is not the Character of SOCRATES, the divine Moralist and Father of ancient Wisdom."—No indeed: and here lay the Wickedness of the Poet's Intention, and the Danger of his Art: in imposing Fictions for Realities on the misled Multitude; and putting a Fool's Coat on the Father of ancient Wisdom. 'Tis true, the People laughed at the *ridiculous Sophist*; but when the ridiculous Sophist came to drink the Poison, what think you became of the Father of ancient Wisdom?

But then he tells us,[124] that as the comic Poet introduced foreign Circumstances into the Character of SOCRATES, and built his Ridicule upon these; "So has the Reasoning of SPINOZA made many Atheists; [95] he has founded it indeed on Suppositions utterly false, but allow him these, and his Conclusions are unavoidably true. And if we must reject the Use of Ridicule, because, by the Imposition of false Circumstances, things may be made to seem ridiculous, which are not so in themselves; why we ought not to reject the Use of Reason, because, by proceeding on false Principles, Conclusions will appear true which are impossible in Nature, let the vehement and obstinate Declaimers against Ridicule determine."[i]

But why so much Indignation against *Declaimers* in one who writes in Defence of *Ridicule,* a Species of *Declamation?* Then as to *rejecting* the Use of Ridicule, a very material Distinction is to be made: As a *Mode of Eloquence* nobody attempts totally to reject it, while it remains under the Dominion of Reason: But as a *Test of Truth,* I hope the Reader hath seen sufficient Reason totally to reject it.

Neither will the Parallel by any means hold good, which the Gentleman hath attempted to draw between the Abuse of *Ridicule* and *Reason.* Because the Imagina[96]tion, to which the Way of Ridicule applies, is apt to form to itself innumerable fictitious Resemblances of Things which tend to confound Truth with Falsehood: Whereas the natural Tendency of Reason is to separate these apparent Resemblances, and determine which are the *real,* and which the *fictitious.* Although therefore SPINOZA hath advanced many Falsehoods in the Way of speculative Affirmation, and founded his Reasonings on these, yet still Reason will be her own

i. Page 106.
124. Ibid.

Correctress, and easily discover the Cheat. But if the Imagination be impressed with false Appearances, and the Passion of Contempt strongly excited, neither the *Imagination* nor the *Passion can ever correct themselves*; but must inevitably be misled, unless *Reason* be called in to rectify the Mistake, and bring back the Passion to its proper Channel.

Nay, so far is the Use of Ridicule, when prior to rational Conviction, from being parallel to Reason, or co-operative with it; that, on the contrary, it hath a strong Tendency to prevent the Efforts of Reason, and to confound its Operations. It is not pretended that human Reason, though the *ultimate*, is yet in all Cases an *adequate* Test of Truth: It is always fallible, often errone[97]ous: But it would be much less erroneous, were every Mode of Eloquence, and Ridicule above all others, kept remote from its Operations; were no Passion suffered to blend itself with the Researches of the Mind. For Ridicule, working on the Imagination and Passions, disposes the Mind to receive and acquiesce in any Opinion without its proper Evidence. Hence Prejudice arises; and the Mind, which should be *free* to examine and weigh those *real* Circumstances which PROVE SOCRATES to be indeed a divine Philosopher, is drawn by the *prior* Suggestions of *Ridicule* to receive and acquiesce in those false Circumstances, which PAINT him as a *contemptible Sophist*.

To conclude: 'Tis no difficult Matter to point out the Foundation of this Gentleman's Errors concerning Ridicule. They have arisen solely from his mistaking *the Passion of Contempt* for a *judicial Faculty:* Hence all those new-fangled Expressions of—"the Faculty of Ridicule"—"the Sense of Ridicule"—and "the feeling of the Ridiculous:" In the Use of which he seems to have imposed upon himself new Phrases for Realities, and Words for Things. I cannot better illustrate this Remark, than [98] by transcribing a Passage from the incomparable LOCKE.[125]—"Another great Abuse of Words is, the taking them for Things. To this Abuse Men are most subject, who confine their Thoughts to any one System, and give themselves up to the firm Belief of the Perfection of any received Hypothesis; whereby they come to be persuaded, that the Terms of that Sect

---

125. John Locke, *An Essay Concerning Human Understanding*, III.xiv.14. Cf. above, p. 10, n. 14.

are so suited to the Nature of Things, that they perfectly correspond with their real Existence. Who is there that has been bred up in the Peripatetic Philosophy, who does not think the ten Names, under which are ranked the ten Predicaments, to be exactly conformable to the Nature of Things? Who is there of that School, that is not persuaded, that *substantial Forms, vegetative Souls, Abhorrence of a Vacuum, intentional Species, etc.* are something real?"—"There is scarce any Sect in Philosophy has not a distinct Set of Terms that others understand not. But yet this *Gibberish*, which, in the Weakness of human Understanding, serves so well to palliate Men's Ignorance, and cover their Errors, comes by familiar Use amongst those of the same Tribe, to seem [99] the most important Part of Language, and of all other the Terms the most significant."[k] And now to save the Trouble of Repetition, the Reader is left to determine how far "the *Faculty of Ridicule* feeling the Incongruity"—and "the *Sense of Ridicule* always judging right"—may with Propriety be placed among the learned *Gibberish* above-mentioned.

'Tis strange this Gentleman should have erred so widely in so plain a Subject; when we consider, that he hath accidentally thrown out a Thought,[126] which, if pursued, would have led him to a full View of the Point debated: "The Sensation of Ridicule is not a bare *Perception* of the Agreement or Disagreement of Ideas; but *a Passion* or *Emotion* of the Mind *consequential to that Perception.*"[l]

SECTION XI

To return therefore to the noble Writer. As it is evident, that *Ridicule* cannot in general without Absurdity be applied as a Test of Truth; so can it least of all be [100] admitted in *examining Religious Opinions,* in the Discussion of which, his Lordship seems principally to recommend it. Because, by inspiring the contending Parties with *mutual Contempt*, it hath a violent Tendency to destroy *mutual Charity,* and therefore to prevent *mutual Conviction.*

k. Locke *on Hum. Understanding,* B. iii. c. 10. § 14.
l. P. 103.
126. Mark Akenside, *The Pleasures of Imagination* (1744), p. 103; note to III.248.

To illustrate this Truth, let us consider the following Instance, which seems clear and full to the Point.

There is not perhaps in any Language a bolder or stronger Ridicule, than the well-known Apologue[127] of *The Tale of a Tub.*[128] Its manifest Design is to recommend the *English Church,* and to disgrace the two Extremes of *Popery* and *Puritanism.*[m] Now, if we [101] consider this exquisite Piece of Raillery as a Test of Truth, we shall find it impotent and vain: For the Question still recurs, whether MARTIN be a just Emblem of the *English, Jack* of the *Scotch,* or *Peter* of the *Roman Church.* All the Points in Debate between the several Parties are taken for granted in the Representation: And we must have Recourse to *Argument,* and to that alone, ere we can determine the Merits of the Question.

If we next consider this Master-piece of Wit as a Mode of *Eloquence,* we shall find it indeed of great *Efficacy* in confirming every Member of the *Church of England* in his own Communion, and in giving him a thorough Distaste of those of *Scotland* and *Rome:* And so far as this may be regarded as a Matter of *public Utility,* so far the Ridicule may be laudable.

But if we extend our Views so as to comprehend a larger Plan of *moral Use*; we shall find this Method of Persuasion is such, as Charity can hardly approve of: For by representing the one of these Churches under the Character of *Craft and Knavery,* the other under that of *incurable*

---

m. Some indeed have pretended otherwise. Thus Mr. *Wotton,* in his *Reflections on Learning,* says, "It is a designed Banter upon all that is esteemed sacred among Men."[129] And the pious Author of the *Independent Whig* affirms it was "the sole *open* Attack that had been made upon *Christianity* since the Revolution, except the *Oracles of Reason,* and was not inferior in Banter and Malice, to the Attacks of *Celsus,* or *Julian,* or *Porphyry,* or *Lucian.*"[130] p. 399. Where by the Way, the Oddity of the *Contrast* is remarkable enough; that he should pronounce the *Tale of a Tub* to be a *Libel on Christianity,* while it is in Fact *a Vindication of our Ecclesiastical Establishment*; and at the same Time entitle his own Book *a Vindication of our Ecclesiastical Establishment,* while in Fact it is *a Libel on Christianity.*

127. An allegorical story intended to convey a useful lesson; a moral fable (*OED*).

128. I.e., Jonathan Swift, *A Tale of a Tub* (1704).

129. William Wotton, *A Defense of the Reflections Upon Ancient and Modern Learning* (1705), p. 48.

130. Arthur Mainwaring, *The Independent Whig,* sixth edition (1732), p. 284; no. 46, "Of High-Church Atheism" (30 November 1720).

Madness, it must needs tend to inspire every Member [102] of the *English* Church who believes the Representation, with such *Hatred* of the one, and *Contempt* of the other, as to prevent all *friendly Debate* and *rational Remonstrance.*

Its effect on those who hold the Doctrines of CALVIN,[131] or of *Rome,* must be yet worse: Unless it can be proved, that the Way to attract the Love, and convince the Reason of Mankind, is to shew that we hate or despise them. While they revere what we deride, 'tis plain, we cannot *both* view the Subject in the same Light: And though we deride what appears to us *contemptible,* we deride what to them appears *sacred.* They will therefore accuse us of misrepresenting their Opinions, and abhor us as *unjust* and *impious.*

Thus although this noted Apologue be indeed a Vindication of our *English* Church, yet it is such as had been better spared: Because its natural Effect is to create Prejudice, and inspire the contending Parties with mutual Distaste, Contempt, and Hatred.

But if the Way of Ridicule is thus wholly to be rejected in treating every *controverted* Subject; it will probably be asked, "Where then is it to be applied? Whether it is reasonable *to calumniate and blacken* [103] *it without Distinction?* And whether it is not Impiety, thus *to vilify the Gifts of our Maker?*"

And 'tis certain, that to do this, were absurd and impious. As on the other hand, there is an equal Absurdity and Impiety in confounding that Order of Things which the Creator hath established, and endeavouring to raise *a blind Passion* into the *Throne of Reason.* One Party or other in this Debate hath certainly incurred the Censure: The Censure is severe, and let it fall where it is deserved. I know none that endeavour to vilify and blacken Ridicule without Distinction, unless when it presumes to elevate itself into a *Test of Truth:* And then, as a Rebel to the Order and Constitution of Nature, it ought to be resolutely encountered and repelled, till it take Refuge in its own inferior Station.

The proper Use of Ridicule therefore is, "to disgrace *known* Falsehood:" And thus, negatively at least, "to enforce *known* Truth." Yet this

---

131. Jean Calvin (1509–64); French theologian and reformer, notorious for his rigorous development of the doctrine of predestination.

can only be affirmed of certain Kinds of Falsehood or Incongruity, to which we seem to have appropriated the general Name of *Folly:* And among the several Branches of this, chiefly [104] I think, to AFFECTA-TION. For as every *Affectation* arises from a false Pretence to *Praise,* so a *Contempt incurred* tends to *convince* the Claimant of his *Error,* and thus becomes the natural Remedy to the Evil.

Much more might be said on this Head. We might run through numerous Divisions and Subdivisions of *Folly:* But as the Task would be both insignificant and endless, I am unwilling to trouble the Reader with such elaborate Trifles.

It seems an Observation more worthy of our Attention and Regard; that *Contempt,* whence Ridicule arises, being a *selfish Passion,* and nearly allied to *Pride,* if not absolutely founded on it; we ought ever to keep a strict Rein, and in general rather curb than forward its Emotions. Is there a more important Maxim in Philosophy than this, that we should gain a Habit of controuling our Imaginations and Passions by the Use of Reason? Especially those that are rather of the selfish than the benevolent Kind? That we should not suffer our Fears to sink us in Cowardice, our Joys in Weakness, our Anger in Revenge? And sure there is not a Passion that infests human Life, whose Consequences are so generally pernicious as those [105] of *indulged Contempt.* As the common Occurrences of Life are the Objects which afford it Nourishment, so by this means it is kept more constantly in Play, than any other Affection of the Mind: And is indeed the general Instrument by which Individuals, Families, Sects, Provinces, and Nations, are driven from a State of mutual Charity, into that of Bitterness and Dissention. We proceed from Raillery to Railing; from Contempt to Hatred. Thus if the Love of Ridicule be not in itself a Passion of the malevolent Species, it leads at least to those which are so. Add to this, that the most ignorant are generally the most contemptuous; and they the most forward to *deride,* who are most incapable or most unwilling to *understand.* Narrow Conceptions of Things lead to groundless Derision: And this Spirit of Scorn in its Turn, as it cuts us off from all Information, confirms us in our preconceived and groundless Opinions.

This being the real Nature and Tendency of Ridicule, it cannot be worth while to descant much on its Application, or explore its Subserviency to the Uses of Life. For though under the severe Restrictions of Reason, it may be made a proper Instru[106]ment on many Occasions, for disgracing *known Folly*; yet the Turn of Levity it gives the Mind, the Distaste it raises to all candid and rational Information, the Spirit of Animosity it is apt to excite, the Errors in which it confirms us when its Suggestions are false, the Extremes to which it is apt to drive us, even when its Suggestions are true; all these conspire to tell us, it is rather to be wished than hoped, that its Influence upon the whole can be considerable in the Service of *Wisdom* and *Virtue*.

Lord SHAFTESBURY himself, in many other Parts of his Book, strongly insists on the Necessity of bringing the Imagination and Passions under the Dominion of Reason. "The only Poison to *Reason,* says he, is *Passion:* For *false Reasoning* is soon redressed, where Passion is removed."[n] And it is difficult to assign any Cause that will not reflect some Dishonour on the noble Writer, why he should thus strangely have attempted to privilege this Passion of *Contempt* from so necessary a Subjection. Let it suffice, in Conclusion, to observe; that Inconsistencies must ever arise and be persisted in, when a roving Fancy, con[107]ducted by *Spleen*[133] and *Affectation,* goes in Quest of idle Novelties, without subjecting itself to the just Restraints of *Reason*.

Upon the whole: This new Design of *discovering* Truth by the *vague* and *unsteady Light* of Ridicule, puts one in Mind of the honest *Irishman,* who applied his *Candle* to the *Sun-Dial,* in order *to see how the Night went.*

n. *Wit and Humour,* Part ii. § 1.[132]
132. Shaftesbury, *Characteristicks,* vol. I, p. 58.
133. Violent ill-nature or ill-humour; irritable or peevish temper (*OED,* 6).

ESSAYS
ON THE
Characteristics, etc.

ESSAY II
On the Obligations of Man to Virtue, and the
Necessity of religious Principle

Having considered the noble Writer's two first Treatises, so far as they regard the *Use of Ridicule,* we now come to his *Soliloquy,* or *Advice to an Author.* And here, bating only a few accidental Passages, which will be occasionally pointed out hereafter, we shall have little more to do, than to approve and admire: The whole Dissertation being, in its general Turn, one con[110]tinued Instance of its Author's Knowledge and refined Taste in Books, Life, and Manners. I could dwell with Pleasure on the Beauties of this Work, if indeed they needed an Explanation: But that noble Union of Truth and Eloquence which shines through the whole, as it supersedes, so it would disgrace any Attempt of this Kind. To the Work itself therefore I recommend the Reader.

The noble Writer having thus prepared us for the Depths of Philosophy, by enjoining an unfeigned and rigorous *Self-Examination;* proceeds to that highest and most interesting of all Subjects, *The Obligations of Man to the Practice of Virtue.* And here it will probably appear, that with a Variety of useful Truths, he hath blended several plausible Mistakes, which, when more nearly viewed, seem to be attended with a Train of very extraordinary Consequences. What he hath given us on this Subject, lies chiefly in the two Treatises, which compose his second Volume:

But as he frequently refers us to the other Parts of his Writings, where he hath accidentally treated the same Points in a more explicit Manner; so the same Liberty of comparing one Passage with an[111]other, will, I apprehend, be judged reasonable by the candid Reader. Thus we shall more effectually penetrate into his true Scope and Intention; and draw off, as far as may be, that Veil of *Mystery*, in which, for Reasons best known to himself, he hath so often wrapped his Opinions.

SECTION II

'Tis no uncommon Circumstance in Controversy, for the Parties to engage in all the Fury of Disputation, without precisely instructing their Readers, or truly knowing themselves, the Particulars about which they differ. Hence that fruitless Parade of Argument, and those opposite Pretences to Demonstration, with which most Debates, on every Subject, have been infested. Would the contending Parties first be sure of their own Meaning (a Species of Self-Examination which, I think, the noble Writer hath not condescended to mention) and then communicate their Sense to others in plain Terms and Simplicity of Heart, the Face of Controversy would soon be changed: And real Knowledge, instead of imaginary Conquest, would be the noble Reward of literary Toil. [112]

In the mean Time, a History of *Logomachies*° well executed, would be no unedifying Work. And in order to open a Path to so useful an Undertaking, I will venture to give the present Section as an Introduction to it: For sure, among all the Questions which have exercised the Learned, this concerning *the Obligations of Man to Virtue* hath given Rise to the greatest Profusion of loose Talk and ambiguous Expression. The Argument hath been handled by several of great Name: And it might possibly be deemed Presumption to differ from any of them, had they not so widely differed among themselves. Much hath been said, and various have been their Opinions concerning our *Obligations* to *Virtue*; but little hath been said in any definitive Manner, on the previous and fundamental Question, *What Virtue is*. By which I do not mean, what Actions are called

o. A Strife about Words.

Virtuous, for, about that, Mankind are pretty well agreed, but, *what makes Virtue to be what it is*. And till we have determined this with all possible Precision, we cannot determine "upon what Foundation Man[113]kind are obliged to the Practice of it." Our first Enquiry therefore must be, concerning the *Nature* of *Virtue:* In the Investigation of which, the Moralists of most Ages seem to have been remarkably defective.

Let us first consider what our noble Author hath said on this Subject. He tells us, "The Mind cannot be without its Eye and Ear; so as to discern Proportion, distinguish Sound, and scan each Sentiment and Thought which comes before it. It can let nothing escape its Censure. It feels the soft and harsh, the agreeable and disagreeable in the Affections; and finds a *foul* and *fair*, an *harmonious* and a *dissonant*, as really and truly here, as in any musical Numbers, or in the outward Forms and Representations of sensible Things. Nor can it withold its Admiration and Extasy, its Aversion and Scorn, any more in what relates to one, than to the other of these Subjects. So that to deny the common natural Sense of a *sublime* and *beautiful* in Things, will appear an *Affectation* merely to any one who considers duly of this Affair."[p] The [114] Perception of this Beauty he calls the *moral Sense* or *Taste*; and affirms, that Virtue consists in "a perfect Conformity of our Affections and Actions with this supreme Sense and Symmetry of Things." Or, to use his own Words, "The Nature of Virtue consists in a certain just Disposition or proportionable Affection of a rational Creature towards the *moral Objects of Right and Wrong*."[q]

The next Writer I shall mention is the learned and amiable Dr. CLARKE.[3] He thinks it necessary to reject this Idea of Virtue, which the noble Writer had established; and as a surer Foundation, than what mere *Affection, Sense,* or *Taste* could produce, lays the Basis of Virtue in *Reason:* And insists, that its true Nature lies in "a Conformity of our Actions, with certain eternal and immutable Relations and Differences of

p. *Inquiry concerning Virtue,* Part iii. § 3.[1]
q. *Inquiry concerning Virtue,* Part iii. § 1.[2]
1. Shaftesbury, *Characteristicks,* vol. II, p. 17.
2. Ibid., p. 23.
3. Samuel Clarke (1675–1729); Cambridge metaphysician, moralist, and defender of rational theology.

Things. That from these, which are necessarily perceived by every rational Agent, there naturally arise certain *moral Obligations,* which are of themselves incumbent on all, antecedent to all positive Institution, and to all Expectation of Reward or Punishment."ʳ [115]

After these, comes an ingenious and candid Writer,[5] and in Opposition to both these Schemes of Moral, fixes the Nature of Virtue in "a Conformity of our Actions with *Truth.*"[6] He affirms, that "no Act, whether Word or Deed, of any Being, to whom moral Good and Evil are imputable, that interferes with any *true* Proposition, or *denies* any thing to be as it is, can be *right.* That, on the contrary, every Act is right which does not contradict Truth, but treats every thing as being what it is."ˢ

There are, besides these, several other philosophical Opinions concerning the Nature of Virtue: as, that it consists in following *Nature*—in avoiding all *Extremes*—in the Imitation of the *Deity.* But these are still more loose and indeterminate Expressions, if possible, than the former. If therefore the first should appear vague and ineffectual, the latter must of Course fall under an equal Censure.

Now it will appear, that all the three Definitions of Virtue, which Lord SHAFTESBURY, Dr. CLARKE, and Mr. WOLLASTON have given us, in designed Opposition to [116] each other, are equally defective; "Because they do not give us any more particular or determinate Ideas, than what we have from that *single Word,* which with so much fruitless Labour they attempt to define."

Let us first examine the noble Writer's Definition in this View. He says, that "Virtue consists in a Conformity of our Affections with our

---

r. Clarke's *Demonst.* passim.[4]

s. Wollaston's *Rel. of Nat.* § 1. passim.[7]

4. Not in fact a quotation, but a summary of the central thesis of Clarke's *A Demonstration of the Being and Attributes of God* (1705).

5. William Wollaston (1659–1724); moral philosopher whose *The Religion of Nature Delineated* (1722) offered an influential rationalistic account of morality and natural religion.

6. Not a precise quotation from *The Religion of Nature Delineated*; but cf. p. 9 for a similar sentiment.

7. Again, not a precise quotation from Wollaston, but instead a *précis* of an important aspect of his doctrine in *The Religion of Nature Delineated.*

natural Sense of the Sublime and Beautiful in Things, or with the moral Objects of Right and Wrong."—Now, what new Idea do we gain from this pompous Definition? Have we not the same general Idea from the Word *Virtue*, as from the more diffused Expression of *the Sublime and Beautiful of Things?* And cannot we gather as much from either of these, as from the subsequent Phrase, the *moral Objects of Right and Wrong?*"[8]— They are all general Names, relative to something which is yet unknown, and which is no more explained by the pretended Definition, than by the Word which is attempted to be defined. Indeed, when his Lordship further affirms, that to relieve the Needy, or help the Friendless, is an Instance of this Sublime and Beautiful of Things, we then [117] obtain a more determinate Idea, with Regard to that particular Case. But still we are as much as ever at a Loss for a general *Criterion* or *Test*, by which the Virtue of our other Actions is to be determined. To say, therefore, that Virtue consists in acting according to the *fair*, the *handsome*, the *sublime*, the *beautiful*, the *decent*, the *moral Objects* of *Right* and *Wrong*, is really no more than ringing Changes upon Words. We might with equal Propriety affirm, "that *Virtue* consists in *acting virtuously*." This Deficiency Mr. WOLLASTON clearly saw. "They, says he, who reckon nothing to be *(morally)* good, but what they call *honestum*, may denominate Actions according as that is, or is not the Cause or End of them: But then, what is *honestum?* Something is still wanting to measure Things by, and to separate the *honesta* from the *inhonesta*."[t]

Dr. CLARKE's Definition seems not to include any thing more precise or determinate, than the noble Writer's. He affirms, that "Virtue consists in a Conformity of our Actions with right Reason, or the eternal and immutable Relations and Dif[118]ferences of Things." Here then a parallel Question ariseth, "What is *right Reason*, and what these *eternal Relations* which are affirmed, by the learned Writer, to be the Test or Criterion

t. *Rel. of Nat.* p. 22.[9]

8. Not a precise quotation from *Characteristicks*, but rather Brown's formulation of what he takes to be Shaftesbury's notion of virtue. However, see the beginning of Book I, part 3, section 1 of *An Inquiry* for wording which comes close to that of Brown (Shaftesbury, *Characteristicks*, vol. II, p. 23).

9. Wollaston, *Religion*, pp. 15–16.

of Virtue?" And 'tis observable, that when he comes to prove the Truth and Reality of these *Relations,* he is forced to resolve it into a *self-evident* Proposition. "These Things, saith he, are so notoriously plain and *self-evident,* that nothing but the extremest Stupidity of Mind, Corruption of Manners, or Perverseness of Spirit, can possibly make any Man entertain the least Doubt concerning them."[v] Thus too, his ingenious *Advocate,* when pushed by his Adversary to declare, whether he perceives the Truth of these Relations by *Proof* or *Intuition,* confesses "they may be looked upon as *self-evident.*"[w] Here then we may observe a strong Coincidence between the noble Writer's System of Expression, and this of Dr. CLARKE: For as the one affirms, that the *Sublime* and *Beautiful* of Things is *self-evident,* so the other affirms the same of the *Fit* and *Reasonable.* And as the *Sublime* and [119] *Beautiful* give us no more determinate Ideas, than the *Virtuous,* so neither can we obtain any additional Information from the *Fit* and *Reasonable.* We are equally at a Loss to know what is *fit* and *reasonable,* as to know what is *virtuous:* Therefore the *one* can never be an adequate Definition of the other. Here too, Mr. WOLLASTON plainly saw the Want of Precision. As to those, he saith, "who make *right Reason* to be a Law—it is true, that whatever will bear to be tried by right Reason, is right; and that which is condemned by it, wrong:—But the Manner in which they have delivered themselves, *is not yet explicit enough.* It leaves Room for so many Disputes and *opposite right Reasons,* that nothing can be settled, while every one pretends that *his* Reason is right."[x]

Now it will doubtless appear a Circumstance of Singularity, that Mr. WOLLASTON, who saw the essential Defects of these two Definitions, should himself offer a *third,* which is precisely liable to the same Objection. "Virtue, saith this learned Writer, consists in a Conformity

---

v. *Demonst.* p. 50.[10]

w. Balguy's *Tracts,* 2^d Part of *Mor. Goodness,* p. 10.

x. *Rel. of Nat.* p. 23.[11]

10. These are Brown's paraphrases of Clarke's doctrine, not actual quotations from *A Demonstration of the Being and Attributes of God.* However, cf. Samuel Clarke, *A Demonstration of the Being and Attributes of God* (1705), p. 175 for some proximate wording.

11. Wollaston, *Religion,* p. 16.

of our Actions with Truth; in treating every [120] thing as being what it is."[12] Well: be it so. Yet the Question still recurs, what is *moral Truth?* And this demands a *Definition* no less than *Virtue*, which was the Thing to be defined. Had Lord SHAFTESBURY lived to see this new Theory proposed, how naturally would he have retorted Mr. WOLLASTON's Objection? "You, Mr. WOLLASTON, reckon nothing to be *morally Good*, but what you call *Truth:* And you may indeed denominate Actions, according as that is, or is not, the Cause or End of them: But then, what is *Truth?* Something further is still wanting to measure Things by, and to separate *Truth* from *Falsehood*."—Thus too would Dr. CLARKE have naturally replied:

> 'Tis true, that whatever will bear to be tried by *Truth*, is right; and that which is condemned by it, wrong: But the Manner in which you have delivered yourself, is not yet explicit enough. You have rather confounded my Definition, than given a new one of your own: All that you have added, is an Impropriety of Speech. I speak of the *Rectitude* of Actions, you of the *Truth* of Actions; which I call an Impropriety of Speech, [121] because *Truth* relates to *Affirmations*, not to *Actions*; to what is *said*, not to what is *done*. But supposing the Propriety of your Expression, what further Criterion have you gained? You confess, that *Truth* is discovered by *Reason* only; for you say, that *to deny Things to be as they are, is the Transgression of the great Law of our Nature, the Law of Reason.*[y] If so, then Reason is as good a Guide as Truth: We can as certainly know what is *right Reason*, as what is *Truth*. If therefore my Definition is defective, yours must be so too. If mine leaves Room for so many Disputes and *opposite right Reasons*, that nothing can be settled, while every one pretends that his Reason is *right*; yours must of Necessity be liable to the same Objection, must leave Room for so many Disputes and *opposite Truths*, that nothing can be settled, while every one pretends that his Idea of *Truth* is the *right* one. Truth, then, can never be a better Criterion than Reason, because our Idea of *Truth* must always *depend* upon our *Reason*. [122]

y. *Rel. of Nat.* p. 15.
12. A paraphrase of Wollaston's general position on the relation of truth to virtue rather than a precise quotation; although cf. Wollaston, *Religion*, pp. 9 and 18.

Thus it should seem, that our three celebrated Writers have not given the Satisfaction which might have been expected in an Affair of such philosophical Importance. Their common Attempt is to define the Nature, or fix the Criterion of Virtue: To this End, the first affirms, it consists in a a Conformity of our Actions to the *Fair* and *Handsome,* the *Sublime* and *Beautiful* of Things: The Second, the *Fitness, Reasons,* and *Relations* of Things: The Third, the *Truth* of Things. But inasmuch as these general Terms of *Beauty, Fitness, Truth,* convey not any more determinate Idea, than that of *Virtue,* which they are brought to define; the several pretended Definitions are therefore *inadequate* and *defective.*^z [123]

What then is *Virtue?* Let us consider its true Nature in the following Section.

SECTION III

There are few among Mankind, who have not been often struck with Admiration at the Sight of that Variety of Colours and Magnificence of Form, which appear in an Evening *Rainbow.* The *uninstructed* in Philosophy consider that splendid Object, not as dependent on any other, but as being possessed of a *self-given* and *original Beauty.* But he who is led to know, that its Place and Appearance always varies with the Situation of the *Sun*; that when the latter is in his Meridian, the former becomes an inconsiderable Curve skirting the Horizon; that as the Sun descends, the Rainbow rises; till at the Time of his *Setting,* it encompasses the Heavens

z. Let it be observed once for all, that the Definitions here censured as defective, are little more than direct Transcripts of what the old *Greek* Philosophers, and *Tully* after them, have said on the same Subject. To shew how generally this Kind of Language infects the Writers on Morality, we need only transcribe the following Passage from a Follower of the noble Writer.[13] "We need not therefore be at a Loss, said he, for a *Description* of the sovereign Good.—We may call it *Rectitude* of Conduct.—If that be too contracted, we may enlarge, and say, 'tis—to live perpetually selecting and rejecting according to *the Standard of our Being.* If we are for still different Views, we may say, 'tis—to live in the Discharge of *Moral Offices*—to live *according to Nature*—To live *according to Virtue*—to live according to *just Experience* of those Things which happen around us." Three Treatises by *J. H.* Treat. 3^d. p. 207.

13. James Harris (1709–80); philosopher and musical patron; Shaftesbury's nephew. The quotation comes from Harris, *Treatises,* p. 207.

with a glorious Circle, yet *dies* away when he *disappears*; the Enquirer is then convinced, that this gay Meteor did but shine [124] with a *borrowed* Splendor, derived from the Influence of that mighty *Luminary*.

Thus, in like Manner, though the *Beauty, Fitness, Truth*, or VIRTUE, of all those Actions which we term *morally Good*, seem at first View to reside in the several Actions, in an original and independent Manner; yet on a nearer Scrutiny we shall find, that, properly speaking, their Nature ariseth from their *Ends* and *Consequences*; that as these *vary*, the Nature of the several Actions *varies* with them; that from these alone, Actions gain their *Splendor*, are denominated *morally Good*, and give us the Ideas of *Beauty, Fitness, Truth*, or *Virtue*.

The first Proofs in Support of this Opinion shall be drawn from those very Writers who most zealously oppose it. And here 'tis first remarkable, that "while they attempt to fix their several Criterions of absolute, independent Beauty, Fitness, and Truth; they are obliged to admit *Exceptions*, which effectually destroy what they design to establish." The following Instance, from one of these celebrated Writers, is equally applicable to the other two. [125]

Mr. WOLLASTON speaks in the following Manner: "To talk to a Post, or otherwise treat it as if it was a Man, would surely be reckoned an *Absurdity*, if not *Distraction*. Why? Because this is to treat it as being what it is not. And why should not the converse be reckoned as bad; that is, to treat a Man as a Post? As if he had no Sense, and felt not Injuries which he doth feel; as if to him Pain and Sorrow were not Pain; Happiness not Happiness."[a] Now, you see that on his Scheme of absolute irrelative Truth, the Absurdity of *talking to a Post* is precisely of the same Nature with that of *injuring a Man*: For in both Cases, we treat the Post and the Man, as being *what they are not*. Consequently, on this Philosophy, if it be morally Evil to *injure* a *Man*, 'tis likewise morally Evil to *talk* to a *Post*. Not that I suppose Mr. WOLLASTON would have maintained this Consequence. He knew that the First of these Absurdities would only deserve the Name of *Folly*; that the latter, of a *Crime*. As therefore he

---

a. *Rel. of Nat.* p. 15.[14]
14. Wollaston, *Religion*, pp. 10–11.

allows that Truth is equally violated in either Case; as there is something *highly* [126] *immoral* in the one, and *nothing immoral* in the other, here is an Exception which overturns his Principle: which proves that the Morality or Immorality of Actions depends on something *distinct* from mere abstract, irrelative *Truth.*

The same Exception must be admitted on Dr. CLARKE's System of Expression. For sure, 'tis neither *fit* nor *reasonable,* nor agreeable to the Relations of Things, that a Man should talk to a Post. Yet, although it be admitted as *irrational* and *absurd,* I do not imagine, any of Dr. CLARKE's Defenders would say it was *immoral.* So again, with regard to Lord SHAFTESBURY, 'tis clear there can be nothing of the *Sublime* or *Beautiful* in this Action of talking to a Post: On the contrary, there is (to use his own Manner of Expression) an apparent Indecency, Impropriety, and *Dissonance* in it. Yet, although his Admirers might justly denominate it *incongruous,* they would surely be far from branding it as *vile.* Here then the same Exception again takes place, which demonstrates that *Virtue* cannot consist either in *abstract Fitness* or *Beauty;* but that something further is required in order to constitute its Nature. [127]

Possibly therefore, the Patrons of these several Theories may alledge, that Actions which relate to *inanimate Beings* only, can properly be called no more than *naturally* beautiful, fit, or true: But that *moral* Fitness, Beauty, or Truth, can only arise from such Actions as relate to Beings that are *sensible* or *intelligent.* Mr. BALGUY expresly makes this Exception: He affirms, that "moral Actions are such as are knowingly directed towards some Object intelligent or sensible."[b]

And so far indeed this Refinement approaches towards the Truth, as it excludes all *inanimate* Things from being the Objects of moral Good and Evil. Yet even this Idea of moral Beauty, Fitness, or Truth, is highly

---

b. *First Treat, on Moral Goodness,* p. 28.[15]

15. John Balguy (1686–1748); Church of England clergyman and moral philosopher, who in 1726 had published an attack on Shaftesbury, *A Letter to a Deist, Concerning the Beauty and Excellence of Moral Virtue.* Balguy's own writings reject the foundation of morality on sense or instinct, and seek instead to ground virtue on reason. The quotation is taken from the second edition of Balguy's *The Foundation of Moral Goodness* (1731), p. 28.

indeterminate and defective: Because innumerable Instances may be given, of Actions directed towards Objects sensible and intelligent, some of which Actions are manifestly *becoming, fit,* or *true,* others as manifestly *incongruous, irrational,* and *false,* yet none of them, in any Degree, *virtuous* or *vicious, meritorious* or *immoral.* Thus to speak to a Man in a Language he understands, is an Action *becoming, fit,* or *true*; [128] 'tis treating him according to the Order, Relations, and Truth of Things; 'tis treating him according to *what he is.* On the contrary, to speak to him in a Language he understands not, is an Action neither *becoming, fit,* nor *true*; 'tis treating him according to *what he is not*; 'tis treating him *as a Post.* But although the first of these Actions be undeniably becoming, fit, or true, who will call it *Virtue?* And though the latter be undeniably incongruous, irrational, and false, who will call it *Vice?* Yet both these Actions are directed towards a Being that is sensible and intelligent. It follows therefore, that an Action is not either morally Good or Evil, merely because it is conformable to the Beauty, Fitness, or Truth of Things, even though it be directed towards an Object both *sensible* and *intelligent*; but that something still further, some more distinguishing and characteristic Circumstance is necessary, in order to fix its real Essence.

What this peculiar Circumstance may be, we come now to enquire. And the first Lights in this Enquiry shall be borrowed from these very celebrated Writers, whom we have here ventured to oppose. [129] For such is the Force and Energy of Truth, that while they are attempting to involve her in a Cloud of Metaphysics, she breaks through the mystic Veil they had prepared and woven for her with so much Art, and diffuseth a Stream of genuine Lustre, which the most obdurate Prejudice can only withstand by winking hard.

And first, though the *noble* Writer every where attempts to fix an original, independent, moral Beauty of Action, to which every thing is to be referred, and which itself is not to be referred to any thing further:[c] Yet when he comes to an Enumeration of those *particular* Actions, which may be called morally Beautiful, he always singles out such as have a

---

c. *Essay on Wit—Soliloquy—Enquiry—Moralists—Miscellanies*—passim.[16]
16. Brown's paraphrases of Shaftesbury's thought on the beauty of virtue.

direct and necessary Tendency to *the Happiness of Mankind.* Thus he talks of the Notion of *a public Interest,*[d] as necessary towards a proper Idea of Virtue: He speaks of public Affection in the same Manner; and reckons Generosity, Kindness, and Compassion, as the Qualities which alone can render Mankind truly Virtuous. So again, when he fixes the Bounds of the social Affections, he evidently refers [130] us to the same End, of human Happiness. "If Kindness or Love of the most natural Sort be immoderate, it is undoubtedly vicious. For thus over-great Tenderness *destroys the Effect of Love*; and excessive Pity renders us incapable of giving Succour."[e] When he fixes the proper Degrees of the *private Affections,* he draws his Proof from this one Point, "that by having the Self-Passions too intense or strong, a Creature becomes miserable."[f] Lastly, when he draws a Catalogue of such Affections, as are most opposite to Beauty and moral Good, he selects "*Malice, Hatred* of *Society—Tyranny—Anger—Revenge—Treachery—Ingratitude.*"[g] In all these Instances, the Reference to human Happiness is so particular and strong, that from these alone an unprejudiced Mind may be convinced, that the Production of *human Happiness* is the great universal Fountain, whence our Actions derive their *moral Beauty.*

Thus again, though the excellent Dr. CLARKE attempts to fix the Nature and Essence of Virtue in certain Differences, Relations, and Fitnesses of Things, to which [131] our Actions ought ultimately to be referred; yet in enumerating the several Actions which he denominates *morally Good,* he mentions none, but what evidently promote the same great End, "the Happiness of Man." He justly speaks of the *Welfare* of the *Whole,* as being the *necessary* and most *important* Consequence of *virtuous* Action. He tells us, "that it is *more fit* that GOD should regard the *Good*

d. *Enqu.* B. i. p. 2. § 3.[17]
e. *Enqu.* B. i. p. 2. § 3.
f. Ibid.
g. Ibid.[18]

17. Cf. Shaftesbury's opinion that "in this Case alone it is we call any Creature *worthy* or *virtuous,* when it can have the Notion of a publick Interest, and can attain the Speculation or Science of what is morally good or ill, admirable or blameable, right or wrong" (Shaftesbury, *Characteristicks,* vol. II, p. 18).

18. Ibid., pp. 16–20.

of the *whole* Creation, than that he should make the Whole continually miserable: That all Men should endeavour to promote the *universal Good* and *Welfare* of all; than that all Men should be continually contriving the *Ruin* and *Destruction* of all."ʰ Here again, the Reference is so direct and strong to *the Happiness of Mankind,* that even from the Instances alledged by the worthy Author, it appears, that a Conformity of our Actions to this great End, is the very Essence of *moral Rectitude.*

Mr. WOLLASTON is no less explicit in this particular: For in every Instance he brings, *the Happiness* of Man is the single End to which his Rule of Truth verges in an unvaried Manner. Thus in the Passage [132] already cited, though he considers the *talking to a Post* as an *Absurdity,* he is far from condemning it as an *immoral* Action: But in the same Paragraph, when he comes to give an Instance of the Violation of *moral* Truth, he immediately has recourse to *Man;* and not only so, but to the *Happiness* of Man. "Why, saith he, should not the Converse be reckoned as bad; that is, to treat a *Man* as a Post; as if he had no *Sense,* and *felt* not *Injuries,* which he doth *feel;* as if to him *Pain* and *Sorrow* were not *Pain; Happiness* not *Happiness."* At other Times he affirms, that "the *Importance* of the Truths on the one and the other Side should be diligently *compared."*ⁱ And I would gladly know, how one Truth can be more important than another, unless upon this Principle, and in Reference to *the Production of Happiness.* Himself indeed confirms this Interpretation, when he speaks as follows: "The Truth violated in the former Case was, B had a Property in that which gave him such a Degree of *Happiness:* That violated in the latter was, B had a Property in that which gave him a *Happiness* vastly *superior* to the other: [133] The Violation *therefore* in the latter Case was *upon this Account* a vastly *greater* Violation than in the former."ᵏ

---

h. *Demonst.* p. 45, &c.[19]
i. *Rel. of Nat.* p. 19.[20]
k. *Rel. of Nat.* p. 21.[21]
19. Samuel Clarke, *A Discourse Concerning the Unchangeable Obligations of Natural Religion,* fourth edition (1716), p. 38.
20. Wollaston, *Religion,* pp. 10–11.
21. Ibid., p. 15.

These Evidences may seem sufficient: But that all possible Satisfaction may be given in a Circumstance which is of the greatest Weight in the present Question, these further Observations may be added.

As therefore these celebrated Writers give no Instances of moral Beauty, Fitness, or Truth, but what finally relate to the Happiness of Man; so if we appeal to the common Sense of Mankind, we shall see that the Idea of Virtue hath never been universally affixed to any Action or Affection of the Mind, unless where this Tendency to produce Happiness was at least *apparent*. What are all the Black Catalogues of Vice or moral Turpitude, which we read in History, or find in the Circle of our own Experience, what are they but so many Instances of *Misery produced?* And what are the fair and amiable Atchievements of *Legislators, Patriots,* and *Sages* renowned in Story, what but so many Efforts to raise Mankind from Misery, and establish the public Happiness on a sure Foundation? [134] The first are *vicious, immoral, deformed,* because there we see Mankind *afflicted* or *destroyed:* The latter are *virtuous, right, beautiful,* because here we see Mankind *preserved* and *assisted.*

But that *Happiness* is the last Criterion or Test, to which the moral Beauty, Truth, or Rectitude of our Affections is to be referred, the two following Circumstances *demonstrate:* First, "those very Affections and Actions, which, in the ordinary Course of Things, are approved as virtuous, do change their Nature, and become vicious in the strictest Sense, when they contradict this fundamental Law, of the greatest public Happiness." Thus, although in general it is a Parent's Duty to prefer a Child's Welfare, to that of another Person, yet, if this natural and just Affection gain such Strength, as to tempt the Parent to violate the *Public* for his Child's *particular* Welfare; what was before a *Duty,* by this becomes immoderate and *criminal.* This the noble Writer hath allowed: "If Kindness or Love of the most natural Sort be *immoderate,* it is undoubtedly *vicious.*"[l] And hence, he says, "the Excess of motherly [135] Love is owned to be a vicious Fondness."[m] The same *Variation* takes Place with regard to every other Relation between Man

l. *Enq. on Virtue.*[22]
m. *Enq. on Virtue.*[23]
22. Shaftesbury, *Characteristicks,* vol. II, p. 16.
23. Ibid., p. 16.

and Man. Insomuch, that the superior Regards which we owe to our Family, Friends, Fellow-Citizens, and Countrymen—Regards which, in their proper Degree, aspire to the amiable and high Names of *domestic* Love, *Friendship, Patriotism*—when once they desert and violate the grand Principle of *universal Happiness*, become a *vicious* Fondness, a mean and odious *Partiality*, justly stigmatized by all, as ignominious and *unworthy*.

Secondly, with such uncontrouled Authority does this great Principle command us; that "Actions which are in their own Nature, most shocking to every *humane* Affection lose at once their moral Deformity, when they become subservient to the general Welfare; and assume both the Name and the Nature of Virtue." For what is more contrary to every gentle and kind Affection that dwells in the human Breast, than to shed the Blood, or destroy the Life of Man? Yet the ruling Principle above-mentioned, can reconcile us [136] even to *this*. And when the Necessity of public Example compels us to make a Sacrifice of this Kind; though we may lament the *Occasion*, we cannot condemn the *Fact:* So far are we from branding it as *Murder*, that we approve it as *Justice:* and always defend it on this great Principle alone, *that it was necessary for the public Good.*

Thus it appears, that those Actions which we denominate Virtuous, Beautiful, Fit, or True, have not any absolute and independent, but a relative and reflected Beauty: And that their Tendency to produce Happiness is the only Source from whence they derive their Lustre. Hence therefore we may obtain a just and adequate Definition of Virtue: Which is no other than "the[n] Conformity of our Affections with the [137] public Good:" Or "the voluntary Production of the greatest Happiness."

n. The Gentlemen above examined seem to have mistaken the *Attributes* of Virtue for its *Essence*. Virtue is procuring Happiness: To procure Happiness is *beautiful, reasonable, true*; these are the Qualities or Attributes of the Action: But the Action itself, or its *Essence,* is procuring Happiness.

The Reader who is curious to examine further into this Subject, may consult the *Prelim. Dissert. to Dr.* Law's *Translation of* King's *Origin of Evil:* Together with several Passages in the Translator's *Notes,* where he will find *Sense* and *Metaphysics* united in a very eminent and extraordinary Degree.[24]

24. William King, *An Essay on the Origin of Evil*, tr. Edmund Law (1731), "Preliminary Dissertation. Concerning the Fundamental Principle of Virtue or Morality," pp. xi–xxxiii.

SECTION IV

It may possibly seem strange that so much has been thought necessary to be opposed to these metaphysical *Refinements* concerning the Nature of Virtue: But in Reality, 'tis a Point of the utmost Consequence: For these Refinements have given rise to a plausible Objection, which hath been retailed in a popular Manner by a late wordy Writer; whose least merit it is to have supplied our modish Coffee-house Philosophers with such a Variety of fashionable Topics, that they have never felt the least Want of that antiquated Assistance derived from Knowledge, Parts, and Learning.

This Gentleman, taking Advantage of these metaphysical Refinements, and particularly of the noble Writer's imaginary Scheme of *absolute, irrelative* Beauty, "the Hunting after which (he elegantly affirms) is not much better than a wild Goose Chase;"[o] attempts from hence to demonstrate, for the *Benefit* of his *Country,* [138] that we are utterly mistaken, when we "look upon Virtue and Vice as permanent Realities, that must ever be the same in all Countries and all Ages."[p] And thus he prosecutes his Argument.

The Worth or Excellence of every thing, he says, varies according to Fancy or Opinion. "Even in human Creatures, what is beautiful in one Country, is not so in another.—Three hundred Years ago, Men were shaved as closely as they are now; since that, they have wore Beards.—How mean and comical a Man looks, that is otherwise well-dressed, in a narrow-brimmed Hat, when every Body wears broad ones: And again, how monstrous is a very great Hat, when the other Extreme has been in Fashion for a considerable Time?—The many Ways of laying out a Garden judiciously are almost innumerable; and what is called Beautiful in them, varies according to the different *Taste* of Nations and Ages."[q]

o. *Fable of the Bees,* vol. i. p. 380. oct. Ed.[25]
p. *Fable of the Bees,* p. 372.[26]
q. P. 376.[27]
25. Mandeville, *Fable,* vol. I, p. 331.
26. Ibid., p. 324.
27. Ibid., p. 328.

Thus capricious and uncertain, he tells us, are our Ideas of natural Beauty; and these he brings home to the Point of Morals. "In Morals there is no greater Certainty: Plurality of [139] Wives is odious among *Christians,* and all the Wit and Learning of a great Genius in Defence of it, has been rejected with Contempt. But Polygamy is not shocking to a *Mahometan.* What Men have learnt from their Infancy enslaves them, and the Force of Custom warps Nature, and at the same Time imitates her in such a Manner, that it is often difficult to know, which of them we are influenced by. In the East formerly, Sisters married Brothers, and it was meritorious for a Man to marry his Mother. Such Alliances are abominable: But it is certain, that whatever Horror we conceive at the Thoughts of them, there is nothing in Nature repugnant against them, but what is built upon Mode and Custom. A religious *Mahometan* may receive as great an Aversion against Wine."ʳ Hence, with great Stretch of Reasoning he concludes, "that Virtue and Vice are not permanent Realities," but vary as other Fashions, and are subject to no other Law, than that of *Fancy* and *Opinion.*

And so far indeed, this Gentleman seems to have argued justly, while he contends [140] that mere *Approbation* and *Dislike,* the mere Idea of *Beauty* and *Deformity, Truth* or *Rectitude,* without Reference to some further *End,* can never constitute a real or permanent Foundation of *Vice* or *Virtue.* For, as he hath observed, there *have* indeed been considerable Differences of Opinion upon *some Kinds* of moral Beauty and Deformity, in the different Nations and Ages of the World: And each Age and Nation hath ever been alike positive in asserting the Propriety of its own. Therefore, unless we have some further Test, some other distinguishing and characteristic Circumstance to refer to, besides that of mere *Approbation* and *Dislike,* how shall we ever know, which of these *anomalous* Opinions are *right* or *wrong?* If we have nothing further to appeal to, than the mere Propriety of *Taste,* though each may be thoroughly satisfied of the Justness of his own; yet he ought in Reason to allow the same Right of Choice to the rest of Mankind in every Age and Nation: And thus

r. *Fable of the Bees,* p. 377, 379.[28]
28. Ibid., pp. 330–31.

indeed, *moral* Beauty and Deformity, *Virtue* and *Vice,* could have no other Law, than that of *Fancy* and *Opinion.*

But when the great End of public Happiness is ultimately referred to, as the *one,* [141] *uniform* Circumstance that constitutes the *Rectitude* of human Actions; then indeed, *Virtue* and *Vice* assume a more *real* and *permanent* Nature: The common *Sense,* nay, the very *Necessities* of Mankind, will urge them to make an unvaried and just *Distinction:* For *Happiness* and *Misery* make too strong an Appeal to all the Faculties of Man, to be borne down by the *Caprice* of Fancy and Opinion. That it was either an accidental or a designed Inattention to this great Principle of *Happiness,* that gave this coarse Writer an Occasion to call in Question the permanent *Reality* of Vice and Virtue, the following Considerations may sufficiently convince us.

Should any one ask, whether *Health* and *Sickness* are two different Things, no Doubt we should answer in the Affirmative: And would surely suspect any Man's Sincerity, who should tell us, that what was accounted Health in one Age or Nation, was accounted Sickness in another. There are likewise such Things as wholesome Food and Poisons: Nor would we entertain a much better Opinion of him who should affirm, that *all* depends upon *Fancy,* that *Bread* or *Milk* are nourishing or destructive, [142] that *Arsenic* and *Sublimate* are wholesome or poisonous, as *Imagination* and *Opinion* dictate. On the contrary we know, their Nature with Respect to Man, is *invariable:* The one, universally wholesome, the other, poisonous. Further: we know there have been Debates among Physicians, about *Regimen* and *Diet:* That some have maintained the Wholesomeness of *Animal,* others of *vegetable* Food: Some recommended the Drinking of *Water,* others of *Wine.* Yet none was ever so weak as to conclude from these different Opinions about wholesome *Diet,* that the nourishing Qualities of *Bread,* or the noxious ones of *Arsenic,* were not *permanent* Realities with regard to Man; or, that the first could be made *poisonous,* the latter, *wholesome,* by Dint of *Fancy* and *Opinion.*

Now, the Case we are debating is exactly parallel. For sure, the *Happiness* and *Misery* of Mankind are Things as distinct as *Health* and *Sickness:* Whence it follows, that certain Actions, under the same Circumstances, must universally produce Happiness or Misery, as naturally as Food produceth Health, or Poison, Sickness, and Death. We have already seen, that what[143]ever tends to the Good of all, is by the consent of all, denominated *Virtue*; that whatever is contrary to this great End, is universally branded as *Vice*; in the same Manner, as whatever nourishes the Body is called *Food*; whatever destroys it, *Poison*. Accordingly, we find the Agreement among Mankind as uniform on the one Subject, as on the other. All Ages and Nations having without Exception or Variance maintained, that Humanity, Fidelity, Truth, Temperance, and mutual Benevolence, do as naturally produce Happiness, as Food gives Health to the Body: That Cruelty, Treachery, Lying, Intemperance, Inhumanity, Adultery, Murder, do as naturally give Rise to Misery, as Poison brings on Sickness and Death.

But hath not this Author given such Instances as prove, that what is detested as *Vice* in one Country, is applauded as *Virtue* in another? That *Polygamy* and *incestuous Marriages* have been in some Nations reputed *lawful,* in others *meritorious?* And if one Virtue or Vice be imaginary or *variable,* doth it not clearly follow that *all* are so?

Now a Man of a common Turn of Thought would be apt to make a very dif[144]ferent Inference. If from the *Variety* of Opinions among Mankind as to *some* Virtues or Vices, he concluded *these* were *variable*; then from the universal *Agreement* of Mankind with regard to *other* Virtues and Vices, he would conclude *these* were *fixed* and *invariable*. The *Consent* of Mankind in the *one*, proves as much as their *Disagreement* in the *other*. And 'tis evident that both their Consent and Disagreement arise from the same Principle: A Principle which destroys the Tenets, which this Author labours to establish. For, to resume our Illustration, as the various Opinions concerning the superior Wholesomeness of this or that kind of *Diet,* does not change the Nature of *Bread* or *Poison*; so neither can the various Opinions concerning *Polygamy* or *Incest,* affect or change the Nature of *Benevolence* and *Generosity, Adultery* and *Murder.* 'Tis plain, these various Opinions have been formed "upon such Actions only, as are not universally and clearly connected with the Happiness or Misery of Mankind."[29] As these Actions have been deemed productive of the *one* or the *other,* they have been regarded as *Virtues* or *Vices:* But this Variety of

---

29. Not a quotation from Mandeville, but a paraphrase of what Brown takes to be his essential position.

Opinions does no [145] more unsettle the Nature of those Actions, whose *Tendency* is clear and *certain*; than the Debates on the superior Wholesomeness of animal or vegetable *Diet* can change the Nature of *Bread* and *Poison*. Hence it appears, that Virtue and Vice are permanent Realities, and that their Nature is fixed, certain, and *invariable*.

Thus one Extreme produceth another. For the noble Writer and this Gentleman, through a strong Dislike of each other's Systems, have *both* endeavoured to prove *too much*, and in Consequence have proved *nothing*. The one, contending for the permanent *Reality* of Virtue, and, not content to fix it on its proper Basis, attempts to establish certain *absolute* and *immutable* Forms of Beauty, without Regard to any *further End*; and thus, by laying a chimerical Foundation, *betrays* the Cause which he so generously defends. The other, intent on destroying the permanent Reality of Virtue and Vice, and perceiving how weak a Basis the noble Writer had laid for their Establishment, after proving *this* to be imaginary, as wisely as honestly infers, there is no real one in Nature. We now see the Folly of these Extremes: That as on the [146] one Part, *Virtue* and *Vice* are Things merely *relative* to the *Happiness* of Man; so on the other, while Man continues what he is, all those *Relations* which concern his *Happiness,* and arise from his present Manner of Existence, are likewise *permanent* and *immutable*.

SECTION V

But this idle Objection against the permanent *Reality* of Virtue and Vice, is not the only one which the Writer last mentioned hath laboured, for the Destruction of Religion and Virtue. For the main Drift and Intention of his Book is to prove no less a Paradox than this, that "private Vices are public Benefits." Now, till this Objection be removed, our Idea and Definition of Virtue can never be thoroughly established. For if *private Vices* be *public Benefits,*[30] then private *Virtues* are public *Mischiefs*. And if so, what becomes of our *Definition?*

30. This phrase supplied the subtitle of Mandeville's *Fable of the Bees* and crystallized its central insight, that public prosperity is nourished by the appetites and passions in individuals which we normally censure as vicious.

Now, the first notable Circumstance in this formidable Assertion of Dr. MANDEVILLE, is its utter Inconsistency with all that he hath advanced in order to destroy the Reality of Vice and Virtue. For if indeed [147] these be mere *Names,* the Creatures of Fancy and Opinion, how can they be attended with any *uniform* Effects? How can they be either public *Benefits,* or public *Evils?*—If on the contrary, they really produce certain uniform Effects, as he hath attempted to prove, how can they be mere *Non-Entities,* the Creatures of Fancy and Opinion? Here lies a gross and palpable Incoherence: Take which of his two Theories you please, the other absolutely destroys it. If Vice be a public *Benefit,* it must be a permanent *Reality:* If it is not a permanent *Reality,* it cannot be a public *Benefit.*

Let us now examine the Foundations on which he hath built this strange Hypothesis. His Book may be analysed into four different Principles, which he hath variously combined, or rather jumbled together, according as each in their Turn would best serve his Purpose.

The first Principle he lays down, or rather takes up, *i.e.* for granted, is, "that Man is a compound of evil Passions:" In other Words, "that the Gratification of the natural Appetites is in itself a Vice."[31] There are in his Book, at least a hundred [148] Pages of the lowest common-place Declamation, all founded on this one Principle, brought from the *solitary Caves* and *Visions* of the *Desart.* Thus the Desire of being esteemed by others, he stigmatizes with the Name of *Pride:* The natural Desire of social Converse between the two Sexes, he distinguisheth by a *grosser* Appellation. In a word, through the whole Course of his Argument, he *supposes* that every *selfish* Appetite (that is, every Appetite which hath regard to *ourself*) is in its own Nature vile and abominable. This the candid Reader will probably think a little hard upon human Nature: That no Man can be *virtuous,* while he endeavours to be *esteemed,* while he loves to quench his Thirst, minister to Posterity, or eat his Dinner. On the Weight of these plain Instances, the Value of this first Principle may be safely left to any Man's impartial Trial.

---

31. Again, not precise quotations from Mandeville, but rather Brown's re-statements of what he takes to be central Mandevillean principles: cf., e.g., "*I believe Man . . . to be a compound of various Passions*" (Mandeville, *Fable,* vol. I, p. 39).

Having thus branded every Gratification of the natural Appetites; he gains from hence a proper Foundation for the second *Pillar* of this *Temple* of Vice. For he acquaints us with great Solemnity, that, of all other Vices, that of *Luxury* is most beneficial to a State: And that if this were [149] banished the Nation, all Kinds of manual Occupations would immediately languish and decay.ˢ He says indeed, that *Pedants* make Objections to this Vice of Luxury, and tell you, that it *enervates* a People: But he adds, that "since he has seen the World, the Consequences of Luxury to a Nation, seem not so dreadful to him as they did."ᵗ Had he left the Matter here, we should have been at a Loss to know how he would have made out this strange Tale: But the Riddle is cleared up at once, when we hear him say, that "every thing is Luxury, that is not immediately necessary to make Man subsist as he is a living Creature."ᵛ

We should have been startled perhaps had he assured us, that he had a *Wind-mill* which laid *Eggs*, and bred *young* ones: But how easily had he reconciled us to his Veracity by only saying, that by a *Wind-mill* he meant a *Goose*, or a *Turkey*?

Thus, when he affirms that Luxury produceth public Happiness, we stand ready for some deep and subtile Speculation, to support so wondrous a Paradox. But when he poorly tells us, "that every thing is [150] Luxury that is not immediately necessary to make Man subsist as he is a living Creature;" we laugh not so much at his Impudence, as at our own Folly in giving Ear to so idle a Prater,³³ whose wide-mouthed Paradoxes so soon dwindle into a little harmless Nonsense; and when we thought we had him reforming States, and new-modeling Philosophy, he was all the while playing at *Crambo.*³⁴

---

s. *Fable of the Bees,* passim.

t. Ibid. p. 247.

v. Ibid. p. 108.³²

32. Mandeville, *Fable*, pp. 118 and 107.

33. An idle, prolix, and sometimes pompous talker (*OED*).

34. A game in which one player gives a word or line of verse to which each of the others has to find a rhyme; used contemptuously for a foolish or vacuous pastime (*OED*).

Lest it should be suspected, that the Features of this Man's Folly are here aggravated, take a Copy of his Countenance in one Instance out of many that might be given. "The Consequences, saith he, of this Vice of Luxury to a Nation, seem not so dreadful to me as they did"—For "clean Linen weakens a Man no more than Flannel."ʷ Now from these Passages laid together, it appears; first, that Luxury is a Vice; secondly, that to wear clean Linen is Luxury; and, therefore, it comes out as clear as the Day, "that *to wear clean Linen* is a Vice."

Seriously; the Sophistry here employed, is one of those Insults that can be safely offered only to an *English* Under[151]standing; which though none of the brightest is always ready to reflect the present Object. Did ever any Man before—except only a Set of wrong-headed Enthusiasts, whose Visions he is here obliged to adopt—did ever any Man maintain, that to use the Bounties of Nature, or enjoy the Conveniences of Life was a criminal Indulgence? Did ever any Man maintain, that *he* could be *viciously* luxurious, who neither *hurt* his *Neighbour* nor *himself?* At this Rate, by an arbitrary Use of Words, and putting one Expression for another, we might boldly advance the most palpable Contradictions, and maintain, that Dr. M—D—LE was a Man of Modesty and Virtue.

Thus far we have seen this Writer endeavouring to throw the *false* Colours of *Vice* upon the *natural Passions,* and such a *Use* of the Gifts of Nature as is really *Innocent.* In examining his two remaining Principles, we shall find him acting a Part the very *reverse*; and with the same Effrontery, endeavouring to throw the *false* Colours of *public Utility* on such *Actions* and *Affections* as are really *criminal* and *destructive.* [152]

To this Purpose he boldly selects some of the most flagrant Crimes; and assures us, that without their happy Influence the Public would suffer exceedingly. Who had ever dreamt, that Mankind receives Benefit from *Thieves* and *House-breakers?* Yet he tells us, that "if all People were strictly honest, half the Smiths in the Nation would want Employment."ˣ

---

w. *Fable of the Bees,* p. 119.[35]
x. *Fable of the Bees,* p. 82.[36]
35. Mandeville, *Fable,* vol. I, p. 119.
36. Ibid., pp. 86 and 87.

Highwaymen too, and *Robbers* are useful in their Generation.[37] For "if a Miser should be robbed of Five hundred or a thousand Guineas,[y] it is certain, that as soon as this Money should come to circulate, the Nation would be the better for the Robbery, and receive the same and as real a Benefit from it, as if an Archbishop had left the same Sum to the Public."[z] [153]

He is abundantly rhetorical on "the large Catalogue of solid Blessings that accrue from, and are owing to intoxicating Gin."[a] Insomuch, that if the Drunkenness and Frenzy arising from the excessive Use of this salutary Liquor were curbed by the Magistrate, he seems to foretel the most fatal Consequences to the public Wealth and Welfare.

Here then he enumerates several real Crimes, which are *necessarily* attended with *great Evils*; and these he demonstrates, are *accidentally* productive of *some Good*. And this indeed is the only Part of his Argument, that is attended with any Degree of Plausibility: For here, it must be owned, there is Room for a dishonest Mind to *confound*, though by no Means to *convince* an impartial Reader. Because the Consequences of these Crimes being of a various and *discordant* Nature, some having the Appearance of *Good*, and others of *Ill* to Society; a *rhetorical* Display of the *former* may possibly induce a superficial Enquirer, who is caught by a Glare of Eloquence, to doubt whether *these* do not really *predominate*. But a moderate Share of Attention [154] will convince us, that this is impossible. Because all the real Vices he mentions, though they be accidentally

---

y. There is a common Error with regard to *Misers*, on which this pretended Argument is built. They are generally accounted the greatest Enemies of *Society*, because they *hoard* the *Wealth* which ought to *circulate*. Now, to give even a *Miser* his due, this is really a groundless Charge: For they seldom *hoard* more than certain useless Papers or Parchments, in the Shape of *Notes*, *Bonds*, and *Mortgages*: While the Wealth which they thus *hoard* in *Imagination*, circulates *freely* among all Ranks of People. The Guilt of the Miser's Passion lies in its being essentially destructive both of Justice and Benevolence.

z. *Fable of the Bees,* p. 83.

a. *Fable of the Bees,* p. 89.[38]

37. A phrase drawn from the contemporary language of Biblical commentary; cf., e.g., Anon., *An Exposition on the Old and New Testament, in Five Volumes,* fourth edition, 5 vols (1737), vol. V, commentary on Acts 21:4.

38. Mandeville, *Fable,* vol. I, p. 89 ff.

productive of some Good; yet 'tis such as might effectually be obtained without them. Thus the Money taken wrongfully by Stealth or Robbery, is only of Service to the Public by its Circulation: But Money may circulate without Stealth or Robbery; and therefore 'tis neither the Stealth nor Robbery that is of Service to the Public. On the other part, there are great and substantial Evils, which these Crimes, and these alone give Rise to. On this Occasion one might be very large on the Terrors and Distress, the Murders, and consequent Miseries, which the Villanies patronized by this Writer do necessarily produce. One who was Master of Dr. MANDE-VILLE's Town-Rhetoric and *Town-Experience,* might draw a striking Picture of honest and industrious Families rowzed from Sleep at Midnight, only to be plundered and destroyed; of the horrid Attempts of abandoned Wickedness, let loose from Fear by the Security of Darkness; the Shricks of ravished Maids and Matrons; the dying Groans of Brothers, Fathers, Husbands, weltring in their Blood; the [155] Cries of innocent and helpless Orphans weeping over their murdered Parents, deprived at once of all that were dear to them, of all that could yield them Consolation or Support; and suffering every vile Indignity, that unrelenting Villainy can suggest or perpetrate. And how, think you, does this Scene of domestic Horror change its original Nature, and rise at length into a public Blessing? Why, because the Adventurers, having made off with their Booty, may possibly "lay it out upon a *Harlot,* or squander it in a *Night-cellar,* or a *Gin-shop.*"[b] And thus the Money circulates through the Nation. But, in the mean Time, our Philosopher hath forgot the helpless Family reduced to Beggary by the Prowess of his *nocturnal Heroes:* He hath forgot that the fond and indulgent Parent might no less probably have laid out the Money in the temperate Maintenance and liberal Education of his Children, which is now squandered in unprofitable *Riot* and *Excess:* That these Destroyers of other Men's Happiness and their own, had they been employed in honest Labour, in the Cultivation of *Lands,* or the Improvement of *Manufactures,* might [156] have done substantial Services to the Public and themselves, without the guilty *Alloy* of unprovoked Mischief. From

b. *Fable of the Bees,* p. 84, 85.[39]
39. A *précis* rather than a quotation; but cf. Mandeville, *Fable,* vol. I, p. 87 ff.

these Circumstances impartially compared, 'tis evident, that the only essential Consequence of private Vice, is public Misery: And thus our Author's new fashioned System of Morals falls back again into nothing.

His fourth Principle is much less plausible. Indeed he never applies to this, but when reduced to the last Necessity: When therefore every other Foundation fails him, he attempts to impose upon his Reader's Negligence or Simplicity, by representing Vice as a *Cause*, where in Reality 'tis a *Consequence*. Thus he tells us, "Great Wealth and foreign Treasure will ever scorn to come among Men, unless you'll admit their *inseparable Companions*, Avarice and Luxury: Where Trade is considerable, Fraud will *intrude*. To be at *once well-bred* and *sincere*, is no less than a Contradiction: And therefore whilst Man advances in Knowledge, and his Manners are polished, we must expect to see at the same Time his Desires enlarged, his Appetites refined, and his *Vices increased*."[c] [157] So again, having been driven from his other strong Holds by certain impertinent Remarkers, whom he wisely dismisseth with an Air of Superiority and Contempt, he takes Refuge in the same ambiguous Phrases: As that "Vice is *inseparable* from great and potent Societies, in the same Manner as *dirty Streets* are a necessary Evil, inseparable from the *Felicity* of *London*."[d]

Now, though this happy *Simile* may work Wonders in a *Coffee-House*, amongst those who see every *dirty Alley* pregnant with Demonstration; yet, 'tis to be hoped, more serious Readers may distinguish better. And be enabled to tell him, that before they grant his Position, *that private Vice is public Benefit*, they expect he should prove, "that the Dirt in *London* Streets, is the Cause or Instrument whereby *London* becomes a populous and flourishing City:" A Proposition almost as remote from common Apprehension, as that *Tenterden Steeple* is the *Cause* of *Goodwin Sands*.[42]

c. *Fable of the Bees*, p. 201.[40]
d. *Fable of the Bees*, Preface, p. 9, &c.[41]
40. Mandeville, *Fable*, vol. I, p. 185.
41. Ibid., p. 12.
42. A Kentish proverb deriving from the story that the Goodwin Sands (quicksands near the coastal town of Deal) were once solid ground in the possession of Earl Godwin, but that the Bishop of Rochester employed the revenue assigned to maintain the sea defenses to endow and build Tenterden church, thus allowing the encroachment of the sea and the formation of the quicksands; see Thomas Fisher,

Thus, we see how dextrously he puts the Change upon the unwary Reader; and while he pretends to exhibit an *essential Cause,* slurs him off with an *accidental Consequence.* [158]

Into these four Principles, all evidently *False* or *Foreign* to the Purpose, his whole Book may be justly analysed. Nor is there one Observation in the Compass of so many hundred Pages, which tends to support the pernicious Falsehood that disgraceth his *Title-Page,* but what will naturally resolve itself into one or other of these wretched *Sophisms.* 'Tis therefore unnecessary to lead the Reader through all the *Windings* of this immense *Labyrinth* of Falsehood, 'tis enough, to have given the *Clue* which may safely conduct him through them.

SECTION VI

Having at Length gained an Adequate Idea of Virtue, and found that it is no other than "the voluntary Production of the greatest public Happiness;" we may now safely proceed to consider, "upon what Foundations Mankind are *obliged* to the Practice of it?"

And here we shall find another metaphysical *Cloud* resting upon *this* Path, in itself plain and easy to all Mankind. For the very Notion of *Obligation* to Virtue hath been as much confounded by moral Wri[159]ters, as the Idea of *Virtue* itself. And here we might travel through another System of *Logomachies;*[43] while one asserts, that we are obliged to *love* and *pursue* Virtue, because *she* is *beautiful*; another, because Virtue is *good*; another, because Virtue is *good in itself*; a fourth, because Virtue is *Truth*; a fifth, because it is *agreeable to Nature*; a sixth, because it is agreeable to the *Relations of Things.*

But 'tis supposed that the intelligent Reader, from a review of the first Section of this Essay, may be convinced, that all these *amusing* Expressions amount to no more than this, "that there is some Reason or other

---

The Kentish Traveller's Companion (Rochester, 1776), pp. 159–60. The proverb had been used in earlier eighteenth-century political polemic: cf., e.g., Charles Hornby, *A Caveat Against the Whiggs* (1710), p. 55.

43. Contentions about words (rather than, by implication, realities) (*OED*).

why we ought to practise Virtue; but that the particular Reason doth not appear, notwithstanding all this refined Pomp of Affirmation." And as it hath already been made evident, that the *Essence* of Virtue consists in a Conformity of our Affections and Actions, with the greatest *public Happiness*; so it will now appear, that "the only *Reason* or *Motive,* by which Individuals can possibly be *induced* or *obliged* to the Practice of Virtue, must be the *Feeling* immediate, or the *Prospect* of future *private Happiness.*" [160]

Doubtless, the noble Writer's Admirers will despise and reject this, as an unworthy Maxim. For so it hath happened, that in the Height of their Zeal, for supporting his Opinions, they generally stigmatize *private Happiness,* as a Thing scarce worth a wise Man's enquiring after. Indeed, the many ambiguous Phrases of their Master have contributed not a little to this *vulgar Error.* For in one Place, he brands the modern Philosophers and Divines with the Name of Sophisters and Pedants, for "rating Life by the Number and Exquisiteness of the pleasing Sensations."[e] At other Times he speaks of *Pleasure,* with all the Contempt of an antient *Stoic.*[f] In the same high Style of the *Athenian Porch,*[46] he passeth Judgment on the Hopes of the Religious: "They have made Virtue so mercenary a Thing, and have talked so much of its *Rewards,* that one can hardly tell what there is in it, after all, which can be *worth* rewarding."[g] So again, he derides those "modern Projectors, who would new frame the human Heart; and have a mighty Fancy to reduce all its Motions, [161] Balances, and Weights to that one Principle and Foundation of a cool and deliberate *Selfishness:* And thus, Love of one's Country, and Love of Mankind, must also be *Self-love.*"[h]

e. *Wit and Hum.* Part iii. § 4.[44]
f. *Moral.* Part iii. § 3.[45]
g. *Wit,* Part ii. § 3.[47]
h. *Wit,* Part ii. § 3.[48]
44. Shaftesbury, *Characteristicks,* vol. I, p. 77.
45. Ibid., vol. II, pp. 239–47.
46. The public ambulatory (or *Stoa Poikile*) in the agora of ancient Athens, in which the philosopher Zeno of Citium discoursed with his followers, and from which their school derived its name of Stoic; hence a metonymy for Stoic philosophy itself.
47. Shaftesbury, *Characteristicks,* vol. I, p. 61.
48. Ibid., p. 74.

Now ere we proceed further, it may be necessary to remark, that in some Degree there hath been a *Strife about Words* in this particular too. For these Expressions of *Selfishness* and *Disinterestedness* have been used in a very *loose* and *indeterminate* Manner. In one Sense a *Motive* is called *disinterested*; when it consists in a pure *benevolent* Affection, or a Regard to the *moral Sense*. In another, no Motive is *disinterested:* For even in acting according to these Impulses of Benevolence and Conscience, we gratify an Inclination, and act upon the Principle or *immediate Feeling* of *private Happiness*. Thus when we say, "We love Virtue for Virtue's Sake;" 'tis only implied, that we find immediate Happiness from the Love and Practice of Virtue, without Regard to external or future Consequences.

Another Source of mutual Misapprehension on this Subject hath been "the In[162]troduction of *metaphorical* Expressions instead of *proper* ones." Nothing is so common among the Writers on Morality, as "the Harmony of Virtue"—"the Proportion of Virtue." So the noble Writer frequently expresseth himself. But his favourite Term, borrowed indeed from the Antients, is "the BEAUTY of Virtue."—*Quae si videri posset, mirabiles excitaret amores*[i]—Of this our Author and his Followers, especially the most ingenious of them,[k] are so *enamoured,* that they seem utterly to have forgot they are *talking in Metaphor,* when they describe the Charms of this *sovereign Fair*. Insomuch, that an unexperienced Person, who should read their *Encomiums,* would naturally fall into the Mistake of him, who asked

i. Cicero.[49]

k. Mr. Hutcheson.[50]

49. Brown misquotes from memory a celebrated passage of Cicero's *De Officiis,* I.v: "Formam quidem ipsam, Marce fili, et tamquam faciem honesti vides, 'quae si oculis cerneretur, mirabiles amores,' ut ait Plato, 'excitaret sapientiae'"; "You see here, Marcus my son, the very form and as it were the face of moral goodness; 'and if,' as Plato says, 'it could be seen with the physical eye, it would awaken a marvellous love of wisdom.'"

50. Francis Hutcheson (1694–1746); moral philosopher who, under the influence of Robert, Viscount Molesworth, had developed Shaftesbury's "moral sense" philosophy in works such as *An Inquiry into the Original of our Ideas of Beauty and Virtue* (1725) and his *Essay on the Nature and Conduct of the Passions and Affections* (1728); appointed Professor of Moral Philosophy at the University of Glasgow, 1729, assuming office in 1730.

the Philosopher, "Whether the Virtues were not living Creatures?"[1] Now this *figurative* Manner, so essentially interwoven into philosophical Disquisition, hath been the Occasion of great Error. It tends to mislead us both with regard to the Nature of Virtue, and our Obligations to the Practice of it. For first, it induceth a Persuasion, that Virtue is *excellent* without Regard to any of [163] its Consequences: And secondly, that he must either want Eyes, or common Discernment, who doth not at first Sight fall in Love with this *matchless Lady.*

Therefore setting aside, as much as may be, all ambiguous Expressions, it seems evident, that "a Motive, from its very Nature, must be something that affects *ourself.*" If any Man hath found out a Kind of Motive which doth not affect *himself,* he hath made a deeper Investigation into the "Springs, Weights, and Balances" of the human Heart, than I can pretend to. Now what can possibly affect *ourself,* or determine us to Action, but either the Feeling or Prospect of *Pleasure* or *Pain, Happiness* or *Misery?*

But to come to the direct Proof: 'Tis evident, even to Demonstration, that no *Affection* can, in the strict Sense, be more or less *selfish* or *disinterested* than another; because, *whatever* be its *Object,* the *Affection* itself is *still* no other than a *Mode* either of *Pleasure* or of *Pain*; and is therefore *equally* to be referred to the *Mind* or *Feeling* of the *Patient,* whatever be its *external Occasion.* Indeed, a late Writer of Subtilty and Refinement hath attempted to [164] make a Distinction here. He says, "It hath been observed, that every Act of Virtue or Friendship is attended with a secret *Pleasure*; from whence it hath been concluded, that Friendship and Virtue could not be disinterested. But the Fallacy of this is obvious. The virtuous Sentiment or Passion *produces* the Pleasure, and does not *arise* from it. I feel a Pleasure in doing good to my Friend, *because* I love him;

1. Senecae Epist. cxiv.[51]

51. A paraphrase of the opening of Seneca, *Epistulae Morales,* CXIII.i: "Desideras tibi scribi a me, quid sentiam de hac quaestione iactata apud nostros: an iustitia, fortitudo, prudentia ceteraeque virtutes animalia sint"; "You ask me to write to you with my opinion concerning this question debated amongst our friends, namely whether or not justice, fortitude, prudence, and the other virtues are living beings."

but I do not love him for the Sake of that Pleasure."[m] Now to me, the
Fallacy of *this* is obvious. For in Fact, neither the *Passion,* nor the *Pleasure,* are either the *Cause* or the *Consequence* of each other; they neither
produce nor *arise* from each other; because, in Reality, they are the *same
Thing* under *different Expressions.* This will be clear, if we state the Case
as follows: "To *love* my Friend, is to *feel* a *Pleasure* in *doing him Good.*"
And conversely; "to feel a *Pleasure* in *doing Good* to my Friend, is to *love
him.*" Where 'tis plain that the *Terms* are *synonymous.* The *Pleasure* therefore is the very *Passion itself*; and neither *prior* nor *posterior* to it, as this
Gentleman supposeth. [165]

Again, that the Pleasures arising from Benevolence, and the moral
Sense, are strictly *Selfish,* in this Sense of the Word, like every other Enjoyment, seems evident from some parallel Concessions of the noble
Writer. For these seemingly disinterested Pleasures he perpetually sets
on a Level with the Perceptions of natural Beauty, Order, Harmony, and
Proportion. These last are, by all, acknowledged to be of the selfish Kind;
therefore the other are so too; being only a *higher Order of the same,* and
expresly called so by the noble Writer.[n]

The Reasons why the great universal Principle of *private Happiness*
hath not been so clearly seen in the *Benevolent,* as in the *Self-Passions,*
seem to be these. First, Ambiguous Expressions, such as have been remarked above. 2*dly,* Perhaps some Degree of *Pride,* and Affectation of
Merit; because *Merit* seems to appear in what is called *Disinterest.* 3*dly,*
And perhaps principally, because in the Exercise of the benevolent
Passions, the Happiness is essentially *concomitant* with the Passion itself, and therefore is not easily separated from it by the *Imagination,* so as
to be considered [166] as a *distinct End.* Whereas in the Passions called
Selfish, the Happiness sought after is often *unattainable,* and therefore
easily and necessarily distinguished by the Imagination as a *positive
End.* This Circumstance of Union however, as is judiciously remarked

m. Hume's *Essays, Mor.* and *Polit.* p. 125.[52]
n. *Moralists,* Part ii.
52. David Hume, "Of the Dignity or Meanness of Human Nature" (Hume, *Essays,* pp. 85–86).

by one of the noble Writer's Followers,° proves the great Superiority and Excellence of the benevolent Affections, considered as a Source of Happiness, beyond the Passions and Appetites, commonly called the *Selfish*.

But although these Observations be necessary, in order to clear up an Affair, which hath been much perplexed with philosophical, or *unphilosophical* Refinements; yet, on a closer Examination, it will appear, in the most direct Manner, from the noble Writer himself, that "there is no other Principle of human Action, but that of the *immediate* or *foreseen* Happiness of the Agent:" That all these amusing Speculations concerning the *Comely, Fit,* and *Decent*; all these *verbal* Separations between *Pleasure, Interest, Beauty,* and *Good,* might have been sunk in one *precise* and plain Disquisition, concerning such Actions and Affections as [167] yield a *lasting,* and such as afford only a *short* and transient *Happiness.* For thus, after all, his Lordship explains himself: "That *Happiness* is to be pursued, and, in Fact, is always sought after; that the Question is not, who *loves himself,* and who *not*; but who *loves* and *serves himself* the *rightest,* and after the *truest* Manner.—That 'tis the Height of *Wisdom,* no doubt, to be *rightly Selfish*"—"Even to leave Family, Friends, Country, and Society—in good Earnest, *who would not,* if it were *Happiness* to do so?"ᵖ

These Expressions are so strongly pointed, as to leave no further Doubt concerning the noble Writer's Sentiments on this Subject. Indeed, they are the natural Dictates of common Sense, unsophisticated with false Philosophy. In every subsequent Debate therefore, wherein his Lordship's Opinions are concerned, we may safely build on this as an acknowledged and sure Foundation, "that the Motives or natural Obligations of Man to the Practice of Virtue, can only arise from a Sense of his *present,* or a Prospect of his *future Happiness.*" [168]

o. Three Treatises, by *J. H.* Treat. 3ᵈ. *On Happiness,* p. 189.[53]
p. *Wit and Hum.* Part iii. § 3.[54]
53. James Harris (see above, p. 96, n. 13).
54. Shaftesbury, *Characteristicks,* vol. I, pp. 76 and 74.

SECTION VII

Now this Conclusion will carry us to another Question of a very interesting and abstruse Nature: That is, "How far, and upon what Foundation, the uniform Practice of Virtue, is *really* and *clearly* connected with the Happiness of every Individual?" For so far, as we have seen, and no further, can every Individual be naturally moved or obliged to the Practice of it.

This is evidently a Question of *Fact:* And as it relates to the *Happiness of Man,* can only be determined by appealing to his *Constitution.* If *this* be indeed *uniform* and *invariable*; that is, if every Individual hath the same Perceptions, Passions, and Desires; then indeed the Sources of Happiness must be *similar* and *unchangeable.* If, on the contrary, different Men be differently constituted; if they have *different* Perceptions, Passions, and Desires; then must the Sources of their Happiness be equally *various.*

It should seem therefore, that "while Moralists have been enquiring into human Happiness, they have generally con[169]sidered it, as arising from one *uniform* and *particular* Source, instead of tracing it up to those various Fountains whence it really springs; which are indefinitely various, combined, and indeterminable." And this seems to have been the most general Foundation of Error.

If we speak with Precision, there are but three Sources in Man, of Pleasure and Pain, Happiness and Misery: These are *Sense, Imagination,* and the *Passions.* Now the slightest Observation will convince us, that these are associated, separated and combined in Man, with a Variety almost infinite. In some, the Pleasures and Pains of *Sense* predominate; Imagination is dull; the Passions inactive. In others, a more delicate Frame awakens all the Powers of Imagination; the Passions are refined; the Senses disregarded. A third Constitution is carried away by the Strength of Passion: The Calls of Sense are contemned; and Imagination becomes no more than the necessary Instrument of some further Gratification.

From overlooking this plain Fact, seems to have arisen the Discordance among Philosophers concerning the Happiness of Man. And while *each* hath attempted to exhibit [170] one favourite Picture, as the *Paragon* or *Standard* of human Kind; they have *all* omitted some Ten thousand other Resemblances which actually subsist in Nature.

Thus, most of the *Epicurean* Sect, tho' not the Founder of it, have discarded *Benevolence* and *Virtue* from their System of *private* Happiness. The modern Patronizers of this Scheme,[55] Mr. HOBBES, Dr. MANDEVILLE, and several *French* Writers, after heaping up a Collection of sordid Instances, which prove the *sensual* Inclinations and *Selfishness* of Man, leap at once to their desired Conclusion, that the pretended public Affections are therefore no more than the same low Passions in Disguise. That *Benevolence* makes no Part of Man's Nature; that the human Kind are absolutely unconnected with each other in Point of Affection: And that every Individual *seeks* and *finds* his *private* Happiness in and *from himself alone.*

The noble Writer, on the contrary, viewing the brighter Parts of human Nature, through the amiable Medium of the *Socratic* Philosophy; and fixing his Attention on the *public Affections,* as the Instruments both of public and private Happi[171]ness; rejects the *Epicurean's* Pretences[56] with Disdain: And fully conscious of the high Claims and Energy of Virtue, affirms that the *private Affections* are, by no means, a Foundation for *private Happiness:* That, on the contrary, we must universally promote the

55. Thomas Hobbes (1588–1679); mathematician and philosopher. Bernard de Mandeville (1670–1733); Dutch physician turned moral philosopher. Both men were exponents of an unillusioned, materialistic view of human nature, although their arguments rest on very different premises. By "several *French* Writers" Brown is probably referring to the followers of François de Marsillac (1613–80), duc de la Rochefoucauld, whose *Maximes* give expression to an astringent view of human motivation which dissolves all appearances of altruism into the underlying reality of self-love.

56. Brown is here using Epicurean in its looser modern sense to denote the advocates of materialist hedonism (although Hobbes and Mandeville would not have accepted that as a summary of their ethical philosophy). Epicureanism could also take the milder form of a philosophical outlook that focused upon achieving wellbeing (not necessarily equated with carnal self-indulgence) in this world rather than the next.

Welfare of others, if we would effectually secure our own: And that in every Case, "*Virtue* is the *Good,* and *Vice* the *Ill* of every one."[q]

'Tis plain, no two Systems of Philosophy can be more *discordant* than these; yet each of them have obtained a Number of Partizans in all Ages of the World. The Question relates to a *Fact,* and the Fact lies open to the *personal Examination* of all Mankind. Whence then can so strange an Opposition of Sentiments arise?

This seems to have arisen, not from a *false,* but a *partial* View and Examination of the Subject. The *Stoic* Party dwell altogether on the *social* or *public,* the *Epicurean*[58] no less on the *private* or *selfish* Affections: On these respectively they declaim; so that according to the one, Mankind are naturally a Race of *Demi-Gods*; according to the other, a Crew of *Devils. Both* forgetting, [172] what is unquestionably the Truth, that these *social* and *private* Affections are blended in an endless Variety of Degrees, and thus form an infinite Variety of Inclinations and of Characters. Many of the particular Facts, therefore, which these two Sects alledge, are true: But the *general* Consequence they draw from these *particular* Facts, is groundless and imaginary. Thus, 'tis true, that Mankind reap high Enjoyments from the Senses, Imagination, and Passions, without any regard to the public Affections: But the Consequence which the *Epicurean* would draw from hence, that "therefore the public

q. *Enquiry concerning Virtue,* passim.[57]

57. A paraphrase of Shaftesbury's thinking in the "Inquiry," as exemplified by passages such as the following: "if by the natural Constitution of any rational Creature, the same Irregularitys of Appetite which make him ill *to Others*, make him ill also *to Himself*; and if the same Regularity of Affections, which causes him to be good in *one* sense, causes him to be good also in *the other*; then is that Goodness by which he is thus useful to others, a real Good and Advantage to himself. And thus *Virtue* and *Interest* may be found at last to agree" (Shaftesbury, *Characteristicks*, vol. II, p. 9). The quotation is the final sentence of the work (Shaftesbury, *Characteristicks*, vol. II, p. 100).

58. Two schools of ancient Greek philosophy. The Stoic school was founded at Athens *c.* 300 B.C. by Zeno of Citium, and taught that virtue was best pursued through detachment from the external world. The Epicurean school was also founded in Athens at approximately the same time by Epicurus, whose philosophy embraced, rather than rejecting, the senses (although not in the spirit of mere sensuality which came to be associated with Epicureanism).

Affections are never, in any Case, a Source of private Happiness;" this is entirely void of Evidence: It supposeth Mankind to be *one uniform* Subject, while it is a Subject infinitely *various*; that every Individual has the same Feelings, Appetites, Fancies, and Affections, while, in Fact, they are mixed and combined in an endless Variety of Degrees. So, on the contrary, it must appear to every impartial Observer, that "the Exercise of the public Affections is a Source of the highest Gratification to many Individuals." But the *Stoic's* Conclusion, that "therefore the [173] uniform Exercise of the public Affections, in Preference to every other, is the only Source of Happiness to every Individual;" this is a Conclusion equally void of Evidence. For, like its opposite Extreme, it supposeth Mankind to be one uniform Subject, while, in Fact, it is a Subject indefinitely various. It supposes that every Individual has the same Feelings, Appetites, Fancies, and Affections, while, in Reality, they are mixed and combined in an endless Variety of Degrees.

Let us now assign the most probable Foundation, on which these *narrow* and *partial* Systems have been so commonly embraced. For, that two Theories so opposite, and so devoid of all rational Support, should have made their Way in the World, without some *permanent* Cause beyond the Instability of mere *Chance*, seems hardly credible.

It should seem therefore, that "while the Patronizers of these two Systems have attempted to give a general Picture of the human Species, they have all along taken the Copy from themselves: And thus their Philosophy, instead of being a true History of Nature, is no more than the [174] History of their own *Imaginations* or *Affections*."—This Truth may receive sufficient Confirmation from the Lives and Conduct of all the old Philosophers, from the *elegant* PLATO walking on his rich *Carpets*, to the *unbred* CYNIC snarling in his *Tub*.[59] As every Man's *Constitution* led him, so he adopted this or that Sect of *Philosophy*, and reasoned concerning *Fitness*, *Decency*, and *Good*. Read the Characters of CATO and

---

59. A reference to Diogenes the Cynic (fl. 4th c. B.C.), whose philosophy entailed an extravagant simplicity of life and a repudiation of civilized customs. He is said to have lived in an earthenware tub in the sanctuary of the mother of the gods at Athens.

CESAR,[60] and you will clearly discover the true Foundation on which the one became a rigid *Stoic,* the other, a gross *Epicurean.* The first, yet a *Boy,* discovered such an *inflexible* Adherence to the Privileges of his Country, that he refused his Assent to what he thought a Violation of them, though threatened with immediate Death.[r] The *latter,* yet unpractised in the Subtilties of Philosophy, and under the sole Dominion of natural Temper, discovered, at his first Appearance in the World, such Traits of *Art, Spirit,* and *Ambition,* that SYLLA declared, he saw something more formidable than MARIUS rising in him.[s] To bring down the Observation to modern Times; 'tis evident, that the Patronizers [175] of these two Systems inlist themselves according to the secret Suggestions of their

r. Plutarchi *Cato Utic.*[61]

s. Suetonii *Julius Cesar.*[62]

60. Marcus Porcius Cato "of Utica" (95–46 B.C.); Roman statesman of inflexible integrity, and an ideal of rectitude in eighteenth-century England as a result of Addison's wildly successful dramatization of the final phase of his life, *Cato: A Tragedy* (1713). Gaius Julius Caesar (102–44 B.C.); preeminent Roman general and statesman, whose personal rule marked the end of the Roman Republic.

61. "While Cato was still a boy, the Italian allies of the Romans were making efforts to obtain Roman citizenship. One of their number, Pompaedius Silo, a man of experience in war and of the highest position, was a friend of Drusus, and lodged at his house for several days. During this time he became familiar with the children, and said to them once: 'Come, beg your uncle to help us in our struggle for citizenship.' Caepio, accordingly, consented with a smile, but Cato made no reply and gazed fixedly and fiercely upon the strangers. Then Pompaedius said: 'But thou, young man, what sayest thou to us? Canst thou not take the part of the strangers with thy uncle, like thy brother?' And when Cato said not a word, but by his silence and the look on his face seemed to refuse the request, Pompaedius lifted him up through a window, as if he would cast him out, and ordered him to consent, or he would throw him down, at the same time making the tone of his voice harsher, and frequently shaking the boy as he held his body out at the window. But when Cato had endured this treatment for a long time without showing fright or fear, Pompaedius put him down, saying quietly to his friends: 'What a piece of good fortune it is for Italy that he is a boy; for if he were a man, I do not think we could get a single vote among the people'" (Plutarch, "Cato the Younger," II.1–4).

62. Gaius Marius (157–86 B.C.); Roman soldier and statesman; served as consul seven times; the leader of a popular and reforming party; eventually challenged and eclipsed by the aristocrat leader Sulla (or Sylla), who had previously served under Marius in the Jugurthine War. For Sulla's observation about Julius Caesar, see Suetonius, "Divus Iulius," I.3 and Plutarch, "Caesar," I.2.

several Passions. 'Tis well known, that the Writer of the *Fable of the Bees* was neither a *Saint* in his Life, nor a *Hermit* in his Diet: He seems to have been Master of a very considerable *Sagacity,* much Knowledge of the World, as it appears in populous *Cities,* extremely sensible to all the grosser *bodily* Enjoyments; but for *Delicacy* of Sentiment, Imagination, or Passion, for an exquisite *Taste* either in *Arts* or *Morals,* he appears to have been *incapable* of it.—The noble Writer is known to have been of a Frame the very Reverse of this: His *Constitution* was neither more nor less opposite to Dr. MANDEVILLE's, than his Philosophy. His sensual Appetites were weak; his Imagination all alive, noble, and capacious; his Passions were accordingly refined, and his public Affections (in *Fancy* at least) predominant. To these Instances, a moderate Share of Sagacity and Knowledge of the World may add others innumerable, in observing the Temper and Conduct of the Followers of these two Systems; who always take Party according to the Biass of their own Constitution. Among the *Epi*[176]*cureans* we ever find Men of high Health, florid Complexions, firm Nerves, and a Capacity for Pleasure: Of the *Stoic* Party are the delicate or sickly Frames, Men incapable of the grosser sensual Enjoyments, and who either *are,* or *think* themselves *virtuous.* Now from these accumulated Proofs we may be convinced, that "they who give us these *uniform* Pictures of a Subject so *various* as *Mankind,* cannot have drawn them from *Nature:* That, on the contrary, they have copied them from their own *Hearts* or *Imaginations*; and fondly erected *themselves* into a general Standard of the *human Species.*"

But although these Observations may afford sufficient Proof, that the *Stoic* and *Epicurean* Pictures of Mankind are equally partial; yet still it remains to be enquired how far, upon the whole, the human Kind in Reality leans towards the *one* or the *other:* That is, "how far, and in what Degree, the uniform Practice of Virtue constitutes the Happiness of Individuals?" Now the only Method of determining this Question, will be to select some of the most striking *Features* of the human Heart: By this Means we may *approach* towards a real [177] *Likeness,* though from that infinite Variety which subsists in Nature, the *Draught* must ever be inadequate and *defective.*

To begin with the lowest Temperature of the human Species; "there are great Numbers of Mankind, in whom the *Senses* are the chief Sources of Pleasure and Pain." To the Harmony of Sounds, the Beauty of Forms, the Decorum of Actions, they are utterly insensible. They are sagacious and learned in all the Gratifications of Sense; but if you talk to them of the public Affections, of Generosity, Kindness, Friendship, Good-will, you talk in a Language they understand not. They seem, in a Manner, unconnected with the rest of their Kind; they view the Praises, Censures, Enjoyments and Sufferings of others, with an Eye of perfect Indifference. To Men thus formed, how can Virtue gain Admittance? Do you appeal to their *Taste* of Beauty? They have none. To their acknowledged Perceptions of *Right* and *Wrong?* These they Measure by their private *Interest.* To the Force of the public *Affections?* They never felt them. Thus every Avenue is foreclosed, by which *Virtue* should enter. [178]

The next remarkable Peculiarity is, "where not the Senses, but *Imagination* is the predominant Source of Pleasure." Here the Taste always runs into the elegant Refinements of polite Arts and Acquirements; of Painting, Music, Architecture, Poetry, Sculpture: Or, in Defect of this truer Taste, on the false Delicacies of Dress, Furniture, and Equipage. Yet Experience tells us, that this Character is widely different from the virtuous one: That all the Powers of Imagination may subsist in their full Energy, while the *public Affections* and *moral Sense* are weak or utterly inactive. Nor can there be any necessary Connexion between these different Feelings; because we see Numbers immersed in all the finer Pleasures of Imagination, who never once consider them as the Means of *giving Pleasure* to *others,* but merely as a *selfish* Gratification. This the noble Writer seems to have been aware of; and, not without great Address, endeavours to convert the Fact into a Proof of his main Theory, though, in Reality, it affords the strongest Evidence against him. "The *Venustum,* the *Honestum,* the *Decorum* of Things, will force its Way. They, who refuse to give it Scope in the [179] nobler Subjects of a rational and moral Kind, will find its Prevalency elsewhere, in an inferior Order of Things—as either in the Study of common *Arts,* or in the Care and Culture of mere mechanic *Beauties.*—The *Specter* still will *haunt* us, in *some Shape or other;* and when driven from our cool Thoughts, and frighted from the *Closet,* will meet us even at Court, and fill our Heads with Dreams of Grandeur, Titles, Honours, and a false Magnificence and Beauty."[t] All this is ingenious and plausible: And the very elegant Allusion, of "the Specter still haunting us in some Shape or other," seems at first View to imply, that even the most obstinate Endeavours to get rid of the Force of moral Beauty, are ineffectual and vain. But a nearer Examination will convince us, that the noble Writer applies here to *Eloquence,* rather than *Argument*; and puts us off with a *Metaphor* instead of a *Reason*. For the Pleasures of Imagination, whether they run in the Channel of polite Arts, Furniture, Planting, Building, or Equipage, are indeed no *Specters,* but independent *Realities* fairly existing in the Mind: They have [180] no immediate or necessary Connexion with the Happiness of Mankind, which is often and *designedly* violated in order to gain the Possession of them. 'Tis true, the Pleasures of Imagination and Virtue are often *united* in the same Mind; but 'tis equally true, that they are often *separate*; that they who are most sensible to the *one,* are entire Strangers to the *other*; that one Man, to *purchase* a fine *Picture,* will *oppress* his Tenant; that another, to *relieve* his distressed Tenant, will *sell* his Statues or his Pictures. The Reason is evident: The one draws his Pleasure from *Imagination*; the other from *Affection* only. 'Tis clear therefore, that "where *Imagination* is naturally the predominant Source of Pleasure," the Motives to Virtue must be very *partial* and *weak,* since the chief Happiness ariseth from a Source entirely distinct from the *benevolent Affections*.

Another, and very different Temperature of the Heart of Man is that "wherein neither Sense nor Imagination, but the Passions are the chief Sources of Pleasure and Pain." This often forms the *best* or the *worst* of Characters. As it runs either, First, Into the Extreme of Selfish[181]ness, Jealousy, Pride, Hatred, Envy, and Revenge; or, 2*dly,* Into the amiable Affections of Hope, Faith, Candour, Pity, Generosity, and Good-will; or, 3*dly,* Into a various Mixture or Combination of these; which is undoubtedly the most common Temperature of human Kind.

t. *Wit and Hum.* Part iv. § 2.[63]
63. Shaftesbury, *Characteristicks,* vol. I, p. 87.

Now to the first of these Tempers, how can we affirm with Truth, that there is a natural Motive or Obligation to Virtue? On the contrary, it should seem, that, if there be any Motive, it must be to *Vice*. For 'tis plain, that from the Losses, Disappointments, and Miseries of Mankind, such vile Tempers draw their chief Felicity. The noble Writer indeed, in his Zeal for Virtue, considers these black Passions as *unnatural,* and brands them as a Source of *constant Misery.*ᵛ And sure it would be matter of Joy to all good Men, to find his Proofs convincing. But if indeed this be not a true Representation of the Case, I see not what Service can be done to the Interests of *Virtue,* by *disguising* Truth. 'Tis not the Part of a Philosopher to write *Panegyrics,* but to *investigate* the real State of human Nature; and the only Way of doing [182] this to any good Purpose, is to do it *impartially:* For with regard to human Nature, as well as Individuals, "Flattery is a Crime no less than Slander."

When therefore the noble Writer calls these Affections *unnatural,* he doth not sufficiently explain himself. If indeed by their being unnatural, he means, that "they are such in their Degrees or Objects as to violate the public Happiness, which is the main Intention of Nature;" in this Sense, 'tis acknowledged, they are *unnatural.* But this Interpretation is foreign to the Question; because it affects not the *Individual.* But if, by their being *unnatural,* he would imply, that they are "a Source of constant Misery to the Agent;" this seems a Proposition not easy to be determined in the Affirmative.

For the main Proof which he brings in Support of this Assertion is, "that the Men of *gentlest Dispositions,* and *best of Tempers,* have at some time or other been sufficiently acquainted with those Disturbances, which, at ill Hours, even small Occasions are apt to raise. From these slender Experiences of Harshness and ill Humour, they fully know and will con[183]fess the ill Moments which are passed, when the Temper is ever so little galled and fretted. How must it fare therefore with those, who hardly know any

v. *Enquiry.*⁶⁴

64. Cf., e.g., "Where there is this *absolute* Degeneracy, this *total* Apostacy from all Candour, Equity, Trust, Sociableness, or Friendship; there are few who do not see and acknowledg the Misery which is consequent" (Shaftesbury, *Characteristicks,* vol. II, p. 48).

better Hours in Life; and who, for the greatest Part of it, are agitated by a thorow *active Spleen,* a close and settled Malignity and Rancour?"ᵂ

Now, this Instance is by no means sufficient to support the Affirmation. For 'tis plain, that in the Case of the "Men of gentlest Dispositions, and best of Tempers, occasionally agitated by ill Humour," there must be a strong Opposition and Discordance, a violent Conflict between the habitual Affections of Benevolence, and these accidental Eruptions of Spleen and Rancour which rise to obstruct their Course. A Warfare of this Kind must indeed be a State of complete Misery, when all is Uproar within, and the distracted Heart set at Variance with itself. But the Case is widely different, where "a thorow active Spleen prevails, a close and *settled* Malignity and Rancour." For in this Temper, there is no parallel Opposition of contending Passions: Nor therefore any similar Founda[184]tion for inward Disquiet and intense Misery. So much the noble Writer himself is obliged to own elsewhere. "Is there that sordid Creature on Earth, who does not prize his own Enjoyment?—Is not *Malice* and *Cruelty* of the *highest Relish* with some Natures?"ˣ Again, and still more fully to the Purpose: "Had we Sense, we should consider, 'tis in Reality the *thorow* Profligate, the very *complete unnatural Villain* alone, who can any way *bid* for *Happiness* with the honest Man. True Interest is wholly on the one Side or the other. All between is Inconsistency, Irresolution, Remorse, Vexation, and an Ague-fit."ʸ Neither is this Acknowledgment peculiar to himself: "To be *consistent* either in Virtue or in Vice," was the farthest that some of the most penetrating among the Ancients could carry the Point of *Morals.*ᶻ Thus where the *selfish* or *malevolent* Affections happen to prevail, there can be no internal *Motive,* or natural *Obligation* to *Virtue.*

w. *Enquiry,* B. ii. Part ii. § 3.⁶⁵
x. *Moralists,* Part i.⁶⁶
y. *Wit and Hum.* Part iv. § 1.⁶⁷
z. See Arrian. *Epict.* lib. iii. c. 15.⁶⁸
65. Ibid., p. 97.
66. Ibid., p. 129.
67. Ibid., vol. I, p. 82.
68. The Bithynian soldier and statesman Arrian (*c.* 89–*c.* 145 A.D.), who became a Roman senator, consul, and archon of Athens, is our sole source for the thought of the Stoic philosopher Epictetus. Brown refers to a maxim in Arrian's *Discourses of Epictetus,* III.xv.13: "You must be one person, either good or bad."

On the contrary, where the amiable Affections of Hope, Candour, Generosity, and [185] Benevolence predominate, in this best and happiest of Tempers, Virtue hath indeed all the Force and Energy, which the noble Writer attributes to her Charms. For where the Calls of Sense are weak, the Imagination active and refined, the public Affections predominant; there the *moral Sense* must naturally reign with uncontrouled Authority; must produce all that Self-Satisfaction, that Consciousness of merited Kindness and Esteem, in which, his Lordship affirms, the very Essence of our Obligation to Virtue doth consist. This shall with Pleasure be acknowledged, nay asserted, as "the happiest of all Temperaments," whenever it can be *found* or *acquired*. To a Mind thus formed, Virtue doth indeed bring an *immediate* and *ample Reward* of perfect Peace and sincere Happiness in all the common Situations of Life. It may therefore be with Truth affirmed, that a Temper thus framed, is indeed naturally and internally obliged to the uniform Practice of Virtue.

There are, besides these, an endless Variety of Characters formed from the various Combinations of these essential *Ingredients*; which are not designed as a full [186] *Expression* of all the Tempers of Mankind: They are the Materials only, out of which these Characters are formed. They are no more than the several Species of *simple Colours* laid, as it were, upon the *Pallet*; which, variously *combined* and associated by the Hand of an experienced Master, would indeed call forth every striking *Resemblance*, every changeful Feature of the *Heart* of *Man*.

Now, among all this infinite Variety of Tempers which is found in Nature, we see there cannot be any uniform Motive or Obligation to Virtue, save only "where the Senses are weak, the Imagination refined, and the public Affections strongly predominant." For in every other Character, where either the Senses, gross Imagination, or selfish Passions prevail, a natural Opposition or Discordance must arise, and destroy the uniform Motive to Virtue, by throwing the Happiness of the Agent into a different Channel. How seldom this sublime Temper is to be found, is hard to say: But this may be affirmed with Truth, that every Man is not *really* possessed of it in the Conduct of Life, who *enjoys* it in *Imagination*, or *admires* it in his Closet, as it lies in the *En*[187]*quiry concerning Virtue*. A Character of this supreme Excellence must needs be *approved* by most: And the *Heart* of Man being an unexhausted Fountain of *Self-Deceit*, what it *approves*, is forward to think itself possessed of. Thus a lively *Imagination* and unperceived *Self-Love*, fetter the Heart in certain *ideal* Bonds of their own creating: Till at Length some turbulent and furious Passion arising in its Strength, breaks these fantastic Shackles which Fancy had imposed, and leaps to its Prey like a *Tyger* chained by *Cobwebs*.

SECTION VIII

From these different Views of human Nature, let us now bring this Argument to a Conclusion.

The noble Writer's Scheme of Morals therefore, being grounded on a Supposition, which runs through the whole Course of his Argument, that "all Mankind are naturally capable of attaining a *Taste* or *Relish* for *Virtue*, sufficient for every Purpose of social Life," seems essentially defective. For, from the Enquiry already made into the real and various Constitution [188] of Man, it appears, that a great Part of the Species are naturally incapable of this *fancied* Excellence. That the various Mixture and Predominancy of *Sense, Imagination*, and *Passion*, give a different Cast and Complexion of Mind to every Individual: That the *Feeling* or *Prospect* of Happiness can only arise from this Combination: That consequently, where the benevolent Affections and moral Sense are weak, the selfish Passions and Perceptions headstrong, there can be no internal Motive or natural Obligation to the *consistent* Practice of Virtue.

The most plausible Pretence I could ever meet with, amidst all the Pomp of Declamation thrown out in Support of this *All-Sufficiency* of a *Taste* in Morals, is this. "That although the Force and Energy of this Taste for Virtue appears not in every Individual, yet the Power lies dormant in every human Breast; and needs only be called forth by a *voluntary Self-Discipline*, in order to be brought to its just Perfection. That the Improvement in our Taste in Morals is parallel to the Progress of the Mind in every other Art and Excellence, in *Painting, Music, Architecture*, [189] *Poetry:* In which, a *true* Taste, however *natural* to Man, is not born with him, but formed and brought forth to Action by a proper *Study* and *Application*."

The noble Writer hath innumerable Passages of this Kind: So many indeed, that it were Labour lost to transcribe them.[a] And one of his Followers hath affirmed in still more emphatical Expressions, if possible, than his Master, that "the Height of *Virtuoso-ship* is Virtue."[b]

Now this State of the Case, though at first View it carries some Degree of Plausibility, yet, on a closer Examination, destroys the whole System. For if, as it certainly is, the *Capacity* for a Taste in *Morals,* be similar to a *Capacity* for a Taste in *Arts;* 'tis clear, that the most assiduous Culture or Self-Discipline can never make it even *general,* much less *universal.* One Man, we see, hath a Capacity or Genius for Painting, another for Music, a third for Architecture, a fourth for Poetry. Torture each of them as you please, you cannot infuse a Taste for any, but his own *congenial* Art. If you at[190]tempt to make the Poet an Architect, or the Painter a Musician, you may make a pretending *Pedant,* never an accomplished *Master.* 'Tis the same in Morals: Where the benevolent Affections are naturally strong, *there* is a *Capacity* for a high *Taste* in Virtue: Where these are *weak* or *wanting,* there is in the same Proportion, *little* or *no Capacity* for a *Taste* in Virtue. To harangue, therefore, on the superior Happiness attending the Exercise of the public Affections, is quite foreign to the Purpose. This superior Happiness is allowed, where the public Affections can be *found* or *made* predominant. But how can any Consequence be drawn from hence, so as to influence those who never felt the Impulse of public Affection? Are not the Pleasures of Poetry, Painting, Music, sublime, pure, and lasting, to those who *taste* them? Doth it therefore follow, that all Mankind, or any of them, can be harangued into a *Taste* and *Love* of these elegant Arts, while the very Capacity of receiving Pleasure from them is *wanting?* Thus in Morals, where a similar Incapacity takes Place through the natural Want of a lively Benevolence, no Progress can ever be made in the *Taste* or *Relish* for virtuous En[191]joyment. Though

a. *Charact.* passim.

b. *Letters of Hydaspes to Philemon,* Let. vi.[69]

69. A slight misquotation from Henry Coventry, *Philemon to Hydaspes; Relating a Second Conversation with Hortensius upon the Subject of False Religion,* second edition (1745), p. 13, which reads: "*Virtue* alone is the Truth and Perfection of *Virtuosoship.*"

therefore you should prove, as indeed one of Lord SHAFTESBURY's Followers hath done, "that Virtue is accommodate to all Places and Times, is *durable, self-derived,* and *indeprivable,*"ᶜ whence he concludes, it has the best Title to the Character of the sovereign Good; yet all the while, the main Point in Debate is taken for granted, that is, "whether the Possession of it be any *Good* at all." Now to those who receive no Increase of *internal* Happiness from it, it cannot be a *Good:* And where there is a natural *Defect* of benevolent Affection, it can give no *internal* Happiness: Consequently, though it have all the other Characters of the *Summum Bonum,* though it be *durable, self-derived,* and *indeprivable,* it can never, by such, be regarded as the *sovereign Good.*

'Tis pleasant enough to observe the Argumentation of the Writer last mentioned. After describing "the fairest and most amiable of Objects, the true and perfect Man, that Ornament of Humanity, that godlike Being, without Regard either to Pleasure or Pain, uninfluenced either by Prosperity or Adversity, superior to the World, [192] and its best and worst Events"—He then raiseth an Objection—"Does not this System border a little upon the Chimerical?"—On my Word, a shrewd Question, and well worth a good Answer; and thus he clears it up.—"It seems to require, said I, a Perfection to which no Individual ever arrived. That very Transcendence, said he, is an Argument on its behalf. Were it of a Rank inferior, it would not be that Perfection which we seek. Would you have it, said I, beyond Nature? If you mean, replied he, beyond any particular or individual Nature, most undoubtedly I would."ᵈ 'Tis not therefore to be wondered at, that this Gentleman, wrapped up in *Visions* of ideal Perfection, should express "his Contempt of those superficial Censurers, who profess to refute what they want even Capacities to comprehend."ᵉ Doubtless he means those *groveling* Observers, who draw their Ideas of Mankind "from particular or individual Natures," and have not yet risen

---

c. Three Treat. by *J. H.* Treat. 3ᵈ. *On Happiness.*[70]
d. Three Treat. by *J. H.* Treat. 3ᵈ. *On Happiness,* p. 215.[71]
e. Ibid. p. 108.[72]
70. Harris, *Treatises,* p. 121.
71. Ibid., pp. 214–16.
72. Ibid., p. 108.

to "the *beatific Vision*[f] of the perfect Man." Indeed, the Gentleman frankly owns, "that [193] Practice too often *creeps,* where Theory can *soar.*"[g] And this I take to be a true Account of the Matter.

Thus, as according to these Moralists, the *Relish* or *Taste* for Virtue is similar to a Taste for Arts; so what is said of the Poet, the Painter, and Musician, may with equal Truth be said of the Man of Virtue—*Nascitur, non fit.*[74] Hence it is evident, that the noble Writer's System, which supposeth all Men capable of this exalted Taste, is chimerical and groundless.

But even supposing all Men capable of this refined Taste in Morals, there would arise an unanswerable Objection against the Efficacy of this refined Theory. Though it were allowed, that all Mankind have the same delicate Perception of *moral,* as some few have of *natural* Beauty, yet the Parallel would by no means hold, that "as the *Virtuoso* always pursues his Taste in Arts *consistently,* so the Man of *Virtue* must be equally *consistent* in *Action* and *Behaviour.*" For the *Virtuoso* being only engaged in mere *Speculation,* hath no opposite Affections to counteract his Taste: He [194] meets with no Obstructions in his Admiration of Beauty: His Enthusiasm takes its unbounded Flight, not retarded by any Impediments of a discordant Nature. But the Man of *Virtue* hath a different and more difficult Task to perform: He hath often a numerous Train of Passions, and these perhaps the most violent to oppose: He must labour through the surrounding Demands and Allurements of selfish Appetite: Must subdue the Sollicitations of every the most natural Affection, when it opposes the Dictates of a pure Benevolence. Hence even supposing the most refined Taste for Virtue common to all, it must ever be retarded in its Progress, often baffled and overthrown amidst the *Struggle* of contending *Passions.*

This seems to be a full and sufficient Reply to all that can be urged in Support of this fantastic System from a View of *human Nature.* But as the noble Writer hath attempted to confirm his Theory by some

f. Ibid.[73]

g. Three Treat. by *J. H.* Treat. 3[d]. *On Happiness,* p. 108.

73. Harris, *Treatises,* p. 214.

74. "[The poet] is born, not made"; proverbial. Cf., Pliny the Elder, *Natural History,* XVII.i.

collateral Arguments of another Kind, it may be proper here to consider their real Weight.

He urges, therefore, the Probability at least, if not the certain Truth of his Hypothesis from hence, "That it would be an [195] Imputation on the Wisdom of the Deity to suppose that he had formed Man so imperfect, that the true Happiness of the Individual should not always coincide with that of the whole Kind."[h] And beyond Question, the Assertion is true: But the Consequence he draws from it, "that therefore human Happiness must always consist in the immediate Feeling of virtuous Enjoyment," is utterly groundless. This Inference seems to have been drawn from a View of the *Brute* Creation; in which, we find, *Instincts* or *immediate Feelings* are the only Motives to Action; and in which, we find too, that these immediate Propensities are *sufficient* for all the Purposes of their Being. In this Constitution of Things the Creator's Wisdom is eminently displayed; because, through a Defect of *Reason* or *Reflexion,* no other kind of Principle could possibly have taken Place. But the Conclusion drawn from thence, "that Man must have a similar Strength of Instinct implanted in him, in order to direct him to his supreme Happiness," this is without Foundation: Because the Deity hath given him not only *present* Per[196]ceptions, but *Reason, Reflexion,* and a *Foresight* of *future* Good and Evil, together with a sufficient Power to obtain the one, and avoid the other. As therefore Man hath sufficient Notices of the *moral Government* of GOD, which will at length produce a perfect Coincidence between the *virtuous* Conduct and the *Happiness* of every Individual, it implies no essential Defect of Wisdom in the Creator, to suppose that he hath not given this *universal* and *unerring* Biass towards Virtue to the whole human Species. Man is enabled to pursue and obtain his proper Happiness by *Reason*; Brutes by *Instinct.*

Again, the noble Writer often attempts to strengthen his Argument, by "representing the *external Good* which naturally *flows* from *Virtue,* and the *external* Evils which naturally *attend* on Vice."[i] But sure this is rather deserting than confirming his *particular* Theory; which is, to prove that

h. *Enquiry.*
i. *Enquiry,* B. ii. P. i. § 3.

Happiness is *essential* to *Virtue*, and *inseparable* from it: "That Misery is *essential* to *Vice*, and inseparable from it."—Now, in bringing his Proofs from Happiness or Misery of the *external* Kind, he surely deserts his original Intention: Be[197]cause these *Externals* are not *immediate*, but *consequential*, not *certain*, but *contingent:* They are precisely of the Nature of *Reward* and *Punishment*; and therefore can have no Part in the Question now before us; which relates solely to "that Happiness or Misery arising from the inward State of the *Mind, Affections,* and *moral Sense,* on the Commission of Vice, or the Practice of *Virtue.*" And this hath been already considered at large.

However, that nothing may be omitted which can even remotely affect the Truth; we may observe, in passing, that after all the laboured and *well-meant* Declamation on this Subject, 'tis much easier to prove, "that *Vice* is the Parent of *external* Misery, than that *Virtue* is the Parent of *external* Happiness." 'Tis plain, that no Man can be vicious in any considerable *Degree*, but he must suffer either in his *Health*, his *Fame*, or *Fortune*. Now the Generality of Moralists, after proving or illustrating this, have taken it for granted, as a certain Consequence, that the external Goods of Life are, by the Law of Contraries, in a similar Manner annexed to the Practice of Virtue. But in Reality the Proof can reach no further than to shew [198] the happy Consequences of *Innocence,* which is a very different Thing from *Virtue*; for *Innocence* is only the *abstaining* from *Evil; Virtue,* the actual Production of *Good.* Now 'tis evident indeed, that by *abstaining* from *Evil* (that is, by *Innocence*) we *must* stand clear of the Miseries to which we expose ourselves by the *Commission* of it: And this is as far as the Argument will go. But if we rigorously examine the external Consequences of an *active* Virtue, in such a World as this; we shall find, it must be often maintained at the Expence both of *Health, Ease,* and *Fortune*; often the Loss of Friends, and Increase of Enemies; not to mention the unwearied Diligence of *Envy,* which is ever watchful and prepared to blast distinguished Merit. In the mean time, the *innoxious* Man sits unmolested and tranquil; *loves* Virtue, and *praiseth* it; avoids the *Miseries* of *Vice,* and the *Fatigues* of *active* Virtue; offends no Man, and therefore is beloved by all; and for the rest, makes it up by fair *Words* and civil Deportment. "Thus *Innocence,* and not *Virtue; Abstinence* from *Evil,* not the *Production* of Good, is the furthest Point to which Mankind in general can be carried, from [199] a Regard to the *external* Consequences of Action."

But whenever Appearances grow too strong against the noble Writer's System, he takes Refuge in an—*apage Vulgus!*—[75] As he had before allowed, that "the Vulgar may swallow any sordid Jest or Buffoonry," so here he frequently suggests, that among the same Ranks, "any kind of sordid Pleasure will go down." But "as it must be a finer Kind of Wit that takes with the Men of Breeding," so in Morals "the *Relish* or *Taste* for Virtue, is what naturally prevails in the higher Stages of Life: That the *liberal* and *polished* Part of Mankind are disposed to treat every other Principle of Action as groundless and *imaginary:* But that among these, the *Taste* in Morals, if properly cultivated, must needs be sufficient for all the Purposes of Virtue."[k]

In reply to this, which is perhaps the weakest Pretence of all that the noble Writer hath alledged, we need only observe, that those who are born to *Honours, Power,* and *Fortune,* come into the World with the [200] same *various* Mixture and *Predominancy* of *Sense, Imagination,* and *Affections,* with the *lowest* Ranks of Mankind. So that if they really enjoy better Opportunities of being compleatly virtuous, these must arise not from their internal *Constitution,* but their external *Situation* in Life. Let us examine how far this may give a Biass either towards Vice or Virtue.

Now 'tis plain that, with regard to the *Senses* or bodily *Appetites,* the Possession of Power and Fortune must be rather hurtful than favourable to Virtue. Wealth gives Opportunity of *Indulgence,* and Indulgence naturally *inflames.* Hence the Habits of *sensual* Inclination must in general be stronger in the *Lord* than the *Peasant:* Therefore, as nothing tends so much to imbrute the Man, and sink every nobler Affection of the Mind, as a servile Attendance on sensual Pleasure; so in this Regard, the Possession of Power and Fortune is rather *dangerous* than favourable to Virtue.

The same may be affirmed in respect to the *Passions* or *Affections.* Can any thing tend so much to render any Passion ungovernable, as to know

k. See Misc. 3[d]. c. 2. and many other detached Passages.[76]
75. "Begone, you rabble!"
76. Shaftesbury, *Characteristicks,* vol. III, pp. 100–15.

that we *need not* govern it? That our Power, Riches, and Au[201]thority, raise us *above Controul?* That we can hate, oppress, revenge, with *Impunity?* Are not the *Great,* of all others, most obnoxious to *Flattery?* Does not this tend to produce and nourish an *overweening* Opinion of *themselves,* an unjust *Contempt* of *others?* And is not *true Virtue* more likely to be *lost* than improved, amidst all these surrounding Temptations?

The *Imagination* indeed is often refined, and *Reason* improved, in the higher Ranks of Life, beyond the Reach of the *mere Vulgar.* But they are little acquainted with human Nature, who think that *Reason* and *Imagination,* among the Bulk of Mankind, are any thing more than the *Ministers* of the *ruling Appetites* and *Passions:* Especially where the Appetites and Passions are inflamed by the *early* and *habitual* Possession of Honours, Power, and Riches.

But still it will be urged, that the *Great* are under the Dominion of a powerful Principle, which is almost unknown among the *Vulgar:*—The Principle of HONOUR—which is a perfect *Balance* against all these surrounding Difficulties, and a full *Security* to *Virtue.* [202]

With regard to this *boasted* Principle, a very material Distinction must be made. By *Honour,* is sometimes meant "an Affection of Mind determining the Agent to the Practice of what is right, without any Dependence on other Men's Opinions." Now this is but the *moral Sense,* under a new Appellation: It ariseth too, not from any particular *Situation* of Life, but from the natural *Constitution* of the Mind. Accordingly, it is not confined to any one Rank of Men, but is seen promiscuously among the *Great* and *Vulgar.* 'Tis therefore entirely beyond the present Question, which only relates to such Circumstances as are peculiar to *high Life.*

The other, and more common Acceptation of the Word *Honour,* and in which alone it belongs peculiarly to the *Great,* is "an Affection of the Mind determining the Agent to such a Conduct, as may gain him the *Applause* or *Esteem* of those whose good Opinion he is fond of." Now this Love of *Fame,* and Fear of *Disgrace,* though, as a *secondary* Motive to Action, it be often of the highest Consequence in Life; though it often *counterfeits,* sometimes even *rivals* Benevolence itself; yet as [203] a *principal* Motive, there cannot be a more *precarious* Foundation of Virtue. For the *Effects* of this Principle will always depend on the *Opinions* of others: It will always take its particular Complexion from *these,* and must always *vary* with them. Thus 'tis a Matter of mere *Accident,* whether its Consequences be *good* or *bad, wholesome* or *pernicious.* If the *applauded Maxims* be founded in *Benevolence,* the Principle will so far lead to *Virtue:* If they be founded in *Pride, Folly,* or *Contempt,* the Principle will lead to *Vice.* And, without any designed Satire on the *Great,* it must be owned, the latter of these hath ever been the *predominant* Character of *Honour.* It were false indeed to affirm, that the Principle hath no Mixture of *benevolent* Intention; yet 'tis equally clear, that its *chief* Design is not so much to secure the *Happiness* of *all,* as to maintain the *Superiority* of a *few:* And hence this Principle hath ever led its Votaries to abhor the Commission, not so much of what is *unjust,* as of what is *contemptible.* Thus it is clear, that the Principle of *Honour,* as distinguished from *benevolent* Affection and the *moral Sense,* can never be a [204] sufficient Foundation for the *uniform* Practice of *Virtue.*

These are the main Arguments by which the noble Writer hath attempted to support this imagined *All-sufficiency* of the *Relish* or *Taste* in *Morals.* Had human Nature been indeed that *uniform* and *noble* Thing, which he seems to have *thought* it, he had surely been right in fixing the *Obligations* of *Man* to *Virtue,* on so generous and amiable a Principle. But as on Examination it appears, that he hath all along supposed this human Nature to be *what it is not,* his System is *visionary* and *groundless;* and his applauded Theory only fit to find a Place with the boasted Power of the great old *Geometer,* when he said—δος που στω, καὶ την γην κινησω.[1]

Most full indeed and clear to this purpose are the Words of the noble Writer himself: Who, in his *miscellaneous* Capacity, and in a *merry* Mood, seems to have spoken more of Truth, than I believe he would care to stand to.—"Such has been of late our dry Task. No wonder if it carries, indeed, a *meagre* and *raw* Ap[205]pearance. It may be looked on in Philosophy, as worse than a mere *Egyptian* Imposition. For to make Brick without Straw or Stubble, is perhaps an easier Labour, than to prove Morals without a World, and establish a Conduct of Life, without the

---

1. Give me but a *Place* to set my Foot on, and I will move the whole Earth.[77]
77. Attributed to Archimedes (*c.* 287–212 B.C.).

Supposition of any thing living or extant besides our *immediate Fancy,* and World of *Imagination.*"ᵐ

These Sallies might possibly have seemed difficult to account for, had not the noble Writer himself saved us the Labour of this Task. For he elsewhere tells us, that "all sound *Love* and Admiration is ENTHUSI-ASM: The Transports of Poets, Orators, Musicians, Virtuosi; the Spirit of Travellers and Adventurers; Gallantry, War, Heroism; all, all Enthusiasm! 'Tis enough: I am content to be this new ENTHUSIAST."ⁿ—And thus in another Place he describes the Effects of this high Passion: That "*Enthusiasm* is wonderfully powerful and extensive:—For when the Mind is *taken up in Vision,*—its Horror, Delight, Confusion, Fear, *Admiration,* or *whatever Passion* belongs to it, or is uppermost on this Occasion, will have something *vast,* [206] *immane,* and, as Painters say, BEYOND LIFE. And this is what gave Occasion to the Name of *Fanaticism,* as it was used by the Ancients in its original Sense, for *an* APPARITION *transporting the* MIND."ᵒ

SECTION IX

Having sufficiently evinced the *flimzy,* though curious, Contexture of these *Cobweb* Speculations *spun* in the *Closet,* let us now venture abroad into the World; let us proceed to something applicable to Life and Manners; and consider what are the real Motives, by which Mankind may be sway'd to the *uniform* Practice of *Virtue.*

And first, in Minds of a *gentle* and *generous* Disposition, where the sensual Appetites are weak, the Imagination refined, and the benevolent Affections naturally predominant; these very Affections, and the *moral Sense* arising from them, will in all the common Occurrences of Life secure the Practice of Virtue. To these fine Tempers thus happily formed,

m. Misc. iv. c. 2.[78]
n. *Moralists,* sub fin.[79]
o. *Letter on Enthusiasm.*[80]
78. Shaftesbury, *Characteristicks,* vol. III, p. 129.
79. Ibid., vol. II, pp. 223–24.
80. Ibid., vol. I, p. 34.

the inward Satisfaction of a virtuous Conduct exceeds that of every outward Acquisition; and affords to its Pos[207]sessor a more true and lasting Happiness, than Wealth, or Fame, or Power can bestow.

Secondly, Where the same Degrees of public Affection subsist, but stand opposed by sensual or selfish Passions of equal Violence, even here the Agent may rise to very high Degrees of Virtue, but not without the Aids of *Discipline* and *Culture*. Yet 'tis observable, that the Virtues of such a Temper are rather *conspicuous* than *consistent:* Without some strengthening Assistance, the Progress of the Mind towards Perfection is often broke by the Sallies of disordered Passion.

There is yet another Character, essentially different from these, but seldom distinguished, because generally taken for the *first*. Many esteem themselves, and are esteemed by others, as having arrived at the most *consummate Virtue*, whose Conduct never merits a higher Name than that of being *innoxious*. This is generally the Case of those who love *Retreat* and *Contemplation*, of those whose Passions are naturally *weak*, or carefully *guarded* by what the World calls *Prudence*. Now, as in the last mentioned Character, a *Curb* from *Irregularity* was requisite, so here a *Spur* to *Action* is equally [208] necessary for the Support and Security of Virtue.

As we descend through more common and inferior Characters, the internal Motives to virtuous Action grow less and less effectual. *Weak* or *no* Benevolence, a moral Sense proportionably *dull*, strong sensual *Appetites*, a clamorous Train of *selfish* Affections, these mixed and varied in endless Combinations, form the real Character of the *Bulk* of Mankind: Not only in *Cottages*, but in *Cities, Churches, Camps,* and *Courts*. So that some stronger Ties, some Motives more efficacious are necessary, not only for the Perfection of *Virtue*, but the Welfare, nay, the very Being of *Society*.

'Tis not denied, nay, 'tis meant and insisted on, that among all these various Characters and Tempers, the Culture of the benevolent Affections ought to be assiduously regarded. For though we have seen that the Design of introducing an universal high *Relish* or *Taste* for Virtue be *visionary* and *vain*, yet still a lower, or a lower Degree may *possibly* be instilled. We have only attempted to prove, that the Capacity for this high Taste in Morals is not universally or essentially interwoven with the human [209] Frame, but dispensed in various Degrees, in the same Manner as the Capacity for a Taste in *inferior* Beauties, in *Architecture, Painting, Poetry,* and *Music.*

To remedy this *Defect* of *unerring* Instinct in Man, by which he becomes a Creature so much less consistent than the Brute Kinds, Providence hath afforded him not only a Sense of *present,* but a Foresight of *future Good* and *Evil.*

Hence the Force of human Laws, which being established by common Consent, for the Good of all, endeavour, so far as their Power can reach, by the Infliction of Punishment on Offenders, to establish the general Happiness of Society, by making the *acknowledged Interest* of every *Individual* to coincide and unite with the *public* Welfare.

But as human Laws cannot reach the *Heart* of Man; as they can only inflict *Punishment* on Offenders, but cannot bestow *Rewards* on the Obedient; as there are many Duties of *imperfect* Obligation which they cannot recognize; as *Force* will sometimes *defy,* and *Cunning* often *elude* their Power; so without some further Aids, some Motives to Action more *universally* interest[210]ing, Virtue must still be left betrayed and deserted.

Now as it is clear from the Course of these Observations, that nothing can work this great Effect, but what can produce "an entire and universal Coincidence between private and public Happiness;" so is it equally evident, that nothing can effectually convince Mankind, that their own Happiness universally depends on *procuring,* or at least *not violating* the Happiness of others, save only "the lively and active Belief of an all-seeing and all-powerful GOD, who will hereafter make them happy or miserable, according as they designedly promote or violate the Happiness of their Fellow-Creatures." And this is the *Essence* of RELIGION.

This, at first View, should seem a Motive or Principle of Action, sufficient for all the Purposes of Happiness and Virtue. Indeed the Bulk of Mankind seem agreed in this Truth. Yet refining Tempers, who love to quit the common Tracks of Opinion, have been bold enough to call even this in Question. Among these, the noble Writer hath been one of the most diligent: [211] It will therefore be necessary to consider the Weight of his Objections.

To prevent Misinterpretation, it may be proper to observe, that Lord SHAFTESBURY sometimes talks in earnest of the *Nobleness* and *Dignity* of *Religion*. But when he explains himself, it appears, he confines his Idea of it to that Part which consists solely in Gratitude to, and Adoration of the supreme Being, without any Prospect of future Happiness or Misery. Now, though indeed this be the noblest Part, yet it is beyond the Reach of all, save only those who are capable of the most *exalted* Degrees of Virtue. His Theory of *Religion* therefore is precisely of a Piece, with his Theory of the *moral Sense*; not calculated for Use, but Admiration; and only existing in the Place where they had their Birth; that is, as the noble Writer well expresseth it, in *a Mind taken up in Vision*.

He sometimes talks, or seems to talk, in earnest too, on the *Usefulness* of *Religion,* in the common Acceptation of the Word. With Regard to which 'tis only necessary to observe, that whatever he hath said on this Subject I readily assent to: But this is no Reason why it may not be necessary to ob[212]viate every thing he hath thrown out to the contrary, to prejudice common Readers against Religion, through the Vanity of being thought *Original.* To *invent* what is *just* or *useful,* is the Character of *Genius:* 'Tis *Folly* only and *Impertinence* to broach *Absurdities.*

First, therefore, he often asserts, that "the Hope of future Reward and Fear of future Punishment is utterly unworthy of the free Spirit of a Man, and only fit for those who are destitute of the very first Principles of common Honesty: He calls it *miserable, vile, mercenary:* And compares those who allow it any Weight, to *Monkies* under the Discipline of the Whip."[p]

In Answer to these general Cavils (probably aimed principally at *Revelation*) which are only difficult to confute, as they are vague and fugitive, let it be observed, first; that whatever can be objected against *religious* Fear, holds good against the Fear of *human* Laws. They *both* threaten the Delinquent with the Infliction of Punishment, nor is the Fear of the one more unworthy, than of the other. Yet the noble Writer [213] himself often speaks with the highest Respect of *Legislators,* of the Founders of *Society* and *Empire,* who, by the Establishment of wise and wholesome Laws, drew Mankind from their State of natural Barbarity, to that of cultivated Life and social Happiness: Unless indeed he supposes that ORPHEUS

---

p. *Wit and Humour—Enquiry—&c.*[81]
81. Shaftesbury, *Characteristicks*, vol. II, p. 32.

and the rest of them did their Business *literally* by *Taste* and a *Fiddle*.[82]
If therefore the just Fear of *human* Power might be inforced without insulting or violating the *Generosity* of our Nature, whence comes it, that
a just Fear of the *Creator* should so miserably degrade the Species? The
religious Principle holds forth the same Motive to Action, and only differs from the other, as the Evil it threatens is infinitely greater, and more
lasting.

Further: If we consider the religious Principle in its true Light, there is
nothing in it either *mean, slavish,* or *unworthy.* To be in a *Fright* indeed, to
live under the Suggestions of *perpetual Terror* (in which, the noble Writer
would persuade us, the religious Principle consists) is far from an amiable
Condition. But this belongs only to the *Superstitious* or the *Guilty.* The
first of these are *falsely* religious; and to the last, I [214] imagine the noble
Writer's most zealous Admirers will acknowledge, it *ought* to belong. But
to the rest of Mankind, the *religious* Principle or *Fear* of GOD is of a quite
different Nature. It only implies a lively and habitual Belief, that we shall
be hereafter miserable, if we disobey his Laws. Thus every wise Man, nay,
every Man of common Understanding, hath a *like Fear* of every *possible
Evil*; of the destructive Power of natural Agents, of *Fire, Water, Serpents,
Poison:* Yet none of these Fears, more than the religious one, imply a State
of *perpetual* Misery and Apprehension: None of them are inconsistent
with the most generous Temper of Mind, or truest Courage. None of
them imply more than a *rational Sense* of these several Kinds of Evil; and
from that Sense, *a Determination to avoid them.* Thus the noble Writer
himself, when it answers a different Purpose, acknowledges that "a Man
of Courage may be *cautious* without real Fear."[q] Now the Word *Caution,*
in its very Nature, implies a Sense of a Possibility of Evil, and from that
Sense a Determination to avoid it: Which is the very [215] Essence of the
religious Principle or the *Fear* of GOD.

And as to the other Branch of religious Principle, "the Hope and Prospect of higher Degrees of future Happiness and Perfection:"—What is

q. *Inquiry,* B. ii. Part ii. § 3.[83]
82. In Greek mythology, Orpheus was a legendary poet and so accomplished a
player on the lyre that wild beasts were held spellbound by his music.
83. Shaftesbury, *Characteristicks,* vol. II, p. 83.

there of *mean, slavish,* or *unworthy* in it? Are all Mankind to be blown up into the *Mock-majesty* of the *kingly* Stoic, seated on the Throne of *Arrogance,* and *lording* it in an *empty* Region of Chimaera's? Is not the Prospect of Happiness the great universal Hinge of human Action? Do not all the Powers of the Soul centre in this one Point? Doth not the noble Writer himself elsewhere acknowledge this?[r] And that our Obligations to Virtue itself can only arise from this one Principle, that it gives us real Happiness? Why then should the Hope of a happy Immortality be branded as *base* and *slavish,* while the Consciousness or Prospect of a happy Life on Earth is regarded as a just and honourable Motive?

The noble Writer indeed confesseth, that "if by the Hope of Reward, be understood the Love and Desire (he ought to have said, the *Hope*) of *virtuous Enjoyment,* it [216] is not derogatory to Virtue."[84] But that in every other Sense, the indulged Hope of Reward is not only mean and mercenary, but even *hurtful* to Virtue and common *Humanity:* "For in this religious Sort of Discipline, the Principle of *Self-Love,* which is *naturally so prevailing* in us (*indeed?*) being no way moderated or restrained, but rather improved and made stronger every Day, by the Exercise of the Passions in a Subject of more extended Self-Interest; there may be reason to apprehend lest the Temper of this kind should extend itself in general through all the Parts of Life."[85]

This, to say the best of it, is the very *Phrenzy* of Virtue. Religion proposeth true Happiness as the End and Consequence of virtuous Action: This is granted. It proposeth it by such Motives as must influence Self-Love, and consequently hath given the best Means of procuring it. Yet, it seems, Self-Love being not restrained, but made stronger, will make Mankind miss of true Happiness. That is, by leading Self-Love into the Path of *true* Happiness, Religion will inevitably conduct it to *false*; by commanding us to *cherish* our *public* Af[217]fections, it will certainly *inflame* the *private* ones; by assuring us, that if we would be happy hereafter, we must be *virtuous* and *benevolent,* it will beyond Question render

r. See above, Sect. VI. of this Essay.
84. Shaftesbury, *Characteristicks*, p. 38.
85. Ibid., p. 33.

us *vile* and *void* of *Benevolence*. But this Mode of Reasoning is common with the noble Writer.

However, at other Times his Lordship can descend to the Level of common Sense; and prosecute his Argument by Proofs diametrically opposite to what he here advanceth. For in proving the Obligations of Man to Virtue, after having modelled the inward State of the human Mind according to his own Imagination, he proceeds to consider the *Passions* which regard *ourselves,* and draws another, and indeed a stronger Proof from *these.*—He there proves[s] the Folly of a vicious Love of Life, "because Life itself may often prove a Misfortune." So of *Cowardice,* "because it often robs us of the Means of Safety."—Excessive *Resentment,* "because the Gratification is no more than an Alleviation of a racking Pain."—The Vice of Luxury "creates a Nauseating, and Distaste, Diseases, and constant Craving." He urges the same Ob[218]jections against intemperate Pleasure of the amorous kind. He observes that Ambition is ever "suspicious, jealous, captious, and uncapable of bearing the least Disappointment." He then proceeds thro' a Variety of other Passions, proving them all to be the Sources of some internal or external Misery. Thus he awakens the same Passions of *Hope* and *Fear,* which, in a religious View, he so bitterly inveighs against. Thus he exhibits a Picture of future *Rewards* and *Punishments,* even of the most *selfish* Kind: He recommends the Conformity to Virtue, on the Score both of present and future *Advantage:* He *deters* his Reader from the Commission of Vice, by representing the Misery it will produce. And these too, such *Advantages* and such *Miseries,* as are entirely distinct from the mere Feeling of virtuous Affection or its contrary: From the Considerations of Safety, Alleviation of *bodily* Pain, the Avoidance of *Distaste,* and *Diseases.* Now doth not his own Cavil here recoil upon him? "That in this Sort of Discipline, and by exhibiting such Motives as these, the Principle of Self-Love must be made stronger, by the Exercise of the Passions in a Sub[219]ject of more extended Self-Interest: And so there may be Reason to apprehend, lest the Temper of this Kind should extend itself in general through all the Parts of Life." Thus the Objection proves

s. *Inquiry,* B. ii. Part ii. § 3.[86]
86. Ibid., pp. 93–100.

equally against both: In Reality, against neither. For, as we have seen, the *Sense* or *Prospect* of Happiness, is the only possible Motive to Action; and if we are taught to believe that *virtuous Affection* will produce *Happiness*, whether the expected Happiness lies in *this* Life, or *another*, it will *tend*, and *equally* tend, to produce *virtuous* Affection. The noble Writer, therefore, and his Admirers, might as well attempt to remove Mountains, as to prove that the *Hope* and Prospect of a happy Immortality, can justly be accounted more servile, mercenary, or *hurtful*, than the View of those transient and earthly Advantages, which his Lordship hath so rhetorically and honestly display'd, for the Interest and Security of *Virtue*. In Truth, they are precisely of the same Nature, and only differ in Time, Duration, and Degree. They are both established by our Creator for the same great End of Happiness. And what GOD hath thus *connected*, [220] it were *absurd*, as well as *impious*, to attempt to *separate*.[t]

There is yet another Circumstance observable in human Nature, which still further proves, that the Hope of a happy Immortality hath no Tendency to produce selfish Affection, but its contrary. For let the *stoical* Tribe draw what Pictures they please of the human Species, this is an undoubted Truth, "that *Hope* is the most universal Source of human *Happiness:* And [221] that Man is never so sincerely and heartily *benevolent*,

---

t. Hence we may see the Weakness and Mistake of those *falsely religious*, who fall into an *Extreme* directly *opposite* to this of the noble Writer; who are *scandalized* at our being determined to the Pursuit of Virtue through any Degree of Regard to its happy Consequences in this Life; which Regard they call *worldly, carnal, prophane*. For it is evident, that the religious Motive is precisely of the same Kind; only *stronger*, as the Happiness expected is *greater* and more *lasting*. While therefore we set the *proper* and *proportioned* Value upon each, it is impossible we can act irrationally, or offend that GOD who established *both*.

This naturally leads to a further Observation, which shews the Danger, as well as Folly, of *groveling* in *Systems*. Virtue, we see, comes recommended and enforced on three Principles. It is attended with *natural* and immediate *Pleasure* or Advantage:—It is commanded by human *Laws:*—It is enjoined by *Religion*.—Yet the *Religionists* have often decry'd the first of these Sanctions: The *fanatical Moralists*, the *last:* And even the *second* hath not escaped the Madness of an *enthusiastic* Party; which however, never grew considerable enough in this Kingdom, to merit Confutation.[87]

87. An echo of the priestly admonition in the form of solemnization of matrimony, "Those whom God hath joined together let no man put asunder."

as when he is truly *happy* in himself." Thus the high Consciousness of his being numbered among the Children of GOD, and that his Lot is among the Saints; that he is destined to an endless Progression of Happiness, and to rise from high to higher Degrees of Perfection, must needs inspire him with that Tranquillity and Joy, which will naturally diffuse itself in Acts of sincere Benevolence to all his Fellow-Creatures, whom he looks upon as his Companions in this Race of Glory. Thus will every noble Passion of the Soul be awakened into Action: While the joyless Infidel, possessed with the gloomy Dread of Annihilation, too naturally contracts his Affections as his Hopes of Happiness decrease; while he considers and despiseth himself, as no more than the Beasts that perish.

The noble Writer indeed insinuates, that there is "a certain Narrowness of Spirit, occasioned by this Regard to a future Life, peculiarly observable in the *devout* Persons and *Zealots* of almost every religious Persuasion."ᵛ In reply to which, 'tis only necessary to affirm, what may be [222] affirmed with Truth, that with Regard to *devout* Persons the Insinuation is a *False-hood*. It was prudently done indeed, to join the *Zealots* (or *Bigots*) in the same Sentence; because it is true, that *these*, being under the Dominion of *Superstition*, forget the true Nature and End of *Religion*; and are therefore scrupulously exact in the Observation of outward *Ceremonies*, while they neglect the superior and *essential* Matters of the Law, of *Justice, Benevolence,* and *Mercy*.

And as to the Notion of confining the Hope of future Reward to "that of virtuous Enjoyment only:" This is a *Refinement* parallel to the rest of the noble Writer's System; and, like all Refinements, contracts instead of enlarging our Views. 'Tis allowed indeed, that the Pleasures of Virtue are the highest we know of in our present State; and 'tis therefore commonly supposed, they may constitute our chief Felicity in another. But doth it hence follow, that no other Sources of Happiness may be dispensed, which as yet are utterly unknown to us? Can our narrow and partial Imaginations set Bounds to the Omnipotence of GOD? And may not our Creator vouchsafe us such Springs of yet untasted Bliss, as shall [223]

v. *Enquiry,* B. i. Part iii. § 3.[88]
88. Shaftesbury, *Characteristicks,* vol. II, p. 34.

exceed even the known Joys of Virtue, as far as *these* exceed the Gratifications of Sense? Nay, if we consider, what is generally believed, that our Happiness will arise from an Addition of new and higher Faculties; that in the present Life, the Exercise of Virtue itself ariseth often from the *Imperfection* of our State; if we consider these Things, it should seem highly probable, that our future Happiness will consist in something quite beyond our present Comprehension: Will be "such as Eye hath not seen, nor Ear heard, neither hath it entered into the Heart of Man to conceive."[89]

SECTION X

But beyond these Objections, the noble Writer hath more than once touched upon another, which merits a particular Consideration. For he affirms, that "after all, 'tis not merely what we call *Principle*, but a *Taste*, which governs Men." That "even Conscience, such as is owing to religious Discipline, will make but a slight Figure, where this Taste is set amiss."[w] [224]

The Notion here advanced is not peculiar to himself. He seems to have drawn it from a much more considerable Writer,[91] who hath endeavoured to support the same Proposition by a great Variety of Examples.[x] Several Authors of inferior Rank have borrowed the same Topic, for popular

---

w. *Misc.* iii. c. 2.[90]

x. BAYLE, *Pens. sur une* Comete.

89. Isaiah 64:4; cf. 1 Corinthians 2:9.

90. Shaftesbury, *Characteristicks*, vol. III, p. 108.

91. Pierre Bayle (1647–1706); French Protestant scholar and philosopher; lived as a refugee in Rotterdam from 1681, where he published his *Dictionaire historique et critique* (1695–97). His first major work was the *Pensées diverses sur la comète* (1682), in which he used the dismay caused by the sighting of comets in Europe during the winter of 1680–81 as a pretext for examining the prevalence of superstition in European society generally. In part a disinterested contribution to the psychology of credulity, the *Pensées diverses* was also a work of profound religious skepticism which advanced what for the times was the almost unthinkable proposition, that a society of atheists might be orderly and virtuous, and which invoked Spinoza to illustrate the possibility of a virtuous atheist.

Declamation. Nay, one hath gone so far as to assert, "that Man is so unaccountable a Creature, as to act most commonly against his Principle."[y]

The Objection, indeed, carries an Appearance of Force: Yet on a near Examination it entirely vanisheth.

It must be owned, that in most Countries, a considerable Part of what is called *Religion,* deserves no other Name than that of *Absurdity* made *sacred.* And it were strange indeed, should *Bigotry* and *false* Religion produce that Uprightness of Heart, that Perfection of Morals, which is the genuine Effect of *Truth.*

It must be owned, that with Regard to religious Principle, as well as moral Practice, every Man has the Power of being a *Hypocrite.* That Knaves, in order to be [225] accounted *honest,* may appear *devout.* And we may reasonably suppose, if we consider the innumerable Artifices of Villainy, that the outward Profession of Religion becomes a frequent *Disguise* to an *atheistical* and *corrupted* Heart.

But though these Circumstances may sufficiently account for the Appearance in many particular Cases, yet, with Regard to the *general* Fact, *here* seems to lie the proper Solution of the Difficulty. "That even where true Religion is known, professed, and in Speculation *assented* to, it is seldom so thoroughly *inculcated* as to become a Principle of Action." We have seen that Imagination is the universal Instrument of human Action; that no Passion can be strongly excited in the Soul by mere Knowledge or Assent, till the Imagination hath formed to itself some kind of Picture or Representation of the Good or Evil apprehended.[z] Now the Senses and their attendant Passions are continually urging their Demands, through the immediate Presence of their respective Objects: So that nothing but the *vivid Image* of some greater Good or Evil in Futurity can possibly resist and [226] overbalance their Sollicitations. The *Idea* therefore of future Happiness and Misery must be strongly impressed on the Imagination, ere they can work their full Effects, because they are *distant* and

---

y. *Fable of the Bees.*[92]
z. See above, Essay I. § 3.[93]
92. Mandeville, *Fable,* vol. I, p. 167.
93. See above, pp. 31–49.

unseen: But this *Habit* of *Reflexion* is seldom properly fixed by *Education*; and thus for want of a proper Impression, "religious Principle is seldom *gained,* and therefore seldom operates."

But where a sincere and lively Impression takes Place; where the Mind is convinced of the Being of a GOD; that he *is,* and is a *Rewarder* of them that diligently seek him; where the *Imagination* hath gained a Habit of connecting this great Truth with every Thought, Word, and Action; there it may be justly affirmed, that Piety and Virtue cannot but *prevail.* To say, in a Case of this Nature, that Man will not act according to his Principle, is to contradict the full Evidence of known Facts. We see how true Mankind commonly are to their Principle of *Pride,* or mistaken Honour; how true to their Principle of *Avarice,* or mistaken Interest; how true to their Principle, of a Regard to *human* Laws. Why are they so? Because they have strongly and habi[227]tually connected these Principles in their Imagination with the Idea of their own Happiness. Therefore, whenever the religious Principle becomes in the same Manner habitually connected in the Imagination, with the Agent's Happiness; that is, whenever the religious Principle takes Place at all, it must needs become infinitely more powerful than any other; because the *Good* it promiseth, and the *Evil* it threatens, are infinitely greater and more lasting. Hence it appears, that the Corruption of Mankind, even where the purest Religion is *professed,* and in Theory *assented* to, doth not arise from the *Weakness* of religious Principle, but the *Want* of it.

And indeed on other Occasions, and to serve different Purposes, the noble Writer and his Partisans can allow and give Examples of all that is here contended for. Nothing is so common among these Gentlemen, as to declaim against the terrible Effects of *priestly Power.'* Tis their favourite Topic, to represent Mankind as groaning under the Tyranny of the *sacred Order.* Now what does this Representation imply, but "the Force of religious Principle improperly directed?" If Mankind can be [228] swayed by religious Hope and Fear, to resign their Passions and Interests to the *Artifice,* or Advantage of the *Priest,* why not to the *Benefit* of *Mankind?* ' Tis only impressing a different Idea of *Duty:* The Motive to Action is in both Cases the same, and consequently must be of equal Efficacy. Thus if religious Principle were void of *Force,* the Priesthood must be void of

Power. The Influence therefore of the Priesthood, however dishonestly applied, is a Demonstration of the Force of *religious Principle.*

This therefore seems to be the Truth. Although, by timely and continued Culture, the religious Principle might be made more universally predominant; yet even as it is, though not so thoroughly inculcated as to become generally a consistent Principle of Action; in Fact it hath a frequent and *considerable,* though *partial* and imperfect Influence. None but the thoroughly Good and Bad act on continued or consistent Principles; all the intermediate Degrees of Good and Bad act at different Times on various and inconsistent Principles; that is, their *Imaginations* are by turns given up to *Impressions* of a *different,* or [229] even *contrary* Nature. This explains the whole Mystery: For, hence it appears that the consistent or inconsistent Conduct of Men depends not on the Nature of their Principles, but on having their Principles, whatever they are, *counteracted* by opposite ones. Although therefore, through a Failure of timely Discipline, Numbers of Men appear to be of that capricious Temper as not to be steddy to any Principle, yet still the religious one will *mix* with the rest, and naturally *prevail* in its *Turn.* This is certainly a common Circumstance among the *looser* and more *inconsiderate* Ranks of Men; who, although by no Means uniformly swayed by the Precepts of Religion, are yet frequently struck with Horror at the Thought of Actions *peculiarly* vile, and deterred by the Apprehension of an all-seeing GOD from the Commission of Crimes *uncommonly atrocious.*

Here then lies the essential Difference between the Efficacy of *Taste,* and *religious* Principle: That the first, being a Feeling or Perception dispensed in various Degrees, and in very weak ones to the Bulk of Mankind, is incapable, even through the most assiduous Culture, of becoming an universal [230] or consistent Motive to Virtue: But the religious Principle, arising from such Passions as are common to the whole Species, must, if properly inculcated, *universally* prevail.

'Tis evident therefore, that in the very first Dawns of Reason, religious Principles ought to be impressed on the Minds of Children; and this early Culture continued through the succeeding Stages of Life. But as the noble Writer hath strangely attempted to ridicule and dishonour Religion in every Shape; so here, he hath endeavoured to throw an Odium on this Method of religious Discipline, by representing it as the Enemy to true Morals and practical Philosophy, as it fetters the Mind with early Prejudices.

> Whatever Manner in Philosophy happens to bear the least Resemblance to that of *Catechism,* cannot, I am persuaded, of itself seem very inviting. Such a smart Way of questioning ourselves in our Youth, has made our Manhood more averse to the *expostulatory* Discipline: And though the metaphysical Points of our Belief, are by this Method with admirable Care and Caution instilled into tender Minds; yet the Manner of this *anticipating* Philosophy may make [231] the Afterwork of Reason, and the inward Exercise of the Mind at a riper Age, proceed the more heavily, and with greater Reluctance.—'Tis hard, after having by so many pertinent Interrogatories and decisive Sentences, declared *who* and *what* we are; to come leisurely in another, to enquire concerning our *real Self* and *End,* the Judgment we are to make of *Interest,* and the Opinion we should have of *Advantage* and *Good:* Which is what must necessarily determine us in our *Conduct,* and prove the leading Principle of our Lives."[a]

In reply to this *most philosophical* Paragraph, let it be observed; that it is not the Design of Religion to make *Sophists,* but *good Subjects* of Mankind. That Man being designed, not for *Speculation,* but *Action,* religious Principle is not to be instilled in a *philosophical,* but a *moral* View: Therefore with Regard to *Practice,* nothing can be more fit and rational than to impress acknowledged *Truths* at an Age when the *Recipient* is incapable of their *Demonstrations*; in the same Manner as we teach the *Me*[232]*chanic* to *work* on *Geometric* Principles, while the Proofs are *unknown* to him.

But then, the *Prejudices of Education*—yes, these are the great *Stumbling-block* to a modern *Free-thinker:* It still runs in his Head, that all Mankind are born to dispute *de omni scibili.*[b] Let therefore this *minute* Philosopher reflect, first, that a *Prejudice* doth not imply, as is generally supposed, the

---

a. *Advice, &c.* Part iii. § 2.[94]
b. On all Subjects.[95]
94. Shaftesbury, *Characteristicks,* vol. I, pp. 189–90.
95. Literally, "about everything knowable."

Falsehood of the Opinion instilled; but only that it is taken up and held without its proper *Evidence*. Thus a Child may be prejudiced in Favour of Truth, as well as Falsehood; and in him neither the one nor the other can properly be called more than an *Opinion*. Further: The human Mind cannot remain in a State of *Indifference*, with regard either to *Opinion* or *Practice:* 'Tis of an *active* Nature; and, like a *fertile* Field, if by due Cultivation it be not made to produce good *Fruit*, will certainly spring up in *Tares* and *Thistles*.⁹⁶ Impressions, Opinions, *Prejudices*, of one kind or other a Child will inevitably contract, from the Things and Persons that *surround* him: And if rational Habits and Opinions be not infused, in order to *anticipate* Absurdities; [233] Absurdities will rise, and *anticipate* all rational Habits and Opinions. His *Reason* and his *Passions* will put themselves in *Action*, however untoward and inconsistent, in the same Manner as his *Limbs* will make an Effort towards progressive *Motion*, however awkward and absurd. The same Objection therefore that lies against in stilling a *salutary Opinion*, will arise against *teaching* him to walk *erect:* For this, too, is a kind of "*anticipating* Philosophy:" And sure, a Child left to his own *Self-Discipline*, "till he could come *leisurely* to enquire concerning his *real Self* and *End*," would stand as fair a Chance to *grovel* in Absurdity, and bring *down* his Reason to the sordid *Level* of Appetite, as to *crawl* upon all *four*, and dabble in the *Dirt*. Thus the noble Writer's Ridicule would sweep away the whole System of Education along with the religious Principle: Not an Opinion or Inclination must be controuled, or so much as controverted; "lest by this *anticipating* Philosophy, the Work of Reason, and the inward Exercise of the Mind, at a *riper* Age, should proceed the more heavily, and with greater Reluctance." The Caprice of Infancy must rule us, till the very [234] *Capacity* of Improvement should be *destroyed*; and we must turn *Savages*, in order to be made perfect in the *sovereign Philosophy!*

'Tis no difficult Matter therefore to determine, whether a Child should be left to the Follies of his own *weak* Understanding and *nascent* Passions; be left to imbibe the Maxims of corrupt Times and Manners;

---

96. Matthew 13:24–30.

Maxims which, setting aside all Regard to their speculative Truth or Falsehood, do lead to certain Misery; or, on the other hand, shall be happily conducted to embrace those religious Principles, which have had the Approbation of the best and wisest Men in every Age and Nation; and which are known and allowed to be the only Means of true Happiness to Individuals, Families, and States.

This therefore ought to be the early and principal Care of those who have the Tuition of Youth: And they will soon find the happy Effects of their Instruction. For as the Child's Understanding shall improve, what was at first instilled only as an *Opinion,* will by Degrees be embraced as *Truth:* Reason will then assume her just Empire; and the great, universal, religious Principle, [235] a rational Obedience to the Will of GOD, will raise him to his utmost Capacity of moral Perfection; will be a wide and firm Foundation, on which the whole Fabric of Virtue may rise in its just Proportions; will *extend* and *govern* his *Benevolence* and *moral Sense*; will strengthen them, if weak; will confirm them, if strong; will supply their Want, if naturally defective: In fine, will direct all his *Passions* to their proper *Objects* and *Degrees*; and, as the great *Master-spring* of Action, at once *promote* and *regulate* every Movement of his *Heart.*

It must be owned, the noble Writer's Caution against this "anticipating Philosophy" hath of late been deeply imbibed. In Consequence of it, we have seen *religious Principle* declaimed against, ridiculed, lamented. The Effect of this hath been, an abandoned Degree of Villainy in one Class of Mankind; a lethargic Indifference towards Virtue or Vice in another; and in the third, which boast the Height of modern Virtue, we seldom see more than the first natural Efforts, the mere *Buddings* of Benevolence and Honour, which are too generally blasted ere they can ripen into *Action.* This Contempt of Religion [236] hath always been a fatal *Omen* to *free* States. Nor, if we may credit Experience, can we entertain any just Hope, that this fantastic Scheme, this boasted *Relish* for Beauty and Virtue, can ever give Security to Empire, without the more solid Supports of religious Belief. For it is remarkable, that in the Decline of both the *Greek* and *Roman* States, after Religion had lost its Credit and Efficacy, this very *Taste,* this *sovereign Philosophy* usurped its Place, and became the common Study and Amusement (as it is now among ourselves) both of the

Vile and *Vulgar*. The Fact, with Regard to *Greece*, is sufficiently notorious; with Regard to *Rome*, it may seem to demand a Proof. And who would think, that QUINTILIAN in the following Passage was not describing our own Age and Nation? "Nunc autem quae velut propria philosophiae asseruntur, passim tractamus *omnes:* Quis enim modo de JUSTO, AEQUO, ac BONO, non et VIR PESSIMUS loquitur?"ᶜ—*What was formerly the Philosopher's Province only, is now invaded by all: We find every wicked and worthless Fellow, in these Days, haranguing on* VIRTUE, BEAUTY, *and* GOOD. What [237] this *Leprosy* of *false* Knowledge may end in, I am unwilling to say: But this may be said with Truth, because it is justified by Experience; that along with the Circumstance now remarked, every other *Symptom* is rising among us, that hath generally attended the dark and troubled *Evening* of a *Commonwealth*.

Doubtless, many will treat these Apprehensions with *Derision:* But this *Derision* is far from being an Evidence of their Falsehood. For no People ever fell a Sacrifice to themselves, till *lulled* and infatuated by their own Passions. *Blind Security* is an essential Characteristic of a People devoted to Destruction. The Fact is equally undeniable, whether it ariseth from the moral Appointment of Providence, or the Connexion of natural Causes. Though this is seen and acknowledged by those who are conversant with the History of Mankind; yet 'tis hard to convey this Evidence to those who seldom extend their Views beyond their own short Period of Existence; because they see the Prevalence of the *Cause* assigned, while yet the pretended *Consequence* appears not. But they who look back into ancient Time are convinced, that the *public* Effects [238] of *Irreligion* have never been sudden or *immediate*. One Age is *falsely* polite, *irreligious,* and *vile*; the next is sunk in *Servitude* and *Wretchedness*. This is analogous to the Operation of other Causes. A Man may be intemperate for twenty Years, before he feels the Effects of Intemperance on his Constitution. The Sun and Moon raise the Tides; yet the Tides rise not to their Height, till a considerable Time after the Conjunction of these two Luminaries.

---

c. *Quint. Proaemium.*[97]

97. Quintilian, *Institutio Oratoria*, I.proemium.16. Brown supplies a loose, but serviceable, translation of the Latin.

We cannot therefore justly decide concerning the future *Effects* of Irreligion, from its present State. The *Examples* of former Times are a much better *Criterion:* And these are such, as ought to make every Man among us, that regards Posterity, tremble for his Posterity while he reads them.

For this is but too just an *Epitome* of the Story of Mankind. That TYRANNY and SUPERSTITION have ever gone Hand in Hand; mutually supporting and supported; taking their Progress, and fixing their Dominion over all the Kingdoms of the Earth; overwhelming it in one general Deluge, as the Waters cover the Sea. Here and there a happy Nation *emerges*; breathes for a while in the enlightened Region of KNOW[239]LEDGE, RELIGION, VIRTUE, FREEDOM: Till in their appointed Time, IRRELIGION and LICENTIOUSNESS appear; *mine* the Foundations of the *Fabric*, and sink it in the general Abyss of IGNORANCE and OPPRESSION.

Possibly the fatal Blow may yet be averted from us. 'Tis surely the Duty of every Man, in every Station, to contribute his Share, however *inconsiderable*, to this great End. This must be my Apology for opposing the noble Writer's fantastic System; which by exhibiting a false Picture of human Nature, is, in Reality an *Inlet* to *Vice*, while it seems most *favourable* to *Virtue*: And while it pretends to be drawn from the *Depths* of *Philosophy*, is, of all others, *most unphilosophical*.

ESSAYS

ON THE
Characteristics, etc.

ESSAY III
On revealed RELIGION, and CHRISTIANITY

SECTION I

In the Course of the preceding *Essay,* we have seen the noble Writer assuming the Character of the professed *Dogmatist,* the *Reasoner* in *Form.* In what remains to be considered, concerning *revealed Religion* and CHRISTIANITY, we shall find him chiefly affecting the *miscellaneous* Capa[242]city; the Way of *Chat, Raillery, Innuendo,* or *Story-telling:* In a Word, that very Species of the present modish Composition, which he so contemptuously ridicules; "where, as he tells us, Justness and Accuracy of Thought are set aside as too constraining; where Grounds and Foundations are of no Moment; and which hath properly neither *Top* nor *Bottom, Beginning* nor *End.*"[a] In this, however, his Lordship is not quite so much to blame as might be imagined. In his Critical Progress, he had treated this *dishabille*[2] of Composition, as the Man in the Fable did his Pears;[3] unconscious he

---

a. See above, *Essay* i. § 2.[1]

1. See above, p. 29.

2. Literally "undress," but here used to denote informality or casualness.

3. A reference to the Aesopian fable "Of the Priest and the Pears," which in a contemporary translation is given as follows: "A Certain greedy Priest going out of his Country to a Wedding, to Which he had been invited, found an Heap of Pears in the Road, of Which He touched not One indeed; but rather having Them in

should be ever afterwards reduced to diet on them himself. The Truth of the Matter is, that the broken Hints, the ambiguous Expression, and the Ludicroserious of the gentle Essayist, perfectly secure him from the rough Handling of the Logical-Disputer.

Indeed the noble Author has a double Advantage from this *Cloud,* in which the *Graces* so frequently secure their Favourite. He not only eludes the Force of every Argument the Defenders of Christianity alledge in it's Support, but even pleads the Privilege of [243] being ranked in the Number of *sincere* Christians. He takes frequent Occasions of expressing his Abhorrence of *idle Scepticks* and *wicked Unbelievers* in Religion: He declares himself of a more resigned Understanding, a ductile Faith, ready to be moulded into any Shape that his spiritual Superiors shall prescribe. At other Times, and in innumerable Places, he scatters such Insinuations against *Christianity,* and that too with all the Bitterness of *Sarcasm* and *Invective,* as must needs be more effectual in promoting *Irreligion,* than a formal and avowed Accusation. For in the Way of open War, there is fair Warning given to put Reason upon Guard, that no pretending Argument be suffered to pass without Examination. On the contrary, the noble Writer's concealed Method of *Raillery,* steals insensibly on his Reader; fills him with endless Prejudice and Suspicion; and, without passing thro' the *Judgment,* fixeth such Impressions on the Imagination, as *Reason,* with all its Effects, will be hardly able afterwards to efface.

These inconsistent Circumstances in his Lordship's Conduct, have made it a Question among some, what his real Sentiments were concerning Religion and *Christianity.* [244] If it be necessary to decide this Question, we may observe, that a disguised Unbeliever may have his Reasons for making a formal Declaration of his Assent to the Religion of his

---

Derision, He sprinkled them with Urine, for He resented that Meats of this Kind should be offer'd in the Journey, who was going to sumptuous Dainties. But when He had found in the Way a certain Brook so increased with the Showers, that We [sic] be not able to pass over It without Danger of Life, He resolved to return Home: But returning fasting He was oppress'd with so great Hunger, that unless he had eat those Pears, Which He had sprinkled with urine, when He could not find any thing else, He had been dead with Hunger" (*Fabulae Aesopi Selectae,* tr. H. Clarke, second edition [1737], p. 82; emphases removed).

Country: But it will be hard to find what should tempt a real *Christian* to load *Christianity* with Scorn and *Infamy*. Indeed, the noble Writer, to do him Justice, never designed to leave us at a Loss on this Subject. For he hath been so good, frequently to remind his Reader, to *look out* for the true Drift of his *Irony*, lest his real Meaning should be mistaken or disregarded.

Here then lies the Force of his Lordship's Attack on *Christianity*; "In exciting Contempt by Ridicule." A Method which, as we have already seen,[b] tho' devoid of all rational Foundation, is yet most powerful and efficacious in working upon vulgar Minds. Thus the Way of *Irony*, and false Encomium, which he so often employs against the blessed Founder of our Religion, serves him for all Weapons; the deeper he strikes the Wound, the better he shields himself.

We are not therefore to be surprized, if we find the noble Writer frequently affecting a Mixture of *solemn Phrase* and *low* [245] *Buffoonry*; not only in the same *Tract*, but in the same *Paragraph*. In this Respect, he resembles the facetious Drole I have somewhere heard of, who wore a *transparent Masque:* Which, at a Distance, exhibited a Countenance wrap'd up in profound Solemnity; but those who came nearer, and could see to the Bottom, found the native Look distorted into all the ridiculous Grimace, which Spleen and Vanity could imprint.

SECTION II

But as *natural* Religion is the only Foundation of *revealed*; it will be necessary, e'er we proceed to the last, to obviate any Insinuations which the noble Writer may have thrown out against the Former.

As to the Expectation of future Happiness considered, as the natural Consequence of virtuous Action; his Lordship hath not, that I know of, either affirmed, or insinuated any thing against it's Reasonableness. But with Regard to the other Branch of Religion, "the Belief of a future State of Misery or Punishment, considered as the appointed Consequence of

b. *Essay* i. passim.[4]
4. See above, pp. 25–88.

Vice," this he [246] hath frequently endeavoured to discredit in such a Manner, as would be no small Degree of Guilt to transcribe, were it not to shew at once the Impiety and Falsehood of his Affirmations.

In his Letter on *Enthusiasm,* he hath obliged us with several Passages of this Kind. These, it must be owned, are so obscure, that we must be content, to refer them rather to the Reader's equitable Construction, than urge them as direct Proofs.

The Apprehension and *Fear* of something *supernatural,* so universal among Mankind, he seems all along to deride, as a visionary and *groundless Pannic.*[c] He adds that, "while some Sects, such as the *Pythagorean* and latter *Platonick,* joined in with the Superstition and Enthusiasm of the Times; the *Epicurean,* the *Academic* and others, were allowed to use all the Force of Wit and Raillery against it."[d] To convince us how much he approves the Conduct of these libertine Sects, he boldly follows their Example. He assures us that "such is the Nature of the liberal, polished and refin'd Part of Mankind; so far are they from the mere Simplicity of [247] Babes and Sucklings; that, instead of applying the Notion of a future Reward or Punishment, to their immediate Behaviour in Society; they are apt much rather, thro' the whole Course of their Lives, to shew evidently, that they look on the pious Narrations to be indeed no better than Children's Tales, and the Amusement of the mere Vulgar."[i] He confirms these Opinions by assigning the Reason why Men of Sense should stand clear of the Fears of a Futurity: "GOD is so *good,* as to exceed the very best of us in *Goodness:* And after this Manner we can have no Dread or Suspicion *to render us uneasy*; for it is *Malice only,* and *not Goodness,* which can make us afraid."[k]

Is this the *Philosopher* and *Patriot,* the Lover of his Country and Mankind! *This* the Admirer of ancient Wisdom, of venerable Sages, who

c. *Let. on Enthus.* passim.
d. Ib.[5]
i. *Misc.* iii. c. 2.[6]
k. *Let. on Enthus.*[7]
5. Shaftesbury, *Characteristicks,* vol. I, p. 12.
6. Ibid., vol. III, p. 108.
7. Ibid., vol. I, pp. 24–25.

founded "Laws, Constitutions, civil and religious Rites, whatever civilizes or polishes Mankind."[1]

> *Tu Pater et Rerum inventor! Tu patria nobis*
> *Suppeditas praecepta!*[9]

This, sure, is unhinging Society to the [248] utmost of his Power: For the Force of *religious Sanctions* depends as much on their being believed, as the Force of *human Laws* depends on their being executed. To *destroy* the *Belief* of the *one* therefore, is equivalent to suspending the *other*.

But as the present Debate concerns not the *Utility*, but the *Truth* of *Religion*; 'tis chiefly incumbent on us, to shew, that the noble Writer's *Opinion* and *Reasoning*, on this Subject, are void of all Foundation.

'Tis observable therefore, First, that his Lordship, in other Places, allows that "If there be naturally such a Passion as Enthusiasm, 'tis evident, that Religion itself is of the Kind, and must be therefore natural to Man."[m] And in his *Letter on Enthusiasm*, even while he derides the Proneness of Mankind to the *conscientious Fear*, he adds, "that tho' Epicurus thought these Apprehensions were *vain*, yet he was forced to allow them in a Manner *innate*."—From which Concession, a *Divine*, methinks, might raise a *good Argument* against him, for the *Truth* as well as *Usefulness* of Religion."[11] Now as some may possibly be at a Loss to determine here, [249] whether the noble Writer be in *Jest* or *Earnest*, the Argument he hints at is plainly this: That if we look round the Works of Nature, we shall find an Analogy established, which seems a Proof, that this natural Fear which *presseth* so universally on the human Mind, hath a real and proportioned Object. The Argument hath been urged by many of great Name, in Favour of the *Hope* of future *Good*; and 'tis surely of equal Force, whatever

---

l. *Moralists*, P. i. § 3.[8]

m. *Misc.* ii. c. 1.[10]

8. Shaftesbury, *Characteristicks*, vol. II, p. 120.

9. A quotation from the address to Epicurus at the beginning of Book III of Lucretius's *De Rerum Natura*, which translates: "You are our father, the discoverer of truths, you supply us with fatherly precepts" (ll. 9–10).

10. Shaftesbury, *Characteristicks*, vol. III, p. 23.

11. Ibid., vol. I, p. 31.

that Force may be, when apply'd to the *Fear* of future *Ill*. For we see thro' the whole Creation, every Animal of whatever Species, directed by it's Nature or the Hand of Providence, to fear and shun it's proper and appointed Enemy. We find these Apprehensions universally suited to the Nature and Preservation of every Species among Birds, Beasts, Fishes, Insects. Nor is there one *Fear*, tho' sometimes *excessive* in it's *Degree*, that is *erroneous* with Regard to it's *Object*. The *religious Fear*, therefore, which *forceth itself* so universally on the human Mind, in every Age and Nation, ignorant or knowing, civilized or barbarous; hath *probably* an Object suited to it's Nature, ordained for the Welfare of the human Species. At least, this Argu[250]ment must ever be of Weight with those, who draw their Ideas of future Existence from the *Instincts, Hopes,* and *Expectations* of the human Mind.

Indeed, on the noble Writer's refined Scheme of Morals, in which the natural Affections of the Mind are represented, as all-sufficient for the Purposes of human Happiness, this Argument must lose it's Force; because, on this Supposition, the religious Fear is *supernumerary* and *useless:* But then this shews the Supposition itself to be *monstrous, absurd,* and contrary to the established Course of Nature; because Nature gives no Power or Passion, but to some proper and appointed End: The very *Existence* of the Passion, therefore, is a Proof of it's Necessity.

Now, if indeed the religious Fear be *necessary,* as, we presume, hath been sufficiently proved in the preceding Essay; then, from hence will arise a strong and convincing Proof, that the Object of religious Fear is *real*. For we find thro' the whole Extent of created Being, that the Author of Nature hath annexed to all his Designs and Purposes, the proper Means or Objects, by which they may be fulfilled. [251] As therefore the religious Fear is not only interwoven with the Frame of Man, but *absolutely necessary* to his *Happiness,* it's Object must be *real*; because, if *not,* you suppose the Creator to have given a NECESSARY *Passion,* without it's *proper* and *appointed Object*; which would be a Contradiction to the *universal* and *known Constitution* of Things.

On this Occasion, we may observe the Weakness of the *Epicurean* System, concerning *Providence:* For that Sect hath ever deny'd, that the Deity concerns himself with the *moral* Conduct of Man. But from the wise and benevolent Constitution of the natural World itself, a strong Proof ariseth in Support of GOD's *moral* Government of it, and of the Truth of the *Fears* and *Expectations* of the human Mind. For if we allow that he regards and preserves the natural Order and Symmetry of the Creation; that he hath formed this immense System of Being, and secured it's Continuance and Welfare, by certain Laws, necessary to the Happiness of his Creatures; then we must on the same Foundation conclude, that he hath likewise established such *Motives* and *Laws* of *Action,* as may determine [252] *Man* to prosecute the same End. It were an Imputation on the Wisdom of the Deity, to conceive him as *doing* the *one,* and *omitting* the *other:* Unless *Mind* and *Morals* be less worthy of his Regard, than *Matter* and *Motion.*

But still the noble Writer proceeds in the Spirit of Derision, to expose the Absurdities and Mischiefs this misguided religious Principle hath occasioned; he often expatiates on the *superstitious Horrors,* and *furious Zeal* which have had their Source in this *Principle*; and thence, in the Way of Insinuation, concludes it *irrational* and *groundless.*

The Facts, it must be owned, are notorious and undeniable: But the Consequence is no less evidently chimerical and vain. Lord SHAFTES-BURY himself hath observed, that in Failure of a *just Prince* or *Magistrate,* Mankind are ready to submit themselves even to a *Tyrant:* "Like new-born Creatures, who have never seen their *Dam,* they will fancy one for themselves, and apply (as by Nature prompted) to some like Form for Favour and Protection. In the Room of a *true Foster-Father* and *Chief,* they will take [253] after a *false one*; and in the Room of a legal Government and just Prince, obey even a Tyrant."ⁿ And hence he draws a strong Proof of the Force of the *social* or *herding* Principle, even from *despotic* Power itself. Again he hath remarked, that "*Heroism* and *Philanthropy* are almost one and the same; yet by a small Misguidance of the Affection, a Lover of Mankind becomes a Ravager; a Hero and Deliverer becomes an Oppressor and Destroyer."° 'Tis the same in Religion. Where the human

---

n. *Wit. and H.* P. iii. § 1.[12]
o. Ib. § 2.[13]
12. Shaftesbury, *Characteristicks,* vol. III, p. 68.
13. Ibid., p. 71.

Mind (ever restless in it's Search for the great Center of created Being, on which alone it can perfectly repose itself) seeks, but cannot find the *true* GOD, it naturally sets up a *false one* in his Place: Here too, Mankind, "like new-born Creatures, who have never seen their *Dam,* will fancy one for themselves, and apply (as by Nature prompted) to some like Form for Favour and Protection. In the Room of a *true Foster-Father,* they will take after *a false one*; and in the Room of an *all-perfect* GOD, worship even an *Idol.*"[14] The religious Principle, thus misguided, breaks forth indeed, into Enor[254]mities the most pernicious and destructive: Hence indeed, "by a small Misguidance of the Affection, a *Lover of Mankind* becomes a *Ravager*; a *Saint,* an *Oppressor* and *Destroyer.*" But as from the Abuse of the *social* Principle, so here, in that of the *religious* one, no other Consequence can be justly drawn, but that it is *natural* and *strong.*

But further, the noble Writer finds the Notion of future Punishment, *inconsistent* with his Idea of *divine Goodness.* Therefore, says he, "We can have no Dread or Suspicion to make us uneasy: For it is *Malice only,* and not *Goodness,* which can make us afraid."[P]

Yet, on another Occasion, his Lordship can affirm, and justly, that, "a Man of *Temper* may resist or *punish without Anger.*"[16] And if so, why may not divine *Goodness* make us *afraid?* For as divine Goodness regards the greatest Happiness of all it's Creatures; so, if Punishment be *necessary* to that End, divine *Goodness* will *therefore* ORDAIN PUNISHMENT. To this Purpose, a Writer of distinguished Rank and Penetration:[17]

> In Reality, Goodness is the natu[255]ral and just Object of Fear to an ill Man. Malice may be appeased or satiated: Humour may change: But Goodness is as a fixed, steady immoveable Principle of Action. If either of the Former holds the Sword of Justice, there is plainly

p. *Enq.* B. ii. Part ii. § 2.[15]

14. Shaftesbury, *Characteristicks*, vol. III, p. 68.

15. Ibid., vol. II, pp. 80–93.

16. Ibid., p. 83.

17. Joseph Butler (1692–1752); bishop of Bristol, and then Durham; clergyman and moral philosopher who sought to blend elements of moral sense philosophy with more traditional ideas of conscience and of the rational distinction between right and wrong.

Ground for the greatest of Crimes to hope for Impunity. But if it be Goodness, there can be no possible Hope, whilst the Reasons of things, or the Ends of Government call for Punishment. Thus every one sees how much greater Chance of Impunity an ill Man has, in a partial Administration, than in a just and upright one. It is said, that the Interest or Good of the Whole, must be the Interest of the universal Being; and that he can have no other. Be it so. This Author (Ld. *S.*) has proved that Vice is naturally the Misery of Mankind in this World: Consequently it was for the Good of the Whole, that it should be so. What Shadow of Reason then is there to assert, that this may not be the Case hereafter? Danger of future Punishment (and if there be Danger, there is Ground of Fear) no more supposes Malice, than the present Feeling of Punishment does.^q [256]

Thus the noble Writer's Derision and Argumentation are equally chimerical and impious; as it appears, that the natural Fears and Expectations of the human Mind are at least founded in Probability.

SECTION III

His Lordship's Opinions being so little favourable to *natural Religion,* we cannot wonder, if we find him, on every possible Occasion, throwing out Insinuations and virulent Remarks, in Order to disgrace *revealed.* The First that will deserve our Notice, are such as tend to invalidate the *Credibility* of *Scripture History.*

He tells us, "He who says he believes *for certain,* or is *assured* of what he believes, either speaks *ridiculously,* or says in Effect, he believes strongly, but *is not* sure: So that whoever is not conscious of Revelation, nor has certain Knowledge of any Miracle or Sign, can be no more than *sceptick in the Case:* And the best Christian in the World, who being destitute of the Means of Certainty, depends only on History and Tradition for his Belief of these particulars, is at best but a *sceptick* Christian."^s [257]

q. Dr. *Butler's* Sermons, Preface, p. 21.[18]
s. *Misc.* ii. c. 2.[19]
18. Joseph Butler, *Fifteen Sermons,* fourth edition (1749), p. xxi.
19. Shaftesbury, *Characteristicks,* vol. III, p. 47.

Now it should seem, that the Dexterity of this Passage lies in a new Application of two or three Words. For, by "*certain* and *assured*" he means *more*, by "*Scepticism*" he means much *less*, than it is ever used to signify. And thus (as in Dr. *Mandeville's* Philosophy already[t] criticized) wherever we have not *Demonstration*, 'tis plain we must needs be *Sceptics*.

But if indeed we must be *Sceptics* in *revealed Religion*, on this Account; the same Consequence will follow, with Regard to every other Kind of Knowledge that depends on *human Testimony*. We must be *Sceptics* too, in our Belief of every *past* Transaction; nay of every thing transacted in our own Times, except only of what falls within the narrow Circle of our proper *Observation*. The Manners of *Men*, the Site of *Countries*, the Varieties of *Nature*, the Truths of Philosophy, the very Food we eat, and Liquids we drink, are all received on the sole Evidence of human Testimony. But what Name would he merit among Men, who in these Instances should say, "he does not believe for certain, or is not assured of what he believes," till in every Case he [258] should be impelled by the Force of *Demonstration*, or the Evidence of *Sense?*

And indeed, on other Occasions, where *Christianity* is not concerned, the noble Writer can speak in a very different, and much juster Manner. For thus he appeals to Nature, in *Proof* of the Wisdom and Goodness of the Creator. "Thus too, in the System of the *bigger* World. *See there* the mutual Dependency of things: The Relation of one to another; of the Sun to this inhabited Earth; and of the *Earth* and *other Planets* to the *Sun!* The *Order, Union,* and *Coherence* of the *whole!* And know, my ingenious Friend, that by this *Survey* you will be obliged to own the *universal System,* and *coherent Scheme* of things; to be *established on* ABUNDANT PROOF, capable of *convincing* any fair and just Contemplator of the Works of Nature."[u] His Lordship's Argument is surely just. Yet, is there one to be found among five Hundred of those, who are thus *convinced* of

---

t. See above, *Essay* ii.[20]
u. *Moralists,* P. ii. § 4.[21]
20. See above, pp. 89–158.
21. Shaftesbury, *Characteristicks,* vol. II, p. 162.

the wise Structure of the Universe, who have ever taken a *Survey* of this immense System, except only in the *Books* and *Diagrams* of *experienced Philosophers?* [259] How few are capable even of comprehending the *Demonstrations,* on which the Truth of the *Copernican* System[22] is established; or receiving, on any other Proof than that of *human Testimony,* "the Relation of the *Earth* and *other Planets* to the *Sun,* the *Order, Union,* and *Coherence* of the *whole?*" It cannot be supposed, that even the noble writer himself ever went thro' the tedious Process of *Experiment* and *Calculation,* which alone can give absolute *Certainty* in this extensive Subject. Yet we find, he is not in any Degree, "sceptical in the Case;" but very rationally determines, that the Wisdom of the Deity in "this universal System, is *established* on *abundant Proof,* capable of *convincing* any *fair* and *just* Contemplator of the Works of Nature."

It appears then, that a Confidence in the Veracity of others is not peculiar to the Belief of *revealed Religion:* The same takes Place in almost every Subject. More particularly, we see, that in the *History of Nature,* as in that of *Revelation,* the Evidence of human *Testimony* is the only Sort of Proof that can be given to Mankind: And whoever allows this Proof, as being "*abundant* and *convincing*" in the *one,* and dis[260]allows or despiseth it in the *other,* how self satisfied soever he may be in his own *Imagination,* is neither a *fair* nor a *just* Contemplator of the Works and the Ways of *Providence.*

If therefore any Objection lies against the Credibility of the *Scripture History,* it must consist in maintaining, not "that human Testimony is insufficient to support it," but "that in Fact, it is not sufficiently supported by the Evidence of human Testimony." If so; this Defect must arise, either from a Want of *External Evidence:* Or Secondly, because the Facts, Doctrines, and Composition of the Bible, are such, that no Testimony whatever can convince us that it is a *divine Revelation.*

---

22. Mikolaj Kopernik, called Copernicus (1473–1573); Polish astronomer who was the first to suggest that the sun was the fixed point around which the planets revolved. Although Copernicus probably formulated the theory of heliocentrism between 1508 and 1514, the final version of the theory was published only in 1543 in *De revolutionibus orbium coelestium libri sex.*

With Regard to the first of these, "the Testimony on which the Authenticity of the Gospel History is founded:" This the noble Writer hath attacked by a long Chain of Insinuations, in his last *Miscellany.*ʷ Where, in the Way of *Dialogue,* he hath indeed amply repaid the Treatment, which in the preceding Chapter he charges upon the *Clergy.* For here he hath introduced two of that *Order,* who, to use his own "Ex[261]pression, are indeed his very legitimate and obsequious *Puppets,* who cooperate in the most officious Manner with the Author, towards the Display of his own proper Wit, and the Establishment of his private Opinion and Maxims.ˣ Where after the poor Phantom or Shadow of an Adversary, has said as little for his Cause as can be imagined, and given as many Opens and Advantages as could be desired, he lies down for good and all; and passively submits to the killing Strokes of his unmerciful Conqueror."ʸ

To these Gentlemen the noble Writer assigns the *herculean* Labour, of proving the Necessity of an absolute *Uniformity* in Opinion. *A hopeful Project indeed!* as his Lordship calls it elsewhere. No Wonder he comes off *Conqueror,* in such a Debate. But here lies the Peculiarity of his Conduct: That while he pretends only to prove, that the Scripture cannot be a Foundation for Uniformity of Opinion *in all things*; he hath thrown out such Insinuations, as evidently imply, that there can be no Foundation for believing the Truth of *any thing* the Gospel History contains. He says, he [262] began by desiring them

> to explain the Word *Scripture,* and by enquiring into the Original of this Collection of antienter and later Tracts, which in general they comprehended under that Title: whether it were the *apocryphal* Scripture, or the more *canonical?* the *full* or *half-authorized?* the *doubtful* or the *certain?* the *controverted* or *uncontroverted?* the *singly* read, or that of *various* Reading? the Texts of *these* Manuscripts or of *those?* the

---

w. *Misc.* v. c. 3.[23]
x. Ib. c. 2.[24]
y. Ib.[25]
23. Shaftesbury, *Characteristicks*, vol. III, pp. 182–209.
24. Ibid., p. 179.
25. Ibid., p. 180.

Transcripts, Copies, Titles, Catalogues, of *this* Church and Nation, or of *that other?* of this Sect and Party, or of another? of those in one Age called Orthodox, and in Possession of Power, or of those who, in another, overthrew their Predecessor's Authority; and, in their Turn also, assumed the Guardianship and Power of holy things? For how these sacred Records were guarded in those Ages, might easily (he said) be *imagined,* by any one who had the least insight into the History of those Times, which we called *Primitive,* and those Characters of Men, whom we styled Fathers of the Church.ᶻ [263]

Here, as his Lordship drags us into the *beaten Track* of *Controversy,* the best Compliment that can be paid the Reader, is to carry him thro' it by the shortest Way. The stale Objections here raked together by the noble Author have been so often, and so fully refuted, by a Variety of excellent Writers, that, to many, it may seem a needless Task, even to touch upon the Subject.ᵃ

However, for the Satisfaction of those who may think it necessary, a summary View of the Evidence is here subjoined,

The Authenticity, therefore, of the Books of the *new Testament,* appears to be founded on the strongest moral Evidence, because from the earliest Ages, we find them ascribed to the Apostles and Evangelists, whose Names they bear. Thus St. PAUL's Epistles are mentioned by St. PETER, and cited by CLEMENS ROMANUS,²⁸ who lived in the Reign of

---

z. *Misc.* v. c. 3.²⁶

a. *Du Pin, Le Clerc, Tillemont, Whitby, Lardner, Phil. Lipsiensis,* &c. and very lately Mr. *Jortin,* in his learned Remarks on *Ecclesiastical History.*²⁷

26. Shaftesbury, *Characteristicks,* vol. III, pp. 195–96.

27. Brown here supplies a select reading list of those who had written against freethinking and deism. Louis Ellies Dupin (1657–1719); French ecclesiastical historian. Jean Le Clerc (1657–1737); Swiss–Dutch theologian, suspected of socinianism and Spinozism. Louis-Sébastien Le Nain de Tillemont (1637–1698); French ecclesiastical historian. Daniel Whitby (1638–1726); Church of England clergyman and author. Nathaniel Lardner (1684–1768); Presbyterian minister and patristic scholar. "Phileleutherus Lipsiensis" ["a freedom-loving man of Leipzig"], i.e., Richard Bentley (1662–1742); preeminent classical scholar, religious polemicist, and enemy of freethinking. John Jortin (1698–1770); ecclesiastical historian and literary critic.

28. St. Clement I (fl. 1st c. A.D.); first apostolic Father, pope from 88 to 97, or from 92 to 101; supposed third successor to St. Peter; a contemporary of the Apostles and a witness of their preaching.

CLAUDIUS, even before St. PAUL was carried Prisoner to ROME. POLY-CARP and IRENAEUS[29] were for some Time contemporary with St. JOHN: They both cite [264] the four Gospels, and affirm they were all wrote by the Apostles and Evangelists, whose Names they bear. JUSTIN MAR-TYR and CLEMENS ALEXANDRINUS, confirm their Accounts in the following Century: And the great ORIGEN, with whom I shall close the Catalogue, and who lived in the Reign of SEVERUS, in his Book against CELSUS[30] hath cited *all* the *Gospels,* and *most,* if not *all* the *Epistles,* under the Names they now bear: And the Words of the several Citations perfectly agree with those of the new Testament, now in Use. Such a full Proof of the Genuineness of these sacred Records, as is not to be parallel'd, concerning any other Book, of *equal* or even of much *less Antiquity.*

The *internal* Proof of their Genuineness, arising from their *Style* and *Composition,* is no less eminent and particular. The Genius of every Book, is so perfectly agreeable to the Character and Education of it's respective Author; every Custom described or alluded to, either *Jewish, Greek,* or *Roman,* so entirely suited to the *Times*; every Incident so *natural,* so *occasional,* so *particular,* so perfectly *identify'd,* that it were the very [265] extreme of Ignorance and Folly, to raise a Doubt on this Subject.

That the Gospel-History hath been transmitted to us, *pure* and *uncorrupted,* we have no less Reason to believe. 'Tis well known how zealous the primitive Christians were in the Preservation of the Scriptures: We know, they regarded them as their chief and dearest Treasure; and often laid down their Lives, rather than deliver the sacred Records to their

---

29. St. Polycarp (fl. 2nd c. A.D.); bishop of Smyrna, who formed a link between the apostolic and patristic periods; his *Letter to the Philippians* is important because of the early testimony it provides of the existence of other New Testament writings. St. Irenaeus (*c.* 120/140–*c.* 200/203 A.D.); bishop of Lyon; said when a child to have heard Polycarp preach.

30. St. Justin Martyr (*c.* 100–*c.* 165 A.D.); important early Christian apologist. St. Clement of Alexandria (150–211/15 A.D.); Christian apologist and missionary; theologian to the Greeks. Origen, or Oregenes Adamantius (*c.* 185–*c.* 254 A.D.); the most important theologian and biblical scholar of the early Greek church. Lucius Septimius Severus Pertinax (145/146–211 A.D.); Roman emperor from 193 until his death. Celsus (fl. 2nd c. A.D.); anti-Christian philosopher and polemicist.

Enemies, who used every Art of Terror, to seize and destroy them. Again, the Scriptures were not then locked up from the Laity, as now in the *Roman* Church: But Copies were taken, dispersed, and became immensely numerous. They were universally read at the Times of public Worship, in different Nations of the World. To this we may add, that as *now,* so *then,* different Sects and Parties subsisted, who all appealed to Scripture for Proof of their several Opinions; and these, 'tis evident, must have been so many *Checks* upon each other, to the general Exclusion of Mistake and Fraud.[b] [266]

This being the real State of the Case; let us now consider the noble Writer's Questions. He asks, whether by Scripture be understood "the apocryphal or more canonical? the full or half-authorized? the doubtful or the certain? the controverted or uncontroverted?" These Questions are nearly synonymous, and one short Reply will clear them all. There are many Books, concerning which there never was *any Doubt.* There are some, concerning which the Doubts have been fully *cleared up.* There are others, concerning which the Doubts have been *confirmed.* Of the first Kind are *all* the *Gospels,* and *most* of the *Epistles:* Of the second, are the Epistle to the *Hebrews,* the *second* of *Peter, second* and *third* of *John,* that of *Jude,* and the *Apocalypse:* Of the third Kind, are the *apocryphal* Books; therefore indeed so called.

The noble Author goes on. "The *single* read, or that of *various* Reading?" [267] My Lord, if by single read you mean a Book in which there are no various Readings, there are none *single read:* Nor, probably, was there ever any Book *single read,* that went thro' more than one Edition: at least, before the Invention of *Printing.* And as the Scriptures were oftener transcribed than any other Book, so, a greater Variety of Readings

---

b. The JEWS and SAMARITANS were *Checks* upon each other in the same Manner, for the Preservation of the Purity of the *Pentateuch.* The *Samaritan Pentateuch* was printed in the last Century: And, "after *Two thousand Years* Discord between the Two Nations, varies as little from the other, as any *Classic* Author in less Tract of Time has disagreed from itself, by the *unavoidable Mistakes* of so many *Transcribers.*"[31] See *Phil. Lipsiens.*

31. [Richard Bentley], *Remarks Upon a Late Discourse of Free-Thinking* (1713), p. 54.

must naturally take Place. But I must inform your Lordship, from the learned Phileleutherus Lipsiensis, that this is the most illiterate of all Cavils: For that in Fact, we have the *Sense* of those ancient Authors most *entire,* where the various Readings are most numerous: As, of those Authors where the Varieties are *fewest,* the Sense is most mutilated or obscure.ᶜ But if by *single read,* your Lordship means an authentic Text collected and composed out of the various Readings, I beg leave to inform you, there is no such in the Protestant Churches. They have been too modest to attempt any such Thing. Nor does the *Truth* suffer by it: For as the learned Critic, just before quoted, observes, the most faulty Copy of the new Testament now in [268] being, does not obscure one moral Doctrine or one Article of Faith.

Again the noble Writer goes on, in a Profusion of synonymous Terms: "The Transcripts, Copies, Titles, Catalogues, of this Church or that? of this Sect or Party, or another? of those in one Age called orthodox, or those who in another Age overthrew them?"[33] What unexperienced Person would not imagine from hence, that *different* Churches, Sects, or Parties, had *each* of them a Bible different from the rest? Yet 'tis certain, that however these Parties differed in Opinions, we find from their Writings now subsisting, that they all appealed to one common Scripture for their Support.

c. For a full View of this Argument, See *Phil. Lipsiens.*[32]

32. Richard Bentley, *Remarks Upon a Late Discourse of Free-Thinking* (1713), pp. 53–54, 56, and 63–66; especially: "In Profane Authors (as they are call'd) whereof One Manuscript only had the luck to be preserv'd, as *Velleius Paterculus* among the *Latins,* and *Hesychius* among the *Greeks;* the Faults of the Scribes are found so numerous, and the Defects beyond all redress; that notwithstanding the Pains of the Learned'st and acutest Critics for Two whole Centuries, those Books are still and are like to continue a mere Heap of Errors. On the contrary, where the Copies of any Author are numerous, though the *Various Readings* always increase in Proportion; there the Text by an accurate Collation of them made by skilful and judicious Hands is ever the more correct, and comes nearer to the true words of the Author" (Ibid., pp. 65–66). See also: "it is Fact undeniable, that the Sacred Books have suffer'd *no more alterations than Common and Classic Authors:* it has been the common Sense of Men of Letters, that numbers of Manuscripts do not make a Text *precarious,* but are useful nay necessary to its Establishment and Certainty" (Ibid., p. 74).

33. Shaftesbury, *Characteristicks,* vol. III, pp. 195–96.

The noble Writer takes his Leave by paying a Compliment to these primitive Writers called the Fathers of the Church. "How these sacred Records were *guarded* in those Ages, might be easily *imagined*,"[34] &c.— But to *imagine*, is a much easier Task than to *prove*; especially when Imagination is helped forward by Inclination. *Guarded* indeed they were, as we have seen, from Interpolation and Falshood. But if he means to insinuate, that they were *guard*[269]*ed* from *Inspection* and *Criticism*, he does great Injustice to Christianity. For whatever Marks of secular Views may be discovered in the Conduct of the ancient Christians in the succeeding Ages, we may safely bid Defiance to the noble Writer's Admirers, to shew any thing of this Kind in the Characters of those to whose Testimony we have here appealed; and on whose Testimony, joined to that of their numerous and ingenuous Contemporaries, the Authenticity of the Gospel-History depends. They were far from acting or writing with a View to temporal Advantage; they were struggling under the Weight of heavy Persecutions; had no Motives to preach or write, but the great Expectation of Happiness hereafter, founded on a firm Belief of that holy Religion, which they propagated with an Effect *almost,* if not *indeed, miraculous.*

On this Occasion I cannot but observe a strange Insinuation thrown out elsewhere by the noble Writer; which, however, is so glaring a Falshood, that he finds himself obliged to disavow it, even while he labours to impress it on his Reader's Imagination, in all the Colours of Eloquence. "If, [270] saies he, the collateral Testimony of other ancient Records were destroyed, there would be less Argument or Plea remaining against that natural Suspicion of those who are called Sceptical, that the holy Records themselves were no other than the pure Invention or artificial Compilement of an interested Party, in Behalf of the *richest Corporation,* and most *profitable Monopoly* in the World."[k] Now if his Lordship be indeed in earnest in urging this Insinuation, he must believe, that *one Set* of Men *preached,* and *wrote,* and endured *Bonds* and *Imprisonment, Torments* and

k. *Misc.* v. c. 1.[35]
34. Shaftesbury, *Characteristicks,* vol. III, p. 196.
35. Ibid., p. 144.

Death; to the End that *another Set* of Men, some *three* or *four Hundred Years* after, might enjoy the *rich Corporations* and *profitable Monopoly* of *Church Preferments.* How far this may be a Proof of the noble Writer's *Sagacity,* I shall leave others to determine. But if he *believes not* the Insinuation, as indeed he seems to *disbelieve* it, then we cannot surely hesitate a Moment concerning the Measure of his *Sincerity.*

The Gentleman therefore who makes so ridiculous a Figure in the supposed Con[271]versation, had he not been a poor *obsequious Puppet,* might have returned one general and satisfactory Answer to all these extraordinary Questions. He might have desired his Lordship "to chuse which he should like *best* or *worst* among all these controverted Copies, various Readings, Manuscripts, and Catalogues adopted by whatever Church, Sect, or Party." Nay, he might have desired him to chuse any of the almost infinite Number of Translations made of these Books in distant Countries and Ages: And taking that to be the Scripture he appealed to, might safely have relied on it, as amply sufficient for all the great Purposes of *Religion* and *Christianity.*

SECTION IV

Since therefore the *Scripture History* appears to be supported by *higher Degrees* of human Testimony, than any other ancient Writing; the only Objections of real Weight against it, must be drawn from it's *internal Structure:* from the Facts it *relates,* the Doctrines it *inculcates,* or the Form of it's *Composition.*

The *Facts* related, being as it were the Foundation of all, will naturally come first [272] under Consideration. "Now these, say the Enemies of Christianity, are *miraculous* or *out of Nature,* and therefore absurd: For *as they can prove nothing,* so it is impossible that Accounts of this Kind could be so essentially mingled with a Religion that should come from God."

On this Foundation the noble Writer hath taken frequent Occasion to deride what he calls the "Mockery of Miracles;"[1] particularly those of our

---

1. *Misc.* ii. c. 2.[36]
36. Shaftesbury, *Characteristicks,* vol. III, p. 46.

Saviour.^[m] Here we shall find him striking at the very Basis of all revealed Religion, while he asserts, that, even supposing the Truth of the Facts, "Miracles cannot witness either for God or Men, nor are any Proof either of Divinity or Revelation."^[n] But that his Argument may be fairly represented, let it appear in his own Words. "The Contemplation of the Universe, it's Laws and Government, was (I aver'd) the only Means which could establish the sound Belief of a Deity. For what tho' innumerable Miracles from every Part assailed the Sense, and gave the trembling Soul no Respite? What tho' the Sky should suddenly open, and all kinds of Prodigies appear, Voices be heard, or [271] Characters read? What would this evince more, than that there was certain Powers could do all this? But what Powers; whether one or more; whether superior, or subaltern; mortal, or immortal; wise or foolish; just or unjust; good or bad: This would still remain a Mystery; as would the *true Intention,* the *Infallibility* or *Certainty* of whatever *these Powers asserted.*"^[o]

'Tis remarkable, that the noble Writer pretends here only to shew, that Miracles are no Proof of the *Existence* of God: Yet in the Conclusion of his Argument, he brings it home to the Case of *Revelation:* To "the true *Intention,* the *Infallibility* or *Certainty* of whatever *these Powers* asserted."This is clearly the Scope of his Argument: And so indeed hath it been understood by his *Under-workmen* in *Infidelity,* who have with great Industry retailed this Objection. As it is a Circumstance of the last Importance in Regard to the Truth of *Christianity,* it cannot be an unseasonable Task, to shew in the fullest Manner the Vanity and Error of this trite Cavil.

But instead, of considering *single Acts* of supernatural or *miraculous Power,* as be[272]ing performed in Attestation of any *particular Doctrine,* (which hath been the general Way of treating this Question) 'tis my

---

m. Ib. c. 3.^[37]
n. *Moralists,* Part ii § 5. passim.^[38]
o. Ib.^[39]

37. Shaftesbury, *Characteristicks,* vol. III, pp. 60–81.
38. The phrase in quotation marks is a summary of the tendency of that chapter; but cf., e.g., Ibid., vol. II, p. 188.
39. Ibid.

Design to consider as one Object, "that vast *Series* and *Concatenation* of miraculous Acts, recorded in the Old and New Testament, wrought thro' a long Succession of Ages, for the *carrying on, Support,* and *Completion* of the *Christian Dispensation.*"

With this View therefore let us first consider the means by which Mankind are justly convinced of the *Being* of a *God.* Now this Conviction, 'tis allowed by all, ariseth from a *Union* of *Power, Wisdom,* and *Goodness,* displayed in the visible Creation. From this *Union* alone arises the Idea of an *all-perfect Being:* so that a Failure in any of these three essential Circumstances would *destroy* the Idea of a *God.* The *Goodness* of the Deity is seen in the designed End or Purpose of the Creation, which is, "The Happiness of all his Creatures:" His *Wisdom* is seen, in the proper Means employed for the Accomplishment of this great End: His *Power* fulfills what Goodness had intended and Wisdom contrived, by putting these Means in Execution. Hence then alone we obtain the Idea of a *Divinity,* from a *Union* of perfect *Goodness, Wisdom,* and *Power.* [273]

'Tis likewise, I think, acknowledged by all *Theists,* that, as to the divine Power, it may work it's Intentions, either by a continued and uninterrupted Superintendency, or Agency on Matter, or by impressing certain original and permanent Qualities upon it. Which of these two Kinds of Operation may really prevail in Nature, is perhaps beyond the Reach of human Knowledge, clearly to determine. The *Newtonian* Philosophy indeed renders it highly probable, that the *continued Agency* of *God* prevails. But a Determination in this Subject is indeed of no Consequence; since, which soever of these Methods be ordained, the *divine Power* is equally display'd, while it ministers to the Ends of *Goodness* and *Wisdom.*

'Tis equally plain, that, if the divine Goodness should determine to raise Mankind to *higher Degrees* of *Knowledge* and *Virtue,* than what they could attain to by the pre-established Laws of Nature; or to free them from *Defects* and *Miseries,* occasioned by any incidental and *voluntary* Corruptions, *posterior* to their *Creation;* 'tis equally plain, I say, that an Exertion of *supernatural Power* for the Accomplishment [274] of *this End,* would be a *Display, Proof,* or *Revelation* of the *Divinity,* entirely similar to that which arises from the Works of Nature. For both *here,* and in the Works of *Nature,* the Proof of the Divinity ariseth, not from mere uniform Acts of Power, but from the *Subserviency* of divine *Power* to this one great End, the *Production* of human *Happiness*. Here then, the noble Writer's Objection is essentially defective: What he affirms is either *false*, or *foreign* to the Question. For if we suppose (and the present Question is put upon this Footing only) that the miraculous or supernatural Effects are evidently subservient to similar Ends of *Wisdom* and *Goodness*, as appear in the Works of the Creation; then sure, we have equal Reason to conclude, and be convinced, that they are the Effects of *one* Power;—of one *superior* and *immortal* Power;—of one Power, *wise, just,* and *good*;— In a Word, of that Power which first brought Nature into Being, established Laws for the Welfare of his Creatures; and when the Happiness of his Creatures requires an Interposition, gives still further Evidences of his *Goodness, Wisdom,* and *Om*[275]*nipotence*, by controuling those Laws which himself had established.

Let us now apply these Principles to the *Christian* Dispensation. "This, we say, was a Scheme of Providence, which still continues operating; whereby the Deity determined to raise fallen and corrupted Man to higher Degrees of *Knowledge, Virtue,* and *Happiness,* than what by Nature he could have attained." In this Design, the *divine* GOODNESS is eminently display'd.

The Means, whereby this great Design was accomplished, was "by separating a peculiar People from the rest of Mankind; not for their own Sakes, but for the Sake of all; by preserving them amidst their Enemies; by leading them forth into a distant Country; by establishing there the Worship of the *one* God, in Opposition to the Idolatries of surrounding Nations: 'Till, when the Fulness of Time should come, and Mankind be capable of receiving a more perfect Revelation, a Saviour JESUS CHRIST should be sent, to free Mankind from the Power of Ignorance and Sin; to bring Life and Immortality to Light, and communicate to [276] all Men the most perfect practical Knowledge of the true God, and of every moral Duty." In this Dispensation is no less eminently displayed the *divine* WISDOM.

But what less than Omnipotence itself could secure the perfect Execution of a Plan so *mighty* and *extensive?* Which reaching thro' the Compass of many, and distant Ages, must combat the *Power,* controul the *Prejudices,* and work it's Way thro' the *discordant Manners* and *Opinions* of all the Kingdoms of the Earth. On this Account the immediate Exertion of divine Power was necessary for it's *Proof, Support,* and *Completion.* Accordingly, we find it's omnipotent Author, carrying on this Scheme of *Wisdom* and *Goodness,* with a *mighty Hand,* and an *out-stretched Arm.*

> He sent a Man before his People, even Joseph, who was sold to be a Bond-Servant: He increased his People exceedingly, and made them stronger than their Enemies. He sent Moses his Servant, and Aaron: And these shewed his *Tokens* among them; and *Wonders* in the Land of *Ham.* He sent Darkness, and it was dark; and turned their Waters into Blood. Their Land brought forth Frogs, yea, even in their [277] King's Chambers. He gave them Hailstones for Rain, and Flames of Fire in their Land. He spake the Word, and the Locusts came innumerable, and devoured the Fruit of their Ground. He smote all the first-born in their Land, even the chief of all their Strength. He brought forth his People from among them: He spread out a Cloud to be a Covering, and Fire to give them Light in the Night-Season. He rebuked the *Red-Sea* also, and it was dried up; so he led them thro' the Deep as thro' a Wilderness. At their Desire he brought Quails, and filled them with the Bread of Heaven. He opened the Rock of Stone, so that Rivers ran in dry Places.—Yet within a while they forgat his Works, and tempted God in the Desert: Then the Earth opened, and swallowed up *Dathan,* and covered the Congregation of *Abiram.* They joined themselves unto *Baal-Peor,* and provoked him with their own Inventions; so the Plague was great among them: Then, being chastised, they turned to their God. He led them over *Jordan*; the Waters divided to let them pass. He discomfited their Enemies: At his [278] Word the Sun abode in the midst of Heaven; and the Moon stood still, and hasted not to go down for a whole Day. So he gave the Kingdoms of *Canaan* to be an Heritage unto his People; that all the Nations of the World might know that the Hand of the Lord is mighty, and that they might fear the Lord continually.[40]

Here then we see, that this mighty Series of miraculous Acts recorded in the *Old Testament,* being *the very Means* of *preserving* and *separating* the Israelites from the *rest* of Mankind, and at the same time designed

40. Psalms 105:17–45.

to *impress* them with a *lasting Idea* of the uncontroulable and *immediate Power* of *God*; were generally *awakening* Instances of *Omnipotence*, often of *Justice* and *Terror*, in the Punishment of *cruel* EGYPTIANS, *rebellious* JEWS, and *idolatrous Nations*.

In pursuing this vast Concatenation of divine Power thro' the Series of Miracles recorded in the *New Testament*, and wrought for the same End, the *Completion* of *Christianity*, we shall find them of a very *different* Nature and *Complexion:* Yet still, admirably suited to accomplish the *same* designed *Ends* of *Providence*. For now the *Fulness* [279] *of Time* was come, in which the Wisdom of the Deity ordained the immediate Establishment of a Religion of perfect *Purity* and boundless *Love*. Accordingly, the Series of miraculous Acts wrought for this great End, were such as must naturally *engage* Mankind to a *favourable Reception* of *Christianity*; were the very *Image* and Transcript, expressed the very *Genius* of that most *amiable* Religion they were brought to *support* and *establish*; in a Word, were continued Instances of *Omnipotence*, joined with *unbounded Charity*, divine *Compassion* and *Benevolence*.

The Birth of JESUS was proclaimed by a glorious Apparition of superior Beings, who declared the End of his coming in that divine Song of Triumph, "Glory to God in the highest, and on Earth Peace, Good Will towards Men!"[41] His Life was one continued Scene of divine Power, Wisdom, and Beneficence. He gave Eyes to the Blind; Ears to the Deaf; and Feet to the Lame: He raised the Dead to Life, rebuked the raging Elements, and made the Winds and Seas obey him. When to fulfill the Decrees of Heaven, and complete the great Work of Man's Redemption, he submitted to an ignominious Death, the [280] Vail of the Temple was rent in twain: A general Darkness[42] involved, and an Earthquake shook, the City. The same Omnipotence by which he wrought his Miracles, raised him from the Grave; and after a short stay on Earth, during which he strengthened and confirmed his desponding Followers, translated him

41. Luke 2:14.
42. For a later discussion of the preternatural darkness which accompanied the Crucifixion, see the conclusion of chapter 15 of Gibbon's *Decline and Fall* (*Decline and Fall*, vol. I, pp. 512–13).

to Heaven. And now, a new and *unexpected* Scene of divine and miraculous Power opened on Mankind, for the full Establishment of *Christianity*. The Spirit of God came down, and dwelt with the Apostles; they were all filled with the Holy Ghost, and spake with other Tongues, as the Spirit gave them Utterance. They were invested with supernatural Power to heal Diseases; were impowered to strike dead the deceitful ANANIAS and SAPPHIRA; and when imprisoned, were delivered by the immediate Hand of GOD. By these Means, Christianity gained a numerous Train of Proselytes among the JEWS; but the great Work of converting the Gentiles was not yet begun. To this End the Apostle PAUL was destined; and converted to Christianity by an amazing Act of supernatural and divine Power. In this important Ministry he was frequently preserved [281] by the miraculous Care of Providence; did himself perform stupendous Acts of Power and Beneficence; by these Means converting Multitudes among the Gentiles, and planting Christianity in the most knowing and polished Nations of the Earth.

To this irresistible Chain of Evidence, arising from the miraculous Exertion of divine Power, we may add another *collateral* Proof, arising from the *miraculous* Emanations of divine *Fore-knowledge,* recorded in the Bible, and delivered in PROPHECY thro' a Series of Ages, all *centering* in the same Point, the foretelling the *Completion* of this immense Plan of *Wisdom* and *Goodness.* These *Predictions* were fulfilled in the Advent, Life, Death, and Resurrection of our *Saviour*; who himself foretold the Success of his Apostles among the Gentiles, and the final Dissolution of the Jewish Polity. This came to pass in the Destruction of the *Temple:* And when a bitter Enemy to Christianity attempted to make void the Decrees of Heaven in rebuilding this *Temple,* (the only Circumstance of Union that could ever make the JEWS *once more a People*) the very Foundations were rent in Pieces by an [282] Earthquake, and the mad Assailants against *Omnipotence* buryed in the Ruins.

From this mighty *Union,* therefore, ariseth a Proof similar to that which we obtain from the Works of Nature. For as in *these* we see the Happiness of the Creation *intended, plann'd,* and *produced,* and from hence discover the Agency of the Deity: So in the Progress and Completion of *Christianity* we find a parallel Display of the divine Attributes: We see the Advancement of Man's Happiness *determined* by divine GOODNESS, *plann'd* by divine WISDOM, *foretold* by divine KNOWLEDGE, *accomplished* by divine POWER: and hence, as in *Nature,* obtain a full *Manifestation, Proof,* or *Revelation* of the DEITY.

As this seems to be the true Light, in which the Evidence arising from the Scripture-Miracles ought to be placed, it may be proper now to add a few Observations on what hath been offered on this Subject, both by the *Defenders* and the *Adversaries* of *Christianity.*

I. As to the Degree of Proof or Evidence arising from a *single Miracle* in Support of any *particular Doctrine*; whatever Force it may carry, 'tis a Point, which we [283] are by no Means at present concerned to determine: Because, as we have seen, in the Progress of the Christian Dispensation, there is a vast *Series* or *Chain,* all *uniting* in one common End. It might be considered, in the same Manner, by those who write in Proof of the Being of a God, "What Evidence of his Being would arise from a single *Vegetable* or *Animal,* unconnected with the rest of the Creation." But however satisfying a single Fact of this Kind may be to impartial Minds, it were surely weak to argue on this Foundation *only,* while we can appeal to that mighty *Union of Design* which appears in the Works of Nature. It should therefore seem, that the Defenders of Christianity have generally set this Evidence in too *detached* and *particular* a Light: For tho' the Proof arising from a single Miracle, in Support of a particular Doctrine may be of sufficient Force to convince an equitable Mind; yet sure, 'tis infinitely stronger and more satisfactory, if we *view at once* the whole *Chain* of Miracles, by which the great Scheme of *Christianity* was propagated, as *one* vast *Object:* Because in this View, we discover innumerable Circumstances of *mutual Relation* and [284] *Agreement,* similar to those which are Proofs of *final Causes* in the natural World: In a Word, we discover that *Union of Design,* that Concurrence of infinite *Goodness, Wisdom,* and *Power,* which is the sure Indication of the *Divinity.*

II. If in a Dispensation thus proved to be from God by all these concurring Signatures of Divinity, any *incidental Circumstances* should be found, which are *unaccountable* to *human Reason*; 'tis the Part of human Reason to *acquiesce* in this *mysterious* and *unknown* Part, from what is *clear* and *known.* Because in a System or Dispensation planned by *infinite* Wisdom, there *must* of Necessity be something which *finite* Wisdom cannot comprehend. This the noble Writer allows with Regard to the Works of Nature. "If, saith he, in this *mighty Union,* there be such Relations of Parts one to another as are not easily discovered; if on this Account, the *End* and *Use* of Things does not every where appear, there is *no Wonder*; since 'tis indeed no more than what *must happen* of *Necessity.* Nor could supreme Wisdom have otherwise ordered it. For in an Infinity of things thus relative, *a Mind* [285] *which sees not infinitely, can see nothing fully.*"[f]

III. Hence therefore may be evinced the Vanity of this Cavil, "that nothing can be proved to be a divine Revelation which is not discoverable by human Reason; since whatever is reasonable needs no Miracle to confirm it, and whatever is beyond the Reach of Reason cannot be made to appear reasonable by any Miracle whatsoever."[g] Hence, I say, the Vanity of this Cavil is evident. Because, as in Nature, so in Revelation, the full Evidence of Divinity is founded, not on single detached Circumstances, but on a mighty *Union* or *Concatenation* of Facts, implying the most perfect *Wisdom, Power,* and *Goodness.* This Foundation being once laid, if any thing *incidental* in either Case appears unaccountable as to it's *End* or *Use,* it is naturally and properly involved, or taken in as *a Part* of this *immense Design,* which thro' it's vast Extent, must needs be *incomprehensible* to *human Reason.*

f. *Moralists,* P. ii. § 4.[43]

g. An Objection urged by *Tindal, Morgan,* and others.[44]

43. Shaftesbury, *Characteristicks,* vol. II, p. 163.

44. Matthew Tindal (1657–1733); freethinker and religious controversialist. Thomas Morgan (*d.* 1743); theological and medical writer; a self-professed "Christian Deist"; ejected from the priesthood shortly after 1720 on grounds of heterodoxy. Brown refers to the arguments of, respectively, Matthew Tindal, *Christianity as Old as the Creation* (1730) and Thomas Morgan, *The Moral Philosopher* (1737). See also Hume's more feline version of this *topos* of freethinking: "So that, upon the whole, we may conclude, that the *Christian Religion* not only was at first attended with miracles, but even at this day cannot be believed by any reasonable person without one. Mere reason is insufficient to convince us of its veracity: And whoever is moved by Faith to assent to it, is conscious of a continued miracle in his own person, which subverts all the principles of his understanding, and gives him a determination to believe what is most contrary to custom and experience" (*An Enquiry Concerning Human Understanding* [1748], sect. X, part 2).

IV. As to the Objection, "that Miracles may be wrought by inferior or sub[286]altern Beings:" This vanishes at once with Regard to the *Christian* Dispensation, on the Evidence as here stated. For as the miraculous Acts of Power recorded in the Bible were wrought for the Support and Accomplishment of a Dispensation full of *Goodness* and *Wisdom,* we have the same Proof that they were the Work of the *supreme God,* as we have, *that Nature is so.* 'Tis true, that in either Case, for aught we know, *inferior* or *subaltern* Beings may have been commissioned by the *Supreme,* as *immediate Agents.* But this Possibility, in either Case, can be a Matter of no Consequence to us, while it is manifest that the *delegated* Beings, whatever they might be, acted in full *Subserviency* to the *Goodness, Wisdom,* and *Omnipotence* of the *one eternal* GOD.

V. To the noble Writer's Objection, "that, while we labour to unhinge Nature, we bring Confusion on the World, and destroy that Order from whence the one infinite and perfect Principle is known."[h]—the Reply is easy and convincing. For while the supernatural Power is directed to advance the Happiness of Mankind, 'tis so [287] far from destroying any Principle from whence the one perfect Being is known; that, on the contrary, it gives us still clearer and more satisfying Notices of the divine Providence. 'Tis allowed on all Hands, that there are Imperfections in the Creation: And tho' there may be, and doubtless are, good Reasons unknown to us, why these should not in every Instance be removed by a particular Exertion of supernatural Power; yet when the divine Wisdom sees fit thus to interpose, for the further Advancement of his Creatures' Happiness; can any thing be more irrational than to say, that "this is bringing Confusion on the World?" The only Question is, "Whether *Happiness* shall be destroyed for the sake of a pre-established *Law;* or a pre-established *Law* be *suspended* for the sake of *Happiness?*" In other Words, whether *Power* shall be subservient to *Goodness,* or *Goodness* yield to *Power?* A Question which no sound *Theist* can be left at a Loss to answer. As therefore the Exertion of divine Power, *in Nature,* is for the Production of *Happiness;* the *miraculous* Exertion of Power, for the further *Advancement* of Man's *Happiness,*

h. *Moral.* P. ii. § 5.[45]
45. Shaftesbury, *Characteristicks,* vol. II, p. 189.

is so far from "bring[288]ing Confusion on the World, either the Chaos and Atoms of the *Atheists,* or the Magick and Daemons of the POLYTHE-ISTS,"[46] that it is even the clearest *Proof,* or *Revelation* of the DIVINITY.

VI. Without this apparent Subserviency to the Designs of Wisdom and Goodness, all Accounts of miraculous Facts must be highly improbable. Because we have no Reason to believe that the Deity will ever counteract the established Laws of Nature; unless for the Sake of advancing the Happiness of his Creatures.

VII. On this Account, most of the pretended Miracles recorded in the *Heathen* Story, are highly *improbable.* For it doth not appear, they were ever said to have been wrought in any *Series* or *Chain:* they never were *directed* to the Accomplishment of any *one End,* thro' *different Periods* of Time: Were frequently far from being *beneficent*: Seldom accommodated even to any *rational* Purpose; but generally, mere pretended Acts of *arbitrary* and *unmeaning Power.* Thus they are essentially distinguished from the Scripture Miracles; and are utterly destitute of that INTERNAL [289] *Evidence* which ariseth from an *Union* of *Design.*

VIII. Hence we may clearly discover the Reason, why the wiser Heathens ridiculed the *Jews,* even to a *Proverb,* for their extravagant Regard to *Miracles.* They knew their own to be *absurd* and *irrational*; this at once prevented them from enquiring into the real Nature of the *Jewish* Miracles; and at the same Time, led them to *deride* and *reject* these boasted *Wonders,* as being no better than their own.

IX. But on the Evidence as here stated, the Scripture Miracles become even *probable,* from the Circumstances under which they are recorded. As they are beneficent: As they were wrought thro' *different Periods* of Time in *Support* of *one* Dispensation full of *Wisdom* and *Goodness:* As it is highly improbable that this Dispensation could have been *completed* in all it's immense *Variety* of *Circumstances* without such an immediate *Interposition* of divine *Power.*

X. And now we shall plainly see the Reason why we reject the Accounts of Miracles given by Heathen Writers, while we believe the other Parts of their Story; and yet cannot reject the *Jewish* and *Chris*[290]*tian*

46. Ibid.

Miracles, without rejecting at the same Time the whole History in which they are contained. For in the first Case, as the Miracles are *useless, unmeaning,* and *unconnected* with the rest of the Facts, it appears they are merely political. But the *Jewish* and *Christian* Miracles make an essential Part of the several Events related; they are strongly connected with this great HISTORY *of* PROVIDENCE, and are indeed *the very Means* by which *Providence* completed it's gracious *Purpose,* "the Establishment of Christianity." We cannot therefore reject these *miraculous* Accounts without rejecting all the *natural Events* with which they are thus intimately *interwoven:* And this we cannot do, without destroying every received Principle of Assent, and shaking the Faith of all ancient History.

I cannot conclude this Argument without transcribing a noble Passage from the Book of *Wisdom,* where several of these Truths are finely illustrated: And which may convince us, how just an Idea the JEWS entertained of *miraculous Interposition,* beyond what their Enemies have industriously represented. The Writer, after recounting the stupendous Chain of Miracles [291] wrought for the Deliverence of the chosen People, concludes thus. "In all things, O Lord, thou hast magnified and glorified thy People, and hast not despised to assist them in every Time and Place.—For every Creature in it's Kind was fashioned a new, and served in their own *Offices enjoyned them,* that thy Children might be kept without Hurt.—For the things of the Earth were changed into things of the Water, and the thing that did swim went upon the Ground. The Fire had power in the Water, contrary to his own Virtue; and the Water forgat his own Kind, to quench.—Thus the Elements were *changed* among themselves by *a Kind of Harmony,* as when one *Tune* is *changed* upon an *Instrument* of Music, and *the Melody still remaineth.*"[47]

Thus he nobly expresseth the *Subserviency* of the *Elements* to the *divine Will:* And under the Image of a musical Instrument, which the skilful Master *tunes, changes,* and *directs* to the *one* Purpose of *Harmony,* he aptly and beautifully represents the *whole Creation* as an *Instrument* in

47. Wisdom of Solomon 19:18–22.

the Hands of GOD, which he *orders, varies,* and *con*[292]*trouls,* to the *one unvary'd End* of HAPPINESS.

SECTION V

Having vindicated the Scripture *Miracles* from the noble Writer's Objections; and shewn that they are so far from being *useless* or *absurd,* that the grand Scheme of Providence could neither have been *evidenced* nor *accomplished* without them; we have destroyed the chief Foundation on which his Lordship hath attempted to fix his Cavils against Christianity on another Subject; I mean, that of *Enthusiasm*; which naturally offers itself next to our Consideration. As this is the noble Writer's favourite Topic, we may reasonably expect to see him shine in it: And in one Respect indeed he does. He never touches on the Subject, but he riseth above himself: His Imagination kindles; he catches the Fire he describes; and his Page glows with all the Ardors of this high Passion.

It will, I presume, be unnecessary to make any Remarks on the large and eminent List of *Enthusiasts,* Poets, Orators, Heroes, Legislators, Musicians, and Philo[293]sophers, which his Lordship cites from PLATO. He may call them *Enthusiasts,* if it seem good to him; and may justly rank himself in the Number too, if by that Name be understood no more, than a Man of uncommon Strength or Warmth of Imagination; for this indeed is the requisite Foundation of Excellence, in any of the Characters here enumerated.

The only Circumstance we are concerned *calmly* to examine, is that of *religious Enthusiasm:* Chiefly, to point out the essential Qualities and Characteristics which distinguish *this* from *divine Inspiration:* Hence to prove, that our *Saviour* and his *Apostles* were not *religious Enthusiasts,* as the noble Writer hath suggested.

'Tis indeed, as his Lordship observes, "a great Work to judge of Spirits, whether they be of God."[48] We shall willingly join him in this Principle too, "that in order to this End, we must antecedently judge our own Spirit, whether it be of Reason or sound Sense, free of every byassing Passion,

---

48. Shaftesbury, *Characteristicks,* vol. I, p. 35.

every giddy Vapour, or melancholy Fume. This is the first Knowledge, and previous Judgment; to understand ourselves, and know what [294] Spirit we are of. Afterwards we may judge the Spirit in others, consider what their personal Merit is, and prove the Validity of their Testimony by the Solidity of their Brain."[49] On this Principle then let the Cause be determined.

In examining this Subject, therefore, we shall find, First, that in *some* Respects, *Enthusiasm* must, from it's Nature, always resemble *divine Inspiration*. Secondly, that in others it hath generally attempted a further Resemblance, but hath always betrayed itself. Thirdly, that in other Circumstances it is diametrically opposite to divine Inspiration, and void even of all seeming Resemblance.

First, *Enthusiasm* must, from it's very Nature, in some Respects always resemble divine *Inspiration*. They both have the *Deity* for their Object; and consequently must both be attended with a devout Turn of Mind. They must both be subject to strong and unusual Impressions; the one *supernatural*; the other *praeternatural,* that is, beyond the ordinary Efforts of Nature, tho' really produced by Nature; *these,* thro' their uncommon Force, will often resemble, and not easily be distinguished from *those* [295] which are the real Effect of *supernatural* Power: This Circumstance deserves a particular Attention: For these two Qualities which are common to both, have induced many to reject the very Notion of divine Inspiration, as mere Enthusiasm. Whereas we see, that, supposing such a thing as divine *Inspiration,* it cannot but resemble *Enthusiasm* in these two Characters.

But tho' it were strange, if *Counterfeits* did not hit off some Features of their genuine *Originals*; yet it were more strange, if they should be able to adopt them all, by such a perfect Imitation as to prevent their being detected.

There are, therefore, secondly, other Circumstances in which *Enthusiasm* hath generally attempted a further Resemblance of divine *Inspiration,* but in these hath always betrayed itself *spurious.*

The first of this Kind is, "A Pretence to, and Persuasion of the Power of working *Miracles.*" This Persuasion must needs be natural to the Enthusiast; because he imagines himself in all things highly favoured of

49. Ibid.

Heaven: The Notion of a Communication of *divine Power* will therefore be among the chief of his *Deliriums.* [296] In this the Enthusiast hath been detected, *sometimes* by the *Absurdity* of the Miracle attempted, *always* by his *Inability* to perform what he proposed. There is scarce an *Absurdity* so great, but what hath some Time or other been aimed at by Enthusiasts, in the Way of miraculous Power. Their Attempts have ever been void of all *rational Intention,* void of *Beneficence,* void of *common Discernment:* And hence manifestly the Effects of a heated Imagination. That they have always failed in their Attempts is no less known. But these are Truths so willingly allowed by the Enemies of Religion, that we need not enlarge on them. On the contrary, we have seen, the Miracles of the Gospel are *rational, beneficent, united* in one great *End*; performed before *Numbers,* before *Enemies*; recorded by *Eye-Witnesses.* His Lordship indeed objects or insinuates, that the Testimony even of Eye-Witnesses cannot in this Case be a Foundation for Assent, unless we know them to have been "free both from any particular Enthusiasm, and a general Turn to Melancholy." But with Regard to the Miracles of the Gospel, we know that many were converted by them, from their former [297] Prejudices; and therefore could not possibly be under the Influence of the *Christian* Enthusiasm, supposing it such. And as to their being free from *Melancholy*; for this we may safely appeal to the rational and consistent Accounts given by the sacred Penmen. Melancholy and Enthusiasm must ever produce inconsistent Visions. For a Proof that the Scripture Miracles are not of this Nature, we appeal to what hath been already said on this Subject in the preceeding Section.

But there is *one* miraculous Gift, *the Gift of Tongues,* which hath more generally been supposed the peculiar Effect of Inspiration. We have an Account of this Kind recorded in holy Writ.[i] And this Account the noble Writer hath thought it expedient to turn to Ridicule; by representing this supposed miraculous Gift, as the mere Effect of strong *Melancholy,* and natural *Inebriation.* To this Purpose, having observed from Dr. MORE, that "the Vapours and Fumes of Melancholy partake of the Nature of Wine;" he adds, "One might conjecture from hence, that the malicious

---

i. *Acts* ii.

Opposers of early Christianity were not un[298]versed in this Philosophy; when they sophistically objected against the apparent Force of the divine Spirit speaking in divers Languages, and attributed it *to the Power of new Wine.*[k] Agreeably to this insinuated Charge, he tells us of "A Gentleman who has writ lately in Defence of revived Prophecy, and has since fallen himself into the prophetic Ecstasies." The noble Writer adds, "I saw him lately under an *Agitation* (as they call it) *uttering Prophecy* in a pompous *Latin Style,* of which, out of his Ecstasy, it seems, *he is wholly incapable.*"[l]

Here we may see, how ready some People are to strain at a *Gnat,* and yet swallow a *Camel.*[52] The noble Writer ridicules the Gift of Tongues from *divine Inspiration,* as absurd and impossible: Yet he believes, you see, or *affects* to believe, that this Man could speak *Latin* by the sole Force of *Imagination* and *Enthusiasm.* A compendious Method this, of learn-ing Languages! I have somewhere met with a very rational Remark, That whereas it was charged by FESTUS upon St. PAUL, "that *Learning* had made him *mad,*" this No[299]tion inverts the Charge; for thus "*Madness* may make a Man *learned.*"

But leaving his Lordship's Admirers to determine which is the greater Miracle, a *Gift* of Tongues from *God,* or a Gift of Tongues from *Melan-choly*; 'tis our Part to shew the essential Characters of Distinction between the *Reality* of *one,* and the *Pretences* of the *other.* Now this will appear most evident, if we compare them, both in their *Manner,* and their *End.* As to the *Manner* of this *new prophecying Sect,* the noble Writer himself tells us, it was that of *Ecstacy* and *Convulsion*; and that he saw this Gen-tleman under an *Agitation* when he had the *Gift of Tongues.* As to the *End* pretended in this miraculous *Gift*; it appears there was really *none:* For the *pompous Latin Style* was uttered among a People who, in general, under-stood the *English* Language *only:* It could therefore serve to no *rational*

---

k. *Misc.* ii. § 2.[50]

l. *Let. on Enthu.* § 6.[51]

50. Shaftesbury, *Characteristicks,* vol. III, p. 43. Henry More (1614–87); philoso-pher, poet, and theologian; one of the "Cambridge Platonists," and a man whose writings prepared the way for latitudinarianism.

51. Ibid., vol. I, p. 29.

52. Matthew 23:24.

Purpose. On the contrary, it appears that the miraculous Gift of Tongues conferred on the Apostles, was *rational* both in its *Manner* and it's *End.* There is not the least Hint of it's having been attended with *Ecstasies* or *Convulsions;* nay, it appears from [300] the Account, that it could not have been so attended: And from the *Occasion* it appears how proper it was, with Regard to it's *End.* The Recital is noble and rational: Let it answer for itself. "And there were dwelling at Jerusalem, JEWS, devout Men, out of *every Nation* under Heaven.—And they were all amazed, and marvelled, saying one to another, Behold, are not all these which speak, *Galileans?* And how hear we *every* Man in *our own Tongue,* wherein we were born? *Parthians,* and *Medes,* and *Elamites,* the Dwellers in *Mesopotamia,* and in *Judea,* and *Cappodocia,* in *Pontus* and *Asia, Phrygia* and *Pamphylia,* in *Egypt,* and in the Parts of *Libya* about *Cyrene:* And Strangers of *Rome; Jews* and *Proselytes, Cretes* and *Arabians;* we do *hear them speak in our Tongues the wonderful Works of God!*"[53] How just an Effort of divine Power! which should at once give *Instruction* to those who most wanted it; and be the *natural Means* of conveying and *dispersing* the glad Tydings of the *Gospel,* to *every Nation under Heaven!*—It should seem probable, therefore, that the Men who "mocked and said, these Men are full of new Wine," were the *Natives of* [301] *Judea.* For PETER, we find, immediately arose, and addressed himself to these in particular. "Ye Men of *Judea,*" &c. And it was natural for them to entertain this Suspicion; because they neither understood what the Apostles uttered, nor could imagine how they should obtain a Knowledge of so many various Tongues. They must, therefore, naturally suspect, that the Apostles were uttering *unmeaning Sounds:* And this they regarded as the Effect of *Wine.*

Another remarkable Circumstance, in which Enthusiasts have often pretended to resemble the divinely inspired, is "the Gift of Prophecy." Which, indeed, is no more than another Kind of Miracle. In this too, Enthusiasm hath always betrayed itself. First, and principally, with regard to the Event. The frequent Attempts of this Kind, and their perpetual *Failure,* need not here be enumerated: They are known sufficiently. This cannot be charged on the *Apostles* with the least Appearance of Reason:

53. Acts 2:5–11.

For it is a Gift they hardly ever pretended to. Our *Saviour* indeed foretold many and great Events—the Defection of PETER; his own Sufferings, Death, Resurrection, and Ascension; the Descent of the Holy Spirit, the [302] Persecution of his Disciples, the Propagation of his Religion among the Gentiles, the approaching Miseries and final Destruction of *Jerusalem.* Now all these Events were clearly accomplished: So far, therefore, are they from proving him an *Enthusiast,* that they demonstrate him possessed of *divine Fore-Knowledge.*

But besides the *Event,* there is a notable Circumstance in the *Manner,* which hath ever distinguished *real* from *pretended, true* from *false* Prophecy: And which the noble Writer's groundless Affirmations have made it necessary to insist on.

He says, "I find by present Experience, as well as by all Histories sacred and prophane, that the Operation of this Spirit is every where the *same* as to the *bodily Organ.*"ᵐ In Confirmation of this he cites a Passage from the Gentleman who was subject to the prophetic Ecstasies, which informs us "that the ancient Prophets had the Spirit of God upon them under Ecstasy, with divers strange Gestures of Body denominating them Madmen (or Enthusiasts) as appears evidently, says he, in the Instances of *Balaam, Saul, David,* [303] *Ezekiel, Daniel,*"ⁿ &c. And he adds, the Gentleman "proceeds to justify this by the Practice of the apostolic Times, and by the Regulation which the Apostle himself applies to these seemingly irregular Gifts."ᵒ In this Instance it is not unpleasant to observe the different Views of his Lordship, and the Gentleman he refers to, in their Endeavours to establish this pretended Fact. The *one* was zealous to fix a Resemblance between the *old* and the *new* prophetic Manner, in order to strengthen the Credit of the *revived* Prophecy: The *other's* Intention plainly was, by that very *Resemblance,* which he was willing should pass for *real,* to destroy the Credit of the *Scripture* Prophecies, well knowing that the other deserved none.

m. *Let. on Enth.* § 6.[54]
n. *Ib.*
o. *Ib.*[55]
54. Shaftesbury, *Characteristicks,* vol. I, p. 28.
55. Ibid.

But so it happens, that the noble Writer's Friend proves as bad an *Historian,* as he was a *Prophet:* And fails as miserably in relating *past* Events, as in foretelling *future.* The Truth is, that both his Lordship and the Gentleman seem to have been in a *Fit of Enthusiasm,* and have therefore been induced to mingle a little *pious Fraud,* thro' a Zeal for their respective *Theories.* [304] For in Reality, this pretended Resemblance is utterly fictitious. There is not the least Hint in Scripture, that any of the Persons mentioned as true Prophets, were ever subject to these *Ecstatic, convulsive* Motions, which the enthusiastic Gentleman and his Tribe were always seized with. As to the Regulation made by the Apostle PAUL; whoever consults the Place[P] will find, there is no Mention made of *Ecstasies, Convulsions,* or extraordinary *bodily Motions.* And 'tis clear, that our Saviour always delivered his Prophecies on every *incidental* Occasion, under all the *common Circumstances* of human Life; *calm, serene,* and with *unaffected Deliberation.* So that the whole Charge is a bold, continued Falshood, void of Truth, and even the Appearance of it.

Indeed, from the Instances which the noble Writer cites from VIRGIL and LIVY,[56] 'tis evident that the old *heathen Pretenders* to Prophecy were affected in the same *convulsive* Manner, as the *modern Christian* Enthusiasts. His Lordship might have cited twenty more from ancient Writers. And what can be rationally inferred from them? What but this—"That this *convulsive* [305] *Agitation* of the bodily Organs is a Circumstance that effectually *betrays Enthusiasm*; and distinguisheth it from the real *Inspirations* recorded in *holy Writ.*"

These are the Circumstances in which Enthusiasm will generally *seem* to *resemble* real Inspiration: tho' on a nearer Scrutiny, these very Circumstances will always *detect* it. We come now to enumerate those other Qualities peculiar to Enthusiasm, in which it bears no Resemblance to divine Inspiration, and in which they are, at first View, clearly distinguished from each other. And here it is remarkable, that, as the noble Writer *dwells* on the *former,* so he scarce ever *touches* on these following Characters of *clear distinction.* This peculiar Conduct can hardly be

---

p. 1 *Corinth.* c. xiv.

56. Virgil, *Aeneid,* VI.47–51 and 77–80; Livy, XXXIX.13 and 18; cf. Shaftesbury, *Characteristicks,* vol. I, pp. 29–30.

judged *accidental:* For a Man of Wit can easily improve a *partial* Resemblance into a *complete* one: But to have added other *Features,* of absolute *Dissimilarity,* would have weakened the *Likeness,* and consequently have disgraced the *intended Representation.*

The chief Qualities, which clearly, and at first View, distinguish *Enthusiasm* from divine *Inspiration,* I find enumerated by the [306] fine Writer of *the Letter on St. Paul's Conversion.* These are, "*Heat* of Temper, *Melancholy, Credulity, Self-Conceit,* and *Ignorance.*"[57] So far as these relate to St. PAUL, the Reader is referred to the excellent Work here cited. 'Tis our Part to consider them as they may affect our Saviour, and the rest of his Apostles. And a brief Consideration may suffice: For all (except the last) are so repugnant to their Characters, that the very Mention of them refutes the Imputation.

With Regard to the first of these Qualities, "uncommon Heat of Temper," 'tis of all others most abhorrent from our *Saviour's* Character. He is every where sedate, cool, and unmoved, even under the most bitter Circumstances of Provocation:[q] He every where appears a perfect Model of Benevolence, Meekness, and mild Majesty. The same Temper generally prevails among his Apostles: More particularly we may observe of the *Evangelists,* who are the *immediate Evidences,* that in their Writings they discover the most perfect *Coolness.* Had they been of a fiery Disposition, they had [307] not failed to load the Enemies of their crucified Lord, with the bitterest *Sarcasms.*

With as little Reason can *Melancholy* be charged on the Founders of Christianity. Our *Saviour* came, "eating and drinking:" So entirely *open, unreserved,* and *social,* that he was branded by his Enemies, as *a Friend of Publicans and Sinners.* Another Circumstance, besides the Passion for *Solitude,* hath ever distinguished *Melancholy:* That is, "an *Over-Fondness* and *Desire* to *suffer* in the apprehended Cause of Truth, beyond the just and rational *Ends of Suffering.*" Now this is diametrically opposite to the

q. See Dr. *Law's* Life of *Christ:* Where his Character is described at large.[58]

57. George Lyttelton, *Observations on the Conversion and Apostleship of St. Paul* (1747), p. 52.

58. Edmund Law, *A Discourse Upon the Life and Character of Christ* (Cambridge, 1749), pp. 5–72.

Character of our Saviour and his Apostles: For even JESUS himself was in an *Agony* at the Apprehension of his approaching Sufferings. So far were his Disciples from being tainted with this Melancholy, that they discovered *unmanly Fear*; for *they all forsook him and fled.*⁵⁹ 'Tis true, they afterwards endured the severest Trials with unshaken Constancy; yet still, with the *resigned* Spirit of *Martyrs*; not the *Eagerness* and *fanatic Vaunts* of all known *Enthusiasts.*ʳ [308]

The Charge of *Credulity* hath no better Foundation. To our Saviour himself it is in it's very Nature utterly *inapplicable*. His Disciples have been often charged with *Credulity*. But on impartial Examination it will appear, that the Charge is groundless. For this is an unvarying Circumstance in the Credulity of an Enthusiast, "that it never admits a Doubt." But it is evident from the united Accounts of the Gospel-History, that they often, nay always *doubted* of our Saviour's *Death*, tho' himself foretold it. 'Tis equally evident, they not only doubted of, but almost disbelieved his Resurrection, till overcome by irresistible Evidence. These Circumstances afford another collateral Proof, that the Apostles were not Enthusiasts: Because it is essentially of the Nature of Enthusiasm, "to run on headlong in the *open* Channel of the *First conceived Opinion*." Now 'tis evident, they *changed* their *first Opinion* concerning the *temporal* Dominion of CHRIST, into the firm Belief of his *Death*, *Resurrection*, and *spiritual* Kingdom: We cannot therefore justly charge them with that *Credulity*, which is the Characteristic of *Enthusiasm.*ˢ [309]

---

r. For a remarkable Instance of this, see a Story relating to SAVANOROLA. *Charact. Misc.* ii. c. i. in the Notes.⁶⁰

s. See this Point treated with great Particularity of Proof, in a Pamphlet intitled, *"A Discourse proving that the Apostles were no Enthusiasts."* By *A. Campbel*, S. T. P.⁶¹

59. Matthew 26:56; Mark 14:50.

60. Shaftesbury, *Characteristicks*, vol. III, p. 26, n. *. Girolamo Savonarola (1452–1498); preacher, reformer, and martyr; after the overthrow of the Medici in 1494, the leader of the republic of Florence; excommunicated and eventually burned at the stake on 23 May 1498 after a perfunctory ecclesiastical trial conducted by papal commissioners.

61. Archibald Campbell, *A Discourse Proving that the Apostles were no Enthusiasts. Wherein the Nature and Influence of Religious Enthusiasm are Impartially Explain'd* (1730).

The next Circumstance, *Self-Conceit,* which hath ever been one of the most distinguishing Qualities of Enthusiasm, is so distant from the Character of JESUS and his *Apostles,* that it hath never, I believe, been laid to their Charge. The Enthusiast is perpetually boasting of immediate *Converse* and *Communication* with the *Deity;* and overflows with a Contempt of all, who are not of his own System. In our Saviour we discover the most unfeigned *Humility* and *Compassion* towards all Men. When urged to shew his *Pretensions* to a divine Mission, so far is he from resolving them into *inward Feelings, Impulses,* or *Notices* from God (the constant Practice of every Enthusiast) that, on the contrary, he calmly appeals to his Works and Doctrines;[t] adding, in a Strain the *Reverse* of all *Enthusiasm,* that "in what we bear Witness only to ourselves, our Witness cannot be established as a Truth."[u] The same Turn of Mind appears in the Apostles. They affect no Superiority themselves, nor express or [310] discover any Contempt or *spiritual Pride* with Regard to others.

The last Quality common to Enthusiasts, is that of *Ignorance.* This hath been sometimes charged on our Saviour himself: often on his Apostles with an Air of Triumph. But so it is, that *seeming Objections* against Truth become often the *strongest Evidence* in Support of it. This will eminently appear in the present Case, if we consider "that Ignorance or Want of Letters, when joined with Enthusiasm, must always produce the most *inconsistent* Visions, *whimsical* Conduct, and *pernicious* Doctrines." These Effects, *Ignorance* and *Enthusiasm* have wrought wherever they appeared, in every Age and Nation. Nor can it indeed be otherwise: For a *lettered* Enthusiast may be supposed to have an *internal Balance,* which must in some Degree *counteract* and *regulate* his Visions; while the *unlettered* is subject to no Controul, but must become the Sport and Prey to the *delirious* Flights of an *unreined Imagination.*

Now, that the Apostles and Evangelists were *unlearned,* must needs be granted: And tho' the noble Writer hath taken upon him to deride them on this Account; yet [311] this very Circumstance, compared with their Conduct and Writings, clears them at once from the Charge of Enthusiasm.

t. *Mat.* vii. 16.
u. *John* v. 31.

So far were they from the *ravings* of this Passion, common to all *ignorant* Enthusiasts, that we may defy the Enemies of *Christianity* to produce any Instance either of Speech or Practice, that hath the smallest Tincture of *Extravagance.* Their Conduct was regular and exemplary; their Words were *the Words of Truth and Soberness.*[62]

As to the Charge of Ignorance against our Saviour, the Enemies of Christianity have been more *cautious:* Yet it hath been insinuated. And indeed, that he had not the common Aids of *human Learning,* is not only *acknowledged,* but *insisted* on. Could *ignorant* and *blind Enthusiasm* then have produced the sublime *religious Doctrines* and *moral Precepts* which the Evangelists have *recorded* from his Mouth? With as much Truth it might be affirmed that the *Creation* is the Produce of *Chance.* With Reason then may we ask the noble Writer this Question, "Whence then had this Man *such Wisdom,* seeing he spake as never Man spake?" And the Answer sure is *one* only, "That as it was not from *Man,* it must [312] have been from GOD." For even the Enemies of Christianity have born Witness to it's Excellence, even when they intended to disgrace it: While with fruitless Labour they have attempted to prove, "that the most exalted *Truths* and *Precepts* of the *Gospel* may be found *scattered* among the Writings of the *heathen Sages.*"

From these concurrent Circumstances, therefore, we obtain a full *internal Proof,* that the *Founders of Christianity* were not *Enthusiasts,* as the noble Writer hath, by the most laboured and repeated Insinuations, attempted to represent them.

SECTION VI

Since therefore we have appealed to the *religious* and *Moral* Doctrines of *Christianity,* as a concurrent Proof of it's *divine Original*; it will be necessary now to examine what the noble Writer hath alledged or suggested against this most *essential* Part of our Religion.

And first, it appears from the general Turn of the *Characteristics,* that the noble Author regards *religious Establishments* as being quite at a distance

---

62. Acts 26:25.

from *Philosophy* [313] and *Truth*, with which he tells us, in ancient Times they never interfered: He therefore derides every Attempt to make them *coalesce*. Thus he tells us, "Not only *Visionaries* and *Enthusiasts* of all Kinds were tolerated by the Ancients; but, on the other Side, Philosophy had as free a Course, and was permitted as a Balance against Superstition.—Thus Matters were happily balanced; Reason had fair Play; Learning and Science flourished. Wonderful was the Harmony and Temper which arose from all these *Contrarieties*."[w] Such therefore being his Lordship's Idea of a *public Religion,* which he ever opposes to *private Opinion* and Philosophy; 'tis no Wonder he should insinuate the Folly of Christianity, which promiseth to all it's Proselytes, "that they shall know the *Truth,* and the Truth shall make them *free*."[64]

But notwithstanding the noble Writer's Partiality to the System of ancient Paganism, which he had deeply imbibed from his familiar Converse with ancient Writers; no unprejudiced Mind can hesitate a Moment, in determining the superior Excellence of the *Christian* Religion, compared with these [314] *well-meant,* but defective Schemes of *heathen Policy*. For, as gross Error, and Misapprehension of the divine Nature and Attributes, was deeply interwoven with ancient Paganism; so, 'tis well known, that in Fact, the most horrid Enormities were committed *upon Principle,* under the Authority and Example of their pretended Gods. Lord SHAFTESBURY himself owns, what indeed it were folly to deny, that the *Imitation* of the *Deity* is a *powerful* Principle of Action.[x] If so, it follows, that to communicate a just Idea of the divine Perfections to all Mankind, must tend to *secure* their *Virtue,* and *promote* their *Happiness*. 'Tis therefore equally *ungenerous* and *impolitic,* to suffer Mankind to live in *Ignorance* and *Idolatry*. Hence 'tis evident, that *Reformations* in Religion are not the ridiculous Things his Lordship would represent them; and that *Christianity,* if indeed it *reveals* the *Truth,* is a Religion in it's Tendency much more *beneficial* to Mankind than ancient *Paganism*.

w. *Let. on Enthus.*[63]
x. *Enq. on Virtue.*[65]
63. Shaftesbury, *Characteristicks,* vol. I, p. 12.
64. John 8:32.
65. Shaftesbury, *Characteristicks,* vol. II, pp. 28–29.

'Tis no difficult Task to assign the original Cause of this so different and even *opposite Genius* of the *pagan* Systems from that [315] of *Christianity*. In early and ignorant Ages, the Necessity of religious Belief and religious Establishments was seen by the Leaders of Mankind: On this Account they instituted the most *salutary* Forms and Doctrines, which their unexperienced Reason could suggest. As Nations grew wiser and more polished, they saw the Weakness and Absurdity of these established Systems; but thro' a Regard, and perhaps a *mistaken* one, to the *public Good*, were unwilling to discover these Defects and Absurdities to the People. Hence probably the Rise of *exoteric* and *esoteric* Doctrines. For the furthest that human Policy dared to go, was to reveal the Truth to a *few initiated:* While the Bulk of Mankind, even in the *wisest* and politest *Ages*, continued the *Dupes* to the *Prejudices* and *Superstitions* of the most *ignorant* ones. On the contrary, it was a main Design of the Christian Dispensation, to dispel this Cloud of Ignorance, which excluded Mankind from all Participation of *divine Truth*; to reveal those just and sublime Ideas of the *Divinity*, which are the noblest, as they are the surest Foundation, not only of *Piety* but of *Morals:* And which, so far as they can affect either [316] *Piety* or *Morals* (such is the Triumph of *Christianity* over the laboured Researches of *false Wisdom*) are no less *intelligible* to the *Peasant* than the *Philosopher*. On this Account, Christianity was perfect (*relatively* perfect) in it's first Delineation: All Attempts to change or add to its Doctrines, have but discovered their own Absurdity: And Experience every Day more and more convinceth us, that the only Method of obtaining a pure and uncorrupt System of practical Religion and moral Precepts, is to search for them in the uncommented Pages of the Gospel.

Thus, what was the Effect of *Necessity* among the *Heathens*, the noble Writer very partially attributes to *Choice:* He mistakes a *Defect* for an *Excellence:* And blindly prefers the Weakness of *Man*, to the Wisdom of GOD.

Another Cavil frequently urged or insinuated by his Lordship against *Christianity*, seems to have been the natural Consequence of the last-mentioned. He much admires the Pagan Religions, as having been *sociable*, and mutually *incorporated* into each other: And often represents *Christianity*, as of an *unsociable, surly*, and *solitary* Complexion, [317] tending to *destroy* every other but itself. The Consequence of this, he tells us, hath been "a new Sort of Policy, which extends itself to another World, and hath made us leap the Bounds of natural Humanity; and out of a *supernatural Charity*, has taught us the Way of plaguing one another most devoutly."ʸ Now with Regard to this pretended *unsociable* Temper of *Christianity*; it must be owned indeed, that our Religion tends to swallow up and destroy every other, in the same Manner as *Truth* in every Subject tends to destroy *Falsehood:* That is, by *rational Conviction*. The same Objection might be urged against the *Newtonian Philosophy*, which destroyed the *Cartesian Fables:*⁶⁷ Or against the *Copernican System*, because the clumsy *Visions* of *Ptolemy and Tycho-Brahe*⁶⁸ vanished before it. The same might be urged against the Usefulness, of the great *Source of Day*, because it *dims* and *extinguishes* every inferior Lustre: For the glimmering Lamps of human Knowledge, lighted up by the Philosophers, served indeed to conduct them as *a Light shining in a dark Place*; but these must naturally be sunk in a superior Lustre, when [318] *the Sun of Righteousness should arise*. The Gospel therefore is so far *unsociable*, as to discredit *Error*; and is incompatible with *this*, as *Light* with *Darkness:* But not so *unsociable*, as to *compel* the erroneous. As to the religious Debates, then, which Christianity hath occasioned, and the Wars and Massacres consequent upon them, which the noble Writer so justly detests; Christianity stands clear of the Charge, till it can be shewn that it countenanceth the inhuman Principle of Intolerance: And this, it's bitterest Enemies can never do. 'Tis true, that if we be so irrational as to take our Idea of Christianity from the Representations of Enthusiasts and Bigots, nothing can

y. *Let. on Enthu.*⁶⁶
66. Shaftesbury, *Characteristicks*, vol. I, p. 12.
67. The gravitational theories formulated by Sir Isaac Newton (1642–1727) discredited the vorticist theories associated with the French philosopher René Descartes (1596–1650).
68. Copernicus, see above, p. 169, n. 22. Ptolemy (*c.* 100–*c.* 170 A.D.); Egyptian astronomer and mathematician who elaborated a theory that the heavenly bodies revolved around the earth, which was stationary. Tycho Brahe (1546–1601); Danish astronomer whose observations and innovations in practical astronomy corroborated the Copernican theory, but who himself was unwilling finally to break with geo-centrism.

appear more absurd and mischievous: As, in like Manner, if we consider the *Heavens* under the perplexed Revolutions and malignant Aspects[69] of the old Astronomers and Astrologers, nothing can be more unworthy either of divine Wisdom or Goodness. But how can these false *Images* affect the noble *Simplicity,* and *Benignity* of the *Gospel,* or the *Solar System?* To the *Works* and the *Word* of God, we must repair, for a true Idea of their undisguised Perfection: And there we shall read their divine Author, in [319] the brightest Characters of Wisdom and Goodness. So far therefore is Christianity from encouraging Wars and Massacres, on Account of a Difference in Opinion, that it's divine Founder hath expressly warned his Followers against the Suggestions of this horrid Temper:[z] Nor can these fatal Consequences ever arise among *Christians,* till they have divested themselves of *Christian Charity,* and[a] mistaken the very Principles of their Profession.

But the noble Writer proceeds to still more bitter Invectives, if possible, against *Christianity.* For he often insinuates, that the Prospect of Happiness and Misery in another Life, revealed in the Gospel, tends to the Destruction of all *true Virtue.*[b] Indeed we cannot much Wonder that his Lordship should treat Christianity in this Manner, when we consider what he hath thrown out against Religion in general, in this Respect. These Cavils have already been considered at large: Whatever therefore he hath insinuated against our Religion in *particular,* will naturally be refer'd to, and effectually be refuted by these more *general* Observations.[c] However, there are [320] two or three Passages on this Subject so remarkable, that they may seem to deserve a separate Consideration.

After having ridiculed and branded Christianity, as destroying the *disinterested* Part of Virtue, he tells us "The *Jews* as well as Heathens were

---

z. *Luke* ix.[70]
a. *Ib.*
b. *Wit and H.* p. ii. § 3.[71]
c. See above, *Ess.* ii. § 9.[72]
69. Terms of art drawn from, respectively, Ptolemaic astronomy and judicial astrology.
70. Possibly Luke 9:23–25.
71. Shaftesbury, *Characteristicks,* vol. I, pp. 60–64.
72. See above, pp. 141–50.

left to their Philosophy to be instructed in the sublime Part of Virtue, and induced by *Reason* to that which was never enjoyn'd them by Command. No Premium or Penalty being inforced in these Cases, the disinterested Part subsisted, the Virtue was a free Choice, and the Magnanimity of the Act was left intire."[d]

Here, again, the noble Writer hath got to his *Peculiarities*. What other Title this Passage may deserve, we shall soon discover. For, first, supposing his Assertion true, what he notes in the *Jewish* and *Heathen* Religions as an *Excellence*, had certainly been a *Defect*. For are not *Hottentots*, wild *Indians*, and *Arabs*, "left to their Philosophy, to be induced by Reason to that which was never enjoined them by Command? No Premium or Penalty [321] being inforced in these Cases, the disinterested Part subsists, the Virtue is a free Choice, and the Magnanimity of the Act is left entire." Thus the noble Writer would again debase us into Savages;[e] and, rather than not disgrace Christianity, would put the State of *Palestine*, *Greece*, and *Rome*, on a Level with that of the *Cape of Good Hope: Blindly* (or shall we say, *knowingly?*) disparaging, what he elsewhere so justly applauds, "Laws, Constitutions, civil and RELIGIOUS Rites, whatever *civilizes* or *polishes* rude Mankind."[f]

But in Fact, neither the JEWS nor *civilized Heathens* were ever tainted with this *Phrenzy*. They saw the Necessity of religious Belief; and as they saw it's Necessity, so they inforced it. With Regard to the JEWS, the noble Writer contradicts himself within the Compass of ten Lines: For there he says, "their Religion taught no future State, nor exhibited any Rewards or Punishments, *besides such as were temporal*." This is the very Truth. Here then he owns a *temporal Sanction* of Premium and Penalty, *Reward* and *Punishment:* Yet in the Passage above cited, and [322] which stands close by the other in the Original, he says, "there was no Premium or Penalty inforced, no Reward or Punishment!" His Lordship deals as *fairly* and *consistently*

d. *Wit. and H.* p. ii. § 3.[73]
e. See above, *Essay* ii. § 10.[74]
f. *Moralists*, Part i. § 3.[75]
73. Shaftesbury, *Characteristicks*, vol. I, p. 64.
74. See above, pp. 150–58.
75. Shaftesbury, *Characteristicks*, vol. II, p. 120.

by the civilized Heathens: For, could he indeed have forgot the distinguished Rank, which, in the *Elysian Fields,* was assigned to those who *fell* to save *their Country?*

> *Hic* Manus *ob* PATRIAM *pugnando vulnera passi—Omnibus his nivea cinguntur tempora vitta.*^g

And now let the Impartial determine, whether the noble Writer's Observation hath more of *Sagacity* or of *Truth* in it.

But the Christian Doctrines relating to an *hereafter,* are to undergo a yet severer *Inquisition* from the noble Writer: They are to be tortured and *mangled* on the *Rack,* of *Wit* shall I say, or of *Buffoonry?*

> The Misfortune is, we are seldom taught to comprehend this SELF, by placing it in a distinct View from it's Representative or *Counterfeit.* In our *holy* Religion, which, for the greatest Part, is adapted to the very meanest Capacities, 'tis not to be expected that a Speculation of this [323] Kind should be openly advanced. 'Tis enough that we have Hints given us of a *nobler* SELF, than that which is commonly supposed the Basis and Foundation of our Actions. *Self-Interest* is there taken as it is vulgarly conceived—In the same Manner as the celestial Phaenomena are in the sacred Volumes generally treated according to common Imagination, and the then current System of Astronomy and natural Science; so the moral Appearances are in many Places preserved without Alteration, according to *Vulgar Prejudice.*—Our real and genuine *Self* is sometimes supposed that *ambitious* one, which is fond of Power and Glory; sometimes that *childish* one, which is taken with *vain Shew,* and is to be invited to Obedience by Promise of *finer Habitations, precious Stones,* and *Metals,* shining *Garments, Crowns,* and other such *dazling Beauties,* by which another Earth, or material City is represented.^h

This Passage contains two insinuated Charges of a very different Nature. The one is *true,* but no *Objection:* The other would indeed be an *Objection,*

g. *Eneid.* lib. vi.⁷⁶
h. *Solil.* Part iii. § 1.⁷⁷
76. "Here is the band of those who suffered wounds, fighting for the fatherland; . . . the brows of all bound with a snowy fillet" (Virgil, *Aeneid,* VI.660 and 665).
77. Shaftesbury, *Characteristicks,* vol. I, pp. 174–75.

but that it is [324] absolutely *groundless*. 'Tis true "that our Religion is for
the greatest Part adapted to the very meanest Capacities; and that the celestial Phaenomena are in the sacred Volumes generally treated according
to *common Imagination*," &c. And would the noble Writer indeed have had
it otherwise? Would he indeed have had them spoken of, according to the
Philosophical Construction of the Universe, rather than the received Notions of Mankind? With how little Reason, we may soon be convinced, if
we consider, First, that the *End* of *Revelation* was not to make Mankind
Proficients in Philosophy, since the Situation of the Generality can never
admit it: And had the Scriptures supposed this, (as indeed such a Conduct
would have supposed it) this very Circumstance had been an Argument
of their Falsehood. Secondly, even Philosophers themselves, tho' intimately
acquainted with the Construction of the Universe, do still *descend* to the
Level of Mankind, when they speak of the Phaenomena of Nature: The *Sun*
sets and *rises,* as it did three thousand Years ago: The *Moon changes, wains,*
is *new,* and *old:* The *Stars* are *in the Firmament,* the *Sun* [325] still *rules the*
Day, and the *Moon* the *Night.* The Reason is evident: Because *astronomical*
Discoveries have not the least Influence on the *Practice of Mankind:* Because,
altho' the *natural Appearances* of things are merely *relative* to the *Imagina-*
tion only, yet they are, for that very Reason, necessary to be referred to, as
the *Imagination* is the great *universal Instrument* of *Life* and human *Action.*

An Objection therefore to the Scriptures on this Account, betrays either a gross *Misapprehension* of human Nature, or the most unpardonable *Insincerity*; yet we find Objections of this kind frequently urged: as
if, because the sacred Penmen were impowered by God to reveal to us a
certain Measure of *religious* and *moral* Truth, suited to our present State,
they must therefore be endued with *Omniscience*; in order to make all
Men not only *good Subjects,* but good *Astronomers* too!

But tho' it were *Folly* to object against the *sacred Penmen,* because they
appear not to have been *omniscient*; yet I cannot conclude this Argument,
without producing a remarkable Instance, wherein their very *Ignorance* of
these *speculative* and *unnecessary* [326] *Truths* becomes a convincing Proof
of their VERACITY: A Circumstance which much more nearly concerns
us. We read in the Book of *Joshua,* "And he said in the Sight of *Israel,* SUN,
stay thou in *Gibeon,* and *thou* MOON, in the Valley of *Ajalon:* And the *Sun*

abode, and THE MOON STOOD STILL,—and hasted not to go down for a whole Day."[i] Here, the *standing still* of these Luminaries is related in such a Manner as concurs with the common Appearances of things; and yet consists with the best Discoveries in Astronomy, tho' unknown to the Writer. For we are now assured that, if *the Sun stood still,* it must have been by suspending the diurnal Rotation of the Earth: The *standing still of the Moon* was therefore the *necessary Consequence.* This the Writer appears not to have known: Yet he relates the *Fact,* tho' it was of no Importance with Regard to that Event for which the Miracle was wrought. It is therefore of singular Force in proving the *Veracity of the Writer,* because, had it not been true in Fact, it is *a Circumstance which could never have occurr'd to him.*

The noble Writer's other Charge relating to the *moral Representations* of the [327] Scriptures, would indeed be of Weight, if it were founded in Truth: But so far from this, that he hath utterly *reversed* the Fact. For in Reality, these *sensible* Representations of *visible* Beauty and Glory, are only *occasionally* or *accidentally* hinted; while the whole *Weight* and *Energy* of the *Gospel* is employed in inforcing the Idea of *moral Perfection,* of our *nobler* SELF, of *Self-Interest* in the *higher* Sense, of the Necessity of extirpating every meaner Passion, and cherishing the great one of *unbounded Love,* as the necessary and only Discipline that can qualify us for future Happiness. 'Tis evident that the noble Writer lays the principal Stress of his Charge, on the *Apocalypse*; a Work in it's whole Turn *strictly allegorical,* and therefore necessarily conversant in *Imagery* and *visible Representation.* To this he hath most *perversly* added a figurative Expression of St. PAUL, who writing to a People among whom the *Prize-Races* prevailed, represents the Christian *Progress* as a *Contest* of this Kind; and shews it's Superiority over the Former, "because, saith he, they labour to obtain a *corruptible,* but we an *incorruptible* Crown."[79] In the mean [328] Time he hath omitted the many *Discourses, Parables, Maxims,* of our Saviour, in which he perpetually exhorts his Disciples to endeavour after unfeigned Virtue and universal Benevolence, as the only Means that can bring them to future *Perfection.* He hath forgot too the repeated Exhortations of St. PAUL, who sets CHARITY so high above

i. *Joshua* x.[78]
78. Joshua 10:12–13.
79. 1 Corinthians 9:25.

every other Gift or Possession, and adds, the Reason of it's Preheminence, "because it shall never fail."[80] 'Tis true indeed, as the noble Writer observes (with what Intention, 'tis no difficult Matter to determine) "that our holy Religion is for the greatest Part adapted to the very meanest Capacities:"We may add, "and to the very worst of Dispositions too." And 'tis one of it's chief Glories, that it is so. Therefore we find it inforcing *every Motive* that can work on *every Mind:* Which must surely be acknowledged as the Character of *the Religion* that should come from him *who knew what was in Man*. But if the noble Writer would further insinuate, that the Idea of future Happiness ought to be *confined* to that of *virtuous* Enjoyment, whereas the *Christian* Religion doth not so *confine* it; we have already seen, that, from [329] the Nature of things, this Refinement is *visionary* and *groundless*.[k]

We now come to the Examination of a Passage more *extraordinary* and *original* than any yet produced. The noble Writer tells us, "I could be almost tempted to think, that the true Reason why some of the most *heroic Virtues* have so little Notice taken of them in our *holy Religion,* is, because there would have been no Room left for *Disinterestedness,* had they been entitled to a Share of that infinite Reward, which Providence has *by Revelation* assigned to other Duties. *Private Friendship,* and *Zeal* for the *Public* and *our Country,* are Virtues purely *voluntary* in a *Christian*. They are no essential *Parts* of his *Charity*. He is not so tied to the Affairs of *this Life*; nor is he obliged to enter into such Engagements with this *lower World,* as are of *no Help* to him in acquiring a *better*. His *Conversation* is in *Heaven*. Nor has he Occasion for such *supernumerary Cares* and Embarrassments here on Earth, as may *obstruct his Way* thither, or retard him in the careful Task of working out his own Salvation."[l] [330]

We have already seen, that the real Nature of Virtue consists "in procuring or promoting the greatest public Happiness:" And that this Truth is often, *occasionally,* acknowledged by Lord *Shaftesbury* himself. Consequently, the *highest* or most *heroic Virtue,* is that which tends to *accomplish* this great *End:* Nor can any *pretended* Virtue be either *great* or *heroic* that tends to *obstruct* or *destroy* it.

k. See above, *Essay* ii. § 9.[81]
l. *Wit. and H.* Part ii. § 3.[82]
80. 1 Corinthians 13:8.
81. See above, pp. 141–50.
82. Shaftesbury, *Characteristicks,* vol. I, pp. 62–63.

On this plain Principle, self-evident to unbyassed *Reason,* let us examine the Passage now before us. And first, as to *private Friendship,* which, the noble Writer says, "is a Virtue purely voluntary in a Christian:"—Let us consider how far it may be regarded as a Virtue *at all.*—Now, on strict Enquiry we shall find, that the extreme Degree of Friendship recommended and applauded by the Ancients, and here patronized by the noble Author, is essentially *repugnant* to *true Virtue: In Friendship* they placed the *Chief Happiness:*—And if this consists in the supreme Love of *one,* it must needs *diminish,* if not *extinguish,* the Love of *all;* because our chief or whole *Attention* must be *employed,* our every *View* and *Design centered* in giving Pleasure or *procuring* [331] *Happiness* to one *Individual.* And this is the very fairest Light it can be view'd in.

For we shall further see, how little it generally partakes of the Nature of true Virtue, if we consider whence it hath it's Rise. This is universally allowed to be "a Similarity of *Disposition, Will,* and *Manners.*" This Circumstance demonstrates, that in general it must be *contrary* to Virtue. For hence, the *general* Good must be often sacrificed to gratify the Will of *one.* Of this dreadful Effect, Instances might be produced almost innumerable. Let one suffice. "Between TIBERIUS GRACCHUS and C. BLOSIUS, a *dear and perfect Friendship* subsisted: The latter being seized for aiding the former in his Conspiracy, was brought before the *Consuls.* He pleaded his Friendship to GRACCHUS in Excuse for his Crime." He was then asked, "What, suppose he had bid you *fire the Capitol,* would you have done it?" To this he boldly replied, "He never would have laid me under such a Necessity; but if he had, *I would have obey'd him.*"[m] A *thorough Friend* sure: But a *vile Citizen;* notwithstanding the [332] artful Gloss of an ingenious Modern, who hath attempted to make out the Innocence of his Intentions.[n]

'Tis true, the Advocates for this *Attachment* sometimes assert, that it cannot consist but with *Virtue.* That it *ought not,* is certain: That it *cannot,* or *doth not,* is a groundless Conceit; unless they chuse to make this

m. Cic. *Laelius.*[83]
n. See Montaigne's *Essay* on this Subject.[84]
83. Cicero, *Laelius de Amicitia,* XI.
84. Cf. Montaigne, "De l'amitié," in which Montaigne seeks to defend Blosius from the charge of being seditious (Montaigne, *Essays,* pp. 212–13).

Circumstance a Part of the Definition, which were idle Sophistry. But if by Friendship be meant, what indeed is always meant, "a violent Love and Attachment to another on Account of a Similarity of Manners;" this, 'tis certain, hath often, nay most commonly subsisted without Virtue: Among *Savages, Robbers, Heroes,* and *Banditti.* In LUCIAN's Tract on Friendship[85] we find, that out of Twelve notable Instances alledged, near half the Number were supported at the Expence of *Justice* or *Humanity;* either by the Commission of Rapine, Adultery, or Murder, or by aiding the Escape of those who ought to have suffered for these enormous Crimes. Will any one alledge the Emperor TIBERIUS or his Favourite SEJANUS as Patterns of Virtue?[86] Yet their Friendship was so remarkable, [333] that, in Honour of it, Altars were dedicated to *Friendship* by a *senatorial Decree.* Nay, some of the applauded Instances appealed to, by the noble Author in his Comment on this Passage, are even notorious in this Respect. Such were THESEUS and PIRITHOUS,[87] equally remarkable for *Friendship, Rapes,* and *Plunder.* And such Instances may still be found in every *savage* Country; where the strongest Friendships are commonly formed: Where Men thus *leagued,* go upon bold Adventures; and hazard and give up Life for each other without Reluctance, while they *ravish* their Neighbours *Wives,* and *carry off* their *Cattle.*

With as little Reason can it be urged, that Friendships in general are *disinterested,* so as to aspire to the Name of *Merit.* For *Merit,* if it exists, can only arise from *Virtue:* And Virtue, we have seen, doth not essentially

85. Lucian, *Toxaris, or Friendship*; a conversation between a Scythian, Toxaris, and a Greek, Mnesippus, in which each extols the capacity for friendship shown by their countrymen by reference to five examples, making a total of ten "notable Instances," rather than Brown's twelve.

86. Tiberius Claudius Nero Caesar (42 B.C.–37 A.D.); emperor from 14 A.D.; stepson of Augustus; after an initial period of good government his reign degenerated into tyranny, as most memorably narrated in the *Annals* of Tacitus. Lucius Aelius Sejanus (*d.* 31 A.D.); Praefect of Praetorians under Tiberius, and after the emperor's withdrawal to Capri, preeminent in Rome; executed on suspicion of treason.

87. In Greek mythology Theseus was the son of Aegeus, who after many adventures became king of Athens, and befriended Pirithous, king of the Lapithae, with whom he descended into Hades to help carry off Persephone. For this crime Theseus was imprisoned in Hades until rescued by his friend Heracles.

belong to Friendship. Nay, in LUCIAN's Tract,[88] 'tis warmly debated between the contending Parties, whether *Affection* or *private Advantage* hath a more considerable Share in this applauded *Union*. Indeed the *civilized* and haughty *Greek* stands upon the Punctilio of *Honour,* and piques himself on the Notion of *Disinterest:* [334] But the *undisguised Scythian* insists that mutual *Advantage and Support* are the ruling *Motives*. However, in Conclusion they fairly agree, in comparing a set of fast Friends to GERYON[89] with *three Heads* and *six Hands,* enabled thro' this Increase of Strength, to overturn all Opposition.[o] But suppose *Affection* the ruling Principle, as unquestionably it often is; where is the *Merit,* while *confined* to *one* Person? Nay, it must rather lean towards *Demerit,* because it appears, 'tis rather *dangerous* than *favourable* to *public Affection* and *Virtue*. 'Tis evident then, that the *friendly Affection* is no more *meritorious* than the *conjugal, paternal,* or *filial Affection;* which being of a *contracted* Nature, are often consistent with great Baseness of Mind, and destructive of a more enlarged Benevolence.[p] And [335] what Degree of

o. Luciani *Toxaris*.

p. Thus a Writer of distinguished Abilities:[90]

> Many Instances occur in History and daily Experience, of Men, not ashamed to commit base and selfish Enormities, who have retained a Tenderness for their Posterity by the strong and generous Instinct of Nature. The Story of *Licinius Macer,* who was Father to *Calvus* the great Orator, is very remarkable, as related by a Roman Annalist. Having gone thro' the Office of Praetor, and governed a Province, he was accused, upon returning Home, of Extortion and Abuses of his Power. The very Morning of his Tryal he strangled himself, after having sent Word to *Cicero,* who was preparing to plead against him, that, being determined to put an End to his Life before Sentence (tho' the Penalty did not extend to taking it away) the Prosecution could not go on, and his Fortune would be saved to the Benefit of his Son.

—*Considerations on the Law of Forfeiture,* p. 32.

88. Lucian, *Toxaris,* VII.

89. In Greek mythology, the son of Chrysaor, who was himself born from the spilled blood of Medusa. Geryon was a monster with three heads and three torsos, who tended cattle on an island in the stream Oceanus with his herdsman Eurytion and his dog Orthrus. The tenth labor of Heracles was to slay Geryon and seize his cattle.

90. Charles Yorke, *Some Considerations on the Law of Forfeiture, for High Treason* (1745), pp. 19–20. Charles Yorke (1722–70), a man of notable talents marred by fatal weaknesses of character, attained the high office of Lord Chancellor for only three days, before dying either by his own hand, or of a burst blood vessel brought on by retching after over-indulgence at the table. For his connections with Brown, see the "Introduction," p. xii, n. 10.

Merit or *Disinterest* there is in Regards of this Nature, when separate from more extensive ones, we may learn from the noble Writer himself, who says, "there is a *Selfishness* in the Love that is paid to a *Wife,* and in the Attendance on a *Family,* and all the little Affairs of it, which, had I my full Scope of Action in the Public, I should hardly have submitted to:"ˢ

So far then is clear, That *Friendship,* or "a violent Affection founded on a Similarity of Disposition and Manners," is more likely to produce *Vice* than *Virtue;* as it tends to fix such Habits of Mind as must lessen our Concern for the *general Good.* And in Fact, every one's Experience will point out to him Numbers of Men, naturally benevolent *to all,* but so strongly byassed and *drawn in* by *particular* Attach[336]ments, that their *Regards* and *Beneficence* are centered wholly on a *select Few;* while the rest of Mankind pass unheeded and unassisted, and have no Share in their Benevolence, further than what *Self-Deceit* throws out, in *unmeaning Wishes* for their Welfare.

'Tis no less evident, that, thro' the natural Advantages of this partial Alliance, Mankind must ever be prone to embrace it, in Exclusion of more extensive Affections, where no such Advantages can follow. It would therefore have been a *Defect* in the *Christian* Religion, to have enjoined or even recommended it in this Extreme. Accordingly we find, in the Gospel, every Attachment of this Kind, however natural and alluring it may be, set very little above the *lowest Selfishness,* and justly represented as entirely consistent with it. "If ye do good to them which do good to you, what thank have ye? Do not the Publicans even the same?"ʳ

Besides; there is something so extraordinary in the noble Writer's Scheme of "enjoining Friendship," as sufficiently exposeth it's own Weakness. Friendship, his [337] Lordship allows, can only arise "from a Consent and Harmony of Minds."ˢ How then could Christianity have *enjoyned* us the Practice of this *supposed* Virtue? What must it have *enjoyned* us? Why, to

---

s. Ld. S's *Let. to Mr. Molesworth,* Let. ix.[91]

r. *Mat.* v.[92]

s. In the Note.

91. Shaftesbury, *Letters from the Right Honourable the late Earl of Shaftesbury, to Robert Molesworth* (1721), p. 30.

92. Matthew 5:46.

go in Quest of a *Mind* resembling our own. It might with equal Propriety have enjoyned us to go in Quest of a *Face* resembling our own: And with as much Reason, for all the Purposes of *true Virtue.*

But if by *Friendship* be meant, what indeed is *not* generally meant, "A particular Love and Esteem for the virtuous or worthy," in which Sense alone it can have any Tendency to produce true Virtue; then we may justly affirm, that it is recommended in the Gospel, both by *Example* and by *Precept.* It is naturally involved in that all-comprehensive Command of *universal Charity:* For tho' many have been zealous in their Friend-ships, while they were insensible to publick Affection; yet, such is the Temperament of human Nature, that no Instance was ever known, of a Man zealous for the Happiness *of all,* yet remiss in or incapable of a *true Friendship* for *the worthy.* It is recommended by St. PAUL, [338] who says, that "peradventure for a *good Man,* one would even *dare to die.*"[93] It is recommended by our Saviour's Example, who selected a beloved Disci-ple as his bosom *Friend,* whose Writings are the overflowings of a Heart filled with the purest and most unbounded Love."[t] Above all, it is recom-mended by our Saviour in that noble and divine Passage; "Who is my Mother or my Brethren? Even *he that doth the Will of my Father* which is in Heaven, he is my *Brother,* and *Sister,* and *Mother.*"[u]

So much for the spurious Virtue of *private Friendship:* Let us next consider the noble Writer's Charge against *Christianity,* on Account of it's not enjoyning "a Zeal for the *Public* and our Country:" For this too, it seems, "is a Virtue purely *voluntary in a Christian.*" Now all the Absur-dities which load his Charge with Regard to *Friendship,* fall with equal Weight on this groundless Imputation. For if by "Zeal for the Publick and our Country," be meant, a Zeal that is inconsistent with the Rights and common Welfare of Mankind, 'tis so far from being a *Virtue,* that, as in the case of *Friendship,* it is really a [339] *Crime,* because it tends to pro-duce the most fatal Consequences. And an Army of victorious Warriors

t. St. *John.*
u. *Matt.* xii.[94]
93. Romans 5:7.
94. Matthew 12:48–50.

returning triumphant on this vile Principle, however graced with the flattering Title of *Heroes*, and Ensigns of *Glory*, are in Truth no better than a Band of *publick Robbers:* or, as our *great Poet*, a Christian and a Lover of Mankind, finely expresseth it,

> *An impious Crew*
> *Of Men conspiring to uphold their State,*
> *By worse than hostile Deeds; violating the Ends*
> *For which our Country is a Name so dear.*ᵂ

Now 'tis evident beyond a Doubt, that at the Time when our Saviour appeared, this destructive *Partiality*, this avowed Conspiracy against the common Rights of Mankind was universally prevalent among the most civilized Nations. The JEWS were not exempted from this common Excess. "*Inter ipsos Fides obstinata, adversus alios hostile Odium,*"⁹⁶ was their Character among the Heathens. The *Greeks* and *Romans* committed and boasted of the most cruel Enormities, conquered and inslaved innocent Nations, plundered Cities, and laid [340] waste Kingdoms, thro' this absurd and *impious Love* of their *Country*; a Principle no better in many of it's Consequences, than the most horrid and accursed *Bigotry*. It had therefore been an essential Defect, nay rather a mischievous Absurdity, in the Christian Religion, to have enjoyned, encouraged, or countenanced a Partiality unjust in itself; to which, from Views of private Advantage, Mankind must ever be prone; and which, at the Time when Christianity began to spread, was indeed the reigning and *predominant Error*.

But if by "Zeal for the Publick and Love of our Country" be meant, such a Regard to it's Welfare as shall induce us to sacrifice every View of private Interest for it's Accomplishment, yet still *in Subordination* to the *greater Law* of *universal Justice*, this is naturally, nay necessarily involved in the Law of *universal Charity*. The noble Writer indeed affirms, "it is no essential Part of the Christian's Charity." On the contrary it is a *chief Part* of the Christian's Charity. It comes nobly recommended by the Examples

---

w. *Sampson Agonistes.*⁹⁵
95. Milton, *Samson Agonistes*, ll. 891–94.
96. "Extremely loyal with one another, but showing only hatred and enmity towards others" (Tacitus, *Histories*, V.v).

of JESUS and St. PAUL: The one wept over the approaching Desolation of his Country:[97] The other declared [341] his Willingness to be cut off from the Christian Community, if by this Means he might save his Countrymen.[98] And that it necessarily ariseth from the Principle of universal Love will be evident, if we consider the *Nature* and *Situation* of *Man*. His *Nature* is such, that he inevitably contracts the *strongest* Affection for those with whom he converseth most *intimately*; and whose *Manners* and *Relations, civil* and *religious,* are most nearly connected with *his own*. His *Situation* is such, that he seldom hath an Opportunity of doing good Offices to any Society of Men, save only those of his *own Country*; all others being naturally removed beyond the narrow Sphere of private Beneficence. Hence the great Precept of universal Charity doth essentially involve "a Zeal for the Publick and Love of our Country:" At once it *curbs* the *Exorbitance* of this natural Partiality, and *carries* it to it's full *Perfection*.

The Necessity of this great *Regulating* Principle will further appear, if we consider, that with Regard to the Conduct of separate States and Kingdoms towards each other, no Sanctions of human Law can ever take place. In this respect all Nations must ever be in a State of Nature. There was [342] therefore a more particular Necessity, on this Account, of regulating their Conduct towards each other, by the great Law of *universal Charity*.

It may seem strange that the noble Writer should be ignorant of these Truths. But after the Imputations he hath here thrown on *Christianity*, it will surely appear *more strange* that he was *not ignorant* of them: And that these bitter Sarcasms were thrown out against the clear Convictions of his own Mind. Yet nothing is more evident, as will now appear. That he understood the Nature of *Christian Charity,* is indisputable: He defines it, and properly, in the Note annexed to the Passage here refer'd to. In another Place, he calls it "the Principle of *Love,* the greatest Principle of our Religion."[x] In a following Paragraph he calls it "that divine Love which

---

x. *Moralists,* Part ii. § 3.[99]

97. Luke 21:20–24.

98. Brown paraphrases Romans 9:3; "For I could wish that myself were accursed from Christ for my brethren, my kinsmen according to the flesh: . . . ."

99. Shaftesbury, *Characteristicks,* vol. II, p. 157.

our Religion teaches."[y] But what is of all *most remarkable*; he sets it, under the new and whimsical Denominations of *Good-Nature* and *Friendship to Mankind,* far above *private* Friendship and Love of our *Country.* Take the Passages as they lie in the noble Writer. "Can any *Friendship* be so *heroic,* [343] as that towards *Mankind?* or *particular* Friendship well subsist, without such an enlarged Affection?"[z] Again. "*Theocles* had almost convinced me, that to be a Friend to any one in particular, 'twas necessary first to be a Friend to Mankind."[a] Lastly, and above all. "And can your *Country,* and what is *more, your* KIND, require less Kindness from you, or deserve less to be consider'd, than even *one* of these *Chance-Creatures?—O Philocles,* how little do you know the Extent and Power of *Good-Nature,* and to what an *heroic Pitch* a Soul may *rise,* which knows the thorow Force of it; *and distributing it rightly,* frames in itself an *equal, just, and universal Friendship?*"[b] Here then we see the former Paragraph utterly reversed. For "*universal Love* is now the only *heroic* Principle:" And "*private Friendship* and the Love of *our Country* are only commendable, as they make *subordinate Parts* of it."

To this astonishing and wilful Perversion of the Moral Principles of *Christianity,* we may add the subsequent Part of the same invenomed Paragraph. For he pro[344]ceeds to *insinuate,* as if *Christian Charity* were no *active* Principle; but such as leads it's Proselytes to a State of mere *Contemplation* and *Inaction,* without Regard to *social* Life, and the Affairs of this *lower World.* We may defy the noble Writer's most zealous Admirers to find any other rational Construction for the following Passage. "The Christian, he says, is not obliged to enter into such *Engagements* with this *lower World,* as are of no Help to him in acquiring *a better. His Conversation* is *in Heaven.* Nor has he Occasion for such *supernumerary Cares,* and *Embarrassments* here on Earth, as may *obstruct his Way* thither, or *retard* him in the *careful Task* of working out *his own Salvation.*"[104] Unexampled Prevarication! thrown out against that

y. *Ib.*[100]
z. Ib. § 1.[101]
a. Ib. § 2.[102]
b. Ib. § 1.[103]
100. Shaftesbury, *Characteristicks,* vol. I, p. 158.
101. Ibid., vol. II, p. 135.
102. Ibid., p. 139.
103. Ibid., p. 137.
104. Ibid., vol. I, p. 63.

Religion which enjoyns an *active* Virtue, a *Regard* to the *present* Happiness of Man in *every possible Relation,* as the only Way to obtain Felicity hereafter: Against that Religion, whose *Founder* did not *idly harangue* in a *Closet* upon *Beauty, Virtue,* and *Decorum,* amidst the *Indolence* and *Pride* of Life; but *practised* the Divine *Truths* he *taught,* and *"went about doing Good,"* a[345]mongst the meanest and most despised of his Fellow Citizens.

To be unmoved on this Occasion were *Stupidity;* not to confess it, *Cowardice. Error* should be exposed with *Calmness;* but *Dishonesty* merits our Abhorrence.

Yet from these Cavils tho' groundless, and Misrepresentations tho' *voluntary,* we may draw an Observation which highly recommends *Christianity.* We may hence see the superior Excellence and Dignity of it's moral Precepts, above the most *applauded* among the Heathen: And how nobly, by one great Principle, it rectifies every little Partiality to which the human Heart is subject. For this is clear; that in one Age or Nation, *Friendship* hath been *idolized* as the supreme Virtue; in another, *Hospitality;*[c] in a Third, the Love of our *Country;* [346] in a Fourth, enthusiastic *Contemplation;* in a

c. Indeed the noble Writer, pursuing the same kind Intention to Christianity, pretends that the Law of *Hospitality,* or *Regard* to *Strangers,* among the *ancient Heathens,* was *equivalent* (nay he gives a very disingenious Suggestion, as if it was far *superior*) to *Christian Charity.* "Such, says he, was ancient *Heathen Charity,* and pious Duty towards the whole of Mankind; both those of different Nations *and different Worships.*"[105] (*Misc.* iii. c. 1. *in the Notes*) For Instances of this, he is forced to go back as far as *Homer,* who indeed hath given us some fine Pictures of ancient Manners of this kind, in his *Odyssey.* The noble Writer might have found others, in no Respect inferior, in the Old Testament, recorded long before *universal Charity* was ever thought of, in the Stories of *Abraham* and *Lot.* The Truth is the *Guest* or *Stranger* was held *sacred,* because he was under the *Protection* of his *Host:* It was therefore deemed *criminal,* to violate a *Trust* thus *reposed.* But it happens unfortunately for his Lordship's Argument, that in these Old Times *Rapine* and *Plunder* were as much in Vogue as either *Friendship* or *Hospitality,* and equally creditable. These *phantom* Appearances of *Virtue* are still to be seen in the *Arabian Deserts* as frequently as ever. If a Traveller comes to the Door of a wild *Arab's* Tent at Night, he is received with so boundless an *Hospitality,* that the *Host* would expose himself, his Wife, and Children to certain Destruction to save the Life of his *Guest.* Had this *hospitable Savage* met the Traveller in the Deserts at Noon, he would have *strip'd* him to the Skin, and on the least Resistance laid him *dead at his Feet.* And this was the true Extent of the noble Writer's boasted *Heathen Charity.*

105. Shaftesbury, *Characteristicks,* vol. III, p. 95, n. *.

Fifth, the *Austerities* of the Hermit; in a Sixth, the *external Practice* of Religion; in a Seventh, which is the *fashionable* Peculiarity of *our own* Times, *occasional Acts* of Humanity and Compassion, while the more *extensive* and *Publick* Views of Beneficence are *neglected* or even *derided.* How different, how superior, is the great Christian Principle of *universal Love!* Which rising gradually, by a Progress thro' all the [347] less enlarged Affections towards Parents, Children, Friends, Country, and spreading till it embraceth all Mankind, and every Creature that hath Life, forms that *perfect Virtue* in which human Weakness is most prone to be *defective,* and which implies and includes every moral Perfection. *Christianity* alone hath *kindled* in the Heart of Man this *vital* Principle; which *beaming* there as from a *Center,* like the great *Fountain* of *Light* and *Life* that sustains and chears the attendant Planets, renders it's Proselytes indeed *"burning and shining Lights,"* shedding their *kindly Influence* on all around them, in that just *Proportion,* which their *respective Distances* may demand.

SECTION VII

The preceding Remarks may sufficiently obviate every Cavil of the noble Writer against the *essential* Parts of *Christianity.* But as his Lordship hath casually interspersed several Random Insinuations, we must be content to receive them as they happen to appear, since they are of that disjointed Kind as to be incapable of Connection. [348]

In a marginal Note, he gives an Account of the Migration of the *Israelites* from *Egypt,* under the Conduct of MOSES. He thinks proper to reject the clear Account which the *Jewish Legislator* himself gives, "That they departed, in order to worship the true God;" and preposterously prefers what TACITUS and JUSTIN[106] have said on that Subject; who affirm indeed, but without Proof, "that the *Jews* were driven out of *Egypt* on Account of their *Leprosy."*[d] This Partiality might of itself appear *mysterious* enough, when we consider the particular and consistent Account given us by the very Leader of the Expedition: For, what should we think of the Man, who

d. *Misc.* ii. c. 1. Notes.[107]
106. St. Justin Martyr (*c.* 100–*c.* 165 A.D.); important early Christian apologist.
107. Shaftesbury, *Characteristicks,* vol. III, p. 35, n. ‡.

should prefer the random Conjectures of an ignorant Modern, to XENOPHON's *Retreat*,[108] or CAESAR's *Commentaries?* But the noble Writer's Partiality will appear still more unaccountable, if we consider the following Passage of STRABO;[109] a Writer as much beyond TACITUS in Candour, as beyond JUSTIN (if indeed JUSTIN and not TROGUS POMPEIUS,[110] be answerable for this Slander) in true Judgement. This Author, STRABO, second to none in Antiquity, [349] speaks thus: "MOSES, an *Egyptian* Priest, retreated along with a number of *religious Followers*. For he affirmed and taught, that the *Egyptians* were mistaken, who imaged the Deity under the Forms of the Brute-Creation; as likewise the *Libyans* and *Greeks,* who represented the *Gods* under the *human Shape*. He held that alone to be *God,* which comprehends every living Creature, the Earth, and Sea; which is called *Heaven,* the *World,* or the *universal Nature*; whose *Image,* who that is in his right Mind, would dare to form out of any *earthly* Materials? *Rejecting* therefore all use of *Images,* he determined to dedicate to him a Temple worthy of his Nature, and worship him without Images.—On this Principle he persuaded and brought over many *well-disposed* Men, and led them forth into that Country *where now* Jerusalem *is built.*"[e]

e. Μωσῆς γάρ τις τῶν Αἰγυπτίων ἱερέων—ἀπῆρεν ἐκεῖσε—ἔφη γὰρ ἐκεῖνος καὶ ἐδίδασκεν, ὡς οὐκ ὀρθῶς φρονοῖεν οἱ Αἰγύπτιοι θηρίοις εἰκάζοντες καὶ βοσκήμασι τὸ θεῖον, οὐδ᾽ οἱ Λίβυες· οὐκ εὖ δὲ οὐδ᾽ οἱ Ἕλληνες, ἀνθρωπομόρφους τυποῦντες· εἴη γὰρ ἓν τοῦτο μόνον θεὸς τὸ περιέχον ἡμᾶς ἅπαντας καὶ γῆν καὶ θάλατταν, ὃ καλοῦμεν οὐρανὸν καὶ κόσμον, καὶ τὴν τῶν ὄντων φύσιν. τούτου δὴ τίς ἂν εἰκόνα πλάττειν θαρρήσειε νοῦν ἔχων ὁμοίαν τινα τῶν παρ᾽ ἡμῖν; ἀλλ᾽ ἐὰν δεῖν πᾶσαν ξοανοποιίαν, τέμενος ἀφορίσαντας καὶ σηκὸν ἀξιόλογον τιμᾶν ἕδους χωρίς·—Ἐκεῖνος μὲν οὖν τοιαῦτα λέγων ἔπεισεν εὐγνώμονας ἄνδρας οὐκ ὀλίγους, καὶ ἀπήγαγεν ἐπὶ τὸν τόπον τοῦτον, ὅπου νῦν ἐστι τὸ ἐν τοῖς Ἱεροσολύμοις κτίσμα. Strabo, l. xvi.[111]

108. Xenophon's *Anabasis* is a narrative of the expedition of Cyrus against his brother, Artaxerxes II, king of Persia, in which Xenophon himself served. The expedition culminated in the disastrous defeat of Cunaxa, after which Xenophon coordinated the difficult retreat to the Euxine of the remnants of the Greek forces. Caesar's *Commentaries* are the Roman general's terse accounts of his campaigns from 58 to 52 B.C., first in the subjugation of Gaul, and second in the Roman Civil War leading up to his defeat of the republican forces under Pompey at Pharsalus.

109. Strabo (*c.* 64 B.C.–19 A.D.); a Greek Stoic and traveller, whose *Geographica* describes the physical geography of the major countries of the Roman world, as well as describing their history, economic development, and customs.

110. Pompeius Trogus (fl. 1st c. A.D.); Roman historian whose work survives only in the epitome of Justin.

111. Strabo, XVI.ii.35–36.

A noble Testimony, sure, from [350] a Heathen Writer: *Less* he could not say, if he was well informed; and, unless he had embraced the *Jewish* Religion, he could not have said *more*.

There is another Passage (*Misc.* v. c. 1.)[112] which discovers somewhat of unfair dealing in the noble Writer. In the Margin, he prettily enough criticizes the Preface to St. Luke's Gospel. But in the Text he hath paraphrased the Evangelist's Expression, in a Manner so distant from any thing St. Luke either wrote or *meant*, as must not a little astonish every candid Reader. St. Luke says, "*It seemed good* to him to write in Order the Things that he knew."[113] To which the noble Writer adds, "As there were many, it seems, long afterwards, who did; and undertook accordingly, to write in Order and *as seemed good to them, &c.*"—What shall we say of the noble Writer on this Occasion? Why, this only; "That [351] inasmuch as it *seemed good to him* to interpret this Preface of St. Luke, he therefore thought himself at Liberty to interpret it *as it seemed good to him*."

There are three more Subjects which his Lordship hath thought fit to represent in the Manner which *seemed good to him*. These are, first, the divine Foreknowledge communicated to Joseph in the Interpretation of Pharaoh's Dreams.[114] Secondly, the Rise of *Bigotry*, or religious *Intolerance* and *Persecution*. Thirdly, and principally, The Relation which the *Jewish* Institutions bear to the *Egyptian*.[f] In all these, the noble Writer hath employed every Art of *Insinuation* and *Address*, that he might throw an Odium on the *Mosaic* Dispensation. These Passages might well merit a particular Consideration, had I not been happily prevented by my most learned Friend,[116] who hath fully exposed their Weakness in that inestimable Treasure of

---

f. See *Misc.* ii. c. 1.[115]

112. Shaftesbury, *Characteristicks*, vol. III, pp. 139–65; esp. p. 150.

113. Luke 1:1–4.

114. Genesis 41:1–45.

115. Shaftesbury, *Characteristicks*, vol. III, pp. 19–41.

116. William Warburton (1698–1779), bishop of Gloucester, had originally followed a legal career before taking orders in 1723. He had attacked Shaftesbury in his *A Critical and Philosophical Enquiry into the Causes of Prodigies and Miracles* (1727), and more recently had pursued his crusade against deists and freethinkers in his major work, *The Divine Legation of Moses Demonstrated* (1738–41). For Warburton's dealings with Brown, see the "Introduction," above, pp. x–xiii.

all true Knowledge, *The divine Legation of* MOSES. Thither the Reader is referr'd; where he will find these Questions treated [352] with that *Reach* and *Mastery* so peculiar to the Author of that great Work.[g]

It may now be necessary to examine the third Chapter of the noble Writer's second Miscellany; where he makes it his Pretence, "to prove the Force of *Humour* in Religion."[117] Of which it may be said, that it is the truest Piece of *Random-Work,* the most genuine *Farce,* that is perhaps to be met with in any Writer of whatever Age or Nation. He *divides* it (as every *Farce* ought to be *divided*) into three *Acts.* In its Progress we are carry'd into a very *Fairy-Land* of *Thought,* if not more properly a *confused Chaos.* For first, he sets about with great Solemnity to prove, "that *Wit and Humour* are corroborative of Religion, and promotive of true Faith:"[118] To prove this, a Story is told, by which it appears, that *not Wit and Humour,* but *good Humour* or *Easiness of Temper* is thus *corroborative* and *promotive:* Then, in Conclusion, *Wit and Humour* come in again, to overturn all that hath been done, and shew that *good Humour* hath suffered itself to be ridiculously *imposed upon.* [353]

Tho' it doth not appear that our modern Advocates for *Wit and Humour* are so *nearly interested* in their Fate as they seem to *think* themselves; yet it must be owned their Generosity is so much the more to be applauded, in thus *pleading* the Cause of *Clients* who *never employed them.* However, taking for granted what seems to be the real Foundation of their Writings on this Subject, "that *talking* in Praise of *Wit and Humour* is a Proof of their being *possessed* of them, and that consequently they are *Parties in the Cause*;" I shall not *envy* the noble Writer *any Man's Admiration,* who may think proper to esteem him a *Wit,* on account of the *grotesque* Appearances he assumes throughout this present *Miscellany.* 'Tis my Intention only to convince the plain Reader, that this *supposed Wit* is by no means *Philosophical.*

The first *Head* therefore, he tells us, is "to make it appear, that Wit and Humour are corroborative of Religion and promotive of true Faith."

---

g. With Relation to the first of these Points, see the *Div. Leg.* Vol. ii p. 164. For the second, see *ib.* Book ii. § 6. For the third, see Book iv. § 6. passim.

117. Shaftesbury, *Characteristicks*, vol. III, p. 60.

118. Ibid., p. 62.

To this Purpose he tires us with a Story, not the most elegantly plann'd, in my Apprehension, of a "Club of *merry* Gentlemen, who in a travelling Expedition meeting with sorry Roads and [354] worse Fare, laugh'd themselves into a Belief, that both Roads, Accommodations, and Cookery, were perfectly good." What follows is the Moral or Application of this curious Conceit. "Had I to deal with a malicious Reader, he might perhaps pretend to infer from this Story of my travelling Friends, that I intended to represent it as an easy Matter for People to persuade themselves into what Opinion or Belief they pleased."[119]

Now without troubling ourselves to enquire how far this Story is a Proof of the noble Writer's fundamental Maxim, "That Ridicule is a Test of Truth;" let us proceed to the intended *Moral*; which seems evidently calculated to throw a false Light on *religious Belief*; by representing it as the mere Effect of *Prejudice, Self-Imposition,* and *Deceit*. To rescue it, therefore, from this insinuated Calumny, we need not *deny*, but *insist*, that the Passions, false Interests, and Prejudices of Mankind must indeed for ever hang as a Byass upon their Opinions. But it must be farther observed too, that these Passions and false Interests will at least as often prejudice them *against* Religion, as *in its Favour*. 'Tis true, there are Preju[355]dices in Favour of Religion, arising from *Education*; but there are Prejudices against it too, arising from *vicious Passions*. Some are *sanguine* in their *Hopes,* and hence, while their Conduct is virtuous, *wish*, and therefore *believe* Religion to be *true:* Others are *sanguine* in their *Hopes,* but *abandoned* in their Conduct, and therefore *live* themselves into a Belief that Religon is *false*. Some, thro' a Dread of Annihilation, persuade themselves beyond the Strength of Evidence: Others, thro' the Prevalence of a suspicious cast of Mind, reject even what is probable. Thus Passions and Prejudices work powerfully indeed; but they work both *for* and *against* *Religion*. It should seem then, that the noble Writer's Moral, which he aims at *Religion*, may with equal Force be apply'd to *Infidelity:* For it is but supposing a Man given up to *Vanity* or *Vice,* and we shall soon "see him enter into such a Plot as this against his own Understanding, and endeavour by all possible Means to persuade both himself and others of

119. Shaftesbury, *Characteristicks*, vol. III, pp. 62–64.

what he thinks *convenient* and *useful* to DISBELIEVE."[120] 'Tis idle there-fore to insist on the Prejudices either *for* or *against* Religion: they will both naturally [356] arise; and it is the Part of Reason to controul them. But we may safely leave it to any one's Determination, which Temper of Mind is the most *amiable,* that which entertains Prejudices *in Favour* of *Religion,* or *against it.*

The noble Writer proceeds to his *second* Head; but seems at the same time conscious how little it was to any good Purpose. However, in Failure of *Truth* and *Method,* he again hath recourse to what he seems to think *Wit and Humour;* and which, for aught I know, may pass for such among his Admirers. "However, says he, lest I should be charged for being worse than my Word, I shall endeavour to satisfy my Reader, by pursuing my Method proposed; if peradventure he can call to Mind what that Method was. Or if he cannot, the Matter is not so very important, but that he may safely pursue his Reading, without further Trouble."[121]

But tho' it was prudently done in the noble Writer, to throw the Sub-ject of his *second* Head into *Shades;* yet for the Sake of Truth, we must drag it into *Light.* It was therefore to prove "That *Wit and Humour* are used as the proper Means of [357] promoting true Faith, by the holy Founders of Religion."[122] But when we come to the Point, for *Wit and Humour,* by Virtue of a certain Dexterity of Hand, the Reader is again unexpectedly presented with *good Humour* in their Stead. This, it will be said, is nimble dealing; but what of that, so long as it may tend to disgrace *Christianity* and its *Founder?* The noble Writer's Application, therefore, is still more Extraordinary. "The Affection and Love which procures a true Adherence to the new religious Foundation, must depend either on a real or *counterfeit Goodness* in the *religious Founder:* Whatever *ambi-tious Spirit* may *inspire him;* whatever *savage Zeal* or *persecuting Principle* may lie *in Reserve,* ready to disclose itself when Authority and Power is once obtained; the *first Scene* of *Doctrine,* however, fails not to pre-sent us with the agreeable Views of *Joy, Love, Meakness, Gentleness,* and

120. Shaftesbury, *Characteristicks,* vol. III, p. 64 (where however the final word is "believe").

121. Ibid., p. 71.

122. Ibid., p. 62.

Moderation."[123]—To speak my inmost Sentiments of this Passage, it is of too black a Nature to deserve a Reply. There are certain Degrees of *Calumny* so *flagrant,* as injured Truth disdains to answer; and this is of the Kind. On this Occasion, there[358]fore, we shall leave the noble Writer to the Reflections of every *honest Man*; in Conformity to the Example of that blessed Person, "*who, when he was reviled, reviled not again.*"[h]

The next Circumstance in holy Writ, that falls under his Lordship's Animadversion, is what he calls "The famous *Entry* or *high Dance* perform'd by DAVID in the Procession of the sacred Coffer."[125] In which he hath again represented Things *as it seemed good to him.* Here, by confounding *ancient,* with *modern Manners* (in such a Way as is quite unworthy of his Character, and suited only to the Genius of a *Coffee-house* Freethinker) he hath endeavoured to bring down the *solemn Procession* of a grand *religious Festival,* to a Level with the Merriments of an Apish *Dancing-Master.* This Representation may very probably pass current among many of his Admirers; so that it had been necessary to set the Matter in its true Light; but that here too, I am happily prevented by a judicious Writer, who hath done all imaginable Justice to the Argument; and effectually ex[359]posed the noble Writer's Weakness and Insincerity.[i]

His Lordship now proceeds to the Story of the Prophet JONAH, which he hath burlesqued and turned to Farce with that Delicacy, so peculiar to himself. The Story itself is indeed authenticated by our SAVIOUR's mention of it, as emblematical of his own Death and Resurrection. Its Moral is excellent; being an illustrious Display of the divine Mercy to penitent and returning Sinners, exemplify'd in GOD's remitting the Punishment denounced, and sparing a devoted City on its sincere Repentance; as also of the Frailty and Imperfection of the best of Men, set forth in the Prophet's Behaviour on the Occasion. To this we may add "the Propriety

h. See above § 3. of this *Essay.* p. 269.[124]
i. See Dr. Leland's *Answer to the Moral Philosopher,* p. 291, &c.[126]
123. Shaftesbury, *Characteristicks*, vol. III, p. 71.
124. 1 Peter 2:23. See above, pp. 174–75.
125. Shaftesbury, *Characteristicks*, vol. III, pp. 72–73.
126. John Leland (1691–1766); Presbyterian minister and theological writer, primarily against the deists. Brown has in mind a passage from Leland's *The Divine Authority of the Old and New Testament Asserted,* 2 vols (1739–40), vol. I, pp. 291 ff.

of the Miracle recorded," which was itself an extraordinary and most awakening "Instance of Punishment *inflicted on Disobedience,* and *remitted on Repentance;*" and therefore bearing a *strong Relation* to the *Event* for which it was wrought; being peculiarly *adapted,* when made known to the *Ninevites,* to in[360]duce them to hearken to the Prophet's Preaching, to *believe* what he *denounced* and *promised,* and rouze them at once into a *Fear* of GOD's *Justice,* and a *Reliance* on his *Mercy.*

Such then being the real Nature of the Fact; the Secret of the noble Writer's polite Representation lies in his burlesquing the Circumstances of the *supposed Dialogue* between GOD and the Prophet; an easy Task for any one who is disingenuous or ignorant enough to represent as strictly *litteral,* what is evidently *parabolical;* according to the frequent and known Manner of *Composition* in the earliest Ages.[k] This his Lordship seems to have been aware of: "Whatsoever of this Kind may be *allegorically* understood, or in the Way of *Parable* or *Fable,* &c."[127] Now had he treated the Scripture Story with the same Candour which he affords to other ancient Writers, he would not have abused this Passage in so unworthy a Manner. A Writer of no Abilities, if provided only with a sufficient Quantity of Spleen and false Con[361]ceit, might easily ridicule his favourite Piece, "The Judgment of HERCULES:"[128] And to a raw Imagination, disgrace that instructive Fable, by burlesquing the supposed Conference between the *Goddesses* and the *Heroe.* VIRGIL hath in Fact been so served. And if Works of mere Invention, and of the heroic Kind, studiously contrived to avoid every thing low, obscure, or equivocal, are subject to this Abuse; can we wonder, if the succinct History of an ancient Fact, recording the Dispensations of Providence, a Matter very obscure in itself, and relative to ancient Manners so distant from our own, should be liable to the false and dishonest Lights of Buffoonry? We may further observe that the noble Writer's Ridicule sometimes falls on divine Providence itself: "His *Tutor had good Eyes,* and a *long Reach;*

k. See the *Div. Leg.* Vol. ii. where a full Account is given of the Origin and Progress of this kind of Writing.

127. Shaftesbury, *Characteristicks,* vol. III, p. 75.

128. Ibid., pp. 211–39.

he *overtook* the Renegade at Sea, &c."[129]—Could an *Epicurean*[130] have used more indecent Language?

His Lordship goes on, to ridicule "the *Descriptions, Narrations, Expressions,* and *Phrases*"[131] of holy Scripture: But these we shall pass over at present, as they will deserve a separate Consideration. He touches once more on the *Patriarch* ABRAHAM; [362] and they who are curious enough to look for the Objection, may find a full Answer to it, in the Place here referred to.[1]

The next, and only remaining Circumstance worthy of Notice in this Miscellany, is a *pretended Translation* from PLUTARCH: In which the noble Writer deals as honourably by that Author, as before by GORGIAS or ARISTOTLE.[m] But here too, I am prevented by the learned PHILELEUTHERUS LIPSIENSIS: However, as his Lordship's Conduct is *remarkable* on this Occasion, it may not be improper to exhibit a View of it in the great Critic's Words; who, it must be owed, hath chastised the noble Writer somewhat *roughly,* and *Aristarchus*-like.

He (Mr. COLLINS) quotes the Place as it is translated forsooth in the *Characteristics,* a Book writ by an anonymous, but, whoever he is, a very whimsical and conceited Author. *O wretched* Grecians (*so that Author renders* PLUTARCH) *who bring into Religion that frightful Mien of sordid and vilifying Devotion, ill-favoured Humiliation and* [363] *Contrition, abject Looks and Countenances, Consternations, Prostrations, Disfigurations, and, in the Act of worship, Distortions, constrained and painful Postures of the Body, wry Faces, beggarly Tones, Mumpings,*[133] *Grimaces, Cringings, and the rest of this Kind.*—Thus far that nameless Opiniatre:[134] And our worthy Writer (Mr. COLLINS) introduces

l. *Div. Leg.* Vol. ii. p. 620.

m. See above, *Essay* i. § ix.[132]

129. Ibid., p. 74.

130. Literally, a follower of the doctrines of Epicurus, which however in the eighteenth century had been misinterpreted as advocating atheism and materialist hedonism of the most vulgar kind. See above, p. 122, n. 56 and p. 123, n. 58.

131. Shaftesbury, *Characteristicks,* vol. III, p. 75.

132. See above, pp. 75–77.

133. Facial grimacings, or grumblings communicated by facial expressions.

134. From the French; an opinionated person, with a negative connotation of being incorrigibly so; slightly archaic in 1751.

it with a grave Air, *that* PLUTARCH *thus satirizes the public Forms of Devotion; which yet are such, as, in almost all Countries, pass for the true Worship of God.*—This would partly be true, if those were really the Words of PLUTARCH: But as not one Syllable of them is found there, what must we think of this *Couple* of *Corrupters* and *Forgers?* There is nothing in all this, but their own *Disfigurations* and *Distortions* of the Original; their own *Mumpings,* and *beggarly Tones,* while they pretend to speak in PLUTARCH's Voice.—PLUTARCH having observed, that Superstition alone allows no Ease nor Intermission, even in Sleep; their Dreams, adds he, do as much torment them then, as their waking Thoughts did before; *they seek for Expiations of those* [364] *Visions nocturnal; Charms, Sulfurations, Dippings in the Sea, Sittings all Day on the Ground.*

O Greeks, *Inventors of* Barbarian *Ills, whose Superstition has devised Rowlings in the Mire and in the Kennels, Dippings in the Sea, Grovelings and Throwings upon the Face, deformed Sittings on the Earth, absurd and uncouth Adorations.* This is a verbal Interpretation of that Place—and now I dare ask the Reader, if he has seen a more flagrant Instance of *Unfaithfulness* and *Forgery,* than this of our two Writers? *Humiliation* and *Contrition,* known Words in your *English Liturgy,* are to be traduced here under PLUTARCH's Name. Where do those and their other Phrases appear in the Original? or where do the Rites, he really speaks of, appear in your Form of Worship? who among you *rowl themselves in Mire, or wallow in Kennels?* a Ceremony fit only to be enjoyned to such *crackbrained* and *scandalous* Writers.[n]

The remaining Part of this random Essay, is so completely vague and unintelligible, that although it be evidently de[365]signed, as a continued Sneer at *Christianity,* 'tis impossible to pick so much as an *Objection,* or even an *Idea* out of it. 'Tis therefore below Criticism. To conclude; when I see the noble Writer debase himself in this strange Manner, exercising at once the *lowest Derision,* and inflicting the *deadliest Wounds on Religion and Christianity*; I must own, the Appearance he makes, call up to my

---

n. *Phil. Lipsiens.* p. 210 *&c.*[135]

135. [Richard Bentley], *Remarks Upon a Late Discourse of Free-Thinking,* eighth edition, enlarged (1743), pp. 209–13.

Imagination a Remark of his own, "That there cannot be a Sight more shocking and contemptible, than that of a Man acting at once the Part of a *Merry-Andrew,* and an *Executioner.*"°

It may be necessary, finally, to obviate his Lordship's perpetual Sneer at the *Mysteries* of our Religion. These, when particular Topics fail him, are the standing Objects of his Raillery. To cite particular Passages of this Kind, were needless, because they are innumerable. The plain Implication of all his gross Banter, is, "That because in the *Christian* Dispensation, there are some things, which surpass human Comprehension, *Christianity* is therefore *absurd* and *ridiculous.*"

With Regard to this Cavil, therefore, [366] 'tis not my Intention to insist on proving the "Difference between Things being *above* Reason and Things being *contrary* to Reason; or that Propositions may be true, though they are *above* our Reason, so long as they are not *contrary* to it." Full enough has been said on this Subject, and by no body better than by the excellent Mr. *Boyle.*[137] 'Tis a Question of more Importance to decide, "Why any thing *mysterious* should be admitted into a Religion, *revealed* for the *Use* of Man?" And in Answer to this, we need only observe, that revealed Religion being designed for Man's *Use,* its *essential* Doctrines are plain, *intelligible* to all, *accommodated* to the Nature and Faculties of the *human* Kind. But as this System not only reveals to us our *Duty,* but all *Motives* too which may induce us to practise it; so, in Order to *inforce these,* and *convince* us of the *Truth* of their divine Original, it was necessary, that a *History of Providence,* or GOD's *Dispensation,* should be revealed along with them. Hence something *mysterious* must needs arise; unless you suppose Man *infinite* in Knowledge. For as this System reveals to us several Particulars (so far as they stand connected with *Piety* [367] and *Morals*) which relate to the Nature of GOD, the State of other, and superior Beings, the original Condition of Man, the Interposition of Providence for

o. *Wit.* and *H.* Part i. § iii.[136]

136. Shaftesbury, *Characteristicks,* vol. I, p. 43.

137. Robert Boyle (1627–1691); natural philosopher and theologian; founder by testament of the "Boyle Lectures" for the defense of Christianity against atheists and others, an early series of which was given by Richard Bentley. Brown alludes to Boyle's *A Discourse of Things Above Reason* (1681).

his Redemption, the Change of his Nature and Faculties, through the future Periods of his Existence; in all which Circumstances, his present Reach of Thought could give him no Information; 'tis evident, that in these Accounts, many Subjects must be *touched upon,* and *other Systems* of *Being* occasionally *glanced at,* the full Knowledge of which, must be far beyond his present Comprehension. Now so far as these Truths and Facts, though *imperfectly revealed,* have any Tendency to *enlighten* his Mind, as to the general *Plan of Providence,* or stand connected in any other Manner with *Religion* and *Virtue,* so as to *encourage* and *promote* them, they must surely be admitted as Circumstances of great *Propriety* and *Use.* Or even supposing some of them to be of *none,* yet if they stand so essentially *connected* with others *which are,* so that the one cannot be destroyed without the other; this very Circumstance of *essential Union,* effectually destroys every Objection against their being of divine Original. [368]

There may be, likewise, and undoubtedly are some few Mysteries of another Kind in the *Mosaic* Dispensation: Such, I mean, as may seem, to some Apprehensions, not so easily reconcileable to the *moral* Attributes of GOD: Of which Kind there are *some* too, in the Constitution of the natural World. Now here in *Revelation,* as in *Nature,* 'tis the Part of human Reason to acquiesce in this *mysterious* and *unknown* Part, from what is *clear* and *known.*[p] Of this Kind, perhaps, is the Expulsion of the *Canaanites* under *Joshua,* which the noble Writer hath taken such Pains to vilify.[q] He might with as much Reason insult the Creator, for the Admission of *Storm, Famine,* or *Pestilence.* For as in Nature, so in *revealed* Religion, we are not to judge of the *whole* Constitution or Dispensation of Things, from *small* and *seeming* Exceptions: On the Contrary, 'tis the Part of Wisdom to determine concerning these *seeming* Exceptions from a full View of the *whole* Dispensation. If *this* evidently tend to Good, the unprejudiced Enquirer into *Nature* and *Revelation* attributes the Doubt and Dark[369]ness, which may involve any particular Part, to his own *Incapacity* and *Ignorance.* And justly; for as the noble Writer

---

p. See above, § iv. of this *Essay.*[138]
q. *Advice,* P. iii. § iii.[139]
138. See above, pp. 176–88.
139. Shaftesbury, *Characteristicks,* vol. I, pp. 203–24.

hath told us on this very Occasion, "In an *Infinity* of Things thus *relative,* a Mind, which sees not *infinitely,* can see nothing *fully.*"ʳ

Let us therefore, while as yet we see but *as through a Glass and darkly,*[141] contemplate the Works of God with Reverence and Submission. Let us wait the happier Hour, when *we shall know even as we are known:*[142] when we shall be raised to a more enlarged Comprehension of our Creator's immense Designs; and the whole intelligent Creation shall joyn, in confessing and adoring the unerring Rectitude of all his Dispensations.

SECTION VIII

Hitherto we have seen the noble Writer buffooning and disgracing *Christianity,* from a false Representation of its *material* Part: we shall now consider what he hath thrown out against the *Composition, Style,* and *Manner* of the sacred [370] Scriptures; for on this too, he has thought it expedient to *point* his *Raillery.*

He tells us, in the *ironical Tone,* "that the Scriptural Descriptions, Narrations, Expressions, and Phrases, are in themselves many Times exceedingly pleasant, entertaining, and facetious.—That our Saviour's Style,—his Parables, Similies, Comparisons,—his Exhortations to his Disciples, the Images under which he often couches his Morals and prudential Rules—carry with them a certain *Festivity, Alacrity,* and good Humour so remarkable, that I should look upon it as impossible not to be mov'd in a *pleasant Manner* at their Recital."ˢ To these general Cavils he hath added a *Simile* in another Miscellany, which, as is usual with all fanciful Writers, is to stand for an Argument. He says "'tis no otherwise in the grammatical Art of Characters, and *painted Speech,* than in the Art of *Painting* itself. I have seen, in certain Christian Churches, an ancient Piece or two, affirm'd on the solemn Faith of priestly Tradition, to have

r. *Mor.* Part ii. § iv.[140]
s. *Misc.* ii. c. 3.[143]
140. Shaftesbury, *Characteristicks*, vol. II, p. 163.
141. 1 Corinthians 13:12.
142. Ibid.
143. Shaftesbury, *Characteristicks*, vol. III, pp. 75–76.

been angelically and divinely wrought, by a supernatural [371] Hand and sacred Pencil. Had the Piece happen'd to be of a Hand like RAPHAEL's, I could have found nothing *certain* to oppose to this Tradition. But having observed the whole *Style* and *Manner* of the pretended heavenly Workmanship to be so indifferent, as to vary in many Particulars from the Truth of Art, I presum'd within myself to beg Pardon of the Tradition, and assert confidently, that, if the Pencil had been *Heaven-guided,* it could never have been so *lame* in it's Performance."ᵗ This ingenious Conceit, in the subsequent Paragraph, he very *clearly,* tho' *slyly,* applies to the holy Scriptures.

'Tis the Province of *Wit* to form *Comparisons*; of *Philosophy,* to *detect* their *Weakness,* when they are obtruded on us as a *Test* of Truth. On Examination therefore I will venture to say, the noble Writer's *Parallel* will be found highly irregular and defective.

For there is an *essential* Difference between *Paintings* and *Writing,* both in their *End* and *Execution.* Paintings, with Regard to their End, are things of mere *A*[372]*musement* and *Taste:* Consequently all their Value lies in the *Exquisiteness* of the *Art,* and the *fine Hand* of the Master. 'Tis likewise a Species of Art, that lies chiefly among the *Few*; the Bulk of Mankind (or in the noble Writer's more elegant Phrase, *the mere Vulgar*) being *incapable,* thro' a Want of *Leisure,* of gaining any Proficiency in this *Taste*; or of acquiring that curious Discernment in *Ordonnance,*¹⁴⁵ *Drawing,* and *Colouring,* which is at once the Pride and Pleasure of the *Virtuoso-Tribe.*

But with Respect to Language the Affair is otherwise: It's *Ends* are *various.* From the Four different Kinds of literary Composition, as explained above,ᵘ there must arise a correspondent Variety of Style, the *Poetical,* the *Oratorial,* the *Historical* and *Didactic.* The First of these Kinds alone partakes of the Nature of *Picture,* and therefore can alone be properly compared with it; as they are both referr'd to the *Imagination,* for the End of *Pleasure:* The other three Species of Composition, tending chiefly to *Utility,* by the Means of *Persuasion* or *Instruction,* draw their prime Value from

t. *Misc.* v. c. 1.¹⁴⁴
u. See *Essay,* i. § 3.
144. Shaftesbury, *Characteristicks,* vol. III, pp. 140–41.
145. Plan or method of artistic composition (OED).

Plainness, Clearness, and *Pre*[373]*cision:* From being adapted, not to the *Taste* of the *fastidious Critic,* but to the *Capacities* of those who are the intended Objects of *Perswasion* or *Instruction.* Here then, the noble Writer's Parallel is essentially defective: Since it was the Intention of *Providence,* in the sacred Scriptures, to condescend to what his Lordship's Quality and refined Wisdom intitle him to disdain, even *to instruct the mere Vulgar:* Whereas the End of *Painting,* is only *the Amusement of the Few.*

In Regard to the *Execution,* we shall find as wide a Difference. There is, in Philosophical strictness, but one *unvary'd Language* or *Style* in *Painting;* which is "such a Modification of *Light* or *Colours* as may imitate whatever Objects we find in Nature." This consists not in the *Application* of *arbitrary Signs;* but hath it's Foundation in the *Senses* and *Reason* of Mankind; and is therefore *the same* in every Age and Nation. But in the literary *Style* or *Language,* the Matter is far otherwise. For Language being the *voluntary* Application of *arbitrary* Signs, according to the Consent of different Men and Nations, there is no *single uniform Model of Nature* to be [374] followed. Hence *Gracefulness* or *Strength* of Style, *Harmony* or *Softness, copious* Expression, *terse* Brevity, or *contrasted* Periods, have by turns gained the Approbation of particular Countries. Now all these *supposed* Beauties of Speech are *relative, local,* and *capricious;* and consequently unworthy the Imitation of a divine Artist; who, to fit the Speech he *ordains,* to the great Work of *universal Instruction,* would, we may reasonably suppose, strip it of every *local, peculiar,* and *grotesque* Ornament; and convey it unaccompany'd by all, but the more *universal* Qualities common to every Tongue.

The noble Writer, then, might with some shew of Reason have objected to the *Style* of Scripture, had the Writers boasted it's *Elegance,* as MAHOMET did that of his *Koran,* and defy'd all his Opposers to write any thing approaching it in this Respect. But the sacred Penmen discover no *Design* or *Desire* of excelling as *fine* Writers: On the contrary, St. PAUL says, "they came not with the Power of human Speech,"[146] and gives a Reason for it which does Honour to his Mission. [375]

146. A paraphrase of 1 Corinthians 2:1. The reason St. Paul offers for his eschewal of eloquence is: "And my speech and my preaching was not with enticing words of man's wisdom, but in demonstration of the Spirit and of power: that your faith should not stand in the wisdom of men, but in the power of God" (1 Corinthians 2:4–5).

Tho' this Scrutiny alone might be sufficient to detect and discredit the Wantonness of the noble Writer's Comparison; yet it will further lead us to a full Disclosure of the Truth; by shewing *that* to be the peculiar Characteristic of the Scripture *Composition,* which hath ever held the first Rank among the Qualities of human Writings; I mean, that of *unadorned* SIMPLICITY.

As much hath been said by many Writers on the Subject of *Simplicity,* with very little Precision; and particularly by the noble Writer, who seems to separate the *simple* Manner from the *Sublime,* as if they were *incompatible;*[x] and indeed in his own Compositions preposterously deserts the *one,* when ever he attempts the *other:*[y] It may be necessary here to fix the Idea of a *just* SIMPLICITY. This may be said to consist "in *Truth* and *Weight* of SENTIMENT, cloathed in such IMAGES and STYLE, as may most effectually *convey* it to the Reader's Mind." If any of these Circumstances be wanting; if the SENTIMENT be *false* or *trifling,* if the IMAGES or STYLE be such as tend rather to *fix the Attention on* [376] *themselves,* than on the *Sentiment* they are employed to *convey,* the *just Simplicity* is destroyed. This, as might be proved by a large Induction of Particulars, is the Circumstance in which the best Critics of Antiquity placed the supreme Excellence of Writing. And, in this Use of the Term, it appears, that not only the *familiar,* the *narrative,* the *didactic,* but the *pathetic,* and *sublime* Manner too, are so far from being inconsistent with *Simplicity,* that they are then only in their Perfection, when *founded on it.*

'Tis true indeed, that the sacred Records are, as the noble Writer calls them, "*multifarious,* and of different Characters, varying according to the Situation, Intention, and natural Capacity of the Writers."[z] Yet amidst all this Variety of Manner, the reigning Quality of *Simplicity* is so *uniform* and *conspicuous,* that the boldest Enemy of *Christianity* will not be forward to hazard the Credit of his *Taste,* by calling it in Question.

---

x. *Advice,* Part ii. § 2.[147]
y. See the *Moralists,* passim.
z. *Misc.* v. c. 1.[148]
147. Shaftesbury, *Characteristicks,* vol. I, pp. 142–62.
148. A summary of Shaftesbury, *Characteristicks,* vol. III, pp. 141–45.

If we examine them in this Light, we shall find, that, according to the Division made above,[a] they consist of Four different Kinds, the *poetic, oratorial, historical,* [377] and *didactic* Forms. The poetic lies chiefly in the Book of *Psalms,* of *Job,* and several detached Passages in the *Prophets,* particularly of *Isaiah.* They contain many noble Efforts of *unmixed Poetry* or *pure Imitation*; yet *these,* being all centered in *one Intention,* that of *extolling* the Works, and celebrating the Power, Wisdom, and Goodness of the *Deity,* do generally partake of the Character of *Eloquence,* being chiefly of the *lyric* Kind.[b] In all these, the great Character of *Simplicity* is so strongly predominant, that every Attempt to *embellish* them, by adding the supernumerary Decorations of *Style* in *Translation,* hath ever been found to *weaken* and *debase* them.

As to the *oratorial* or *pathetic* Parts, innumerable might be produced, equal if not superior to any recorded by prophane Antiquity. In these, the leading Character of *Simplicity* is no less remarkable. Our SAVIOUR's *Parables* and Exhortations are generally admirable in this Quality: Filled with unfeigned Compassion for the Weakness and Miseries of Man, they breathe nothing but the purest Benevolence. St. PAUL's last Conversation with his Friends [378] at *Ephesus,* on his Departure for *Jerusalem*;[c] his Discourses on the *Resurrection* and on *Charity*; his Reproofs, his Commendations, his Apologies, especially that before AGRIPPA,[d] are wrote in the noblest Strain of Simplicity. And as a perfect Model of this Kind, we may give the Story of JOSEPH *and his Brethren,*[152] which for Tenderness, true *Pathos,* and unmixed Simplicity, is beyond Compare superior to any thing that appears in ancient Story.

a. *Essays* i. § 3.[149]
b. See *Essay* i. § 3.
c. *Acts,* c. xx.[150]
d. *Ib.* c. xxvi.[151]
149. See above, pp. 32–49.
150. Acts 20:17–38 (the conversation is with the elders of Ephesus, but in fact takes place at the nearby town of Miletus).
151. Acts 26:1–32.
152. Genesis 37:1–36.

But as the most important Part of Scripture lies in the *historical* and *preceptive* Part; especially in the *new Testament,* whence chiefly our Idea of *Duty* must be drawn; so we find this uniform and *simple* Manner eminently prevailing throughout, in every *Precept* and *Narration.* The History is conveyed in that artless Strain which alone could *adapt* it to the *Capacities* of *all Mankind*; the Precepts delivered by our SAVIOUR are drawn from the Principles of *common Sense,* improved by the most exalted Love of GOD and *Man*; and either expressed in clear and direct Terms, or couched under such *Images* and *Allusions,* as are every where to be found *in Nature,* such as *are,* [379] and *must ever be* universally *known,* and *familiar* to all Mankind;[e] in which, we may further observe, his Manner of teaching was greatly superior even to the noble Writer's justly applauded SOCRATES, who for the most part drew his *Images* and Allusions from the *less known* ARTS and MANNERS of the *City,* tho' indeed not without Reason. He did not aim at the Instruction of Mankind, but of the more literate Part of his fellow Citizens. His proper End was rather reforming the Minds of those who had been ill taught, than instructing those who had never learnt. To return; thro' all this Variety of striking Allusion and moral Precept, the *Style* ever continues the same, *unadorned, simple,* and, even by the noble Writer's own Confession, "*vehement* and *majestic;*"[f] yet never drawing the Reader's Attention on itself, but on the divine *Sentiments* it *conveys.*

To this we may further add, that these several Kinds of Composition are mixed and united with such Propriety and Force, as is scarce to be equalled in any other Writings. [380] The poetical Parts are heightened by the great Strokes of *Eloquence* and *Precept*; the *pathetick,* by the noblest *Imagery,* and justest *Morals*; and the *preceptive* is strengthened and

---

e. See Newton on *Daniel*;—Mr. Jortin's *Discourses*;—Dr. Law's *Life of* CHRIST.[153]
f. *Misc.* ii. c. 3.[154]

153. Sir Isaac Newton, *Observations Upon the Prophecies of Daniel, and the Apocalypse of St. John* (1733); John Jortin, *Discourses Concerning the Truth of the Christian Religion* (1746); Edmund Law, *A Discourse Upon the Life and Character of Christ* (Cambridge, 1749).

154. Shaftesbury, *Characteristicks*, vol. III, p. 76.

inforced by all the Aids of *Poetry, Eloquence,* and *Parable*; calculated at once to engage the *Imagination,* to touch the *Passions,* and command the *Reason* of Mankind.

'Tis true, this unadorned *Simplicity* so conspicuous in the Scripture Composition, hath often given Offence to puerile Critics. The noble Writer hath but revived the Objection; it was weakly urged by CELSUS in the Infancy of the Christian Religion.[g] At the Period when *Letters* revived in *Europe,* the *florid* Taste was so prevalent in *Italy,* under the Pontificate of LEO the Tenth,[156] that the Composition of the Scriptures was on this Account held in general Contempt; and one of the fine Gentlemen in Literature,[h] of those Days, is known to have declared, "that he dared not to read the *Bible,* lest it should *endanger his Style.*"[157] We may easily form a Judgment of the Taste of that Age from [381] this one Circumstance, "that their most elaborate and celebrated Compositions were all wrote in a *dead Language:*" For thus they became mere *Imitators,* even to a Degree of *Servility.* And 'tis sufficient for the Defenders of the *Bible* to observe, that along with *it,* every other great Model of antient Writing fell into the same Disgrace at the above-mentioned Period; while the

g. Origen *contra Cels.* l vii.[155]
h. Cardinal PIETRO BEMBO.
155. This allegation is not mentioned by Origen in book VII of *Contra Celsum*; but cf. VI.12.
156. Giovanni de'Medici (1475–1521); Pope Leo X from 1513 until his death; a pacific ruler under whose pontificate Rome became the cultural capital of Europe.
157. Brown presumably derived this anecdote concerning Pietro Bembo (1470–1547) from Bayle's *Dictionary,* where it can be found in note F to the article "Bembus," and where it is traced to an unattributed comment in a work by a German author, Thomas Lanzius: "Advertite, auditores, inepti hominis impietatem cum pari stultitia conjunctam. Is siquidem Epistolas omnes Pauli palam condemnavit, easque deflexo in contumeliam vocabulo Epistolaccias est ausus appellare, cum amico autor esset ne illas attingeret, vel, si coepisset legere, de manibus ejiceret, si elegantiam scribendi & eloquentiam adamaret"; "Take note, you who listen to me, of the equal impiety and folly of this impertinent man. Since indeed he openly condemned all the epistles of St. Paul, and contemptuously dared insultingly to refer to them as 'epistolets,' telling a friend to have nothing to do with them or, if he should begin to read them, soon to throw them aside, if he were truly devoted to elegance of style and eloquence."

general Taste and Attention was turned from weight of *Sentiment,* and strength of *Image* and *Expression,* to the *local* and *capricious* Decorations of *Style* and *Language.* But the Reign of this false Taste was of short Duration; so that for a long Time past, the comparative Merit of ancient Writers hath been *weighed* in a juster *Scale.*

Now if we examine the Writers whose Composition hath stood the Test of Ages, and obtained that highest Honour, "the concurrent Approbation of distant Times and Nations," we shall find that the Character of *Simplicity* is the *unvarying* Circumstance, which alone hath been able to gain this universal Homage from Mankind. Among the *Greeks,* whose Writers in general are of the *simple* Kind, the divinest Poet,[i] [382] the most commanding *Orator,*[k] the finest *Historian,*[l] and deepest *Philosopher,*[m] are, above the rest, conspicuously eminent in this great Quality. The *Roman* Writers rise towards Perfection according to that Measure of true *Simplicity* which they mingle in their Works. Indeed they are all inferior to the *Greek* Models. But who will deny, that LU-CRETIUS, HORACE, VIRGIL, LIVY, TERENCE, TULLY, are at once the *simplest* and *best* of *Roman* Writers? Unless we add the noble *Annalist,*[n] who appeared in after Times; who, notwithstanding the *political Turn* of his Genius, which sometimes *interferes,* is admirable in this great Quality; and by it, far superior to his Contemporaries. 'Tis this one Circumstance that hath raised the venerable DANTE, the Father of modern Poetry, above the succeeding Poets of his Country, who could never long maintain the *local* and *temporary* Honours bestowed upon them; but have fallen under that just Neglect, which *Time* will ever decree to those who desert a *just Simplicity* for the *florid* Colourings of Style, contrasted Phra[383]ses, affected Conceits, the mere *Trappings* of Composition, and *Gothic* MINUTIAE. 'Tis this hath given to BOILEAU the most lasting Wreath in *France*; to SHAKESPEAR and MILTON in *England*;

i. Homer.
k. Demosthenes.
l. Xenophon.
m. Aristotle.
n. Tacitus.

especially to the last, whose Writings are more *unmixed* in this Respect; and who had formed himself entirely on the *simple* Model of the best *Greek* Writers, and the *sacred* Scriptures.° [384]

As it appears from these Instances, that *Simplicity* is the only universal Characteristic of just Writing; so the superior Eminence of the sacred Scriptures in this prime Quality hath been generally acknowledged. One

o. Mr. DRYDEN somewhere observes "that MILTON never sinks so far below himself, as when he falls on *some Track of Scripture.*" 'Tis equally true, that he never *rises* so far *above himself,* as when he falls on some *Track of Scripture.*[158] 'Tis easy to guess what was the Drift of Mr. DRYDEN's Remark. But the Observations made above[159] (*Essay* i. § 3) will easily reconcile these seeming Contradictions. When MILTON adopts the *poetical* Parts of Scripture, he *rises* above himself. But by an *injudicious Application* of the *historical* or *didactic* Parts, he *often falls indeed.*

This naturally leads us to an Observation on Mr. HUME's Essay "*on Simplicity and Refinement in Writing.*" He hath attempted to fix a certain *Union* of these two Qualities, which, he says, constitutes the most perfect Form of Composition. It were to be wished he had given us some better *Reasons* in support of this *Opinion,* which itself seems to be a mere *Refinement.* The Progress of his Argument is remarkable.— He draws all his Instances from *Poets*; and having given some Examples of Poets who are both *simple* and *unpoetical* in the Extreme, he arbitrarily throws the Censure on the too great Degree of *Simplicity,* instead of fixing it where he ought, *viz.* on the too great Mixture of the *historical, oratorial,* or *argumentative* Species. In Proof of this, we need only alledge the Examples of HOMER, PINDAR, and CALLIMACHUS, where *Simplicity,* and at the same Time *Sublimity* and the *true poetic Forms,* are in their last *Perfection.* Thus all he proves is, "that a *Poet* ought not to be *unpoetical.*"— Next, he puts VIRGIL and RACINE on a *Level,* as having attained the nearest to this *imagined Union* of *Simplicity* and *Refinement.* Here he obligeth us again to call his Taste in Question: For every Page of RACINE is full of *Turns,* both of *Phrase* and *Sentiment:* Whereas we scarce meet with three Instances of this Kind in all VIRGIL's Writings.—He then gives us his Idea of *Simplicity:* "Those Compositions which have the Recommendation of Simplicity, have *nothing surprizing* in the Thought, when divested of that *Elegance of Expression,* and *Harmony of Numbers,* with which it is cloathed."—From these extraordinary *Premises,* we are naturally prepared to expect his *Conclusion,* "that CATULLUS and PARNEL are his *favourite* Authors!"[160]

158. The remark occurs in Dryden's "A Discourse Concerning the Original and Progress of Satire" (1693), in the course of a review of the deficiencies of modern epic poetry in comparison to the works of Homer and Virgil: "'Tis true, he [Milton] runs into a flat of thought, sometimes for a hundred lines together, but 'tis when he is got into a track of scripture" (*John Dryden: Selected Criticism,* eds. James Kinsley and George Parfitt [Oxford: Oxford University Press, 1970], p. 218).

159. See above, pp. 32–49.

160. Hume, *Essays,* pp. 191–96.

of the greatest Critics in Antiquity, himself conspicuous in the *sublime* and *simple* Manner, hath born this Testimony to the Writings of Mo-ses and St. Paul.[P] And by Parity of Reason we must conclude, that had he been conversant with the other sacred Writers, his *Taste* and *Candour* would have allowed them the same Encomium. [385]

But we need not have Recourse to Authorities, for the Proof of the superior Weight and Dignity of the sacred Scriptures, in this great Quality. 'Tis evident to Demonstration from the following Circumstance. It hath been often observed, even by Writers of no mean Rank, that "the Scriptures suffer in their Credit by the *Disadvantage* of a *literal Version*, while other ancient Writings enjoy the *Advantage* of a *free* and *embellished Translation*." But in Reality these Gentlemen's Concern is ill-placed and groundless. For the Truth is, "That most other Writings are indeed *impaired* by a *literal Translation*; whereas, giving only a due Regard to the *Idioms* of different Languages, the sacred Writings when *literally translated*, are then in their full Perfection." Now this is an *internal* Proof, that in all other Writings there is a Mixture of *local, relative, exterior* Ornament; which is often lost in the Transfusion from one Language to another. But the *internal* Beauties which depend not on the *particular* Construction of *Tongues*, no *Change* of *Tongue* can destroy. Hence the *Bible-Composition* preserves its native Beauty and Strength, [386] alike in every Language, by the sole Energy of unadorned Phrase, natural Images, weight of Sentiment, and *great Simplicity*.

'Tis in this Respect, like a rich Vein of *Gold*, which, under the severest Trials of Heat, Cold, and Moisture, retains its original *Weight* and *Splendor*, without either Loss or Alloy; while baser Metals are corrupted by Earth, Air, Water, Fire, and assimilated to the various Elements thro' which they pass.

This Circumstance then may be justly regarded as sufficient to vindicate the Composition of the sacred Scriptures; as it is at once their chief *Excellence*, and greatest *Security*. 'Tis their *Excellence*, as it renders

---

p. Longinus.[161]

161. Longinus, *On the Sublime*, IX.9. The genuineness of these scriptural references had been questioned even in the eighteenth century.

them *intelligible* and *useful to all*; 'tis their *Security*, as it prevents their being disguised by the *false* and *capricious* Ornaments of *vain* or *weak* *Translators*.

We may safely appeal to Experience and Fact for the Confirmation of these Remarks on the superior Simplicity, Utility, and Excellence of the Style of holy Scripture. Is there any Book in the World, so perfectly adapted to all Capacities? that contains such *sublime* and *exalting* Precepts, convey'd [387] in such an *artless* and *intelligible* Strain? that can be read with such Pleasure and Advantage, by the lettered *Sage* and the unlettered *Peasant?* To whom then would the noble Writer send Mankind for religious and moral Instruction? To the divine PLATO, it may be supposed; or, more probably, to the *inraptured* Strains of PHILOCLES and THEOCLES.[162] And sure, Mankind must reap much Instruction and Advantage from the *puffed Epithets* and *fustian Style* of a *philosophical Romance*. We may reasonably hope indeed, soon to see (nay, do we not already see?) the happy Effects of this high Discipline. For in Fact, the noble Writer's *Characteristics* are now the standing *Oracle* in the *Office*, the *Shop*, nay, as I am informed, sometimes even in the *Cobler's Stall*. We need not wonder therefore, that in these new Habitations of *Taste, sublimed Phrase*, and *abstruse Philosophy*, the *simple* Strains of the Gospel are *damned* and *discarded*.

To return then to the noble Writer's Comparison (if indeed we have departed from it) these united Observations may convince us, that the only circumstance in Painting, which can with any Propriety be compared to literary *Style*, is that of [388] *colouring*. And on this principle we may farther confirm all that hath been said on the superior Excellence of the *simple* Manner. For 'tis well known, and the noble Writer knew it, that while the Masters in this fine Art confined the Pencil to the genuine Forms of *Grace* and *Greatness*, and only superadded to these the temperate Embellishments of a *chastised* and *modest* colouring, the Art grew towards its *Perfection:* but no sooner was their Attention turned from *Truth, Simplicity*, and *Design*, to the gaudy Decorations of a rich

162. Both persons in Shaftesbury's dialogue "The Moralists" (Shaftesbury, *Characteristicks*, vol. II, pp. 101–247).

and luscious *Colouring*, than their Credit declined with their Art: and the experienced Eye, which contemplates the *old* Pictures with *Admiration*, surveys the *modern* with Indifference or *Contempt*.

To conclude. We see there are two Kinds of *Composition*, essentially opposed to each other. The *one* turns the Attention on *itself*; the *other*, on *the Truths it conveys*. The first may be justly compared to a *Sun-Beam play-ing* on the *Surface* of the Water, which *attracts* and *dazzles* the Beholder's Eye by its own *useless Splendor*. The last is like a *Sun-Beam* darting to the Bottom; which, while itself is *unseen*, or [389] *unobserved, communicates* its brightness, and *illumines every Object on which it falls*.

How far the *first* of these may belong to the noble Writer, let oth-ers determine. 'Tis sufficient to have proved, that the *last* is the *unvaried* Style and Manner of the *sacred Scriptures*.

SECTION IX

It would have been strange, had his Lordship emptied so much of his Gall on *Christianity*, without bestowing a Share on its *Ministers*. It may therefore be expected, that something should be said on his Treatment of the *English Clergy*.

So far as his Spirit of Satire may have been provoked by the persecut-ing and intolerant Principles of some of the *Clergy* in his Time, 'tis highly commendable. It matters not in what Rank, Order, or Profession, the En-emies of *Freedom* may appear. What shape or Pretence soever they may assume, 'tis a work of true Charity to stigmatize and disgrace them, as the Enemies of Mankind.

But it appears too evidently, that the noble Writer's *Spleen* arose from another Foundation. For his Satire is not so often [390] pointed against them, as being the *Enemies of Freedom*, as the *Friends of Christianity*. With a view of disgracing them in this Regard, he hath ridiculed and abused their *Writings*, their *Preaching*, and even their *Persons*. It will only be necessary to select a few Instances of this kind, from an infinite Number; in all which, the *Delicacy* of the *Raillery* is so *conspicuous*, as to need *no Illustration*.

In his *Soliloquy*, he hath paid his Compliments to the *Writings* of the *Clergy*, under the Title of "Candidates for Authorship of the sanctify'd

Kind." "These, he says, may be termed a sort of *Pseudo-Ascetics,* who can have no real Converse either with themselves or with Heaven." "And although the Books of this sort, by a common Idiom, are called *good Books,* the Authors for certain are a *sorry Race*"—"*A Saint-Author, of all Men, least values Politeness.*—He is above the Consideration of that, which in a narrow Sense, we call *Manners:* nor is he apt to examine any other Faults, than those which he calls *Sins.*"q [391]

Thus he deals with the Clergy, when they are *dull* enough to write *seriously* on the most *interesting Subjects.* But if any of the Order happens to fall into a gayer turn of Composition, the Charge is renewed under another Form. Then, "the *burlesque* Divinity grows mightily in vogue; and the cry'd up Answers to Heterodox Discourses are generally such as are written in Drollery—*Joy* to the Reverend Authors, who can afford to be thus gay, and condescend to correct us in this *Lay-Wit.*"r

Their *Preaching* is another standing Subject of Derision: and ridiculed they must be, whether they *divide* their Discourse, or *divide it not.* If the first, then the following stroke of Raillery is prepar'd for them: "Come we now (as our *authentic Rhetoricians* express themselves) to our *second Head.*"s If the latter, then "our religious *Pastors* have changed their Manner of distributing to us their *Spiritual Food*—they have run into the more savory way of *learned Ragout* and *Medley.* The elegant Court-Divine exhorts in *Miscel*[392]*lany,* and is ashamed to bring his *two's* and *three's* before a fashionable Assembly.*"t

The *Defenders* of *Christianity* are baited in their Turn. "For Example, let a *zealous Divine* and *flaming Champion* of our *Faith,* when inclined to shew himself in Print, make choice of some *tremendous Mystery* of

q. *Solil.* Part i. § 1.[163]
r. *Misc.* v. c. 2.[164]
s. *Misc.* ii. c. 3.[165]
t. *Misc.* ii. c. 3.[166]
163. Ibid., vol. I, p. 104.
164. Ibid., vol. III, pp. 178–79.
165. Ibid., p. 70.
166. Ibid.

Religion, opposed heretofore by some *damnable Heresiarch*"—"A Ring is made, and Readers gather in Abundance. Every one takes Party and encourages his own Side. *This shall be my Champion!—This Man for my Money!—Well hit on our Side!—Again, a good Stroke!—There he was even with him!—Have at him next Bout!—Excellent Sport!*"ᵘ

The same *familiar Elegance* of Composition, joyned with a surprising Effort in the noble Writer's *own Sublime,* runs through the following Paragraph; where he compares a Controversy in *Divinity,* to a Match at *Foot-Ball.* "So have I known a *crafty Glazier,* in time of Frost, procure a FOOT-BALL, to draw into the Street the *emulous Chiefs* of the *robust* [393] *Youth.* The *tumid Bladder* bounds at every KICK, *bursts* the *withstanding* CASEMENTS, the *Chassys, Lanterns,* and all the *brittle vitreous* WARE. The *Noise* of *Blows* and *Out-cries* fills the WHOLE NEIGHBOURHOOD; and the Ruins of Glass cover the *stony Pavements:* till the *bloated battering Engine, subdued* by Force of FOOT and FIST, and *yielding up its Breath* at many a *fatal* CRANNY, becomes lank and harmless, sinks in its Flight, and can no longer uphold the Spirit of the contending Parties."ʷ

Not content with these *severe Strokes* of Raillery, the noble Writer prepares a more deadly Blow at the Clergy; even no less than ruining their Fortunes among the *Fair-Sex.* And here the discerning Reader will readily guess, that his Ridicule must be needs levelled at their *Persons.* He introduces, or drags in, the Story of OTHELLO and DESDEMONA; represents the one as a *miraculous* Story-teller, the other as a *credulous* Hearer. He then adds, "But why the Poet, amongst his *Greek* Names, should have chosen one which denoted the Lady *superstitious,* I can't [394] imagine; unless, as Poets are sometimes Prophets too, he should figuratively, under this dark Type, have represented to us, that, about a hundred Years after his time, the Fair Sex of this Island should, by *other monstrous Tales,* be so seduced, as to turn their Favour chiefly on the *Tale-Tellers;* and change

u. *Misc.* i. c. 2.¹⁶⁷
w. *Misc.* i. c. 2.¹⁶⁸
167. Shaftesbury, *Characteristicks,* vol. III, p. 9.
168. Ibid., p. 11.

their natural Inclination for fair, *candid,* and *courteous Knights,* into a Passion for *a mysterious Race of black Enchanters.*"ˣ

I cannot think this *elegant* Passage deserves a particular Reply. 'Tis supposed, the noble Writer designed it only as a Proof, "That the *Saint-Author* of all Men *least values Politeness;*"¹⁷⁰ as a Proof how *incapable* he was of *violating his own Rule,* or exercising any Degree of "that *gross* sort of *Raillery,* which is so *offensive in good Company.*"ʸ

Indeed all the *delicate* Paragraphs here cited are much of the same nature; and afford an undeniable Proof, how great a Master his Lordship was, in the true *refined* Manner of *Attic* Wit. I shall only add, that if, according to the noble Writer's projected Scheme of Confutation, the [395] *English Clergy* should ever be *baited* in the way of *Puppet-show* at *Bart'l'mew-Fair;*¹⁷² I would recommend the above Passages, with many parallel ones in the *Characteristics,* to the Managers of the *Drama;* as being admirably suited to the *Genius* of their *wooden* DROLE, whether he should chuse to *swagger* in the *Sock,* or *strut* in the *Buskin.*¹⁷³

Were the Clergy disposed to return these Compliments *in Kind,* it may be questioned whether his Lordship's Admirers would acquit them of *coarse Manners.* But however some of that Body may *blindly hate,* and others as *blindly admire* the Author of the *Characteristics;* yet the best and wisest of the Profession, so far as I have been able to learn from their Conversation, would probably rather chuse to return his Salutations in the following Manner.

Notwithstanding the superior Airs of *Contempt,* which on all Occasions your-Lordship is pleased to assume, we cannot think you of such

x. *Solil.* Part ii. § 3.¹⁶⁹
y. *Wit. and H.* Part i. § 2.¹⁷¹

169. Shaftesbury, *Characteristicks,* vol. I, p. 214. The name Desdemona derives from the Greek word δεισιδαιμονια, meaning "fear of the gods" or, more neutrally, "religious sentiment."

170. Ibid., p. 104.

171. Ibid., pp. 41–42.

172. In the early modern period a large fair was held in Smithfield on 24 August (St. Bartholomew's Day), characterized by carnal self-indulgence and burlesque puppet theater. Ben Jonson's *Bartholomew Fair* (1614) offers a satiric portrait of the fair and its activities.

173. In ancient Greece and Rome the sock was a light shoe worn by comic actors (*OED,* 3), the buskin a high thick-soled boot worn by tragic actors (*OED,* 2); used metonymically therefore for comedy and tragedy respectively.

Ability, as you seem to appear in your own Eyes: neither can we think this overweening Opinion of your self, this Disdain of all who adopt not your peculiar Tenets, is any Proof of real Wisdom, since yourself have taught us [396] to believe, "that as we grow *wiser,* we shall prove *less conceited*."[174] Though we scorn to *revile* you, yet we judge ourselves *well intitled* to tell you *the Truth* on every Subject. We regard, therefore, a fine *Imagination,* an extensive *Knowledge,* and a commanding *Judgment,* as three Qualities independent of each other. In the first, we think you *eminent*; in the second, considerable; in the last, we must be excused, if we think you *neither eminent nor considerable:* And on this Account we can allot you *no high Rank,* in the Scale of *true Genius.* Suitable to this, your *Taste* in *Arts* is much superior to your *Talents* for *Philosophy.* The only *Chain* of *Reasoning* you have exhibited, is found in your *Enquiry concerning Virtue:* nor is even this fastened to the *Throne of Truth,* but hangs trembling from a *shadowy* and *aerial* Fabric, blown up by a sportive Imagination. You have indeed obtained the Character of an *original Writer* in *Philosophy:* how little you deserve this must needs be known to all who are versed in the *Greek Schools*; for thence the *rational Part* of your System is chiefly drawn. What you *borrow,* you often *embellish,* [397] sometimes *disguise,* never *strengthen:* but when you attempt to become *original,* you only convince us how ill qualified you are for such a Task. Accordingly, we find in the general turn of your Writings, *meagre Sentiments* studiously adorned by a *glare* of *Words,* and a *waste* of *Imagery:* with these you amuse the common Reader; like the unqualified Painter, who, unable to reach the Beauties of a just and *vigorous Expression,* covers a lifeless Figure with *gaudy Draperies.* And we cannot but think, that had you studied the Writings of that great and excellent Man whom you so weakly deride,[y] your Volumes, whatever they had lost in *Bulk,* would have gained in *weight* and *splendor.*

y. *Mr.* Locke. *See* Advice, &c. Part iii. § 1.[175]

174. Shaftesbury, *Characteristicks,* vol. I, p. 224.

175. Brown refers to Shaftesbury, *Characteristicks,* vol. I, p. 186 where, in the course of an attack on the rebarbative language of modern philosophy, Shaftesbury quotes, more or less accurately and as a sample from "a renown'd modern Philosopher," the following passage from Locke, *An Essay Concerning Human Understanding,* II.xiii.22: "For I desire any one so to divide a solid Body, of any dimension he pleases, as to make it possible for the solid Parts to move up and down freely every way within the bounds of that Superficies, if there be not left in it a void space, as big as the least part into which he has divided the said solid Body."

With regard to the Buffoonries, which you have occasionally exercised on Christianity, in what you call "your Random Essays;"[176] they are so much below the Character of *the Philosopher*, that it is matter of Surprize to us, that you could think they can become the *Man of Wit*. It is true, among those whom you most despise, the *mere Vulgar*, they have gained you the Character of an *inimitable* Author; [398] among Readers of that Rank "who are ready to swallow any low Drollery or Jest;"[177] among those whom you have elsewhere described, "who, while they pretend to such a Scrutiny of other Evidences, are the readiest to take the Evidence of the greatest Deceivers in the World, *their own Passions.*"[z] But whatever these Passages may be in their *Consequences*, we cannot but think them, in their own *Nature*, even *contemptible*. For, to use your own *Attic* Phrase, "to *twitch, snap, snub* up, or *banter*, to torture *Sentences* and *Phrases*, and turn *a few Expressions into Ridicule*, is not sufficient to constitute what is properly esteemed *a Writer.*"[a] On this Account we look upon these boasted Passages in your Book, to be of that Kind which are calculated only "*to create Diversion* to those who look no further;"[b] and in which, as you elsewhere observe, "the most *confused Head*, if *fraught with a little Invention*, and provided with *Common-Place-Book Learning*, may exert itself to as much Advantage, as the most *orderly* and *well-settled Judgment.*"[c] We cannot therefore express any [399] Esteem either for the *Scurrilities* of the *coarse* JESTER, or the *trim Delicacy* and *Self-Admiration* of the *literary* NARCISSUS.

But, *my Lord*, there lies a heavier Charge against you, than that of *bad Writing*. We mean, the *Indecency* and *Immorality* of *your Conduct*,

z. *Mor.* P. ii. § 1.[178]
a. *Misc.* v. c. 2.[179]
b. *Misc.* i. c. 1.[180]
c. *Ibid.*[181]
176. Shaftesbury, *Characteristicks*, vol. III, p. 7.
177. A misquotation of Shaftesbury, *Characteristicks*, vol. I, p. 8: "The Vulgar, indeed, may swallow any sordid Jest, any mere Drollery or Buffoonery; but it must be a finer and truer Wit which takes with the Men of Sense and Breeding."
178. Shaftesbury, *Characteristicks*, vol. II, pp. 130–31.
179. Ibid., vol. III, p. 167.
180. Ibid., p. 6.
181. Ibid., p. 5.

in your *Manner* of attacking *Christianity*. You would be thought a *Lover* of your *Country*; yet you pour *Contempt* upon its *Laws* and *Institutions*. You allow the Propriety of a *religious Establishment*; yet you take every Occasion to *deride* it. You contend for a *public Leading* in Religion; yet you perpetually insinuate, that Mankind are *led by the Nose*. You say, "The *Public* ought not to be *insulted to its Face*;" yet your Writings are one *continued Insult* upon its *Opinions*. Our excellent and unrivaled Constitution allows a perfect *Freedom* of *Enquiry*; had you then argued *ingenuously* and *fairly* against *Christianity*, without attempting *Ridicule*; whatever Opinion we might have entertained of your *Head,* we might at least have thought favourably of your *Heart*. But in direct Opposition to this Rule, you always *ridicule*, scarce [400] ever *argue*; you endeavour to instil *illegal Opinions*, without bringing any Evidence to support either their *Usefulness* or *Truth:* You give these *crude Buffoonries* to the World in *Print*; and is not this *insulting the Public to its Face?*—In this Instance, we must think you *a bad Citizen*; and to be ranked among those, whom a Writer, by no Means prejudiced in Favour of Religion, thus justly stigmatizes: "Who, I hardly know for what End, have written against the Religion of their Country; and without pretending to substitute any thing better, or more practicable, in its Place, would deprive us of our happy Establishment, merely, as it should seem, for the Pleasure of pulling down and doing Mischief."[e] Besides this, *my Lord,* we must take the Liberty to say, that you betray such frequent Marks of *Insincerity* and *designed Misrepresentation* in your Treatment of *Christianity,* as but ill consists with that *Reverence* which you owe to *Truth* and to *yourself*; such as becomes not *a* MAN, much less a *Man* whom the Public consent hath distinguished by the Title of RIGHT HONOURABLE. [401]

What your particular Motives may have been to this Treatment of *Christianity,* you best know. The most *excusable Temptation* to this strange Conduct, that we can assign, must have been the *natural Prevalence* of *Spleen*. For, as you observe, "all *splenetic* People have a necessary Propensity to Criticism and Satire."—"The Spirit of Satire

---

e. *Enquiry into* Homer's *Life and Writings,* § 6.[182]
182. Thomas Blackwood, *An Enquiry into the Life and Writings of Homer* (1735), pp. 77–78.

rises with the *ill Mood*; and the chief Passion of Men thus *diseased* and thrown *out of good Humour,* is to find *Fault, censure, unravel, confound,* and leave nothing without *Exception* and *Controversy.*"f

Far be it from us to derogate from your *private Virtues*; tho' we cannot but wish, that in your Treatment of *Christianity,* you had given better Proofs of that *universal Charity,* which you so *warmly profess*; even while you are reviling *that Religion* where alone it is to be found.—There is another Circumstance, that sure the more humane Part of your Admirers would hesitate upon; we mean, that *extreme Contempt* you express for those you call the *mere Vulgar.* Your Regard seems solely centered in establishing your *peculiar System* among those you call "Men of *Fashion* and *Breeding*;" [402] while you give up *the Vulgar,* that is (to speak with due Reverence of the Works of God) the Bulk of your *Fellow-Creatures,* as a proper Prey to the supposed Delusions and Tyranny of those, whom you brand as the Enemies of Mankind. How this *Contempt* for the greatest Part of your *Species* can consist with true *Virtue* or *Charity,* we are at a Loss to comprehend. 'Tis certain, *Christianity* would have taught you otherwise. Nay, *my Lord,* a great *Roman,* as much your Superior in *Station,* as in *Genius* and *active Virtue,* would have told you, "that true Goodness extends itself to the *Multitude*; that Virtue is not disdainful or proud; but regards all Ranks of Men, and consults their Welfare; which it could not do, if it *despised the Vulgar.*"g *Christianity* hath nobly heightened this Principle; and recommends the *Weak,* the *Poor,* the *Ignorant,* as the proper Objects not only of our *Charity,* but *Instruction.* And however mortifying it may be to proud Minds, we must say, that we frequently meet with Men in the lower Ranks of Life, sometimes even in *Cities,* often in *Cottages,* who when [403] *instructed* in the Principles of true *Christianity,* are superior in *Knowledge, Worth,* and *Happiness,* to those who hold them in Contempt.

With Regard to your Treatment of *ourselves:* It gives us no Concern. For in one Word, Calumnies thrown on whole Bodies of Men,

f. *Misc.* ii. c. 3.[183]
g. Cicero, *Lael.*[184]
183. Shaftesbury, *Characteristicks,* vol. III, p. 68.
184. A summary of Cicero's arguments concerning friendship in *Laelius de Amicitia.*

are *unmeaning* and *self-confuted*. "You may therefore proceed in your Invectives; bestowing as free Language of that Kind, as your *Charity* and superior *Breeding* will permit. You may liberally deal your *courtly Compliments* and *Salutations* in what Dialect you think fit; since for our own Part, neither the the Names of *Bigots, Impostors, Pedants, Formalists, Gladiatorian Penmen, Flaming Champions of the Faith, Black Tribe,* or *Black Enchanters,*[h] will in the least scandalize us, while the Sentence comes only from *the Enemies of our Master.* On the contrary, we rather strive with ourselves to suppress whatever Vanity might naturally arise in us, from such Favour bestow'd. For whatever may, in the Bottom, be intended us, by such a Treatment, [404] 'tis impossible for us to term it other than *Favour*; since there are certain *Enmities,* which it will be ever esteemed a real Honour *to have merited.*"[i]

You have indeed wisely and artfully endeavoured to *intimidate* us from exposing the Folly of your *Insults* on *Religion* and *Christianity*; by representing such an Attempt as being in itself *Contemptible.* For thus you are pleased to speak: "It must be own'd, that when a Writer of any Kind is so *considerable* as to deserve the Labour and Pains of some *shrewd Heads* to refute him in Public, he may, in the Quality of *an Author,* be justly congratulated on that Occasion. 'Tis supposed necessarily, that he must have writ with some kind of *Ability* or *Wit.*"[k]

To obviate this Remark, is the only further Trouble we shall give your Lordship on the present Occasion. And here without any particular Application to yourself, we must beg Leave to offer the plain Reason why we think your Observation, however plausible and commonly received, is yet entirely groundless. Indeed, with regard to Writings of

---

h. Names bestowed on the English Clergy throughout the *Characteristics.*[185]

i. See *Misc.* v. c. 3.[186]

k. *Misc.* i. c. 2.

185. *Bigots*—Shaftesbury, *Characteristicks*, vol. II, pp. 71 and 124; *Impostors*—Shaftesbury, *Characteristicks*, vol. I, p. 94 (much less frequent than the noun "Imposture"); *Pedants*—a very common Shaftesburyan term of abuse, but see, e.g., Shaftesbury, *Characteristicks*, vol. I, p. 42, vol. II, p. 105, and vol. III, p. 10; *Formalists*—Shaftesbury, *Characteristicks*, vol. I, p. 9; *Gladiatorian Penmen*—Shaftesbury, *Characteristicks*, vol. III, p. 9; *Flaming Champions of the Faith*—Shaftesbury, *Characteristicks*, vol. III, pp. 8–9; *Black Tribe*—Shaftesbury, *Characteristicks*, vol. I, p. 214; *Black Enchanters*—Shaftesbury, *Characteristicks*, vol. I, p. 214.

186. Shaftesbury, *Characteristicks*, vol. III, p. 204.

mere *Speculation* or *Criticism,* which affect not the Happiness of [405] Mankind, "if Authors write ill they are despised" and forgotten. At least, as the *Satirist* observes, they ought to be so:[1] And on this Account, many Parts of the *Characteristics* will, probably, pass for ever *uncensured* by us.

But there are other Kinds of bad Writing, which will ever bid fair to *live* and be *admired.* We mean, such as *minister* to the *low Passions* and *Vices* of Mankind; among which, RIDICULE *on* RELIGION is of all others the most favourite Topic. And even where these Affections do not prevail, the generality of Men, thro' the Weakness of Nature, are easily misled in Matters even of the nearest Concernment, by *Sophistry* or *Buffoonry;* by a *Hint,* a *Sarcasm,* or an *Allusion.* Now in this Case, 'tis surely a proper and *rational,* tho' perhaps no *easy* Task, to *detect Misrepresentation,* and lead Mankind back again to the Paths of *Truth* and *Happiness.* For the Effects of *Ridicule* on the *Mind,* resemble those of *Venom* on the *Body;* which, [406] tho' struck into the Blood by a *puny Reptile,* may yet *demand,* nay even *baffle* the Power of the *strongest Medicines.* How then can you affirm that an Effect of this Kind "*implies* either *Ability* or *Wit,*" if *Buffoonry* and *Sophistry* can do the Business? And that they *may,* we have your Lordship's *full Acknowledgment;* for, to adopt and conclude with your own Expression, "In the same Manner as a *malicious* CENSURE, *craftily* worded and pronounced with *Assurance,* is apt to pass with Mankind for *shrewd* WIT; so a *virulent* (or a *visionary*) MAXIM, in *bold* Expressions, tho' without any *Justness* of Thought, is readily received for *true* PHILOSOPHY."[m]

FINIS

---

1. *Quel Demon vous irrite, & vous porte à medire?*
   Un Livre vous deplait: Qui vous force à le lire?
   Laissez mourir un Fat dans son Obscurité.
   Un Auteur ne peut il pourrir en Sureté?
   Boileau, Sat. ix.[187]

m. *Moralists,* P. ii. § 5.[188]

187. "What devil irritates you, and leads you to curse? A book displeases you; who obliges you to read it? Allow a conceited fool to die in his proper obscurity. Can't an author rot in peace?" (Boileau, *Satire* IX, ll. 87–90).

188. Shaftesbury, *Characteristicks,* vol. II, p. 181.

*An Estimate of the Manners
and Principles of the Times*
(1757)

* "Though built of Pontic pine, the daughter of a noble forest, and though you boast of your race and your useless name [yet the fearful sailor puts no faith in your gilded stern]" (Horace, *Odes*, I.xiv.11–13). In this poem Horace compares the Roman state, lately emerged from the tempest of civil wars into the relative calm of the principate of Augustus, to a battered ship in danger of being swept out to sea again. The epigraph therefore recalls a moment of Roman national danger relevant to the analysis of the predicament of the British state that Brown will advance in *An Estimate*.

AN

ESTIMATE

OF THE

MANNERS

AND

PRINCIPLES

OF THE

TIMES

By the AUTHOR of
ESSAYS on the CHARACTERISTICS, &c.

Quamvis Pontica Pinus,
Silvae Filia nobilis,
Jactes & Genus & Nomen inutile.*

The Second Edition.

LONDON,
Printed for L. DAVIS, and C. REYMERS, in *Holborn*;
Printers to the ROYAL SOCIETY.
MDCCLVII.

ADVERTISEMENT

The *leading Principles*, which run thro' the following *Estimate*, make a small Part of a much more extensive Work, planned on the general Subject of *Manners*. In the mean time, the Writer thought it not amiss to offer his Sentiments on the present State and Situation of his Country, at a *Crisis* so important and alarming.[1]

1. For an account of the domestic and international situation in 1757, see the "Introduction" (above, pp. xv–xvii).

Contents

PART III
Of the Sources of these Manners and Principles

PART I

A

DELINEATION

OF THE

RULING MANNERS

AND

PRINCIPLES

PART I

A

DELINEATION

OF

The RULING MANNERS and PRINCIPLES

SECT. I

The Design

Superficial, though zealous, Observers, think they see the Source of all our public Miscarriages in the particular and accidental Misconduct of Individuals. This is not much to be wondered at, because it is so easy a Solution. [12]

This pretence, too, is plausibly urged upon the People by profligate Scribblers, who find their Account in it. It is a sort of Compliment paid the Public, to persuade them, that they have no Share in the Production of these national Misfortunes.

But a candid and mature Consideration will convince us, that the Malady lies deeper than what is commonly suspected: and, on impartial Enquiry, it will probably be found springing, not from varying and incidental, but from permanent and established Causes.

It is the observation of the greatest of political Writers, that "it is by no means Fortune that rules the World: for this we may appeal to the *Romans,* who had a long Series of Prosperities, when they acted upon a

259

certain Plan; and an [13] uninterrupted Course of Misfortunes, when they conducted themselves upon another. There are general Causes, natural or moral, which operate in every State; which raise, support, or overturn it."*

Among all these various Causes, none perhaps so much contributes to raise or sink a Nation, as the Manners and Principles of its People. But as there never was any declining Nation, which had not Causes of Declension peculiar to itself, so it will require a minute Investigation into the lead[14]ing Manners and Principles of the present Times, to throw a just Light on the peculiar Causes of our calamitous Situation.

To delineate these Manners and Principles without Aggravation or Weakness, to unravel their Effects on the public State and Welfare, and to trace them to their real though distant Sources, is indeed a Task of equal Difficulty and Importance.

It may be necessary therefore to apologise even for the Attempt: as being supposed to lie beyond the Sphere of him who makes it. To this it can only be replied, that a common Eye may *possibly* discover a lurking Rock or Sand, while the able and experienced Mariners overlook the Danger, through their Attention to the Helm, the Sails, or Rigging. [15]

He will be much mistaken, who expects to find here a Vein of undistinguishing and licentious Satire. To rail at the Times at large, can serve no good Purpose; and generally ariseth from a Want of Knowledge or a Want of Honesty. There never was an Age or Nation that had not Virtues and Vices peculiar to itself: And in some Respects, perhaps, there is no Time nor Country delivered down to us in Story, in which a wise Man would so much wish to have lived, as in our own.

Notwithstanding this, our Situation seems most dangerous: We are rolling to the Brink of a Precipice that must destroy us.

---

* "Ce n'est pas la Fortune qui domine le Monde: on peut le demander aux Romains, qui eurent une suite continuelle des Prosperités quand ils se gouvernerent sur un certain Plan, & une suite non interrompue de revers lors qu'ils se conduisirent sur un autre. Il y a des Causes generales, soit morales, soit physiques, qui agissent dans chaque Monarchie, l'elevent, la maintiennent, ou la precipitent."— *Grandeur,* &c. *des Romains,* c. 18.[2]

2. Montesquieu, *Considérations,* p. 235.

At such a Juncture, to hold up a true Mirroir to the Public, and let the Nation see *themselves* as the Authors of their own [16] Misfortunes, cannot be a very popular Design. But as the Writer is not sollicitous about private Consequences, he can with the greater Security adopt the Words of an honest and sensible Man.

> Most commonly, such as palliate Evils, and represent the State of Things in a sounder Condition than truly they are, do thereby consult best for themselves, and better recommend their own Business and Pretensions in the World: But he who, to the utmost of his Skill and Power, speaks the Truth, where the Good of his King and Country are concerned, will be most esteemed by Persons of Virtue and Wisdom: And to the Favour and Protection of such, these Papers are committed.* [17]

SECT. II

Of the Spirit of Liberty

Before we enumerate the concurrent Causes of our present Misfortunes and Decline; let us, by way of Contrast, muster the few remaining Virtues we have left; to which, in part, it is owing, that our Misfortunes are not heavier, and our Decline more rapid.

Among these, the first and most important, is the Spirit of Liberty. This, happily, still subsists among us: Not indeed in its genuine Vigour; for then, it would work its genuine effects. Yet, that the Love of Liberty is not extinguished, appears from the *united Voice* of a *divided People*. It still animates their Conversation, and invigorates their Addresses: tho' [18] in their Conduct it appears no more. But it is remarkable, that in Proportion as this Spirit hath grown weak in *Deeds,* it hath gained Strength in *Words*; and of late run out, into unbounded License.

This, however, appears beyond a Doubt: that we all wish to continue free; tho' we have not the Virtue to secure our Freedom. The Spirit of Liberty

---

* Dr. *Davenant,* on Trade.[3]

3. Charles Davenant, "On the Protection and Care of Trade," in Davenant, *Works,* vol. I, p. 459.

is now struggling with the *Manners* and *Principles*, as formerly it struggled with the *Tyrants* of the Time. But the Danger is now greater, because the Enemy is *within*; working secretly and securely, and destroying all those *internal Powers*, from which alone an effectual Opposition can arise.

Wherever this Spirit of Liberty subsists in its full Vigour, the Vigilance and Power of impotent Governors are vain: A Nation can neither be surprised nor com[19]pelled into Slavery: When this is extinguished, neither the Virtue nor Vigilance of Patriots can save it. In the Reign of JAMES the Second, *Great Britain* was free, tho' a despotic Prince was on the Throne: At the Time when CESAR fell, *Rome* was still inslaved, tho' the Tyrant was no more.

This great Spirit hath produced more full and complete Effects in our own Country, than in any known Nation that ever was upon Earth. It appears indeed, from a Concurrence of Facts too large to be produced here, that whereas it hath been ingrafted by the Arts of Policy in other Countries, it shoots up here as from its natural Climate, Stock, and Soil. From this Distinction, if laid in Nature, two or three Consequences will fairly arise. Its Effects must, of course, be more vigorous [20] and full. It's Destruction, by external Violence, will probably be no more than temporary. It's chief Danger must arise from such Causes, as may poison the Root; or attack, and destroy the natural Spirit itself: These must be such Causes, as can steal upon, and subdue the *Mind:* that is, they must be "some Degeneracy or Corruption of the Manners and Principles of the People."[4]

SECT. III

Of the Spirit of Humanity

Let us now trace the Spirit of Liberty through such of its Effects, as are not yet destroyed by opposite Principles and Manners.

The first that occurs, is *Humanity.* By this, is not meant that Smoothness and refined Polish of external Manners, by which the present Age

---

4. Not apparently a quotation from another work, but for a parallel passage, cf., e.g., Philip Skelton, *Ophiomaches: or, Deism Revealed* (1749), p. 399. Brown occasionally uses inverted commas for emphasis rather than to indicate the presence of a quotation.

affects to be distinguished: [21] for this, it is apprehended, will belong to another Class. By *Humanity*, therefore, is meant, "that Pity for Distress, that Moderation in limiting Punishments by their proper Ends and Measures, by which this Nation hath always been distinguished."

The Lenity of our Laws in capital Cases; our Compassion for convicted Criminals; even the general Humanity of our Highwaymen and Robbers, compared with those of other Countries; these are concurrent Proofs, that the Spirit of Humanity is natural to our Nation.

The many noble Foundations for the Relief of the Miserable and the Friendless; the large annual Supplies from voluntary Charities to these Foundations; the frequent and generous Assistance given to the Unfortunate, who cannot be admitted into these [22] Foundations; all these are such indisputable Proofs of a national Humanity, as it were the highest Injustice not to acknowledge and applaud.

SECT. IV

Of the civil Administration of Justice

Another Virtue, and of the highest Consequence, as it regards the immediate and private Happiness of Individuals, yet left among us, is the pure Administration of Justice, as it regards private Property.

Many Causes may be assigned, for the Continuance of this public Blessing. The Spirit of Liberty and Humanity beget a Spirit of Equity, where no contrary Passion interferes: The Spirit of Commerce, now predominant, begets a kind of regulated Selfishness, which tends at once to the Increase and Preservation of Property. The Difficulty of corrupting Juries under the [23] Checks of their present Establishment, in most Cases prevents the very Attempt. And the long-continued Example of a great Person on the Seat of Equity,[5] hath diffused an uncorrupt Spirit through the inferior Courts, and will shine to the latest Posterity.

---

5. I.e., the office of Lord Chancellor, which was held by Philip Yorke (1690–1764), first earl of Hardwicke, from 1737 to 1756, when he resigned his office to accompany his friend and ally the Duke of Newcastle into opposition (cf. above, p. 2, n. *).

SECT. V

Of the Ruling Manners of the Times

Having made this prefatory Estimate of those remaining Manners which may demand Esteem and Applause, let us now proceed to the ruling Manners of the Times; from which this Age and Nation derives its present and particular Complexion.

It may be necessary to remark, that this designed Estimate extends not to the comparative Excellence of Manners and Prin[24]ciples, considered in every View, and in all their Variety of near and remote Effects. It relates not to the immediate Happiness or Misery, which Individuals, Families, or Nations, may derive from the Force of prevailing Principles and Manners. These Effects branch out into an Infinity of intricate Combinations, which cannot be comprehended in the present, but will make a material Part of some future Enquiry. This Estimate, therefore, confines itself to such Consequences only, as affect the *Duration* of the *public State:* So that the leading Question will be, "How far the present ruling Manners and Principles of this Nation may tend to its Continuance or Destruction."

In Consequence of this Restriction, the Manners and Principles of the common People will scarce find a Place in the Account. For though the Sum total of a Na[25]tions immediate Happiness must arise, and be estimated, from the Manners and Principles of the Whole; yet the Manners and Principles of those who *lead,* not of those who *are led*; of those who *govern,* not of those who *are governed*; of those, in short, who *make* Laws or *execute* them, will ever determine the Strength or Weakness, and therefore the Continuance or Dissolution, of a State.

For the blind Force or Weight of an ungoverned Multitude can have no steady nor rational Effect, unless some *leading Mind* rouse it into Action, and *point* it to it's proper *End:* without this, it is either a *brute* and random *Bolt,* or a *lifeless Ball* sleeping in the *Cannon:* It depends on some superior *Intelligence,* to give it both *Impulse* and *Direction.*

Indeed, were the *People* remarkably corrupt, they might properly make a Part [26] of this Enquiry: But in most of those important Circumstances to which this Estimate refers, they are in general much more irreproachable than their Superiors in Station; especially, if we except the lower Ranks of those who live in great Towns. It will therefore be unnecessary to mark the Character of their Principles or Manners, unless where they appear evidently poisoned by the Example or other Influence of the higher Ranks in Life.

Now the slightest Observation, if attended with Impartiality, may convince us, that the Character of the Manners of this Age and Nation, is by no means that of *abandoned Wickedness* and *Profligacy*. This Degree of Degeneracy, indeed, is often imputed to the Times: But, to what Times hath it *not* been imputed? Present Objects are naturally magnified to the hu[27]man Eye, while remote ones, though larger in Dimensions, vanish into nothing. Hence the Speculative and Virtuous, in every Age, confining their Views to their own Period, have been apt to aggravate its Manners into the highest Degree of Guilt; to *satyrize,* rather than *describe*; to throw their respective Times into one dark Shade of *Horror,* rather than mark their peculiar *Colour* and *Complexion*.

Here, a large Field of Comparison and Debate would open, were it necessary or even expedient to enter upon it. We might cast our Eye upon the Manners of ROME, CARTHAGE, and many other States, in their last declining Period; where we should behold such tragic Scenes of Cruelty, Impiety, and Oppression, as would confound the most sanguine Advocate for the Manners of Antiquity. But, in Truth, [28] there can be no Occasion for this Display of *Profligacy:* For if the previous Estimate, already given, be just; if the Spirit of *Liberty, Humanity,* and *Equity,* be in a *certain Degree* yet left among us, some of the most essential Foundations of abandoned Wickedness and Profligacy can have no Place: For these are *Servility, Cruelty,* and *Oppression.* How far we may be from this last Period of Degeneracy, it were Presumption to affirm: At present, it is certain, we are not arrived at it. Whenever this fatal Time approaches, it will come distinguished by its proper and peculiar Characters; and whoever shall estimate such Times, will find himself under the same Circumstance with the great Historian, who, in the profligate Period of declining ROME, tells us he had nothing to relate, but "false Accusations, bloody Proscriptions, treacherous Friendships, [29] and the Destruction of the Innocent."*

---

* "Saeva jussa, continuas accusationes, fallaces amicitias, perniciem innocentium." *Tacit. Annal.* l. iv.[6]

6. Tacitus, *Annals*, IV.33.

This, we may truly affirm, is far from the Character of the Manners of our Times: which, on a fair Examination, will probably appear to be that of a *"vain, luxurious,* and *selfish* EFFEMINACY."

This will be evident from a simple Enumeration of acknowledged Facts: many of them indeed, in Appearance, too trite to merit Notice, and too trifling for Rebuke; were they not, in their Tendency, as fatal to the Stability of a Nation, as Maxims and Manners more apparently flagitious.

As the first Habits of Infancy and Youth commonly determine the Character of the [30] Man, we might trace the Effeminacy of modern Manners, even to the unwholesome Warmth of a Nursery. As soon as the puny Infant is suffered to peep from this Fountain of *Weakness* and Disease, he is confirmed in the Habits already contracted, by a mistaken Tenderness and Care. The "School Boy's Satchel, and shining Morning-Face,"[7] once the Characteristic of the Age itself, are now only to be seen among the Sons of Villagers and Peasants; while the Youth of Quality and Fortune is wrapt up from the wholesome Keenness of the Air: And thus becomes incapable of enduring the natural Rigours of his own Climate.

'Tis odds, indeed, but the Prevalence of Fashion places him in some public School, where the learned Languages are taught: And, to do Justice to the Times, the most considerable among these Semi[31]naries were never more ably supplied than at present. But whatever be the Master's Ability, the Scholar's can in general reach no farther than to *Words*;[8] this first Stage of Education, therefore, can only be preparatory to a higher; without which, the other is defeated of its Purpose.

Here, then, lies an essential Defect in modern Education. The Pupil is not carried on from *Words* to *Things*. The *Universities*, where the Principles of *Knowledge* should be imbibed, are growing daily thinner of young Men of Quality and Fortune. Instead of being initiated in *Books*, where the Wisdom of Ages lies reposed, our untutored Youth are carried into the *World*; where the ruling Objects that catch the Imagination, are the Sallies of Folly or of Vice. [32]

7. *As You Like It,* II.vii.145–46.
8. Cf. Pope, *Dunciad,* IV.149–50.

Thus like *Plants* hastily removed from their first Bed, and exposed to the Inclemencies of an unwholesome Air, without the Intervention of a higher and more enlarged *Nursery,* where stronger Shoots might be obtained, our rising Youth are checked in their *first Growths,* and either *die away* into Ignorance, or, at most, become *Dwarfs* in Knowledge.

But here, it must not be disguised; that an Abuse, through Time, hath insensibly crept upon the *Universities* themselves, and greatly impaired their Use and Credit. The public Fountains of Instruction are at length dried up; and the *Professorships,* founded as the Means of general Instruction, degenerated into gainful *Sine-cures.*[9] Instead of these, where, by a proper Choice, every Department would naturally be filled with Ability in its respective Science; the *private* Lectures of *College-Tutors* have usurped [33] and occupied their Place. Thus the great Lines of Knowledge are broken, and the Fragments retailed at all Adventures, by *every Member* of a College, who chuseth to erect himself into a *Professor of every Science.* What can be the Consequence of this Practice, but a *partial* and *superficial Instruction?* 'Tis true, there are in this Sphere, who would do Honour to the highest Academical Station: But what an Accession of Lustre, Fame, and Knowledge, would our Universities receive, were these *few,* now confined to the narrow Sphere of *particular* Colleges, ordained and *appointed* to *illuminate* the *whole.*

Neither would it reflect any Dishonour on our Universities, if the few young Men of Fashion yet found there, were laid under the same Restraints of moral and literary Discipline, with those of inferior Quality. [34]

The next Error that presents itself to Observation, is that of sending our ignorant Youth abroad.[10] A Mind stored with Taste and Knowledge,

---

9. For later similar censure of the University of Oxford, cf. Smith, *Wealth of Nations,* p. 761 and Gibbon, *Autobiographies,* pp. 70–73. However, the recent history of the University finds that this strain of criticism "stands up neither to the evidence left by individual undergraduates of their studies nor to the surviving records in college archives" (*The History of the University of Oxford: Volume V The Eighteenth Century,* eds. L. S. Sutherland and L. G. Mitchell [Oxford: Oxford University Press, 1986], p. 476).

10. The practice of including a period of travel on the continent to finish the education of a young man—the "Grand Tour"—had by 1757 begun to be criticized as merely an expensive opportunity for debauchery. Whereas Richard Lassels had

will indeed naturally refine that Taste, and increase that Knowledge, by seeing and *judging* of foreign Countries. For thus he acquires a large Addition of new Experiences and Examples, which may confirm or rectify his prior Observations. On the contrary, we may affirm, with Truth, that no Circumstance in Education can more surely tend to strengthen Effeminacy and Ignorance, than the present premature, and indigested *Travel.* For as the uninstructed Youth must needs meet with a Variety of Example, good and bad, vile and praise-worthy, as his Manners are childish, and his Judgment crude, he will naturally imbibe what is most consentaneous with his puerile Habits. Thus, while Wisdom and Virtue can find no Place [35] in him, every Foreign Folly, Effeminacy, or Vice, meeting with a correspondent Soil, at once take Root and flourish.

But suppose him *not* of that Rank or Fortune, which may demand or admit of the grand Tour; he is then brought up to *London,* and initiated in the Pleasures of the Metropolis. Here then let us view him, inspired with every fashionable Ambition; while we take an impartial Estimate of those Amusements, or rather Employments, which attract the Attention of the Town, and form the Genius and Character of the present and rising Generation.

The first and capital Article of Town-Effeminacy is that of *Dress:* which, in all its Variety of modern Excess and Ridicule, is too low for serious Animadversion. Yet in this, must every Man of every Rank and Age employ his Mornings, who pretends to keep *good Company.* The wisest, the most [36] virtuous, the most polite, if defective in these exterior and unmanly Delicacies, are avoided as *low People,* whom *Nobody knows,* and with whom one is *ashamed to be seen.*

---

argued that the Tour instilled "the *Elements* and *alphabet* of breeding" (*The Voyage of Italy* [Paris, 1670], "Preface to the Reader"), in 1778 Johnson would grumble to Boswell: "Time may be employed to more advantage from nineteen to twenty-four almost in any way than in travelling; when you set travelling against mere negation, against doing nothing, it is better to be sure; but how much more would a young man improve were he to study during those years. . . . How little does travelling supply to the conversation of any man who has travelled?" (Boswell, *Life of Johnson,* p. 714).

How would he have been derided in the Days of ELIZABETH, when a great Queen rode on Horseback to *St. Paul's*, who should have foretold, that in less than two Centuries no Man of Fashion would cross the Street to Dinner, without the effeminate Covering and Conveyance of an *easy Chair?*

Yet thus accoutred, the modern Man of Fashion is *conveyed* to Company. Wherever he goes, he meets the same false Delicacy in all: Every Circumstance of modern Use conspires to sooth him into the Excess of Effeminacy: Warm Carpets are spread under his Feet; warm Hangings [37] surround him; Doors and Windows nicely jointed prevent the least rude Encroachment of the external Air.

Vanity lends her Aid to this unmanly Delicacy: Splendid Furniture, a sumptuous Side-board, a long Train of Attendants, an elegant and costly Entertainment, for which Earth, Air, and Seas, are ransacked,[11] the most expensive Wines of the Continent, the childish Vagaries of a whimsical Desert,[12] these are the supreme Pride of the Master, the Admiration or Envy of his Guests.

Luxury is not idle in her Province, but shares with her Sister Vanity, in the Labours of the Day. High Soups and Sauces, every Mode of foreign Cookery that can quicken Taste, and spur the lagging Appetite, is assiduously employed. The End of Eating is not the allaying of natural Hun[38]ger, but the Gratification of sordid and debasing Appetite. Hence the most inflaming Foods, not those which *nourish*, but those which *irritate*, are adopted; while the cool and temperate Diets that purify the Blood, are banished to inferior Tables. To this every Man of Taste now aspires, as to the true *sçavoir vivre*.[13]

Do you expect in these fashionable Meetings, to hear some Point of Morals, Taste in Arts or Literature, discoursed or canvassed? Alas! these are long since expelled from every modish Assembly. To speak any

11. For earlier, more positive accounts of the eighteenth-century global trade in luxuries, cf. *The Spectator* 69 (19 May 1711; *Spectator*, vol. I, pp. 292–96) and Pope, *The Rape of the Lock*, I.121–48.

12. A course of fruit or sweetmeats served at the end of a supper.

13. Knowledge of how to live.

thing that carries Weight and Importance, is an Offence against Good-breeding. The supreme Elegance is, to trifle agreeably.

But as Insipidity of Conversation is soon worn out, and as Intemperance in Wine is [39] not of the Character of refined Luxury; so, to prevent the Stagnation of Folly, some awakening Amusement is naturally sought for.

We read in ancient Story, that in the most polished Court of the most refined Period, a Reward was proclaimed to him, who should invent a new Pleasure.[14] This may justly be styled, the last wretched Effort of bungling and despairing Luxury.—The great Desideratum is at length found: A Pleasure which absorbs the whole Man; a Pleasure in which there is no Satiety; which cloys not by Use, but gains new Vigour from Enjoyment. The Vulgar only can need to be informed, that the Pleasure here alluded to, is that of GAMING. [40]

But as the present increasing Splendor of Dress, Equipage, Furniture, Entertainments, is enormously expensive; what can so naturally create a Lust of Gold, as the vain Ambition of Equality or Superiority in this System of effeminate Shew? Hence, *Rapacity* attends *Profusion*; till the Spirit of Avarice glides secretly into the Soul; and impels the Man of Fashion to that *Gaming,* as a *Trade,* which he had before adopted as a *Pleasure.* But as we read that CAESAR's Lust was only the *Servant* of his *Ambition,*[15] so this Lust of Gold is no more than the *Handmaid* to vain *Effeminacy.*

Thus we see *Gaming* established on the two great Pillars of *Self Interest* and *Pleasure:* and on these Foundations seems to rest the midnight Riot and Dissipation of modern Assemblies. [41]

But tho' Gaming be now the capital Pleasure, as well as Trade, of most Men of Fashion; yet other incidental Amusements intervene at vacant Times. Neither can it be affirmed with Truth, that all are immersed in this fashionable Folly. Nor let any one imagine, that he stands clear of the ruling Manners of the Times, because not infected with the Rage of *Gaming.* Let us then proceed to examine the other reigning Amusements

14. Attributed to the Persian king Xerxes; cf. Hume's essay "The Epicurean" (Hume, *Essays,* p. 139).
15. Suetonius, "Divus Iulius," XLIX–LII.

of the Age; and see how far they are, or are not, subject to the Charge of *unmanly* Delicacy.

A Knowledge of Books, a Taste in Arts, a Proficiency in Science, was formerly regarded as a proper Qualification, in a Man of Fashion. The Annals of our Country have transmitted to us the Name and Memory of Men, as eminent in Learning and Taste, as in Rank and For[42]tune. It will not, I presume, be regarded as any kind of Satire on the present Age, to say, that among the higher Ranks, this literary Spirit is generally vanished. *Reading* is now sunk at best into a Morning's *Amusement*; till the important Hour of Dress comes on. Books are no longer regarded as the Repositories of Taste and Knowledge; but are rather laid hold of, as a gentle Relaxation from the tedious Round of Pleasure.

But what kind of Reading must *that* be, which can attract or entertain the languid Morning-Spirit of modern Effeminacy? Any, indeed, that can but prevent the unsupportable Toil of *Thinking*; that may serve as a preparatory *Whet* of *Indolence,* to the approaching Pleasures of the Day. Thus it comes to pass, that weekly Essays, amatory Plays and Novels, politi[43]cal Pamphlets, and Books that revile Religion; together with a general *Hash* of these, served up in some *monthly Mess* of *Dulness,*[16] are the meagre *literary Diet* of Town and Country.

True it is, that amidst this general Defect of Taste and Learning, there is *a Writer,* whose Force of Genius, and Extent of Knowledge, might almost redeem the Character of the Times.[17] But that Superiority, which attracts the Reverence of the *Few,* excites the Envy and Hatred of the *Many:* And while his Works are translated and admired *Abroad,* and patronized at *Home,* by those who are most distinguished in Genius, Taste, and Learning, himself is abused, and his Friends insulted for his Sake, by

16. The 1750s saw a great increase in the number of literary periodicals, in which recent publications were reviewed and summarized: "Excluding newspapers, there were more than 30 different periodicals published in London in 1745. By 1755, that number had increased to more than 50, and by 1765 to more than 75" (Frank Donoghue, *The Fame Machine: Book Reviewing and Eighteenth-Century Literary Careers* [Stanford: Stanford University Press, 1996], p. 2). Notable among them were the *Monthly Review* (founded 1749) and the *Critical Review* (founded 1756).

17. I.e., William Warburton; cf. above, p. 219, n. 116.

those who never read his Writings, or, if they did, could neither *taste* nor *comprehend* them: while every [44] little aspiring or despairing Scribler eyes him as CASSIUS did CESAR, and whispers to his Fellow,

> Why Man, he doth bestride the narrow World
> Like a *Colossus*; and we petty Men
> Walk under his huge Legs; and peep about,
> To find ourselves dishonourable Graves.[18]

No wonder then, if the Malice of the *Lilliputian* Tribe be bent against this dreaded GULLIVER; if they attack him with *poisoned Arrows,* whom they cannot subdue by *Strength.*[19]

But in Justice to the present Age, another Observation must be added. As Excess of Delicacy hath destroyed our *Force of Taste*; it hath at least had one laudable Effect: for along with this, it hath carried off our *Grossness* of *Obscenity.* A strong Characteristic, this, of the Manners of the Times: The untractable [45] Spirit of Lewdness is sunk into gentle Gallantry, and *Obscenity* itself is grown *effeminate.*

But what *Vice* hath lost in *Coarseness* of Expression, she hath gained in a more easy and general *Admittance:* In ancient Days, *bare* and *impudent Obscenity,* like a common Woman of the Town, was confined to *Brothels:* Whereas the *Double-Entendre,* like a modern fine Lady, is now admitted into the *best Company*; while her *transparent Covering* of Words, like a *thin* fashionable *Gawze* delicately thrown across, *discloses,* while it seems to *veil,* her *Nakedness* of Thought.

No wonder, if these leading Characters of false Delicacy influence our other Entertainments, and be attended with a low and unmanly Taste in *Music.* That divine [46] Art,[20] capable of inspiring every thing that is great or excellent, of rouzing every nobler Passion of the Soul, is at length

---

18. *Julius Caesar,* I.ii.135–38.

19. An allusion to the events of Swift's *Gulliver's Travels,* Part I, chapters 1 and 7. When the Lilliputians eventually want to get rid of Gulliver they entertain the idea of shooting him with poisoned arrows; but they do not do so to begin with.

20. On which Brown would soon write at greater length in his *A Dissertation on the Rise, Union and Power . . . of Poetry and Music* (1763).

dwindled into a Woman's or an Eunuch's effeminate Trill. The chaste and solemn Airs of CORELLI, of GEMINIANI, and their best Disciples; the divine and lofty Flights of CALDARA and MARCELLO; the elegant Simplicity of BONONCINI; the manly, the pathetic, the astonishing Strains of HANDEL,[21] are neglected and despised: While instead of these, our Concerts and Operas are disgraced with the lowest Insipidity of Composition, and unmeaning *Sing-Song*. The Question now concerns not the Expression, the Grace, the Energy, or Dignity of the Musick: We go not to admire the *Composition*, but the *Tricks* of the *Performer*; who is then surest of our ignorant Applause, when he runs through the Compass of the *Throat*, [47] or traverses the *Finger-board* with the *swiftest Dexterity*.

While *Music* is thus debased into Effeminacy, her Sister-Art of *Painting* cannot hope a better Fate: For the same Dignity of Manners must *support*; the same Indignity *depress* them. Connoisseurs there are, indeed, who have either *Taste* or *Vanity:* Yet even by these, the Art is considered as a Matter of *Curiosity*, not of *Influence*; a Circumstance which proves their Taste to be spurious, undirected, or superficial. But with regard to the public Eye; this is generally depraved. Neither the comic Pencil, nor the serious Pen of our ingenious Countryman,* have been able to keep alive the Taste of Nature, or of Beauty. The fantastic and grotesque have banished *both*. Every House of Fashion is [48] now crowded with Porcelain Trees and Birds, Porcelain Men and Beasts, cross-legged Mandarins and Bramins, perpendicular Lines and stiff right Angles: Every gaudy *Chinese*

---

* Mr. *Hogarth's* Treatise on the Principles of Beauty.[22]

21. Arcangelo Corelli (1653–1713); Italian violinist and composer. Francesco Geminiani (1687–1762); Italian violinist, composer, teacher, and writer on musical subjects. Antonio Caldara (1670–1736); Italian composer of operas and oratorios. Benedetto Marcello (1686–1739); Italian composer and writer on musical subjects whose *Il teatro alla moda* (1720) is an amusing satire on early eighteenth-century fashions in musical drama. Giovanni Bonincini (1670–1747); Italian composer of opera, and Handel's chief rival in the musical world of London during the 1720s. George Frideric Handel (1685–1759); German-born English (after 1715) composer in a variety of forms (opera, oratorio, and instrumental compositions); the dominant figure in English music in the first half of the eighteenth century.

22. William Hogarth (1697–1764); English artist particularly celebrated for his moral and satiric engravings. His aesthetic credo, *The Analysis of Beauty*, had been published in 1753.

Crudity,[23] either in Colour, Form, Attitude, or Grouping, is adopted into fashionable Use, and become the Standard of Taste and Elegance.

Let us then search the Theatre for the Remains of manly Taste: And *here*, apparently at least, it must be acknowledged we shall find it. A great Genius[24] hath arisen to dignify the Stage; who, when it was sinking into the lowest Insipidity, restored it to the Fulness of its ancient Splendor, and, with a Variety of Powers beyond Example, established *Nature, Shakespear*, and *Himself*.

But as the Attractions of the Theatre arise from a Complication of Causes, be[49]yond those of any other Entertainment; so while the judicious Critic admires his original Excellencies, it may well be questioned whether the Crowd be not drawn by certain secondary Circumstances, rather than by a Discernment of his real Powers. Need we any other Proof of this, than the Conduct of his fashionable Hearers? who sit with the same Face of Admiration at LEAR, an OPERA, or a PANTOMIME.

These seem to be the main and leading Articles of our unmanly Winter-Delicacies. And as to our Summer-Amusements, they are much of the same *Make*, only *lighter*, and if possible more *trifling*. As soon as the Season is grown so mild, as that the Man of Fashion can stir abroad, he is seen lolling in his *Post-Chariot*, about the Purlieus[25] of the Town. The manly Exercise of *Riding* is generally disused, as [50] too coarse and indelicate for the fine Gentleman. The Metropolis growing thin as the Spring advances, the same Rage of Pleasure, Dress, Equipage, and Dissipation, which in Winter had chained him to the Town, now drives him to the Country. For as a vain and empty Mind can never give Entertainment to

23. A reference to the taste for "chinoiserie," a style of interior design and furniture influenced by those of China. It had first appeared in Versailles during the 1670s, before spreading more widely over northern Europe. Sir William Chambers's *Designs of Chinese Buildings* (1757) was an important primer for the movement, one based (as many were not) on first-hand experience.

24. David Garrick (1717–79); actor and playwright; the dominant theatrical personality in London during the mid-eighteenth century. Brown had been introduced to Garrick by Warburton, and Garrick had taken a leading part in Brown's *Barbarossa* (Garrick, *Correspondence*, vol. I, p. 65).

25. I.e., the outskirts or suburbs of the town; as used at this time, with a possible pejorative connotation of squalor or ill-repute.

itself; so, to avoid the Taedium of Solitude and Self-Converse, *Parties* of Pleasure are again formed; the same Effeminacies, under new Appearances, are acted over again, and become the *Business* of the Season. There is hardly a Corner of the Kingdom, where a *Summer Scene* of public *Dissipation* is not now established: Here the Parties meet till the Winter sets in, and the separate Societies are once more met in *London*.

Thus we have attempted a simple Delineation of the ruling Manners of the Times: [51] If any thing like Ridicule appears to mix itself with this Review, it ariseth not from the *Aggravation*, but the natural *Display* of *Folly*.

It may probably be asked, Why the ruling Manners of our Women have not been particularly delineated? The Reason is, because they are essentially the same with those of the Men, and are therefore included in this Estimate. The Sexes have now little other apparent Distinction, beyond that of Person and Dress: Their peculiar and characteristic Manners are confounded and lost: The one Sex having advanced into *Boldness*, as the other have sunk into *Effeminacy*. [52]

SECT. VI

Of the Principles of Religion, Honour, and public Spirit

Most Writers, who have attempted to prove the Efficacy of Principle, have supposed it to be the great and universal Fountain of Manners: They who have espoused the opposite System, observing this Theory to be at variance with Fact, have rashly concluded that Principle is void of all real Influence.

The Truth seems to lie between these two Opinions. Principles cannot be the Fountain of Manners, because Manners precede Principles: That is, in our Progress from Infancy, Habits of *Acting* are *prior* to Habits of *Thinking*. Yet on the other Hand, Principles, early and deeply ingrafted in the Mind, may grow up with [53] Manners; may be at variance with Manners; may yield to Manners; or, gathering Strength by Cultivation, may check, controll, or destroy them.

This Distinction is proper for many Reasons. One is evident: It shews the Propriety of treating of the Manners *first*, and *then* the Principles of the Times.

The Principles here to be estimated, are such only as tend to counter-work the *selfish Passions*. These are, the Principle of *Religion,* the Principle of *Honour,* and the Principle of *public Spirit.* The first of these has the *Deity* for it's Object; the second, the *Applause* of Men; the third, the *Approbation* of *our own Heart.* Let us examine the present Influence of these several Principles on the Manners already delineated. [54]

Did the Writer court the Applause of his polite Readers (if any such peradventure may honour him with their Regard) he would preface this Part of his Subject with an Apology, for the Rudeness of hinting at *religious Principle.* To suppose a Man of Fashion swayed in his Conduct by a Regard to *Futurity,* is an Affront to the Delicacy and Refinement of his *Taste.* Hence the Day set apart by the Laws of his Country for religious Service, he derides and affronts as a *vulgar* and *obsolete* Institution:[26] Should you propose to him the Renewal of that *Family Devotion,* which concluded the guiltless Evening Entertainments of his Ancestry? You would become an Object of his Pity, rather than Contempt. The sublime Truths, the pure and simple Morals of the Gospel, are despised and trod under foot. Can we wonder, if that Pro[55]fession which asserts these Truths, and preaches these Morals, be treated with a similar Contempt? But Irreligion knows no Bounds, when once let loose: and Christianity herself hath been obliquely insulted within those *consecrated* Walls, where *Decency* and *Policy,* in the Absence of *Reason* and *Virtue,* would for ever have held her in *legal Reverence.*

But notwithstanding the general Contempt of Religion among the fashionable World, the uninformed Reader is not to imagine, that the present Age is deep in the *Speculations* of *Infidelity.* No such Matter: for that would imply a certain *Attention* to these Subjects; a certain Degree of Self-Converse and Thought; and this would clash with the ruling Manners of the Times. Indeed there have not been wanting laborious

26. Not so regarded by all, however. As late as the 1790s the agricultural writer Arthur Young would be scandalized when the President of the Board of Agriculture, Lord Sheffield, obliged him to travel to Woburn Abbey on a Sunday to discuss business with the Duke of Bedford (Arthur Young, *Autobiography,* ed. M. Betham-Edwards [1898], pp. 395 and 469). Traveling on the Sabbath was also deplored by Vicesimus Knox (*Personal Nobility* [second edition, 1793], p. 275).

Husbandmen, who have pain[56]fully sown their Tares;[27] not in the Night Season, but in broad Day-light. These have at length shot up into a large and fruitful Crop of *irreligious implicit* FAITH: For implicit Faith is *Belief* or *Disbelief,* without Evidence; and *why* they disbelieve, I trow, few of the present Age can tell. They have other Attentions, than the meagre Sophisms of Irreligion; and are therefore well content with the *Conclusions,* without the *Premises.* This Distinction will lead us to the plain Reason, why in an Age of Irreligion, so capital a Book as the Writings of Lord BOLINGBROKE,[28] met with so cold a Reception in the World. Had they appeared under the inviting Shape of "ESSAYS *philosophical and moral,"* they might have come within the Compass of a Breakfast-reading, or amused the Man of Fashion while under the Discipline of the *curling Tongs:* But five *huge Quarto* Volumes (like [57] five *coarse* Dishes of Beef and Mutton) tho' fraught with the very *Marrow* of Infidelity, what *puny* modern *Appetite* could possibly *sit down to?*

In Confirmation of these Truths, we may conclude this Part of our Subject with a not incurious Anecdote. A certain Historian of our own Times,[29] bent upon *Popularity* and *Gain,* published a large Volume, and omitted no Opportunity that offered, to disgrace Religion: A large Impression was published, and a small Part sold. The Author being asked, why he had so larded his Work with Irreligion, his Answer modestly implied, "He had done it, that his Book might sell."—It was whispered

---

27. Cf. Matthew 13:24–30.

28. Henry St. John (1678–1751), viscount Bolingbroke; statesman, Jacobite, political and moral philosopher. Bolingbroke's philosophical writings had been published posthumously in five volumes in 1754, edited by the notorious deist David Mallet. Dr. Johnson's indignation at this way of proceeding was recorded by Boswell: "Sir, he [Bolingbroke] was a scoundrel and a coward: a scoundrel, for charging a blunderbuss against religion and morality; a coward, because he had not resolution to fire it off himself, but left half a crown to a beggarly Scotchman, to draw the trigger after his death!" (Boswell, *Life of Johnson,* p. 145).

29. David Hume. The four installments of Hume's *History of England* were published in 1754, 1757, 1759, and 1762. The second installment of 1757 contains no apology for the first installment, although Hume's comments on religion there are more guarded. For the context and Hume's enraged response to Brown's allegation, see E. C. Mossner, *The Life of David Hume* (Edinburgh and London: Thomas Nelson, 1954), pp. 307–9.

him, that he had totally mistaken the Spirit of the Times: that no Allurements could engage the *fashionable* Infidel World to travel through a large Quarto: And that as the [58] few Readers of Quarto's that yet remain, lie mostly among the serious Part of Mankind, he had offended his best Customers, and ruined the Sale of his Book. This Information had a notable Effect: for a second Volume, as large and instructive as the first, hath appeared; not a Smack of Irreligion is to be found in it; and an Apology for the *first* concludes the whole.

This being the State of religious Principle, let us next examine how it fares with the *Principle* of *Honour*. By this is meant, "The Desire of Fame, or the Applause of Men, directed to the End of public Happiness." Now this great Ambition, which in other Times or Nations hath wrought such wonderful Effects, is no longer to be found among us. It is the Pride of *Equipage*, the Pride of *Title*, the Pride of *Fortune*, or the Pride of *Dress*, that [59] have assumed the Empire over our Souls, and levelled *Ambition* with the *Dirt*. The honest Pride of *Virtue* is *no more*; or, where it happens to exist, is overwhelmed by inferior Vanities. A Man who should go out of the common Road of Life, in Pursuit of Glory, and serve the Public at the Expence of his Ease, his Fortune, or his Pleasure, would be stared or laughed at in every fashionable Circle, as a silly Fellow, who meddled with Things that did not belong to him: As an Ideot, who preferred Shadows to Realities, and needless Toil to pleasurable Enjoyment. The laurel Wreath, once aspired after as the highest Object of Ambition, would now be rated at the Market-price of its Materials, and derided as a *three-penny Crown*.[30] And if its modern Substitutes, the *Ribbon* or the *Coronet*,[31] be eagerly sought for, it is not that they are regarded as the *Distinctions* [60] of *public Virtue*, but as the *Ensigns* of *Vanity* and *Place*.

But what implies or proves the general Extinction of the Principle of Honour, is a peculiar Circumstance, which at first View seems to

---

30. Cf. Swift's famous comparison of the rewards paid to a victorious Roman general with the rewards lavished on the Duke of Marlborough by Queen Anne in *The Examiner* no. 16 (23 November 1710).

31. The emblems of, respectively, membership of an order of chivalry (such as the Order of the Garter), and of the possession of a title of nobility.

challenge Praise. It hath been weakly attributed to the moderate and for-giving Spirit of these Times, that no Age ever so patiently suffered its ruling Follies to be laughed at. But this, in truth, is a superficial and inad-equate Representation, as well as Solution, of the Fact. We not only suffer our ruling Vices and Follies to be ridiculed, but we cordially join in the Laugh. Was there ever a juster Picture drawn, than of modern *Effemi-nacy* and *Nonchalance* in the Characters of FRIBBLE and Lord CHALK-STONE?[32] Did ever dramatic Characters raise louder Peals of Laughter and Applause, even among those [61] who sat for the Likeness? They hear with Pleasure, they acknowledge the Truth of the Representation, they laugh at the Picture of their own Follies; they go home, and *with-out a Blush repeat them.* The Truth is, therefore, that we can see and own our Vices and Follies, *without being touched with Shame:* a Circumstance which ancient Times justly regarded as the strongest Indication of de-generate and incorrigible Manners.

It appears then, that the Principle of Honour is either lost, or totally corrupted: That no generous Thirst of Praise is left among us: That our Ambitions are trifling and unmanly as our Pleasures: That Wealth, Titles, Dress, Equipage, Sagacity in Gaming or Wagers, splendid Furniture and a Table, are the sole Fountains, from which we desire to draw Respect to ourselves, or Applause from others: We as[62]pire to Folly, and are proud of Meanness: Thus, the Principle of *Honour* is perverted, and dwindled into *unmanly Vanity.*

---

32. Both characters in plays by David Garrick. Although a "fribble" was a term in use from the mid-seventeenth century to denote a frivolous person (*OED*, 1), "Frib-ble" was the name given to "a surly Cuckold" by Thomas Shadwell in his comedy *Epsom Wells* (1672). The name was revived for a type of hen-pecked and cuckolded husband by Addison in *The Spectator* no. 295 (7 February 1712), before Garrick used the name for an effeminate character in his farce *Miss in Her Teens* (1747). The name went on to enjoy a vigorous afterlife on the mid-century stage and in mid-century poetry; cf. Timothy Brecknock, *The Important Triflers* (1748), p. 9; Whirligig Bolus, *The Quackade* (1752), pp. 37 and 55; Anon., *The Female Parliament* (1754), pp. 40 and 52; Anon., *Chit-Chat*, 2 vols (1755), vol. II, p. 185; Mary Davys, *The Accomplish'd Rake* (1756), "Dedication;" Phanuel Bacon, *The Tryal of the Time Killers* (1757), p. 46. Lord Chalkstone is a character added to the fifth edition of David Garrick's *Lethe. A Dramatic Satire* (1757; first published, 1745).

Can it be imagined, that, amidst this general Defect of *Religion* and *Honour,* the great and comprehensive Principle of *public Spirit,* or *Love of our Country,* can gain a Place in our Breasts? That mighty Principle, so often feigned, so seldom possessed; which requires the united Force of upright *Manners,* generous *Religion,* and unfeigned *Honour,* to support it. What Strength of Thought or conscious Merit can there be in effeminate Minds, sufficient to elevate them to this Principle, whose Object is, "the Happiness of a Kingdom?" To speak therefore without Flattery, this Principle is perhaps less felt among us, than even those of Religion and true Honour. So infatuated are we in our Contempt of this powerful Principle, that we deride [63] the Inhabitants of a *Sister-Kingdom,*[33] for their *national Attachments* and *Regards.* So little are we accustomed to go, or even *think,* beyond the beaten Track of private Interest, in all Things that regard our *Country*; that he who merely does his *Duty* in any conspicuous Station, is looked on as a Prodigy of public Virtue. But in other Times and Nations, when this Principle was in Force, Enterprises were formed, and Deeds done, which it would now be thought Phrenzy to attempt. Think what a Friend will do for a Friend; a Sister for a Brother, a Lover for his Mistress, a Parent for his Child; even *that,* in all its Fulness of Affection, in other Times and Nations, hath been the Aim and the Work of public Virtue, *doing* or *suffering* for its *Country's Welfare.*

Domestic Affections are not yet generally extinguished: There are kind Fa[64]thers, kind Mothers, affectionate Children, Sisters, Brothers: Humanity to Distress, we have already marked as another Character of the Times: But whether our very Effeminacy be not one of its Sources, might probably be a Question more *curious* in its Progress, than *agreeable* in its Solution.

However that be, let us be modest in our Claims, and confess, that our Affections seldom reach farther than our Relations, our Friends, or Individuals in Distress. Happy (in the present) it is for us, that they reach so far. Happy were it for us, or our Posterity, that they were of more inlarged

---

33. Presumably Ireland, Scotland having ceased to be a separate kingdom after the Act of Union of 1707.

Extent. In the mean Time, let us with due Abasement of Heart acknowledge, that the *Love* of our *Country* is no longer felt; and that, except in a few Minds of uncommon Greatness, the Principle of *public Spirit* EXISTS NOT. [65]

It is not affirmed or implied, in this general Review, that *every Individual* hath assumed the Garb and Character of false Delicacy, and uncontrouled Self-Love: As in *manly* Ages, some will be *effeminate*; so, in *effeminate* Times, the *manly* Character will be found: As in Times of Principle, some will be void of Principle; so, in Times when Principle is derided, in some superior Minds Principle will be found. But from the general Combination of Manners and Principles, in every Period of Time, will always result one ruling and predominant Character; as from a confused Multitude of different Voices, results one general Murmur, and strikes the distant Ear; or from a Field covered with Flocks, Herds, or Armies, though various in themselves, results one general and permanent Colour, and strikes the distant Eye: [66]

> Nam saepe in Colli tendentes pabula laeta
> Lanigerae reptant Pecudes, quo quamque vocantes
> Invitant Herbae gemmantes Rore recenti;
> Et satiati Agni ludunt, blandeque coniscant:
> Omnia quae nobis *longe confusa* videntur,
> Et veluti in viridi *Candor consistere* Colli.*

It is enough, then, if from a proper *Point of View*, we have fixed the *ruling Colour* of the Manners and Principles, for on this will depend the *ruling Character* of the *Times*.

As it appears, therefore, from this Delineation, that SHOW and PLEASURE are the main Objects of Pursuit: As the general Habit of *refined*

---

* Lucretius, l. ii.[34]

34. "For often on a hill, cropping the rich pasture, woolly sheep go creeping towards where the grass, glittering with fresh dew, tempts and invites each of them; and the full-fed lambs play and butt in fun, all of which we see from a distance blurred together, as a kind of whiteness at rest on a green hill" (Lucretius, *De Rerum Natura*, II.317–22).

Indulgence is *strong,* and the Habit of *induring* is *lost:* As the general Spirit of *Religion, Honour,* and *publick Love,* are weakened or vanished; as [67] these Manners are therefore left to their own Workings, uncontrouled by *Principle*; we may with Truth and Candour conclude, that the ruling Character of the present Times is that of "a *vain, luxurious,* and *selfish* EFFEMINACY."

PART II

OF THE

PUBLIC EFFECTS

OF

THESE MANNERS

AND

PRINCIPLES

PART II

OF THE

PUBLIC EFFECTS

OF

These MANNERS and PRINCIPLES

SECT. I

What constitutes the Strength of a Nation

Hitherto we have done little more than *delineate* the ruling Manners and Principles of the Times: we must now assume a severer Tone, and *reason* upon the *Facts* thus established. [72]

There are three leading Circumstances on which the *internal Strength* of every Nation most essentially depends: These are, the *Capacity, Valour,* and *Union,* of those who *lead* the People. The first may be called, "the *national Capacity*; the second the *national Spirit of Defence*; the third, the national *Spirit of Union*."

The next Step, therefore, will be, to consider all that Variety of Respects, in which the ruling Manners and Defect of Principle, already delineated, must naturally weaken or destroy these Sources of *internal* Power.

As this Enquiry will of course lead to a particular View of those several Ranks, Departments, Employments, or Professions, into which such a Nation is divided; [73] it is presumed, that no Instances alledged, or Facts alluded to, will be weakly construed into the Wantonness of licentious Satire. Every Profession is honourable, when directed to its proper End, the Publick Welfare: And the Intention of this Estimate is not to *defame*; but to *enquire* how far the several *Departments* or *Professions*, on which the internal Strength of this Nation depends, are *properly* or *improperly* directed.

SECT. II

Of the national Capacity

Let us then first enquire, how far the false Delicacy and Effeminacy of present Manners may have weakened or destroyed the *national Capacity*. [74]

It was a shrewd Observation of a good old Writer, "How can he get Wisdom, whose Talk is of Bullocks?"* But *Rusticity* is not more an Enemy of Knowledge, than *Effeminacy:* With the same Propriety therefore it may now be asked, "How can he get Wisdom, whose Talk is of *Dress* and *Wagers, Cards* and *Borough-jobbing*,² *Horses, Women,* and *Dice?*" The Man of Fashion is indeed cut off from the very Means of solid Instruction. His late Hours occasion a late rising; and thus the Morning, which should be devoted to the Acquisition of *Knowledge*, is devoted to *Sleep*, to *Dress*, and *Ignorance*.

How weak then must be the national Capacity of that People, whose leading [75] Members in *public Employ* should, in general, be formed on such a Model? If instead of a general Application to Books, instead of investigating the great Principles of *Legislation*, the Genius of their national Constitution, or its Relations and Dependencies on that of others, the great Examples and Truths of *History*, the Maxims of generous and upright *Policy*, and the severer Truths of *Philosophy*, on which all these are founded;—if instead of these, they should seldom rise in *political* Study higher than the securing of a *Borough*; instead of *History*, be only read in

* Book of Wisdom.¹
1. Ecclesiasticus 38:25.
2. A pejorative term for the trade in parliamentary seats for boroughs, commonly practiced prior to 1832 and the passage of the Great Reform Bill.

Novels; instead of *Legislation*, in *Party Pamphlets*; instead of *Philosophy*, in *Irreligion*; instead of manly and upright *Manners*, in trifling *Entertainments, Dress*, and *Gaming*:—If this should ever be their ruling Character, what must be expected from such esta[76]blished *Ignorance*, but *Errors* in the first Concoction?[3]

In a Nation thus circumstanced, it is odds but you would see even some of its most public and solemn Assemblies turned into Scenes of unmanly Riot; instead of the *Dignity* of *Freedom*, the *Tumults* of *Licentiousness* would prevail. Forwardness of young Men without Experience, intemperate Ridicule, dissolute Mirth, and loud Peals of Laughter, would be the ruling Character of such an Assembly.

This Reflexion, some how or other, calls up the Memory of a Circumstance or two, peculiar to the public Meetings of the *Athenians*. In the Court of *Areopagus*,[4] so little was *Ridicule* regarded as a *Test of Truth*,[5] that it was held an unpardonable Offence, for any Member to *laugh* while [77] the Assembly was sitting.—Another wise and prudent Regulation was the Practice of the *Cryer* in the *Senate*; who, before Business began, called out aloud, "*Who will speak that is turned of Fifty?*"

It is true, that in every Assembly of this Kind, the public Measures will generally be determined by the *Few*, whose Superiority is approved and acknowledged: By the *Few*, who have been so unfashionable as to

3. A phrase drawn from the old physiology, which analyzed digestion into three processes: first concoction, digestion in the stomach and intestines; second concoction, the process whereby the chyme so formed is changed into blood; and third concoction, secretion; hence, by extension, in the initial stage or at the very beginning (*OED*, 1 b and c).

4. The Areopagus is the Hill of Ares in Athens, to the west of the Acropolis, where after the synoecism the Council of State held its meetings, and which later, under the constitutions of Draco and Solon, gave its name to the court which, meeting on that hill, heard cases of murder, malicious wounding, arson, and poisoning. In addition, the Court of the Areopagus had the responsibility to guard the laws, to exercise oversight of education, to censor public morals, and in an emergency to assume dictatorial powers.

5. A reference to Shaftesbury's principle, that nothing is "proof against *Raillery*, except what is handsom and just" ("On the Freedom of Wit and Humour," pt. IV, sect. 1, *Characteristicks*, vol. I, p. 80).

despise the ruling System of Effeminacy: and before they had appeared on a *higher Stage*, had *laboured* and *shone* in a *College*. But what an Increase of *national Capacity* must arise, if those *Master-Spirits* were aided, and their Plans of Government examined and improved, by Men of the like *Application* and *Ability?* [78]

But if, in any Nation, the Number of these superior Minds be daily decreasing, from the growing Manners of the Times; what can a Nation, so circumstanced, have more to fear, than that in another Age, a general Cloud of Ignorance may overshadow it?

How much, or how little, in this Particular, *we* resemble the declining State of the *Roman* Republic, let any one determine from the following Passage: Where the great Author, after celebrating the general *Ability* of those who were *formerly* in public Station, concludes thus: "Nunc contra, plerique ad honores adipiscendos, et ad rempublicam gerendam, *nudi* veniunt atque *inermes,* nulla cognitione rerum, nulla scientia ornati."* [79]

Let us next consider the natural Effects of these effeminate Manners, on *Fleets* and *Armies*. And here, 'tis supposed, it will be readily acknowledged, that the Conduct and Fate of Fleets and Armies depend much on the Capacity of those that lead them, through every Rank of Office. Chiefly, indeed, of those who are *highest* in Command; but in Part too, of those who fill the *lower* Stations: the more, because they in inferior Rank *aspire,* and by Degrees *ascend,* to the highest.

Now, I apprehend, it would be ill taken, to *suppose,* that the fashionable and *prevailing Manners* abound not in the *Army* and *Navy*. The Gentlemen of these Professions are even *distinguished* by their Taste in *Dress,* their Skill at *Play,* their Attendance on every *Amusement,* pro[80]vided it be but *fashionable*. And sure, it must be by Miracle, if this trifling and effeminate Life conduct them to *Knowledge,* or produce *Capacity*. It were unjust to deny, that Men of Ability in this Order, are *yet* among us. But it would be Matter of great Pleasure and Expectation to the Public, to find *Ignorance,* in this *Profession,* either *uncommon* or *disgraceful*.

---

* Cic. de Oratore, l. iii.[6]

6. "Nowadays, on the contrary, men usually come to the pursuit of office and to positions in the government quite naked and unarmed, not equipped with any acquaintance with affairs of state, or knowledge" (Cicero, *De Oratore*, III.xxxiii).

Would these Gentlemen please to look into History, they would find, that in *polished Times,* few have ever distinguished themselves in *War,* who were not eminent or considerable in *Letters.* They would find PISIS-TRATUS, PERICLES, ALCIBIADES, DION, AGESILAUS, EPAMINON-DAS, among the *Greeks:* in the *Roman* List, both the SCIPIO's, CATO the elder and the younger, LUCULLUS, POMPEY, BRUTUS, CESAR, distinguished in *Letters* as in *War.*[7] [81]

'Tis true, indeed, that in barbarous Ages, there want not Instances of unlearned Leaders, who have done mighty Actions in Battle. But we must observe, that these were, at least, practised in their own Profession. It is farther to be observed, that in such Times, the Fate of War depends little on *Stratagem* or *Discipline.* But it is chiefly to be observed, that no general Rule can be drawn from a few Instances. A Man of great natural Talents takes mighty Strides in any Science or Profession: He is self-taught: While the common Run of Men, whom Nature hath destined

---

7. Pisistratus (*d.* 527 B.C.); Athenian soldier and statesman, and encourager of literature. Pericles (*c.* 500–429 B.C.); great Athenian statesman and orator. Alcibiades (*c.* 450–404 B.C.); cultured, but also corrupt, Athenian soldier and statesman; friend of Socrates. Dion (409–354 B.C.); brother-in-law to Dionysius I, ruler of Syracuse, to whom he is said to have introduced his friend Plato; defender of Plato's philosophy; the subject of a life by Plutarch. Agesilaus (*c.* 444–361 B.C.); king of Sparta. Epaminondas (*c.* 420–362 B.C.); great Theban military commander. Publius Cornelius Scipio Africanus Major (*c.* 236–*c.* 183 B.C.); Roman consul who concluded the second Punic War with his victory over Hannibal at Zama. Publius Cornelius Scipio Africanus Minor (*c.* 185–129 B.C.); Roman consul and adopted grandson of the above; concluded the third Punic War by destroying Carthage in 146 B.C.; great orator and patron of literature. Marcus Porcius Cato (234–149 B.C.), "Cato the Censor"; the embodiment of traditional Roman morality in its most severe form. Marcius Porcius Cato (95–46 B.C.), "Uticensis"; great-grandson of the above; a statesman of unbending rectitude, and one of the leading republican opponents of Julius Caesar; see above, p. 125, n. 60. Lucius Licinius Lucullus (*c.* 114–57 B.C.); Roman consul and statesman; enthusiast for Hellenic learning and owner of the library of the Pontic kings, which he had looted during the third Mithridatic War. Gnaeus Pompeius (106–48 B.C.); Roman statesman, and greatest Roman general before Julius Caesar. Marcus Junius Brutus (?78–42 B.C.); ardent supporter of republican principles; one of the leading conspirators against Julius Caesar. Gaius Julius Caesar (?102–44 B.C.); the preeminent commander and statesman of the late Roman republic, who composed narratives of his military campaigns, and also a number of minor works on grammar and astronomy which have not survived.

to travel on to Improvement by the beaten Track of Industry, through a blind and ill-understood Imitation of his superior Conduct, must for ever fall the Victims of their *Vanity* and *Ignorance.*

Here then we find another ruling Defect in the national Capacity of an effemi[82]nate People. How few can arise, amidst this general *Dissipation* of Manners, capable of conducting its Fleets and Armies? Or even suppose a Man of Application and Ability possessed of the chief Command; yet, in Case he falls in Battle, how small must be the Chance that the next in Succession, upon whom his Command naturally devolves, can be *equal* to the Importance of his *new Station?*

There is another *Profession,* which, under this Article of the *national Capacity,* the vulgar Reader will naturally expect to find considered. I mean, that of the *Clergy.* But the general Defect of religious Principle among the higher Ranks, hath rendered this order of Men altogether useless, except among those in *middle Life,* where they still maintain a certain Degree of Estimation. The Contempt with which not *they,* but their [83] *Profession* is treated by the *Ignorant* and *Profligate,* is equally common indeed to *high* and *low* Life: A Circumstance, which may be an Occasion of *Pride* in the *one,* but ought rather to be Matter of *Humiliation* to the other. 'Tis true, a modern Writer felicitates the present Times, and makes it their Boast, that "the Clergy have lost their Influence."* By which he evidently means, that Religion hath lost its Influence. Yet of this, at least, one of the Order may decently remind his Countrymen; that when the *English Protestant Clergy,* and that Christianity which they teach, were most *honoured* and respected at *Home, England* was then most honoured and respected *Abroad.*[9]

---

* See Mr. *Hume's* Essays.[8]

8. A misquotation from David Hume's essay "Whether the British Government Inclines More to Absolute Monarchy, or to a Republic," first published in 1741, where Hume reflects on recent changes in men's opinions: "Most people, in this island, have divested themselves of all superstitious reverence to names and authority: The clergy have much lost their credit: Their pretensions and doctrines have been ridiculed; and even religion can scarcely support itself in the world" (Hume, *Essays,* p. 51).

9. Glossed by Brown himself in vol. II as a reference to the reigns of Elizabeth (1558–1603) and Anne (1702–14), and also to the events of 1688; see below, p. 299, n. 22.

And although the present fashionable Contempt that is thrown upon their [84] *Profession,* preclude the Clergy from the *Opportunity,* had they the *Will,* to practice that Christian Duty of "overcoming Evil with Good;"[10] yet they need not blush to find, that they have *fallen* with the *Fame,* the *Manners,* and *Principles* of their Country: nor can the worthy Part of them, sure, aspire to *truer Glory,* than to have become the *Contempt* of *those,* who are become the *Contempt of* EUROPE.

But while I defend and *honour* the *Profession,* I mean not to flatter the *Professors.* As far, therefore, as the Influence of *their* Conduct and Knowledge can be supposed to affect the *national Capacity;* so far, they seem falling into the same unmanly and effeminate Peculiarities, by which their Contemporaries are distinguished: Such of them, I mean, as have Opportunity of conversing with what is called *the World,* [85] and are supposed to make a Part of it. In their Conduct, they *curb not,* but *promote* and encourage the trifling Manners of the Times: It is grown a fashionable thing, among these Gentlemen, to despise the Duties of their Parish; to wander about, as the various Seasons invite, to every Scene of false Gaiety; to *frequent* and *shine* in all *public* Places, their own *Pulpits* excepted.

Or if their Age and Situation sets them above these puerile Amusements, are we not to lament, that, instead of a manly and rational Regard to the Welfare of Mankind, the chief Employment of many a clerical Life is, to slumber in a *Stall,*[11] haunt *Levees,* or follow the gainful Trade of *Election-jobbing?*[12]

If false Pleasure and Self-Interest thus take Possession of the Heart, how can we ex[86]pect that a Regard for Religion and Christianity should find a *Place* there?

In Consequence of these ruling Habits, must we not farther lament, that a general Neglect of *Letters* is now creeping even upon this Profession, which ought to maintain and support them? Instead of launching into the *Deeps* of Learning, the fashionable *Divine* hardly ventures on the

---

10. Romans 12:21.

11. A stall is one of a row of seats in the choir of a church reserved for the use of canons or other senior clergy (*OED*, 5).

12. The practice of influencing the outcome of an election for personal gain (*OED,* "jobbing," *n.*², 2). Cf. above, p. 286, n. 2.

Shallows. The great Works of *Antiquity,* the Monuments of ancient Honour and Wisdom, are seldom *opened* or *explored:* and even mere *modern* Books are now generally read at *second Hand,* through the false Mediums of bald *Translations* or sorry *Abstracts.*

This seems to be the real State of the *clerical* Profession, so far as it hath Influence on the *national Capacity.* [87]

The Writer pretends not in any Case to impose his Opinions; but submits them to the Consideration of the Public. There is a wide Difference between the *Remonstrances* of *Reason,* and the *Insults* of *Malice* or *Contempt.*

SECT. III

Of the national Spirit of Defence

Having seen how the Manners of the Times have levelled the national *Capacity*; let us next enquire how it fares with the national Spirit of *Defence.*

As this Part of our Subject naturally involves a larger Number of the Community than the last, it will be necessary, here, to take a larger Compass.

The national Spirit of *Defence* then, to speak with Precision, will always be com[88]pounded of the national bodily *Strength, Hardiness, Courage,* and *Principle.*

The *common People* of this Nation seem possessed of the *three* first of these four Qualities, in a Degree sufficient to form an effectual and national Spirit of Defence. And though they who are selected for public *Service* be commonly most *profligate* in Manners, yet as their *Sphere* of Action is *confined,* they commonly have a proportioned *kind of Principle,* which works its Effect in Battle. In the Land Service, they are zealous for the *Honour* of their *Platoon,* their *Company,* their *Regiment.* At Sea, there is the same Emulation, whose *Gun,* whose *Ship,* whose *Squadron,* shall be best *served* and *fought.* It is well known there are no better fighting Men upon Earth.[13] They seldom turn their Backs upon their Enemy, unless

---

13. Cf. Samuel Johnson's essay of 1760, "The Bravery of the *English* Common Soldiers," where he notes that "Our nation may boast, beyond any other people in the world, of a kind of epidemic bravery, diffused equally through all its ranks. We can shew a peasantry of heroes, and fill our armies with clowns, whose courage may vie with that of their general" (Johnson, *Selected Essays,* p. 535).

when their Offi[89]cers shew the Way; and even then, are easily rallied; and return to the Charge with the same Courage.

Thus our *Villages* and *Ports* are an effectual Fund of Supplies for the national Spirit of Defence, in its inferior Departments.

But if we rise, or rather *descend,* to an impartial View of those who are called the *better Sort,* we shall find such a general Defect in the Spirit of *Defence,* as would alarm any People who were not lost to all Sense of *Danger.*

Our effeminate and unmanly Life, working along with our Island-Climate, hath notoriously produced an Increase of *low Spirits* and *nervous Disorders,* whose [90] natural and unalterable Character is that of *Fear.*

And even where this Distemper *is not,* the present false Delicacy of the fashionable World effectually disqualifies them from *enduring Toil,* or *facing Danger.*

Enthusiastic Religion leads to *Conquest*; rational Religion leads to rational *Defence*; but the modern Spirit of *Irreligion* leads to *rascally* and abandoned *Cowardice.* It quencheth every generous Hope that can enlarge the Soul; and levels Mankind with the Beasts that perish.

Can the Debility of modern Honour produce the manly Spirit of Defence? Alas, if ever it is put in Action by any thing beyond the *Vanity* of *Shew*; it is rouzed by an *Affront,* and dies in a *Duel.* [91]

How far this dastard Spirit of Effeminacy hath crept upon us, and destroyed the national Spirit of Defence, may appear from the general *Panic* the Nation was thrown into, at the late *Rebellion.*[14] When those of every Rank above a Constable, instead of arming themselves and encouraging the *People,* generally fled before the *Rebels*; while a Mob of ragged Highlanders marched unmolested to the Heart of a populous Kingdom.

Nay, so general was this cowardly and effeminate Spirit, that it was not confined to the *Friends* of Liberty and *Britain:* In *England,* it infected even their *Enemies:* who, while the hardy *Scots* risqued their Lives

---

14. A reference to the Jacobite Rebellion of 1745, when the advance to Derby of an army of highlanders under Charles Edward Stuart caused consternation in London. For Brown's part in resisting the Jacobites at Carlisle, see the "Introduction," p. ix and n. 2.

in a strange Country, amidst the Inclemencies of a severe Season, sat like Cowards by the Chimney Corner, tamely [92] wishing the Success of that Mischief, which their effeminate Manners durst not propagate.

It hath been urged indeed, as a Proof that the national Spirit of Defence is not yet extinguished, that we raised such large Sums during that Rebellion, and still continue such plentiful Supplies for the Support of our Fleets and Armies. This is weak Reasoning: For will not *Cowardice*, at least as soon as *Courage*, part with a Shilling or a Pound, to avoid *Danger?* The capital Question therefore still remains, "Not who shall *Pay*, but who shall *Fight?*"

Money, it is true, hath of late more than ever, been among *us* regarded as the main *Engine of War:* How truly, let our *Success* tell the World.—This Point will [93] hereafter be treated more at large.* In the mean Time, it cannot be amiss to observe, that *a little* of the active *Spirit* of *Courage* would do well, in order to *give Play* to this boasted *Engine*, which otherwise may sink into a *dead* and *unactive Mass.*

For a natural Display, therefore, of the Genius of the Times, commend me to the frank Declaration of an *honest* Gentleman, during the impending Terror of a *French* Invasion.[16] "For my Part, I am no *Soldier*; and therefore think it no Disgrace, to own myself *a Coward. Here* is my Purse, at the Service of my Country: If the *French* come, *I'll pay:* but—take me, *if I fight.*" [94]

How many modern fine Gentlemen, notwithstanding the warlike Weapon at their Side, would make the same *Declaration*, had they the same *Sincerity?*

There is another Circumstance in modern Manners, the Consideration of which must not be omitted because at first View it bids fair for

* See Part the Third.[15]

15. See below, pp. 315–44.

16. Fears of an invasion by France in 1756 had been strong enough to throw the ministry into a panic concerning the weakness of the nation's defenses. In May of that year William Pitt and George Townshend had secured the passage in the Commons of a bill for establishing a national militia, but it had been voted down in the Lords. As a result, the British government had been reduced to the humiliating expedient of hiring German mercenaries from Hesse and Hanover to guard the homeland.

the Spirit of Defence among the *Great:* I mean, the Spirit of *deliberate Self-murder:* For this ran high in ancient GREECE and ROME, when the Spirit of *Defence* was *strong.*

For the clearing of this Point, it must be premised and confessed, that something *like* the Principle of *Honour,* that is, the *Dread* of *Infamy* and *Shame,* appears the leading Motive in both Instances. [95]

But a farther Dictinction is to be made, with Regard to the different Objects of this *Fear:* And for this, we must refer to a former Section.* There we have seen, that the ruling *Pride* of a *modern* man of Fashion, lies in the Parade of *Dress, Gaming, Entertainments,* and *Equipage:* whereas, on the contrary, the *Ambition* of an old *Roman,* was, to excel in *military Virtue.* Now this Dictinction at once clears up the Question we are upon, and confirms much of what hath been advanced on modern Principles and Manners. The *Roman* killed himself, because he had been unfortunate in *War;* the *Englishman,* because he hath been unfortunate at *Whist:* The *old* Hero, because he had *disgraced* his *Country;* the *modern,* because he dares not shew his Head at *Arthur's:*[18] That, [96] because he was deprived of his *Glory;* this, of his *Ortolans* and *Champaigne:* The first was encouraged by a *mistaken* Principle of Religion; the latter, by his being *void* of all Religion: The one, because he had lost a *Battle* or a *Province;* the other, because the Bailiff hath seized his *Equipage:* The *Roman* was impelled to *Self-Destruction* by the Strength of *warlike Honour;* the *Briton,* by *despicable* and *effeminate Vanity.*

Where then shall we seek for the genuine Spirit of Defence? Where, in Truth, should we most seek for it, but among those who are our *Defenders* by *Profession?*

But, "what Probability is there, that the Spirit of Defence should be strong in any Profession, when the Members of that Profession are all chosen, without [97] prior Culture or Preparation, from a People among whom the Spirit of Defence is lost?" The Truth implied in this Question is so evident in itself, that it is hard to go about to prove it. Can a mere

* Part i. Sect 6.[17]

17. See above, pp. 275–82.
18. A London club.

Change of *Dress* or *Title*, or the buckling on a military *Weapon*, infuse Strength, Hardiness, Courage, or Honour? These are Qualities that must either be natural, which seldom happens; or they must be infused by an early and continued Discipline; or else, they come not at all. Schools and Seminaries of this Kind we have none; or none that are in any Degree attended to. The young Men designed for the military Profession are bred up to the same effeminate Maxims and Manners, which their Fathers are proud of: Can we wonder, if these shoot into Action, and form parallel Characters? Well might we wonder if they *did not*. [98]

So then, if it appear by our present Success in War, that our naval and military Spirit of Defence is strong, it must be evident at the same Time, that this great Spirit is infused by some Means altogether supernatural.

In the mean Time, what becomes of the four great natural Hinges, on which the true Spirit of Defence must hang, *Strength, Hardiness, Courage,* and *Principle?*

Can the modern System of false Delicacy nerve the Warrior with Hardiness and Strength? These Qualities, I believe, are hardly *boasted,* as making any Part of the modern warlike Character. It is a prudent as well as a modest Part, indeed, not to throw these rough and antiquated Weights [99] into the present military Scale: For every common Eye would detect the false Pretension.

But tho' brutal Strength and unpolished Hardiness be gone, are not our *Army* and *Navy* the great *Schools* of *Courage* and *Honour;* where these shining Qualities are of Course obtained?—Truly, it hath long been so affirmed: So long, that the *Affirmation* hath, till of late, passed for *Proof.* But the Nation is now beginning to grow *sceptical* in this Point; and require something more than *Affirmation,* for the Support of an Article of such *Importance.*

Let us first weigh the Probability of this, from the Nature of Things and Men. True *Courage* and a Principle of *Honour,* if they be not the rare and generous Growths of *Nature,* are the Effect of [100] *early* and *continued Habits.* Tho' *grown* Gentlemen may learn to *Dance;* yet, their Movements will be none of the most *graceful:* And tho' grown Gentlemen repair to the School of Courage and Honour: yet, with all their pre-conceived Maxims of false Delicacy, their trifling Ambitions, and effeminate

Manners about them, I ween, they are like to make a *sorry Progress*. Long before this, the Mind hath taken its *decisive Cast* of *Thought*, and can but rarely be brought back from its first *Obliquities*.

But suppose the Possibility of this sudden Infusion: It is to be feared, the Consequence would fail us. It is true, that when *Armies* take the *Field*, and *Fleets* put to *Sea*; when Sieges are undertaken, and Battles fought, and Glory is the Prize of Toil and Danger;—then indeed, [101] Armies and Navies become the Schools of Courage and warlike Honour: Here is a strong and continued Bias put upon the Mind of every Individual, of Force to conquer it's earliest Obliquities. But where nothing of this happens; where *Land Officers* in the Capital are occupied in *Dress, Cards*, and *Tea*; and in Country Towns divide their Time between Milleners *Shops* and *Taverns*; and *Sea Officers*, even in Time of War, instead of annoying the Enemies Fleets, are chiefly busied in the gainful Trade of catching *Prizes*;[19]—in such a Case, the Army must of necessity be the *School*, not of *Honour*, but *Effeminacy*; the *Navy* the School of *Avarice*, to the *Ends of Effeminacy*.

How far these general Reasonings are confirmed by a Series of *recent Events*, the World is left to judge. It is not the [102] Writer's Intention to make personal Applications, but to trace acknowledged *Facts* to their *Principles* and *Consequences*.

SECT. IV

Of the national Spirit of Union

These accumulated Proofs may convince us, that the national Spirit of *Defence* is not less weakened than the national *Capacity*, by the Manners and Principles of the Times. Let us next weigh their various Effects on the national Spirit of *Union*.

It may be proper to preface this Part of the Estimate, by observing, that whereas a national *Capacity* and Spirit of *Defence* are not necessarily affected by a national Form of *Government*; the national Spirit of [103] *Union*, on the contrary, is naturally *strong* under *some* Forms, and naturally *weak* under *others*.

19. Cf. below, p. 473, n. 8.

It is naturally *strong* in *absolute Monarchies*; because, in the Absence both of Manners and Principles, the *compelling* Power of the *Prince* directs and draws every thing to one Point; and therefore, in all common Situations, effectually supplies their Place.

But in *free Countries* it is naturally *weak,* unless supported by the generous Principles of Religion, Honour, or public Spirit: For as in most Cases, a full national Union will require, that the separate and partial Views of private Interest be in some Degree sacrificed to the general Welfare; so where Principle prevails not, the national [104] Union must ever be thwarted or destroyed by selfish Views and separate Interests.

Another Circumstance must be remarked, by which, in free Countries, the national Union will accidentally be often checked, but not destroyed: I mean, by the Freedom of *Opinion* itself, urged into Act by the very Strength of generous and prevailing *Principle.*

This Distinction leads us to observe what may perhaps be deemed an Oversight or Inaccuracy of the celebrated MONTESQUIEU. He hath often given it as his Opinion, that *Factions* are not only natural, but necessary to *free* Governments: And this general Rule he gives without Restriction. Thus he speaks of *Rome.* "On n'entend parler dans les auteurs, que des divisions qui perdirent [105] Rome: mais on ne voit pas que ces Divisions y étoient *necessaires,* qu'elles y avoient toujours été, & qu'elles y *devoient toujours etre.*"*

How far this Proposition is *true* or *false,* the Distinction made above will lead us to discover. When the Spirit of Union is checked, and Divisions arise, from the Variety and *Freedom* of *Opinion* only; or from the contested Rights and Privileges of the different Ranks or Orders of a State, not from the detached and selfish Views of Individuals; a Republic is then in its *Strength,* and gathers Warmth and Fire from these Collisions. Such was the State of ancient *Rome,* in the simpler and more disinterested Periods of that Republic.

---

* Grandeur des Rom. l. ix.[20]

20. "One hears talk amongst authors of nothing but the divisions which ruined Rome; but one overlooks that these divisions in Rome were necessary, that they had always existed there, and that they must always exist there" (Montesquieu, *Considérations,* ch. IX, p. 156).

But when Principle is weakened and Manners lost, and Factions run high from [106] selfish Ambition, Revenge, or Avarice, a Republic is then on the very Eve of its Destruction: And such was the State of Rome, in the Times of MARIUS and SYLLA, POMPEY and CESAR, ANTHONY and AUGUSTUS.[21]

Therefore, before we can determine whether the *Factions* that divide a *free* Country be *salutary* or *dangerous,* it is necessary to know what is their *Foundation* and their *Object.* If they arise from *Freedom* of Opinion, and aim at the public Welfare, they are *salutary:* If their Source be *selfish* Interest, of what kind soever; they are then *dangerous* and *destructive.*

It was necessary to make these Distinctions, before we could say with Precision, how far, in our own Country, a *national Spirit of Union,* is in reality a *national* GOOD. [107]

The Point therefore to be examined, is, "how far our national Spirit of Union is weakened or destroyed by selfish Views of Good, by separate Interests, and Defect of Principle?"

Now, if the Delineation already given of our ruling Manners and Principles be true, the Consequence must needs follow, that our national Spirit of Union must be shaken by them.

Neither shall we need to cast about, for evident Facts that will confirm this Theory. Glaring Proofs will meet us at every Turn; and not only make good this Conclusion, but throw new Light on the Delineation already made.

The Restraints laid on the royal Prerogative at the Revolution,[22] and the Acces[108]sion of Liberty thus gained by the People, produced two Effects with Respect to Parliaments. One was that, instead of being

---

21. Three episodes of civil conflict at Rome marking the demise of the republic and its transformation into a principate, the first occurring in 89–86 B.C., the second in 49–45 B.C., and the third in 42–30 B.C.

22. Following the abdication and exile of James II and the accession of William and Mary in 1688, in December 1689 Parliament passed *An Act Declaring the Rights and Liberties of the Subject and Settling the Succession of the Crown*, in which certain rights belonging to the subject (such as freedom to petition the monarch) and certain restrictions on the actions of the monarch (such as the prohibition of maintaining a standing army in time of peace and of taxation by royal prerogative, as well as the abolition of the royal dispensing power) were enshrined in statute law.

occasionally, they were thence-forward *annually* assembled: The other was, that whereas on any trifling Offence given, they had been usually *intimidated* or *dissolved*, they now found themselves possessed of new *Dignity* and *Power*; their Consent being necessary for raising the *annual Supplies*.

No Body of Men, except in the simplest and most virtuous Times, ever found themselves possessed of Power, but many of them would attempt to turn it to their own private Advantage. Thus the Parliaments finding themselves *of Weight*, and finding at the same Time that the Disposal of all *lucrative Employments* was vested in the *Crown*, soon bethought themselves, [109] that in Exchange for *their* Concurrence in granting Supplies, and forwarding the *Measures* of *Government*, it was but equitable that the Crown should *concur* in vesting *Them*, or their *Dependants*, with the *lucrative Employs* of State.

If this was done, the Wheels of Government ran smooth and quiet: But if any large Body of Claimants was dissatisfied, the political Uproar began; and public Measures were obstructed or overturned.

William the *third* found this to be the national Turn; and set himself, like a Politician, to oppose it: He therefore silenced all he could, by Places or Pensions: And hence the Origin of MAKING of PARLIAMENTS. [110]

But the Art, as yet, was but in its *infant* State. The ruling Principles, which had brought about the REVOLUTION, had not as yet lost their Force: And the first Essays of Art are always rude: Time only, and Variety of Trial and Experiment, can form them into perfect Systems.

In the mean Time, this new Principle of Self-Interest began to work deeper every Day in its Effects. As a Seat in Parliament was now found to be of considerable selfish Importance, the Contention for *Gain*, which had begun in *Town*, spread itself by Degrees into the *Country*. *Shires* and *Burroughs*, which in former Times had *paid* their Representatives for their Attendance in Parliament, were now the great Objects of *Request*, and *political Struggle*. [111]

And as the *Representatives* had already found their Influence, and made their Demands on the *Crown*; so now, the *Constituents* found *their* Influence, and made *their* Demands on the *Representatives*.

Thus the great Chain of political Self-Interest was at length formed; and extended from the *lowest Cobler* in a *Burrough*, to the *King's first Minister*.

But a *Chain* of *Self-Interest* is indeed no better than a *Rope* of *Sand:* There is no *Cement* nor *Cohesion* between the Parts: There is rather a mutual *Antipathy* and *Repulsion*; the Character of *Self-Interest* being in a peculiar Sense, that of "*teres atque rotundus;*"[23] wrapt up wholly in *itself*; and unconnected with others, unless for its own Sake. Here then, we see even this Chain itself ready to [112] fall in Pieces, and on any sudden Thwart or Concussion, break into an Infinity of Factions.

Besides this, the lucrative Employs of our Country not being near so numerous as the Claimants are, in every Degree of political Power and Expectation; the Spirit of selfish Faction arose of course in its Strength, from unsatisfied Demands, and disappointed Avarice.

It hath much been debated, whether the Ministers or the People have contributed more to the Establishment of this System of Self-Interest and Faction. On Enquiry it would probably appear, that at different Periods the Pendulum hath swung at large on both sides. It came down, in former Times, from the Minister to the Representative, from the Representative to [113] the managing Alderman, from the Alderman to the Cobler. In later Times, the Impulse seems to have been chiefly in the contrary Direction: From the Cobler to the managing Alderman; from him, to the Member; from the Member, to the *great Man* who ruled the Burrough; and thence to the Minister. Thus, what was formerly, in the Minister, an Act of *supposed Prudence,* has of late grown into an Act of *supposed Necessity.* The *Cobler* by this Time had found his *Strength,* so the Pressure went *upwards,* till it came upon the *Ministry.*

To suppose that the Servants of the Crown never attempted Measures that were known to be bad, nor ever *made* Parliaments, in order to carry their Attempts into Action, would be ridiculous: But on the other hand it is equally true, [114] what MACHIAVEL somewhere delivers as a Maxim, "That an ill-disposed Citizen can do no great Harm, but in an ill-disposed City."[24] Bribery in the Minister supposes a corrupt People.

23. "Smoothed and rounded" (Horace, *Satires*, II.vii.86).
24. "A bad citizen cannot do much harm in a republic that is not corrupt" (Machiavelli, *The Discourses*, III.8, p. 426).

And, to venture a plain, tho' perhaps an unpopular Truth on this Occasion; it must be owned that a Minister is not therefore *certainly* corrupt in his *Intention*, because he *makes* a Parliament by indirect and corrupt *Means*. This Conduct, however indefensible, may arise from two opposite Causes. He may be *afraid* of the *Virtue* of a Nation, in its *opposing bad* Measures: Or he may not dare to *rely* on the *Virtue* of a Nation, in *supporting* him in *good ones*.

There was a noted Minister in this Kingdom,[25] who, during his long Reign, [115] seems to have put these two Maxims in Practice, as Occasion offered. For if it was his Maxim, "that every Man had his Price." It was his Maxim too, "That he was obliged to bribe the Members, not to vote *against*, but *according* to their *Conscience*."

However, this is not meant as a Vindication of his Measures. On the contrary, they seem generally to have aimed no higher than to secure present Expedients, to oblige his Friends and Dependants, and provide for his own Safety. His Capacity, even when he meant well, seems to have been too narrow to comprehend any *great Plan* of Legislation; and perhaps his Character might be drawn in these few Words, "That while he seemed to *strengthen* the *Superstructure*, he *weakened* the *Foundations* of our *Constitution*." [116]

But however defective Ministers may have been in making the public Welfare the *main Object* of their Views, we may be satisfied by this Estimate of Things from the *Revolution* to the present Times, that the Nation have at least marched "*Passibus aequis*."[26] And tho' this Work is not intended either as a Defence or an Accusation of Ministers; yet for the

25. A reference to Sir Robert Walpole (1676–1745), the dominant English politician of the earlier eighteenth century. From the early 1720s he had acted as George I's chief minister, and had been retained by George II in the same role until his downfall in 1742. Walpole's mastery of the House of Commons, and hence his long tenure of office, was popularly attributed to his use of secret service funds to buy votes. For Hollis's balanced view of Walpole, cf. Blackburne, *Memoirs*, vol. I, pp. 183–84.

26. "With equal steps;" an allusion to Virgil's description of Aeneas and his family fleeing Troy on the evening of its destruction by the Greeks: "dextrae se parvus Iulus | implicuit sequiturque patrem non passibus aequis' (*Aeneid*, II.723–24); "Little Iulus clasps his hand in mine, and follows his father with unequal steps."

sake of Truth it must be said, that the eternal Clamours, of a selfish, and a factious People, against every Ministry that rises, puts one in Mind of those *Carthaginian* Armies, which being at once cowardly and insolent, ran away at Sight of an Enemy, and then *crucified* their *General,* because he did not gain the *Victory.*[27]

To return therefore to our Subject, (if, indeed, we have departed from it) evident [117] it is, that the want of Principle hath at length firmly established a System of political Self-Interest among us, which must at all times break out into Factions; and prevent the great Effects which a national Spirit of Union would produce. Former Times, we plainly see, have been fatally infected with this selfish Spirit. Present Times, *in this respect,* are *sacred*; and therefore we speak not of them. But if the ruling Manners and present want of Principle in this Kingdom be not checked in their Carriere;[28] we must expect that future Times will be more selfish, and therefore more factious, than those former ones, we have already described.

For Vanity, Luxury, and Effeminacy, (increased beyond all Belief within these twenty Years) as they are of a *selfish,* so are they of a craving and unsatisfied Na[118]ture: The present Rage of Pleasure and unmanly Dissipation hath created a Train of new Necessities, which in their Demands outstrip every possible Supply.

And if the great Principles of Religion, Honour, and public Spirit are weak or lost among us, what effectual Check can there be upon the Great, to controul their unbounded and unwarranted Pursuit of lucrative Employments, for the Gratification of these unmanly Passions?

And whenever this happens, what can we expect as the Consequence, but a general Anarchy and Confusion? what, but that disappointed *Avarice* will kindle *Faction?* That national Union must be thwarted by selfish Regards? That no public Measure, however salutary, can be carried into Act, [119] if it clash with any foreseen private Interest?

27. Brown seems to have in mind the crucifixion of the defeated Carthaginian general Hannibal by Mathos, one of the leaders of a rebellious mercenary army (Polybius, I.lxxxvi.5–6).

28. An archaic spelling of "career," here meaning the course over which something passes (*OED*, 1b).

Nay, is it not the Duty of every Well-wisher to his Country, to consider, not only how soon this *may be,* but how far *it is* our present Situation?

What other Effect can naturally arise from the Vanity, Dissipation, and Rapacity of a dissolute People? For in a Nation so circumstanced, 'tis natural to imagine, that next to Gaming and Riot, the chief Attention of the great World must be turned on the Business of *Election-jobbing,*[29] of securing *Counties,* controuling, bribing, or buying of *Burroughs,* in a word, on the Possession of a great Parliamentary Interest? [120]

But what an Aggravation of this Evil would arise, should ever those of the highest Rank, tho' prohibited by Act of Parliament, insult the Laws by interfering in Elections, by solliciting Votes, or procuring others to sollicit them; by influencing Elections in an avowed Defiance of their Country, and even *selling* vacant *Seats* in Parliament to the *best Bidder?*

Would not this be a faithful Copy of degenerate and declining *Rome?* "Ea demum Romae libertas est, non Senatum, non Magistratus, non Leges, non Mores Majorum, non Instituta Patrum vereri."[30]

And what, can we suppose would be the real Drift of this illegitimate Waste of Time, Honour, Wealth, and Labour? might not [121] the very Reason publickly assigned for it, be this, "That they may strengthen themselves and Families, and thus gain a *lasting Interest* (as they call it) for their Dependants, Sons and Posterity?" Now what would this imply but a supposed Right or Privilege of demanding lucrative Employs, as the chief Object of their View? And whence can this supposed Privilege of Demand derive its Force, but from a foreseen Power, and determined Purpose, of kindling Faction, and obstructing all public Measures, in case of Disappointment and Disgust?

We see then, how the political System of Self-Interest is at length compleated; and a Foundation laid in our Principles and Manners for *endless Dissentions* in the State. [122]

Thus *Faction* is established, not on *Ambition,* but on *Avarice:* on *Avarice* and *Rapacity,* for the Ends of *Dissipation.*

29. See above, p. 286, n. 2.

30. "In the end liberty in Rome has come to mean that a man has no respect for the senate, for the magistrates, for the laws, for ancestral customs, or for the institutions of our forefathers" (Livy, V.vi.17).

Need we point out particular Facts, in Confirmation of these Truths? Is not the Nation even now labouring under this fatal Malady? Is not the deadly *Bow-string*[31] already stretched, and the *Public* gasping and expiring under the Tugs of opposed and contending Parties?

"Distractam, laceratamque Rempublicam—magis *quorum in manu sit, quam ut incolumis sit* quaeri."* [123]

SECT. V

Of the Consequences of National Disunion

It is not enough to have shewn in what Manner our Defect of Principle and ruling Manners have compleated the Ruin of the national Spirit of Union: If we would obtain a full View of our Subject, it is a necessary tho' disagreeable Task, to trace this *Disunion* thro' its *particular Effects*.

Now these will always vary along with the Character of the People thus divided. If the Nation be *warlike*, and the Spirit of Defence be *strong*, the Danger will generally arise from *within*. If the Nation be *effeminate*, and the Spirit of Defence be *weak*, the Danger will generally arise from *without*. [124]

The first of these was the Situation and Fate of the ancient Military Republics. That of *Corinth* was destroyed by the Faction of the *Praetor* DIAEUS and his Party.[33] The *Athenian* Commonwealth was again and again shaken and overturned by the Weight of opposing Parties: insomuch that the History of this *Republic* may justly be styled the History

---

* Liv.[32]

31. A reference to what was reputed to be the preferred mode of assassination—strangulation using a bow-string—in the ruling dynasties of Persia and the near East, particularly the Ottoman empire; cf., e.g., *The Craftsman*, 159 (19 July 1729); Charles de Sainte-Maure, *A New Journey* (1739), p. 198; O. G. de Busbecq, *Travels into Turkey* (1744), p. 45; F. I. Espiard de la Borde, *The Spirit of Nations* (1753), p. 272; Egmond van der Nijenburg, *Travels Through Part of Europe*, 2 vols (1759), vol. II, p. 356.

32. "The state was distracted and torn apart, and the question was rather who was to hold power, than how the state was to be made safe" (Livy, II.lvii.3).

33. Diaeus of Megalopolis (fl. *c.* 150 B.C.); *strategos* of the Achaeans; inveterate opponent of Roman expansion.

of *Faction*. When degenerate Manners had destroyed the Purity of the *Spartan* Constitution and Laws of Lycurgus, Agis attempted to restore them, but was murdered in the generous Attempt by a Faction headed by the *Ephori*.[34] The *Roman* Commonwealth, in its later Periods, was thrown into perpetual Convulsions by ambitious and warlike Faction, and died at last of the Malady. And, to pass by many other Proofs that might be [125] alledged, what Rivers of Blood have been spilt in *our own Country*, among contending Factions, while the Spirit of Arms and Honour remained among us?

But to give every Period of Manners it's due Character, it is confessed that in the present *effeminate* tho' *factious* Times, we have no Danger of this kind to fear. For as our Manners are degenerated into those of Women, so are our Weapons of Offence.

But as this *Home-Security* arises only from the common *Impotence*; it is probable, that other Nations may soon know of what Materials we are made; and therefore our Danger is likely to arise from *without*.

Let us then examine what Effects this national Spirit of *Disunion* must have upon [126] us, as we stand affected by any *foreign Enemy*.

It weakens the *Consistency* of all public Measures: So that no great national Scheme of Thought can be carried into Action, if it's Accomplishment demands any long Continuity of Time.

It weakens not only the *Consistency*, but the *Vigour* and Expedition of all publick Measures: So that while a divided People are contending about the Means of Security or Defence, a united Enemy may surprize and invade them.

These are the apparent Consequences of national Disunion: There is another not so obvious, and therefore more likely to be fatal. [127]

We have seen that in a Nation circumstanced like *ours*, the great Contention among those of Quality and Fortune will probably lie in the Affair of *Election Interests:* That next to effeminate Pleasure and Gaming,

---

34. Lycurgus was the legendary lawgiver of ancient Sparta, whose austere constitutional design for the Spartan state was praised by Xenophon and Plutarch. Agis IV (fl. 240 B.C.), king of Sparta and social reformer. The ephors were a body of five Spartan magistrates who exercised control over the kings of Sparta.

this (for the same End as Gaming) will of Course be the capital Pursuit: that this Interest will naturally be regarded as a kind of *Family-Fund,* for the Provision of the younger Branches: and that it's Force must arise from this Principle, that in Case the Head of the Family is not *gratified* in his lucrative Demands, he and his Dependants will raise a *Combustion* in the State.

Viewing the Affair, then, in this Light; we shall see that, besides the general ill Influence of Faction, this Principle of Disunion must farther tend to weaken or de[128]stroy both the National *Capacity* and the national Spirit of *Defence.*

For, in a Nation so circumstanced, thro' the Strength of this Principle, many high and important Posts, in every public and important Profession, must of Course be filled by Men, who instead of *Ability* and *Virtue,* plead this *Interest* for their *best Title.*

Thus in a Time when Science, Capacity, Courage, Honour, Religion, Public Spirit, are rare; the remaining *Few* who possess these Virtues, will often be shut out from these Stations which they would fill with Honour; while every public and important Employ will abound with Men, whose *Manners* and *Principles* are of the *newest Fashion.*

'Tis acknowledged there are Exceptions to the Truth of this Remark. Nay, were [129] it necessary, the Writer could gratify his Vanity, by ranking some of these Names in the Number of his Friends. But notwithstanding these Exceptions, the general Observation will maintain it's Truth.

How indeed can it be otherwise, while the Consciousness of this Principle has any Place in the Mind? Is not the Parliament-Interest of every powerful Family continually rung in the Ears of it's Branches and Dependants? And does not this inevitably tend to relax and weaken the Application of the young Men of Quality and Fortune, and render every Man who has Reliance on this Principle, less qualified for those Stations *which* BY THIS VERY PRINCIPLE he *obtains?* For why should a Youth of Family or Fashion (thus he argues with himself) "Why should *He* submit to the Drudgery of Schools, Colleges, Aca[130]demies, Voyages, Campaigns, Fatigues, and Dangers, when he can rise to the highest Stations by the smooth and easy Path of Parliamentary Interest?"

'Tis granted, indeed, that the Sons and Relations of Men of Quality and Fortune, have not only an equal, but even a prior Claim to all high Employments in the State, provided only, they are *qualified to fill them honourably*.

We may truly add to this, that in that Period of a State, when Capacity, Courage, and Honour, form its ruling Character; those of high Quality and Degree, are generally of all others the most capable, most couragious, most honourable.

On the contrary, where Effeminacy and selfish Vanity form the ruling Character of [131] a People; there we may be no less certain, that those of high Rank and Quality will in general be of all others most vain, most selfish, most incapable, most effeminate.

The Reason is permanent, and the same in both Cases: "Because in every Period of every State, the Influence of the *leading People*, soon or late, will form it's *leading Character*."

How far these Truths are verified by present Facts, it were *needless*, perhaps *dangerous*, particularly to say. Let it therefore be left to the candid Consideration of every honest and impartial Man, how far several recent Events, by which both the Honour and outward Strength of this Nation have been impaired, have arisen from the prevailing Principle here delineated. [132]

We may conclude this Subject with a general Remark, which, together with the Result of these Observations, may form a general Maxim: That "when Factions arise from the Excess of military Spirit and the ambition of Dominion, they increase the national Capacity and Spirit of Defence: On the contrary, where Factions arise from selfish Effeminacy, the national Capacity and Spirit of Defence will certainly be weakened or destroyed."* [133]

---

* We must not omit to observe, that there are two Professions which, even in the most selfish and effeminate Times, will generally maintain their proper Vigour: These are the Professions of *Law* and *Physic*. For as their Object is the Security of the *Property* and *Health* of Individuals, the most selfish and effeminate of Mankind will always be more attentive to the Preservation of *these*, in proportion as they are *less attentive* to the public Welfare, and lost to all generous Affections and Regards. Thus even in the most selfish and effeminate Times, the ablest *Lawyers* and *Physicians* will generally be at the Head of their Profession.

Such are the Effects of this prevailing Principle of Self-Interest and Disunion, in *high Life*. But if we take into the Account all that despicable Train of political Managers, Agents, and Burrough-Jobbers, which hang like Leeches upon the Great, nor ever quit their Hold till they are full gorged; we shall then see this reigning Evil in it's last Perfection. For here, to Incapacity and Demerit, is generally added *Insolence*. Every low Fellow of this Kind looks upon the Man of Genius, Capacity, and Virtue, as his natural Enemy. He regards him with an evil Eye; and hence undermines or defames him; as one who thwarts his Views, questions his Title, [134] and indangers his Expectations. He must have had little Experience in the World, who has not, among *every Order*, met with flagrant Characters of this Kind, and Instances of this Truth.

Thus the public Body is *again* weakened, or rather *mutilated* in all its Limbs. And that national Spirit of *Disunion* which our Principles and Manners have produced, comes not only attended with it's proper and *immediate Effects*, but hath completed the Ruin of the national *Capacity*, and the national Spirit of *Defence*.

SECT. VI

An Objection, drawn from the Manners of the French Nation, considered

We might here close our Estimate of the public Effects of the ruling Manners [135] and Principles of the Times; were not the Theory here established on a Number of concurrent Facts, apparently liable to an Objection.

This ariseth from the ruling Manners of the *French* Nation: Which being as *vain* and *effeminate* as our own, and the very Archetype from which our own are drawn, should of Course involve that Nation in the same Consequences, the same Defect of national *Capacity*, *Defence* and *Union*: But as these Principles of national and internal Strength are, on all hands, acknowledged to maintain their proper Vigour in *France*, where the ruling Manners are effeminate; therefore, say the Patronizers of our modern Manners, *these* cannot be the Cause of our national Miscarriages and Defects. [136]

'Tis granted, then, that their Manners are of the same Kind: But on Examination it will appear, that whereas *ours* (as we have seen) are suffered to go on to all their proper and natural Effects; *theirs*, on the contrary, are checked and counteracted in their Effects, by a variety of Causes and Principles wholly dissimilar.

Their effeminate *Manners* affect not their national *Capacity*, because their Youth are assiduously trained up for all public Offices, civil, naval, military, in Schools provided at the national Expence: Here the Candidates for public Employ go thro' a severe and laborious Course of Discipline, and only expect to *rise* in *Station*, as they *rise* in *Knowledge* and *Ability*. [137]

Their effeminate Manners affect not their national Spirit of *Defence*, because they are controuled by the Principle of military *Honour*. This, for some Ages, hath been early instilled into every rising Generation; and is at length become so strong and universal, as to form the *national Character*. It spreads through every Rank; inspires even the meanest in the Kingdom; and pervades and actuates the whole Machine of Government, with a Force little inferior to that of public *Virtue*.

It were no incurious Subject, to investigate this peculiar Principle to it's first Causes: But *that* lies beyond the Intention of the present Design. It may be called a *peculiar*[35] Principle, in *France*, because it is *unconnected*, nay even at *Variance* with it's Manners; and in no other Country did this [138] Principle ever subsist in it's Strength, when *other* Principles were *weakened*, and *Manners lost*.

It may seem, perhaps, at first View, to have arisen from the civil Wars that rent the Kingdom[36] in the Time of HENRY *the Great*, to have been transfused from thence into the gallant Reign of LOUIS,[37] and thence heightened and delivered down to present Times.

But tho' it received great Heightenings in these two Reigns, yet it produced signal and peculiar Effects, before the first of these Periods. In

35. Here not used to mean "odd" or "remarkable" (*OED*, 1a and 5), but rather to identify a characteristic which belongs to one person, place, or group rather than another (*OED*, 2b).

36. The French Wars of Religion, which began in 1562 and raged bitterly for over thirty years, were eventually calmed only by the apostasy of Henri IV ("Henry the Great") on 25 July 1593, and his coronation at Chartres on 27 February 1594.

37. Louis XIV (1638–1715), who became king of France in 1643.

Proof of this, we need only alledge the famous Route called the *Battle of Spurs*,[38] when HENRY *the Eighth* of *England* invaded *France*. On this Occasion, the Body of the *French* Army giving Way thro' some sudden Panic, the Officers kept their Ground, and rather [139] chose to be slain or taken Prisoners, than give Countenance to such an ignominious Flight.

This Principle, so remarkable at this Day among the FRENCH, *we* stigmatize with the Name of *false Honour.* Such as it is, it were to be wished we had more of it. It aims not, indeed at *generous* Ends, beyond a *certain Sphere:* But it is plausible, polite and splendid, in the Pursuit even of it's ungenerous Ends. In short, the Honour, like the Religion of *France,* is not *void* of Benevolence, but *confines* its Benevolence, within a *certain Pale.* 'Tis *false* Honour, as it regards *other* Nations; as it regards *their own Country,* it is *true.*

As this Principle in *France,* secures the national Spirit of Defence, so the *Power* [140] *of their Monarch,* aided by this Principle, secures their national Spirit of *Union.* In consequence of this, the World has accidentally seen their vast Plan of Power (formed by the great *Colbert*[39] almost a Century ago) carried on, tho' with frequent Interruptions, and in a great Degree now accomplished, thro' a Variety of Reigns, Wars and Administrations. The *Monarch's* Power gives *Unity* and *Steddiness,* the Principle of *Honour* gives *Vigour,* to every *Movement* of the State.

Thus, in Contradiction to all known Example, *France* hath become powerful, while she seemed to lead the Way in Effeminacy: And while she hath allured her neighbour Nations, by her own Example, to drink largely of her *circaean* and *poisoned Cup* of *Manners,*[40] hath secured her own *Health* by the *secret Antidote* of *Principle.* [141]

Forced by this, the Character of the *French* Nation, tho' inconsistent, is respectable: They have found, or rather invented, the Art of uniting

---

38. An encounter between French and invading English forces at Guinegate, in the Pas de Calais, on 16 August 1513; so called because of the speed of the French withdrawal when attacked.

39. Jean-Baptiste Colbert (1619–1683); controller general of finance and secretary of state for the navy under Louis XIV.

40. In book X of *The Odyssey* the sorceress Circe turns the companions of Odysseus into swine by means of poisonous drugs.

all Extremes: They have Virtues and Vices, Strengths and Weaknesses, seemingly incompatible. They are effeminate yet brave: insincere, yet honourable: hospitable, not benevolent: vain, yet subtile: splendid, not generous: warlike, yet polite: plausible, not virtuous: mercantile, yet not mean: In Trifles serious, gay in Enterprize: Women at the Toilet, Heroes in the Field: profligate in Heart; in Conduct, decent: Divided in Opinion, in Action united: In Manners weak, but strong in Principle: *Contemptible* in *private* Life; in *public, Formidable.* [142]

SECT. VII

Of the most probable Tendency of these Effects

Notwithstanding this apparent Objection, therefore, the Principles here advanced maintain their Force. And thus we see, how our *effeminate Manners* and *Defect* of *Principle* have weakened the national Capacity, and Spirit of Defence; and by giving a new Turn to our national *Disunion,* have still farther aggravated these ruling Evils in the State.

What then is the most probable Consequence of this *national Debility?*

'Tis from an *outward Enemy,* as hath been observed, that Danger is most to be apprehended. [143]

The FRENCH, in Land Armies, are far our Superiors: They are making large and dreadful Strides towards us, in *naval Power.* They have more *than disputed* with us the Empire of the *Mediterranean.* They are driving us from our Forts and Colonies in *America.*[41]

---

41. Brown here makes general reference to the military and naval reverses suffered by British forces during the early years of the Seven Years' War. The conflict had been precipitated by French attempts to prevent the westward expansion beyond the Allegheny Mountains of English settlements in North America. Accordingly the French had sought to construct a series of forts along the Ohio and Mississippi rivers, linking French territories in Canada and Louisiana. Initial clashes in the spring of 1754 had culminated in the calamitous defeat of British forces under General Braddock at Monongahela on 6 July 1755. Disaster in the new world was matched by calamity in the old, where the British had just lost Minorca to the French. On 14 March 1757 Admiral Byng had been executed by firing squad on his own quarterdeck following a court martial in which it had been found that he had shown culpable reluctance to engage the French fleet then investing the British naval base at Minorca.

These are the steddy Effects of *their* Principles and Union; of *our* Deficiency in *both*.

These Causes reach to, and operate, even in the *new* World. *Their Governors* of Colonies are actuated by *Honour* and their *Monarch's Power: Ours,* too commonly, by *Self-Love* and uncontrouled *Rapine. Their* Zeal and Policy direct them to make *Converts* and *Friends* of the *Indian Nations:*[42] *Our* Irreligion prevents [144] the *one*; our dishonest Treatment, the *other*. For by the best Accounts, our Colonies have in general copied, and even outgone us, in every *fashionable Degeneracy*.

Should the *French,* then, possess themselves of *North America,* what Eye can be so weak, as not to see the Consequence? Must not a naval Power come upon us, *equal,* if not superior to our own?

Thus by a gradual and unperceived Decline, we seem gliding down to Ruin. We laugh, we sing, we feast, we play: We *adopt* every *Vanity,* and *catch* at every *Lure,* thrown out to us by the *Nation* that is *planning* our *Destruction*; and while Fate is hanging over us, are *sightless* and thence *secure*. Were we but as *innocent* as *Blind,* we should, in our *Fond*[145]*ness* for *French* Manners, compleatly resemble the *Lamb* described by the *Poet*:

> The Lamb thy Riot dooms to bleed to Day,
> Had he thy Reason, wou'd he skip and play?
> Pleas'd to the last, he crops the flow'ry Food;
> And *licks* the *Hand* that's *rais'd* to *shed his Blood*.[43]

---

42. French forces in the early 1750s were supported by large numbers of Indian auxiliaries.

43. Pope, *An Essay on Man,* I.81–84.

PART III

OF THE

SOURCES

OF

THESE MANNERS

AND

PRINCIPLES

PART III

OF THE

SOURCES

OF

These MANNERS and PRINCIPLES

SECT. I

Of a general Mistake on this Subject

The publick Effects of our Manners and Principles here enumerated, begin now to appear too manifest in our public Miscarriages, to be any longer derided. The Nation stands aghast [150] at it's own Misfortunes: But, like a Man starting suddenly from Sleep, by the Noise of some approaching Ruin, knows neither whence it comes, nor how to avoid it.

In Proof of this, we need only look into the late Instructions from Constituents to Representatives. These, we see, seldom look farther than the immediate and incidental Occasion of each particular Misconduct: While the grand general Principles in which these Misconducts have been chiefly founded, are neither seen, nor suspected: Nay, an impartial Enquiry will probably convince us, that while they strike at the Shoots and Branches, they feed the Root from whence these Misconducts have been originally derived.

For it seems to be the ruling Maxim of this Age and Nation, that if our Trade and [151] Wealth are but increased, we are powerful, happy, and secure: And in estimating the real Strength of the Kingdom, the sole

Question for many Years hath been, "What Commerce and Riches the Nation is possessed of?" A Question, which an ancient Lawgiver would have laughed at.

There never was a more fatal Error more greedily embraced by any People.

SECT. II

Of the Effects of exorbitant Trade and Wealth, on Manners

By Wealth is understood, every kind of useful Possession; or Money, which is it's Sign, and may be converted into it.

By Commerce is understood the Exchange of Wealth, for mutual Benefit. [152]

The Effects of Commerce on Manners have by most Writers, I think, been considered as *uniform.* Even the sage and amiable MONTESQUIEU says only, in general Terms, "That Commerce polishes Manners, but corrupts Manners."* Whereas, from a candid View of it's Nature and Effects, we shall probably find, that in it's first and middle Stages it is beneficent; in it's last, dangerous and fatal.

If we view Commerce in its first Stages, we shall see, that it supplies mutual Necessities, prevents mutual Wants, extends mutual Knowledge, eradicates mutual Prejudice, and spreads mutual Humanity.

If we view it in its middle and more advanced Period, we shall see, it provides [153] Conveniencies, increaseth Numbers, coins Money, gives Birth to Arts and Science, creates equal Laws, diffuses general Plenty and general Happiness.

---

* L'Esprit des Loix, l. xx. c. 1.[1]

1. An over-compressed expression which sounds like nonsense, but which Montesquieu explains more fully: "On peut dire que les lois du commerce perfectionnent les moeurs, par la même raison que ces mêmes lois perdent les moeurs. Le commerce corrompt les moeurs pures: c'était le sujet des plaintes de Platon; il polit et adoucit les moeurs barbares, comme nous le voyons tous les jours"; "It can be said that the laws of commerce bring manners to a point of perfection, for the same reason that these same laws destroy manners. Commerce corrupts pure manners: this was the subject of Plato's complaints; it polishes and softens barbaric manners, as we see every day" (Montesquieu, *De l'Esprit des Loix*, XX.1).

If we view it in it's third and highest Stage, we shall see it change it's Nature and Effects. It brings in Superfluity and vast Wealth; begets Avarice, gross Luxury, or effeminate Refinement among the higher Ranks, together with general Loss of Principle.

Concerning the two first Stages of Commerce, I shall have no Dispute with the present Times: It's Benefits are generally acknowledged. The dangerous Effects of it's Exorbitance or Excess have not yet been sufficiently developed. [154]

That Commerce in it's Excess brings a general Superfluity of Goods, that this general Superfluity settles in particular Hands into vast Wealth, will be readily acknowledged.

The next Step is, to consider how vast Wealth naturally produces Avarice, Luxury, or Effeminacy, according to the Genius or Circumstances of the People among whom it comes.

Industry, in it's first Stages, is *frugal*, not *ungenerous:* It's End being that of Self-Preservation and moderate Enjoyment, it's little Superfluities are often employed in Acts of Generosity and Beneficence. But the daily Increase of Wealth by Industry, naturally increases the *Love* [155] of Wealth. The Passion for Money, being founded, not in Sense, but Imagination, admits of no Satiety, like those which are called the natural Passions. Thus the Habit of saving Money, beyond every other Habit, gathers Strength by continued Gratification. The Attention of the whole Man is immediately turned upon it; and every other Pursuit held light when compared with the Increase of Wealth. Hence, the natural Character of the Trader, when his final Prospect is the Acquisition of Wealth, is that of *Industry* and *Avarice*.

What is true, in this Respect, of *trading Men*, is true of *trading Nations*. If their Commerce be that of Oeconomy in the Extreme, if the last Object of their Pursuit be Wealth for it's own Sake, if the Leaders of such a People be *commercial*, the Cha[156]racter of that People, and it's Leaders, will be found in *Industry* and *Avarice*.

But if a trading Nation hath a large *Territory*, sufficient to create a *Landed Interest*, Commerce will produce very different Effects.

For as it multiplies Inhabitants, and brings in Wealth, it naturally increases the Value of landed Estates. Barren Grounds are cultivated, and cultivated Spots are made more fertile. Hence a vast Accession of Income to the Nobility and Gentry.

These Ranks of Men being not bred up to Habits of Industry; on the contrary, their increased Rents coming in unsought for, and their Time being often a Load upon them, thro' want of Capacity and Employment, the Habit of *Indulgence* comes on, and grows of Course. Addi[157]tional Wealth gives the Power to gratify every Desire that rises, Leisure improves these Desires into Habits; thus Money is at length considered as no more than the Means of Gratification; and hence the genuine Character of a rich Nobility or Gentry, is that of Expence and Luxury.

But the first Essays of Luxury, like those of every other Art, are coarse and rude: The natural Character of Luxury, therefore, is to refine by Degrees: Especially, when assisted by Commerce, it advances apace into Refinement. For Commerce searches every Shore and Climate for it's Supplies; and Art is studious, because rewarded, in arranging and applying these Materials to the most exquisite and delicate Use. Thus every coarser Mode of Pleasure is by Degrees despised; new Habits of higher Indulgence come on: [158] gross Luxury is banished, and Effeminacy takes it's Place.

But Luxury, in this *last* Period, being exhausted in it's Course; and turned, for want of new Objects of Indulgence, into Debility and Languor, would expire or sleep, were it not awakened by another Passion, which again calls it into Action. Nothing is so natural to effeminate Minds, as *Vanity*. This rouzes the luxurious and debilitated Soul; and the Arts of pleasurable Enjoyment are now pushed to their highest Degree, by the Spirit of delicate Emulation.

Thus the whole Attention of the Mind is centred on *Brilliancy* and *Indulgence:* Money, tho' despised as an *End*, is greedily sought as a *Means:* And *Self*, under a dif[159]ferent Appearance from the trading Spirit, takes equal Possession of the Soul.

Thus as the Character of a State altogether commercial in the highest Degree, is that of Industry and Avarice; so, in a Nation of extended Territory, where Commerce is in it's highest Period, while it's trading Members retain their Habits of Industry and Avarice, the natural Character of it's landed Ranks, it's Nobility and Gentry, is that of "a vain, luxurious, and selfish Effeminacy."

We speak here of the simple and proper Effects of Trade and Wealth, uncontrouled by opposite Manners or Principles; which, it is to be observed, never existed probably, at least in the mixed State, in their full Extent: Individuals there are, and will be, in almost every State and Period, who are [160] influenced by dissimilar Manners or Principles: There are Traders who are generous; Nobles and Gentry whose ultimate Passion is for Gold: But such Exceptions affect not the general Principle: And tho' these incidental Mixtures *Weaken* the different Colours of different Ranks or States, yet still the different Colours remain in their Nature distinct and invariable.

'Tis probable, the Reader will have discovered, that this Reasoning is strengthened by, or rather built upon, the Examples of two neighbour Nations; one wholly commercial, that of *Holland:* The other a mixed State, compounded of a commercial and landed Interest; I mean *our own.* And to say the Truth; no two Nations perhaps ever existed, which approached so near to the full and proper Effects of the Causes here alledged. [161]

It will appear immediately why the Genius of the Republic of *Holland* is here analysed into its first Principles; which are simply, those of Industry and the Love of Gain.

In the mean Time, we may justly conclude from this Argument, that the exorbitant Trade and Wealth of *England* sufficiently account for it's present *Effeminacy.*

SECT. III

Of the Effects of exorbitant Trade and Wealth, on the religious Principle

Such therefore are the ruling Manners which may naturally be expected in a Nation thus circumstanced, unless they be [162] counteracted by opposite Principles: 'Tis now Time to consider the natural Effects of exorbitant Trade and Wealth, on all those salutary Principles by which these effeminate Manners can most effectually be controuled.

Let us still carry the two characteristic States of *Holland* and *England,* in our Eye.

Whether, then, we view the commercial State, where the Love of Money rules; or the mixed State, where vain Effeminacy predominates;

we shall find both these national Characters have but a bad Aspect and Influence on every Kind of Principle. Let us first consider that of Religion. [163]

Avarice seems not, in it's own Nature, prone to destroy *speculative* religious Belief; but effectually to extinguish *active* religious Principle.

It tends not to destroy speculative Belief, because this Effect must be a Work of Application, Time, and Labour: Now the Labour of Avarice is naturally bent on it's main Object, *Money*; therefore, to waste this Labour on the Propagation of the unprofitable and fruitless Doctrines of Irreligion, must ever be contrary to it's ruling Character.

But Avarice naturally tends to the Destruction of active religious Principles; because this is chiefly a Matter of *habitual Impression*; and therefore, in order to accomplish it's Destruction, nothing more is [164] necessary than to *forget*. Now this requires no positive Act or Labour of the Mind, but is the natural Result from an attentive Pursuit of the favourite Object, *Money*.

Hence, in a mere commercial State, actuated by the Love of Gain, Religion is not railed at or disputed against, but only *neglected* and *forgot*. And thus, the *genuine Trader,* who never questioned the Articles of his national Faith at home, scruples not to forswear *Christianity,* and tread upon the Cross in *Japan,*[2] and returns the same good *Christian* as he went.

But in the mixed State, where national Effeminacy forms the *primary,* and Avarice only the *secondary* Character, the Effects of exorbitant Trade and Wealth on religious Principle, will be widely different. [165]

---

2. This is the ceremony of *Yefumi,* employed by the Japanese to detect Christians who were forbidden in Japan. The origin of the practice is described by George Psalmanazaar, *An Historical and Geographical Description of Formosa* (1704): "the *Dutch* advised the Emperor to distinguish *Christians* from all other *Foreigners* by this Test *viz.* by making an Image of Christ Crucified . . . and requiring all *Foreigners* to trample upon this Image: For, said they, If these *Foreigners* be *Christians* they will not trample upon it; and all others who do trample upon it, are certainly no *Christians.* . . . the *Hollanders* make no scruple to trample upon the Crucifix whenever they are required to do it" (pp. 316–17). The ceremony had been referred to by Swift in Part III, chapter 11 of *Gulliver's Travels* (1726).

Lord *VERULAM* hath somewhere observed, that "Times of Atheism are civil Times."[3] He had been much nearer the Truth, had he affirmed, that "Civil Times are Times of Atheism." He mistook the Cause for the Effect.

This Effect of national Luxury and Refinement, in producing national Irreligion, is not difficult to account for. In some Periods of a State, Opinions controul Manners; but in most Periods, Manners controul Opinions. Where the ruling Manners coincide with the common Good, as in the middle Periods of a State, there we commonly find that a rational and beneficent System of Religion prevails: This comes to pass, because the Principles of the received Religion contradict not the ruling Manners. [166]

But in the State and Period of Luxury or Refinement, active religious Principle is lost thro' the attentive Pursuit of *Pleasure*; as in the commercial State, it is lost thro' the attentive Pursuit of *Gain*.

And *speculative* Belief, in this Period, must naturally be lost along with *practical*; because *Leisure* and *Literature* having opened the Field of *Disputation*, Vice as well as Virtue will of course arm herself with every Weapon of Preservation and Offence. Luxury therefore will generally list[4] under the Banner of Irreligion; because Religion condemns her Manners; Irreligion suffers, or approves them.

To confirm the Truth of this Reasoning, we need only observe, that in the Period of refined Luxury, *few* but they who are in[167]volved in the *Vices,* are involved in the *Irreligion* of the Times.

One Exception, however, must be made, with Regard to the *Writers* against Religion. For *these,* though they *promote,* yet are not often *involved* in the common Degeneracy. This Fact hath been regarded as unaccountable: that *sober* Men of Morals apparently *unblameable,* should madly unhinge the great Principle of Religion and Society, without any visible Motive or Advantage. But by looking a little farther into human Nature, we shall easily resolve this seeming Paradox. These Writers are

3. In his essay "Of Atheisme," Francis Bacon lists the "*Causes* of *Atheisme,*" one of which is "*Learned Times,* specially with Peace, and Prosperity: For Troubles and Adversities doe more bow Mens Mindes to *Religion*" (Bacon, *Essayes,* p. 53).

4. I.e., enlist.

generally Men of Speculation and Industry; and therefore though they give themselves up to the Dictates of their ruling Passion, yet that ruling Passion commonly leads to the Tract of *abstemious* Manners. That Desire of *Distinction* and *Superiority,* so na[168]tural to Man, breaks out in a thousand various and fantastic Shapes, and in each of these, according as it is directed, becomes a Virtue or a Vice. In Times of Luxury and Dissipation therefore, when every Tenet of Irreligion is greedily embraced, what Road to *present Applause* can lie so open and secure, as that of disgracing religious Belief? Especially if the Writer help forward the Vices of the Times, by *relaxing Morals,* as well as *destroying Principle.* Such a Writer can have little else to do, but to new model the Paradoxes of ancient *Scepticism,* in order to *figure it* in the World, and be regarded by the Smatterers in Literature and Adepts in Folly, as a Prodigy of Parts and Learning. Thus his *Vanity* becomes deeply criminal, and is execrated by the Wise and Good, because it is gratified at the Expence of his Country's Welfare. But the *Consolation* which degenerate Manners receive from his fatal Tenets, is [169] repaid by eager *Praise:* And *Vice* impatiently drinks in and *applauds* his hoarse and boding Voice,[5] while like a *Raven,* he sits croaking universal Death, Despair, and Annihilation to the human Kind.

Thus, where Manners and Religion are opposed, nothing is so natural, as that the *one* should bear down the *other.* If Religion destroy not the ruling Manners, *these* will gather Strength, and destroy Religion.

Especially, in a Country where Freedom is established, and Manners lost through the Exorbitance of Wealth, the Duration of religious Principles can be but short. Despotism arms itself with Terror; and by checking the open and avowed *Profession,* checks in a certain Degree the *Progress* of *Impiety.* Whereas it must be [170] acknowledged and lamented, as one of the unalterable Defects of a free Government, that *Opinion* must have its Course. The Disease is bad; but the Cure would be fatal. Thus Freedom is compelled to admit an *Enemy,* who under the Pretence and Form of an *Ally,* often proves her *Destroyer.*

---

5. Cf. Lady Macbeth's words on hearing of the imminent arrival of Duncan: "The raven himself is hoarse, | That croaks the fatal entrance of Duncan | Under my battlements" (*Macbeth,* I.v.38–40).

SECT. IV

Of the Effects of exorbitant Trade and Wealth, on the Principle of Honour

In the mixed State, where Luxury and Effeminacy form the ruling Character of a People, the Excess of Trade and Wealth naturally tends to weaken or destroy the Principle of *Honour*, by fixing the Desire of Applause, and the Fear of Shame, on improper and ridiculous Objects. Instead of the Good of others, or the Happiness of [171] the Public, the Object of Pursuit naturally sinks into some unmanly and trifling Circumstance: The Vanity of Dress, Entertainments, Equipage, Furniture, of course takes Possession of the Heart.

But in the pure commercial State, where the Love of Gain predominates among the higher Ranks, the Desire of Applause and Fear of Shame are not *perverted*, but *extinguished*. The Lust of Gold swallows up every other Passion: and a Nation of this Character can without Emotion stand the Laughter and Contempt of *Europe*, and say with the Miser,

> Populus me sibilat; at mihi plaudo
> Ipse Domi, simulac Nummos contemplor in Arca.[6]

In whatever Shape, therefore, the Passion for Applause appear, whether it assume [172] the fantastic Form of Vanity, the more solemn one of Pride, or the steady and elevated Desire of rational Esteem; we shall find this Excess of national Avarice tends to its Extinction. A great Writer indeed hath told us, that "Vanity creates Industry;"* which is true:

---

* L'Esprit des Loix, l. xix. l. 9.[7]

6. "The people hiss me, but at home I applaud myself, once I gaze on the money in my chest" (Horace, *Satires*, I.i.66–67).

7. Once again, Brown compresses into blank paradox a series of thoughts which Montesquieu develops with more nuance and suppleness: "La vanité est un aussi bon ressort pour un gouvernement, que l'orgueil en est un dangereux. Il n'y a pour cela qu'à se représenter, d'un côté, les biens sans nombre qui résultent de la vanité: de là le luxe, l'industrie, les arts, les modes, la politesse, le goût; et, d'un autre côté, les maux infinis qui naissent de l'orgueil de certaines nations: la paresse, la pauvreté, l'abandon de tout, la destruction des nations que le hazard a fait tomber entre leurs

Notwithstanding this, we have seen above, that Industry in the Excess naturally begets Avarice; and Avarice in the Excess works a total Change in the Soul, and expels that Vanity which gave it birth.

The same great Writer hath told us, "that Pride destroys Industry;"* the Reverse of which holds equally true: "that Industry destroys Pride:" We speak here of Pride in the blameable Sense, as when it riseth into blind and overbearing *Insolence.* [173] Industry in the moderate Degree tends to destroy this contemptuous Spirit, by introducing Knowledge and Equality: and in this Respect, as in most others, is attended with excellent Effects.

But the Spirit of Trade in its Excess, by introducing Avarice, destroys the Desire of *rational Esteem.* In Confirmation of this, we need only cast our Eyes on the HOLLANDERS and CHINESE, among whom the trading Spirit is almost in its unmixed Perfection: The one is the most *mercenary,* the other the most *thieving* of all Nations.

SECT. V

Of their Effects on public Spirit

This Part of our Subject needs little Investigation. For both in the commercial [174] and mixed State, it appears, that exorbitant Trade and Wealth tend naturally to turn all the Attention of Individuals on *selfish* Gratification.

---

mains, et de la leur même. La paresse est l'effet de l'orgueil; le travail est une suite de la vanité: l'orgueil d'un Espagnol le portera à ne pas travailler; la vanité d'un Français le portera à savoir travailler mieux que les autres"; "Vanity is as good a motivation for a government, as pride is a dangerous one. One needs only to consider, on the one hand, the uncountable benefits which arise from vanity: luxury, industry, arts, fashions, politeness, taste; and, on the other, the infinite evils which are born of the pride of certain nations: idleness, poverty, disregard for everything, the destruction of nations which have fallen into their hands by chance, and from that their own destruction. Idleness is an effect of pride; work is a consequence of vanity: the pride of a Spaniard will induce him not to work; the vanity of a Frenchman will induce him to know how to work better than others" (*De l'Esprit des Loix,* XIX.9).

* Ibid.

Therefore they must of course generally tend to destroy the Principle of public Spirit: because *this* implies, that our Attention and Regard is turned on *others*.

In the commercial State, Avarice represents *Wealth*, in the mixed State Effeminacy represents *Pleasure*, as the *chief Good*. Both these Delusions tend to the Extinction of public Spirit.

These Delusions create a new Train of Wants, Fears, Hopes, and Wishes: All these terminating in selfish Regard, naturally destroy every Effort of generous and public Principle. [175]

SECT. VI

Farther Remarks on this Subject

In Consequence of these Remarks, some farther Distinctions will arise.

Thus, the religious Principle will *seem* to exist in the commercial State, where Avarice forms the national Character; while in the mixed State where Luxury and Effeminacy predominate, it is evidently destroyed. The Reason is, that in the first, although active Principle is lost, speculative Belief is not controverted: Whereas, in the latter, not only active Principle is lost, but Religion itself (if such a State be free) is publickly insulted and derided. Thus in *Holland*, Religion *seems* yet to exist; while in *England* it is evidently destroyed. [176]

On the contrary, the Principle of Honour will seem to exist in the mixed State, where luxurious Effeminacy forms the primary Character of the Nation; while in the commercial State, where Avarice predominates, the Principle is evidently no more. The Reason is, that in the former, the Love of Applause and Fear of Shame are not wholly destroyed, but perverted, and turned upon unworthy Objects; while in the latter, the Passion itself is totally extinguished. Thus the faint Appearance of Honour yet remains in *England*, while in *Holland* it is manifestly destroyed.

But as modern *Dutch* Religion, and modern *English* Honour, seem no more than the Ghosts of departed Principles, so they have precisely those Effects, which [177] may reasonably be expected from such shadowy Non-Entities.

Again: The Colours or Characters of Industry and Avarice will naturally be *strong* in the commercial State: because, being almost wholly unmixed with Manners of a dissimilar Nature, the ruling Genius of the State is left uncontrouled, to its proper Operations and Effects.

But in the mixed State, where Industry and Love of Gain form the Character of the *secondary* Ranks; Dissipation and Effeminacy, of the *higher*; there the two separate Characters, by the Force of incidental Coalition and Example, will always influence each other in a certain Degree. Some ambitious Traders will aspire to luxurious Effeminacy: Some, of the higher Orders, will descend to Industry and Mer[178]chandise. Thus each Rank must be tinctured with a Colour different from its own; and hence, the general Colour or Character of each of these Ranks, will, in some measure be controuled and *weakened*.

This Circumstance is favourable to the mixed State, beyond that which is purely commercial; as it checks in a certain Degree the Virulence of the Excess; and produceth a national Character in some Measure approaching that of more moderate Trade and Wealth.

Hence too it follows, that a State purely commercial, when once arrived at the Period of exorbitant Wealth, will naturally degenerate *faster* than that which is compounded of Commerce and Luxury. For whatever Causes check the ruling Man[179]ners in their *Degree,* will check them in their *Consequences.*

But beyond this, there is another Reason, why the State purely commercial will degenerate faster than the mixed State. In the commercial State, the ruling Manners go Hand in Hand with the Exorbitance of Wealth; because the Love of Gain, which forms the leading Character, being likewise the leading Motive, must be even prior to this Exorbitance in the Order of our Ideas; and therefore, in its Effects, must be at least contemporary.

But in the mixed State, there will always be a short Period between the national Exorbitance of Wealth, and the national Increase of luxurious Effeminacy: because Manners, once got into a certain Track, are not at once thrown out of it. [180] There must be a short Period, before the leading Parts of the Nation can *feel* their Increase of Wealth; and after this, another Period, before new and more refined Modes of Pleasure can be invented.

Hence a neighbouring Republic[8] seems to have well nigh filled up the Measure of its Iniquities; while *ours,* as yet, are only rising towards the *Brim.*

Lastly; though the ruling Manners of such a mixed State are luxurious and effeminate, yet its public Measures will be *commercial.* First, because Commerce is the Hand-Maid of *Wealth,* and therefore of *Pleasure.* Secondly, because the Idea of national Strength as well as Happiness being degenerated into that of Wealth and external Good, Commerce will above all Things be naturally encouraged, because it is the Means of procuring them. [181]

SECT. VII

A Review of the Argument

Thus our present exorbitant Degree of Trade and Wealth, in a mixed State like that of *England,* naturally tends to produce luxurious and effeminate Manners in the higher Ranks, together with a general Defect of *Principle.* And as the internal Strength of a Nation will always depend chiefly on the Manners and Principles of it's leading Members, so these effeminate Manners and this Defect of Principle operate powerfully, and fatally, on the national Conduct and Affairs. They have produced a general Incapacity, have weakened the national Spirit of Defence, have heightened the national Disunion: And this national Disunion, besides it's proper and immediate Effects, being founded in [182] Avarice for the Ends of Dissipation, hath again weakened the small Remainder of publick Capacity and Defence; and thus seems to have fitted us for a Prey to the Insults and Invasions of our most powerful Enemy.

SECT. VIII

An Objection considered

Tho' this Estimate may appear *just* to those who take an enlarged View of Things in their Principles and Consequences; yet I am not ignorant

8. I.e., Holland.

of certain Maxims, generally approved, and hardly even disputed among modern Politicians, which if true, would weaken or overturn these accumulated Proofs.

The capital Maxim, which seems to include the rest, is this; "That vast Trade [183] and Wealth, above all things make a Nation powerful and invincible, as they increase it's Numbers, enable it to pay it's Fleets and Armies, provide continual Supplies for War; and thus, in the End, tire out and defeat every Enemy, whose Wealth and Commerce are inferior."

The Examination of this Maxim will throw many strong collateral Lights upon our main Subject.

First it affirms, "That Trade and Wealth make a Nation strong, because they make it populous." This indeed is true of the first and second Periods of Trade and Wealth: That it is true of the *third* or *highest* Period, of which *England* is now possessed, may very reasonably be questioned. In the first Period, Industry is chiefly [184] employed in cultivating the Lands, in encreasing, manufacturing, and exchanging the Produce of the Mother Country. These Branches of Trade call for vast additional Numbers of Hands; and hence an Increase of Numbers naturally ariseth.

The same Effect takes Place in the second Period of Trade; so far as home Productions are *exchanged* for foreign ones. This Stage of Commerce brings on a fresh Demand of Artificers of new and various Kinds, produces and Increase of Labour, and therefore of Inhabitants.

But in the third or highest Period of Trade, of which *England* is now possessed, there are very extensive Branches of Commerce, which bring no new Accession of Numbers to the Commonwealth. I mean, [185] all those Branches of Commerce, where *Money* is sent and exchanged for *foreign* Goods. This Species of Trade occasions little Increase of *Labour*, and therefore less of *Numbers*; except only of those few who navigate the Vessels thus employed, to their respective Ports. And as this kind of Trade will always grow and predominate, in proportion as a Nation becomes more luxurious and effeminate, so for this Reason the highest Stage of Trade is not naturally attended with the highest Increase of Labour, nor consequently of *Numbers*, as is commonly imagined. Besides this, in the refined Period, additional Art and Experience in

Labour prevent, in some Measure, the Increase of Numbers. By the Invention of Machines, an equal Degree both of Tillage and Trade is carried on by fewer Hands, than in the simpler Periods; and therefore the Increase of Numbers is [186] by no means proportional to the Increase of Commerce and Wealth.

But these are far from being the only Considerations worth our Notice on this Subject. For when we speak of any Stage of Trade, we must in Reason take in *every* Circumstance which naturally attends it. There are other Causes, therefore, why Numbers increase not, but rather naturally *diminish,* in the highest Period of Trade and Wealth.

For *first,* the Vanity and Effeminacy which this exorbitant Pitch of Wealth brings on, lessens the Desire of Marriage.

Secondly, the Intemperance and Disease which this Period of Trade naturally produceth among the *lower Ranks* in great [187] Cities, bring on in some Degree an Impotence of Propagation.

Thirdly, This Debility is always attended with a Shortness of Life, both in the Parents and the Offspring; and therefore a still farther Diminution of Numbers follows on the whole.

Matter of Fact confirms these Reasonings; and lies open to every Man's Observation. Since the first Increase of Tillage and Home-manufactures, the Increase of Inhabitants hath been great in *England:* Since the vast Increase of foreign Commerce, the Increase of Numbers is hardly perceivable. Nay, there is great Reason to believe, that upon the whole, the Nation is less populous than it was fifty Years ago, tho' it's Trade perhaps is doubled. Some trading Towns indeed are better [188] peopled, but others are thinned by the Flux of Commerce. The Metropolis seems to augment in its Dimensions: But it appears, by the best Calculations, that it's Numbers are diminished; And as to the Villages thro' *England,* there is great Reason to believe, they are in general at a Stand, and many of them thinner of Inhabitants than in the Beginning of this Century. 'Tis hard to obtain Certainty in this Particular, without a general Examination and Comparison. But it appears by the Registers of some *Country* Parishes, which I have looked into, that from the Year 1550 to 1710, the Number of Inhabitants increased gradually; the two Extremes being to each other, as

57 to 72; and that from 1710 to the present Time, the Number has been at a Stand, if not rather diminished.⁹ [189]

But suppose, what there is no Reason to believe, that our present Excess of Trade and Overflow of Wealth have in some Degree increased our *Numbers*, yet it will probably appear, that they have as much, at least, impaired our *bodily Strength*.¹⁰ For as *Temperance* is the ruling Character of the middle Stage of Commerce, so is *Intemperance* of the highest. Hence, Health and Strength prevail in the first; Disease and Debility in the latter. This is universally confirmed by Fact: Villages abounding with Health; commercial Cities with Disease. So that an Army taken from the Villages, with equal Commanders, Arms, and Discipline, would drive the same Number of debilitated Gin-drinkers, like a Flock of Geese before them. [190]

The Author of the *Fable of the Bees* made his Boast, that the Wisdom of the Legislature had, upon his Plan, adopted the Encouragement of this pernicious Liquid:¹¹ But the same Wisdom hath upon Trial been obliged to *discourage* the Use of this malignant Spirit; as they found that it ruined the Health, and shortened the Lives, of half the lower Ranks in *London*.

And all good Men hope, that the Time will come, when this infernal Potion will be laid under such Discouragements, as may amount to a general Prohibition. The Necessity of such a Reformation grows greater every Day, not only in *London*, but throughout the Kingdom. For in some

9. The population of Britain increased very slowly from 1681 (when it was just over 5,000,000) to the mid-1720s (when it reached approximately 5,600,000). At that point it dipped for five years or so, before resuming its gentle upward trend. In 1757, the population of Britain was approximately 6,100,000 (E. A. Wrigley, "British population during the 'long' eighteenth century, 1680–1840," in *The Cambridge Economic History of Modern Britain*, vol. I [Cambridge: Cambridge University Press, 2004], pp. 57–95; statistics drawn from table 3.1, p. 64).

10. Fertility rates in Britain increased "considerably" during the early part of the eighteenth century; adult mortality "improved sharply," but infant mortality remained broadly constant (ibid., pp. 69 and 79).

11. For Mandeville's comments on gin, see Remark "G" in *The Fable of the Bees* (Mandeville, *Fable*, vol. I, pp. 86–93). Hogarth's paired prints, "Beer Street" and "Gin Lane," both published in 1751, contrast the healthy consequences of drinking beer with the calamities which arise from the prostrate inebriation produced by drinking gin.

Villages in *England* there is now a greater Quantity of Gin consumed than of Ale. [191]

But to quit these inferior Considerations, tho' they all unite in confirming the Theory here advanced; the Weight of the Reply lies indeed in another Circumstance: For altho' we should admit (what is not true) that our present Exorbitance of Trade and Wealth increased our Numbers and bodily Force, yet as the real and essential Strength of a Nation consists in the manners and Principles of it's *leading Part*; and as our present Excess of Trade and Wealth hath produced such fatal Effects on these Manners and Principles; no Increase of Numbers in the inferior Ranks can possibly make amends for this internal and capital Defect. Such a Nation can, at best, only resemble a large *Body*, actuated (yet hardly actuated) by an incapable, a vain, a dastardly, and effeminate *Soul*. [192]

But the Maxim we are engaged to obviate, alledges farther, that "This exorbitant Increase of Trade and Wealth enables a Nation to pay it's Fleets and Armies, and afford continual Supplies for War." Yet, even this Part of the Maxim, in it's modern Acceptation, is far beyond the Truth.

For under the present Stage of Trade, the Increase of Wealth is by no means equally or proportionally diffused: The Trader reaps the main Profit: after him, the Landlord, in a lower Degree: But the common Artificer, and still more the common Labourer, gain little by the exorbitant Advance of Trade: It is true, their Wages are increased; but so are the Prices of Provisions too: and therefore they are no richer than before. [193] Now Taxes and public Supplies are raised upon the Consumer: and as it appears from hence, that only a few of the Consumers are made richer by the Exorbitance of Trade, it follows, that not the Nation in general, but a select Number of Individuals only, are made more capable of contributing to those Supplies, which are levied without Distinction on the *whole*. Would they who reap the plenteous Harvest of foreign Trade, generously allot their proportional and extraordinary Gains to the Service of the Public, we should then indeed be furnished with a *new* Argument in Favour of Commerce in it's highest Pitch.

Farther: As the labouring Ranks are little or nothing enriched by the exorbitant Degree of Trade, so it often happens that even the higher Ranks, and the Nation in general, are not *more*, nay perhaps *less* en[194]abled to contribute to the public Supplies, than when possessed of Wealth in a more moderate Degree. For we have seen, in the Progress of this Estimate, that the natural Effect of an Increase of Wealth, is an Increase of Luxury, Vanity, and Expence; which, if it outrun the Increase of Wealth, as in it's Nature it tends to do, instead of Riches will bring on public Poverty. For the Ability or Wealth of a People, considered in their Capacity for raising Supplies, consists not in the Largeness of their Income, but in the Proportion of their Expences to their Income: It consists not in "what they *have,*" but "what they can *Spare?*" Hence it appears, that a Nation may be at once very *rich,* and very *poor*; rich in Income, but poor thro' Extravagance. And as national Extravagance is the natural Effect of an Overflow of Wealth, so national Indigence [195] is it's most natural and final Consequence. How far this is our present Situation, can hardly be necessary to affirm.

To this Argument it may possibly be objected, that if great Wealth is but among us, new Imposts will naturally *force* it into Circulation: That the more the Artificers and Labourers are taxed, the more their Wages will increase, and consequently their Ability to bear the increasing Taxes: And that as to the higher Ranks, exorbitant Wealth *enables* them still better to endure additional Imposts, because these deprive the Great of nothing but the Superfluities of Vanity and Luxury.

To this it is replied, that in Case of additional Taxes, tho' the Poor *must* indeed increase their Wages in order to subsist, yet this Increase never takes Place, till [196] they are compelled by the last *Necessity* and *Want:* The natural Consequence of which must be Murmurs, Sedition, and Tumults. With Regard to the higher Ranks, a parallel Reply may suffice: For in the refined Period, when Manners and Principles are lost, the Luxuries of Life become *Necessaries* among the Great; and therefore will be as obstinately adhered to, and quitted with the same Reluctance, as Food and Cloathing by the *Poor.* The Consequence therefore must be the same; a general Discontent and Disaffection to the Government, among the higher Ranks of Life.

Is not all this confirmed by evident Facts; There is at present in this Nation a Mass of Wealth at least twelve Times more than the publick Debt: Yet we are reduced to the sad Necessity of plunging [197] deeper every

Day. What is the Reason? No Ministry dares to provoke and exasperate a luxurious and selfish Nation, by demanding such Sums, as every one has the *Power* had he but the *Will*, to bestow.

But beyond all this, will any Man of Sense assert, that the Circumstance of *paying* an Army or a Fleet, is the one thing that will decide a War? 'Tis true, indeed, Provisions, Arms, Ammunition are necessary; and therefore *Wealth*, because it procures them. But will a General or Admiral therefore gain the Victory, only because his Men are furnished with Provisions, Arms, and Ammunition? If not, what can Trade or Wealth do, towards making a Nation victorious? Again, therefore, let me remind my Countrymen, that the capital Question still remains, not "who shall *pay*, but who shall *fight?*" [198]

There is a trite Observation on Foot, indeed, drawn from the best political Writers ill understood, that "the Principles of War are wholly changed; and that not the Nation who has the best *Troops*, but the longest *Purse*, will in the End obtain the Victory." This, in the modern Application of it, is a most dangerous Maxim. It naturally tends to extinguish military Skill, as well as Honour: and will inevitably sink the People that maintains it, into a Nation of defenseless and Money-getting Cowards.

It must be confessed that Doctor DAVENANT, the most able Writer on these Subjects, hath affirmed, "That now, the whole Art of War is in a Manner reduced to Money; and now-a-days, that Prince who can best find Money to [199] feed, cloath, and pay his Army, not he that hath the most valiant Troops, is surest of Success and Conquest."* This Declaration, which is now stolen and retailed for new, by every modern Dabler in Politics, has had the usual Fortune of these kind of Thefts, to be misunderstood: as may appear from the general Tenor of the Doctor's Writings. To shew this, two Instances, out of many may suffice. Even when speaking on the Benefits of foreign Trade, he warns us, as if he had foreseen all that has befallen, or is likely to befall us. For he says, "If a trading and rich People are grown soft and luxurious, their Wealth will invite over

---

* Ways and Means, p. 27.[12]

12. Charles Davenant, *An Essay Upon Ways and Means of Supplying the War*, third edition (1701), p. 27.

to them Invaders from Abroad, and their being *effeminate* will make the Conquest easy."* And [200] again, in Terms yet stronger: "In succeeding Times our Manners may come to be depraved; and when this happens, all Sorts of Miseries will invade us: The whole Wealth of the Kingdom will not be sufficient for it's Defence."†

Thus, what he and other sensible Writers have affirmed under proper Restrictions, and upon Supposition that a Nation maintained it's Manners and Principles, is now advanced absolutely, and without Restriction, as if Manners and Principles, military and naval Skill and Courage, had no Part, or at least no essential Part, in the Success of War.

These shallow Politicians, therefore, might well be put in Mind of the Maxim of a warlike Prince, when his Ministers [201] dissuaded him from attacking a wealthy Enemy, because he wanted Money to pay his Troops: "My Enemies, said he, are rich, luxurious, and effeminate; my Troops are valiant and hardy; my Officers brave and honourable; they shall plant *my* Standard in my Enemy's Country, and then *my Enemy shall pay them*."[15]

We have lately seen this military Conduct followed by a brave King, in the Electorate of *Saxony:*[16] We ourselves have formerly pursued it on

---

* Dav. on Trade, v. ii. p. 13.[13]

† Ibid. p. 317.[14]

13. Charles Davenant, *Discourses on the Public Revenues, and on Trade, Discourse I: That Foreign Trade is Beneficial to England*, in Davenant, *Works*, vol. I, p. 353.

14. Ibid., *Discourse III: On the Plantation Trade*, in Davenant, *Works*, vol. II, p. 76.

15. Untraced.

16. Frederick II (known as "the Great") (1712–86), king of Prussia since 1740, was one of Britain's allies in the Seven Years' War. On 29 August 1756, Prussian forces had invaded Saxony, the Saxon army surrendering on 17 October after the Battle of Lobositz (1 October). On 18 February 1757, Pitt had risen in the House to urge full British support for Prussia, a commitment which translated into a yearly subsidy of £700,000, thus bankrolling Frederick's military adventures. In the spring of that year Prussian forces invaded Bohemia, and on 6 May defeated an Austrian army under the walls of Prague. On 18 June, largely as a result of his own tactical blunders, Frederick was heavily defeated by the Austrians at Kolin. It was his first defeat after eighteen straight victories in the field. However, later in the year he exacted full revenge, with a technically superb defeat of superior French and Imperial forces at Rossbach on 5 November (10,000 enemy casualties to only 500 Prussians), the defeat of a numerically superior Austrian army at Leuthen on 5 December, and

the Plains of *Agincourt* and *Cressi:*[17] The *French* are now pursuing it on the Plains of *America:*[18] And if we hold to our dastardly Maxim, they will pursue it on the Plains of *Salisbury.*

Thus the boasted modern Maxim which we proposed to obviate, seems void of [202] Truth in every Branch of it: As it appears from this View, that without the internal Strength which Manners and Principles produce, the most exorbitant Trade and Wealth can never be the Foundation of a successful War; or give us any rational Prospect, either of *Victory* or *Self-Defence.*

SECT. IX

Another Objection considered

Such then are the natural Effects of exorbitant Trade and Wealth, unless counteracted by opposite Manners or Principles. The History of our own Nation would confirm these Truths in a most striking and particular Manner, were it within the proposed Limits of this Estimate, to enter so large a Field of Enquiry. We should there see, that Manners and Principles [203] have always prevailed, and baffled the most sanguine Attempts of Wealth, when set in Competition with them. This System would be found supported by a vast Variety of Events, from the Reign of *Elizabeth* to the present Times. But this might perhaps be regarded as a Research rather curious than necessary; since a single Reflection on the present State of the Kingdom may seem to stand in the Place of a thousand Proofs.

At present, therefore, we shall not touch on this Enquiry; but rather proceed to remove another Objection, which may seem to overturn the Theory here proposed.

For it is urged, that *France* is an Exception to the Truth of these Remarks: inasmuch as, in the midst of a large and extensive Commerce,

---

the capitulation of Breslau on 20 December. The king of Prussia was also a hero of Thomas Hollis, who in 1759 had a medal struck in his honor (Blackburne, *Memoirs*, vol. I, p. 80).

17. Famous English victories over the French, in 1415 and 1346 respectively.

18. See above, p. 312, n. 41.

which brings in a [204] vast Accession of Wealth, she stills retains her Principles and Power.

The Fact objected is true: but the Consequence follows not; because the Trade of *France* is limited and controuled by such Accidents, as prevent it's most dangerous and ruinous Effects on Government.

The *Poverty* of its *Noblesse* or leading Ranks, who are often possessed of sounding[19] Titles without any Realities annexed, as it prevents them from reaping that Increase of Wealth which naturally ariseth to a rich Landed Gentry from an Increase of Commerce, so it naturally drives them to the Profession of *Arms,* as the necessary Means of Support: This strengthens and supports their Monarchy; which, finding it's Advantage from this Disposition to [205] Arms, naturally gratifies this military Spirit in it's *Noblesse,* and gives it Exercise and Encouragement by frequent Wars.

Hence the national Spirit of the *French Noblesse* hath long been military, in the highest Degree.

With Regard to Commerce, it's Growth in *France* hath been but late: Meeting therefore with this established Spirit of Arms in the leading Ranks, it hath not as yet been able to controul it. Commerce indeed is encouraged; but so encouraged, as not to destroy the leading Principle of their Monarchy. To this End, the Ranks of the Kingdom are kept essentially distinguished; and while the People are allured to Trade by every Kind of Motive, the *Noblesse* or Gentry are, in Honour, prohibited from Commerce. It was indeed [206] formerly proposed in *France,* that the *Noblesse* should be drawn down to Trade: But, whether thro' deep and consummate Policy, or thro' the Principle of Honour itself, working blindly for it's own Preservation, the dangerous Proposal was *weakly* or *wisely* rejected. Whenever this Overture meets with Acceptance and Success, tho' it may seem for a while to give Vigour to their State, yet from that Period we may date the Downfall of *France.* Their effeminate Manners, now controuled by *Oeconomy* and the Love of *Glory,* will, like ours, degenerate into *Profusion* and the Love of *Gold.*

19. I.e., resounding.

On the contrary; Trade, tho' encouraged, is by the ruling Principle of this great Monarchy, kept within it's proper Limits; and while the Merchant traverseth Seas in Pursuit of *Gain,* the Gentleman does the [207] same in Pursuit of *Glory.* Thus the two incompatible Provinces are kept distinct; and hence, while the *French* vie with us in *Trade,* they tower above us in *Principle.*

Nay their very trading Settlements among foreign Nations are actuated by this ruling Principle in such a Manner, as to give a Splendor to their Monarchy and Commerce in the most barbarous Climates.* Thus, while *we* are poorly influenced by a sorry and mercantile Maxim, [208] first broached by a trading Minister, "that the *Interest* of a Nation is it's *truest* Honour;" the *French* conduct themselves on an opposite and higher Principle, "that the *Honour* of a Nation is its truest Interest."

In Confirmation of what is here advanced, we need only cast our Eyes on the Fortune and Fate of *France,* during the present Century. In the last War, she was exhausted, tho' victorious: in the former, she was both beaten and exhausted: In both these Instances, it was weakly thought by every superficial Politician in *England,* that because we had exhausted the Men [209] and Money, we had destroyed the Power of *France.* Experience hath told us the Reverse: The Spirit of Honour and Union working at the Root, soon restored those Branches that War had swept away, and have at length shot them into their former Vigour and Luxuriancy.

Hence then, we may learn an important Truth: "That no incidental Events can make a Nation *little,* while the Principles remain that made it *great.*"

---

* Numerous Proofs might be given of this: At present it may suffice to take one from a very fine Book lately published. "It is usual among the *French* of *Alexandria* to shew an extreme Respect for their Consul. In order to make him more considerable in the Eyes of the *Turks,* and of the other Nations, they endeavour to give an high Idea of his Person, and to illustrate his Birth in such a Manner, that it is not their Fault, if he is not considered as issued from the Blood Royal. If by Chance he take a Tour to *Rosetto,* he carries a white Flag at the Mast of his Pinnace; and when he goes out of the Port, as likewise when he returns into it, he is saluted by a general Discharge of the Cannon of the *French* Vessels." NORDEN's Travels in *Egypt* and *Nubia,* Vol. i. p. 29.[20]

20. Frederik Ludvig Norden, *Travels in Egypt and Nubia,* 2 vols (1757), vol. I, p. 47.

SECT. X

Conclusion

From these accumulated Proofs, then it seems evident, that our present effeminate Manners and Defect of Principle have arisen from our exorbitant Trade and Wealth, left without Check, to their na[210]tural Operations and uncontrouled Influence. And that these Manners, and this Defect of Principle, by weakening or destroying the national Capacity, Spirit of Defence, and Union, have produced such a general Debility as naturally leads to Destruction.

We might now proceed to confirm these Reasonings, by Examples drawn from History. For there is hardly an ancient or modern State of any Note recorded in Story, which would not in one Respect or other, confirm the leading Principles on which this Argument is built.

In these, throughout their several Periods, we should see *Trade* and *Wealth*, or (what is in this respect equivalent) *Conquest* and *Opulence*, taking their Progress: At one Period, polishing [211] and strengthening; at another, refining, corrupting, weakening, destroying, the State that gave them Entrance: Working indeed in different Ways, and under a Variety of Appearances; by Avarice, by Faction, by Effeminacy, by Profligacy; by a Mixture and Combination of all these Evils: sometimes dividing a Nation against itself; at others, quelling it's Spirit, and leaving it an easy Prey to the first Invader: Sometimes checked by a rising Patriot, or counterworked[21] by national Misfortunes: In one Country corrupting Manners; in another, Principles; in a third, both Manners and Principles: rendering one People blind, another cowardly, another treacherous to itself: Stealing secretly and insensibly on one Nation; overwhelming another in sudden Destruction. [212]

But to enlarge on these Subjects in that vague and undistinguishing Manner, which most Writers have pursued in treating them, tho' it might carry the *Appearance* of Reasoning, would in Truth be no more than *Declamation* in Disguise. And to develope and unravel the Particularity of

21. I.e., undermined.

Causes and Effects, thro' all their Variety of Combination and mutual Influence, as it would extend this Estimate beyond it's designed Limits, must be left to make a Part of some future Enquiry.

The *Character, Effects,* and *Sources* of our Manners and Principles, being thus laid open, the Writer had it in his Thoughts to have proceeded to the Consideration of "*their most practicable Remedies.*" But as the Closet-*Projects* of retired and speculative Men, often *are,* and always are *re*[213]*guarded,* as *chimerical*; he was therefore unwilling, at present, to hazard the Discredit of such an Attempt.

However, lest his Attempt should be deemed more visionary than perhaps it is, he judged it not improper to hint at some of the leading Principles on which it is built. And with this View, the following Reflections are submitted to the Consideration of the Public.

The World has been long amused with a trite and hacknied Comparison between the Life of Man, and that of States; in which it is pretended that they both proceed in the same irrevocable Manner; from Infancy to Maturity, from Maturity to Death: A Comparison, perhaps as groundless as it is common. The human Body contains, in its very Texture, the [214] Seeds of certain Dissolution. That is, tho' you set aside all the possible Accidents arising from Intemperance, from the Influence of the Elements, the Climate, and every other external and contingent Cause the human Frame itself, after a certain Period, would grow into Rigidity; the Fluids would decrease, the Solids accumulate, the Arteries *ossify,* the Blood stagnate, and the Wheels of Life stand still.

But in Societies, of whatever Kind, there seems no such necessary or essential Tendency to Dissolution. The human Body is *naturally* mortal; the political, only so by *Accident:* Internal Disorders or Diseases may arise; External Violence may attack or overpower: but these Causes, tho' always to be expected, are wholly incidental: the first is precisely of the same Nature as Intemperance, the second as [215] the Influence of the external Elements, on the human Body. But there appears nothing in the internal Construction of any State, that tends inevitably to Dissolution, analogous to those Causes in the human Frame, which lead to certain Death.

This Observation seems confirmed by History: Where you see States, which, after being sunk in Corruption and Debility, have been brought back to the Vigour of their first Principles: But you must have recourse to Fables, for medicated Old Age, restored to Infancy or Youth.

If this be true, it seems not altogether chimerical, tho' confessedly difficult, to bring about the Reformation of a State. To lay down general Rules, in such a Case, would be like giving a *Panacea*; the very [216] *Empiricism*²² of Politics. The Remedies must be suited to the Disease.

We have seen, that the ruling Evils of our Age and Nation have arisen from the unheeded Consequences of our Trade and Wealth. That these have produced effeminate Manners, and occasioned Loss of Principle: That these have brought on a national Debility. But would the lessening this exorbitant Trade and Wealth bring back Manners and Principles, and restore the Nation's Strength?—I very much Question the Event.

But whatever the Consequences might be at *Home*, those *Abroad* would certainly be fatal. The *French* are every Day gaining upon us in Commerce; and if ours should lessen, theirs would increase to our Destruction. [217]

Thus are we fallen into a kind of Dilemma: If our Commerce be maintained or increased, its Effects bid fair to destroy us: If Commerce be discouraged and lessened, the growing Power of our Enemy threatens the same Consequence.

There seems, then, no other Expedient than this, "That Commerce and Wealth be not discouraged in their *Growth*; but checked and *controuled in their Effects*."

And even in attempting this, Care must be had, lest in controuling the Effects of Commerce, we should destroy Commerce itself.

We see how strongly the natural Effects of Trade and Wealth, are controuled in [218] *France*, by proper Checks and counteracting Principles: Yet mere Imitation is always a narrow, and often an ineffectual Scheme. Besides, as our Constitution is of a superior Nature, so our Manners and Principles must be adapted to it, ere it can obtain it's proper Strength.

The Virtues yet left among us, and enumerated above,* may be a possible Foundation for such a Change.

---

* See Part I. Sect. 2, 3, 4.²³

22. Used here with its pejorative meaning of ignorant and unscientific practice or quackery (*OED*, 1).

23. See above, pp. 261–63.

There are two different Kinds of Remedies, which might in due Time be applied. The first are radical, general, and lasting: The latter, palliative, particular, and temporary.

The first seem totally impracticable at *present:* For as they suppose a Change of [219] Manners and Principles, this may justly be regarded as an impossible Event, during the present Age; and rather to be wished than hoped for, in the next.

The palliative, particular, and temporary Remedies, may seem more practicable at this Juncture. I mean, those which are of the coercive Kind; which work by opposed Passions, or by destroying the Opportunities or Occasions of Evil. Where the ruling Mischiefs lie among the People, these Remedies, with proper Care, may easily be administered. Thus we have lately seen the salutary Effects of a new Kind of Police, established by a useful Magistrate in the City of *London*;[24] by which, the reigning Evil of *Street-Robberies* hath been almost wholly suppressed; altho' we may reasonably suppose, the Disposition towards them remains as strong as ever. [220]

But where the ruling Mischief desolates the Great, there, even the palliative Remedies cannot easily be applied: The Reason is manifest: A coercive Power is wanting: They who should cure the Evil are the very Delinquents: And moral or political Physic is what no distempered Mind will ever administer to itself.

Necessity therefore, and *Necessity alone*, must in such a Case be the Parent of Reformation. So long as degenerate and unprincipled Manners can support themselves, they will be deaf to Reason, blind to Consequences, and obstinate in the *long* established Pursuit of *Gain* and *Pleasure*. In such Minds, the Idea of a Public has no Place; and therefore can never be a Curb to private Gratification: Nor can such Minds be ever awakened from their [221] fatal Dream, till either the Voice of an abused People rouse them into Fear; or the State itself totter, thro' the general Incapacity, Cowardice, and Disunion of those who should support it.

---

24. The allusion is to Henry Fielding (1707–54), who after his appointment as JP for Westminster in 1748 established the "Bow Street Runners," a small body of thieftakers.

Whenever this compelling Power, *Necessity*, shall appear; then, and not till then, may we hope that our Deliverance is at hand. Effeminacy, Rapacity, and Faction, will then be ready to resign the Reins they would now usurp: One common Danger will create one common Interest: Virtue may rise on the Ruins of Corruption; and a despairing Nation yet be saved, by the Wisdom, the Integrity, and unshaken Courage, of SOME GREAT MINISTER.[25]

FINIS

25. An allusion to William Pitt the Elder (1708–78). In the summer of 1756 the collapse of Newcastle's continental diplomacy and his evident inadequacy as a war leader had led him to make overtures to Pitt, then the most effective speaker in the Commons, and a man whose Patriot platform was proving popular in the country at large and devastating in the House. Eventually, after several months of maneuvering and false starts, by the summer of 1757 Pitt and Newcastle were working in harness, the latter as First Lord of the Treasury, but the former as the dominant figure in both the Cabinet and the Commons.

*An Estimate of the Manners
and Principles of the Times*, vol. II
(1758)

A N

ESTIMATE

OF THE

MANNERS

A N D

PRINCIPLES

OF THE

TIMES

By the AUTHOR of
ESSAYS on the CHARACTERISTICS, &c.

Tu, ne cede Malis; sed contra audentior ito.*

VOL. II.

LONDON:
Printed for L. DAVIS and C. REYMERS,
against *Grays-Inn-Gate, Holborn*;
Printers to the ROYAL SOCIETY.
MDCCLVIII.

Contents

PART I

ADDITIONAL REMARKS

ON THE

RULING MANNERS

AND

PRINCIPLES

PART I

ADDITIONAL REMARKS

ON

The RULING MANNERS and PRINCIPLES

SECT. I

The Design of this VOLUME

Had the first Volume of this Work met with a less favourable Reception in the World, a second had not been offered to its Perusal.

There are certain Subjects, in which the Public are little concerned; and in [10] which they are certainly no competent Judges. But in those Topics which relate to the moral or political Happiness of Man, the general Voice of a People is perhaps the best Criterion of Truth and Falsehood.

I shall not dwell at present on the Proof of this. I only speak my Opinion; and this, no farther than to apologize for these additional Remarks, which are in Part thrown out in Consequence of that Belief.

The Author easily foresaw, that a Work of this Nature, whose very Existence depended on the severest Impartiality, must give Offence to many Individuals: that by some he must be reckoned arrogant and assuming, by others imprudent, and blind to his own Interests; that by one Set he should be stigmatized as a Republican, by another as a Tory: That some should allow the Substance of the Work to be good, but affirm it to be stolen; others, that the [11] Substance was his own, but altogether good for nothing. That he should by Turns be stigmatized as the Friend of

353

arbitrary Rule, and seditious Democracy; as an insolent Abuser of those in Power, a servile Flatterer of those who have none; that every contradictory Charge should be heaped upon him, which blind Partiality, effeminate Manners, profligate Principles, selfish Cunning, political Servility, and Depravity of Heart could suggest, was from the first his Expectation (not his Fear) because it was his determined Purpose, to combat these Enormities.

With much Calmness therefore hath he heard of these various Accusations, and leaves those who chuse, at their full Liberty to believe any of them, or all. In the mean time, he wraps himself up in the Integrity of his Intentions, and in those undeserved Honours which have been done [12] his little Work, both in his own and in foreign Countries.

He hath heard too, of certain written Criticisms on his *Estimate:* But if he does not read, how can it be expected he should answer them? Yet this he believes, from the Report of some of his Friends, that if his temporary Critics had applied to him for Occasions of Censure or Reproof, he could have furnished them with a juster Catalogue than what they have produced against him in their still-born Essays. As therefore these Gentlemen, it seems, profess themselves the Servants of the ungrateful Public, it must needs be agreeable to them, that an Author should alleviate their despised Labours, and set himself to criticise his own Writings.

This therefore is declared to be the simple Intent of the present Volume: And [13] that his Readers may more clearly comprehend the main Drift of a Work which, from its Nature, cannot admit of Form, he thinks it expedient to premise the several Classes, under which his Remarks will fall.

First, they will contain *Retractions* of such Mistakes as the Writer thinks he hath committed.

Secondly, of *Proofs* in such Points as were affirmed and not proved.

Thirdly, of *Illustrations* in those Particulars which were hinted, but not explained.

Fourthly, of *Replies* to such capital Objections, as have been made to his general System, by preceding Writers on the same Subject.

Fifthly, of the *Consequences* which may be fairly deduced from his Principles, and [14] thro' a designed Brevity were omitted in the first Volume.

The intelligent Reader will readily comprehend, that these several Topics are not to be collectively considered, in the Order in which they are here laid down; but touched on as they rise successively in the Perusal of the first Volume. To *that* they refer; and therefore any other Disposition of Parts than what is subordinate to the Method there pursued, though it might carry the Appearance of *Order,* would be *Disorder* in the Result.

SECT. II

Remarks on the introductory Section of the first Volume

The very first Paragraph, it seems, wanted an Explanation. For when the Author affirmed that "our Misfortunes had not their Source in the particular [15] and accidental Conduct of Individuals, but arose from permanent and established Causes:" His Affirmation has been wrested into this unmeaning Form, "that no Individuals were delinquent in their respective Stations." The candid Critic will not hastily lay this Charge upon him. For in Truth he meant not to deny, that all may have been delinquent in their Turn. What he insists upon, is this, "That this Failure or Delinquency is not merely personal or accidental; but founded in the established Manners and Principles of the Times; and therefore cannot probably be rectify'd effectually, by any Change of Men, or even of Measures, till these Manners and Principles are controuled." Need we any additional Facts, to prove this Truth?

He spoke too of certain profligate Scribblers, who find their Account in laying all to the Charge of a few Individuals. [16] It hath been asked, "who are these Scribblers?" Indeed, he remembers not their Names; and besides, if he did, the Catalogue would be too large to insert here. Their Characters, however, he can give in a few Words. "All those who dabble on the Surface of the political Deep; who ply their wretched Oar for Bread, hire themselves out to whoever offers them a Fare; and then, like true *Thames-Watermen,* abuse every Man that passes who is better dressed than themselves, or their Retainers."

These Men have been toiling many a Day, to impress the Body of the People with this Opinion, "That if certain Individuals were but removed

from the public Administration, our Affairs would of course go well."
This hath been the Cry so long, that, till of late, the Truth of the Affirmation hath scarce been doubted. The Manners, the Principles, [17]
the Characters, the Conduct, of the higher Ranks and leading Members
of the Community, from whence alone every State will for ever derive
its particular Colour and Complexion, Strength or Weakness; these were
never taken into the Account. Alas, what can it avail, that a Nation hath
a Head, if she have no Hands! But Experience is the best Teacher: She
hath already taught us much on this Topic; and, I fear, will teach us more.

"Among all Causes, none perhaps so much contributes to raise or sink
a Nation, as the Manners and Principles of its People."* Many other
Causes may concur, and may indeed be the immediate Instruments of a
Nation's Ruin; while the original Cause lies hid, or is seen only by those
few, who dare descend and penetrate to the Foundations of political
Happiness and Stability. 'Tis easy to see [18] when an Arch is shrunk; 'tis
quite another Thing to find out the original Cause of its giving Way.

The President MONTESQUIEU hath a fine Observation, which may
well be apply'd to this Subject; though that great Writer hath not so
apply'd it. He says, "that, if any Nation is undone by a particular Event, as
the Loss of a Battle, there must be some general Cause, why the Loss of a
single Battle could undo that Nation."† He adds, "we see that for near two
Centuries the Land Armies of *Denmark* have been almost always beaten

---

* Vol. I. p. 13.[1]

† Grand. des Romains, &c. l. xviii.[2]

1. Cf. above, p. 260.

2. A famous passage from chapter XVIII of the *Considérations*, which Brown
translates serviceably: "Il y a des causes générales, soit morales, soit physiques, qui
agissent dans chaque Monarchie, l'élevent, la maintiennent, ou la précipitent; tous
les accidens sont soumis à ces causes, & si le hazard d'une bataille, c'est-à-dire, une
cause particuliere, a ruïné un Etat, il y avoit une cause générale, qui faisoit que cet
Etat devoit périr par une seule bataille: en un mot l'allure principale entraîne avec
elle tous les accidens particuliers. Nous voyons que depuis près de deux siecles, les
troupes de terre de Dannemarc ont presque toujours été batues par celles de Suede:
il faut qu'independemment du courage des deux Nations & du sort des armes, il y
ait dans le Gouvernement Danois militaire ou civil un vice interieur qui ait produit
cet effet, & je ne le crois point difficile à découvrir" (Montesquieu, *Considérations*,
pp. 235–36).

by those of *Sweden:* Setting aside the natural Courage and the Weapons
of the two Nations, there must be some internal Defect in the military or
civil State of *Denmark,* which could be sufficient to produce that Effect:
And I think it would not be difficult to deve[19]lope it."*'Tis pity he did
not exert his Sagacity in this Enquiry. It was the Fate of *France* to be always beaten by the Allies in the general War which ravaged *Europe,* in the
Beginning of this Century.[3] What might be the ruling Causes of that general Effect, may hereafter be considered. Far different is the Fate of *France*
and *England* at present: And it hath been, and is the Writer's main Intent to prove, that the ruling Cause of this strange Catastrophe lies in the
Manners and Principles of the leading Ranks of this degenerate Nation,
and to trace those Manners and Principles to their respective Sources.

Let me here add another Observation. Political Writers have generally
attributed the Fall of States to some defective, false or improper Principle
woven into the original Constitution of their *Laws.* Now [20] this, in that
Extent in which it is generally affirmed and understood, seems an entire
Mistake. For salutary Principles and Manners will of themselves secure
the Duration of a State, with very ill-modelled Laws: Whereas the best
Laws can never secure the Duration of a State, where Manners and Principles are corrupted. Of these Truths, History affords Instances abundant.
The general Defect, therefore, of political Institutions hath been, their not
effectually providing for the Continuance and Stability of Principles and
Manners; of Religion, Public Spirit, Honour, Temperance, Fortitude. This
Truth will perhaps be readily allowed, as it regards Nations that are deeply
sunk in Effeminacy, and ready to be swallowed up by some warlike Neighbours: But it is no less certain, as it regards the internal Ballance of Power
in any Nation whatever; although Volumes have been written on that
Subject, with[21]out so much as taking this Truth into the Account.† To

---

* Ibid.

† Two of our own Countrymen, Lord *Bolingbroke* and Mr. *David Hume,* (the first
of them esteemed a capital Writer in Politics) have written whole Systems of Policy,
without so much as mentioning, or seeming to regard, this ruling Circumstance.

3. Brown refers to the War of the Spanish Succession (1702–13), in which French
forces were repeatedly defeated by the armies of Britain and the Low Countries
under the command of John Churchill (1650–1722), first duke of Marlborough.

offer one Instance, out of innumerable that might be brought from every Period of History;—It is the sole Force of *Manners* and a *Principle,* that prevents *France* from sinking into the deepest and most abandoned Despotism. This Principle, and it's correspondent Manners give the *French* many of the Blessings of Liberty; while their mere political Constitution savours as much of Despotism as that of many of their Neighbours, who feel all the Rigours of Oppression.

Hence then appears the important Use of investigating the real and particular State of the Manners and Principles of a Com[22]monwealth: Since, altho' it be a Circumstance totally overlooked by many superficial Pretenders to the political Science, and loosely and blindly declaimed upon by others, yet is it the only Method by which we can rationally determine the Strength or Weakness, the Danger or Security of a State.

And here the penetrating MACHIAVEL seems to have erred in his Determinations on this Point. He says, "As good Customs cannot subsist without good Laws, so good Laws cannot be executed without good Customs."*4 The latter Part of the Sentence is a great Truth: The former Part is a vulgar Error. So long as the Causes of corrupt Manners are absent, good Manners preserve themselves without [23] Laws, or with bad Laws. Good Laws are only then necessary, as the Means of Prevention, when corrupt Manners or Customs take Place.

"To rail at the Times at large, can serve no good Purpose; and generally ariseth from a Want of Knowledge, or a Want of Honesty."† No Labour is

---

* Disc. l. i. c. xviii. The several Passages quoted from MACHIAVEL, are generally taken, with very few Alterations, from the Translation published in 1680:5 The Author did not think it necessary to load the Page with the Passages in the Original *Italian*; as it is a Language, which but a few of his Readers may have studied.

† Vol. I. p. 15.6

4. "Just as for the maintenance of good customs laws are required, so if laws are to be observed, there is need of good customs" (Machiavelli, *Discorsi,* I.xviii).

5. I.e., *The Works of the Famous Nicholas Machiavel, Citizen and Secretary of Florence. Written Originally in Italian, and from thence newly and faithfully Translated into English* (1680); Wing M 129. This translation, associated with the Parliamentarian statesman and political theorist Henry Neville, had in fact first been published in 1675.

6. Cf. above, p. 260.

more *useless,* than that of railing at the Times at large, because, as a great Writer hath observed, "no certain Rule can be prescribed, unless we know the Degrees, or Kinds of Corruption."* No Labour is more *easy,* than to rail at large on the Corruptions of the Times, because there are Corruptions in *all* Times. Nothing perhaps is more *difficult,* than to point out the peculiar Colour, and leading Character, of any Times: Because this requires not only a just and extended Discernment [24] of Men and Things as they exist, but as they unite, act, or are acted on, as Causes and Effects. It must likewise be the Result of a severe Impartiality, which can stand aloof, superior to all Connexions; a Quality seldom found, and never approved, but by the Impartial. To the first of these Qualities, *Dulness* or *Refinements* are as dangerous Enemies, as *Attachments* or *Resentments* to the last.

"In some Respects, perhaps, there is no Time nor Country delivered down to us in Story, in which a wise Man would so much wish to have lived, as in our own."† It hath been asked, in what Respects? Let us do Justice to our Age and Country in every Regard. A political Constitution, superior to all that History hath recorded, or present Times can boast: A religious Establishment, which breathes universal Charity and Toleration: A [25] Separation from the Continent, that naturally secures us from the Calamities of Invasion, and the Temptations to Conquest:‡ A Climate,

---

* Machiavel's Disc. B. i. c. 18.[7]

† See Vol. I. p. 15.[8]

‡ MACHIAVEL, speaking on the Stability of a Commonwealth, reasons in the following Manner. "I should think, therefore, a Commonwealth that would stand long, should seat itself in so strong and inexpugnable a Place, that it might not apprehend any sudden Insult; nor make itself so great as to become formidable to its Neighbours. For the common Motives that excite People to make War upon a Commonwealth, are two; either to *conquer* it themselves, or to *secure themselves* against it: And by the aforesaid Expedient, both these Motives are prevented."§ This Reasoning he applies to SPARTA and VENICE: I need not point out to the Reader, how much more applicable it is to BRITAIN.

§ Disc. Pol. l. i. c. 6.[9]

7. "It is, moreover, almost impossible to lay down rules, for the method to be adopted will of necessity depend upon the degree of corruption" (Machiavelli, *Discorsi,* I.xviii).

8. Cf. above, p. 260.

9. "I am firmly convinced, therefore, that to set up a republic which is to last a long time, the way to set about it is to constitute it as Sparta and Venice were

fertile in the substantial Comforts of Life: A Spirit of Liberty, yet un-conquered: A general Humanity and Sincerity beyond any Nation upon Earth: An Administration of Justice, that hath even silenced Envy. These are Blessings which every *Englishman* feels, and ought to acknowledge. Search thro' all [26] the most admired Periods of the most admired Countries, the most flourishing Aera's of *Greece, Italy,* or *France*; and tell me, if in any of these, such an *Union* can be found? A Volume might be written in Proof and Display of this Superiority.

"Notwithstanding this, our Situation seems most dangerous: We are rolling to the Brink of a Precipice that must destroy us."* Because, in the Writer's Opinion, the Manners and Principles that are taking Root among us, will soon poison these generous Plants, and in the End destroy them.

"At such a Juncture, to hold up a true Mirroir to the Public, and let the Nation see *themselves,* as the Authors of their own Misfortunes, can-not be a very popular Design."† This is *improperly,* because *too generally* expressed: 'Tis the [27] leading Part of the Nation chiefly, if not only, that the Writer esteems accountable for the Miseries that threaten us: As ap-pears by the general Tenor of his Work.

"Why then, (it hath been asked) should a Man in private Life stand forth to offend the *Great?*" Indeed, he means not to *give* Offence; but if it *will* be *taken,* he cannot help it.

Schemes of Reformation, 'tis true, are generally regarded as chimerical: And an agreeable Writer, who knew the World, tells us, that "Quarrels with the Age, and Pretences of reforming it, end commonly like the Pains

---

constituted; to place it in a strong position, and so to fortify it that no one will dream of taking it by a sudden assault; and, on the other hand, not to make it so large as to appear formidable to its neighbours. It should in this way be able to en-joy its form of government for a long time. For war is made on a commonwealth for two reasons: (i) to subjugate it, and (ii) for fear of being subjugated by it. Both these reasons are almost entirely removed by the aforesaid precautions; . . ." (Machiavelli, *Discorsi,* I.vi).

* Vol. I. p. 15.[10]
† Ibid.[11]
10. Cf. above, p. 261.
11. Cf. above, p. 260.

of a Man in a little Boat, who tugs at a Rope that is fast to a Ship. It looks as if he meant to draw the Ship to him; but the Truth is, he draws himself to the Ship, where he gets in, and does like the rest of the Crew."* On this pretty Allusion, I [28] have only to remark, that had the State of the *Fact* alluded to been more *philosophical,* the *political* Application had been more *just.* For as in reality the Man in the little Boat, while he is drawn towards the *Ship,* draws the Ship towards *him* in a certain Degree; so the Censor of Manners, though himself may be drawn towards the ruling Manners of the Times, yet if he censures justly, need not despair of drawing the vast political Machine towards his philosophic Barque, in Proportion to it's *Weight,* however inconsiderable. In plain Terms: Though it were Folly to expect, that any Work of this Kind can effect a general Reformation (a Thing which the Author was never so ignorant as to dream of) yet it wants not it's real Use. It tends to preserve the honest Impressions yet left among us; to keep up the Combat against those Vices, Follies, Corruptions, Profligacies, which, if not opposed, would soon overwhelm [29] us: And if the Flame should chance to strike upon a few great and generous Minds, may possibly conspire to rouse a Spirit of public Virtue in this degenerate Kingdom, where it is now weakened or extinct.

SECT. III

Farther Remarks on the Spirit of Liberty

Among the remaining Virtues yet left us, the Spirit of *Liberty* was placed as the main Foundation. A Question naturally riseth here, to which the too general Expression of the first Volume affords no Solution: "Is the Spirit of *Liberty* consistent with an established *Effeminacy,* and Want of

---

* Sir *William Temple.*[12]

12. From the final paragraph of Sir William Temple's "An Essay Upon the Advancement of Trade in Ireland," where the text in fact reads: ". . . I have observed all set quarrels with the Age, and pretences of Reforming it by their own Models, to end commonly like the pains of a Man in a little Boat, who tugs at a Rope that's fast to a Ship; it looks as if he resolved to draw the Ship to him, but the Truth and his Meaning is, to draw himself to the Ship, where he gets in when he can, and does like the rest of the Crew when he is there" (Temple, *Works,* vol. I, p. 121).

Principle? If not, then how can it be affirmed, that this Spirit of *Liberty* can subsist among a People, whose ruling Character is that of *effeminate Manners,* and Defect of *Principle?*" [30]

It seems to me then, that the Spirit of *Liberty* is indeed totally inconsistent with an established *Effeminacy* and Want of *Principle:* Inasmuch as these two Causes, above every other, tend to debase the Mind, and fit it for Subjection. With Regard, therefore, to the latter Part of the Question, the Truth is, that the Spirit of Liberty subsists yet among the *middle,* and some of the *lower* Ranks; but is much weakened, and in many Instances extinguished, among the *higher.* The Reason, I apprehend, why this Virtue abounds more in middle, than in high Life, is, that the first is not yet effectually tainted by the ruling Manners and Principles of the Times. This Distinction accounts for a Fact, which at first View may seem a Contradiction; that the Spirit of Liberty and Effeminacy may subsist together: They do indeed subsist together in the *same Nation,* but not in the *same Ranks.* [31]

"Whereas the Spirit of Liberty hath been ingrafted by the Arts of Policy in other Countries, it shoots up here, as from its natural Climate, Stock, and Soil."* It may not, perhaps, sufficiently gratify the Self-esteem of a true *Englishman,* to be told, that the Root of this fair Plant is no other than a certain Impatience of Controul, arising from a Spirit of Chagrin; which hath, for it's original Cause, the Soil, Food, Winds, and Climate. This, indeed, hath long been my Opinion; and it gave me Pleasure, to find it confirmed by that of Baron MONTESQUIEU; who hath indirectly, at least, affirmed it.† I will add a further Observation; which is, that as this Spirit of Chagrin, and splenetic Turn of Mind, seems the

* Vol. I. p. 19.[13]
† L'Esprit des Loix, l. xiv. c. 13.[14]
13. Cf. above, p. 262.
14. Montesquieu has been discussing in the previous chapter the English disposition towards suicide, which he asserts to be "une maladie du climat," and which he then goes on to associate with the English tenacity of freedom: "Dans une nation à qui une maladie du climat affecte tellement l'âme, qu'elle pourrait porter le dégout de toutes choses jusqu'à celui de la vie, on voit bien que le gouvernement qui conviendrait le mieux à des gens à qui tout serait insupportable, serait celui où ils ne pourraient pas se prendre à un seul de qui causerait leurs chagrins, et où les lois gouvernant plutôt que les hommes, il faudrait, pour changer l'État, les renverser elles-mêmes.

original Cause of *our* Spirit of Liberty; so the gay, chearful, and contented Turn of the [32] *French*, is certainly one ruling Cause of their Slavery. The Truth is, they are happy under it; and therefore no Desire of changing their Condition ever ariseth in their Hearts: For it is Uneasiness alone, that prompts to change. Shift the Inhabitants of each Kingdom into the other's Place, and, in another Generation, the Posterity of the *Slaves* would become *Freemen*; and those of the *Freemen, Slaves*.

Which of the two Nations are happier in their respective States, no impartial Man will be bold to pronounce, as he cannot have Trial of the internal Feelings of other Men. But what a Writer of fine Sense hath said, may surely be applied here; who, speaking of the Condition of the *French*, says, "I do not call it miserable (the Term usually given it) because no Condition is so, but to him that esteems it so: And if a *Paisan*[15] of *France* thinks of no more than his coarse Bread and his Onions, his Canvas Cloaths and [33] wooden Shoes; labours contentedly on Working-Days, and dances or plays merrily on Holidays; he may, for ought I know, live as well as a Boor of *Holland*,[16] who is either weary of his very Ease, or whose Cares of growing still richer and richer, waste his Life in Toils at Land, or Dangers at Sea; and perhaps fool him so far, as to make him enjoy less of all Kind in his Riches, than t'other in his Poverty."*

Que si la même nation avait encore reçu du climat un certain caractère d'impatience qui ne lui permit pas de souffrir longtemps les mêmes choses, on voit bien que le gouvernement dont nous venons de parler serait encore le plus convenable"; "In a nation where an ailment arising from climate so affects the soul that it can carry world-weariness to the point of suicide, one can easily see that the government which would suit best a people who find everything unbearable would be that in which they could not attribute the cause of their uneasiness to any single person, and in which, being a government of laws not of men, it would be necessary, in order to change the state, to overturn the laws themselves. If this same nation has also derived from their climate a certain impatience of temper, which renders them incapable of putting up with the same things for long, one can easily see that the government we have just mentioned is the one that suits them best" (*Esprit des Loix*, XIV.xiii).

* Sir *William Temple*, vol. I. p. 92.[17]

15. I.e., peasant.

16. A Dutch peasant (*OED*, 2a).

17. An accurate quotation from Sir William Temple's "A Survey of the Constitutions and Interests of the Empire, Sweden, Denmark, Spain, Holland, France, and Flanders; with their Relation to England in the Year 1671" (Temple, *Works*, vol. I, p. 92).

But though absolute Rule be compatible with the Happiness of the *French*; I apprehend, that Liberty is the first necessary Ingredient in the Composition of *English* Happiness. As our Temper, resulting from our Food and Climate, naturally urgeth us to the Pursuit of Freedom; so, were we deprived of it, our Sensibility of Servitude must be extreme. [34]

Farther: The fine Writer just now cited, affirms that "the *English* do well to be watchful of their *Liberty*; for if ever they are inslaved, they will be the compleatest *Slaves* upon Earth."* He hath not given the Reasons[19] on which he founds his Affirmation: Yet the Remark, tho' it carries the Appearance of Refinement and Improbability, I believe is just. I would Reason thus upon it. The same ruling Causes which produce that Gayety and Contentment of Heart, which give Birth to Servitude in *France*, and make the People easy under it—the same ruling Causes do naturally produce a gentle Use of Power in those who rule. On the contrary, if that *English* Liberty should be lost, which is the Result of a local Spleen, and that local Spleen should continue in it's Strength, who sees not, that the Exercise of unlimited Power in such a Cli[35]mate, must be barbarous, brutal, and abandoned?

"The Destruction of Liberty (in *England*) by external Violence, will probably be no more than temporary."† Because that local Spleen which gives it Birth, will, in Case of an Overturn, be in perpetual Ferment, till it

---

* L'Esprit des Loix.[18]

† Vol. I. p. 20.[20]

18. A slightly compressed version of Montesquieu's French: "Les Anglais, pour favoriser la liberté, ont ôté toutes les puissances intermediaries qui formaient leur monarchie. Ils ont bien raison de conserver cette liberté; s'ils venaient à la perdre, ils seraient un des peuples les plus esclaves de la terre"; "the English, to promote liberty, have removed all the intermediate powers which moulded their monarchy. They are certainly right to preserve that liberty; if they ever came to lose it, they would be one of the most enslaved peoples on earth" (*Esprit des Loix*, II.iv).

19. In fact, as is clear from the full quotation above, Montesquieu does supply a reason for his opinion, namely the eradication of intermediate powers in the English constitution. Brown seems here to be quoting Montesquieu imperfectly from memory. The fact that he does not supply a reference for the quotation to book and chapter of the *Esprit*, as he sometimes does, supports this inference.

20. Cf. above, p. 262.

brings about it's Restoration. This Climate will for ever form the Complexion of it's Inhabitants. Degenerate *Englishmen,* though *free,* may be subdued by *Foreigners,* though *Slaves:* But the Climate will conquer in it's Turn; the Posterity of those Slaves will throw off the Yoke, and defy the servile Maxims of their Forefathers.

"But it is remarkable, that in Proportion as this Spirit hath grown weak in *Deeds,* it hath gained Strength in *Words*; and of late run out, into un[36]bounded Licence."* It hath grown *weak* in *Deeds,* because it hath grown weak among those whose Province it is to *act:* It hath gained *Strength* in *Words,* because it is strong in those who have only the Privilege to *speak.* It hath of late run out into unbounded Licence, through certain unhappy Causes which might be explained: But the Writer chuseth rather to be silent, than either to say such Things as might seem to aggravate the Evil, or such as would be inconsistent with that inviolable Regard which he will ever maintain for Truth.

SECT. IV

Remarks on the Spirit of Humanity

"The Lenity of our Laws, the many noble Foundations, *&c:* All these are such indisputable Proofs of a National Humanity, as it were the highest In[37]justice not to acknowledge and applaud."† This Remark is not to be limited to the middle Ranks, like that upon the Spirit of Liberty. For, to do Justice to the higher Ranks of this Kingdom, it may be maintained, that, in Point of *Humanity,* they have not their Equals upon Earth.

It may seem improbable, or perhaps incredible, that such a Spirit of *Humanity* should remain in those Ranks among whom the Spirit of *Liberty* is weakened or extinct. Yet the Fact is indisputable. I could point out

---

* Vol. I. p. 18.[21]
† Vol. I. p. 21, 22.[22]
21. Cf. above, p. 261.
22. Cf. above, p. 263.

a certain Transaction,[23] which passed last Year in two great Assemblies, in Regard to a Marriage Settlement, which, if examined to the Bottom, would be an incontestable Proof of what is here advanced: In which, for the sake of making two Individuals happy, a Step was taken, at which our more rigorous Fore[38]fathers would have started, as subversive of all Law, Policy, and Freedom. But I forbear.

However, thus much in general may be affirmed without Offence, that Humanity neither *improved* nor *controuled*, is always *defective* and partial; and *may be* very *dangerous* in its Effects. When once the leading Measures of a Kingdom are drawn from a Regard to *Individuals*, rather than the *Public* State, it is certain, that "the Pillars of that State are shaken."

Let us now consider, whence this Spirit of Humanity may arise, and how it comes to be continued among a People of such a Complexion.

---

23. There seem to be two possibilities. On 1 April 1757, royal assent was given to the following two bills: "For varying certain limitations in a grant made by King *Charles* II. of a duty on coals, to *Charles* late D. of *Richmond*, for enabling the present duke to make a jointure on his intended marriage with Lady *Mary Bruce*. [K. *Charles* II. granted to his son *Charles* D. of *Richmond* and *Lenox*, and his heirs, the sum of 12*d*. on every chaldron of coals shipt at *Newcastle* to be spent in *England*, and also the Yearly sums of 1838 *l*. 12*s*. 6*d*. and 612 *l*. 17*s*. 6*d*. payable to his said majesty on several former demises of the said duty, subject to the yearly payment of 500 *l*. to Sir *Thomas Clarges*, his heirs and assigns, and of 1 *l*. 6*s*. 8*d*. to his majesty and his heirs. The intention of this act is to limit the said coal duty to the male line, in order to support the honour and dignity of the title; and to enable Lady *Mary Bruce*, a minor, on her marriage with his grace, to accept of a grant of 3000 *l*. a year, payable out of the said duty in lieu and bar of her dower, and thirds of his grace's estate.]—For setting a certain yearly sum upon the Right Hon. the Countess of *Euston*, out of certain yearly pensions issuing out of the hereditary revenue of the excise. [K. *Charles* II. granted a yearly pension of 3000 *l*. to each of his three sons, *Charles* Earl of *Southampton*, *Henry* Earl of *Euston*, and *George*, then Earl of *Northumberland*, and their heirs male; by which grant, upon the death and failure of issue male of any of the said sons, his yearly pension was limited over in moyeties to the two remaining sons, and their heirs male respectively. His grace the present Duke of *Grafton* is possessed of one of the three said yearly pensions, and also of a moyety of the other; and the intention of this act is to enable the duke and his grandson and heir apparent the E. of *Euston*, to settle 1500 *l*. a year, part of the said pension, upon the Hon. *Anne Liddel*, only child of the Rt. Hon. Lord *Ravensworth* (with whom his lordship received 40,000 *l*. as a marriage portion) in part of her jointure.]" (*The Gentleman's Magazine*, vol. XXVII [1757], p. 185).

One Cause seems to be the *Excellence* of our *Religion*; which although thrown off and despised by the fashionable World in their Maturity of Age; yet having tinctured the Infant Mind, leaves it's salutary Effects behind it, in spite of every acquired ill Habit. That [39] the Mode of *Christianity* established in this Kingdom is at least inferior to none, seems evident from this one Circumstance, that "every other religious sect esteems and loves it, next to their own."

The Lenity of our *Laws* is another Preservative of the National *Humanity*. Indeed they are drawn in great Part, from the same pure Fountain of Truth with our *Religion*; and therefore may well be expected, in great Part, to produce the same happy Effect.

But that Justice may be done in every View, it must not be disguised, that another Cause, hinted but not explained in the first Volume, hath its Share in this amiable Production. "Humanity to Distress, we have already marked as another Character of the Times: But whether our very Effeminacy be not one of its Sources, might probably be a Question more curious in its Progress, than agree[40]able in its Solution."* Thus, and naturally, the Matter may be explained. Effeminacy begets Cowardice, and a Dread of enduring and suffering of every Kind. Minds thus constituted are easily moved by the *apparent* Sufferings of others: Hence, where opposite Passions prevail not, *Pity* is generally strong in *Women:* And hence Pity, or Humanity, is the natural Growth of an *effeminate Nation:* That is, of a Nation which *resembles Women*.

This farther Distinction is to be made: That so far as Humanity ariseth from Courage tempered by pure Religion, it will be regular, extensive, and consistent: So far as it ariseth from Effeminacy, it will be partial, irrational, and confined: Which of these two is the leading Character of the Humanity of our Times and Nation, I leave others to determine. By comparing it with the Humanity of the last Cen[41]tury, when there was more of Principle, and less of Effeminacy, its Character will be more evident.

---

* Vol. I. p. 16.[24]
24. Cf. above, p. 280.

"These are concurrent Proofs, that the Spirit of Humanity is natural to our Nation."* This was inconsiderately affirmed. The Spirit of Liberty *is,* but that of Humanity *is not* natural to our Nation. The Proof lies in the History of the Country; which tells us, that in ancient Times, before *Christianity* came among us, tho' the Spirit of Liberty was strong, yet the ruling Character of the Nation was that of *barbarous* and *inhuman.* This may serve as an additional Proof, that our present Humanity ariseth from the Causes assigned above.

SECT. V

A Remark on the Inhumanity of the ITALIANS

Let me here, for once, make an Excursion into my more general Plan,[26] that I [42] may bring home an Observation which hath a distant, though not an intimate Connexion with the Subject of the last Section.

The ITALIANS are an effeminate People; yet in the general Opinion, void of Humanity: They are given to Cruelty, Treachery, Assassination. The Question is, then, from what Causes this singular Appearance may arise?

It is commonly affirmed and supposed to be *natural* to the Country. But they who talk thus, I think, mean no more (so far as they mean any thing) than this, that there is some Cause unknown, which produceth this Crime in ITALY, rather than elsewhere.

MACHIAVEL, who knew Mankind, ascribes this Degeneracy in the People, to the Wickedness and ill Example of their Rulers. "If the People of our Times are infamous for Thefts and Robberies, [43] and plundering, and such Kind of Enormities, it proceeds from the Exorbitance and Rapacity of their Governors. ROMANIA[27] (before ALEXANDER the sixth[28]

---

* Vol. I. p. 21.[25]

25. Cf. above, p. 263.

26. I.e., the project of writing "a much more extensive Work, planned on the general Subject of *Manners*" to which Brown refers in the "Advertisement" to vol. I of the *Estimate* (above, p. 254).

27. The Romagna; the district surrounding Rome.

28. Rodrigo de Borja y Doms, Italianized as Rodrigo Borgia (1431–1503); Pope Alexander VI from 1492 until his death; a worldly and corrupt prelate who nevertheless contributed to the peace of Rome by his vigorous suppression of the feuding Orsini and Colonna families.

exterminated those Lords who had the Command in those Parts) was a Place of all Kind of Dissoluteness and Iniquity: Every Day, and every trivial Occasion producing notorious Murders and Rapines: Which was not so much from any *Depravity in the Nature of the People,* as some Persons would have it, as from the Corruption of their Princes: For being poor of themselves, and yet ambitious to live in Splendor and Magnificence, they were forced upon ill Courses; and indeed refused none that could supply them."* This, in some Measure, accounts for the Inhumanity of the People: But we are still at a Loss, as much as ever, [44] how such an *exterminating* Principle came first among the Great.

What follows, then, seems the natural Solution of the Question. When ITALY became divided into a vast Number of petty States, the Contentions and Factions in these States were endless. The Parties were often too small to levy Armies: Hence Conspiracies, Insurrections, Assassinations by Sword or Poison, were the common, because the readiest Way of prosecuting the political Designs either of the Oppressors or the Oppressed.† By this Means, the dreadful Practice of Assassination, by being applied *politically,* lost a great Part of its Horror in the Minds of the Parties who practised it: Thus it naturally crept into private Use; and hath been of Course transmitted from one Generation to another.

Hence appears the great Importance of curbing the Violence and Horrors of *pub*[45]*lic* Contention, by what are called the Laws of War and of Nations. Since the opposite Conduct is not only attended with immediate Cruelties, but, what is worse, is in Danger of striking its Colours

---

* Mach. Disc. Pol. l. iii. c. 29.[29]

† See *Machiavel's* Historical Tracts, passim.

29. A heightened translation of Machiavelli's Italian, which is more accurately rendered as: "Those who talk about the peoples of our day being given up to robbery and similar vices, will find that they are all due to the fact that those who ruled them behaved in like manner. The Romagna, before Pope Alexander VI got rid of the lords who ruled it, exemplified the very worst types of behaviour, for it was apparent to every one that every least occasion was followed by killings and wholesale rapine. It was the wickedness of the princes which gave rise to this, not the wicked nature of man, as people said. For the princes who were poor, yet desired to live like rich men, of necessity had recourse to robberies of one kind or another" (Machiavelli, *Discorsi*, III.xxix).

into *private* Life, and giving even to succeeding Times the Complexion of *Inhumanity*.

We must not leave this Subject, without adding a Remark on MACHIA-VEL himself; who undoubtedly writ under the Influence of this Habit of thinking so peculiar to *Italy*. For we see, in the Passage now cited, that altho' he speaks with Resentment against the private Murders so common in his Days, yet he mentions those *political Assassinations* with a kind of Approbation, for which ALEXANDER the sixth and his Son VALEN-TINE,[30] are so justly infamous thro' all *Europe*. He expressly treats of this Method of acquiring Government; and with all the *Sang froid*[31] of a Man talking on a just and legitimate [46] Subject.* Hence, Conclusions have been drawn much in his Disfavour, as a Man abandoned to all Wickedness; while others have adopted the contrary Opinion, and affirmed, that he pointed out these Ways of iniquitous Policy and Assassination, that he might teach Mankind more effectually to prevent them. Now in Truth, these two Opinions are equally groundless; for on the one Hand, his Writings abound with incontestable Proofs, that he was a Wellwisher to his Country and Mankind: On the other it must be allowed, that he hath rather shewn the Methods of treacherous Policy, than the Ways of preventing them. The Truth is, those iniquitous Practices, which shock *our* Humanity, were familiarized to *his* Imagination by the common Usage of his Country: Hence he treated them, as he did other political Maxims of better Stamp, and only talked [47] the Language of his Times and Nation. Nay it appears from a particular Passage in his Works, that he vindicated this Practice of Assassination, as being in some Cases a Principle of the truest Humanity. CAESAR BORGIA was counted cruel, yet that "Cruelty reduced ROMAGNA, united it, settled it in Peace, and rendered it faithful; so that if well considered, he will appear much more merciful than the

---

* See his Prince, c. viii.[32]

30. Cesare Borgia (1475/76–1507); duca Valentino; natural son of Alexander VI; duke of the Romagna and captain-general of the armies of the church; praised by Machiavelli in *The Prince* (1532).

31. Coolness or self-possession.

32. The subject of chapter VIII of *The Prince* is "Of those who have become Princes through Wickedness."

FLORENTINES, who, rather than be thought cruel, suffered PISTOIA to be destroyed."* These no doubt, are horrid Maxims, and such as could never have arisen in the Mind of such a Man as MACHIAVEL, but from the Cause assigned above. They are the more to be lamented, as they have thrown a Cloud over the Fame of one, who in my Opinion is the greatest political Reasoner upon Facts, that hath appeared in any Age or Country. [48]

SECT. VI

Remarks on the Ruling Manners of the Times

Though the Writer made his best Efforts, in his first Essay, towards a true *Likeness* of the Genius of the Times; and tho' he believes he caught the ruling Features; yet the World should not regard that as a complete Portrait, which, in the Painter's Language, ought only to be styled the *Dead Colour*.[34] The Public therefore is requested to give him a *second Sitting*; that he may add those particular, characteristic, and finishing Touches of Light and Shade, which escaped his Eye; and at the same Time smooth off some of those *Asperities,* which might possibly remain upon the Canvas, from the Rudeness of his *first* Pencil. [49]

'Tis again desired, it may not be forgot, "That this Estimate confines itself to such Consequences only, as affect the Duration of the public State: So that the leading Question is, How far the present ruling Manners and Principles of this Nation may tend to its Continuance or Destruction."†

---

* Prince, c. xvii.[33]

† Vol. I. p. 24.[35]

33. "Cesare Borgia was considered cruel; nonetheless, this cruelty of his brought order to the Romagna, united it, and restored it to peace and loyalty. If we examine this carefully, we shall see that he was more merciful than the Florentine people, who allowed the destruction of Pistoia in order to avoid being considered cruel" (*The Prince*, ch. XVII, "Of Cruelty and Mercy, and whether it is better to be loved than to be feared or the contrary"). Pistoia is a town to the northwest of Florence. Machiavelli had first-hand experience of the disorders in the town arising from feuds between the Panciatichi and Cancellieri families, having been sent there on four occasions in 1501 by the Florentine government.

34. The first or preparatory layer of color in a painting.

35. Cf. above, p. 264.

This is the more necessary to be repeated, because eight Readers out of ten, it is believed, forget it, before they had turned the next Leaf.

"In Consequence of this Restriction, the Manners and Principles of the common People will scarce find a Place in the Account."* If the Manners and Principles of a common People are desperately corrupt, they may hasten the Dissolution of a State. But although they be good, they cannot preserve it, if those of the leading ranks be depraved. [50]

"How far we may be from the last Period of *Degeneracy*, it were Presumption to affirm: At present, it is certain, we are not arrived at it. Whenever this fatal Time approaches, it will come distinguished by its proper and peculiar Characters."† This, and the following Part of the Paragraph, will best be commented on by a Quotation from MACHIAVEL, describing the profligate Period of declining ROME: "Commotions, Discord, Sedition, Assassinations, in Peace; cruelty in War; Princes murthered; *Italy* afflicted; its Cities destroy'd; *Rome* burnt; the *Capital* by it's own Inhabitants demolished; the ancient Temples desolate; religious Ceremonies prophaned; the City full of Adulteries; the Sea covered with Exiles, the Rocks with Blood; infinite Cruelties committed daily in the City; Nobility, Riches, Ho[51]nour, and *especially* VIRTUE, grown to be capital Offences: Informers and Calumniators rewarded; Servants instigated against their Masters; Children against their Parents; and those few who were so unhappy as to have no Enemies, destroyed by their Friends."‡

---

* Ibid.[36]
† Vol. I. p. 28.[37]
‡ Disc. Pol. l. i. c. 10.[38]
36. Cf. above, p. 264.
37. Cf. above, p. 265.
38. Machiavelli is contrasting the healthful commotions of the Roman republic with the, as he sees it, far more noxious upheavals which occurred in the reigns of the emperors who followed the brief interlude of good emperors from Nerva to Marcus Antoninus (96–180 A.D.; cf. Gibbon, *Decline and Fall*, vol. I, p. 103), when Rome was "distraught with wars, torn by seditions, brutal alike in peace and in war, princes frequently killed by assassins, civil wars and foreign wars constantly occurring, Italy in travail and ever a prey to fresh misfortunes, its cities demolished and pillaged. He will see Rome burnted, its Capitol demolished by its own citizens, ancient temples lying desolate, religious rites grown corrupt, adultery rampant throughout the city. He will find the sea covered with exiles and the rocks stained

That the true Character of the Manners of our Age and Country is that of "a vain luxurious, and selfish Effeminacy," the Writer affirms will appear from a simple Enumeration of acknowledged Facts, "many of them indeed, in Appearance, too *trite* to merit Notice, and too *trifling* for Rebuke; were they not, in their Tendency, as fatal to the Stability of a Nation, as Maxims and Manners more apparently flagitious."* On this, he understands, a Sort of Objection hath been raised, that a Work founded on Facts so *trite* and *trifling,* [52] must be as *trite* and *trifling* as the *Facts* it is built on.

Now with Regard to his own Work, he is willing to allow the Objection to hold good, as far as any particular Reader chuseth to think it ought. But with Regard to the Truth of the general Objection, he apprehends it will not hold good, for the following Reasons,

1. Because all Reasonings on every Subject, ought to be founded on *evident* Facts; and the more evident the Facts are, the more certain and conclusive the Reasoning will be. Now an *evident* Fact is, in this Regard, the same as a *trite* one, before it can properly be apply'd in the Way of Argument: That is, it must offer itself clearly and incontestably to the Observation of the Writer and the Reader; whether it be drawn from ancient *Books* or modern *Practice.* [53]

2. A Selection of *leading* Facts once made, may appear more obvious in itself than it really is. When you see Flowers or Shells well disposed in a Variety of *Festons,*[40] the Work may seem easy and obvious; and the more natural and pleasing the Disposition is, the more obvious it may seem: Yet may it have required a more delicate and inventive Fancy than is suspected, to have made this proper Selection, from that

---

with blood. In Rome he will see countless atrocities perpetrated; rank, riches, the honours men have won, and, above all, virtue, looked upon as a capital crime. He will find calumniators rewarded, servants suborned to turn against their masters, freed men to turn against their patrons, and those who lack enemies attacked by their friends" (Machiavelli, *Discorsi,* I.x).

   * p. 29.[39]

39. Cf. above, p. 266.

40. Chains or garlands, usually of flowers, suspended in a curved line between two points.

confused Mass of Forms and Colours which Nature offers to the Eye. To speak without a Figure; there are in modern Manners many Appearances wholly contradictory and dissimilar: The Age hath been branded in general Terms, as *ignorant* and *profligate*; it hath been applauded, as *knowing* and *virtuous*. Praise and Censure have been promiscuously and blindly thrown out: But it is another Thing, to mark the peculiar and predominant Virtues and Vices, and give to [54] each, that Weight and Influence which it hath in Nature. On these Distinctions, indeed, the very Essence of such a Work must depend: A Failure in these necessary Distinctions would be a Defect in the first Conception; and, like a false Outline in a Design, draw after it a Multitude of Errors: For, as a delicate Writer hath observed, "l'Allure principale entraine avec elle tous les Accidens particuliers."*

3. The more *trite* and *trifling* the Facts may seem, the more their Consequences are likely to escape Notice: For Attention is naturally fixed only on things of manifest Importance: Now if indeed, notwithstanding this, "they be in their Tendency as fatal to the Stability of a Nation, as Maxims and Manners *more apparently* flagitious;" then, it may be not only a Task of some Importance, but [55] of some Delicacy too, to trace them to their Consequences and Sources, to point out their mutual Influence as Cause and Effect; and, in the very Plainness and Simplicity of Reasoning, "search out (as a good old-fashioned Writer somewhere hath it) the Verities less exposed to View, and make them so familiar, that they who perceived them not before, may come as it were to touch them."[42]

---

* Grandeur des Romains, c. 18.[41]

41. In chapter XVIII of his *Considérations*, Montesquieu enforces his elevation of general above minute causality by observing that in the affairs of a state "the main direction of travel drags in its wake all individual events" (Montesquieu, *Considérations*, p. 235).

42. Brown slightly misquotes from a letter dated 4 August 1630 from Jean-Louis Guez (1595–1654), seigneur de Balzac, to Cardinal Richelieu, in which Balzac praises the highest kind of orators as those who "search out, in every matter, the verities lesse exposed to view, and to make them so familiar, that they who perceived them not before, may by their relation come as it were to touch them" (*A Supply to the Second Part; or, The Third Part of the Letters of Mounsieur de Balzac* [1654], p. 71).

SECT. VII

On the present ruling Motives to Marriage, and their Effects on Manners and Principles

The Writer observed, "that as the first Habits of Infancy and Youth commonly determine the Character of the Man, we might trace the Effeminacy of modern Manners, even to the unwholesome Warmth of a Nursery."* [56] This, though seemingly a good Aim, was falling short of the Mark: Modern Manners, and Principles too, are not a little sway'd by the present *sordid*[44] and *prevailing* Motives to *Marriage*.

Where Virtue, Sense, Beauty, Birth, an Union of amiable Qualities, are the Motives that determine to Marriage; there, domestic Love and Happiness are the natural Concomitants. Hence a tender and generous Concern for the real Welfare, the Manners and Principles of the Offspring, naturally riseth and prevails in the Parents. Those Qualities which they see and love in each other, they naturally endeavour to transplant into their Posterity.

Now modern Matrimony, in high Life, (and the same wretched Spirit is creeping into the middle Ranks) is the Reverse of all this. Neither Virtue, Sense, [57] Beauty, Birth, or the fairest Union of amiable Qualities, generally determine the Choice of either Sex. Instead of these, the most sordid Views of Wealth, or powerfull Alliance; a total Disregard to the Person chosen; a total Disregard to the domestic Comforts of Life; the most despicable Motives of Avarice, external Shew, Dissipation, or Profligacy; these do now most commonly prevail. Hence naturally arise Indifference or Aversion between the Parties.

In Consequence of this Spirit, and *other Practices* which follow it, Separations and Divorces are now more frequent than ever. In the Year seventeen hundred and fifty-seven, when these Tracts were written, there were at one Time seventeen Divorces depending in one Court of

---

* Vol. I. p. 29.[43]

43. Cf. above, p. 266.

44. Here used in the restricted sense (derived from the Latin *sordidus*) to refer to an action prompted by ignoble motives of monetary gain (*OED*, 5a).

Judicature in this Kingdom: A Circumstance of Infamy, unparallel'd in *English* Story.[45] [58]

These fatal Circumstances conspire to blast our rising Spring. In Families thus disposed, what can we expect, but that the *Education* of the Children must be *neglected,* or, what is worse, *perverted?*

Besides, where neither Mind nor Person are the Objects of mutual Choice, but the vile Consideration of Wealth the leading Motive; there, distempered Bodies, and distempered Minds (being frequently the Inheritors of Wealth) must of course be received, and transmitted to Posterity.

Another necessary Consequence of this low and selfish Principle of Marriage, is the *keeping* of Women, and the Increase of *illegitimate* Children. For where the sordid Views of Avarice determine to Marriage, when those Views cannot be gratified, a cheaper Way of Gratification than that of Marriage will take Place. [59] Now, who sees not, that this growing Practice is a dreadful Drawback upon Manners and Principles? I mean not to affirm, that illegitimate Children are never virtuously brought up: But he must be bold indeed, who dares assert, that the Practice of *keeping* Women leads not, in general, to a *dissolute Education* of the Offspring.

Here then we see how fatally this sordid Motive to Marriage affects the *rising* Generation, and therefore the Duration of the State. *When* and *whence* this low Principle had its Rise, is a Consideration which properly belongs to the third Part of this Work: But, after what hath been advanced, the original Cause so naturally offers itself to the Mind, that I need hardly affirm it to have been, "the exorbitant Increase of Trade and Wealth." In *Scotland, France, Germany,* where the Excess of Trade and Wealth hath not yet [60] corrupted Manners, and honest Poverty is not yet disgraceful, the sordid Views of Gain seldom determine the Choice of either Sex to Marriage. This might stand as a sufficient Proof of the Cause here assigned: But it will appear still more evident, if we can fix the Time of this Principle rising among us, and shew it to be cotemporary with the

---

45. I.e., English history. Modern demographic studies of the patterns and frequency of divorce in England do not extend back into the eighteenth century, so it is at present impossible to confirm or deny Brown's opinion that divorce rates in England during the eighteenth century increased.

exorbitant Increase of *Trade* and *Wealth*. And this, it happens, we are able to do, upon the Authority of a good Writer, who at the same Time that he affirms the *Fact*, seems to have had no Suspicion of the *Cause*.

> Our Marriages are made, just like other common Bargains and Sales, by the mere Consideration of Interest or Gain, without any of Love or Esteem, of Birth or of Beauty itself, which ought to be the true In-gredients of all happy Compositions in this Kind, and of all generous Productions. Yet this Custom is of *no ancient Date* in *England*; and I [61] think I remember, within *less than fifty Years*, the first noble Fami-lies that married into the City for downright Money, and thereby in-troduced by Degrees this public Grievance, which has since ruined so many Estates by the Necessity of giving great Portions to Daugh-ters; impaired many Families by the weak or mean Productions of Marriages, made without any of that Warmth and Spirit that is given them by Force of Inclination and personal Choice; and extinguished many great ones by the Aversion of the Persons who should have continued them.*

Here, we see, the Date of the Fact is settled by clear Evidence: The Rise of this Principle, then, was coincident with the Time when our Trade and Wealth grew *exorbitant*; and may justly be ranked among their earliest *apparent Effects*. [62]

SECT. VIII

Of another Source of improper Education of Youth

The Substance of the following just and sensible Remark was sent to the Author from an unknown Hand.

There is a Mistake in the Disposal of Youth, which generally prevails, and is of pernicious Consequence to the Public. Their Genius is con-sulted *too little*, or their Inclination *too much*, in the Choice of a Profes-sion. Their Genius is consulted *too little*, when it is determined perhaps

---

* Sir *William Temple*, Vol. I. p. 268.[46]
46. An accurate quotation from Sir William Temple's "Of Popular Discontents" (Temple, *Works*, vol. I, p. 268).

from their Birth, what shall be their Profession, without any Regard had to their future Talents or Disposition. Their Inclination is consulted *too much,* when they are allowed to make a Choice for themselves, while their unformed Opinions are swayed by the first glaring Object that [63] catches their Imagination. If the Boy is in the Neighbourhood of some *Clergyman,* who lives with Hospitality and Reputation, the *Ministry* appears to him most *desirable.* If he hath had frequent Opportunities of seeing the Finery, Power, and Parade of *Officers* in their *Quarters,* nothing perhaps appears more charming than the *military Life.* If an *eminent Lawyer* lives within his Observation, the *Law* will seem the ready Road to Wealth and Honour. The fond Parent looks on these as happy Omens of Success: Hence the Child is indulged in an inconsiderate Choice, without any Warning given of the *Duties* and *Difficulties* that attend every Profession. When, therefore, he is possessed of his hasty Wish, and finds himself among *Thorns,* where he expected *Roses,* he grows at once dissatisfied, negligent, and *useless.* Thus are Numbers misplaced in the World; and, by this wrong Position, are rendered obscure or hurtful, [64] when they might have shone and been beneficial to the Public, if fixed in their proper Sphere. Many a dastardly Officer might have exerted himself with Spirit at the Bar: Many a bashful Lawyer might have appeared with Credit in the Pulpit: Many a bold-swaggering Churchman might have been a brave Admiral or General: And many an industrious Alderman is buried in a Country Curacy.[47]

SECT. IX

Farther Remarks on the Universities

Is it not somewhat strange, that the *higher* a young Man's Rank is in our *Universities,* and the more important those Stations are, to which, by that higher Rank, he is ordained; the more he is at Liberty to take his full Range in the fertile Fields of *Idleness* and *Inclination?* Yet this hath long

---

47. Cf., for a general parallel, and some slight echoes of phrasing, Thomas Gray, "Elegy Written in a Country Churchyard," ll. 57–64.

been the State of our Universities; and hath had its Rise, partly from [65] the mistaken Fondness and Vanity of Parents in high Life, who must needs have their Sons distinguished by the Article of *Expence,* even in a *College*; and partly from the Temptations of *Gain* and *Credit* in the *Governors* and *Tutors* of the several Colleges, who thus make their Court to idle Sons and weak Mothers, in Proportion as they suffer their wealthy Pupils to live, and return, laden with *Ignorance* and *Vice.* However, it were not Justice (to some Colleges, at least, in one of our Universities)[48] not to assure the Public, that this fatal Practice is wearing off; and a *rational Subjection* to College Rules expected and required from those of the highest Rank and Station.

The Writer is informed, that much Exception hath been made to what he affirmed concerning the University *Professorships,* and the Possibility of their being rendered useful to the Public. What fol[66]lows, is a Summary of his Sentiments on that Subject.

It was never meant to be affirmed, that the *public Lectures* of Professors should be the only Means of Instruction in the academic Education. This Practice is well known to be very insufficient, in all *foreign* Universities where it takes Place. On the other Hand, neither can the private Lectures of College Tutors be of sufficient Power, for the Reasons assigned in the first Volume.* A Union of these, therefore, seems to be the true and effectual System. *College Tutors* should *instruct* their Pupils; but *College Tutors* themselves ought to be *overseen,* and perhaps *instructed,* by the *Professors* in their several Departments; who ought to be Men of singular Capacity and Eminence, appointed for this great Purpose. The Universities, in this important Circumstance, would do well to consider the State of the great Schools. What a Maim [67] would those of ETON and WESTMINSTER receive, should the Head Masters desert the Duties of their Station, and leave their Boys to the blind Direction of every pert *Assistant?* The *Heads* of Colleges, indeed, might stand here in the Place of the *Professors,* or at least aid them in this important Task: And it were much to be wished,

---

* P. 32, 33.[49]
48. Presumably Cambridge, where Brown was a member of St. John's College.
49. Cf. above, p. 267.

that, instead of a perpetual Attention to Cards, Tea, sumptuous Entertainments, and Parties of Pleasure, these Gentlemen would now and then recollect what was the *original Purpose* of College Government.

Nothing of personal Invective is here intended. The Evil is so general, that it manifestly lies in the Manners of the Times, not in those of Individuals. But this Circumstance makes the Evil so much the heavier, and therefore the rather to be noted, as it tends to prevent all Remedy. [68]

One Remark more shall close my Strictures on this Subject.

To *think* justly, to *write* well, to *speak* agreeably, are the three great Ends of academic Instruction. The Universities will excuse me, if I observe, that *both* are, in one respect or other, defective in these three capital Points of Education. While in CAMBRIDGE the general Application is turned altogether on *speculative* Knowledge, with little Regard to *polite* Letters, *Taste*, or *Style:* in OXFORD, the whole Attention is directed towards classical *Correctness*, without any sound Foundation laid in severe *Reasoning* and *Philosophy:* In CAMBRIDGE and in OXFORD, the Art of *speaking* agreeably is so far from being taught, that it is hardly talked or thought of. These Defects naturally produce dry unaffecting Compositions in the *one*; superficial Taste and puerile Elegance in the [69] *other*; ungracious or affected speech in *both*.

SECT. X

An additional Remark on modern Travelling

To what was observed on this Subject, in the first Volume, this farther Remark must be added.

There is not, perhaps, a more important political Principle than this, "That the ruling Habits of young Men, both in Thought and Action, should be thrown as much as possible into one Channel in every Kingdom, and formed suitable to the Laws, the Customs, the Climate, the *Genius*, of their own *Country*." I have much to say upon this Subject, on a future Occasion: At present I shall only observe, that the pernicious Practice of early Travelling, so much in Vogue at present, stands in [70] direct Opposition to this salutary Principle. The Genius of *our* Country, above all others, is particularly distinguished from that of its Neighbour Nations. To this therefore the Taste and Habits of our rising Youth ought to be severely and unalterably formed, before they be permitted to wander abroad in ignorant Wonder and Curiosity, in those Countries where they imbibe Maxims, political, moral, and religious, essentially opposite to those which are the main Foundations of the Stability of our public State. Thus fraught with mischievous, instead of wholesome Prejudices, our young *Men of Quality* return, at once the Contemners and the Contempt of their own wiser Countrymen.

Certainly, the Legislature could not take a more effectual Step towards restoring Manners and Principles, than by suppressing this most pernicious Practice of *early Travel.* [71]

SECT. XI

Farther Observations on the Manners of the Times

The Writer, speaking of the Ridicule of modern Dress, observed, that "yet in this, must every Man of every Rank and Age employ his Mornings, who pretends to keep *good Company.*"* The vulgar Reader, after this Observation made, may probably be at a Loss to know what is meant by "*Good Company.*" Observe, how we have imported the Idea from *France:* "Les Gens qu'on dit être de *bonne Compagnie,* ne sont souvent que ceux, dont le *vice* est *plus rafiné.*"†

"Thus we see Gaming established on the two great Pillars of Self-Interest and Pleasure: and on these Foundations seems to rest the Midnight Riot and [72] Dissipation of modern Assemblies."‡ This false Taste of Interest and Pleasure hath produced a great Evil, which is now becoming general. Every Man of Fortune hath now a splendid House in Town, where his Forefathers were contented with a temporary Lodging. Here he passeth, at least, half the Year: By which means, the ancient and generous

---

* Vol. I. p. 35.[50]
† Lettres Persanes.[51]
‡ Vol. I. p. 40.[52]
50. Cf. above, p. 268.
51. "Those people who are said to comprise 'good Company' are often only those whose vice is more refined"; Montesquieu, *Lettres Persanes*, letter XLVIII.
52. Cf. above, p. 270.

Hospitality of the Country is neglected, and *derided*; and a Kind of *polished Selfishness* takes Place. The honest Peasant is *racked*[53] to the last Excess; and not only so, but the Villages are immediately drained of their natural Wealth, which is transported to the grand Scene of *Dissipation*; and with Difficulty finds its Way back again, especially to the remoter Provinces.

It may be objected, perhaps, that the old *Hospitality* was not less *expensive* than modern *Town-Entertainments*. But sup[73]posing this true, there were two Consequences good and salutary. First, the Money was mostly expended for the useful Produce of our own Country: Whereas the modern Entertainments generally consist of such *exotic Articles,* as no *Englishman* of *middle* Rank ever heard of. Secondly, while the old Taste continued, the *great* People of course mixed with their *Neighbours* in the Country: This generous Communication naturally created or improved in them a Spirit of Benevolence towards their Countrymen, though their Inferiors. Hence, when they came to Town on the Business of the Public, they naturally brought along with them a Regard to the real Interests of their Friends and Neighbours, whose good or social Qualities they knew and loved. Now, the present prevailing System of Town-Effeminacy leads to the Reverse of all this. The Country Seats are depopulated; their Owners are estranged from those, with [74] whom the true Interest of their Country requires them to have the closest Connexions. A total Forgetfulness of their provincial Duty takes Place: Vain and Effeminate Dissipation is the End; Money, rapaciously sought after, is the Means; no matter whence, at whose Expence, or on what Conditions it comes; whether from the *Farmer's Purse,* or the KING's *Exchequer.*

"A knowledge of Books, a Taste in Arts, a Proficiency in Science, was formerly regarded as a proper Qualification in a Man of Fashion, *&c.*"* Yet even this Taste and Proficiency itself ought to be controuled and regulated: It ought to be considered as a *secondary* and *subordinate* Qualification, subject to the higher Views of *Religion, Morals,* and *civil Policy.* Otherwise, even the *truest Taste* commonly degenerates, and [75] forms a Character of illiberal *Conceit* and *Affectation*; drawing down the Mind

* Vol. I. p. 41.[54]
53. I.e., made to pay high rents.
54. Cf. above, p. 271.

from higher Pursuits, no less than Effeminacy itself: Perhaps, thus circumstanced, it may even be styled a *Species of Effeminacy*. In Proof of this Remark we need only observe, that the best Proficients in *Poetry, Painting, Music, Literature*, when they are *merely such*, whether their Conversation lies among *Books* or in the *World*, equally form useless and ridiculous Characters; the Difference consists but in a few *Externals*, between the *trim literary Fop*, and the *sullen literary Pedant*.

"A general Hash of these, served up in some monthly Mess of Dulness, is the meagre literary Diet of Town and Country."* This relates to two notorious Gangs of *monthly* and *critical* Book-Thieves,[56] hackney'd in the Ways of [76] Wickedness, who, in the Rage of Hunger and Malice, first *plunder*, and then *abuse, maim*, or *murder*, every honest Author who is possessed of ought worth their *carrying off*; yet by skulking among other Vermin in *Cellars* and *Garrets*, keep their Persons tolerably out of Sight, and thus *escape* the Hands of *literary Justice*.

"Our Operas are disgraced with the lowest Insipidity of Composition, and unmeaning Sing-Song."† This is a Subject, as much talked of, and as little understood, as the deepest Mysteries of State. At another Time the Writer will speak at large on this Matter: At present, the full Discussion of it would break the Texture of his main Design. He therefore contents himself with referring the Reader to an *Essay on musical Expression*,‡

---

* Vol. I. p. 43.[55]
† Vol. I. p. 46.[57]
‡ By Mr. *Avison*.[58]

55. Cf. above, p. 271.

56. Brown here refers to mid-century journals such as the *Monthly Review* (founded 1749) and the *Critical Review* (founded 1756), which solely reviewed new publications, often incorporating lengthy extracts. For a study of the impact of these journals on eighteenth-century ideas of authorship and literature more broadly, see Frank Donoghue, *The Fame Machine: Book Reviewing and Eighteenth-Century Literary Careers* (Stanford, CA: Stanford University Press, 1996).

57. Cf. above, p. 273.

58. Charles Avison, *An Essay on Musical Expression* (1752). Charles Avison (1710–70) had been since 1736 organist of St. Nicholas's Church, Newcastle, which possessed the largest organ in the northeast of England. His *Essay*, which controversially praised Geminiani and Marcello above Handel, was not wholly his own work, but contained contributions from Brown himself, Thomas Gray, William Mason, John Jortin, Joseph Barber, and Robert Shafto.

as the most rational Thing he hath met with on this Subject. He may truly say, [77] with his favourite Author, "Ces Matieres demanderoient d'être traitées avec plus d'etendue: mais la Nature de cet Ouvrage ne le permet pas. Je voudrois couler sur une Riviere tranquille; je suis entrainé par un Torrent."*

One Remark however, on the Subject of Music, he desires to be indulged in, because it tends directly to mark the Character of the Times. The *Harpsichord,* an Instrument of Power and Compass, is now going out of Use: The *Guitar,* a trifling Instrument in itself, and generally now taught in the most ignorant and trifling Manner, is adopted in its Place: While the *Theorbo*⁶⁰ and *Lute,* the noblest, because the most expressive and pathetic of all Accompaniments, are altogether laid aside. What is the Reason of this? Because the Guitar is a *Plaything* for a *Child*; the [78] Harpsichord and Lute require *Application.*

"The manly Exercise of *riding* is generally disused, as too coarse and indelicate for the fine Gentleman."† This hath been cavilled at, as being false in Fact; the Writer therefore explains himself. He affirms then, (and appeals—to the *Observation,* shall he say, or to the *Practice,* of all his *polite* Countrymen?) that it is disused, as an Exercise that can give Strength and Vigour. The *Riding,* now in Vogue, extends little farther than to a Morning Saunter in *Hyde-Park*; where People of Fashion, like puny and *starved Exotics,* take the Advantage of a *South-Wall,* to shelter themselves from the wholesome Rigours of the Winter Air; to rekindle the dissipated and extinguished Warmth of Nature, and draw new Life from the Powers of a reflected Sun-beam. [79] Here, it is remarkable, that the Sexes have changed Characters: The Men capering about, on *Hobbys*⁶² of

---

* L'Espirit des Loix.⁵⁹

† Vol. I. p. 49.⁶¹

59. "These subjects deserve to be treated at greater length; but the nature of this work will not allow it. I would prefer to glide on a calm river; I am carried away by a torrent"; the opening words of Montesquieu, *Esprit des Loix,* XX.1.

60. A large lute with a double neck and two sets of tuning pegs, the lower holding the melody strings and the upper the bass strings; very popular in the seventeenth century.

61. Cf. above, p. 274.

62. Small or middle-sized horses; ambling or pacing horses.

thirteen Hands; while the Women are galloping full Speed, on sized and *firey Hunters.*

"It may probably be asked, why the ruling Manners of our Women have not been particularly delineated? The Reason is, because they are essentially the same with those of the Men, and are therefore included in this *Estimate.*"* Besides this, there is another Reason. The Manners of Women depend on those of the Men: They will always be such, as the Men chuse to make them.

"The Sexes have now little other apparent Distinction, beyond that of Person and Dress; their peculiar and characteristic Manners are confounded and lost: The one Sex having advanced in[80]to Boldness, as the other have sunk into Effeminacy."† The Fact noted in the Conclusion of the last Paragraph but one, may stand, among twenty others, for a glaring Proof of this.

But here, a Difficulty may seem to arise: For if the Manners of Women be always such as the Men chuse to make them, whence comes it, that such a System of Manners is now taking Place among our Women, as is despised or detested by all Men?

Now the Solution of this Difficulty lies in the modern Manners of the Men themselves. In Times when Courage, Generosity, Sense, Sensibility, and other kindred Qualities, form the ruling Character of the Men, a sincere and honourable Regard to the fair Sex naturally prevails: Hence in such Times, Modesty, Gentleness, and [81] amiable Demeanour, form the Character of the Women. But when, as at present, the ruling Character of the Men is Effeminacy, Selfishness, Folly, Insensibility, and other kindred Qualities; there, all sincere and honourable Regard for the fair Sex is of course extinguished: The Consequence riseth of itself. The Women, finding themselves neglected by the Men, chuse that System of Manners, which is most agreeable to their own Views and Passions.

But still it may be asked, why do they fix in a System of Manners, which Mankind naturally abhor? This too, with the good Leave of my

---

* Vol. I. p. 51.[63]
† Vol. I. p. 51.[64]
63. Cf. above, p. 275.
64. Cf. above, p. 275.

fair Country-Women, I must (in Quality of *Censor*) be so unpolite as to explain. It is a well known Maxim, that Necessity hath no Law. Hence that *Male-Insensibility*, which *Modesty* cannot *attract*, *Impudence* (if it can) must allure or take by *Violence*. Thus [82] you see, how naturally the Fribbles[65] and the Daffodils[66] have produced the Messalina's[67] of our Time.

Alas! how different is this applauded State, from that antiquated Praise of Britain, "when her *Daughters* were *chaste*,[68] and her *Sons valiant!*"

Blush, *if ye can*, my degenerate Contemporaries!

SECT. XII

Of the ruling Principles of the Times

The three great *Principles* which curb the selfish Passions, and sway the Manners of Men, are those of Religion, Honour, and Public Spirit. The first of these, it was observed, has the *Deity* for its Object; the second, the *Applause* of Men; the third, the *Approbation* of our own *Heart*. The Frame and Situation of Man [83] admits of no other Principle, from whence the Idea of *Duty* can arise.

These Principles operate, by affecting the Mind with certain Kinds of Pleasure and Pain; which, though they may be called *selfish* in one Sense, are *disinterested* in another. *Moralists*, each pursuing his own System of *Thought*, or perhaps of *Words*, will dispute on this Matter, as long as their

65. Cf. above, p. 279, n. 32.

66. Daffodil is the eponymous character in David Garrick's *The Male Coquette* (1757).

67. Valeria Messalina, the wife of the emperor Claudius; notorious for her sexual profligacy.

68. "An Ode to the People of Great-Britain" (1746) praises the middle ages when England's "sons, tho' bold, were wise; the daughters chaste, tho' fair" (*A Collection of Poems in Six Volumes* [1758], vol. III, p. 22). The first verse of the song "English Roast Beef" is another possible source for at least half this praise of the British: "When humming brown beer was the Englishman's taste | Our wives they were merry, our daughters were chaste; | Their breath smelt like roses when ever embrac'd, | Oh the brown beer of old England! and old English brown beer" (*A Complete Collection of Old and New English and Scotch Songs*, 2 vols [1735], vol. II, p. 151).

Ink lasts. But as I write to the World, I quit what is merely speculative, for what relates to Manners and Action. It is enough to observe, that whatever Name these Principles be entitled to, their well-directed Power tends to the general Happiness of Man, their Absence to Disorder and Misery.

On the Subject of *religious Principle,* the Author observed, that "to suppose a Man of Fashion swayed in his Conduct by a Regard to Futurity, is an Affront [84] to the Delicacy and Refinement of his *Taste.*"* As *Taste* hath now generally supplanted *religious Principle,* we have the best Evidence in the World of their comparative Excellence and Effects, in appealing to the comparative Strength and Stability of the public State, in *past* and *present* Times.

"Hence, the Day set apart by the Laws of his Country for religious Service, he derides and affronts as a vulgar and obsolete Institution."† The general Effects of this insolent Abuse are bad enough, even on the Manners of those of the highest Rank and Quality: Nay indeed, the higher their Rank, the worse its Effects; as the Contagion of the ill Example spreads wider, and strikes deeper. Its immediate and particular ill Effect on the Manners and Principles of *Servants* in great Families, is still more dreadful. There is not [85] perhaps, generally speaking, a more graceless and abandoned Crew upon Earth, than the Servants in the Houses of the modern Great.[71] They commonly have the *Vices* of their *Masters,* without the Sense of *Decency* to curb or disguise them. I am told, that in some great Houses, the Place of Rendezvous for the Servants goes by the Name of *Hell*; a Name, perhaps, not ill suited to the Genius of its Inhabitants: But a Name vilely given in Sport, and in Defiance of Divine Justice. How different a Scene does almost every modern great Family afford, from those of the ancient Nobles of our Country, where the *Master* was the *Father, Instructor,* and *Friend* of his Servants, and had a generous

---

* Vol. I. p. 54.[69]
† Ibid.[70]
69. Cf. above, p. 276.
70. Cf. above, p. 276.
71. Cf. Jonathan Swift, *Directions to Servants* (1745).

Regard to their Morals, Principles, and real Welfare? I need hardly tell the World, that they are now generally left to the Workings of unbridled Passions, heightened by Idleness, high Living, and dissolute Example. What can be the Result of this Madness, but [86] Profligacy in its Excess? Or what can come forth from such Scenes of unprincipled Licentiousness, but Pick-pockets, Prostitutes, Thieves, Highwaymen, and Murderers? These are your Triumphs, O SHAFTESBURY, BOLINGBROKE, TINDAL, MANDEVILLE, MORGAN, HUME![72]

"A certain *Historian* of our own Times, bent upon *Popularity* and *Gain*, published a large Volume, and omitted no Opportunity that offered to disgrace Religion, *&c.*" This Anecdote is so curious, and characteristic of the Writer alluded to, that it is fit the World should know it more particularly. When this Gentleman found that his History, though larded with Irreligion, did not sell among the *licentious*; and that the *serious* were shocked at his Treatment of Religion, and on that Account were not Purchasers; he ordered his Agent (but too late) to expunge the exceptionable Pas[87]sages; assigning for the Reason of his avoiding every Thing of this Kind in his second Volume, "that he would not *offend the Godly*." Now this very Man, in Defiance of all Decency, hath for several Years carried on a Trade of Essay-writing; in the Course of which he hath not only misrepresented, abused, and insulted the most essential Principles of *Christianity*, but, to the utmost of his Power, shaken the Foundations of all *Religion*. In these sorry Essays he had no Fear of *offending the Godly*, because he knew the *Godly* were not to be his *Buyers:* But when he finds that his History must *sell* among the *Godly*, or *not sell* at all; *then* comes the Panic upon him; *then*, forsooth, he will not *offend the Godly*. Here, therefore, a *Character* is clearly developed. With St. PAUL, *Godliness* was *Gain:*[73] But with *this* Man, *Gain* produceth *Godliness.*

As this was an Offence against the Public, 'tis fit the Public should know it. Our [88] free and happy Constitution admits not of condign

---

72. All writers against established religion; cf. above, p. 25, n. 3 (Shaftesbury); p. 277, n. 28 (Bolingbroke); above, p. 184, n. 44 (Tindal); above, p. 122, n. 55 (Mandeville); below, p. 184, n. 44 (Morgan).

73. 1 Timothy 6:5.

Punishment for the most profligate Crimes of this Kind: The Reason is, not that such Men *deserve not* Punishment, but that their Punishment would destroy Freedom. *Just Disgrace,* therefore, is the proper Reward of those, who thus vilely destroy the *Consolation* of the *Afflicted,* the *Hopes* of the *Good,* and the *Fears* of the *Wicked.*

Next to the *Writers* of such Books as tend to overturn the fundamental Principles of Religion, their *Publishers* deserve surely to be ranked among the modern Pests of Society. They are at least as bad as an *Apothecary,* who should sell *Arsenic* with an Intent to *kill.* Every Man who is so abandoned as to deal in this pernicious Trade, ought in common Justice to give fair Notice of it to his Fellow Citizens, and write over his Door,

> *And if a Man have need of Poison now,*
> *Here lives a* Caitiff Wretch, *will sell it him.** [89]

Hear the wise and sagacious MACHIAVEL; a Writer never charged with any Tincture of Superstition. "Among all excellent and illustrious Men, they are most praise-worthy, who have been the chief Establishers of Religion and divine Worship: In the second Place, are they, who have laid the Foundations of a Kingdom or Commonwealth.—On the other Side, they are infamous and detestable, who are Contemners of Religion, and Subverters of Government."† What then, are we to think of a Herd of dull Scribblers and their Admirers in our own Country, who during the last fifty Years have passed, with the fashionable World, for the *Oracles* and *Heroes* of the Time?

---

* Romeo.[74]

† Disc. Pol. l. i. c. 10.[75]

74. Shakespeare's lines are in fact: "And if a man did need a poison now, | Whose sale is present death in Mantua, | Here lives a caitiff wretch would sell it him" (*Romeo and Juliet,* V.i.50–52).

75. "Of all men that are praised, those are praised most who have played the chief part in founding a religion. Next come those who have founded either republics or kingdoms. . . . On the other hand, those are held to be infamous and detestable who extirpate religion, subvert kingdoms and republics, make war on virtue, on letters, and on any art that brings advantage and honour to the human race, i.e. the profane, the violent, the ignorant, the worthless, the idle, the coward" (Machiavelli, *Discorsi,* I.x).

Let the just Remark of a wise and good Man, a Lover of Virtue and his Country, [90] conclude this Part of our Subject. "These Men would pass for Wits in our Age, by saying Things, which DAVID tells us, the *Fool* said in *his:* And set up with bringing those Wares to Market, which (GOD knows) have been always in the World, though kept up in Corners; because they used to mark their Owners, in former Ages, with the Name of *Buffoons, Prophane,* or *Impudent* Men; who deride all Form and Order, as well as Piety and Truth; and, under the Notion of Fopperies, endeavour to dissolve the very Bonds of all Society."*

The Principle of *Honour* hath fared as ill among us, as that of Religion. "A Man who should go out of the common Road of Life in Pursuit of Glory,—would be stared or laughed at,—as an Ideot, who preferred *Shadows* to [91] *Realities.*"† This was not *loosely* or *figuratively,* but *strictly* and *literally* affirmed. "Honour (saith a modern Writer) is a *Chimera* without Truth or Being."‡ And again: "So silly a Creature is Man, that, intoxicated with the Fumes of Vanity, he can feast on the Thoughts of the Praises that shall be paid to his Memory in future Ages."§ These Maxims have now generally taken Root among us: Thus *Honour* is despised and neglected as a *Shadow; Wealth* sought after as the grand *Reality.*

Now let us candidly examine, on what Foundation Honour is despised and neglected as a *Shadow.* Every pleasing Impression made on

---

* Preface to Sir *William Temple's* Works.[76]

† Vol. I. p. 59.[77]

‡ Fable of the Bees, Rem. R.[78]

§ Ibid.[79]

76. A slight misquotation from the "Preface" to Sir William Temple's *Observations upon the United Provinces of the Netherlands* (Temple, *Works,* vol. I, sig. B3ʳ).

77. Cf. above, p. 278.

78. "Honour in its Figurative Sense is a Chimera without Truth or Being, an Invention of Moralists and Politicians, and signifies a certain Principle of Virtue not related to Religion, found in some Men that keeps 'em close to their Duty and Engagements whatever they be; . . ." (Mandeville, *Fable,* vol. I, p. 198).

79. "So silly a Creature is Man, as that, intoxicated with the Fumes of Vanity, he can feast on the thoughts of the Praises that shall be paid his Memory in future Ages with so much ecstasy, as to neglect his present Life, nay, court and covet Death, if he but imagines that it will add to the Glory he had acquired before" (Mandeville, *Fable,* vol. I, pp. 213–14).

the Mind is equally a Reality, whatever be its external Occasion. The external Occasion is of no Consequence to the Percipient, but as it affects him with Pleasure: If it has that Effect, [92] it is of the same Import and Consequence, that is, in other Words, it is equally *real,* whether it be a Heap of Gold present to the Eye, or the Applause of Men present to the Imagination. The Mind is *equally* affected, though by different Instruments. It is a Mistake therefore to say, that Honour is a *Chimera,* more than that Wealth is a *Chimera,* provided it affect the Mind with as much Pleasure.

But it will be urged, that Wealth furnisheth us with *solid* and *substantial* Pleasures, which the Possession of Honour cannot give. This, in that Extent in which it is affirmed, is no less a Mistake than the other. Mere Competence can furnish all that is desirable for its own Sake, in the Articles of Eating, Drinking, Cloathing, Lodging: Now, beyond these, most of the Pleasures which Wealth can furnish, are founded in Imagination. And among these, it is remarkable, we must [93] have Recourse chiefly to a *Desire of Distinction,* that is, in other Words, to VANITY, ere we can rouze the Mind to taste or desire additional Degrees of Wealth. Now, what is *Vanity,* but a *Chimera,* if *Honour* be such? The Sense of Honour is the Desire of Applause, through Means whose End is public Happiness: Vanity is the Desire of Applause, through Means which are often, if not generally, destructive of the public Happiness. Thus we see what the Public hath gained (and by what wretched Sophistry they have been misled) in despising *Honour* as a *Chimera,* and courting *Wealth* only as a *Reality.* The Consequence is, as the Writer observed, that "Wealth, Titles, Dress, Equipage, Sagacity in Gaming or Wagers, splendid Furniture and a Table, are the sole Fountains from whence we desire to draw Respect to ourselves, or Applause from others. Thus the salutary Principle of virtuous Honour is perverted, [94] and dwindled into unmanly and pernicious Vanity."*

The Author made no Scruple to declare, that he thought "the Principle of *public Spirit,* or the Love of our Country, is less felt among us, than even

---

* Vol. I. p. 61.[80]
80. Cf. above, p. 279.

those of *Religion* and true *Honour."** This is easily accounted for, according to the natural Course of Things, of Causes and Effects. For the Principles of Religion and virtuous Honour, tho' both of them salutary and excellent, yet they do not so totally disengage the Mind from the Views of Self-Love, as the Principle of pure and genuine Public Spirit. In Times, therefore, when Selfishness forms the ruling Character of a People, that Principle which is at farthest Distance from Self-love, will soonest and most generally lose its Influence. The Principle itself, therefore, being at Variance with the Character of the [95] Times, and its best Supports, *Religion* and *Honour,* being weakened or perverted, what can prevent its total Annihilation?

I know there are a Set of *Dreamers,* who talk in their Sleep on the Fair and Beautiful, and will tell you, in Spite of Experience, that this Annihilation of public Spirit is impossible: because the Love of our Country, being naturally beautiful, is natural to the Mind of Man, and therefore cannot be extinguished. To me, I must confess, it seems far otherwise, from all that I have observed of human Nature: The Affections which are necessary to the *Being,* the *Increase,* and *Preservation* of the Species, are *universal:* Those which are only necessary to the *Well-being* or *Improvement* of the Species, seem to require both *Instruction* and *Habit,* to bring them to their just Perfection. Thus the Desire of the Sexes, and the parental Affection, rise universally of their own Accord: A more extended [96] Benevolence, and the Love of our Country are the Result of Culture and Habit. Without these, the benevolent Affection grows weaker, in Proportion as its Object is farther removed from Self.† But enough, or perhaps too much, of speculative Disquisition.

---

* Ibid. p. 62.[81]

† There is a delicate Observation in one of the Letters of NINON DE L' ENCLOS. Speaking of the Virtue of Women, she gives it as a Maxim of Caution to her Pupil, that there are Seasons when Passion is in Danger of being too strong for Virtue; for, says she, "Our Passions are, as it were, a Part of our *solid Substance*; whereas our Virtue is only *inlaid.*" The Original is more elegant: "N'est qu' une Piece de Rapport."[82]

81. Cf. above, p. 280.

82. Brown slightly misremembers the conclusion of Letter XVI: "Le besoin d'aimer fait dans une femme partie d'elle-même, sa vertu n'est qu'une piece de rapport"; "In a woman the need to love is part of her nature, while her virtue is only a decorative inlay" (*Lettres de Ninon de Lenclos au Marquis de Sévigné, avec sa vie,* 2 vols ["Londres" (i.e., Paris), 1782], vol. I, p. 99).

"Our Affections (at present) seldom reach farther than our Relations, our Friends, or Individuals in Distress."* This, as the Author hath observed above,† is the Reach and Character of modern *Humanity*. It may seem odd, that, while this so generally prevails, public Spirit [97] should be so totally quenched. Yet this Appearance is easily accounted for. When the Humanity of a People is founded in *Principle* of any Kind, it naturally riseth into public Spirit. But where Humanity hath its chief Foundation in *effeminate Manners,* as at present, *there* it amounts to no more than *temporary* Starts of *Pity,* according as Objects of Distress occasionally present themselves. Enlarged Views of Benevolence are quite beyond the Reach of such a People: And hence, this Species of *Humanity,* and a total *Defect* of *public Spirit,* are not only *compatible,* but naturally *connected.*

In Confirmation of this, it is remarkable, that *Ferocity* was the Character of the ROMAN People, when their public Spirit was in its meridian Splendor. *Their* private Connexions and Regards gave Way to the Welfare of their Country, in as remarkable a Degree, as our [98] Attention to the Welfare of our Country gives Way to private Connexions and Regards. *Here,* whenever the private Interest of any Individual clashes with the public Safety, Parties are formed in favour or disfavour of the Individual, not according to the Merits of the Cause, but their Likings or Dislikings of, their Attachments to, their Interests with, their Expectations from, the Man. How contrary to this, the great ROMAN Spirit was, in the Period of public Virtue, let the following Instance stand for Proof.

MANLIUS, surnamed CAPITOLINUS,[85] from the particular Service he had done his Country, was the most renowned and beloved Person of his

---

* Vol. I. p. 64.[83]
† See Page 39. of this Volume.[84]
83. Cf. above, p. 280.
84. Cf. above, p. 367.
85. Marcus Manlius Capitolinus; the Roman commander who held the Capitol against the Gauls in 390 B.C.; he later intervened on behalf of the poorer classes of Roman citizen, was accused of trying to make himself a tyrant, condemned, and executed by being hurled from the Tarpeian Rock.

Age. In Emulation of CAMILLUS,[86] whom the ROMANS had advanced
to a higher Degree of Honour, he attempted to destroy the Liberties of
Rome. He was detected, and seized. Then it was, that the great Ro[99]man
Spirit shone out in its Lustre. He was at once forsaken by all who had so
late adored him. The whole Body of the Nobility, the Tribunes, and the
People laid aside their Enmities, and united in the just Design of punishing his Guilt. His nearest Friends and Relations sympathized with the
Public; and refused him the wonted Consolation of appearing in Mourn-
ing at his Trial. He had saved his *Country*; yet all his Virtues could not
save *him*, when he meditated the Destruction of his Country. He was
tried, condemned, and suffered Death.

This, perhaps, is the strongest Instance upon Record, of the Triumph
of public Spirit over private Humanity.

It might now, in Conclusion, be no incurious Search, to enquire into
the comparative Force and Effects of these three Principles, of Religion,
Honour, and pub[100]lic Spirit. But in a Work of this Kind, every Branch
of every Subject cannot be particularly examined. Perhaps, in brief, their
essential Effects may thus be truly separated and distinguished. *Honour*
will prevent *small* Crimes, and produce *great* Actions: *Religion* will prevent *great* Crimes, and produce *good* Actions: The *Love* of our *Country*,
as it seldom riseth unless when built on Honour and Religion, hath commonly the Force of the other two united; will prevent Crimes *great* and
small, will produce Actions *great* and *good*.

But what is the State of that Nation, in which the first of these is
generally perverted among the Great, the second derided, and the third
extinguished?

What the Effects are, we are now more particularly to consider.

The END *of the* FIRST PART.

---

86. Marcus Furius Camillus; fl. early 4th c. B.C.; Roman statesman and general;
dictator on five occasions; conqueror of Veii; exiled on a charge of having appropriated the plunder of that city; recalled to drive a Gaulish army under Brennus out of
Rome; conqueror of the Volsci and the Aequi.

PART II

Additional Remarks
on the
PUBLIC EFFECTS
of these
MANNERS
and
PRINCIPLES

PART II

ADDITIONAL REMARKS

ON

The PUBLIC EFFECTS of these Manners and Principles

SECT. I

Farther Remarks on the National Capacity

With Regard to the *political Leaders* of the People, in every Department, this Subject may seem to have been sufficiently exhausted, and perhaps too freely treated, in the first Volume. However, a few additional Observations naturally offer themselves.

"But if in any Nation (suppose our own) the Number of these superior [104] Minds be daily decreasing from the growing Manners of the Times; what can a Nation, so circumstanced, have more to fear, than that, in another Age, a general Cloud of Ignorance may overshadow it?"*

The Circumstances, that seem to threaten this Catastrophe, are, First, The general Ignorance of the great World. Secondly, Their Contempt and Ridicule of Letters. Thirdly, Their Neglect of Men of Genius and Learning.

The general Ignorance of the great World (tho' there be a few Exceptions) is no Secret to the *rest* of Mankind, whatever it be to *themselves:* and therefore the Writer cannot be said to *divulge* it. If any of these high

---

* Vol. I. p. 78.[1]
1. Cf. above, p. 288.

Personages doubt the Fact, the Circumstances enumerated in the first Volume may give them all reasonable Satisfaction.* [105]

And if a Writer, so far below their honourable Regard, may presume to point out those Paths of Learning and Knowledge, which they might tread with Credit to themselves, and Use to their Country; I will adventure to lead them into this salutary Track; not on my own weak Authority; but on that of Facts, and the unshaken Experience of Ages.

Let it therefore be remembered here, that the *Permanency* or *Duration* of the State, is the main Object of these Essays. And as it is most evident, that the Character and Conduct of the Great, is the Circumstance on which this *Duration* naturally depends; so if we can fix the leading Character and Conduct of the *Great,* in that State, which hath been remarkably and eminently of the longest Duration; it follows, that *such* a leading Character and Conduct ought, above all others, to be the Object of Imitation among those of high [106] Rank in our own Country; especially, if the Effects of such a leading Character and Conduct on the Duration of a State, can be pointed out and traced.

Now, so it happens, that the State which hath been eminently of the longest *Duration,* is that wherein *Knowledge* and *Learning* has, through all the *Records* of Time, been the *leading Character* of the GREAT.

The Nation of CHINA may be distinguished into *learned* and *illiterate.* The last makes up the Body, or Mass, of the People: The first comprehends all that govern; for no other than the *Learned* are ever employed in the Government.

But to comprehend what this Government of CHINA is, and what the Persons employed in it, there will be a Necessity of knowing what their Learning is, and [107] how it makes them fit for Government; very contrary to what ours in *Europe* is observed to do;† and the Reason of such different Effects from (seemingly) the same Cause.

---

* Vol. I. from page 74, to p. 78.[2]
† See p. 37. of this Volume.[3]
2. Cf. above, pp. 286–88.
3. Cf. above, pp. 286–87.

Their Learning is contained in the Writings of the great and re-nowned CONFUCIUS. The Sum of his Writings seems to be a Body or Digestion of Ethics; that is, of all moral Virtues, either personal, œconomical, civil or political; and framed for the Institution and Conduct of Mens Lives, their Families, and their Governments, but chiefly of the last. That the Means to this End is chiefly, not to will or desire any thing that is not agreeable to the Good and Happiness of other Men, as well as our own.—In short, the whole Scope of all CONFUCIUS has writ, seems aimed only [108] at teaching Men to live well, and to govern well: How Parents, Masters, and Magistrates should rule; and how Children, Servants, and Subjects, should obey.

This is the Learning of the CHINESES; and all other Sorts are either *disused,* or *ignoble* among them.

All their Councils and all their Magistracies are composed of Men, eminent in this useful Knowledge. From these are chosen all their *Chief-Officers* and *Mandarines,* both civil and military: their Learning and Virtue make them esteemed more able for the Execution and Discharge of all public Employments, than Practice and Experience in most other Countries: and when they come into Armies, they are found braver and more generous in exposing their Lives upon all great Occasions, [109] than the boldest Soldiers of their Troops.*

Can we be surprized, if a State, whose Leaders are thus severely formed from their Infancy, to political and virtuous Knowledge, should stand un-moved, the unshaken Wonder of passing Ages; while other Common-wealths are born and die, ere a Comet can revolve round the Sun?

Or could we reasonably be surprized, if a State which hath continued firm and unmoved thro' such a Series of Ages, while supported by such Manners and Principles in its leading People, should in the Course of a few Years seem to *totter,* when these Manners and Principles, founded in a virtuous and learned Education, give Way to the private Avarice, Ambition, and selfish Passions of its Leaders?

---

* Sir *W. Temple,* on Heroic Virtue.[4]

4. A *précis* of a long passage from Sir William Temple's "Of Heroic Virtue" (Temple, *Works,* vol. I, pp. 199–202).

'Tis true, a justly admired Writer ascribes this Permanency to a different Cause; [110] "The strict Complication of Parts in this immense political Structure: so that no single Part can be shaken or removed, without overturning the whole; which is a Weight too great for any earthly Power to move."* 'Tis with Reluctance the Writer differs from one he so much admires. But here, tho' the Fact he affirms be true, he hath fallen short of the *original* Cause. 'Tis true, that the Complication he speaks of, is the *immediate* Cause of the Permanency of the State: But the *peculiar Character, Knowledge,* and *Virtue,* of the *leading Members* of the State, is the great, universal, and powerful *Cement,* which runs thro' the whole Mass, and alone maintains this strict Complication; which, without this *uniting Power,* will of itself dissolve; and the Structure, like that of other States; grow old, and by its own Weight fall to Pieces. But more of this in another Work.† [111]

The second Circumstance that threatens us with a general Overflow of Ignorance, *is the Contempt* and *Ridicule* of *Learning* among the Great. Even the Ridicule of *Pedantry* was, in the last Century, regarded as a Symptom fatal to Letters. "The last Maim given to Learning, has been by the Scorn of Pedantry; which the shallow, the superficial, and the sufficient among Scholars first drew upon themselves, and very justly, by pretending to more than they had, or to more Esteem than what they could deserve; by broaching it (Learning) in all Places, at all Times, upon all Occasions; and by living so much among themselves, or in their Closets and Cells, as to make them unfit for all other Business, and ridiculous in all other Conversations."‡ What Consequences, then, may we not expect and fear, when not Pedantry, but Know[112]ledge and Learning, is the common Object of Contempt among the Great? Or rather, when all

---

* L'Esprit des Loix.[5]
† See the Advertisement prefixed to Vol. I.[6]
‡ Sir *William Temple,* Vol. I. p. 169.[7]
5. Untraced.
6. Cf. above, p. 254.
7. A slight misquotation (Temple originally wrote ". . . what they had could deserve . . .") from "An Essay Upon the Ancient and Modern Learning" (Temple, *Works,* vol. I, pp. 168–69).

Knowledge and Learning, except in Gaming, Wagers, good Eating, Bur-rough-Jobbing,[8] and Intrigue, is ridiculed under the Name and *Masque* of *Pedantry?*

The third Circumstance is, the general Neglect of Men of Genius and Learning. It must be confessed, these do not abound: How should they, at a Time, when literary Patronage and Encouragement is so generally extinguished? For it is but a few disinterested and daring Spirits, in any Age, that will devote themselves to the Labours of Contemplation, when Neglect is the known Reward; or prefer the unfrequented and generous Path of Freedom and Competence,[9] to the wide and easy Road of Ser-vility and Wealth. 'Tis true, there are not wanting Instances of the most respectable Generosity in the Patronage of [113] Letters: The more such Characters ought to be, and will be revered, as departing from the com-mon Degeneracy of their Time and Country. But the general Character of the Age is quite the Reverse of this; and implies a general Want of Ca-pacity in the higher Ranks; because all Men of Knowledge and Letters, love Men of Knowledge and Letters; as all Men of Ignorance despise or hate them. In Proof of this we need only appeal to the present State of our own Country; where the remaining FEW, who regard and promote Genius, Knowledge, Taste, and Learning, are themselves conspicuous in these fine Qualities.

So much with Respect to the *Capacity* of our civil and political Lead-ers: With Regard to that of the *Military,* the Writer observed, that "would these Gentlemen please to look into History, they would find, that [114] in *polished* Times, few have ever distinguished themselves in War, who were not eminent or considerable in *Letters.* They would find PISISTRATUS, PERICLES, ALCIBIADES, DION, AGESILAUS, EPAMINONDAS, among the *Greeks:* In the *Roman* List, both the SCIPIO's, CATO the elder and the younger, LUCULLUS, POMPEY, BRUTUS, CAESAR, distinguished in *Letters* as in War."* Turn your Eyes, *Britons,* from your own fallen and

---

* Vol. I. p. 80.[10]
8. Cf. above, p. 286, n. 2.
9. Sufficiency of means for living comfortably (*OED*, 3a).
10. Cf. above, p. 289.

wretched Country; turn them to the *Continent,* and behold even this illustrious List eclipsed by the unexampled Genius, Magnanimity, Constancy, and Valour, of ONE HERO: And give at least a sincere, though fruitless Proof of your Gratitude to your Deliverer, and of your remaining Sense and Admiration of those Virtues you dare not imitate, in being the first to lead the Way [115] to present Times and to Posterity, in styling him "FREDERIC THE GREAT."[11]

The third Order of Men, on whom, in the Writer's Opinion, the national Capacity depends, is that of the *Clergy.* And on this Subject he observed, that "when the *English* Protestant Clergy, and that Christianity which they teach, were most honoured and respected at Home, *England* was then most honoured and respected abroad."* It hath been asked, When was this? The Reply is obvious to any unprejudiced Mind. In the Reign of ELIZABETH; at the Abdication of JAMES the Second; in the honest and prosperous Days of ANN. I say the *honest* and *prosperous*; because she lived to see Days neither *honest* nor *prosperous.*

"Nor can the worthy Part of them, sure, aspire to truer Glory, than to [116] have become the *Contempt* of *those,* who are become the *Contempt* of EUROPE."† A bigotted and tyrannical Clergy will be feared and idolized in a Country of Slavery and Superstition: A virtuous Clergy will be loved and reverenced in a Country of Freedom and Virtue: The virtuous among a Clergy will be despised or hated (according to their Rank) in a Country of Freedom and licentious Principles and Manners. The first is the Case in most *Papist* Countries; the second, in the *Protestant* SWISS Cantons; the third, in *modern* ENGLAND.

It is not true, what hath been insinuated, that not the *Profession,* but the worthless *Professors* are despised. On the contrary, the worthless Professors are often caressed and promoted, because they fall in with the ruling Vices of the Great: While the worthy Part of the Order are [117] often

---

* Vol. I. p. 83, 84.[12]
† Vol. I. p. 84.[13]
11. Cf. above, p. 336, n. 16.
12. Cf. above, p. 290.
13. Cf. above, p. 291.

kept at Distance, because they scorn to degrade themselves and their Profession by a wicked and shameful Adulation.

"But while I defend and honour the Profession, I mean not to flatter the Professors."* The Truth is, the Clergy are neither better nor worse than other Men, but are naturally carried along in the general Stream of Manners. And hence, it must be owned and lamented, that Religion cannot possibly have that Influence in the luxurious and effeminate Period, which it hath in simpler Times; on Account of that ruling System of Manners in which its Ministers will naturally be involved.

When it is said, "they are neither better nor worse than other Men," it is meant, "so far as they are Men." But in every Period, every *Profession* hath its [118] distinct *Character*; and *theirs* naturally *exempts* them from *some Vices,* and perhaps *exposes* them to *others.*

At the same Time it must be confessed (or, if you please, it shall be maintained) that the Idea of a proper clerical Conduct is carried higher in *Speculation,* than human Nature will in Reality admit. The Laity seem to forget that the Clergy are Men of like Passions with themselves. From this Archetype of *ideal* Perfection, it comes to pass, that any *Ridicule* in this Order of Men is *doubly ridiculous*; any *Crime,* doubly *criminal.* Yet, with all their Defects and Frailties, the Writer is of Opinion, that, among the middle Ranks of this Profession, there is more Regard to Duty, more open and undesigning Hospitality, more unaffected Generosity, as well as Charity and Piety, than in any other Order of Men now in Being. [119]

But with Regard to those who "converse with what is called the *World,* and are supposed to make a Part of it:" These, the Writer still maintains, are *generally* (not universally) given up, the younger Part to Views of *Pleasure*; the elder, to Views of *Gain.*

And the Completion of the Evil is, that these Characters stand in the Sunshine and Glare of Life, exposed to public Observation and Scorn; while the Humble, the Pious, the Learned, the Virtuous, are lost to the unworthy and contemptuous World, in the Obscurity of a peaceful Retreat.

* Vol. I. p. 84.[14]
14. Cf. above, p. 291.

The Weekly Dabblers in Politics, it seems, (some of whom, the Writer is informed, now and then honour him and his Friends with their Abuse) are mighty Sticklers for having the *public Reform* be[120]gin with that of the *Clergy*. And indeed, what should seem more natural at first Sight, than that a Reformation should first prevail among that Body of Men, whose peculiar Province it is, to *reform others?* Yet this Project, plausible as it may appear, can never take Place, under our present Circumstance, except in the Brain of those who skim the Surface of political Speculation.

For, first, a Clergy cannot generally be reformed, till *they* are reformed who generally appoint them. Who appoint the Clergy? Are they not, the GREAT? Are they not those (I take things in the general Aspect) who are most infected with the Manners and Principles of the Times? Now, these will generally *appoint* such as they *approve* and *like*; and they will generally *approve* and *like* those Men, who are of *their own* Manners, Principles, and Character. [121]

Secondly, the Reformation of a Clergy, at such a Period, would not bring on a general Reformation, or cure the ruling Evils of the Times. It might do additional Good among the *middle* and *lower* Ranks, but not generally among the *higher:* Because *there*, a *Clergy*, though reformed, will always be *despised*, where Manners are *luxurious*, and *religious* Principle *extinct*.

SECT. II

The Writer's Apology for himself

"It is grown a fashionable Thing, among these Gentlemen (the Clergy) to despise the Duties of their Parish."* This is too copious a Subject, to be here treated of: And besides, is of too *particular* a Nature, to gain a Place in a Work of this Kind, which treats not of Things [122] in the *Detail*, but in their more *general* Principles.

"To wander about, as the various Seasons invite, to every Scene of false Gaiety."† This Charge, it seems, hath been retorted with Vehemence upon

---

* Vol. I. p. 85.[15]
† Vol. I. p. 85.[16]
15. Cf. above, p. 291.
16. Cf. above, p. 291.

the Writer himself. He understands, it is loudly objected to him, that *he* mixes in public Life, and with the fashionable World, as frequently as most of his Profession; and, *at times,* is seen in Places of the most public Resort and Dissipation.

He admits the Fact: And presents his Apology.

First, Supposing all that is alledged or insinuated, to be true; he apprehends, the Conduct of his Life cannot affect or weaken the Reasoning of his Work.

Secondly, He hath Cause to believe, that they who thus accuse him, are such [123] as themselves frequent those Scenes of fashionable Folly. Now, let but these Gentlemen as loudly and publicly declare against the modern Spirit of Effeminacy and Dissipation, as he hath done; and then the World may possibly believe, that he and they are *there* upon the *same Principle.*

Thirdly, He hath Reason to suspect, that if he writ altogether from the Closet, these Objectors would then assume another Tone. They would say (and indeed with good Reason)

> Yes; we despise the Man to Books confin'd,
> Who from his Study rails at all Mankind.
> The Coxcomb Bird, so talkative and grave,
> Who from his Cage cries Cuckold, Fool, and Knave;
> Tho' many a Passenger he rightly call,
> We hold him no Philosopher at all.*

Lastly, Therefore, if he mixeth in public Life, the candid World will judge [124] for what End he does it, not from the railing of angry Men, but from the *Tenor* of his *Writings*; the best Indications of his Mind and Character. There is an essential Distinction between those who *love* Dissipation, and those who *view,* in order to *expose* it. There is an essential

---

* Mr. *Pope.*[17]

17. A misquotation, presumably from memory, of the opening lines of Pope's *Epistle to Cobham*: "Yes, you despise the man to Books confin'd, | Who from his study rails at human kind; | Tho' what he learns, he speaks and may advance | Some gen'ral maxims, or be right by chance. | The coxcomb bird, so talkative and grave, | That from his cage cries Cuckold, Whore, and Knave, | Tho' many a passenger he rightly call, | You hold him no Philosopher at all" (ll. 1–8).

Distinction between the *Provost* of an Army,[18] who goes out on Duty, and the *Marauders,* whom he hangs upon the next Tree.

To conclude; every Man's Sphere of Observation and Experience should be, as far as possible, of the same Extent with the Objects of his Attention. The Painter, if he would give the Truth, must copy from Nature. The *retailing* Tradesman keeps to his Shop; the *private* Officer to his *Platoon*; the *Sailor* to his *Gun:* But the *Merchant,* the *General,* the *Admiral,* if they be wise, will take a *larger Tour* of Observation. The Writer neither [125] *despises* nor *neglects* the Duties of his private Station: But as he hath taken upon him not only the Task of a *parochial,* but the more important and arduous one of a *national Preacher,* he hopes these Gentlemen will excuse him, if he goes a little out of the *common* Road, and endeavours to *understand* his Subject before he *talks* upon it. With their Leave therefore (nay, without their Leave) he will continue to visit the several Parts of his *larger* District; and intends not to content himself with a narrower Sphere of Remark, than that of his Majesty's Dominions.

SECT. III

Farther Remarks on the national Spirit of Defence

"The national Spirit of Defence will always be compounded of the national bodily Strength, Hardiness, Courage, [126] and Principle.—The common People of this Nation seem possessed of the three first of these four Qualities, in a Degree sufficient to form an effectual and national Spirit of Defence."* Here the Writer left the Matter short: It may truly be affirmed, that the common People of this Kingdom are in little or no Danger of being defective in these three Qualities: Their Climate, their Diet, their Way of Life, to which Necessity inures them, naturally form them strong, hardy, and couragious. The only Enemies they have to fear, are the Creatures of Luxury, *Gin* and *Tea.*

---

* Vol. I. p. 87, 88.[19]

18. The senior officer charged with punishing criminal behavior in an army (*OED,* 5b).

19. Cf. above, p. 292.

"They commonly have a proportioned Kind of Principle, which works it's Effect in Battle."* The Principle here spoken of, is that of Honour. But as to this, the Writer thinks it may be easily [127] destroyed: And will certainly be weakened as modern Maxims gain Ground among them.

SECT. IV

Of the different Genius and Permanency of Popery and Protestantism

Let us now more particularly consider, how far the different Genius of the two religious Systems of Popery and Protestantism, may affect the national Spirit of Defence, and consequently the Duration of every State: A Subject but slightly touched on in the former Volume.

"Enthusiastic Religion leads to Conquest; rational Religion leads to rational Defence; but the modern Spirit of Irreligion leads to rascally and abandoned Cowardice."† [128]

This is a Text, on which the Writer thinks it of particular Consequence to enlarge.

1. Popish Superstition, as well as Fanaticism (of which indeed, in many Instances, Popish Superstition is a Species) is a more active Principle, with Regard to Conquest, than rational Protestantism. The first piques itself on destroying and extirpating the Enemies of God: The latter, re-garding none as the Enemies of God on account of *Error*, aims only at rational Defence.

While Protestantism, therefore, retains its proper *Influence* in the Minds of Men, it may be a Match for Popish Superstition. What it wants in *Fury*, it makes up in *Steadiness*. This Truth our Forefathers have *twice* seen manifested in our own Country. [129]

But here lies the Danger: Mankind are apt to be either blindly *zealous*, or altogether *cool* in Matters of *Religion:* The Reason is, because Mankind

---

* Ibid.[20]
† Vol. I. p. 90.[21]
20. Cf. above, p. 292.
21. Cf. above, p. 293.

are generally led by their *Passions,* in Religion, as in other Things. Hence the peculiar Danger to Protestantism, arising from Popery. For Popery, in it's Nature tending to *inflame* a *Passion,* lays hold of the ruling Weakness of Man: While Protestantism, working only on his nobler Part, his *Reason,* whose Dictates he but seldom regards, is apt to fall away into Neglect and Coldness. Thus we see, taking Man as he is, *Fury* is the natural Character of the one; *Indifference,* of the other.

2. Besides this, Popish Superstition obtains another Advantage over rational Protestantism, arising from *degenerate Manners.* For Popery points out religious Fury and Persecution, as the best *Attonement* [130] for Vice or *Crimes:* Whereas Protestantism urgeth no Pretence of this Kind upon it's Votaries; but, on the contrary, teaches them, that without Morals, Religion is *Mockery* of God. Thus we see, that even the *Vices* of a *Papist* tend to inspire him with *furious Zeal:* Whereas the *Vices* of a *Protestant* urge him, for the sake of a false Peace of Mind, to the Neglect, the designed *Forgetfulness* of all Religion.

Thus, though the persecuting Principle of the Papist doth not preserve the Purity of his Manners; yet even the Degeneracy of his Manners tends to preserve his Principle. This we see confirmed by the general State of Things in our own Country; in which, though the Roman Catholics are carried along in the common Stream of Manners, yet their Principles remain unshaken. [131]

On the other hand, tho' the rational Principles of Protestantism tend to preserve the Purity of Manners; yet, if a Degeneracy of Manners comes on, it certainly tends to destroy the Principle. This, too, we see confirmed by the general State of Things in our own Country; where, as Manners have degenerated, religious Principle hath decayed.

3. Another Circumstance, which tends to preserve and strengthen the blind Zeal and intolerant Principles of Popery, is, the tremendous Penalty annexed in the Imagination to any Departure from them. For as the Papist believes this Departure will expose him to all the Effects of the divine Displeasure; so this Apprehension tends to prevent the natural Excursions of Thought, and chains down the Mind in intellectual Darkness.

On the contrary, the free Principle of Protestantism, not working by *Terror,* en[132]courages the Mind to range abroad in Quest of Truth. No religious Apprehension accompanies the Search: And hence, tho' *Reason* will sometimes fix the Mind in salutary religious Principle, *Passion* will oftener allure and misguide it into the pleasurable Path of Unbelief.

4. Another Cause of the superior Permanency of Popery, ariseth naturally from the last assigned. Where so much Merit is supposed to be in one particular System of Belief, and so much Demerit or Guilt in any Departure from it, there, even the benevolent Passions urge strongly to making Proselytes. It is esteemed little less than saving a Soul, to draw a Man over to the Popish Faith. And, to give all Parties their Due, this hath been often the mistaken and fatal Motive to Persecutions, which have been charged altogether upon unfeeling Cruelty. Now the Genius of Protestantism is essentially opposite to this. [133] As it is too just and generous to *compel,* so, as a natural Consequence, it is often too indolent, even to *persuade.*

5. A fifth Cause of the Permanency of Popish Principle, beyond that of Protestantism, was touched in general Terms in the first Volume. Popish Superstition arms itself with the Weapons of civil Power; and, by checking the open and avowed *Profession,* checks in a certain Degree the Progress of Impiety. Whereas it must be acknowledged and lamented, as one of the unalterable Defects of a free Government, that Opinion must have its Course. The Disease is bad; but the Cure would be fatal. Thus Freedom is compelled to admit an Enemy, who, under Pretence and Form of an Ally, often proves her Destroyer.

6. The last Cause flows naturally, as a Consequence of these which have been as[134]signed. A religious Principle, which is only overwhelmed by the Prevalence of Vice or Passion, but still lies dormant in the Heart, may be easily awakened and recalled into Action: But where the Principle is not *overwhelmed,* but *extinguished* by degenerate Manners, *there* it is seldom, if ever, restored to its former Influence.

Now the Popish Principle, when it seems to lose its Effect, is generally no more than overwhelmed by vicious Manners: The religious Belief being rooted in powerful Passions, remains in the Heart, and thro' any striking or alarming Incident, is again awakened into Action. Thus it manifestly operated, in an Instance recorded by MACHIAVEL. "The Roman Religion would doubtless have been lost before this, had it not been reduced towards its first Principle by St. FRANCIS and St. DOMI- NIC; who, by their Poverty, and Christian-like Examples, re[135]vived it in the Minds of Men, where it was almost effaced; and prevailed, that the Looseness and Depravity of the Prelates and Cardinals did not ruin it: For Men, seeing them live in that Indigence and Poverty, by confess- ing their Sins to them; and hearing them preach, began to learn Meek- ness, Charity, and Obedience."* In this Instance, we see, the Principle was *overwhelmed*, but not *extinguished*.

But where the Principles of rational Protestantism are born down by opposite Manners, there the Power of these ruling Manners tends not only to overwhelm the Effects of the rational Principle, but to destroy the Principle itself. For Reason is easily betrayed or corrupted by Passion: and where rational Principle is not rooted in some opposite Passion of equal Strength [136] with that which bears it down, as soon as Reason is corrupted, the Principle is of Course extinguished, and lost. The *present* State of our own Country is a lamentable Instance of this Truth.

Need I point out the particular Tendency and End of these Rea- sonings? It is plainly this: That if we regard Man as that weak Crea- ture which he always hath been, is, and will be; as a Creature often led by *Passion*, and seldom by *Reason*; there is manifestly an Inequality of Force in these two Species of Religion. Their GENIUS is essentially op- posite: Protestantism calmly presents herself to the *Reason*, Popery seizes the *Passions* of Mankind: And hence, modern Popery set against modern Protestantism, is in Danger of overwhelming it. [137]

---

* Disc. Pol. l. iii. c. 1.[22]

22. A rather free and compressed version of the following passage: "As to reli- gious institutions one sees here again how necessary these renovations are from the example of our own religion, which, if it had not been restored to its starting-point by St. Francis and St. Dominic, would have become quite extinct. For these men by their poverty and by their exemplification of the life of Christ revived religion in the minds of men in whom it was already dead, and so powerful were these new religious orders that they prevented the depravity of prelates and of religious heads from bringing ruin on religion. They also lived so frugally and had such prestige with the populace as confessors and preachers that they convinced them it is an evil thing to talk evilly of evil doing, and a good thing to live under obedience to such prelates, and that, if they did wrong, it must be left to God to chastise them" (Machiavelli, *Discorsi*, III.i).

It may be objected against this Argument, and is frequently maintained, that although the vulgar are led blindfold by Popish Superstition, yet Statesmen are not its Dupes, and therefore it is to be regarded as a mere Creature of the State, and subservient to the Views of Policy. In Reply to this, let it be considered, first, that although Statesmen are often Contemners of the Religion of their Country, yet they are not always so: Secondly, suppose them to be of this Turn, yet, in Popish Countries, the Princes are generally superstitious, and will therefore often sway the Councils of the State, where they have Spirit and Action. Thirdly, they are altogether unacquainted with the Foundations of Politics, who know not, that the Religion of every Country will always strike its ruling Colours deep into the Politics of the Country, in spite of all the [138] Statesmen in the World. And lastly, that even where Superstition is made the Dupe of Ambition, and Schemes of Policy, even *there* it is the most powerful of all Engines in working up the Body of the People to carry into effectual Execution those very Schemes which perhaps were planned by *Atheism*. The Objection thereof is futile; and founded in a total Ignorance of true Politics and human Nature.

To convince the Protestant World, how much Reason there is at present for a general Watchfulness and Union in this Regard, let us confirm what hath been here said on the different Genius of the two Religions, by a short View of the present State of BRITAIN, AMERICA, and the EUROPEAN Continent.

With Regard to our own Country, the Principles of Protestantism have lost [139] their Influence: Insomuch, that it is no Injustice to the higher Ranks of this Kingdom to say, that the main Security of the Church ariseth from its Alliance with the State.[23] There is now among the Great, such a general Indifference and Supineness in, not to say Contempt of, every Thing that regards Religion *only*, as may well alarm those few, who look forward to Posterity. How different a State of Religion is this, from that which prevailed in the Reign of ELIZABETH? When, as BOLINGBROKE[24] justly

---

23. An allusion to the title and theme of William Warburton's *The Alliance between Church and State, or, The Necessity and Equity of an Established Religion and a Test-Law Demonstrated* (1736).

24. Cf. above, p. 277, n. 28.

observes, "the Reformation was established, not only in outward Form, *but in the Hearts of Men.*"* How different from that which prevailed at the grand Period of the Abdication of JAMES the Second?[26] When Protestant Principle took the Lead, even of the Spirit of *civil* Liberty; and [140] effected the most glorious Revolution that History hath yet recorded: A Revolution, which might justly be styled *religious* rather than *political.* That great religious Spirit, which at these illustrious Periods shone so bright, is now quenched in Darkness; and the World beholds the Consequence.

On the other Hand, the Zeal of Popery, in this Kingdom, is active, is indefatigable. It's very State of Separation tends naturally to this Effect. The Reasons assigned above, arising from its particular Genius, maintain its Influence. The Priests are assiduous, from Principle, in making Proselytes, and in urging their Party to make them. There is, at present, a Gentleman in the West of *England,* who openly gives five Pounds to every Person who becomes a Proselyte to the Roman Church; and the additional [141] Bribe of a *Sunday's* Dinner, for every such Person that attends Mass. Allurements of the same Kind are known to prevail in most Parts of the Kingdom, and among those of the highest Rank, though not so openly declared. The Papists *seem* to *approve* our Lenity, in thus supinely letting the Laws sleep: In the mean Time their Numbers increase. But can a Nation use its Eyes, and not see, that they must secretly deride our Folly? Especially when we reflect farther, that they have at their Head, a Pretender[27] to his Majesty's Throne and Kingdoms, who regards the Inhabitants of this Nation, not as his *Subjects,* but his *Cattle.*[28] Who doth

---

* Remarks on the History of England, Let. XVIII.[25]

25. Bolingbroke, *History*, Letter XVIII, pp. 217–18.

26. I.e., in 1688. Note the strongly Whiggish implications of the term "abdication."

27. James Francis Edward Stuart (1688–1766); son of James II; the so-called "Old Pretender."

28. A metaphor with strong connotations in the political language of eighteenth-century Britain. In his *Two Treatises on Government* (1690), Locke had used the image of cattle twice to evoke the miserable conditions of life under despotic monarchs. In the *First Treatise*, § 156, Locke accuses Filmer of characterizing "the Societies of Men . . . as so many Herds of Cattle, only for the Service, Use, and Pleasure of their Prince" (Locke, *Two Treatises*, p. 256). In the *Second Treatise*, § 163, he accuses those who "speak as if the Prince had a distinct and separate Interest

not see, that by this blind Neglect, or, if you please, this mistaken Lenity, (which by the Way ariseth not from our *Generosity,* but our *Contempt* of *Religion* and the *public* Welfare) we are treasuring up a hidden and dreadful Mine,[29] which, on the first Occa[142]sion given, will blow up our Constitution both in Church and State?

The Writer hath no personal Pique to the Gentlemen of the Popish Faith: On the contrary, he knows many of them to be, in private Life, of *amiable* and *respectable* Characters. He is far from presuming to deny even the *Merit* of their *Intentions* in a *religious* Regard: For there is no Doubt, but good Intentions may exist in every religious Sect. He hopes therefore, they will put the same charitable Construction on *his* Intentions, while he lays open the Genius and Tendencies of their System of Belief. He is far from meaning to revive sanguinary Laws: Yet these Gentlemen must excuse him, if, knowing the *ruling* Principles of their Church, he freely explains and urges the Dangers that threaten his Country. [143]

With Regard to the State of Popery and Protestantism on the Continent of AMERICA; this is no less discouraging to the true Protestant. The different Genius of the two Systems operates with the same Universality and Power. The Papists are zealous, watchful, and assiduous; the Protestants are cold, indifferent, and neglectful. The SPANIARDS, in Course of Time, will have converted one half of the vast *Southern* Continent, and murdered the other. The FRENCH join Policy to Zeal; or rather, make Zeal subservient to Policy. They reason, they persuade, they cajole, they terrify the poor INDIAN Nations; and by every Means of Truth, or Falsehood, draw them over to their Party. The Conduct of the ENGLISH is the Reverse of all this. Doubtless many of our *Missionaries* are worthy

---

from the good of the Community" of implicitly conceiving of the people as "an Herd of inferiour Creatures, under the Dominion of a Master, who keeps them, and works them for his own Pleasure or Profit" (Locke, *Two Treatises,* p. 377). In *The Decline and Fall,* Gibbon would list, among the apparent absurdities of hereditary monarchy, the fact that "on the father's decease, the property of a nation, like that of a drove of oxen, descends to his infant son" (Gibbon, *Decline and Fall,* vol. I, p. 187). See also Blackburne, *Memoirs,* vol. I, p. 211.

29. A subterranean passage dug under an enemy position or the wall of a besieged fortress, in which explosives would be detonated in order to gain entrance or to bring about its collapse (*OED,* 3a).

Men: But it must be acknowledged, as the natural Effect and *Defect* of the *Protestant* System, that [144] they are not generally *impelled* by *Zeal,* but *compelled* by *Necessity,* to visit these remote and *inhospitable* Regions. In the mean Time, the Inhabitants of our Colonies are, like ourselves, given up to Views of Gain and Pleasure:[30] The State of Religion is totally disregarded; its Dictates and Principles derided and thrown off. Thus *Popery* advances with dreadful Strides, while *Protestantism* lies immersed in Indolence and Sleep.

Let us next consider the State of the two Religious Systems on the *Continent.*

In the UNITED PROVINCES, we shall see their contrary Genius exerting itself, as if the Pourtrait here given of each had been drawn from hence.

There are very great Numbers of *Roman Catholics* in the *United Provinces*; notwithstanding their Religion, as Sir WILLIAM [145] TEMPLE observes, is not immediately protected by the Laws of the Republic. The same Author has assigned the Reason of this; which is, that the States believe the Roman Catholic Religion must make Men bad Subjects, while it teaches them to acknowledge a foreign Power superior to that under which they live: And accordingly they have made several penal Laws to prevent the Growth of it. But as each Province hath reserved to herself the Liberty of regulating Religion within her own Jurisdiction, these penal Laws of the States General have never been put in Execution. In HOLLAND especially neither PRUDENCE nor POLICY would permit them to exclude so large a Body as the Roman Catholics out of the general Toleration: And accordingly they

---

30. Contrast Burke's very different assessment of the religious character of the American colonists in his speech of 22 March 1775 on "Conciliation with the Colonies": "Religion, always a principle of energy in this new people, is no way worn out or impaired; and their mode of professing it is also one main cause of this free spirit. The people are protestants; and of that kind, which is the most adverse to all implicit submission of mind and opinion. This is a persuasion not only favourable to liberty, but built upon it. . . . the religion most prevalent in our Northern Colonies is a refinement on the principle of resistance; it is the dissidence of dissent; and the protestantism of the protestant religion" (Burke, *Writings and Speeches,* vol. III, pp. 121–22).

are very numerous in the great Towns of that Province, where [146] the Magistrates give them an equal Protection with other Dissenters. At AMSTERDAM, they have not fewer than twenty-four Chapels. There are great Numbers of the same Communion in ROTERDAM, and several other Cities: But they are most numerous in the Villages: Insomuch that a Miller, Smith, or any other Mechanic, being a Protestant, is sure to be a Beggar if he settles in the Country; for the Priests never fail to enjoin their whole Communion to neglect him. This perhaps may seem strange to the *English* Reader, who considers HOLLAND as a reformed Country, and a principal Bulwark of the Protestant Religion: But I speak upon good Grounds; and, amongst many Proofs which I might bring, of the Truth of what I advance, I chuse to instance the Remonstrance made to the States General in 1725, [147] by the Deputies of the General Synod, who represented the Growth of Popery in the most pathetic Terms; and affirmed, that since the Year 1650, the Number of Roman Catholics in the seven Provinces was increased *three hundred and fifty thousand*; of which they had authentic Proofs.*

Thus the Love of *Gain* hath worked as powerfully towards the Increase of Popery in HOLLAND, as the Love of *Pleasure* and *Dissipation* hath done in ENGLAND: Conformable to the Principles laid down in the first Volume.†

With Respect to the rest of EUROPE; its present State tends to prove strongly the general Truths here advanced. We see the Protestant Crowns divided against each [148] other; the Popish Crowns in Union and Confederacy. The RUSS and SWEDE have joined the *Popish* Power in tearing to Pieces his Majesty of PRUSSIA. The EMPRESS QUEEN[33] hath at length thrown off the Masque; hath basely deserted those who had long and often saved her from Destruction; and given a striking Proof of this great

---

* Batavia Illustrata. By O. Burrish, Esq; p. 147, 148.[31]

† Vol. I. p. 163, &c.[32]

31. Onslow Burrish, *Batavia Illustrata: Or, A View of the Policy and Commerce of the United Provinces*, second edition (1742), pp. 147–48.

32. Cf. above, p. 322.

33. I.e., Catherine the Great (1729–96), empress of Russia from 1762. Presumably those who on behalf of Catherine the Great approached Brown in July 1765 to reform the Russian education system had not read this passage.

Truth, That where Pride and Bigotry rule the Heart, *there* human Virtues find no easy Entrance. FRANCE is playing its old Game, and pursuing its established Plan of Power.

Thus the active and zealous Popish Principle is every where working its Way; while the Coldness of Protestantism leaves the Issue of Things to the calm and ineffectual Deliberation of civil Policy; forgetting that *Passion* is the *Soul* of *Action,* and the great *Spur* that hath ever urged Mankind to all that is *Good* or *Wicked.* [149]

If we consider the different Genius of these two Systems, as described above, we cannot wonder at this Difference of Conduct: and to evince, that it is not the Result from Chance, but from established Causes, we shall see the same Spirit working in each, in former Ages. BOLINGBROKE (who was a *great Historian,* tho' but a *poor Reasoner,* and saw Facts in their apparent Connexions, rather than in their *interior* Causes) hath given us the actual State of *Europe* in the Days of JAMES the First; which bears so strong a Resemblance to our own, in Regard to the Genius of the two Religions, that it cannot be thought incurious.

> On the one Side, the whole *Popish* Interest, in the Empire, was *closely united;* and the Cause of FERDINAND was the common Cause of the Party. The Popish Interest, out of the Empire, conspired in the same [150] Cause. The King of POLAND assisted the Emperor in HUNGARY. Troops from ITALY, and a great Army from the *Netherlands,* acted for him in GERMANY.—Even FRANCE, who ought in good Policy to have opposed the House of AUSTRIA, was induced, by the *Bigotry* of her Court, and perhaps by the private Interest of LUINES, to declare for the Emperor against the King of BOHEMIA. On the other Side, the *Protestant* Interest in the Empire was *far from* being *closely united;* and *farther* still from making the Cause of FREDERIC the common Cause of the Party. Even the Princes of the Union had different Views: many of them leaned to the Emperor; none of them could be entirely depended upon: And the Elector of SAXONY, the most powerful of the Protestant Princes of the Empire, was so far from uniting with the others, that [151] he was first privately, and afterwards openly, but all along

very steadily, on the Side of FERDINAND. Out of the Empire, some Assistance might have been expected from the King of DENMARK and the DUTCH: but even *their* Accession must have been *purchased*, at least it must have been made useful, at the Expence of BRITAIN.*

Had the Writer collected these Facts from History, and drawn them thus to one central Point, it might justly have been suspected, that he had thrown a false Light upon them in the Recital, that they might better serve his Purpose: But when we consider this Paragraph as coming from an Author who was dead before the present Aspect of Things took Place, we cannot but acknowledge the permanent *Unifor*[152]*mity* of *Principles*, working the same Effects in the most *distant* Periods of Time.

The Event of this Popish League ought indeed to strike us with *Awe*, tho' not with *Despondency*. FREDERIC of BOHEMIA[35] was swallowed up by the Confederacy: But though no human Eye can pierce the impenetrable Veil of Fate, yet we have Reason to hope from what is past, that the great Prince[36] now combined against, is not designed by Providence as a Sacrifice to bigot Power: Let us rather behold him as the *appointed* guardian Angel of *Truth* and *Liberty*, who with the Swiftness of *Light*, and the Terror of a *Whirlwind*, chears the Friends of *Freedom*, and overwhelms her *Enemies*.

The manifest Inference is this: As it appears from these Reasonings that the Genius of Popery is active, insinuating, [153] furious, unalterable, permanent; the Genius of Protestantism, calm, rational, indolent, fluctuating, perishable; that we ought to be most *watchful* in the Preservation of this invaluable Blessing; and active in the *Support* of *those* who are the great *Supports* of *Protestantism*.

---

* Remarks on the Hist. of *England*, Let. XXII.[34]

34. Bolingbroke, *History*, Letter XXII, pp. 286–87.

35. Frederick V (1596–1632), elector Palatine of the Rhine; king of Bohemia (as Frederick I, 1619–20); director of the Protestant Union.

36. I.e., Frederick the Great.

SECT. V

*How far the Spirit of Duelling is connected with
the manly Spirit of Defence*

"Can the Debility of modern Honour produce the manly Spirit of Defence? Alas, if ever it is put in Action by any Thing beyond the Vanity of Shew; it is rouzed by an Affront, and dies in a Duel."*

But it seems the Opinion of many, that the Spirit of *Duelling*, and that of manly [154] national *Defence* are naturally connected, and of Course rise or fall together. Much might be said on this Subject; at present I shall only mark the Difference of *Principle*, on which these two different Systems of Conduct are founded.

The Principle of *Honour* depends on, and ariseth from, the *Love* of *Glory*, or the *Fear* of *Shame*. Where the Love of Glory is, the Dread of Shame comes of Course: But the Dread of Shame may exist without the Love of Glory; a Truth which is confirmed by Experience, in all *groveling* and *narrow* Minds; and in many that are *Good* too, but not *elevated*.

On this Distinction is founded the essential Difference between a national Spirit of Defence, and the private Habit of Duelling. The national Spirit of *Defence*, so far as it depends on the Principle of *Ho*[155]*nour*, can only be kept up by the *Love* of *Glory*. The mere *Dread* of *Shame* cannot raise this general Passion in a *People*, because, among a People who have lost the national Spirit of Defence, there is *no Shame* attending the *Loss* of it.

But private Duelling arising from the Sense of private Injury, is naturally produced by the Fear of Shame *only*. Glory is seldom thought of in this Instance: and where it is, produces the hateful Character of a *Bully*. It is the *Fear* of *Shame* therefore, and not the *Love* of *Glory*, that supports the Spirit of *Duelling*.

Thus we see, the Principle of Honour works by two different Passions in producing a Nation of *Duellists*, and a *Nation* of *Heroes*. The first are only compelled by the Fear of Shame; the latter are actuated by the Love of Glory. And thus [156] the national Spirit of *Defence* may be *strong*, when

* Vol. I. p. 90.[37]
37. Cf. above, p. 293.

that of *Duelling* is *extinct*; and the Spirit of *Duelling* may *exist*, when that of military *Honour* is *extinguished*.

SECT. VI

A remarkable Consequence arising from this Difference of Principle

These Truths relate to Nations; and the Character of a People. But with Regard to *Fleets* and *Armies*, another Truth offers itself to Observation. Here, "The Love of *Glory* is necessary in the *Leaders*, as a Motive to great and daring *Enterprize:* But among the inferior Ranks, the Fear of *Shame* will be generally of Influence sufficient to compel them to their *Duty*." The Reason is evident: With Regard to the Leaders, as it is im[157]possible to point out to them their particular Track of Duty in every Instance, so their Conduct must be left in general, to the Determinations of their own Mind: *Great Actions* will naturally be attended with *Glory*; but the mere *Omission* of great Actions, where peremptory Orders are not given, is not necessarily attended with *Shame:* Therefore it is the *Love* of *Glory* only, that can urge a *Leader* to *great* and *dangerous Attempts*.

But with Regard to the *inferior* Ranks; *there* the particular Track of Duty is pointed out; which is only this, "Obey the Commands of your Leader." Under this Circumstance, no Evasion can take Place: Every Man must obey, or Infamy overtakes him: And thus the Fear of Shame becomes sufficient. [158]

This Distinction will clearly account for that strange Difference of Conduct in our *British* Troops, during the last, as well as the present War.[38] It hath been remarked, that at Times they have fought like *Lions*; at others, have been timorous as *Hares*. Their Bravery, in particular Instances, hath been brought as a Proof against the Existence of the ruling Principle of *Effeminacy*, which runs through this Work. But whoever views this Matter, according to the Distinctions here pointed out, will at once see the Veil drawn off from this mysterious Appearance of Things.

---

38. I.e., during the War of the Austrian Succession (1740–48) as well as the Seven Years' War (1756–63).

Where did our Troops distinguish themselves in Valour? Was it not at DETTINGHEN? at LA FELDT? and above all, on the dreadful Field of FONTENOY,[39] where honest *Fame* forsook the Standard of the *Victor,* and *wept* over the Banners of the retreating ENGLISH? And [159] who were the *Leaders* on these important Days? They were such as were *inspired* and *actuated* by the *generous Love* of GLORY.

SECT. VII

Of a national Militia

"Will not Cowardice, at least as soon as Courage, part with a Shilling or a Pound, to avoid Danger? The capital Question therefore still remains; not who shall *pay,* but who shall *fight.*"*

A Capital Question, this, indeed; and hard to be resolved among a *mercantile* and *effeminate* People. This naturally leads us to consider what may be expected, feared, or hoped, from the Establishment of a national *Militia.* In which Enquiry, the Writer's sole Intention is, to pursue [160] his leading Principles through all their Consequences; without any Intention of contradicting or offending any Party whatever.

First, An *English* Militia cannot be so *dangerous* now, as in former Times; because the *Commons* are discharged from those slavish military Tenures, which so often brought them into the Field, to butcher each other in former Days, at the Command of a *seditious* or *revengeful* Lord. HENRY the Seventh, through his Hatred to the Nobility, let in this first Dawn of lasting Liberty on the Inhabitants of this Kingdom. The People, though armed, would now want Leaders of Influence, to unite them in Seditious Purposes. Therefore the sudden and short-lived Fury of a

---

* Vol. I. p. 80.[40]

39. All battles fought as part of the War of the Austrian Succession. George II had in person led the British and Hanoverian troops to victory at the battle of Dettingen (27 June 1743); the battle of Laufeldt was a narrow victory in June 1747 for French forces under Maurice de Saxe over an allied army commanded by the Duke of Cumberland; while the French under Saxe had gained a notable victory over Austrian and British forces at the battle of Fontenoy (11 May 1745).

40. Cf. above, p. 294.

Mob, is the worst that can be feared from this Establishment. 'Tis true, an armed Mob is a dreadful Monster to the *Indivi*[161]*dual*, but cannot rise into *public* or *treasonable* Attempts, through want of a uniting Power.

Hence, L I V Y's fine Description of a Mob: "Ex ferocibus universis, singuli metu suo obedientes."[41]

Secondly, The *effeminate* Manners of the Times take away the great *Danger* which formerly arose from a free Militia in more warlike Periods.

But then, on the other Hand, these same Reasons that take away the *Danger,* are fair to destroy the *Usefulness* of a Militia. For we see, their Danger arose from their *Union* and their *Valour:* Now, what is a Militia without these two Qualities?

A *Legal Union* indeed may be acquired; more *rational,* though not so *powerful* [162] as the *slavish*. But without national *Valour, Union* is a dead and unactive Quality.

If the Principles maintained in this Work be true; the Defect of Valour in a national Militia, will not lie among the *private* Men, but among the *Officers*. And indeed, who can seriously believe, that those Gentlemen who find the *Attendance* upon a *Quarter-Sessions* for the Service of their Country, too *severe* a Burthen of Duty upon their enervated Bodies and Minds, will vigorously undertake and go through the *Dangers* and *Fatigues* of warlike Service?

It must therefore be expected as a certain Event, that a Militia will, on its first Institution, and for a long Time be *useless*. But this is not said with a View to discourage the Establishment, but only to [163] prevent groundless Expectations; which being disappointed in the first Establishment of a Militia, might lead the Nation into a Belief, that the Institution could *never* be *useful*.

This Circumstance, therefore, is no Reason why a Militia should not be set on Foot; but rather a good Reason for its speedy Establishment: Because the continued *Exercise* of a Militia, if undertaken with that

41. Again, Brown is slightly misquoting from memory. Livy wrote: "ex ferocibus universis singulos, metu suo quemque, oboedientes fecit"; "they turned from a defiant group to obedient individuals, as each man became alarmed for himself" (Livy, VI.iv.5).

Vigour and *serious Intention* which it deserves, is perhaps the most promising means of *re-kindling,* by slow Degrees, the *military* Spirit among us.

As a rational Encouragement to the Hopes of the Nation, let us cast our Eyes back upon former Times, and hear the impartial Judgement of a great Foreigner, who could have no Views to influence his Opinion. "There is scarce any Body ig[164]norant, that of late Years the ENGLISH invaded FRANCE, and entertained no Soldiers but their own: And yet, tho' ENGLAND had had no Wars of thirty Years before, and had neither Officer nor Soldier who had ever seen a Battle, they ventured to attack a Kingdom where the Officers were excellent, the Soldiers good, having been trained up for several Years together in the *Italian* Wars. This proceeded from the Prudence of the Prince, and the Excellence of that Government, in which, even in Times of Peace, the *Exercise* of *Arms* is *not intermitted.*"*

The main Conclusion I mean to draw from these Observations, is only this. "The Establishment of a Militia must [165] destroy effeminate Manners; or effeminate Manners will render useless a Militia."

SECT. VIII

Farther Remarks on the State of our Armies

"Land-Officers in the *Capital,* are occupied in Dress, Cards, and Tea; and in Country Towns divide their Time between Milleners *Shops* and *Taverns.*"†

This Abuse of Leisure in Time of Peace, hath been one of the leading Causes of that Disgrace, into which the Armies of *Great-Britain* are fallen. On this Subject, as being beyond my Sphere, I will not presume to instruct the military [166] Gentlemen of my Country: At least, if I do, it shall be on the Authority, and in the Words of a great Writer; who speaking of the proper Employments of a Soldier in Time of Peace, wisely expresseth himself as follows.

---

* Mach. Disc. l. i. c. 21.[42]
† Vol. I. p. 101.[43]
42. A broadly accurate translation of Machiavelli, *Discorsi*, I.xxi.
43. Cf. above, p. 297.

He never ought to relax his Thoughts from the Exercises of War; not even in Time of Peace: And indeed, *then* he ought to employ his Thoughts more studiously therein, than in War itself; which may be done two Ways, by the Application of the Body, and of the Mind. As to his bodily Application, or Matter of Action;—he ought to inure himself to Sports: And by hunting and hawking, and such like Recreation, accustom his Body to Hardship, Hunger, and Thirst: And at the same Time inform himself of the Coasts and Situation of the Country; the Size and Ele[167]vation of the Mountains; the Largeness and Avenues of the Valleys; the Extent of the Plains, the Nature of the Rivers and Fens, which is to be done with great Curiosity. This Knowledge is useful in two Respects: For hereby he not only learns to know his own Country, and to provide better for its Defence; but it prepares and adapts him, by observing their Situations, to comprehend the Situations of other Countries, which perhaps may be necessary for him to explore. For the Hills, the Vales, the Plains, the Rivers, and the Marshes (for Example) in TUSCANY, have a certain Similitude and Resemblance to those in other Provinces: So that, by the Knowledge of one, we may more easily imagine the rest. And he who is defective in this, wants the most necessary Qualification for a General: For by knowing the [168] Country, he knows how to beat up his Enemy, take up his Quarters, march his Troops, draw up his Men, or besiege a Town with Advantage. In the Character which Historians give of PHILOPOMENES Prince of ACHAIA, one of his great Commendations is, that in Time of Peace he studied military Affairs; and when he was in Company with his Friends in the Country, he would many Times stop suddenly, and expostulate with them, "If the Enemy were upon that Hill, and our Army where we are, which would have the Advantage of the Ground? How could we come at them with most Security? If we would draw off, how might we do it best? Or if they should retreat, how should we pursue?" So that, as he was travelling, he would propose all the Accidents to which an Army was Subject; he would hear their Opinion, [169] give them his own, and reinforce it with Arguments: And this he did so frequently, that by continual Practice, and a constant Intention of his Thoughts upon that Business, he brought himself to that Perfection, that no Accident could happen, no Inconvenience could occur to an Army, but he could presently redress it. But as to the Exercise of the Mind, he is to do that by Diligence in

History,* and solemn Consideration of the Actions of the most excellent Men: By observing how they demeaned themselves in War; by examining the Grounds and Reasons of their Victories and Losses; that he may [170] be able to avoid the one, and imitate the other.†

These, doubtless, are admirable Instructions; and followed, as I have been informed, by the greatest Captain of this, or any other Age: Yet such is the established Effeminacy, the wretched Affectation of [171] fashionable and trifling Discourse, that now prevails in the Armies of *Great-Britain,* that such a Conduct, though rational and manly in the highest Degree, would be treated with Derision and Contempt. The Writer cannot hope to escape their Ridicule on this Occasion: And doubts not, but he is by this Time set down by most of his military Readers, as a *Pedant* and a *Martinet.*[45]

SECT. IX

The same Subject continued

It may, perhaps, be a Question worth resolving, "whether *gross* Vices or *refined* Vices be more fatal to the Spirit of Defence, and to the *Armies* of any State?" The Writer hopes, that no Critic will be so very uncharitable, as to tax him here, with a Vindication of any Vice whatever: [172] Yet knowing of what

---

* MACHIAVEL is a little incorrect here, in the Division of his Subject: For a great Part of what he had said above is, strictly, an Exercise of the Mind, no less than the Study of History.

† MACHIAVEL's Prince, c. 14. He adds another Circumstance, which perhaps is not so certain in its Effects. He says, "Above all, he is to keep close to the Example of some great Captain of old; and not only to make him his Pattern, but to have all his Actions perpetually in his Mind." Thus, it is true, ALEXANDER did (as it is affirmed) by ACHILLES; CAESAR by ALEXANDER; SCIPIO by CYRUS. And the Principle was just, while the Arms offensive and defensive were of the same Kind. But the Invention of *Gunpowder* hath wrought such a total Change in Arms, Discipline, and the Methods of *Attack* and *Defence,* that an Adherence to the Practice of any ancient Leader would be in Danger of misguiding, rather than instructing any modern Warrior, in the *particulars of Execution:* But in the *general Principles* of *conducting* War and Armies, this Rule may still be applied with Success.[44]

44. Machiavelli, *The Prince*, chapter XIV. The anecdote about Philopoemen is to be found in Livy, XXXV.xxviii.1–8 and Plutarch's "Life of Philopoemen," IV.v–vi.

45. Originally a follower of the system of military drill devised by Jean Martinet, inspector-general of infantry under Louis XIV; by extension, a rigid or merciless disciplinarian (*OED, n.4*, 1 and 2a).

Materials the general Herd of Critics are made, he thinks it not amiss to throw in this Caution. His Resolution, then, of the Question is, that *refined* and *effeminate* Vices are more fatal to an Army than *gross* ones. First, Because, when they once catch, they become more general. Secondly, Because they are equally destructive of military Application and Capacity, with those of a grosser Cast. Thirdly, Because they tend much more than gross Vices, to destroy two of the main Hinges, on which the Spirit of Defence must hang: These are *Hardiness* and *Courage*. Is it necessary to confirm this by Facts? The Facts are at Hand. The Armies of this Kingdom were more *grossly* vicious in Queen ANN's Reign than at present. I need not point out the Consequence. [173]

At the same Time, let it be acknowledged or asserted, that the *personal* Character and Conduct of a Man *grossly* vicious is more *hateful* than of *refined* Vice. Which of these two Kinds of Vice are more criminal in a *moral* or *religious* Light, is again a different Question. We keep here, to the leading Point in View, the *Strength* and *Duration* of a State.

And it is certain (such is the strange Complication of human Circumstances and Affairs) that with Regard to this, several Habits, Qualities, and Actions, which seem innocent in themselves, as they affect or influence *private* Life, are equally or more hurtful than others of a more odious Appearance, if we consider them as they affect the *public* Strength and Welfare. This comes to pass, because the ill Consequences of some Actions are *immediate*; [174] of others, more *distant*. The first strike the *Imagination*, and are seen by all: The latter must be traced up to their Causes by the Use of *Reason*; and to do this, exceeds the Talents of the many. Hence an unequal Judgment often ariseth, concerning moral and political Good or Evil, the *comparative* Merit or Demerit of Actions and Men. Many of the pernicious Effects of Luxury and Effeminacy fall under this Observation: And hence came the poor and wretched Reasonings of two Champions of Luxury and Effeminacy,* whose Principles will be examined in a proper Place.

---

* Doctor MANDEVILLE, and Mr. DAVID HUME.[46]

46. Bernard Mandeville (1670–1733) had argued in his *Fable of the Bees* that the economic well-being of a modern commercial society depended upon the gratification of the human appetites upon which moralists of a civic humanist stripe tended to pass their most severe censures. David Hume (1711–76), in essays such as "Of Refinement in the Arts," had also opposed the traditional critique of luxury as a solvent of virtue, albeit in a more suave manner.

SECT. X

Additional Thoughts on the Navy

"Sea-officers, even in Time of War, instead of annoying the Enemy's [175] Fleets, are chiefly busied in the gainful Trade of catching Prizes."*

There is little Danger, as yet, of the Body of our Fleets being Effeminate: Their way of Life secures them from it. There is a natural Ferocity of Manners attending the Sea-Service, which would always preserve itself, were it not quelled by the Contagion of effeminate Example. The Danger, therefore, ariseth from the *Commanders,* whose present false Ambition and Way of Life naturally leads them to Effeminacy.

It is remarkable in our Navy, (what the Writer speaks, he knows to be Fact) that the young Men bred to the Sea Service, so long as their Conversation lies among the *inferior* Ranks in their Ship, [176] retain or acquire the *Spirit* of *English* Sailors; that is, they grow brave, hardy, and intrepid. But no sooner do they rise to the Rank of *Captains,* but the Example of the Times infects them: False *Elegance* and effeminate *Parade* take Place: *French* Cooks and Valets are sought after: The Commander of the Ship becomes a *Sultan,* who lives in idle State, and hath his Duty done by his *Vizir,* his *First Lieutenant.* Time was, when Matters went otherwise; and the Nation feels the Difference.

At the same Time, it were Injustice to the *Navy,* not to acknowledge, that there are Men in this Department who have done Honour to themselves and their Country; and others rising into Name, who, with due *Encouragement* and *Distinction* given, bid fair to retrieve the Glory of the *British Flag.*

The Act which gave the *Prize* to the *Captors,* had manifestly a bad Tendency: [177] In every particular Case, it was an Allurement to draw off the Captains from the *Duty* of their Country, to the despicable Views of *Privateering.* A worse Effect than this was, it's setting up a false and fatal Principle, the Love of *Money,* instead of the Love of *Glory* or of *Duty.* Rational and true is the Observation of a late political Writer: "We have

* Vol. I. p. 101.[47]
47. Cf. above, p. 297.

destroyed the Principle, which was the Source of our Glory. We have mis-guided the Ambition of our Seamen; we have tempted them with *Wealth* instead of *Reputation*; and we have substituted *Avarice* to *Honour*."*

These are manifest Tendencies to *Ill*; and are generally supposed to have brought upon our Fleets this sordid Spirit of *Prize-catching:* But the Writer is of a different Opinion. This Act seems to have been, not so much the *Cause,* as the *Consequence,* of [178] the present *Rapacity* and *Profusion.* In a virtuous and disinterested Period, as there would have been no Necessity for it, so if it had taken Place, it would have had no Effect: The Reward proposed would not have drawn off a brave and disinter-ested Commander from his Duty. But, I apprehend, they who proposed this Act, seeing and knowing what was the *ruling* Spirit of the *Times,* imagined it more for the Benefit of the Public, that our Fleets should fight for *Gain,* than *not at all.*

The Truth therefore seems to be, that tho' the Act hath a bad Ten-dency; yet it cannot be said to have created, tho' it hath certainly in-creased the selfish Spirit of the Navy. An ill *Act,* like an ill *Citizen,* can do no great Harm, but in an *ill-disposed City.*

How different were both the Conduct and the Police of the ROMANS? Who, in[179]stead of filling the *private* Purses of their *Leaders,* made it a Circumstance of *Infamy,* if, upon their Return from War, they did not enrich the *Coffers* of the *Republic:* Insomuch, that at length it came to pass, that no *Consul* was permitted to Triumph, who had not first put a vast Quantity of Silver or Gold, or some other valuable Commodity, into the PUBLIC TREASURY.

SECT. XI

Of the Marine Society

Since therefore the Degeneracy of our Fleet ariseth evidently from the Commanders: this naturally leads me to say something on the Institution

---

* Letter, by a Country Gentleman.[48]
48. Thomas Potter, *The Expedition Against Rochefort Fully Stated and Considered* (1758), p. 36.

of the *"Marine Society,"*[49] and to consider what *may,* or may not be expected from it. [180]

The Institution is humane, praiseworthy, and excellent, in two Respects.

First, It rescues a Number of wretched *Boys* from *Crimes* and *Misery;* and the *Public* from the *Effects* which these *Crimes* and that *Misery* would have produced.

Secondly, It tends to alleviate that great Evil of *pressing* Men for the Sea-Service.

But notwithstanding these good Effects, it must not be expected, that this Institution, laudable and humane as it is, will ever raise our *Fleets* into their former *Credit;* because it can only affect and strengthen the *Body* of the Fleet, and not the Manners, Principles, and Conduct of the *Commanders.* [181]

SECT. XII

Farther Considerations on the National Spirit of Union

"MONTESQUIEU hath often given it as his Opinion, that Factions are not only natural, but necessary to free Governments."* This Opinion was criticised, and shewn to be in some Sense *erroneous,* because too *general.* It is only taken Notice of here, with a View to observe, that the celebrated Author borrowed this Opinion, with many other important Observations in his Book, from MACHIAVEL's Discourses on LIVY.† But in Justice to the sagacious FLORENTINE, we must observe, that *he* limits the Observation to the Times in which public Spirit was predominant; whereas the other great Writer ex[182]tends it to the later Periods, when selfish Ambition had quenched the Love of their Country; and hence arose his Error.

* Vol. I. p. 104.[50]
† Vol. I. l. i. c. 4.

49. Established in 1756, the purpose of the Marine Society was to attract the sons of poor families, and also able-bodied but otherwise unemployed men, to enlist as seamen; cf. Jonas Hanway, *Motives for the Establishment of the Marine Society* (1757), and his later *A Letter from a Member of the Marine Society* (1757).

50. Cf. above, p. 298.

As these two Authors, in the Writer's Opinion, possess the highest Station in the political Scale; it may be worth while to give a *comparative* Sketch of their different *Characters*.

MACHIAVEL, born and bred in tumultuous and profligate Times, and occupied in the Affairs of a distempered Republic, caught his first Principles of Politics from what he *saw*. MONTESQUIEU, more happy in his Birth and Fortune, enjoying an early Leisure, in a quiet and well-regulated Monarchy, drew his first Principles of Politics from what he *read*. Yet neither was the *first* given up to mere personal *Observation*; nor the last, to mere *Study:* In the Progress of Life, MACHIAVEL ap[183]plied himself to *Books*, and MONTESQUIEU to *Men:* Yet, as was natural, their first Habits *prevailed*, and gave to *each* his distinct and peculiar *Character*.

Hence, tho' *both* saw the internal and secret Springs of Government, (which, in my Opinion, no Writer, but these two, did ever fully comprehend or penetrate) yet they saw them by different *Lights*, and thro' different *Mediums*. MACHIAVEL's leading *Guide*, was *Fact*; MONTESQUIEU's was *Philosophy*. In Consequence of this, *Simplicity* forms the Character of the *one*, *Refinement* that of the *other*. The speculative FRENCHMAN forms a fine *System*, to the Completion of which, he sometimes *tortures* both *Argument* and *Fact:* The plain and downright FLORENTINE builds on *Facts*, independent of all *System*. The polite and disinterested *Sage* is warm in the *Praise of Honesty:* The active and pene[184]trating *Secretary*, above Praise or Censure, gives a bold and striking Picture of the *Ways of Men*. Hence, while the first gains every *Heart*, by the Force of *moral* Sympathy, the latter hath been falsely *detested*, as the *Enemy* of Virtue and Mankind. MACHIAVEL is *negligent*, yet pure and *strong*, scorning the *minuter Graces* of Composition: MONTESQUIEU is *elegant*, yet *nervous*; and to the *Acuteness* of the *Philosopher*, often adds the *Fire* of the *Poet*. Both were the Friends of Freedom, and of Man: Both *superior* to the *Genius* of their *Time* and *Country:* Both, truly *great:* The FLORENTINE *severe* and *great*; the FRENCHMAN, *great* and *amiable*.

"Therefore, before we can determine, whether the Factions that divide a free Country be salutary or dangerous, it is necessary to know what is their Foundation and their Object: If they [185] arise from Freedom of Opinion, and aim at the public Welfare, they are salutary: If their Source be selfish Interest, of what Kind soever, they are then dangerous and destructive."* I cannot give a better Comment on this Truth, than in the Words of BOLINGBROKE.

> As long as the Spirit of Liberty prevailed, a *Roman* sacrificed his own, and therefore, no Doubt, every other personal Interest, to the Interest of the Commonwealth: When the latter succeeded (the Spirit of Faction) the Interest of the Commonwealth was considered no otherwise, than in Subordination to that *particular* Interest, which each Person had espoused. The principal Men, instead of making their Grandeur and Glory consist, as they formerly had done, in that which the [186] Grandeur and Glory of the Commonwealth reflected on them, considered themselves now as *Individuals,* not as *Citizens*; and each would shine with his own Light. To this Purpose alone they employed the Commands they had of Armies, the Government of Provinces, and the Influence they acquired over the Tribes at ROME, and over the Allies and Subjects of the Republic. Upon Principles of the same Kind, inferior Persons attached themselves to these; and that Zeal and Industry, nay that Courage and Magnanimity, which had been exerted formerly in the Service of the Commonwealth, were exerted by the Spirit of Faction, for MARIUS or SYLLA, for CAESAR or POMPEY.†

So stands the Case, with Regard to the *general* Foundations of *Faction,* in most [187] Times and Countries. But there is another Source of Faction, of which we have had most fatal Instances in our own Country, distinct both from that of public Spirit and selfish Interest: I mean that of *erroneous Conscience*; when the *unalienable Right* of governing is supposed to be inherent in any particular Man, or Race of Men. This, though it hath not the *Nature,* hath most of the *Consequences* of *selfish Faction*; and is attended with this additional Evil, that as it is founded in *Principle,* it is more *steady* and *resolved.* The Civil Wars which rent the Kingdom[53]

---

* Vol. I. p. 106.[51]
† Remarks on the History of *England,* Letter II.[52]
51. Cf. above, p. 299.
52. Bolingbroke, *History,* Letter II, pp. 25–26.
53. The so-called "Wars of the Roses" (1455–85).

during the Contentions between the Houses of YORK and LANCASTER, were of this Kind. Of this Kind too, in good Measure, were the Civil Wars, in which CHARLES the First perished: And of this Kind, altogether, have been the consequent Rebellions against the established Government. This Distinction, however, [188] must be remarked in Favour of the free Spirit and Sense of the *Lancastrians* and *Yorkists,* beyond that of the *Stuart* Party; that these last pant for *Thraldom* and *Chains*; but among both the former, the same Men who would have *died* for their respective *Kings,* would have *died* for the *Laws* and the *Liberty* of their Country.

SECT. XIII

The same Subject continued

Let us now proceed to consider more particularly the Causes that have weakened or destroyed the national Spirit of Union, since the great Revolution, which took Place on the Abdication of JAMES the Second.[54]

It hath been one of the Writer's main Intentions, in the Progress of this Work, [189] to point out the natural *Weaknesses* and Defects of a *free* System of Government: He did not at first apprehend, that any Apology could be necessary for this Conduct, because he thought it a clear Point, that the more evidently these *Weaknesses* and *Defects* were *explained,* their proper *Guards* and preventive *Securities* would with the greater Care and Caution be *applied.* Hence he freely expatiated on the Dangers attending a Dissolution of Manners and Principles; hence he hath freely set forth the natural Stability of *Popery* beyond that of *Protestantism*; hence he freely explained the natural Inconveniencies that arose even from such a great Event, as that of the *Revolution* in eighty eight. This, and more, he hath done, that his Countrymen, being aware of the *Delicacy* of that fine *Structure,* which is at once the Pride and Security of its Owners, might use all timely Expedients, to maintain its [190] *Foundations* in their original Strength, and not expose themselves to the dreadful Calamities in which its *Fall* must involve them.

54. In 1688. Once again, the use of the term "abdication" is strongly Whiggish.

But see the Consequence: Because he had affirmed, that, under an arbitrary Government, the Spirit of Union was naturally *strong*, he hath from thence had the Imputation laid upon him, of being a Friend to arbitrary Government: Because he pointed out a new Principle of Faction, which *naturally arose* from the *Revolution*, he hath been accused, as an *Enemy* to that *Revolution:* Because he had asserted, that the *Abuse* of *Freedom* had destroyed religious Principle, he hath been miscalled an ill *Wisher* to *Freedom* itself. So blind are these QUIXOTS in their Adoration of *Liberty*, that they accuse her Physician of *Disaffection* to the favourite *Fair*, merely because he declares her to be *mortal*; tho' [191] at the same Time he holds forth the *Medicines* that might *prolong* her *Life*.

But though he hath Candour enough to believe, that in some, these Accusations arise from sincere Belief, founded in narrow and mistaken Views of Politics; yet he hath ample Grounds to suspect, that in others, Insinuations of this Kind have sprung from the Leaven of Malice and Wickedness, working in its usual Way, against every Thing that is free, fair, and honest. The next Charge against him will probably be founded in what he hath said on the Genius of *Popery* and *Protestantism:* Nor will he be much surprized, if those who naturally rail at what they cannot answer, should blacken him with the Infamy of being a *Papist* in his *Heart*. [192]

In the mean Time, he turns his Back on their Iniquity, and proceeds to his appointed Task.

From the Restraints laid on the Royal Prerogative at the Revolution, and the Power of Parliaments which naturally arose from these Restraints, together with the selfish and lucrative Views, to the Gratification of which these Parliaments soon began to prostitute their growing Power, he drew this Consequence. "WILLIAM the Third, found this to be the national Turn; and set himself, like a Politician, to oppose it: He therefore silenced all he could, by Places or Pensions: And hence the Origin of MAKING PARLIAMENTS."[55]

This, the Writer is informed, hath been perversely misinterpreted into a Satire [193] on King WILLIAM. He therefore thinks it necessary to explain himself.

55. Cf. above, p. 300.

When therefore it is said, "Hence the Origin of making Parliaments," it is not meant, that such Attempts had never been made before. There is hardly a Period in the *English* History, but would give the Lye to such an Assertion. From an Examination of ancient Times it would appear, that the Practice (as was natural) was always most *frequent* when the Government was *weakest:* When the Power and Prerogative of the Crown were high, the desired Effects were wrought without *making Parliaments.* Therefore the evident Meaning of the Passage is this, that the Practice of making Parliaments was now first laid down as a *necessary Principle* of Government; and this was the necessary Consequence of *lessening* the [194] *Prerogative,* where *Parliaments* were *selfish.*

In WILLIAM the Third therefore, it seemed an Act of Necessity: At least, he judged it such, and was heartily tired of it. Insomuch that the Perverseness of his Parliaments, arising from *factious* Conduct, founded in *selfish* and *lucrative* Views, had well nigh tempted him to quit his Throne, to return to his native Country.

We see then, that this Principle of *Faction* was a *natural* Defect, arising from a *noble Change* in the Constitution: Evils infinitely greater were taken away: A general Change of political Principles, with all their various Consequences, was the natural Effect of that Revolution. The *Defects* (or rather Evils) of an *arbitrary* Government *ceased:* The *Defects* of a *free* Government *arose:* And it is the main [195] Purpose of this Estimate, to point out and resist *these.*

"Shires and Boroughs, which in former Times had paid their Representatives for their Attendance in Parliament, were now the great Objects of Request, and political Struggle."*

The following Anecdotes, in Illustration of the Progress of the Evil here spoken of, were given to the Writer, by a learned Friend, whose Profession leads him to Enquiries of this Nature.

It hath long been debated among the learned in the Antiquities of this Kingdom, at what Time the Privilege of the *Commons* of *England,* to share in the *Legislative* Power, first commenced; some placing its Origin

---

* Vol. I. p. 110.[56]
56. Cf. above, p. 300.

as high as the earliest Ages of the *Saxon* [196] Monarchy; others reducing it to the latter End of the Reign of EDWARD I. There is a Mixture of Truth in both Opinions.—For it is most probable, that the Commons of *England,* who were *Proprietors* of Land, had always some Share in the Legislature. And at the same Time it is most certain, that this Right was not reduced to the regular Form it now assumes, till the latter Period.

However important this Privilege may now appear, it was not for a long Time after the Reign of EDWARD I. thought of any great Value, or much sought after; as appears by the great Neglect of Attendance in Parliament in the latter End of the Reign of EDWARD III. and the Beginning of RICHARD II. which was then so remarkable, that it was found necessary to enforce it by an Act of Parliament, which [197] *required Attendance,* under Pain of Amercement.[57]

It is an old Observation, that formerly "the Interest of Parliament was never more predominant, than when Kings wanted Title or Age." Hence the Commons first began to find their Importance in the Reign of RICHARD II. and continued to increase it during the Reigns of HENRY IV. HENRY VI. and HENRY VII. In Consequence of this, it became necessary to regulate Elections; the first Statute relating to which was made in the Reign of HENRY IV. From this period, Endeavours were used to make Parliaments subservient to the Views of the ruling Party, and their Importance in those Days arose, or fell, in Proportion to the Occasions such Party had for their Authority. [198]

As the Times were tumultuous till the Union of the Houses of YORK and LANCASTER,[58] it was common before that Period for *Sheriffs* to omit or excuse the not making Returns for several of the Boroughs within their Counties. Sometimes giving for Reason of their Omission, that the other Boroughs were not able to send any Burgesses because of their *Poverty* or *Inability*; which was never then complained of, or objected to, by the Boroughs themselves; though several Acts of Parliament had been made to compel the Sheriffs to make Returns for all the Boroughs: Nay, several of the Boroughs after they had once or twice sent up their Representatives,

---

57. I.e., a discretionary penalty or fine.
58. On 18 January 1486, with the marriage of Henry VII and Elizabeth of York.

found the Burthen too great, and *procured* perpetual *Exemptions* which remain to this Day. How differently do we value this Right at present? When no Price is thought too great for the Purchase of a Borough; [199] and no Family, how ancient or honourable soever, of any Consequence, but in Proportion to these modern Possessions?

Mark the uniform Effects of the same Principles and Causes, working at the Distance of two thousand Years.

> The Consulship, or any other Office or Dignity, was never conferred by the People of ROME, upon any body but by formal Application: Which Custom was originally very good; because none sought for them, who was conscious of being unfit; forasmuch as to be repulsed, was a dishonourable Thing; and to make himself *fit*, every Man chose to be *virtuous*. But afterwards, the Manners of the People growing so fatally corrupt, this Custom lost its primitive Convenience, and became not only useless, but pernicious: For they who had most Power, not they who had most Virtue and Capacity, [200] pretended to the Magistracy; the Poor and the Virtuous not daring to appear, for fear of a Repulse. But this Inconvenience, like the City itself, was not the Product of a Day: It stole into the Commonwealth, lay concealed, increased, and exerted itself by Degrees, as all other Inconveniences do.—Security, and an unhappy Scarcity of Enemies, was the Occasion, that, in their Creation of Consuls, the People of ROME began to regard *Riches* and *Favour* more than *Ability* and *Virtue*; preferring such Persons as could entertain and treat People handsomely, to such as were grave, and could only conquer their Enemies: Afterwards, from those who were most plausible, they came down, and created such as were most powerful; so that Persons of *Virtue* and *Capacity* were *totally excluded.** [201]

The Writer proceeds: "It hath been much debated, whether the *Ministers* or the *People* have contributed more to the Establishment of this System of Self-Interest and Faction."† Here is an Error, in Expression

---

* Machiavel's Disc. l. i. c. 18.[59]

† Vol. I. p. 112.[60]

59. Brown's customarily heightened rendering of a passage from Machiavelli, *Discorsi*, I.xviii.

60. Cf. above, p. 301.

at least. In Justice to the Body of the *British* People it must be remarked, that by the *People* was, or ought to have been meant, chiefly the higher Ranks of the Nation; except only in *Boroughs,* where the Corruption, here spoken of, runs down through the lowest of the People.

"On Enquiry it would probably appear, that at different Periods the Pendulum hath swung at large on both Sides: It came down in former Times, from the Minister to the Representative, [202] *&c.*—In later Times, the Impulse seems to have been chiefly in the contrary Direction, *&c.*"*—These Changes followed each other according to the natural Operation of Causes and Effects: But tho' the Writer shewed their general Progress, yet he did it not with that Particularity of Circumstance, which so interesting a Subject deserves.

He apprehends, therefore, that there have been three essential Changes of Principle, in the Progress of this great and ruling Evil. It *began* from the *Crown,* at the *Revolution,*[62] from a Principle of *Necessity:* It was *continued,* by succeeding Ministers, and brought to its Crisis by ONE Minister,[63] on a Principle of supposed *Prudence:* It hath since been *continued* on a Principle of supposed *Necessity* again: but [203] that supposed Necessity hath had a Foundation different from that which took Place at the Revolution. For that *first* Necessity arose from the State of the Times, when a new modelled Government, like a new planted Tree, had not yet taken Root in the Minds of the People; and therefore the Storms of Parliamentary Faction were of more dangerous Consequence to its Rise and Growth. But after this System of Self-Interest had been rivetted by *one Minister,* in the Minds of the People, and the *higher Ranks* throughout the Nation, and all Men of *all* Ranks in *Boroughs,* were taught to expect and demand the utmost Penny for their Vote or Interest; then it was, that a new Kind of Necessity commenced; and succeeding Ministers, honest in their Wishes and Intent, were seemingly *compelled* to *that* which their Predecessor had *voluntarily* established. [204]

---

* Vol. I. ibid.[61]
61. Cf. above, p. 301.
62. I.e., in 1688.
63. I.e., Sir Robert Walpole.

SECT. XIV

Remarks on the Conduct of a famous Minister[64]

"There was a noted Minister in this Kingdom, whose Character, perhaps, might be drawn in these few Words, that while he seemed to strengthen the Superstructure, he weakened the Foundations of our Constitution."*

The Writer understands, that some Offence hath been taken at what he affirmed in general Terms, concerning this Minister: He therefore thinks it necessary to explain himself more particularly: Not, indeed, with any *interested* Views of pleasing any *Party*; because he apprehends, that his Sentiments concerning this [205] Minister, are *different* from those of both his *Friends* and *Enemies*.

The real Faults of his Ministry ought the rather to be delineated, because many Men of *Sense* and *Worth, admire* and *maintain* his System: And finding that he was charged with Designs he never formed, they have thence inferred, I suppose, that he was therefore *blameless*.

His Friends are generally accounted, and some of them I know *are*, the real Friends of Liberty: To *these* it cannot be unacceptable, *freely* and FAIRLY to examine the Nature of his Administration. If we are curbed in this Point of Enquiry, our Liberty is lost in its most essential Circumstance. Nor surely can it be taken amiss in that Nation, to criticise a *dead Minister*, where every Man with Impunity can insult the LIVING GOD. [206]

In this Enquiry, therefore, two Things will appear remarkable: One, that his Enemies, in their Discourses, Speeches, and Writings, charged him with Things he was not guilty of: The other, that what was really pernicious in his System, *that* they totally overlooked; and would not, or could not see.

Firstly, therefore, it is not true, that this Minister corrupted the Nation: He found it corrupted to his Hand. It is not in the Power of any *one* Man to taint an upright People. He may put the Wheels in Motion, but cannot create a general Change: His Life is too short, and unequal to the Effect.

---

* Vol. I. p. 114, 115.
64. I.e., Sir Robert Walpole.

Secondly, it is not true, that he ever formed any Design to inslave his Country. He did not wish *so ill* to his Country. More [207] than this: His Genius was *peaceful*, and never led him to this blind and ambitious Project: For he had Sense enough to know, that so daring a Design could never be executed, without involving the Nation in the Horrors of a *civil War*.

These are the atrocious Crimes, with one or both of which he hath been falsely charged by his Enemies. Let us now consider the real Genius and Faults of his Administration.

1. In his private Character, he was *amiable* and *friendly*. Yet even this private Character may justly be regarded as a main Foundation of those Defects, which blotted his Ministry. For,

2. He carried his domestic and friendly Attachments into public Life; and for the Advantage of *Individuals* whom [208] he *loved*, often sacrificed the Interests of that *Public* which he neither *loved* nor *hated:* For his Affections were of the common and confined Kind, and never reached so far as to comprehend his *Country*.

3. Though he had no natural Inclination to corrupt Practices, yet he rather chose to rule by *these*, than to resign his Power. This Conduct was founded in his Temper too: He preferred the immediate interest of his Friends, to the future and distant Welfare of his Country.

4. His *Genius* for Government was of a *confined* Nature; and therefore it may be unfair to charge his Intentions with all the Consequences of his Administration. Tho' he had an acute Eye, so far as its Sphere extended, yet that Sphere was but narrow. He saw Things in their immediate, but not [209] in their remote Effects. He regarded Wealth, as the sole Fountain of national Power, Strength, and Stability: He did not foresee its Influence and Effects. But let me add, that if he had foreseen them, I do not think his Regard to the Public was strong enough to have determined him to a contrary System, against the natural Bent of his own partial and confined Affections.

5. The Consequence of this narrow Ability and Turn of Mind was, the utter Neglect of the Manners and Principles of the Nation, and of all those counterworking *Checks*, which ought to be laid upon a People that is *growing* in Trade, Wealth, and Luxury.

6. Nay, on the contrary, he forwarded the Growth of these pernicious Manners and Principles: Not through the na[210]tural Love of Vice; but

because he saw them favourable to that Parliament Influence, without which he found he could not both gratify his favourite Ends, and maintain himself in Power.

Thus, while Trade and Wealth, the grand *Incentives* to *Vice*, increased; he neglected, nay discouraged the Care of salutary Manners and Principles, the only effectual *Checks* to *Vice*. Thus, while he *enriched Individuals*, he made his *Country poor*. Instead of using his Power, in filling every public Office and Department with Men of Ability and Virtue, he sacrificed Ability and Virtue to Views of Parliament Influence. Thus he established corrupt Principles with a View to strengthen Faction in support of the Crown, till those very Principles have become a Burthen upon the Crown itself: Thus by unnatural and forced Applications, he gave a temporary [211] Motion to the Wheels of State; while the natural, and internal Master-Springs of Government were losing their Elasticity and Power: And thus he greatly contributed to reduce us to that State of political *Dissolution* and *Non-Entity*, under which we groan at present.

This, according to the Writer's Apprehension, is a true Delineation of the Genius of his Ministry. And thus, "while he seemed to strengthen the Superstructure, he weakened the Foundations of our Constitution."[65]

SECT. XV

A Reflection on the future Effects of Parliamentary Influence on the Balance of Power

"But what an Aggravation of this Evil would arise, should ever those of [212] the highest Rank insult the Genius of the Constitution, by solliciting Votes, or procuring others to sollicit them; by influencing Elections in an avowed Defiance of their Country, and even selling vacant Seats in Parliament to the best Bidder?"*

The Writer apprehends, there is a dreadful Evil ready to burst upon this Kingdom, which hath not yet disclosed itself; but will soon come to

---

* Vol. I. p. 120.[66]
65. Cf. above, p. 302.
66. Cf. above, p. 304.

a Crisis, if not checked with Speed and Vigour. This he will take the Liberty to explain with *Candour*. Yet *Prudence* whispers him, on this Occasion, to speak with *Caution*. But though, on this Account, his *Expressions* may be *indirect*, he will take Care that his *Meaning* shall be *clear*. [213]

The Danger which threatened our Constitution, by a too violent Exertion of the Prerogative, under the Reigns of the STUARTS, hath long ceased. Nevertheless, the Convulsions it occasioned in 1641, will not speedily be forgotten: Nor ought the Mischiefs and Confusions arising from a Democracy, raised on the Destruction of the regal and aristocratic Powers, to be slightly reflected on. This Period of the *English* History cannot be too much attended to.

It is generally apprehended now, that our Constitution is again leaning towards a Democracy: The Privilege of raising Money, which is vested in the Commons, gives that House so great a Weight in all Determinations of Importance, that the Crown and the House of Lords seem but [214] as Feathers put in the Scale against Heaps of Gold.

How far this *seeming* State of Things may be supported by *Reality* and *Fact*, is a Point too *delicate* for the Writer to determine. Yet, notwithstanding the Privilege vested in the Commons, of commanding the Purses of their Constituents, it is not difficult to point a Situation, where this Privilege would be nothing but a *Name*. And as in the last Century, the regal and democratic Branches by turns bore down the Constitution, so, in such a Situation as is here *supposed*, the real Danger, tho' hidden, would lurk in the *Aristocratic* Branch; which would be secretly bearing down the Power both of the King and People.

The Matter may be explained in a small Compass. Cannot we put a Case, [215] in which, the Parliamentary Interest of the great Nobility might swallow up the House of Commons? Members might be elected indeed; and elected in Form too. But by whom might they really be elected? By the free Voice of the People? No impartial Man would say it. It were easy to suppose thirty or forty Men of high Quality and Power, who, if united, might go nigh to command a *Majority* in the *lower* House. The Members of that House might seem to be the Representatives of the People: But would be in Truth, a great Part of them, no more than the commissioned Deputies of their respective

Chiefs, whose Sentiments they would give, and whose Interests they would pursue.

Thus, while Power would, in Appearance, be centering in the lower House, [216] it would in reality be lurking in the higher.

This State of Things, should it come to pass, might not perhaps result from any Design in the Aristocratic Branch, to destroy the Constitution. They might have no farther Views than those of Gain, Vanity, or Pleasure. Notwithstanding this, their Conduct might have those Effects, which their Intentions never aspired to; though their own Ruin might be the final Consequence. Let us consider the most probable Effects.

The first fatal Effect that offers itself to Observation is, that the Conciousness of such an increasing and exorbitant Power, which the Lords might acquire in the House of Commons, would *destroy* all honest *Ambition* in the younger *Gentry*. They would know, that the utmost Point [217] they could hope to arrive at, would only be to become the *Deputy* of some great Lord in a County or Borough. All the Intentions of such a Post can be answered by Ignorance and Servility, better than by Genius and public Spirit. People of the latter Stamp, therefore, would not naturally be appointed to the Task: And this, once known, would check the Growth of Genius and public Spirit throughout the Nation. The few Men of Ability and Spirit that might be left, seeing this to be the Case, would naturally betake themselves to such private Amusements as a free Mind can honestly enjoy. All Hope, and therefore by Degrees, all Desire, of serving their Country would be extinguished.

Thus, honest Ambition would naturally and generally be quenched. But even where Ambition *continued*, it would [218] be *perverted*. Not *useful*, but *servile* Talents would be applauded; and the ruling Pride would be, not that of *Freemen*, but of *Slaves*.

These Effects would be bad: But there would be worse in Store. The *Nobility*, by this blind Conduct, would pave the Way for their own Destruction. It might be impossible, absolutely to foretell future Events; but what follows, seems to be according to the natural Progress of Causes and Effects.

It is a known and trite Observation, that Power follows Property.[67] Whoever examines in whose Hands the Weight of Property in this Nation is lodged, will find it to be in the Possession of the Commons. And although a few ambitious Lords should even engross a Majority of Counties and Boroughs; (the last, more generally, are within their Reach) yet these Men would not from hence become [219] possessed of the Property of those Countries, nor therefore of the Weight and Influence which naturally follows it; and which, if it is deprived of its proper and legal Exertion, will break forth in illegal and seditious Attempts. 'Tis easy to foresee, what would be the End of such Measures, when pursued to Extremity. What else, but the Destruction of all Friendship and good Correspondence between the higher and lower Ranks of the Nation, which hath hitherto been supported by their mutual Want of each others Aid?

Now suppose this mutual Friendship and Dependance to be destroyed by these pernicious Measures, and then consider the Consequence. The People would be easily persuaded, that they have nothing left, but an expensive Shadow of their former Constitution: That the greatest Part of their Property is spent in supporting a [220] new System, built on the Ruins of their former Privileges: That the Nation would be better served, the Expence of Government less burthensome, if the Prince were left without the Controul of a Parliament, and from himself should appoint such Persons as are best qualified for the Posts they are to fill; and suppress such Offices as would be found useless and expensive, and of no Consequence to any but the Possessors.

Something of this Kind must inevitably happen, if ever the Power of the Lords should make its Way into the lower House: And let a private Man dare to say, that it will *become* the GREAT, who *ought* to be well read in History, to reflect on what happened in the *Roman* State. *There,* the *Patricians,* while they maintained their proper Character of superior Wisdom, Valour, and Love of their Coun[221]try (the only Characteristics of true Nobility) enjoyed their Power and Privileges, unmolested by the People. But when these noble Qualities were sunk in mean Views and selfish

67. Cf. below, p. 565, n. 97.

Attachments; when degenerate Manners and Lust of Power among the Leaders of the State, had destroyed the Rights of Election; *then,* even *Praetors* and *Consuls* became the mere Creatures of DICTATORS and TRIUMVIRS: These calamitous Events, after a few unsuccessful Struggles of expiring Freedom, terminated in an *arbitrary Monarchy*, under which, the *ancient Nobility* were in no Respect *distinguished,* but by the superior *Calamities,* in which the Cruelty of their Emperors involved them.

Let us now come nearer Home, and from ancient to modern Times; where we shall see similar Causes producing similar Effects. [222]

The State of SCOTLAND, (till the *Union* took Place,[68] and the heritable Jurisdictions were abolished by the Influence of one, to whose Wisdom and Integrity in his high Station, this Kingdom will for ever stand indebted) presents an Instance by no means foreign to our Purpose: And this, I cannot better represent, than in the Words of a late learned Writer.[69]

> The Constitution of SCOTLAND, till incorporated with that of ENGLAND, was in Fact, a Mixture of *Monarchy* and *Oligarchy*. The Nation consisted of a *Commonalty* without the Privilege of chusing their own Representatives; of a Gentry, intitled indeed to represent by Election, but unable to serve the Nation; and of a Nobility who oppressed the one, and despised both. [223]
>
> In this Situation, the Representatives of the Commons, discouraged with their own Insignificancy, either did not attend the Parliament, or surrendered their Privileges when in it. It appears by the Acts of 1457, and 1503, that though the Act of 1427, had given the Freeholders a Power of sending Representatives to Parliament, yet none, or few, were sent.———
>
> The Revolution first brought other Maxims into our (the *Scotch*) Government; and the Union gave other Rights to our Part of the Legislature: So that now, our *Lords* and *Commons* being incorporated

68. In 1707.

69. Brown quotes from Sir John Dalrymple, *An Essay Towards a General History of Feudal Property in Great Britain* (1757), pp. 330–31. Dalrymple did not die until 1789, so when Brown refers to him as a "late" writer, he means one recently published.

with those of the *English,* the Constitution of *Scotland* is settled upon that just Poise, betwixt Monarchy, Aristocracy, and Democracy, which has [224] made the Constitution of ENGLAND the Wonder of Mankind.*

Thus, we see, the Kingdom of SCOTLAND was in great Part rescued from the exorbitant Power of the *Aristocratic* Branch, by its Union with ENGLAND; and its Freedom compleated by the Abolition of the heritable Jurisdictions.† But as Power may be equally usurped and engrossed by *different Ways*; so *Parliamentary Influence* may work the same Effects with *slavish Tenures*; and from a *new Cause,* the Liberties of ENGLAND and SCOTLAND may fall together.

To this Instance of a free Nation groaning under the exorbitant Power of its Nobles, till rescued by its Union with another, let us add a still more striking Ex[225]ample, of a modern free State overturned from its Foundations from the Prevalence of the same Cause.

After the Conclusion of the Peace between the two Northern Crowns, in 1660, some considerable Care and Time was necessary to redress the Disorders occasioned by so terrible a War. DENMARK had been most violently shaken:—The *People* had been in a Manner ruined by the Miseries attending the War: The *Nobility,* though *Lords* and *Masters,* were full of Discontent.

The King thought fit to appoint a Meeting of the three Estates at COPENHAGEN, *viz.* the Nobility, Commonalty, and Clergy:—The Nobility were for exempting themselves from paying Taxes, except only in the Way of vo[226]luntary Contribution. The People held it reasonable, that the necessary Sums of Money should be levied proportionally; and that the Nobility, who enjoyed *all* the *Lands,* should at least pay their *Share* of the *Taxes.*

This Manner of arguing was very displeasing to the Nobles; and begat much Heat, and many Replies on both Sides. At Length a principal Senator stood up, and in great Anger told the President of the City, that the Commons neither understood nor considered the

* History of Feudal Property in *Britain,* p. 274. &c.
† See ibid. p. 246.

Privilege of the Nobility, who at all Times had been exempted from Taxes, nor the true Condition of themselves, who were no other than *Slaves:* [the Word in the *Danish* Tongue, is *unfree*]. This Word *Slaves* put all the Burghers and Clergy in Disorder: On which NANSON, the *Speaker* of the [227] House of Commons, rose out of his Seat, and swore, that the Commons were no Slaves; nor would from thenceforth be called so by the Nobility; which they should soon prove to their Cost.

It was now thought necessary, by the Commons, to consider speedily of the most effectual Means to suppress the intolerable Pride of the Nobility, and how to mend their own Condition. After many Debates, they concluded, that they should immediately wait upon the King, and offer him their Votes and Assistance to be absolute Monarch of the Realm.—They promised themselves, the King would have so great Obligations to them for this Piece of Service, that he would grant and confirm such Privileges, as should put them above the Degree of Slaves. [228] They knew, he had been hitherto curbed by the Nobility to a great Measure; and now saw their own Force, to perform what they undertook. At the worst, they supposed they should only change *many Masters* for *one*; and could better bear Hardships from a *King*, than from *inferior* Persons: Besides the Satisfaction of *Revenge*, on those who had hitherto not only *used* them *ill*, but *insulted* over them so lately. They knew the King, and had seen him bear with an admirable Patience and Constancy, all his Calamities; were persuaded that he was a valiant Prince, who had often exposed his Person for the Sake of the Public; and therefore thought, they could never do enough to shew their Gratitude.

Scarce was this Proposal made, but it was agreed to: and nothing but the [229] Unseasonableness of the Time, it being now near Night, deferred the immediate Execution of it: but all the necessary Measures were taken against next Morning.

All this while, the Nobles either had none, or but small Intimations of the Designs of the Commons. They had been so long used to slight and tyrannize over them, that they were not now sensible of any impending Danger from thence; contemning their Threats as well as their Persons; and imagining they would have repented next Day, and complied with all that should have been demanded of them:

But the Plot was deeper laid than they supposed: for not only the Prime Minister, but some other Members of their own Body, who had Employments depending on the Court, were [230] engaged in it. This Inadvertency, with the Want of requisite Courage on the Occasion, brought upon them the Mischief on a sudden; so that, except two or three, who were more than ordinary doubtful of what might happen, and slipt out of Town that Night, the rest were altogether fearless of Danger, till the very Instant that the Evil was remediless.

SCHACK, the Governor of the Town, urged vehemently, that the Commons should insist to have a Promise under the King's Hand, and make themselves sure of a Reward for so considerable a Present as they were going to make, whilst they had so fair an Opportunity in their Hands: But all his Instances were in vain; they were in the giving Humour, and resolved to do it generously, trusting the King for the Per[231]formance of his Word; a Thing which they have since often, tho' too late, repented of.

The Mischief no sooner appeared to the Nobles, but they saw it was unavoidable: There was no Leisure allowed them to consult; and to deny their Compliance, or even to delay it, was dangerous. They saw, they were no longer Masters; the Commons were armed; the Army and Clergy against them; and they found now too late, that what the Day before they had considered only as the Effort of an unconstant giddy Multitude, was guided by wiser Heads, and supported by Encouragements from Court; nay possibly by some of their own Body.—They were assembled in a fortified Town, remote from their several Countries and Interests (where they had governed like so [232] many Princes) in the Power of those who could, and certainly would be revenged, in Case they proved refractory. The best Way, therefore, was to seem to approve of what they could not hinder.

In the mean time, the Commons grew impatient: The Answer given them was not satisfactory. The Clergy and Burghers therefore, led on by their Bishop and President, proceed without them to the Palace, and were met by the Prime Minister, and conducted by him to the Hall of Audience, whither, after some short Time, the King came to them. The Bishop makes a long Speech, setting forth the Praises of his Majesty, and the Cause of their waiting on him; concluding with an Offer, in the Name of themselves, the two most numerous, and (if he pleased) the most [233] powerful Estates, of an hereditary and absolute Dominion; together with the Assistance of their Hands and Purses, in Case any Body should go about to obstruct so necessary and laudable a Design for the Good of the Country.

But the Nobles were all this while in a grievous Distraction: They saw the Commons were gone to the King without them. Their Messengers brought News back, that their Proposition of entailing the Crown on the Heirs Males, was not pleasing, because a greater Advantage was in Prospect: That this Offer was looked upon to proceed from Persons that would not have bestowed any Thing, if they could have helped it: That it was thought they pretended a Merit in giving only a [234] Part, when it was not in their Power to hinder the taking the whole.

While the Nobles were all together, an Officer comes into the Room, and whispers some of the principal Men, that the City Gates were shut, and the Keys carried to Court. The Governor had sent one BILL, the Town-Major, to put this in Execution; who, as soon as he had done it, came to the House where they were met, and sat down at Table among the Senators. This dismal News of the Officer was presently whispered round the Company: They asked him, what Destiny was appointed them? whether they were there to be massacred, or what else was to be done with them? The Town-Major calmly answered, that he believed there was no Danger towards them: That such violent Measures would not be taken by so [235] gracious a King; though he had indeed given the Orders himself for the shutting the Gates; and that no body was to stir out of Town without Leave. There wanted no more than this Confirmation from the Officer, to overthrow all the Resolution and Consultations of the Nobles: The Dread of losing their Lives took away all Thoughts of their Liberty. They immediately dispatched Messengers, both to the Court and the Commons, to give Notice of their Disposition to comply with what was formerly proposed; assuring them likewise, that they were ready to agree to all that should be asked of them.

Three Days Time was requisite, to prepare Matters for that fatal Hour, wherein they were to make a formal Surrender of their Liberty. The Scaffolds were raised in the Place before the [236] Castle, and adorned with Tapestry: Orders were given for the Soldiery and

Burghers to appear in Arms under their respective Officers: And when all Things were ready, on the 27th of *October* in the Morning, the King, Queen, and Royal Family, mounted on a Theatre erected for that Purpose, and being placed in Chairs of State under Canopies of Velvet, received publickly the Homage of all the Senators, Nobility, Clergy, and Commons.

Thus this great Affair was finished; and the Kingdom of DEN-MARK, in four Days Time, changed from an Estate little differing from *Aristocracy*, to as *absolute* a *Monarchy* as any is at present in the World.* [237]

Thus, we see, DENMARK was *inslaved* by the Inchroachments of the *Nobility* on the *Privileges* of the *Commons*. And can the higher Ranks of this Kingdom be so blindly partial as to imagine, that the *People* of *England* (if ever their essential Privileges should be invaded and torn from them by the fatal Arts of Parliamentary Influence) would tamely sit down under so cruel an Oppression, and not repel so *desperate* an *Evil*, though it were even at the Hazard of a *desperate Remedy?*

These, no Doubt, are ungrateful Remarks, to those whom they most concern. But the Writer continues to wrap himself up in the Integrity of his Intentions; and concludes in the cogent Style of a Person, once reverenced by the Ancestors of the [238] modern Great:—"Am I therefore your Enemy, because I tell you the Truth?"[71]

SECT. XVI

Of the immediate Consequences of national Selfishness and Disunion

"If we would obtain a full View of our Subject, it is a necessary, though disagreeable Task, to trace this Disunion through its particular Effects."†

---

* Account of DENMARK, by MOLESWORTH, Chap. 7.[70]

† Vol. I. p. 123.[72]

70. An edited *précis* of Molesworth's account of the *coup d'état* which established absolute monarchy in Denmark; cf. Molesworth, *Denmark*, pp. 53–64.

71. St. Paul, in Galatians 4:16.

72. Cf. above, p. 305.

The ruling Principle of ministerial or parliamentary Influence had hitherto been declaimed against, as solely tending to destroy our Liberties, by giving too much Power to the Crown. In the Progress of this Work, it hath been shewn to have had other fatal Effects, by destroying the national *Capacity, Valour,* and Spirit of *Union.** [239] 'Tis with the greatest Satisfaction, that the Writer finds the general Sense of the Nation, since the Publication of his first Essay, turned into the same new Channel.

This important Circumstance, therefore, being now generally agreed to, except among those few who expect to be Gainers by the common Calamity, it needs the less to be inforced or inlarged on, in this Volume. The ruinous Effects of this insatiable Thirst of Power and Profit, founded in Parliamentary Influence, together with the notorious Incapacity, Effeminacy, Inaction, and Debility, of those who aspire to the highest and most important Trusts, are at length no longer doubted. All Attention is turned on Gain or Pleasure; Duty is forgot, or laughed at: The main Springs of Government are thus relaxed; and, if a timely Check is not put [240] to this ruling Evil, the Nation, in all Appearance, devoted to Destruction: Insomuch, that the late and present Strife about Places of Profit in *this* Kingdom, puts one in Mind of the *drunken Crew* of the Ship, who were *squabbling* about the *Brandy Casks,* while the *Vessel* was *splitting* on a Rock.

SECT. XVII

Of the most practicable Remedy for this capital Evil

Waving therefore, for the present, many new and material Points of Enquiry, which will naturally offer themselves to Consideration, in the Progress of the first Volume, I shall proceed to consider what may be the first and most practicable Means of restoring the Nation to its natural Strength.

I mean not to enter into a Detail of all those Methods, by which a general Reformation, founded on a general Change of [241] Manners and

---

* Ibid. p. 127, &c.[73]
73. Cf. above, p. 307.

Principles, might be attempted. This were an idle Project under our present Circumstance. All that can be hoped for, in the first Instance, is only to stop the Career of the Nation in its Progress towards immediate Ruin. The Motion of the *Ship* must be *gradually* changed and relaxed, if we would wind her *safely* into *Port:* Too sudden a *Check,* thro' the *Violence* of the *Concussion,* might be *fatal.*

The Writer fears, the very first Circumstance by which alone even a *partial* Reform can be begun, will be regarded as chimerical, if not inhuman. He foresees, the Remedy will prove a nauseous Draught to those who must take it: Not much more palatable, than a Mess of SPARTAN *Black broth.*[74]

It hath been laid down by the best political Writers, as a capital Maxim, that, in [242] order to bring back a State to its first Principles, you must cut off the corrupted Members of the Body Politic. Now, if the Principles advanced in this Work be true, the corrupted Members of OUR Body Politic should seem to be those, who thro' the Force of parliamentary or other Influence are possessed of Places of Trust and Consequence in any public Department of the State, for which they are in any Respect INCAPABLE. These Gentlemen will do the Writer great Injustice, if they charge him with any Design against their *Lives*; but their *Appointments,* he must needs think, they ought to be *deprived of,* because they fulfil not those Conditions on which, and for the Sake of which, these *Appointments* were *given* by their *Country.* To *displace* these Men therefore, as far as the Laws allow; to *prevent* others from creeping in upon the same Principle; and to *bestow* public Offices of Trust and Importance on [243] Men of *Capacity, Courage,* and *Virtue,* is in Effect to cut off the *corrupted* Members of the State, and to restore it to its *first Principles.*

---

74. A legendary dish of the ancient Spartans, probably consisting of pork cooked in blood: "Of their dishes, the black broth is held in the highest esteem, so that the elderly men do not even ask for a bit of meat, but leave it for the young men, while they themselves have the broth poured out for their meals" (Plutarch, "Lycurgus," XII.6). It was said to be an acquired taste: "one of their chief Dishes being the famous *Spartan* Broth, which was black, and not very palatable to those who were not us'd to it" (Temple Stanyan, *The Grecian History. Volume the First* [1707], p. 67).

SECT. XVIII

By what Means this Remedy can be effected

Superficial Writers talk of the Reformation of a State, as if it was a Matter of no more Difficulty, than that of sweeping out a Room, or clearing a China Jar of Cobwebs.

But they who look a little deeper into Things, are soon convinced, that it is a Work of almost insuperable Difficulty. The Reason is this. A State cannot want a general Reform, unless the Great be corrupted: now when these are corrupted, [244] "a coercive Power is wanting: They who should cure the Evil are the very Delinquents; and moral or political Physic, is what no distempered Mind will ever administer to itself."*

If the Shepherds are watchful, the Flock is easily kept within the Fold: But if these be careless of their Charge, "Quis custodiet ipsos Custodes?"[76]

The great *Geometer* said, "Give me but a *Place* to stand on, and I will *move* the *Earth.*"[77] So says the true Politician, "Give me but a *coercive Power,* and I will *reform* the *Great.*"

Such a *coercive Power* (like the Geometer's imaginary Station) is of such Difficulty to be found, that the Writer made no Scruple to declare, "that NECESSITY [245] alone must in such a Case be the Parent of Reformation: So long as degenerate and unprincipled Manners can support themselves, they will be deaf to Reason, blind to Consequences, and obstinate in the long established Pursuit of Gain and Pleasure."†

This compelling Power, therefore, *Necessity,* may be of two different Kinds.

One Kind of *Necessity,* not yet come upon us, though it be too evidently advancing, is "when the State itself totters, through the general

---

* Vol. I. p. 220.[75]
† Vol. I. p. 220.[78]
75. Cf. above, p. 343.
76. "Who will stand watch over the guardians?"; Juvenal, VI.347–48.
77. A remark attributed to Archimedes (*c.* 290 B.C.–*c.* 211 B.C.); ancient Greek mathematician, engineer, and inventor.
78. Cf. above, p. 343.

Incapacity, Cowardice, or Disunion, of those who should support it."* This may properly be called *external Necessity:* Because, whenever it appears, it will come from *without.* The Enemies of our Country will pour in upon us; till the blindest and most [246] incorrigible will be awakened to a Sense of Danger and impending Ruin. *This* NECESSITY will prove a most *severe,* though salutary *Task-master*; and standing with a scorpion *Whip,* over a *dissolute* and *harlot Kingdom, chastise* her into *Labour* and *Amendment.*

The *Second* Kind of *Necessity,* should it ever come upon us, is of such a Genius, as might perhaps happily prevent the Approach of the *first.* 'Tis likewise of a milder Nature; nor would come with those alarming Circumstances of national Ruin, with which the other must be dreadfully attended. This might be called an *internal Necessity*; and would arise, "when the Voice of an abused People should rouze the *Great* into Fear."† If a People thus abused, were less corrupt than their Leaders, who can say, that this Ne[247]cessity would be either dangerous or hurtful? Might not the honest and powerful Voice of such a People awaken the *Great* from their *Dream* of *Folly,* and lead them to adopt those salutary Manners and Principles, which, in a State of too *prosperous Security,* they had blindly *forsaken?*

I am not ignorant, that it hath been made a Point of Debate, whether, in political Matters, the general Voice of a People ought to be held worth much Regard. Right sorry I am to observe, that this Doubt is the Growth of *later Times*; of Times, too, which boast their Love of *Freedom:* But ought, surely, to *blush,* when they look back on the generous Sentiments of *ancient Days,* which Days *we* stigmatize with the Name of *slavish.* [248]

Thus runs the Writ of Summons, to the Parliament of the Twenty-third of EDWARD the First.

"The *King* to the venerable Father in Christ, R. Archbishop of *Canterbury,* Greeting: As the most just Law, established by the provident

---

* Ibid. p. 221.[79]
† Vol. I. p. 221.[80]
79. Cf. above, p. 343.
80. Cf. above, p. 343.

Wisdom of Princes, doth appoint, *that what concerns all, should be* AP-PROVED *by* ALL; so it evidently implies, that *Dangers common* to *all,* should be obviated by *Remedies provided* by *all.*"*

A noble Acknowledgment from an ENGLISH *King,* which ought never, sure, [249] to be *forgotten* or *trod under foot* by ENGLISH Subjects!

There are two manifest Reasons, why, in a degenerate State, and a de-clining Period, the united Voice of a People is, in general, the surest Test of Truth in all essential Matters on which their own Welfare depends, so far as the ENDS of Political Measures are concerned.

First, Because in such a Period and such a State, the Body of a People are naturally the least corrupt Part of such a People. For all *general* Cor-ruptions, of whatever Kind, begin among the *Leaders,* and descend from *these* to the *lower* Ranks. Take such a State, therefore, in what Period of Degeneracy you please, the *higher* Ranks will, in the natural Course of Things, be *farther* gone in the *ruling* Evils than the *lower*; and therefore, the *less* to be *relied* on. [250]

Secondly, A still more cogent Reason is, that the *general Body* of the People have not such a *Bias* hung upon their *Judgment* by the Prevalence of personal and particular *Interest,* as the *Great,* in all Things which re-late to State Matters. It is of no particular or personal Consequence to the general Body of a People, what *Men* are *employed,* provided the *gen-eral* Welfare be accomplished; because nothing but the *general Welfare* can be an Object of Desire to the *general Body.* But it is of much particular and personal Consequence to the Great, what *Men* are *employed*; because, through their Connexions and Alliances, they must generally find either their *Friends* or *Enemies* in *Power.* Their own private *Interests,* therefore, naturally throw a *Bias* on their *Judgments,* and destroy that *Impartiality* which the [251] general *Body* of an *uncorrupt People* doth naturally *possess.*

Hence then it appears, that the united Voice of an uncorrupt People is, in general, the safest Test of *political* GOOD and EVIL; and therefore, the

---

*Thus runs the original Latin. "Rex venerabili in Christo Patri R. eadem Gratia Cantuariensi Archiepiscopo, totius Angliae Primat. Salutem. Sicut Lex justissima, provida circumspectione sacrorum Principum stabilita, hortatur & statuit, ut *quod omnes tangit, ab omnibus approbetur*; sic & innuit evidenter, ut *communibus Periculis* per Remedia *provisa communiter* obvietur."

best Aid and Assistant to an upright Prince, in the Choice of such MIN-ISTERS as may secure to them the GOOD, and divert the EVIL.

But as *Philosophy* may aid and confirm the general Sense of an uncorrupt People in this important Circumstance; so, the Writer leaves it to the Determination of his Country, whether, if ever a GREAT MINISTER* should arise among us, he would not naturally be distinguished by the following characteristic Qualities. [252]

SECT. XIX

Of the Characteristics of a great Minister [81]

He will not only have honest Intentions of Mind, but Wisdom to plan, and Courage to execute.

He will regard the Interests of the Prince and People, as inseparably and invariably united.

He will, to the utmost of his Power, abolish ministerial Influence on Parliaments, and discourage Parliamentary Influence among the Great.

He will endeavour to destroy Party Distinctions; and to unite all Men, in the Support of the common and national Welfare.

In Consequence of this, he will be hated by the corrupt Part of the Kingdom, high [253] and low; because *their* Expectations of Advantage, can only arise from those Distinctions and that Influence which *He* labours to abolish.

The honest and unprejudiced Part of the Nation will adore him, for the contrary Reason.

He will be remarkable, rather for his Knowledge in the great Principles of Wisdom and Virtue, than in the oblique Ways and Mysteries of selfish Cunning.

He may be displaced once, or more than once, by the Power of Faction: But the united Voice of an uncorrupt People will restore him to the Favour

---

* Let it be observed, that there is an essential Distinction to be maintained here, between a *good Minister* and a *great Minister*. They may be *equally upright* in their *Intentions*; but the Difference may lie either in the superior *Ability*, or *Courage* of the *latter*.

81. An anonymized but easily recognizable panegyric on Pitt the Elder.

of the Sovereign; especially in a Time of Danger. And the oftener he is cut down by corrupt Power, the deeper Root he will take in the Affections of the Prince and People, and rise and flourish with renewed Vigour. [254]

His private Life will be consistent with his public Conduct: He will not adopt, but scorn the degenerate Manners of the Times. Above Luxury and Parade, he will be modest and temperate; and his Contempt of Wealth will be as signal as his Contempt of Luxury.

He will be distinguished by his Regard to Religion, Honour, and his Country.

He will not despise, but honour the People, and listen to their united Voice.

If his Measures are not always clear to the People in their *Means*, they will always be so in their *Ends*. In this, he will imitate a great Queen, or her great Minister, "whose Policy was deep, and the Means she employed were often very secret; but the Ends to which this Policy and these Means were directed, *were never equivocal.*"[82] [255]

As a natural and happy Consequence of this Conduct, should he happen either to *err* in a *Design*, or *fail* in its *Execution*, an uncorrupt People will still *confide* in him. They will continue to repose on his general Wisdom and Integrity; will regard him as a kind and watchful Father; yet, tho' *wise*, not *infallible*.

He will look *forward*, rather than to what is *past*; and be more zealous to select and reward those who may do well, than to prosecute those whom, in his own Opinion, he may think Delinquents.

His Principles and Conduct, as they will be *hated* by *vile*, so they will be *derided* by *narrow* Minds, which cannot enlarge their Conceptions beyond the beaten Track of present Practice. Prince MAURICE[83] was

---

82. A reference to Elizabeth I and her secretary of state, William Cecil (1520/21–98), later Lord Burleigh.

83. Maurice (1567–1625), Prince of Orange and Count of Nassau; hereditary stadtholder of the United Provinces of the Netherlands. His campaigns against the occupying Spanish forces met with success from 1590 to 1609, partly as a result of the innovations in discipline and equipment to which Brown alludes (cf. Onslow Burrish, *Batavia Illustrata*, second edition [1731], pp. 188–89). But he was unable to expel the Spanish entirely from the territories the Dutch claimed as their own.

ridiculed in his *first Attempts,* for [256] those very Expedients, by which he drove the SPANIARDS out of his Country.*

If his little or no Influence in Parliament be objected to him, he will answer as HENRY the Great did with regard to *Rochelle,* "I do all I desire to do there, in doing nothing but what I ought."[84]

He will practise "that double Oeconomy, which is so rarely found, or even understood. I mean, not only that inferior Oeconomy, which consists in the Management of the Receipts and Issues of the public Revenue; but that superior Oeconomy, which consists in contriving the great Schemes of Negotiation and Action."

The Laws he frames, will be generous and comprehensive; that is, in Lord VE[257]RULAM's nervous Expression, "Deep, not vulgar: not made upon the Spur of a particular Occasion for the present, but out of Providence of the future; to make the Estate of the People still more and more happy, after the Manner of the Legislators in ancient and heroical Times."[85]

Above all, he will study to restore and secure upright *Manners* and *Principles*; knowing *these* to be the very *Strength* and *Vitals* of *every State.*

As by all these Means, he will put the natural and internal Springs of Government into Action; so he will keep up that Action in its full Vigour, by employing Ability and Merit: And hence, Men of Genius, Capacity, and Virtue, will of Course fill the most important and publick [258] Stations, in every Department of the State.

To fulfil this great Purpose, he will search for Men, capable of serving the Public, without regard to Wealth, Family, Parliamentary Interest, or Connexion.

He will despise those idle Claims, of *Priority* of Rank, or *Seniority* in Station, when they are *unsupported* by *Services* performed in that Rank and Station: He will search for those, wherever they are to be found, whose active Spirits and superior Capacity promise Advantage to the Public.

---

* *Burrish,* Bat. illustrat. p. 189.

84. A remark attributed to Henri IV (1553–1610), king of France.

85. So Bacon praises the achievements of Henry VII as a lawgiver in his *History of King Henry VII*; cf. Bacon, *Works,* 4 vols (1730), vol. III, p. 430.

He will not abuse this Power indulged to him, of superseding superior Rank, by preferring his own Favourites. If he finds the Appearance of Ability and Worth a[259]mong the Friends or Dependents of his Enemies, he will trust them with the Execution of his most important Designs, on the Success of which, even his own Character may depend.

Having no Motive, but the Welfare of his Country; if he cannot accomplish *that,* by such Measures as his Heart approves, he will not struggle for a Continuance in Power, but bravely and peaceably *resign.*

SECT. XX

The Conclusion

Whether such a Character as is here delineated, may ever arise, is a Question which it were superfluous for the Writer to determine: If ever such a Minister appears, he will best be seen by his own Lustre. [260]

There is another Character, belonging indeed to a much lower Walk in Life, which might be no less strange than that which is here delineated. I mean, the Character of a political Writer, not only *intentionally,* but *in fact* IMPARTIAL.

This is a Character which hath never yet existed; nor, probably, will ever appear, in our own Country. However, let us attempt a Sketch of this ideal Pourtrait, for the Use of those who may aspire to Impartiality; and consider, "by what Characteristics HE would be distinguished."

He would chuse an untrodden Path of Politics, where no Party-man ever dared to enter. [261]

He would be disliked by Party-bigots of every Denomination; who, while they applauded one Page of his Work, would execrate the next.

The undisguised Freedom and Boldness of his Manner, would please the Brave, astonish the Weak, disgust and confound the Guilty.

Every Rank, Party, and Profession would acknowledge he had done tolerable Justice to every Rank, Party, and Profession, their own only excepted.

He would be called *arrogant* by those, who call every Thing *Arrogance,* that is not *Servility.*

If he writ in a Period, when his Country was declining; while he pointed out [262] the Means from whence alone honest *Hope* could arise,

he would be charged by scribbling Sycophants with plunging a Nation in
Despair.

While he pointed out the Abuses of Freedom, and their fatal Effects,
he would be blackened by designing Whisperers, as the Enemy of Freedom itself.

The worthless of every Profession would be his sworn Enemies; but
most of all, the worthless of his own Profession.

As he would be reviled and defamed by the *dissolute* Great, without Cause; so he would be applauded by an *honest* People, beyond his
Deservings.

Tho' his Abilities were small, yet the Integrity of his Intentions would
make [263] Amends for the Mediocrity of his Talents.

As such a Writer could have little Pretensions to literary Fame, so he
would not be intoxicated with the Fumes of literary Vanity: But would
think, with SHEFFIELD, that

> One Moral, or a mere well-natur'd Deed,
> Does all Desert in Sciences exceed.[86]

Yet, tho' he scorned the Gildings of false Ambition, and Riches acquired by Adulation; he might not, possibly, be unconscious of that unsought Dignity, that envy'd Superiority to Wealth and Titles, which even
the Love of Wisdom and Virtue give.

Should any of the Great, therefore, affect to disdain him, on account of
his private Station, he might perhaps reply, with PERDITA, [264]

> I was not much afraid; for once or twice
> I was about to speak, and tell him plainly,
> The self-same Sun that shines upon his Palace,
> Hides not his heav'nly Visage from *my* Cottage,
> But looks on *both alike.*[87]

---

86. John Sheffield, Earl of Mulgrave and Duke of Buckingham, "On Mr. POPE
and his POEMS," ll. 21–22.

87. A misquotation of *The Winter's Tale*, IV.iv.443–47, where the lines in fact are:
"I was not much afeard; for once or twice | I was about to speak, and tell him
plainly, | The selfsame sun that shines upon his court | Hides not his visage from
our cottage, but | Looks on alike."

His free and unconquered Spirit would look down with Contempt on Views of Interest, when they came in Competition with Views of Duty.

Nay, were he called to so severe a Trial, he would even dare to make the greatest and the rarest of all honest Sacrifices, that of Friendship itself, to Truth and Virtue.

Should the Sense of his Duty to his Country determine him to a farther Prosecution of his Labours, he would say, [265]

> If such his Fate, do thou, fair Truth, descend,
> And watchful, guard him in an honest End:
> Kindly severe, instruct his equal Line,
> To court no Friend, nor own a Foe, but thine.
> But if his giddy Eye should vainly quit
> Thy sacred Paths, to run the Maze of Wit;
> If his apostate Heart should e'er incline
> To offer Incense at Corruption's Shrine,
> Urge, urge thy Pow'r; the black Attempt confound;
> Oh, dash the smoking Censer to the Ground!
> Thus aw'd to Fear, instructed Man may see,
> That Guilt is doom'd to sink in Infamy.[88]

FINIS

88. Brown here slightly modifies the wording of the concluding lines of his own *An Essay on Satire*, second edition enlarged (1749), p. 29, ll. 517–28.

An Explanatory Defence of the Estimate
of the Manners and Principles of the Times
(1758)

A N

Explanatory Defence

OF THE

ESTIMATE

OF THE

MANNERS

AND

PRINCIPLES

OF THE

TIMES

BEING

An APPENDIX to that Work, occasioned by the Clamours
lately raised against it among certain Ranks of Men.

WRITTEN

By the AUTHOR of the ESTIMATE, in a Series
of Letters to a noble FRIEND.

LONDON:

Printed for L. DAVIS and C. REYMERS,

against *Grays-Inn-Gate, Holborn.*

MDCCLVIII.

AN

EXPLANATORY DEFENCE

OF THE

ESTIMATE, &c.

LETTER I

My LORD,

That Friendship with which you have so long honoured me, was never more clearly proved, or more nobly exercised, than in the free and candid Account you lately gave me, of some Ex[2]ceptions taken against the Estimate, among certain Ranks of Men in Town, more particularly on the Publication of the second Volume, and since the Author's Retirement into the Country.

This Intelligence hath indeed alarmed the Writer; and set him to review his Work with greater Circumspection even than that with which he writ it. 'Tis certain, that no Man can expect to hear the frank Opinions of the World, from the World itself. 'Tis, therefore, an Office of the truest Friendship in your Lordship to communicate all you have heard on this Subject. The Objections which you have so fairly stated, I shall answer in their Order; and with equal Pleasure *vindicate*, where I think myself *right*; or *retract*, where I am *wrong*. [3]

On this Occasion, your Lordship may expect a Series of Letters. This Method will equally alleviate *my* Trouble in *writing*, and *yours* in *reading*.

LETTER II

Before I proceed to your Objections, you will give me Leave, my Lord, briefly to state the main Intent or Scheme of the Estimate; in such a

Manner as may prove a Sort of general Key to the Objections you have made. For I perceive plainly that many of them proceed from a mere Inattention to, or a total Misunderstanding of the leading Principles of the Work.

And that I may give your Lordship a just Idea of its main Design, I will give you a short Account of the accidental *Rise* and *Occasion* of this Work; the leading Principles of which, are indeed no more [4] than a small Part of a much larger Design, of a much more extensive Nature.

The Writer being convinced both from Books and Observation, that the Happiness and Duration of States depends much less on mere Law and external Institution, and much more on the internal Force of Manners and Principles than hath been commonly imagined; and being of Opinion, that the fundamental and leading Causes of the Happiness and Duration of States had not as yet been enquired into or pointed out, with that Particularity of Proof, Circumstance and Illustration, which so important a Subject might demand; had for some Time bent his Thoughts on a Design of considerable Extent, which might be called "A History and Analysis of Manners and Principles in their several Periods." His general Plan begins with the Examination of *savage Life,* and [5] proceeds through the several intermediate Periods of *rude, simple, civilized, polished, effeminate, corrupt, profligate,* to that of final DECLENSION and RUIN.

In the Course of this Plan (too extensive, indeed, for the Mediocrity of the Writer's Talents) a Diversity of Circumstances, almost infinite, have presented themselves. The Rise, Changes, and Progress of Commerce, Arts, Science, Religion, Laws; their mutual Influence, and Effects on each other, and on Manners and Principles; the Characters, Virtues and Vices of Rank, Office, and Profession, in each of the Periods thus delineated; the natural Means by which these Periods generate each other; the Advantages and Disadvantages, Strengths and Weaknesses, which mark and distinguish these several Periods; the most practicable Means of [6] *bringing forward* the *savage* and *rude* Periods towards *polished* Life, and of *bringing back* the *effeminate* and *corrupt* Periods to the same *salutary Medium*; above all, the Regulation and strong Establishment of Manners and Principles to this important End;—these, with other subordinate Articles of Research, proved and illustrated by Facts drawn from History, form the Substance of the Writer's general Design.

On this Design he was intent, when the War broke out[1] between BRITAIN and FRANCE; which being very unsuccessful in its Beginnings, on the Part of BRITAIN; he thought he could not, in his private Station, do a better Service to his Country, than in pointing out what to him appeared the fundamental and *latent Causes* of this ill Success. To this End he singled out so much of his main Design, as immediately [7] related to the present State of his own Times and Country; endeavouring to convince his Fellow Citizens, that "the Source of our public Miscarriages did not lie merely in the particular and incidental Misconduct of Individuals; but in great Part in the prevailing Character of *that Period in which we live*; that is, in the *Manners* and *Principles* of the *Times*."

Hence alone, the Estimate had its accidental Birth: Let it be chiefly remembered then, that the main Subject of this Estimate is solely "the Effects of present Manners and Principles on the Duration of the State." This the Writer insisted on so strongly, and repeated so often, that he thought his Readers would certainly carry it along with them: yet he finds, he was mistaken. [8]

The leading Truths, therefore, which in the Course of his Work he has attempted to prove, are these; That exorbitant Trade hath produced exorbitant Wealth; that this hath naturally produced a high Degree of Luxury, and a general Attention to pleasurable Enjoyment *among the higher Ranks*, among whom the Effects of Luxury must of course *first* appear. That these natural Effects of Wealth have been naturally attended

---

1. Hostilities between Britain and France began in the early 1750s, although a formal declaration of war had to wait until 1756. By 1758, the tide of war was turning in Britain's favor, and the following year—the famous "Year of Victories"—would see a cluster of notable triumphs. In May, Guadeloupe was captured; on 1 August, British regiments were conspicuous at Minden in Ferdinand of Brunswick's great victory over a numerically superior French force under Contades; on 13 September, Wolfe took Quebec (accompanied the following year by Canada in its entirety); and finally in November, a French fleet gathered to escort across the Channel the transports of an invading French army mustered on the Britanny coast was almost entirely destroyed by Hawke in the battle of Quiberon Bay.

with public Consequences which tend to the weakening or Dissolution of the State, by turning that general Attention upon *pleasurable Enjoyment*, which in simpler Times was bent on Views of *Duty*. That hence, a general Defect of Capacity, Fortitude, and Principle, did naturally rise; such as, in its End, must be fatal, if unchecked in its Progress: and that all the leading Ranks were of course infected with these natural [9] Consequences, in some Degree or other, from their very Situation.

That another Evil hath conspired with this; and that as this arose from the Abuse of Wealth, so the other was inflamed by this, and arose from the Abuse of Liberty. That our Constitution, excellent in its Nature, was liable to an Abuse, which arose even from its Excellence. That the Principle of *parliamentary Influence* which was thought or found necessary at the Revolution in Eighty-eight, as a new Principle of Government, had conspired with the Luxury and ruling Manners of the Times, to weaken the national Powers, by raising many Men to Places of the most important Trust, who were in some Respect or other unequal to the Task: And hence the accumulated Danger to the Stability of the Commonwealth. [10]

This is the main Outline of the Author's Design, strip'd of that Particularity and Variety of colouring, which it was necessary to give it, ere it could be made a just and striking Picture of the Times. All that circumstantial Delineation of the ruling Character of each Rank, Condition, Order, or Profession of Men, being indeed no more than what the Writer intended as a Proof in Detail, of these general Principles.

The Reception which the Work hath met with in the World, is a Proof sufficient, how thoroughly the main Body of the Nation is convinced of the general Truth and Utility of the Plan. As to the Execution of it; whoever considers the Nature of the Work; and that in the Course of particular Proof, it was necessary to speak with uncommon Freedom concerning the real State of all Ranks and Orders [11] of Men, will easily see that Numbers must be displeased at a Freedom which was perhaps *new*, but which the very Genius of the Work rendered *necessary*.

What Foundation this particular Displeasure of Individuals may have had in Reason, and what in Passion and Self-Partiality, I will now calmly consider; in weighing those Objections which your Lordship hath laid before me.

LETTER III

You say, my Lord, that "many good and well meaning People have taken Offence, as being involved in the blameable Manners of the Times, and therefore charged with Guilt, as the Enemies of their Country, while they are not conscious of acting *intentionally amiss.*"—[12]

In reply to this, my Lord, let me briefly quote my Vindication from some Passages in the Book itself. "It is not affirmed or imply'd, in this general Review, that every Individual hath assumed the Garb and Character of false Delicacy.—As in manly Ages, some will be effeminate, so, in effeminate Times, the manly Character will be found."—But from "the general Combination of Manners and Principles, in every Period of Time, will always result one ruling and predominant Character."*

Yet altho' it be true, that the Character of guilty Effeminacy belongs not to all; it seems to the Writer, that none are exempt from some Degree or other of those ruling Manners, which, when indulged beyond a certain Degree, constitute the Character of guilty Effeminacy. He cannot acquit his [13] best and worthiest Friends of some Participation with the Defects of their Time and Country. Nor doth he pretend to be exempt from them himself. Alas, if he did, he must be the blindest and most self-ignorant of all Mortals! These Manners are, in a certain Degree, in-wrought into our very Nature by the Force of early Habit; then become, as it were, a Part of us: and we might as well attempt to divest ourselves of the Modes of Speech, as of the Modes of Thought and Action which are peculiar to our Time and Country.†

Thus, as no Period is without its Defects, so by early Habit, we are all necessarily doomed to a Participation of these Defects. Hence, all Characters are imper[14]fect; not only from their internal Frame and Passions;

---

* Vol. i. p. 65.²
† Virtuous and vicious ev'ry Man must be,
　Few in th' extreme, but all in the Degree:
　The Rogue and Fool by Fits is fair and wise;
　And ev'n the best, by Fits, what they despise.³

2. Cf. above, p. 281.
3. Pope, *An Essay on Man*, I.231–34.

but from their external Habits of Education. But where the Scales fairly preponderate on the Side of Reason and Virtue; there, tho' the Character be *imperfect,* it is not *vicious.*

Nay, not only the worthiest are in some Degree necessarily tinctured with the ruling Errors of the Times; but I will go a Step further, my Lord, and affirm, "that Men may be involved in the Manners of the Times, to a Degree that is even pernicious, and yet not be justly stigmatized as immoral or unworthy Characters, so as to become justly the Objects of Hatred or Detestation."

To prove that I am not cooking up a new System in my own Defence, different from the Principles of the Estimate, I must again have Recourse to the Estimate itself. [15] The following Paragraph is decisive. "Several Habits, Qualities, and Actions, which seem innocent in themselves, as they affect or influence *private* Life, are equally or more hurtful than others of a more odious Appearance, if we consider them as they affect the *public* Strength and Welfare. This comes to pass, because the ill Consequences of some Actions are *immediate*; of others, more *distant.* The first strike the *Imagination,* and are seen by all: The latter must be traced up to their Causes by the Use of *Reason*; and to do this, exceeds the Talents of the Many."*

Give the Author Leave now, my Lord, to apply this Truth fairly and candidly in his own Defence: A Use, which he little dreamt, when he writ it, that he should ever have Occasion to apply it to. [16]

When, therefore, the Author charged his Contemporaries with indulging Manners pernicious to the public Welfare, he never intended to charge ALL who thus indulged them, with any designed Immorality or Guilt. These Manners, it appears, do not necessarily imply an immoral Character, in the strictest Sense; because, tho they be attended with distant Consequences which are bad, nay perhaps fatal, yet these Consequences are not always perceived or suspected by those who are involved in them. There is, in this Case, no Idea, no Suspicion of any Violation of Duty; the Consequences are perhaps too distant to be seen by every Eye; and therefore, strictly speaking, no moral Guilt or Demerit can arise. Yet

* Vol. II. p. 173.[4]
4. Cf. above, p. 425.

these Manners (to cite another Passage which may convince you that the Writer's Defence is built on his first Principles) "tho' in Appearance they are too trite to merit Notice, and [17] too trifling for Rebuke, may in their Tendency be as fatal to the Stability of a Nation, as Maxims and Manners more apparently flagitious."*

Now, these Manners, my Lord, which are thus fraught with hidden and unseen Mischief, ought surely to be laid open in all their Consequences, no less than Manners more apparently flagitious. Nay, there is indeed the greater Necessity for such a Developement, because without it, even the worthy and well-intentioned may be drawn in, while they suspect no such Consequence, to adopt a System of Manners destructive to their Country.

Let the following Paragraph (apply'd, indeed, in the Book itself to a different Purpose) serve as a concurrent Proof of what is here asserted. "The more trite [18] and trifling the Facts may seem, the more their Consequences are likely to escape Notice: For Attention is naturally fixed only on Things of manifest Importance. Now, if indeed, notwithstanding this, they be in their Tendency as fatal to the Stability of a Nation, as Maxims and Manners more apparently flagitious; then it may be not only a Task of some Importance, but of some Delicacy too, to trace them to their Consequences and Sources."†

This, my Lord, may be called the *second Degree,* in which the Writer esteems his Country very generally infected with that System of Manners, which he hath attempted to disgrace. But neither in this Degree, does he think that moral Guilt is chargeable on the Delinquents; nor did he ever charge them with it, so as to en[19]deavour to render Individuals the Objects of Hatred and Detestation.

But there is a *third Degree* of Degeneracy, which the Writer esteems the proper Object of severe Censure and Reproof; and that is "When thro' a determined Pursuit of Gain or Pleasure, manifest ill Consequences are willfully overlooked and seasonable Admonitions neglected; or when these

* Vol. I. p. 29.[5]
† Vol. II. p. 54.[6]
5. Cf. above, p. 266.
6. Cf. above, p. 374.

Consequences are seen, and Admonitions attended to; yet deliberately despised, and set at Defiance." Now this Degree of Degeneracy, my Lord, the Author believes and hopes, is not very common: Indeed, the very Tenor of his Work, the very essential Principles on which he set out, imply and affirm the contrary. For if this had been the Representation he had designed to make of his Times and Country, he must have regarded and branded them as *profligate*. Now so [20] far from this, that he hath expressly affirmed, as a fundamental Principle of his Work, that the Character of the Times is NOT that of profligacy. "The slightest Observation, if attended with Impartiality, may convince us, that the Character of the Manners of this Age and Nation, is by no means that of abandoned Wickedness and Profligacy. This Degree of Degeneracy, indeed, is often imputed* to the Times; but to what Times hath it not been imputed?" Again: "If the previous Estimate, already given, be just; if the Spirit of Liberty, Humanity, and Equity, be in a certain Degree yet left among us, some of the most essential Foundations of abandoned Wickedness and Profligacy can have no Place."[†]

Yet, my Lord, tho' these atrocious Crimes have no Place among us, so as to [21] form the Character of a People, the Writer can entertain no Doubt, but there are Characters in every Rank and Station of Life, who may justly deserve the Style of *profligate*. This is often supposed, in the Course of the Estimate; these Characters, with their Effects on the public Welfare, are incidentally touched on: But as the general Tenor and Complexion of the Work supposes, that the general Character of the Times is totally different from this; no candid Reader, sure, will charge the Writer with imputing this Profligacy to any particular Character, unless where it is PARTICULARLY AFFIRMED and IMPUTED.

LETTER IV

Such, then, my Lord, is the general Foundation of the Writer's main Defence: A Defence which, if every one had known his Sentiments of Men

* Vol. I. p. 26.
† Ib. p. 28.[7]
7. Cf. above, p. 265.

and [22] Things, as well as your Lordship, he is persuaded he never could have had Occasion to make. And he hath only to apply these general Principles of Defence, to all those Ranks, Conditions, Orders, and Professions, which he hath scrutinized in his Estimate, in order to clear himself of this capital Objection.

Thus, when he affirms, that the leading Ranks in general are infected with the Manners of the Times, he means not to charge the leading Ranks with a general Profligacy or deliberate Guilt. He believes them involved, from their Situation, in a System of Manners, and in very various Degrees of these Manners, which, if not attended to, and curbed in their Excess, will soon or late endanger the Stability of the Commonwealth. But he believes, at the same Time, nay, and knows it too, that many among these leading Ranks are [23] possessed of Qualities truly amiable. He only thinks, and hath asserted what he thinks, that they extend not their Views to distant or future Consequences; but heedlessly adopt a System of Manners, which, if unchecked in their Progress, will be attended with such Effects as they themselves would tremble to behold.

He regards the Armies of *Great Britain,* as being less grossly vicious than in former Times: He applauds their Valour in particular Instances: But he points out, what all indifferent People acknowledge, that the ruling Character of the Times hath naturally drawn them into a System of Manners, which tends to the Destruction of military Spirit.

Of the same Kind are his Strictures on the Navy. Nay, here he acknowledgeth Instances of the most consummate Bravery. [24] He laments the public Act of their Country, which conspired with the Manners of the Times, and exposed these Gentlemen to the Temptations of Gain, in Preference to Views of Duty.[8] He affirms, that their Remissness is not properly a *personal* Guilt, but the natural Effect of their *Situation,* in such a *Period,* and in such a *Nation;* for that "they are brave, hardy, and

---

8. Apparently an allusion to the suspicion that during the Seven Years' War certain naval actions were not pushed *à l'outrance* in order to preserve as many captured vessels as possible in a serviceable condition. These vessels were then "bought" by the state for its own use, and the proceeds of the sale, or "prize money," was divided among the crews of the victorious vessels in a way that overwhelmingly favored their commanders and, to a lesser extent, their officers.

intrepid, till they rise to the higher Commands; and then the Example and Manners of the Time infect them."[9]

He hath treated his own Profession with the same Freedom and Impartiality: But what is remarkable here, is, that while some cry aloud against him for his ill Usage of his own Profession, others affirm he hath done it more than Justice. For it seems, he hath affirmed that "in the middle Ranks of this Profession there are more good Qualities found than in [25] any other."[10] This indeed he thinks is true; and resolves it, not into the superior personal Virtue of the *Professors,* but into the Nature of the *Profession* itself; which, among the middle Ranks, contains and presents stronger Motives to Virtue, and more effectual Bars to Vice, than any other Profession he knows of. Now, as he judgeth of the Virtues, so doth he judge of the Failings, or, if you will, the Vices of this Order. Personal Vices he never thought of meddling with, but only the Vices of Rank and Profession; especially such as the Manners of the Times inflame. Now, it is manifest, that all those of this Profession, who "converse with the World, and are supposed to make Part of it," without Regard to their *particular Rank,* stand exposed to Temptations, Follies, and Vices, which the more retired Part of the Profession are not exposed to. In such a Case, it is hard to say, where [26] personal and moral Guilt begins; but this he adventures to say, that many well-meaning Men in the Profession may be involved in Manners and Habits which are consequentially pernicious, tho' seemingly innocent. This Conduct is often the Effect of Inattention: doubtless, it is sometimes the Result of deliberate Design: Where the Boundaries lie, the Writer pretends not to determine: neither indeed is it necessary for his main Purpose, that he should determine; because his main Purpose was only to point out and prevent *Consequences:* And Consequences will equally arise, from any supposed System of Conduct, whether that Conduct ariseth from mere *Inattention,* or from moral *Depravity* of Heart.

With Regard to the political Leaders of the People, every Man who reads his Work with an Eye of Candour and Im[27]partiality, will see

9. Cf. above, p. 426.
10. Cf. above, p. 403.

that the general Drift of his Reasoning is of the same Kind. He hath
represented the Great, as being too generally immersed in the Pursuit
of Pleasure, or of Wealth for the Sake of Pleasure; inattentive to the Interests of the Public, but far from being void of private, moral, and personal Virtues. He acknowledges there are kind Fathers, Mothers, Sisters,
Brothers, Friends;* Humanity to Distress he insists on as a ruling Feature
of the Times;† and a general Spirit of Equity, in all Things that relate to
private Property, between Man and Man. These Virtues, yet left among
us, do not only form amiable Characters in the common Intercourses of
private Life; but in his Opinion may form a fair Foundation on which to
build those public Virtues, the Loss of which he affirms and laments.‡ It
is the Idea of a Public that, [28] in his Opinion, is too generally lost: It is
the Force of Religion that is too generally no more: It is the Principle of
virtuous and public Honour, that in his Estimation is too generally dwindled into unmanly Vanity. Thus, while the Manners of the Times are in
many Instances amiable and alluring, as they regard private Life and particular Connexions; the great Bonds of public Strength, the Sinews of the
Commonwealth, the Manners and Principles which should be the Soul
of the State, should unite all its Members into one Body, vigorous, strong,
and terrible to its Enemies, these, in his Opinion, have been relaxed into
Weakness, and Dissolution.

Nay, even the great ruling Evil of parliamentary Influence, whose Effects, on the national Strength, he hath been so bold in disclosing; and at
which, he believes, the Great have taken most Offence;—even this [29]
ruling Evil, he believes, hath made its Progress in many Instances, through
the mere Blindness, and Inattention of the Parties concerned; who bent
only on private Advantage, or perhaps actuated only by the Reputation
and Honour annexed to an extensive Influence (a View no ways blameable

---

* Vol. I. Part I.[11]
† Ib.[12]
‡ Ib.[13]
11. Cf. above, pp. 259–82.
12. Cf. above, pp. 259–82.
13. Cf. above, pp. 259–82.

while consistent with the Welfare of the Public) and not conscious of those Effects which naturally arose from such a Conduct, have often immersed themselves in all the Wretchedness of Party Violence and Borough-jobbing,[14] without any ill Intention to the State. Nay, in many Cases, he makes no Doubt, but the very private *Virtues* of the *Man* have given Birth to the *Vices* of the *Politician*; and a misguided *Love* to Sons, Daughters, Friends, and Dependants, been the Source of political *Servitude* and Attachments, which, in their unseen or unregarded Effects, have been of the most fatal Consequence to the Com[30]monweal; by raising Men to public Offices of Trust and Importance, who were unequal to their Station both in Capacity, public Spirit, and other necessary Qualifications. But altho' he thinks thus of many of his Fellow Subjects, he cannot be so blindly credulous, as to think thus of all: He cannot doubt, but there are some, who would hire themselves out to sale, would obstruct wholesome Measures, would forward bad ones, in order to force themselves into lucrative Employments, and enrich themselves, their Families, and Dependants, tho' the Disorder or the Ruin of the State were the foreseen and certain Consequence. Yet, how many of these Characters may infest the Nation, or where such Characters are to be looked for, he neither hath affirmed, nor even insinuated. His Design was of a far different Nature, "not to make personal Applications, but to trace acknowledged Facts to their un[31]seen Consequences." Whether, therefore, dishonest Intentions were concerned or not, was of no essential Import to his capital Design; which was only to point out the *dangerous Effects* of such a ruling System of *Policy*, whether it was founded in *blameless* or in *wicked Intention*.

On these Foundations then, my Lord, the Author of the Estimate rests his Defence. He affirms, what, indeed, the greater Part of his Readers are well satisfied of, that he never meant to stigmatize or point out personal Defects or Vices, but only those of Rank, of Profession, of the Times. He hath in Consequence of this Principle endeavoured to lay open the peculiar Defects incident to each Rank and Profession; but no where hath he designedly pointed out the particular Men which are

14. Cf. above, p. 286, n. 2.

chargeable with these Defects. So far is he from resolving these general Defects [32] or Vices into personal and deliberate Guilt, that he thinks it possible, that if the leading Ranks and the middle Ranks of the Nation were to change *Places,* they might change *Characters* too: That many of those who are now borne down by the Manners of the Times, might, thro' such a Change of Situation, stand entirely clear of them; and many of those who now stand clear of them, might be overwhelmed by their prevailing Influence. But if the Writer was to estimate the moral Merit or Demerit of private and personal Characters (a Thing which came not within his Design) he would surely go another Way to Work: He would not weigh *Consequences,* so much as *Intentions:* He would consider, who were delinquent thro' *Inadvertence,* and who thro' *deliberate Design.* As he never did this; as nothing of this Kind makes any Part of his Work; as he hath in many Places declared the very contrary; it [33] is evident, that he never meant to charge Individuals with moral Guilt; but, in one Word, "to estimate the Consequences of those Manners and Principles, in which the particular State of the Times hath naturally, in some Degree or other, involved *himself,* his *Friends,* and his COUNTRY."

I foresee, my Lord, an Objection may rise to the Propriety of this Defence. It may be asked, "If these Manners and Principles of the Times are properly treated here with *Gentleness,* why in the Estimate itself are they often treated with *Severity?*"

The Reply to this Objection, my Lord, is easy; and not only consistent with the Nature of the Defence, but indeed essentially founded on it. In this Defence, the author hath considered the Manners and [34] Principles of the Times, as they affect the *Intentions* of those who are involved in them: their Intentions, he supposes, to be in many Instances, void of *deliberate* Guilt: therefore, when he regards them in this Light, he regards them as not chargeable with moral Profligacy, and therefore to be treated with *Gentleness.*

But in the Estimate itself, he considered the Manners and Principles of the Times, solely with regard to their *Consequences.* These, he thought, were pernicious, and fatal: and therefore the Manners and Principles which led to them, were, in his Opinion, to be displayed as being pernicious and fatal; and therefore, in this Regard, to be treated with *Severity.*

It is farther urged, it seems, "that the Writer hath acted with a blame-able Partiality, in painting the ruling Fol[35]lies and Vices of the Times with the utmost, and even aggravated Severity; but hath given few or no Virtues to compensate: whereas an Estimator of the Times ought to have been *impartial*; and should have *commended*, as well as *blamed*."

That Men of Sense and knowledge should raise this objection, is not so easily accounted for. I can only suppose they take Things upon Trust, and have not read the Book. My Lord, the Writer hath given a Catalogue of Virtues, which adorn our Times and Country, so very favourable, that the only candid and decent adversary who hath yet appeared against him, thinks the Picture, in one Circumstance, rather *flattering*.* Hear what the Writer himself adds on this Subject in the second Volume. "Let us do [36] Justice to our Age and Country in every regard: a political Constitution, superior to all that History hath recorded, or present Times can boast: A religious Establishment, which breathes universal Charity and Toleration. A Spirit of Liberty yet unconquered; a general Humanity and Sincerity, beyond any Nation upon Earth: an Administration of Justice, that hath even silenced Envy:—These are Blessings which every *Englishman* feels, and ought to acknowledge."[16]—Sure, my Lord, these are far from general and undistinguishing Invectives against our Times and Country. Beyond this, the Writer hath expressly affirmed, that in every Rank, Order, and Profession, there are Men who stand distinguished by their Capacity and Virtue. This Catalogue he could have drawn out by particular Panegy-ric: but in the View of Things, and with the Intentions with [37] which he writ, a general Acknowledgment was sufficient; and such an *enlarged* Panegyric, however *just*, would have been highly *blameable*. It could have answered but two Purposes; to make himself a *favoured* Writer among the Great, when he meant to be an *honest* one; and to lull the higher Ranks in that *flattering Stupor* in which they were already sunk. The first of these he was not sollicitous about: the second he held *dishonest*. Mankind were to

---

* *Characteristics of the present political State of* Great Britain, p. 203.[15]

15. Robert Wallace, *Characteristics of the Present Political State of Great Britain* (1758).

16. Cf. above, pp. 359–60.

be awakened and alarmed. This could not be done by dwelling on obsequious Representations. Soft and gentle Touches had been ineffectual:
The Success of the Stroke depended on the Strength and Boldness. This
was one of those particular Occasions, when it became his Duty, not
only to *cry aloud*, but to *spare not*. The Diseases of the Times called for
such a Conduct. The Season was favourable: it was the Hour of Sickness,
and the Time to alarm. [38] The national Distresses and Disgraces had
already awakened the Fears of serious Men: This, then, was the Time
to point out the *Causes* of the Mischief, and its *Cure*. These Fears were
not confined to Men of Speculation and the Closet; but public Men and
Ministers saw and avowed the ruling Evils; which were freely and boldly
exposed in the Senate, as they have been by the Writer from the Press.
This was the Time for honest Men of every Rank, to join with those
Men of public Station in so laudable a Work, and to second and support
their Endeavours for a general Reformation. The GREAT, then, were to
be *rouzed* from their *Lethargy*; the PEOPLE led to *see* the *Source* of Danger, and to *prevent* it. The View, therefore, was honest and laudable; the
Means *dangerous only* to *him* that *used* them. The Writer may be found,
indeed, to have judged [39] ill for himself, in the Language of worldly
Prudence; but a Man who risks what is commonly held most dear, from
a conscientious and fixed Resolve to do what he thinks his Duty, may
seem reasonably intitled, at least to the *Excuse* of those who wish to see
good Manners and Principles prevail. Some, no Doubt, may think he
hath acted an imprudent Part, and sacrificed his chief Interests: but it is
a Mistake, my Lord: for he hath ever held his chief Interests to lie in a
Perseverance in the Paths of Duty.

LETTER V

So much for the Writer's general Defence. You tell me next, my Lord,
that some People have found the Appearance of an Inconsistency, "While
he delineates the Times as *selfish*, and yet admits them to be *friendly*,
charitable, and *humane*." [40]

   This Objection ariseth (like most of the rest) from a Misapprehension of his Plan: His Design, was to consider the general Character of his

Contemporaries, as they stand related to the *Public*. Now, in this Light he cannot but regard the general Character of the Times as *selfish*. We have not that real and generous Concern for the national Welfare, which we discover in Behalf of our *Friends*, or *Individuals* in *Distress*. Doth not the following Circumstance demonstrate the Truth of this Character? That while large and generous Subscriptions are carried on for the Relief of all Manner of *private* Distress, most Men grudge what they are called upon to contribute toward the public Exigencies. They pay, when they are compelled to pay, with Murmurs and Reluctance. I mean this of the superior Ranks: The poor Farmer, Labourer, and Mechanic pays, without re[41]pining, the Taxes on his Candles, his Salt, and his Shoes, tho' they are Articles necessary to his Subsistence. But did the higher ranks shew their *public Zeal,* when the Wisdom of the Legislature chose that Article of Luxury, a *Coach* or *Chariot,* as proper to support a moderate Tax? Did each Man *press forward* to take his trifling Share of the general Burthen, and to contribute a Mite from his Abundance? When the Pomp of the loaded Side-board became another Object of a moderate Tax, did the Owners *rejoice* in this Opportunity of contributing to the *Wants* of the *Public?* Yet this was not only *called* by those who projected it, *a Tax upon Honour,* but in Reality it was so; since, in the very Nature of it, it could not be made *compulsory.* Those who knew the Manners of the Age foresaw and foretold the Consequences of it; and, in Fact, the *public Honour* of some among the Great was found, on [42] this Occasion, so equal to their *public Spirit,* that the Tax has produced a mere Trifle. Yet, it seems, the Sense of *Shame* could produce, what public Honour and public Spirit failed to produce; for I am told, that the Revenue arising from one of these taxes received a sudden and most astonishing Increase, from an Order of the House of C.[17] that the Names of those who had paid it should be laid before them. Those who would neither obey the Law, nor support the Public, were afraid of being exposed to the Shame of having discovered that they failed in either: they were content to DO what they were ashamed to have it said they had done. It is, in Truth, owing, in great Part to the same Turn of Thought, that so much Offence hath been

17. I.e., the House of Commons.

taken, amongst the higher Ranks, at the Truths delivered in the *Estimate*. They see, the Representations there made are unfavourable to the Conduct, perhaps of themselves, [43] but at least, of many of their Friends, whose private Qualities they esteem and love: How their *public* Conduct affects the Interests of their *Country,* they seldom enlarge their Views so far as to consider: and hence, a Writer, who separates their *public Conduct* from their *private,* and considers the Actions of Men, ONLY as they regard his Country, cannot possibly fail of incurring their Displeasure. The Reason, my Lord, was assigned in the second Volume: "Enlarged Views of Benevolence are quite beyond the Reach of such a People."[18] [44]

LETTER VI

Your Objections which follow next, are chiefly personal: However, as they have been *made,* they shall be *answered.* You say, my Lord, it hath been asked, "Who appointed this Man a *national* Preacher?"—Now, this Expression is in Truth metaphorical: The literal and proper Manner of putting the Question, if any Doubt arises on the Matter, is this: "Who gave this Man Authority to speak his Thoughts on national Affairs?"—When the Thought is thus divested of Figure, and given in mere literal Expression, you see, that any modest and sensible *Englishman* would blush to ask the Question. It is doubting of that common Right, which every *Englishman* demands, and is *possessed of.* This Privilege the Writer hath exerted in common with Hun[45]dreds of his Time and Nation. By what Motives other Men may have been determined, he leaves to themselves; for his own Part, he spoke, because he thought he saw the ruling Errors of his Country. 'Tis certain, that in Point of *Opinion* he hath a great *Majority* in his Favour: but he never expected to find that *Majority* among those Ranks, where the *ruling Errors* are supposed to *lie.* And if it be true, as the Writer often suggests, that all *national Failures* begin among the higher Ranks, 'tis certain, that a *declining* Nation may slide down to Ruin, before a *national Preacher* be in Form *appointed:* Or if he was, it may be presumed, his System of Manners and Principles would be somewhat

18. Cf. above, p. 396.

curiously *modeled* and *prescribed*; and would be more likely to help forward the ruling Evils, than to cure them. [46]

Let us conclude then, my Lord, that whoever has the *Power*, has likewise the *Right*, to command the national Attention. There never was any Period in any State, where Reformations of some Kind were not wanting. The great Point is, not as is commonly done, and with great Applause, to declaim, in a *vague* Manner, against the Iniquity of the Times, (a Kind of Rhetorick which strikes the *Ear*, but never the *Heart*) but to point out the *ruling Errors* and *Corruptions* with such a Particularity of Circumstance, that every Delinquent, in every Rank, shall see, and be made to feel, his own. This, my Lord, is the Way to awaken, to convince: thus alone the Mind and Conscience is turned upon itself: Few Men are so deliberately vile, as to withstand the Convictions of their own Reason: The great Source of *Wickedness* is *Self-deceit*. But this Method of convincing, the Writer was well aware, [47] is a Task which (however useful to the Public) will bring no Favour to the Individual who undertakes it.

The next Objection you tell me of, my Lord, may seem to wear a little more than this, the Face of Reason. The Objection is, that, "considering the Writer's private Station, he takes too much upon himself in his Censures on the Great; that he is insolent, dogmatical, arrogant, assuming."—With Regard to this, my Lord, the Writer protests, that so far as concerns himself, he is content to be thought as inconsiderable, as every Reader chooseth to make him in his own Eyes. He never obtruded any Authority but that of Reason: He desired the World only to read the Book, and weigh the Truth of it. If to be the Means of conveying some plain and necessary Truths to the World, without attacking the private Character of [48] Individuals, be Insolence, Arrogance and Dogmatism, the Writer stands guilty of the Charge: But if this be not the case, if the Accusation be founded in the mere Want of those frequent and common *Apologies, Reserves, Exceptions, Salvo's*[19] and *Douceurs*,[20] by which

---

19. Dishonest mental reservations; quibbling evasions; consciously bad excuses (*OED*, 2).
20. Softenings or extenuations; compliments (*OED*, 2).

Writers are apt to court the self-love or Malice of the World, and by which every Reader is happily prevented from *applying* any thing to *himself*; The Writer apprehends, that in this Case he is not *assuming*, but that he did his Duty in being explicit and *intelligible*.

There is, in this respect, an essential Difference between *Writing* and *Speaking*. The Speaker's private Rank and Character is necessarily attended to; because from his personal Presence, personal Considerations will (contrary to what is right) intermix themselves. A Writer, it hath been generally supposed, has the Privilege to be exempt from these personal Distinctions and Restraints; and if [49] he loses the Benefits of superior Station on one Hand, on the other the Want of them ought not to be imputed. On the public Stage, all those who address the Publick are, in Rank, equal: Or rather, it is the Province of *Reason*, and not of *Norroy King at Arms*,[21] to determine their Superiority. Are the Follies and Vices attacked, of a public or private Nature? If public, they are of public Cognizance; and the Accuser is not to be told, that he has no Right to accuse, because he is of an inferior Station: It is enough, that he is a Fellow-Member of the Community. If the Happiness of his Country be at Stake, it matters not whether it be endangered by the Defects of the *Great* or *Vulgar*. In such a Case, the Point of *Ceremony* must give way to the *public Welfare*; and the sole Question worth debating is only, whether the Author speaks the Truth in such a *Manner*, as may be [50] of most *effectual Service* to his COUNTRY? He gives in his Evidence and Proof to the great *Court* of Judicature, the *World*; and this he hath a Right to do in the same *unreserved Manner*, whether the Ranks accused wear *Aprons, Bands, Cockades,* or *Coronets*.[22] In a Word, the *Writer* of the *Estimate*, and the private *Man*, are in this Respect, two different Characters. The latter knows his Station, and hopes he conducts himself in it with Humility and Propriety. The Persons of the Great he treats with due Respect, and in Point of Decency, (and perhaps of Dignity

21. More correctly, Norroy King *of* Arms; one of the senior officers of the College of Arms. In 1758, the office was held by William Oldys (1696–1761).

22. Items of dress characteristic of, respectively, deans, clergymen and academics, soldiers, and peers.

too) maintains his Distance: As a Writer, he is a little more familiar with their Vices, when they interfere with the Welfare of his Country; because *these* are not the Objects of his Reverence; not even of his external Reverence, as they have no Place, Rank, or Titles of Honour legally annexed to them (that he knows of) in this [51] Kingdom. As his Censures therefore are *general*, and not *particular*, he thinks, he may arraign the *Vice*, and yet preserve due Respect to the *Man*.

However; tho' he held this Principle of Conduct to be *necessary*, and therefore *just*; yet, like every other Principle, it certainly hath its proper Bounds: Nor does the Writer pretend to erect himself into an absolute Judge of the Propriety of his own Conduct, in every Instance. All that he is sure of, is only this; that what he writ in this Kind, was the pure Result of his preferring Truth and public Utility to the Favour of any Ranks or Individuals whatever: And if, in the Rapidity of Composition, any seeming Excesses of this Kind fell from his Pen; whoever may think they see such Excesses, will do him no more than Justice, if they ascribe them to [52] the Warmth of a well-intentioned Mind, heated with the Importance of its Subject.

LETTER VII

But you add, my Lord, that supposing the Representations just, which the Writer of the Estimate hath given of his Times and Country, it is farther objected, "that as the Book has been translated into foreign Tongues, and made its Way on the *Continent*, it has given Advantage and Encouragement to our Enemies, by painting this Nation as being sunk in Effeminacy."

Alas! my Lord, our Enemies knew our Weakness and Degeneracy before: the national Disgraces had proclaimed it. As to the *Causes* and *Remedies* of this political Degeneracy, the Knowledge of these could only affect ourselves. We [53] might reap Advantage, (if we so pleased) by being led to the Knowledge and Sense of these: Our Enemies had already reaped all the Advantages of Information, from the mere Knowledge of the *Fact*. Is a Nation to go quietly down to Ruin, without one awakening Voice to rouze it from its fatal Lethargy, merely through Fear that our Enemies should take Advantage? They saw we were asleep: they had surprized and attacked us in our Slumber: Sure, it could not be dangerous or hurtful, to awaken from its Dream a Nation so exposed and attacked. Nor could it lessen that Nation in another's Eyes, to see there was one bold enough to attempt it.

But, it seems, "the Alarm was so strong, that it was in Danger of throwing the Nation from a State of blind *Security,* into a State of *Despair.*" [54]

This, my Lord, is the vague Language of undistinguishing Objectors; and savours little of the Knowledge of Human Nature. Would to God, the Feelings of the Guilty were so delicate; but to bring that Part of the Nation which was sunk in blind *Security,* to the opposite Extreme of *Despair,* is, by no Means, an easy Task. There are many intermediate Periods to be gone through, of Doubt, Suspicion, Fear, Despondency, ere the dissolute Mind can arrive at this Extreme. Rouze the Secure and Luxurious as severely as you can, you will hardly awaken them into the *first* Stage of *Doubt.* A Twitch by the Ear, or the Scratch of a Pin, may be felt by a People whose *Sensibility* is *strong*; while their lethargic Leaders, sunk in Indolence of Manners, may be Proof against the Application of red-hot *Pincers.* [55]

This, my Lord, is a clear Reply, with regard to the higher Ranks, and Leaders of the People. With respect to the People themselves, the thinking Part had already been awakened into *Fear,* if not to *Despondency,* by the *public Disgraces.* I repeat it, my Lord, that "the Nation stood aghast at its own Misfortunes; but like a Man, starting suddenly from Sleep, by the Noise of some approaching Ruin, knew neither *whence* it *came,* nor *how* to *avoid* it."* What then was the Consequence of this Book? It was, to investigate the real *Causes* of those national Disgraces which had alarmed us; and, together with the *Causes,* to suggest the *Cure.* Could this tend to drive a People to *Despair?* On the contrary, it naturally led them to a rational and lively *Hope:* For, together with the ruling Evils, the natural Remedy was pointed out. My Lord, the Na[56]tion *saw* the *Remedy*; they have *claimed* it, and already feel its powerful *Effects.*

* Vol. I. p. 150.[23]
23. Cf. above, p. 317.

LETTER VIII

Your Lordship says, it is farther objected, that "if the Substance of the Work was true, whence could such Clamours arise against it, even among any Rank or Party of Men?"

The Objections already stated by your Lordship, afford a Reply, in part, to this general Question.—Worthy Men may have taken Offence at the Work, from a Consciousness of their own innocent Intentions, and a Misapprehension of the Author's main Design: They see not the Consequences of those Manners in which they are involved; and therefore may think it unjust, that these Consequences should be charged upon their Conduct, which is in[57]tentionally blameless.—Farther, that sparing Hand, with which the Author thought it necessary to mingle Panegyric in his Work, hath undoubtedly been the Occasion of much Discontent.—Again, the open and unreserved Manner in which the Estimate is written; the seeming Danger of telling so much political Truth to the World, supposing the Representations true;—All these, my Lord, have been undoubtedly regarded as improper or imprudent Steps; and declaimed against, as such, by Men of good Intentions.

For a Reply to these Objections, your Lordship is referred to the preceding Letters. There are other Causes of Clamour, I apprehend, of a very different Nature; and I will point out these with the same Freedom. [58]

One Source of Clamour hath been the obstinate Blindness of the *dissolute*, in every Rank and Station; who, being determined to proceed in the beaten Track of Pleasure, without Regard to Consequences, do therefore naturally dislike those who display them.

Again, my Lord, the more Truth appears in a Work of this Nature, by which the Interests of Individuals are so nearly affected, the more Enemies the Work must have among a certain Party of Men: I mean all that Party who look no farther than themselves, and are watching to plunder the Public for their own private Emolument. How large a Party this may be, or where they may lie, the Writer leaves to your Lordship to determine. 'Tis enough to observe here, that these Men, seeing their own Plans of selfish Interest [59] obstructed by the open Avowal of the Truths thrown out so freely to the Public in this Estimate, must naturally rise against the Author, and fasten upon him like a Nest of *Hornets*.

Besides these Causes of Offence and Clamour, I will beg Leave to whisper another in your Lordship's Ear: It is a Secret, my Lord, which you Great People are not often given to hear or understand: Many of the Dependants of the Great, and whom they are pleased to call their *Friends,* are in Truth no more than their *Flatterers* in Disguise. They have not that generous Regard to the real Advantage of their Lords and Masters, which they so zealously pretend: Their own Interest is the Compass they steer by: they are therefore glad to take Advantage of the common Partialties of human Nature, to dis[60]grace all Men in the Opinions of those whom they seem to serve, who dare point out to them even the *Semblance* of an *Error*.

LETTER IX

You tell me farther, my Lord, that "a particular Passage hath given much Offence to the Universities and their Friends; in which a general Censure is thrown on the Heads of Colleges."

On this, therefore, the Author thinks it necessary to explain himself more particularly; as no Man entertains a truer Regard to the real Honour and Welfare of these learned Bodies, than himself.

With Regard, therefore, to what he apprehends to be the most material Part [61] of the supposed Charge against these Gentlemen, that is, "their not sufficiently recollecting the original Purpose of College Government;" he finds that his Meaning hath been strangely mistaken or perverted. He was not, in that Passage, questioning the *legal* and *statutable Administration,* but pointing out the *defective Form* of our College-Institutions; and proposing a Method, by which their Defects might in some Measure be remedied, thro' the *voluntary* Care and Superintendance of the *Heads,* in certain Circumstances, to which he believes they *are not obliged* by *Statute*. He had been pointing out the Use and Necessity of a Subordination of *Instructors*; in which, *one* Party should be an *Assistance* and a *Check* to another; and brought the *great Schools,* as Examples (in some Degree) of this proposed Method of Instruction. Whoever considers this

Circumstance here insisted on, will find it of the [62] last Consequence in all public Institutions: It keeps all Parties *alive* and *active* in their respective Spheres; who, without these awakening *Checks,* are apt to slide down into *unsuspected* Negligence. Now, the general Want of these continued and subordinate Checks, are, in his Opinion, a capital Defect in our University Establishments. He therefore took, what he thinks an allowable Freedom, in pointing out this ruling Defect: Which, as it is not generally obviated by the Governors of Colleges, as they do not regard it as a Part of their Office, to instruct either the Tutors or the Pupils, he could not resolve this Omission into any Cause more excusable, than their "not recollecting the *original Purpose* of College Government."

As to the general Causes of this *Inattention,* which in the Writer's Opinion, [63] implies no positive Demerit,* he supposes it to arise from Imperfections common to Men, and to Men of Worth and Probity; as explained in the Beginning of this Defence.† With Regard to certain particular Attentions hinted at, more especially to Cards and Entertainments; if, formerly, some growing Attentions of this Kind fell under his Observation in one of the Universities, such as the worthiest Men might inadvertently fall into, he is informed that they are now ceased. His Remark, therefore, not being applicable to the present Time, becomes a Mistake in Point of Fact; and as such he freely devotes and offers it up, a voluntary Sacrifice to Truth and Justice: leaving it to those who are *infallible,* to upbraid him with the Acknowledgment of an *Error.* [64]

LETTER X

I proceed, my Lord, to your last Objection. It seems, "The Freedom with which the Character of a famous Minister[25] is treated, hath been the Occasion of much Offence to his Friends and Adherents, which form a large and powerful Party in this Kingdom."

* This was manifestly imply'd in the subsequent Paragraph, where the Author declared, he meant no *personal Invective.*
† See Letter III.[24]
24. Cf. above, pp. 469–72.
25. Sir Robert Walpole; cf. above, pp. 301–2 and n. 25.

As to the mere Matter of *Offence*, my Lord, there is no preventing it in certain Cases. But if the Writer was to calculate *Numbers* on this Occasion, he finds the *Majority* would consist of those who think he hath treated the Character of this Minister at least with *sufficient Lenity*. 'Tis certainly a Kind of Presumption in his Favour, that one Part of the Nation thinks he hath allowed *too little*; and others, *too much*, to this deceased Minister. [65]

Be that as it may; the Investigation of this Minister's Principles and Conduct is certainly of national Concern: It is of great Importance to this Kingdom, that it be known whether his political System be *salutary* or *destructive:* therefore the Character of his Administration not only *may*, but *ought* to be freely and fairly canvassed, for the Conviction and Benefit of the Whole.

Had the Writer treated this Minister's Character with Contempt, there had been some Pretence for Blame: As he studiously avoided every thing of this Kind, he cannot but be astonished, that Men of Candour and fair Intentions can be offended at his cool and dispassionate Reasonings on this Subject. He never entertained any personal Dislike to this Minister, his Friends, or Adherents. On the contrary, he knows some of them to be Men of Worth and Honour, the Friends of Liberty and their [66] Country; and for whose Characters, he were both unjust and insensible if he had not the highest Deference: If he differs from these Gentlemen in Point of Opinion, they are satisfied he does it from the Convictions of his own Reason. They know, he proceeds on the same Principles of Liberty with themselves; that he only dissents in his Conclusions; and are too just and generous, to dislike him for throwing out his Sentiments so freely, on a Subject of such Importance.

Is the Writer mistaken in his Opinions concerning the Conduct of this Minister? The Press is open to every body: Why then is *Clamour* spread, instead of rational *Confutation?* To tie down the Nation to this System, to forbid or discourage rational Inquiry into its Tendency, would be to erect a political Tyranny in the State. If it is clear then, that the Writer's Inten[67]tions are honest, the Friends of this Minister will find it equitable to make Allowance for Difference in Opinion. What they contend for in *Religion*, will they deny in *Politics?* Certainly, my Lord, the

Maxims of *arbitrary Power* sit with the worst Grace on the declared Patrons of *Freedom*.

It were perhaps unfair to charge any of the more *generous* Part of this deceased Minister's Friends, with joyning in the Clamours raised on this Occasion. That no candid and equitable Mind can be disgusted at his Conduct, he concludes from the generous Professions of a late Writer, so nearly connected with this Minister, that his Evidence must be allowed above all Suspicion. "This Freedom of Discussion on the Dead of any Rank, or however consecrated by the Authority of great Names, or even by the Esteem of Ages, [68] every Man ought to be at Liberty to exercise. The greatest Men certainly may be mistaken; so may even the Judgment of Ages, which often takes Opinions upon Trust. No Authority, under Divine, is too great to be called in Question: And however venerable Monarchy may be in a State, no Man ever wished to see the Government of Letters, under any Form but that of a *Republic*. As a Citizen of that Commonwealth, I propose my Sentiments for the Revision of any Decree, of any honorary Sentence, as *I think fit:* My Fellow Citizens, *equally free,* will vote according to their Opinions."*—Such are this Gentleman's free and generous Principles on the like Occasion: And the Writer is well persuaded, that this honourable Person is too equitable to refuse that Privilege to another, which he so rationally assumes to himself. [69]

LETTER XI

Others, it seems, my Lord, "think it somewhat strange that a Man should step out of his own Profession, and engage in a Province in which he was no way particularly bound to concern himself."

In reply to this, my Lord, several Considerations may be alleged. The Writer perhaps might content himself with the old Apology of "*Homo sum; humani nihil a me alienum puto.*"[27] He may alledge, that as the Causes

---

* Preface to Mr. WALPOLE's Catalogue of royal and noble Authors.[26]

26. Horace Walpole, *A Catalogue of the Royal and Noble Authors of England*, 2 vols (Twickenham, 1758), vol. I, pp. vi–vii.

27. "I am a man; and I think that nothing human is alien to me" (Terence, *Heautontimorumenos*, I.i.77).

of the Duration of the State are the main Object of his Enquiry, the Pres-
ervation of the *Christian* and *Protestant Religion* become, among other
Things, the natural Objects of his Attention and Pursuit. Above all, my
Lord, he insists, that the *System* of *Policy*, which he recommends and enforces, is not only *religious*, but *moral:* and therefore, to en[70]deavour to
establish this System, is to endeavour to establish the public Happiness of
Mankind on the solid Basis of *Virtue*, which is the *End* of *Religion itself*.
He therefore thinks, that both in *this*, and in the Pursuit of his *greater*
Plan, he is, to the utmost of his Power, serving the Cause and End of Religion and Christianity; the main Drift of his general Design being only
to prove, that the most effectual Way to render Kingdoms *happy, great*,
and *durable*, is to make them *virtuous, just*, and *good*. In this Point he
confirms himself on the Authority of an excellent Prelate, whose political
Researches were of like Tendency. "As the Sum of human Happiness is
supposed to consist in the Goods of Mind, Body and Fortune, I would
fain make my Studies of some Use to Mankind, with Regard to each of
these three Particulars; and hope, it will not be thought faulty or indecent
in any Man, of what [71] Profession soever, to offer his Mite towards improving the *Manners*, Health, and Prosperity of his Fellow-Creatures."*

LETTER XII

Such, then, my Lord, is the Writer's Reply to the several Objections
which you tell me have been urged against his Estimate. How far it may
be satisfactory he pretends not to determine; but leaves every Man to
weigh it with candid Freedom.

Give me Leave now, my Lord, to close this Defence with a few Observations, which may still farther tend to clear the Doubts of those who
have started the Objections.

Let them consider, my Lord, that in a Subject so wide, multifarious,
and compli[72]cated, as that of the Manners and Principles of a wealthy

---

* Dr. *Berkley's Misc.* p. 118.[28]
28. "Advertisement" to *The Querist*, in George Berkeley, *A Miscellany, Containing
Several Tracts on Various Subjects* (1752), p. 118.

and luxurious Nation, there are not perhaps two Individuals of that Nation, whose Opinions do altogether coincide. Every Man that examines such a Subject, proceeds not only on a View of *Facts*, but on a Set of *Principles* too, in some Degree *different* from those of every other. The Body of the Nation, which hath been so partial in Favour of this Estimate, should they compare their particular Opinions, would find them widely different in many Circumstances: and those among the higher Ranks who have dissented, should they enter into the same critical and minute Comparison of each others Thoughts, would find them equally discordant. If so, my Lord; is not here a manifest Reason for mutual Forbearance, where Opinions clash? And who will deny that it was a Task of the greatest Difficulty, to steer thro' such a Sea of [73] Doubt, where (though the Facts lie open to every Man's Observation) every Man forms an Opinion peculiar to himself. The great Outlines, the essential Truths, the leading Principles of such a Work may be acknowledged to be just by Thousands, who, amidst that infinite Variety of Circumstances glanced at in the Course of it, may have particular Opinions different from the Author and each other. All, therefore, that a modest Writer will pretend in such a Case to give, or a modest Reader expect to *find*, will be *a good deal of Truth*, and *a little Error*.

In Consequence of this, my Lord, consider farther, how often and how naturally particular Passages must necessarily be objected to, in such a Work, while the general Truths and leading Principles, on which the Work is founded, are totally overlooked. For every Reader erects him[74]self into a Judge of the *particular* Remarks made, and pronounces on them by the Standard of his own Judgment, formed upon his own Observation and Principles: While, among the Multitude of Readers, even of those who mean well, an extended Discernment of Things, and the Comprehension of a *general Plan*, is not always to be found. How easy a Task then, my Lord, and how natural to weak, to vain, or ungenerous Minds, to throw out Objections to particular *Parts*, without any Regard had to the main *Tenor, Extent*, and *Disposition* of the *Whole*?

Besides the Nature of the Subject, there was a farther Difficulty, arising from the Danger either of *too general*, or *too particular Expression*. Had the Writer declaimed in a vague and undistinguishing Manner, on the Errors and Vices of the Times, he had failed of his main Intent, which

was, to [75] point out *where* the ruling Errors and Vices lay: Had he
singled out *Individuals*, he had justly incurred the Censure of *personal*
Invective. What then was left for him to do? He only saw one proper
Expedient; which was, to give the predominant or leading Character of
the several Ranks concerned; yet to admit (in general Terms) that in each
Rank there were *Exceptions* to this leading Character. The very Intention of his Work forbad him to *dwell* at large on these *Exceptions.** And
besides this main Reason, another presented itself: Had he *professedly*
singled out every Individual in every Rank and Station, whose Conduct
deserved Praise; those who had been passed in Silence, might probably
have upbraided him with personal Reproach. He judged it best, therefore,
in general Terms, to admit *Exceptions,* but to leave [76] it to every Man's
particular Judgment, to determine *where* these *Exceptions* lay.

LETTER XIII

Thus, my Lord, the Writer hath endeavoured to explain and defend
his Estimate; in which he needed not to have been so sollicitous, had
it been true what it seems, hath been insinuated to your Lordship, that
"the Work is not properly his own; that he hath only delivered the Sentiments of other Men, and been the mere Instrument of conveying their
Principles to the Public." But he here assures your Lordship, in the most
solemn Manner, that the whole of this Estimate was the sole Result of
his own Reason, uninfluenced by the Advice, or Direction of any Friend
whatever: And that, indeed, he thought the Subject of so delicate a Nature, that it would have been [77] ungenerous to have involved any Friend
in the personal Consequences which he foresaw it might produce. Had
no disagreeable Effects attended the Publication, he should not have
judged it necessary to make this Avowal; but as the Clamour and Displeasure of certain Ranks have been the Consequence of its Appearance
and Success, he thinks it a Duty incumbent on him to clear every Friend
of this groundless Imputation; and declares, that whatever may appear

* See above, Letter IV. p. 37.[29]
29. Cf. above, pp. 478–79.

in it either inadvertent, or erroneous, the Whole is to be attributed to himself alone; to the Overflowings of his own Zeal, thrown out to the World without Disguise, Expectation, or Fear; and bent, not against *Persons,* but against the predominant Errors, Follies, and Vices of his Time and Country. His Work hath had the Fate which might reasonably be expected: it hath been *read, approved, dissented* from, and [78] *reviled.* For the Conviction of those who have candidly *dissented,* the Publication of these Letters may be of Use: But when the Writer considers, by WHOM his Work hath been *approved,* and by WHOM *reviled,* as the first of these Parties *desire* no Reply, so the latter *deserve* none: They have *both* done his Work all the Honour that is in their Power to give; and he cannot but esteem its Fate to have been *peculiarly happy.* The worst that he wishes to his worst Enemy, is *Honesty* and a *better Mind.*

Upon the whole, my Lord, the Writer can but declare his upright Intentions, and leave the World to judge of their Propriety and Success. He would desire his Countrymen to remember the generous Maxim of a true Politician, "that a Patriot will admit there may be honest Men, and that honest Men may differ:" And that, [79] "where the Heart is right, there is true Patriotism."* He knows, it is the Principle of many good Men, that all Attempts towards *Innovation,* of whatever Kind, are dangerous. For himself, he is of a different Opinion: He thinks that *seeming Innovation* is, in many Cases, no more than the necessary Means of *preventing* a gradual and unsuspected *Change* of Things for the worse, which inevitably steals on in every State, if not checked by timely and resolute Applications.

So far is the Writer from imagining, with the Herd of Politicians, that there is no Virtue nor good Intention in any but those who approve that System of Politicks which He espouses; that on the contrary, he makes no Doubt, but some of the Great, who had not the Courage to combat the ruling Evils of the Times, wished sincerely to compass such an End, but judged the [80] End unattainable. He is, therefore, the more surprised that Individuals should take Offence at this Part of his Work, because it is

* Dr. *Berkley's Maxims.*[30]

30. George Berkeley, *Maxims Concerning Patriotism,* in *A Miscellany, Containing Several Tracts on Various Subjects* (1752), p. 115.

pointed, not against the Conduct of Individuals, but against the common and ruling Errors of the Times. He believes there are upright Men of all Parties, and only wishes they would believe so of one another. His Approbation or Disapprobation is not of *Men,* but *Measures:* And he is well persuaded, that many of those who once thought the present Measures of Government *impracticable,* begin now to see the *Possibility,* as well as the great *Importance* of carrying on the public Affairs, on a higher Principle than that of *venal* Influence.

So sudden and so great is the Change in the Appearance of our public Affairs, in Consequence of this sudden and couragious Check given to the ruling Manners and Principles of the Times, that the Wri[81]ter hath been seriously asked, "Whether the rising Courage of the Nation, our formidable Armaments, and the gallant Spirit of several young Men of Fashion and Fortune, are not so many Confutations of the Principles advanced in the *Estimate?*" Seriously, my Lord, the Writer of the *Estimate* is right glad to be so CONFUTED. Had these Appearances risen before the Publication of his Work, he might justly have been accused of Partiality and Misrepresentation. But as it is confessed, that these Appearances are but now *rising,* he will only desire his Objectors to look back to the *Estimate* itself, and consider whether they are not *rising* on the very Principles there *urged, delineated,* and *foretold.* The Writer did indeed believe, he foresaw, nay he foretold, that "NECESSITY alone could bring back effeminate and unprincipled Minds from their Attachments to Gain and Pleasure."* Nay, he foretold the [82] very Means: "The Voice of an *uncorrupt People,* and a GREAT MINISTER."† Cast your Eye back, my Lord, to no very distant Day, and be You the Judge, what was the *Distress,* and what the *Necessity* of the Time: Had not a general Dissolution of Manners and of Principle disordered, nay, almost unhinged the State? This it was, that united the *Voice,* the *legal Representations,* of an uncorrupted People: That united Voice, *steady,* not *factious*—*loyal,* yet *couragious*—was heard and approved

* Vol. I. p. 220.[31]
† Vol. I. p. 221.[32]
31. Cf. above, p. 343.
32. Cf. above, p. 344.

by a GRACIOUS SOVEREIGN: The *expected Minister* was found; and a *coercive Power* hath thus appeared from the *Throne*, sufficient to controul the Blindness and Folly of the dissolute and thoughtless among the higher Ranks, and to lead them to *salutary Measures* and their own *Safety*.

Mark the Effects of this uniting Power: *private Good* gives Way to *public:* the se[83]veral Ranks assume a Spirit and *Fervor* unknown before: Fear of *Shame*, and Thirst of *Honour*, begin to spread thro' our *Fleets* and *Armies*; and our growing *Youth* seem already to catch the kindling *Fire*. In a Word, the national Strength is awakened, and called forth into Action: The GENIUS of BRITAIN seems rising as from the *Grave:* he shakes himself from the *Dust*, assumes his ancient *Port*, and *Majesty* of Empire, and goes forth in his Might to *overwhelm* our *Enemies*.[33]

I cannot conclude, my Lord, without seriously recommending to your particular Notice and Regard, two Observations, (which contain, indeed, the Substance and End of the *Estimate* itself) arising from the present State of our public Affairs. The first is, that by proper Exertions and well-directed Applications, the ruling *Evils* of an *effeminate Period* may be *controuled:* The Second is, that under our present Constitu[84]tion, the national Affairs may be carried on with *Honour* to the *Crown* and *Success* to the *Kingdom* (a Truth which, not long ago, many serious Men did not believe) on a higher Principle than that of *corrupt Influence*.

However, let us not be intoxicated with the Appearances of Success: The Tree may *blossom*, and yet be *blasted*. The ruling Defects and Evils of the Times are for the present *controuled* indeed, but not *extirpated*. The Remedy, tho' it begins to take Effect, is yet no more than *temporary:* The Distemper *lurks*, tho' the Symptoms begin to *vanish*. Let those who wish well to their Country, then, be watchful, and prepared against a Relapse. 'Tis *something*, to have *check'd* the *Disease* at its *Crisis*; the perfect *Cure* will require the *Attention* and *Labour* of an *Age*.

FINIS

---

33. Broadly reminiscent of Milton's similar encomium in *Areopagitica* (1644) on the English nation as it awoke to its destiny of liberty: "Methinks I see in my mind a noble and puissant Nation rousing herself like a strong man after sleep, and shaking her invincible locks: . . ." (Milton, *Areopagitica*, p. 43).

Thoughts on Civil Liberty,
on Licentiousness, and Faction
(1765)

* "But its liberty declined into vice, and into a violence deserving the curb of law" (Horace, *Ars Poetica*, ll. 282–83). Horace is referring to the Old Comedy of Athens.

THOUGHTS

ON

CIVIL LIBERTY,

ON

LICENTIOUSNESS,

AND

FACTION

By the AUTHOR of
ESSAYS on the CHARACTERISTICS, &c.

——Sed in Vitium Libertas excidit, et Vim
Dignam Lege regi.——*

NEWCASTLE UPON TYNE:
Printed by J. WHITE and T. SAINT,
For L. DAVIS and C. REYMERS, against
Grey's-Inn Gate, Holborn, London;
Printers to the ROYAL SOCIETY.
MDCCLXV.

Contents

THOUGHTS

ON

CIVIL LIBERTY, &c.

SECTION I

The DESIGN

There are two Causes, essentially distinct, though often interwoven, by which a free State may perish. These are, *external* and *internal* Violence: *Invasions* from Abroad, or *Dissentions* at Home: The Rage of foreign *War,* or domestic *Faction.*

After a dangerous and exhausting War, Victory hath at length restored Peace to our bleeding Country.[1] But in vain the [10] Sword of War is sheathed, if in Time of Peace the Poignard of *Licentiousness* and *Faction* is drawn, and madly level'd by many of our Countrymen, at the Breasts of their Fellow-Subjects.

To prevent the fatal Consequences of this deluded or deluding Spirit, is the Purpose of this Essay: In which the Writer will endeavour to trace the present State of Things to its general Foundations: By pointing out the real Basis and genuine Characteristics of true Liberty; by unmasquing the Pretences, and laying open the secret *Sources* and distinctive *Marks* of *Licentiousness* and *Faction.*

As the political Principles here laid down and inforced, will be found strictly connected with Religion and Morals; no Apology will be made for endeavouring to establish the public Happiness of Mankind on the

---

1. The Seven Years' War had been concluded in 1763 by the Treaty of Paris.

solid Basis of *Virtue*, which is the *End* of *Religion itself.*—In this Point the Writer confirms himself on the Authority of an excellent and learned Prelate, whose [11] political Researches were of like Tendency. "As the Sum of human Happiness is supposed to consist in the Goods of Mind, Body, and Fortune, I would fain make my Studies of some Use to Mankind, with Regard to each of these three Particulars; and hope it will not be thought faulty or indecent in any Man, of what Profession soever, to offer his Mite towards improving the *Manners* (I will add, the *Religion*) *Health,* and *Prosperity* of his Fellow-Creatures."*

SECT. II

Of the Nature of Civil Liberty

To some it will doubtless appear a superfluous Labour, to fix the true Idea of *civil Liberty,* in a Country which boasts itself *free.* [12]

Yet the Writer esteems it a necessary though obvious Task: Not only that he may appeal to his Idea of it, thus established; but also, because in the *Conduct* (at least) if not in the *Writings* of his Countrymen, it seems to have been sometimes mistaken.

The *natural Liberty* of Man, considered merely as a solitary and savage Individual, would generally lead him to a full and unbounded Prosecution of all his Appetites. Some Savages there are, though few, who live nearly, if not altogether, in this *brutal* State of *Nature.*

These last Expressions, it must be confessed, are inadequate to their Subject: For such a State of Man is worse than that of Brutes, and in the strict Sense, is also *contrary* to *Nature.* For Brutes are endowed with unerring Instincts, which Man possesseth not: Therefore such a solitary and wretched State is strictly *unnatural*; because it prevents the Exertion of those Powers, which his *Nature* is *capable* of at[13]*taining:* But those *Powers Society* alone can *call forth* into *Action.*

* Dr. *Berkley's* Misc. p. 118.[2]

2. "Advertisement" to *The Querist*, in George Berkeley, *A Miscellany, Containing Several Tracts on Various Subjects* (1752), p. 118. Brown had also used this quotation from Berkeley in his *An Explanatory Defence of the Estimate* (1758); cf. above, p. 491, n. 28.

Man is therefore formed for *Society:* That is, Man is formed for Intercourse with Man: Hence, through the natural Developement of the human Powers, a Variety of new *Wants,* a Necessity for mutual *Aids* and distinct *Properties,* must arise: From these, a new *Accession,* as well as a frequent *Disagreement* and *Clashing* of *Desires* must inevitably ensue. Hence the Necessity of *curbing* and *fixing* the *Desires* of Man in the social State; by such *equal Laws,* as may compel the *Appetites* of each *Individual* to yield to the *common Good* of *all.*

From this salutary *Restraint, civil Liberty* is derived. Every natural Desire which might in any Respect be inconsistent with the general Weal, is given up as a voluntary Tax, paid for the higher, more lasting, and more important *Benefits,* which we reap from *social Life.* [14]

SECT. III

Of Licentiousness and Faction

From the Nature of civil Liberty, thus delineated, the Nature of *Licentiousness* will easily be fixed: Being indeed no other than "Every Desire carry'd into Action, which in any Respect violates those equal Laws, established for the common Benefit of the Whole."

Thus, an *unlimited Indulgence* of Appetite, which in the *savage* State is called *natural Liberty,* in the *social* State is stiled *Licentiousness.*

And *Licentiousness,* when its immediate Object is That of "thwarting the Ends of civil Liberty," is distinguished by the Name of *Faction.* [15]

SECT. IV

Unassisted Laws no permanent Foundation of Civil Liberty

These Remarks are obvious; and clear to every Man possessed of the common Degrees of Understanding. Let us now consider, "What are the *permanent Foundations* of civil Liberty:" That is, in other Words, "What are the effectual Means by which every Member of Society may be uniformly sway'd, impelled, or induced, to sacrifice his private Desires or Appetites, to the Welfare of the Public."—This is a Subject, which deserves a particular Elucidation, because in our own Country, and our own Times, it seems to have been *much* and *dangerously* mistaken.

It hath been affirmed as a first Principle by certain Writers, and hath been artfully or weakly suggested by others, "that the [16] coercive Power of human Laws is sufficient to sustain itself: That the Legislator or Magistrate hath properly no Concern with the private Opinions, Sentiments, or Operations of the Mind: And that *Actions* alone fall under the legal Cognizance of those in Power."

The Author of the *Fable of the Bees*[3] hath boldly laid down this; which, as a ruling Principle, pervades his whole Work. He professes himself the Friend of Liberty: He derides private Virtue, as the Offspring of Flattery, begotten upon Pride: He discards Religion, as a political Fable; he treats the Principle of Honour, as an empty Chimera; he recommends private Vices as public Benefits;* and having thus level'd the whole Fabric of *Manners* and *Principles*; what, do you think, is the grand Arcanum of his Policy, for the Prevention of such Crimes as would indanger the Grandeur and Stability of the State? Why;—"se[17]vere Laws, rugged Officers, Pillories, Whipping-Posts, Jails, and Gibbets."†

This Principle, of the Sufficiency of human Laws to sustain their own Efficacy and Power, without Regard to the Opinions or Principles of Men, hath been, at least, indirectly held forth by other Writers.

An Author, who although a *sincere,* was certainly an *imprudent* Friend of Liberty,[5] speaks in the following ambiguous Stile; which, if not designed to impress the Principle here called in Question, is at least very liable to be interpreted into it.

It is foolish to say, that Government is concerned to meddle with the *private Thoughts* and Actions of Men, while they injure neither the Society, nor any of its Members. Every Man is in Nature and Reason,

---

* *Fable of the Bees*, passim.

† Essay on Charity Schools.[4]

3. Bernard de Mandeville (1670–1733); cf. above, p. 122, n. 55.

4. A misquotation from Remark "O" of *The Fable of the Bees*: "but Men of abandon'd Principles must be aw'd by rugged Officers, strong Prisons, watchful Jailors, the Hangman and the Gallows" (Mandeville, *Fable*, vol. I, p. 164).

5. I.e., Thomas Gordon (*d.* 1750); Whig pamphleteer and classical scholar.

the *Judge* and *Disposer* of his own *domestic Affairs*; and according to the *Rules* of *Religion* and [18] *Equity*, every Man must carry *his own Conscience:* So that neither has the Magistrate a Right to *direct* the *private Behaviour* of Men; nor has the Magistrate, or any Body else, any Manner of Power to *model* People's *Speculations*, no more than their *Dreams*. Government being intended to *protect* Men from the *Injuries* of one another, and not to direct them in *their own Affairs; in* which *no one is interested but themselves*, it is plain, that their *Thoughts* and *domestic Concerns* are *exempted* entirely from its Jurisdiction: In Truth, Men's *Thoughts* are not subject to *their own Jurisdiction*.

Let People alone, and they will *take Care of themselves*, and do it *best:* And if they do not, a sufficient *Punishment* will *follow* their *Neglect*, without the *Magistrate's Interposition* and *Penalties*. It is plain, that such busy Care and officious *Intrusion* into the *personal Affairs*, or *private Actions, Thoughts*, and *Imaginations* of Men, has in it more *Craft* than [19] *Kindness:*—To *quarrel* with any Man for his *Opinions, Humours*, or the Fashion of his *Cloaths*, is an *Offence* taken without being given.—True and impartial Liberty is therefore the Right of every Man, to pursue the *natural, reasonable*, and *religious* Dictates of his own Mind: To *think what he will*, and *act as he thinks*, provided he *acts not* to the *Prejudice* of another.*

These Expressions are crude, inaccurate, and ambiguous; leaving the thoughtful Reader at a Loss for the Author's precise and determined Meaning. For, first, they may possibly imply, "that the Magistrate hath no Right to violate the Laws of what is commonly called *religious Toleration* or *christian Liberty*; but that every Man hath an unalienable Right to worship God in that *Manner* which accords to the Dictates of his own Conscience."—In this Sense they are rational and true: [20] And to this Truth the Writer hath more than once born public Testimony.†

---

* *Cato's* Letters, No. 62.[6]
† See Vol. of Sermons, Serm. 4, 5, 12.[7]

6. A series of quotations taken from the beginning of *Cato's Letters*, no. 62 (*Cato's Letters*, vol. I, pp. 426–28).

7. John Brown, *Sermons on Various Subjects* (1764), pp. 67–90, 91–118, and 311–41.

But, secondly, they may imply, "that Thoughts, Speculations, Opinions, Principles, however received and imbibed by the Mind of Man, have no Connexion with his Actions; at most, no Connexion so necessary and strong as to give the Magistrate a Right to *regulate* them by *any Means* whatever. That no Direction is to be given either to the *grown* or the *infant Mind*; that as every Member of Society hath a Right to hold what Opinions and Principles he pleaseth, so he hath the same Privilege to communicate them to his *Family* and *Children:* That they are to think what they will, because Thoughts and Opinions are a private and personal Affair: That the Magistrate is only concerned to regulate their Actions." [21]

This is not only a possible Interpretation, but in all Appearance, the more natural of the two. For it is not here once suggested by this Author, that *Opinions* have any *Influence* on *Actions*; but rather, that they concern *nobody* but *Him* who *holds* them. 'Tis true, he speaks of them as being *reasonable,* and *religious:* But if they be the mere Result of private and fortuitous Thought, unaided by the Regulations of civil Policy, I see not why they may not more probably be *unreasonable* and *irreligious:* Because they are more likely to be model'd by *ruling Appetites* than *rational Deduction.*

At the same Time, it is but Justice to this Author to say, that he certainly meant not (like the Author of the *Fable of the Bees*) to discard all *moral* Principles as groundless and chimerical; whatever his Intentions were with Regard to *Religion.* But his Expressions are *ambiguous,* and have been laid hold of by Men of the most libertine Opinions: Therefore in [22] whatever Sense they were *written,* it is necessary to oppose them, in that Sense in which they have been *received.*

And farther, this is certain: That the Principle implied in this second Interpretation hath passed into a general Maxim in this Kingdom, among those who pique themselves on *unlimited Freedom* of *Thought.* These Men have long and openly derided every *Regulation* of *Opinion* and *Principle;* have discarded all *moral* and *religious Instruction,* under the despised Idea, of *Prejudice of Education;* have laid it down as their fundamental Maxim, "that you are to think what you will: Only to act honestly." Not attending to that essential Connexion which subsists between *Thoughts, Opinions, Principles,* and Actions.

Doubtless, any Society of Men, aiming at the Establishment of civil Liberty, have a Right to unite themselves on what Conditions they please. But it is the Purpose of this Essay, to prove, by Reasonings confirmed by Facts, that a free Commu[23]nity built on the Maxims above delivered, cannot be of *long Duration:* That the mere *coercive Power* of *human Laws* is not sufficient to *sustain itself:* That there is a strong and unalterable *Connexion* between *Opinions* and *Actions:* That a certain *Regulation* of Principles is necessary to check the selfish Passions of Man; and prevent *Liberty* from degenerating into *Licentiousness:* And that "a certain System of Manners and Principles, mutually supporting each other, and pervading the whole Community, are the only permanent Foundation on which true civil Liberty can arise."

The natural Appetites, Passions, and Desires of Man, are the universal Fountain of his Actions: Without the Impulse which he receives from *those,* he would be at once unfeeling and inactive. Consequently, according to the State and Character of his Desires, his Actions will *naturally* be good or evil; innocent, useful, or destructive. [24]

Were these Desires universally coincident with the Welfare and Happiness of others, no coercive Power would be wanting, as the Means of producing and securing perfect Liberty.

But the acknowledged Necessity of penal Laws affords an incontestable Proof, that the *unbridled Desires* of Man are utterly inconsistent with the Welfare and Happiness of his Fellow Creatures.

Whatever Means, therefore, are most effectual in curbing and *subduing* the selfish *Desires* of Man, are the most effectual Means of *regulating* his *Actions,* and establishing civil Liberty on its most permanent Foundations.

The mere coercive Power of human Laws, without an assistant Regulation of the Passions and Desires, is utterly inadequate to the great Ends either of *private* Happiness or *public* Liberty.

It cannot produce *private* Happiness to the Individual, because while it leaves his Mind open to be *infested* by every *unruly* [25] *Passion* that may arise, it *forbids* him the *Gratification:* Thus it sets the distracted Soul at Variance with itself. The best Consequence that can be hoped for, is a continued Conflict of *Fear* and *Appetite*; of a *Dread* of human *Laws,* warring with inordinate and *selfish Passions*.

It cannot be a *permanent* Foundation of public Liberty; because while the Passions are thus left without an inward Controul, they will often be too strong for *Fear,* even where a legal Punishment is the certain Consequence: For as they are suffered to subsist in their full Vigour, and when kindled in the Soul are blind and headlong, they will often carry away the whole Man; will bear him down in their Gratification, even to unavoidable Destruction.

Still farther, and chiefly: Human Power cannot penetrate the secret Recesses of the Soul, nor reach the dark Intentions of the Heart of Man, nor always be of Weight to combat the Strength of Indi[26]viduals: Hence *Cunning* will often *evade,* and *Force* will often *defy,* the coercive Power of the best-formed Laws. Thus *public Wisdom* must give Way to *private Gratification,* the *Innocent* must become a *Prey* to the *Guilty;* that is, in other Words, *Liberty* must be *destroyed,* and *Licentiousness* must *triumph.*

SECT. V

Virtuous Manners and Principles the only permanent Foundation of civil Liberty

What, then, are the *permanent Foundations,* on which perfect Liberty can arise?—I answer, it can only arise on the Power of such a System of *Manners* and *Principles* effectually impressed on the human Mind, as may be an *inward Curb* to every inordinate Desire; or rather, such as may so frame and model the human Heart, that its ruling Desires [27] may correspond, coincide, or coalesce, with all the great and essential Appointments of public Law.

The Nature of Man admits of this Improvement, though not in a perfect, yet in a considerable Degree. He is born with Appetites suited to his own Preservation, and the Continuance of his Species: Beyond this, he is by Nature at once *selfish* and *social; compassionate* and *resentful; docile,* either to *Good* or *Evil;* and hence, capable of acquiring *new Habits,* new Passions, new Desires, either to the *Welfare* or *Destruction* of his Fellow-Creatures.

Virtuous Manners I call such acquired Habits of Thought and correspondent Action, as lead to a steady Prosecution of the general Welfare.

Virtuous Principles I call such as tend to confirm these Habits, by superinducing the Idea of *Duty*.

Virtuous Manners are a permanent Foundation for civil Liberty, because they [28] lead the Passions and Desires themselves to coincide with the Appointments of public Law. The infant Mind is pregnant with a Variety of Passions: But it is in the Power of those who are intrusted with the Education of Youth, in a considerable Degree, to determine the Bent of the nascent Passions; to fix them on salutary Objects, or let them loose to such as are pernicious or destructive.

Here, then, lie the first Foundations of civil Liberty: In forming the Habits of the youthful Heart, to a *Coincidence* with the *general Welfare:* In checking every rising Appetite that is contrary to This, and in forwarding every Passion that may promote the Happiness of the Community: In implanting and improving Benevolence, Self-Controul, Humility, Integrity, and Truth; in preventing or suppressing the contrary Habits of Selfishness, Intemperance, Pride, Dishonesty, and Falsehood: In teaching the young Mind to *delight,* as far as is possible, in [29] every Virtue for its own Sake: In a Word, in so forming the Pleasures and Displeasures of the opening Heart, that they may coalesce and harmonize with the Laws of public Freedom.

Above all, *This* will give Stability to civil Liberty, if the social Passions of Individuals can be so far extended, as to include the Welfare of the *whole* Community, as their *chief* and *primary* Object. This Affection is distinguished by the Name of *public Spirit,* or the *Love* of our *Country;* the highest Passion that can sway the human Heart, considered as a permanent Foundation of true Liberty.

But in some Minds the selfish Passions are strong, and the social ones weak or wanting: And in the best formed Heart incidental Temptations may arise, and overturn its pre-established Habits: Therefore it is a necessary Measure for the Security of private Virtue and public Freedom, that *virtuous Principles* be likewise implanted in the Heart. Such Principles, [30] I mean, as may *strengthen* the good Habits of Thought and Action already contracted, by superinducing the Idea of *Duty*.

Of these there are but *three,* which can sway the Manners of Men, and confirm the Foundation of civil Liberty. These are *Religion, Honour,* and natural *Conscience*. The first has the *Deity* for its Object; the second, the *Applause* of *Men;* the third, the *Approbation* of our own *Heart.* The Frame and Situation of Man admits of no other *Principle*, from whence the Idea of *Duty* can arise.

The Principle of *Religion* tends to this End of confirming civil Liberty, as it induces the Idea of *Duty;* and urges the Performance of it, on the Belief of a just, omnipotent, and all-seeing GOD; who approves and condemns, will reward or punish, according as our Thoughts and Actions are Good or Evil.

But, as the Means of rendering *Religion*, a firm *Ally* and *Support* of *Liberty*, [31] it is necessary that their *Dictates* should be *coincident:* That is, that the Thoughts and Actions which Religion prescribes as Duties, and forbids as Sins, should coincide with the Dictates and Appointments of public Law. In free Countries, this is the natural State of Religion; which commonly either bends to the established Laws of the Community, or moulds them into its own Genius and Complexion.

The Principle of *Honour* affords a concomitant Support of civil Liberty, when properly directed. It works by a powerful and universal Passion, "our Fondness for the Applause of Men:" But in free Countries, this Principle is much more liable to abuse than that of Religion: Because it is apt be be warped by the fashionable and ruling Manners of the Times: For whatever is fashionable is apt to draw Respect and Applause: Whatever is unfashionable is for the present intitled only to Contempt. Hence the Principle of *Honour* becomes *fluctuating* and *uncer*[32]*tain* in its Nature, and therefore in its *Effects:* A *Regulation* of this Principle, therefore, is of the most important Consequence; because, if left to its own fantastic Dictates, it will often *endanger* instead of *strengthening* the Foundations of public Freedom.

The third Principle, that of natural *Conscience*, which tends to confirm the Establishment of Liberty, is founded in the Approbation of our own Heart. This Principle is in one Respect independent of the other two, but in another Respect seems to stand intimately related to them. It is independent of them, as it neither looks out for the Approbation of God, nor the Applause of Men: It seems intimately related to them, because on a strict Examination of the human Frame, as well as the History of

Mankind, it appears generally to be the Result of the *one*, or *other*, or *both*. We transplant the acknowledged *Approbation* of *Heaven* and the *Applause* of *Men* into our own *Heart*; [33] and from this, through the fertile Power of *Association*, springs a new Principle of *Self-Approbation* and *Self-Reproof*, as an additional *Regulator* of our Thoughts and Actions.

'Tis true, many Writers have resolved the *particular* Dictates of natural Conscience into an *unchangeable* Principle of Right and Wrong, arising universally in the human Heart. There is no Doubt, but the *general* Principle of Self-Approbation or Self-Rebuke ariseth in an *universal* Manner, in some Degree or other: But as it appears from the History of human Nature, that the *particular* Dictates of this Conscience *vary* with the other received Principles of the Mind, it is not necessary to debate or dwell on this speculative Point: We may take it as a Truth confirmed by Facts, that the *particular* Dictates of natural *Conscience* will generally be founded on those of *Religion* and *Honour*. [34]

Hence, then, it appears, that this Principle of Conscience stands in Need of a *Guide*, in the same Degree as those Principles on which it is founded. If it be founded on the *Religion* of a free State, it will generally *coincide* with the Principles of *Freedom:* If its Foundations are laid in the mere Principle of *Honour*, its Dictates will be *fantastic* as those of its Parent; and will therefore require a parallel *Regulation*.

Each of these Principles, singly taken, is of Power, in *some* Degree or other, to strengthen the Basis of civil Liberty. On their *united* Influence, added to the Force of pre-established Habits of Thought and Manners, public Freedom might seem to arise on immoveable and everlasting Foundations.

But as the Nature of Man, even in his most virtuous State, is *imperfect* and *inconsistent;* so, in Spite of the most salutary Institutions, some *Defects* will intrude. Hence, from an unavoidable Alloy of [35] Vice, civil Liberty must ever be *imperfect:* A certain Degree of Licentiousness (that is, of private Will, opposing the Public) will always mix itself, and in some Degree contaminate the Purity of every Commonwealth.

Yet, while virtuous Manners and Principles clearly predominate in their Effects, a State may still be justly called *free*.

But in Proportion as these Manners and Principles decay, and their Contraries rise into Power and Action, public Freedom must necessarily decline. For in that Case, the Passions and Powers of the human Mind are all set in Conspiracy against the Dictates of public Law. Hence unbridled Passions will have their Course; every Man's Heart and Hand will be set against his Brethren; and the general Cement of Society, which bound all together, being thus dissolved; even without any external Violence offered, the Commonwealth through its *internal Corruption* must fall in Pieces. [36]

SECT. VI

An Objection considered

Doubtless, it will be objected (nay, it *hath* been objected) by the Patrons of unlimited Freedom of Thought, that This is indeed a System of *Slavery*; that it is building civil Liberty on the *Servitude* of the *Mind*, and shackling the infant Soul with *early Prejudice*.

In Answer to this plausible Objection, the Writer replies (what he hath elsewhere advanced)* "That a Prejudice doth not imply, as is generally supposed, the Falsehood of the Opinion instilled, but only that it is taken up, and held, without its proper Evidence. Thus the infant Mind may be prejudiced in Favour of *Truth* as well as *Falsehood;* and neither can the one or the other, thus instilled, be properly called more than an *Opinion*."[8] [37]

Farther: The infant Mind cannot remain in a State of Indifference and Inaction, either with Regard to Habits of Conduct, or Principles and Opinions. Habits, Impressions, Beliefs, Principles, of one Kind or other, the growing Mind will inevitably contract, from its Communication with Mankind: If therefore rational Habits and Principles be not infused, in order to preclude Absurdities; it is Odds,[9] but Absurdities will get the Start, and preclude all rational Habits and Opinions. The Passions and the Reason of a Child will put themselves in Action, however wretched

* Sermons on Education, &c. p. 62, &c.

8. A slight misquotation from Brown's third sermon "On the First Principles of Education," in *Sermons on Various Subjects* (1764), p. 62.

9. I.e., it is probable.

and inconsistent; in the same Manner, as his Limbs will make an Effort towards *walking*, however awkward and absurd. The same Objection, therefore, that lies against instilling salutary Habits and Principles, will arise against teaching him to *walk erect:* This being indeed a Violation of the natural *Freedom* of the *Body*, as the other is of the natural *Liberty* of the Passions and [38] the *Mind*. The Consequences, too, are of the same Nature: For sure, a Child left to the Direction of his own Appetites and Reason would stand the same Chance to grovel in Absurdities, as to crawl on Hands and Knees, and wallow in the Mire.

Neither is there any Difference, with Respect to the real and internal Freedom of the Mind, between *Opinions instilled*, and *Opinions caught by Accident*. For in Truth, the Mind cannot be *compelled* to receive any Habit of Thought, Principle, or Opinion. These may indeed be offered to the infant Mind, but the Reception of them is its own voluntary Act; and is equally so, whether they be presented by fortuitous Incidents, or designed Instruction. All the Difference is, that in the first Case such a System of Habits and Opinions will certainly arise, as tend to the Destruction of Society: In the second, such a System of Habits and Opinions may be infused into the free Mind, as [39] will lay a sure and lasting Foundation of public Liberty and Happiness.

Nay, if any Difference could arise, with Respect to the true *Freedom* of the *Mind;* surely, *That Mind* ought, in the Eye of Reason, to be adjudged *most free*, which adopts a System of Thought and Action, founded on the *Wisdom* of the agreeing *Society;* rather than *That* which is suffered to be incurably tainted with the *vague* and *random* Conceptions of *untutor'd Infancy*.—This, at least, is consonant with the old Stoic Principle, that "The wise Man alone is free."*

Much hath been said in our Times, indeed, concerning the Force of *unassisted* human *Reason:* The Writer would not willingly either flatter or degrade its Powers. But to Him it appears, that they are superficially informed of the Frame and Tenor of the human Mind, who think that *mere Reason*

---

* Solus Sapiens liber.[10]

10. For similar sentiments attributed to the Stoics, cf. Cicero, *Paradoxa Stoicorum ad M. Brutum*, Paradox VI, sect. xlii, and Seneca, *Epistulae Morales*, LXXXI.xii.

(as it exists in Man) is more than a Power of dis[40]cerning and chusing the *properest Means* for obtaining his *desired Ends,* whether these Ends be *Good* or *Evil.* The Passions, pre-established Habits, and infused Principles of the Soul are the universal Motives to human Action. Where these point not to an *End desired,* Reason may indolently exercise its Eye; but can never find nor create an Object, of Force sufficient to put the Powers of the Soul and Body in Motion. Hence, human Reason must always receive its particular Cast and Colour from the pre-established Passions, Habits, and Principles; will ever form its ruling Ideas of Good and Evil, Right and Wrong, Just and Unjust, from these great Fountains of human Action.

The History of human Nature confirms this Truth: Hence it is, that this boasted human Reason is indeed so poor and unprofitable a Possession; being warped and moulded into that particular Form, which the varying Accidents of Climate, Soil, established Manners, Religion, [41] Policy, bodily Frame, or prevailing Passions and Principles, chance to give it.

Hence, then, it appears, that the private Freedom of the infant Mind is not *violated* but only *directed* to its *best End,* by early and salutary Instruction. Hence it appears to be the proper Destination of Man, that he shall not be left to the Follies of his own weak Understanding and nascent Passions; that he shall not be left *fortuitously* to imbibe the Maxims of corrupt Times and Manners; Maxims which, setting aside all Regard to their speculative Truth or Falsehood, do lead to the Dissolution of Law and Freedom: But that he shall be conducted voluntarily to adopt those Habits and Principles, which have been consecrated by the Approbation of the best and wisest Men, in every Age and Nation; such, in particular, as are suitable to the Laws, the Customs, the Genius, of his own free Country; such, in a Word, as are a *secure Foundation* of *public Liberty.* [42]

SECT. VII

A Confirmation of these Principles, drawn from the History of free States. First of Sparta.

These Reasonings, founded on the Nature and Constitution of Man, will receive a strong and unanswerable Confirmation from the History of free

States. Hence we shall obtain the clearest Evidences of Fact, that while virtuous Manners and Principles retained their Efficacy and Power, civil Liberty remained unshaken: That as these decayed, Liberty declined: That as soon as these were lost, Liberty was no more; Licentiousness crept in; Faction triumphed; and overwhelmed these degenerate States in one common Ruin.

To this Purpose I shall briefly analyze the Genius of the three most eminent [43] *Republics* that are recorded in Story: Those of SPARTA, ATHENS, and ROME. The Events are sufficiently known to those who are conversant in ancient History: But the fundamental and leading *Causes* of these Events deserve a particular Investigation: They will form a concurrent Proof of the Principles here given.

The Republic of SPARTA claims the first Place; both on Account of its Antiquity, and Perfection. By its Perfection is meant, not the moral Perfection of its *particular Institutions,* but of the *Means* and *Principles* by which *These* Institutions were secured.

The leading Institutions which LYCURGUS[11] fixed as the Essence of his Commonwealth, were these which follow.

1. He established a Senate of *twenty-eight,* as an *intermediate Power* between that of *Prince* and *People* . . . 2. He made an equal Partition of Lands and Goods, among the free Members of the Community . . . 3. He introduced the Use of Iron Money, instead of Gold and Silver . . . 4. He banished or [44] prevented all the Arts of Commerce, Elegance, and Luxury . . . 5. He ordained, that all the Members of the Society should eat together, and partake alike of the same coarse Fare . . . 6. He established an occasional Community of Wives: So that a Wife was not so much the Property of her Husband, as of the Republic, to the End of Population . . . 7. With a parallel View, he ordained a Kind of Community of Children: By This, no Father had the Care of his own Child; which, on its Birth, was immediately delivered over to the Officers of the State; and was either preserved or destroyed according to their Decree . . . 8. A continued Attention to the Preservation of the State, and an unremitted Preparation and Readiness for defensive War, formed the chief Employment of the *Spartan*

11. Cf. above, p. 306, n. 34.

State . . . 9. He committed the Cultivation of their Lands to a large Body of Slaves, who dwelt in the surrounding Country, were deprived of all the natural Rights [45] of Men, and were often laid in Wait for, and butchered in cold Blood by the young Men of SPARTA.*

These were the public and essential Institutions of the Spartan Republic: Many of them strange in their Nature: Yet formed for long Duration, through the Means and Principles on which they were established: Which we shall find to be consistent with, and corroborative of the Principles of civil Liberty above laid down.

The first and best Security of civil Liberty, hath been shewn to consist "in impressing the infant Mind with such Habits of Thought and Action, as may correspond with and promote the Appointments of public Law."—This Security was laid by LYCURGUS, in the [46] deepest and most effectual Manner, by the Mode of *Education* which he prescribed to the *Spartan* Youth.

No Father had a Right to educate his Children according to the Caprice of his own Fancy. They were delivered to public Officers, who initiated them early in the Manners, the Maxims, the Exercises, the Toils, in a Word, in all the mental and bodily Acquirements and Habits, which *corresponded* with the *Genius* of the *State*. Family Connexions had no Place: The first and leading Object of their Affection, was the general Welfare. This Tuition was carefully continued, till they were enrolled in the List of *Men:* To secure the Manners thus acquired, they were prohibited from travelling into other Countries, lest they should catch Infection from ill Example: On the same Foundation, all Visits from Strangers were forbidden.† Thus were they strongly and [47] unalterably possessed with the *Love* of their *Country*.

---

* This Enormity, practised with Impunity by the young Men of Sparta, hath been held unaccountable: But seems to have been allowed on the same warlike Principle with That other Allowance "of stealing Victuals." Both were probably established as the Means of preparing them for the Exercise of *Stratagem* in War.

† Plutarch: in Lycurgo.[12]

12. Plutarch, "Lycurgus," XXVII.3–4.

These severe Manners were confirmed by all the Principles that could strengthen them in the Mind of Man.

The Principle of *Religion* laid at the very Foundation of the State: For LYCURGUS expressly modeled his Commonwealth on the Pretence of a divine Authority. He declared to the People, that its essential Institutions were given him by the Oracle of DELPHI, which he went on Purpose to consult.* Again, after he had modeled his Republic, he repaired once more to the sacred Tripod; and enquired, "whether the God approved of the Laws he had established." The Answer was in the Affirmative: And this Reply LYCURGUS sent to SPARTA.†

This Principle was so intimately blended with that of the State, that their *Kings* were at the same Time the *High Priests* of the Community.‡— The Reli[48]gion and Power of an Oath was so strongly impressed on their Minds, that LYCURGUS trusted the future Execution of his Laws, to *That* Oath which the People took, on his last Departure from the City:§—An Oath, which proves, that the Religion of the Country was not at Variance with the Appointments of the State; because it obliged them never to depart from the Institutions of LYCURGUS.

The Principle of *Honour* was not at Variance, but *co-operated* with and *sustained* That of *Religion*. PLUTARCH is very particular, on their early and continued Encouragement of this Principle. Their Songs (which made a Part of their Education) tended to inflame their Minds with honest Ambition. "Their Subject was generally the *Praise* of such Men as had dy'd in Defence of their Country; or in *Derision* of Those who had shrunk from the public Service. The *old* Men talked high of what they

---

* Plutarch: in Lycurgo.[13]
† Ib.[14]
‡ Ib.[15]
§ Plutarch: in Lycurgo.[16]
13. Ibid., V.3.
14. Ibid., XXIX.2–4.
15. Plutarch nowhere says that the Spartan kings are priests, but Brown perhaps is recalling "Lycurgus" VI.5, where the *rhetra* from the oracle at Delphi states that "honours divine" are due to the Spartan kings. For the sacrosanctity of the Spartan kings, cf. Plutarch, "Agis," XIX.
16. Ibid., XXIX.2–3.

had [49] done: The *younger* Part echo'd back their Song; declaring their Resolution, not to disgrace the Valour of their Forefathers."*

The Principle of natural *Conscience* was so intimately interwoven with those of their *Religion* and *Honour,* that it affords a striking Proof how far natural Conscience depends on these other Principles. If natural Conscience were in itself a well-regulated and *sufficient Guide;* could any Thing have been more odious to its Dictates, than *Prostitution, Adultery, Thieving,* and *Assassination?* Yet all these did the severe *Spartans* practise, not only *without Remorse,* but with *Self-Approbation;* the infant Mind being beforehand modeled to this *preposterous* System of *imagined Duty.* For, on the very ruling Principles of the State, their Daughters were debauched, their Wives were common, their Victuals were stolen, their Slaves were murdered.† [50]

Thus was the famed Republic of *Sparta* strongly fortify'd, by the united and concurrent Power of *Manners* and *Principles,* all pointing to the *same* End, the *Strength* and *Duration* of the *State:* Of Manners and Principles, which in their particular Application, seemed to sacrifice the Happiness of Individuals to the Preservation of the Whole: And while they were most *abhorrent* from the Maxims of *improved* human Nature, *secured* the Institutions of a *savage* Policy.

From this View of the *Spartan* Commonwealth, these farther Remarks may naturally arise.

1. It hath been Matter of Surprize to those who have written on this famed Republic, "by what Means LYCURGUS should be able to perswade the *Spartans,* not only to change the Form of their Government, but to quit their private Possessions, their Manner of Life, the Use of Money, the Advantages of Commerce, the Property of their Wives, [51] the Care of their Children; and adopt a contrary System, so abhorrent from the Desires of civilized Man." And indeed, supposing the *Fact,* it should seem a Paradox utterly unaccountable.—The true Solution seems of a quite different Nature.—PLUTARCH leads me to it.—"There is so much Uncertainty (saith he) in the Accounts which Historians have left us of LYCURGUS,

* Plutarch: in Lycurgo.[17]
† Ib.[18]
17. Plutarch, "Lycurgus," XXI.1–2.
18. Respectively, Plutarch, "Lycurgus," XV.3; XV.7; XVII.3–4; XXVIII.1–4.

that scarce any Thing is asserted by one, which is not contradicted by others. Their Sentiments are quite different as to the Family he came of, the Voyages he undertook, the Place and Manner of his Death: But most of all, when they speak of the Laws he made, and the Commonwealth he founded.—They cannot be brought to agree, as to the very *Age* when he lived.—TIMAEUS conjectures, that there were two of his Name, and in different Times; but that the one being more famous than the other, Men gave to Him the Glory of both their Ex[52]ploits."*—Hence it appears, that the true History of this Lawgiver was lost in the Darkness of fabulous and obscure Ages: And that, as to the Beginnings of this Commonwealth, we have nothing to depend on, but the traditionary Rumours of a barbarous and lying Period. Now this seems to be fairly weighed down by the internal Evidence arising from the Nature of the Establishment itself. For it was indeed "the Establishment of barbarous Manners, carried into Permanency by political Institutions." That Mankind should be *carry'd back* to *This*, from a State of *Humanity* and *Civilization*;—that they should quit private Property, Money, Commerce, Decency, domestic Comforts, Wives and Children, and give them up to the Possession of the Public, is a Contradiction to all the known Powers and Passions of the human Mind. To effect a *Change* of *Government only*, is a Work sufficient for the Abilities of [53] the greatest Legislator: But to overturn all the pre-established Habits of the Head and Heart, to destroy or reverse all the fixed Associations, Maxims, Manners, and Principles, of a whole civilized Community; were a Labour, which might well be ranked among the most extravagant Legends of fabulous GREECE.

On the other Hand, to *bring forward* a Tribe of untaught Savages *one Degree* towards *Civilization,* and *there* to *fix* them;—to assign equal Portions of Land to those among whom Lands laid in Common;—to introduce Iron Money, where *no Money* had been in Use;—to prohibit Commerce, where Commerce was almost unknown;—to make the Girls dance naked in Public, where they had never known the decent Use of Cloaths;—to allow of Theft and Homicide under certain Limitations,

---

* Plutarch: in Lycurgo.[19]
19. Plutarch, "Lycurgus," I.1–2.

where *Both* had been practised without Limitation;—to make Wives at Times a public Property, where promiscuous Concubinage had prevailed; [54] to give Children a public Education, where no Education had taken Place;—These might all seem the natural and practicable Efforts of a *Pagan* Legislator.

Thus, the Formation of the *Spartan* Republic seems clearly accounted for. A Tribe of untaught Savages, were brought forward by LYCURGUS one Degree towards Civilization and Humanity, and There fixed by severe Institutions.

The Fate of AGIS, their patriot King,[20] confirms this Solution. He, with a Degree of public Virtue seldom seen in any Station, attempted to bring back the corrupt State to its first rigorous Institutions. But That which LYCURGUS could establish among untaught Savages, AGIS found impracticable, among a corrupted People. He was seized, imprisoned, and murdered by a Faction, in his Attempt to restore Freedom to a degenerate Republic.

2. If the Argument here alledged be just, concerning the first Institution of this [55] Republic; it follows (what, indeed, seems probable in its own Nature) that the strongest political Institutions may be formed on the savage State of Man. In this Period the Legislator hath few or no prior Institutions to contend with; and therefore can form a System of Legislation consistent with itself in all its Parts. While the Lawgiver who reforms a State already modeled and corrupted, must content himself with such partial Regulations, as the Force of prior Establishments and public Habits will admit.

3. The long united State of this Republic afford a Proof against a political Maxim commonly received, "That Divisions are necessary to a free State;[21] and that inward Tranquillity is a certain Symptom of its

20. Cf. Brown's earlier invocation of this passage of Spartan history in *An Estimate of the Manners and Principles of the Times* (above, pp. 305–6).

21. A principle normally traced to Machiavelli's praise of the beneficial consequences on the manners and virtue of the Romans of the turmoil of the early Roman republic (*Discourses*, Book I, ch. 4). Montesquieu elaborated Machiavelli's insight in chapter VIII of his *Considérations sur les causes de la grandeur des Romains, et de leur decadence* (1734) (Montesquieu, *Considérations*, pp. 145–52).

approaching Ruin." For, from the History of SPARTA, it appears, that during the Space of at least five hundred Years, intestine Divisions were unknown. This common and mistaken Maxim (adopted by almost all poli[56]tical Writers)* hath been founded on a Supposition, that where Opinion is *free,* it must ever be *divided.* The *Spartan* Commonwealth presents a clear Proof of the Reverse: That Opinion may be *free,* yet still *united.* But this *free Union* can only be the happy Effect of an early and rigorous Education; by which the growing Minds of the Community are voluntarily led, by public Institutions, into *one common Channel* of *Habit, Principle,* and *Action* . . . PLUTARCH tells us, that the Effect of this entire Union was so conspicuous in SPARTA, that "the Commonwealth resembled *one* great and powerful Person, *actuated by one Soul,* rather than a State composed of *many* Individuals."†

4. It appears, that the institutions of the *Spartan* Republic were admirably calculated for each other's Support, while [57] their perfect Union was maintained: And further, that when an Inroad was made into any one of them, the Ruin of the Whole was inevitable.

"Its Institutions were admirably calculated for each other's Support, while their perfect Union was maintained." Because they tended strongly to prevent the *first Inroads* of *Temptation* to the *Mind,* the very *first Impulses* of *selfish Passion.* The equal Partition of Lands and Goods took away all Hope of Superiority in Wealth: The Introduction of Iron Money rendered Wealth cumbersome and untractable: The Prohibition of Commerce prevented the Materials of Luxury: The Banishment of elegant Arts prevented the first Conception of them. Their public Meals eaten in common, cut off the Hope, nay, prevented the Desire of all private Indulgence of the Palate, the Disorders of Intemperance. To secure these rigid Institutions, the public Education of their Children was ordained, lest private Pas[58]sion should mix its Alloy, with the rigorous Appointments of the State. Thus the Republic was so round and compact in all its Parts, that it might seem to defy the Attacks of the most powerful Enemy.

---

* Among others, by MACHIAVEL and MONTESQUIEU.

† In Lycurgo.[22]

22. Plutarch, "Lycurgus," XXV.3 and XXX.2.

"But supposing an Inroad made into any one of its capital Institutions, the Ruin of the Whole was inevitable." For its several Parts receiving their Strength from each other, were therefore mutually *dependent;* and the Whole being an austere Contradiction to the natural Appetites of Man, the least Inroad of Indulgence naturally led on to more forcible Temptations. Thus, *Inequality* of Possessions brought in *Wealth* and *Poverty. Wealth* brought in *Luxury: Poverty* gave Birth to *Envy* and *Avarice.* Licentiousness and Faction thus crept in; and the Fall of SPARTA was *inevitable.*

Yet even amidst the *Decays* of this Republic, the Force of a rigorous Education essentially mixed with the Principles of [59] the State, was still conspicuous. The Power of Manners and Maxims thus imbibed was so untractable, even in the declining Periods of the *Spartan* Commonwealth, that PHILOPAEMEN, after many fruitless Attempts to annihilate its Influence, declared, "that the only effectual Method of destroying SPARTA, must be in *dissolving* the *Education* of their *Youth.*"*

This Analysis is clearly confirmed by PLUTARCH in the following Passages.

Since we may blame the Legislators of common Rank, who, through Want of Power or Wisdom, commit Mistakes in the Formation of fundamental Laws; how much more may we censure the Conduct of NUMA, who for the Reputation of his Wisdom only, being called by the general Voice of an unsettled People to be their King, did not in the first Place constitute Laws for the Education of Children, and Discipline of [60] Youth? For Want of which, Men become seditious and turbulent, and live not peaceable in their Families and Tribes: But when they are inured from their Cradle to good Principles, and imbibe from their Infancy the Rules of Morality, they receive such Impressions of Virtue, as convinces them of that Advantage which mutual Concord brings to a Commonwealth. This, with many others, was one of the Policies of LYCURGUS: And was of singular Force in the Confirmation and Establishment of his Laws:—Hence the

---

* Plutarch: in Philopaem.[23]
23. Ibid., "Philopoemen," XVI.5.

Spartans having sucked in these Principles with their Milk, were possessed with a most reverend Esteem of all his Institutions: So that the Fundamentals of his Laws continued in Force for above five hundred Years, without any Violation.*

Such then was the Force of concurrent Manners and Principles, all centering on one Point, impressed on the infant Mind, [61] and continued by a Variety of rigorous Institutions.—Thus, the Strength of the *Spartan* Republic, like the firm-compacted Weight of the *Macedonian Phalanx*,[25] bore down every opposing Power.

SECT. VIII

Of the Republic of Athens

We have seen the Force of Manners Principles in the strong Formation, the *Unanimity*, and *Continuance* of the *Spartan* State. We shall now see the Effects of the *Want* of Manners and Principles, in the weak Establishment, the unceasing *Factions*, and early *Dissolution* of the Commonwealth of ATHENS.

It appears above, that LYCURGUS, probably forming his People in the first and earliest Period of Civilization, was thus enabled to establish a perfect Republic. SOLON, on the contrary, having a *cor*[62]*rupted* People to *reform*, could only institute such a Kind of Government, as their *pre-established* Habits, Vices, and Forms of Polity could admit.

Here we discover the Foundation of that striking Remark of SOLON himself. "That he gave not the *Athenians* the *best* Laws that could be *given*, but the *best* they were *capable* of *receiving*."†

---

* Comparison of NUMA and LYCURGUS.[24]
† Plut. Solon.[26]
24. Plutarch, "Lycurgus and Numa," IV.4–5.
25. A military formation developed by Philip of Macedon, consisting of sixteen ranks of infantry armed with long spears. It was an inflexible unit, vulnerable to attacks on its flanks, and prevailed against the enemy only by weight and discipline. It fell into disuse when its inferiority to the Roman maniple was made evident in the Macedonian defeats at Cynoscephalae (197 B.C.) and Pydna (168 B.C.).
26. Plutarch, "Solon," XV.2.

The first and ruling Defect in the Institution of this Republic seems to have been "the total Want of an established Education, suited to the Genius of the State." There appears not to have been any public, regular, or prescribed Appointment of this Kind, beyond what Custom had accidentally introduced. 'Tis true, that the Parents often had Masters to instruct their Children in the *gymnastic* Arts, and in *Music*. Which last, in the ancient Acceptation of the Word, included *Poem* as well as *Melody:* 'Tis farther true, that the Poems thus taught [63] their Children, included often the great Actions, but withal, the Vices of Gods and ancient Heroes.* Yet in this first and ruling Circumstance, in the Institution of a free State, the Parents were much at Liberty, to do as seemed good to them. Hence, a dissimilar and discordant System of Manners and Principles took Place; while some youthful Minds were imbued with proper and *virtuous* Principles, some with *no* Principles, and some with *vicious* Principles; with such as must, therefore, on the Whole, tend to shake the Foundations of true Freedom.

The second ruling Defect in the Constitution of this Republic, was the Establishment of an unmixed and absolute Democracy. This naturally arose from the *licentious* State of *Manners* and *Principles,* which SOLON found already prevalent among the *People.* A *virtuous* People would have been content to have [64] *shared* the legislative Power with the higher Ranks of the Commonwealth. But a *licentious* People naturally grasped the Whole, as the likeliest Means (in their deluded Eye) of gratifying their own unbridled Passions. From this partial Distribution of Power, the State was blindly ruled by the Dregs of the Community. For *All* who were of Ability to maintain a *Horse*, were admitted to the Rank of *Magistracy:*† And all who were *admitted* to the Rank of *Magistracy* were *excluded* from any Share in the *legislative Power*.‡ Hence it

---

* See a Dissertation on Music and Poetry, Sect. v.[27]
† Plut. in Solon.[28]
‡ Ib.[29]

27. John Brown, *A Dissertation on the Rise, Union, and Power, the Progressions, Separations, and Corruptions, of Poetry and Music* (1763), pp. 46–95.
28. Plutarch, "Solon," 1–2.
29. Ibid., 2–3.

followed, that "All they who possessed the *Legislative Power*, were such as were *not* of *Ability* to *maintain* a *Horse*."—"Do not you despise (said SOCRATES to his Pupil ALCIBIADES, who was afraid to speak in Presence of the *Athenian* People) do not you despise That *Cobler?* I do, reply'd the Youth. Do not you (rejoyned the Philosopher) equally contemn that *Cryer*, and yon [65] *Tent-Maker?* ALCIBIADES confessing that he did; then said SOCRATES, "Is not the Body of the *Athenian People* composed of Men *like these?* And therefore, when you *despise* the *Individuals,* why should you fear the *Whole?*"*—A hopeful Tribe of *Legislators!* and such as might naturally be supposed to give Rise to that Licentiousness, Discord, and Ruin, in which they were soon swallowed up.

From this weak and imperfect Establishment, founded on the Caprices of an ignorant, unprincipled, and *licentious Populace,* all the subsequent *Factions,* which ended in the *Ruin* of this *Republic,* are clearly derived.

Even SOLON, the original Legislator, outlived the Commonwealth he had formed. On his Departure from ATHENS, *Factions* immediately arose. PISISTRATUS, the first ruling Demagogue, *led* the *People*; obtained a Guard; seized the Castle; and *established* a *Tyranny.*† [66]

We need go no farther into the History of this Republic, for a Discovery of the Causes of its final Ruin. It is true, that an imperfect Semblance of Liberty often appeared, amidst the Factions of succeeding Times: It is true, that Wealth and Luxury contributed to hasten the Fall of ATHENS: It is true, that PERICLES and ALCIBIADES,[32] in their Turn, while they seemed to polish the Manners, inflamed the Vices of the Populace; and led them on to the certain Destruction of the State. But for the Ruin of this Commonwealth, we need not have Recourse to the Inroads of Wealth or Luxury, as the Causes of its Dissolution. It resembled

---

* Aeliani Var: Hist. L. ii. C. i.[30]
† Plut: in Solon.[31]
30. Aelian, *Varia Historia,* II.i.
31. Plutarch, "Solon," XXIX–XXX.
32. Pericles (*c.* 500–429 B.C.); preeminent Athenian statesman and orator. Alcibiades (*c.* 450–404 B.C.); Athenian statesman and leader, educated by Pericles; but arrogant, unscrupulous, and dissolute.

a beautiful *Edifice* founded in *Sand* and *Rubbish:* Where an *uneducated,* an *unprincipled,* a *licentious Populace,* ruled the State; That State was destined to the convulsive Struggles of *Faction* while it lived, and then to a *speedy Death.* [67]

SECT. IX

Of the Commonwealth of Rome

Let us now pass to a Review of the Commonwealth of ROME: In the History and Fate of which, we shall find most abundant Proof of the Truths here laid down, concerning the Power of Manners and Principles, in the Preservation or the Dissolution of public Freedom.

MONTESQUIEU remarks finely, in his Discourse on this Republic, that "more States have perished, thro' a Violation of Manners, than thro' a Violation of Laws."* The Reason (though he does not assign it) appears evident on the Principles here given. He who violates established *Manners,* strikes at the general *Foundation;* he who violates *Law,* strikes only at a particular Part of the *Superstructure* of the State. [68]

In the Republic of SPARTA, we have seen the original State of Manners and Principles conspiring strongly to the *Preservation* of the Republic: In that of ATHENS, we have seen the original State of Manners and Principles tending no less clearly to its *Dissolution.*

In analysing the original State of Manners and Principles in the *Roman* Commonwealth, we shall find a different and *intermediate* State of Things; mixing the *Strength* of the *Spartan,* with the *Weakness* of the *Athenian* Institutions; tending first to *enlarge* and *aggrandize* the Republic, and in the End to *corrupt* and *destroy* it.

The Manners and Principles of early ROME, which tended to enlarge and aggrandize the Republic, were 1. A *Love* of their *Country* instilled

---

* Grandeur, &c.[33]

33. A translation of a comment in chapter VIII of Montesquieu's *Considérations sur les causes de la grandeur des Romains, et de leur decadence* (1734): "plus d'Etats ont peri parce qu'on a violé les moeurs, que parce qu'on a violé les Loix" (Montesquieu, *Considérations,* pp. 149–50).

into their rising Youth: Formed chiefly on the Power of *Custom*; and more particularly on the *warlike* Genius of the State. Their Annals abound with so many Instances of this grand Passion, that present Times stand amazed, and with Difficulty credit their Story. [69]

2. This Passion, founded on an *early*, though *not* a *prescribed* Education, was so strengthened by their *religious* System, that till the fatal Entrance of the Doctrine of EPICURUS, no *Roman* was ever known to have violated his Oath.*

3. Their Principle of *Honour* coincided with that of their Religion. It was so strong, at the Time of the first Formation of the Republic, that the Punishment of *Disgrace* was judged sufficient to deter the People from a Violation of the Laws. "When a Delinquent was cited before the People (saith LIVY) the *Valerian* Law ordained only, that he should be branded as *infamous*."†

4. From the Truths laid down above, it appears, that the Principle of natural *Conscience* must of Course co-operate with these, for the Confirmation of civil Freedom. The Force of this Principle is no less conspicuous in the early Periods of [70] *Roman* Liberty: It arose even into a ferocious Pride of Virtue, independent of all outward Testimony, which hath distinguished the great Names of ancient ROME, from Those of every other People upon Earth.

5. To these we must add the *Equality* of Property, the *Mediocrity* of Possession, the *Simplicity* of Life, which prevailed in early ROME; all these were the Outworks that guarded the internal Strength of Manners

---

* See Montesq. Grand. des Rom. C. x. Polyb. L. 6.[34]

† Liv. Hist. L. 10.[35]

34. Cf. Montesquieu, *Considérations*, p. 160; Polybius, VI.lvi.14.

35. "Valeria lex cum eum qui provocasset virgis caedi securique necari vetuisset, si quis adversus ea fecisset, nihil ultra quam 'improbe factum' adiecit. Id, qui tum pudor hominum erat, visum, credo, vinculum satis validum legis: nunc vix serio ita minetur quisquam"; "The Valerian law, having forbidden that he who had appealed should be scourged with rods or beheaded, merely provided that if anyone should disregard these injunctions it should be deemed a wicked act. This seemed, I suppose, a sufficiently strong sanction of the law, so modest were men in those days; now one would hardly make such a threat in earnest" (Livy, X.ix.5–6).

and Principles; and seemed, like the Institutions of SPARTA, to promise an Eternity of Freedom.

But in Spite of all these Foundations of civil Liberty, there were three fatal Circumstances, admitted into the very Essence of the Republic, which contained the *Seeds* of *certain Ruin:* While the *Tree* seemed to *flourish* in its full Growth and Vigour, *These,* like *Canker-Worms,* lay *eating* at the Root.

The first of these was the Neglect of instituting public Laws, by which the [71] *Education* of their Children might have been *ascertained.* This is justly charged by PLUTARCH, as a capital Defect in NUMA's Legislation:* This Defect, when once admitted into the Essence of the State, could not easily be rectify'd in succeeding Times: The Principle could only have been effectually infused, at the general Formation of the whole Mass. In Consequence of this Error in the first Concoction,[37] the supporting Principles of Freedom were vague and fluctuating: For Want of this *preventing* Power, the incidental Vices of a Parent were naturally transmitted to his Children, and thence to future Ages. The rigorous Education of SPARTA was a strong Check to the Proneness of human Nature towards Degeneracy and Corruption: Through This, every incidental Vice dy'd with its first Possessor. While the more lax Institution of the *Roman* Republic, suffered every original Taint in Man[72]ners and Principles to be transfused into, and to contaminate succeeding Times.

The second of these was "Their Principle of *unlimited Conquest.*" Their early Passion for War arose from their *Necessities.* On their first Establishment, they had neither *Territory* nor *Commerce:* They lived by *Plunder:* Hence, the *ruling Genius* of the *State* was *warlike:* Their warlike Genius was *unchecked* by any other Principle: Hence, unremitted Exercises, unceasing Improvements in Discipline, increasing Valour and Ferocity arose. Thus they attempted to subdue, and thus they subdued the World.

But such an Empire is utterly *untenable: Valour* may *acquire,* but cannot *maintain* it. The *Body* of such a State is too enormous to be effectually

* See above, Sect. vii.[36]
36. See above, p. 525, n. 24.
37. Cf. above, p. 287, n. 3.

animated by the *Soul*.[38] This is a Cause of Ruin so clear, that it hath met every Writer's Observation; and therefore needs no farther Proof. [73]

The third Principle of inevitable Destruction, which seems to have been inwrought into the very Essence of the *Roman* Republic, was the fatal Principle of *Change:* This is a Cause not so obvious; and therefore may require a farther Investigation.

Montesquieu hath justly observed, that one Cause of the *Roman Greatness* was "their *adopting* any Institution or Custom of other Nations whom they conquer'd, provided it was better than their own."* It seems to have escaped the Observation of this great Writer, that the same Principle of *Adoption,* carried through every Period of the Republic, led the Way to its final *Ruin*.

For altho' in the early Periods, when Manners were simple, and concurrent Principles were strong, this Spirit of *Adoption* was confined to Customs that were *better* than their own; yet in the succeeding Pe[74]riods, when Manners grew more relaxed, and Principles were weakened, the same Spirit of *Adoption* opened a Door for the Admission of *Customs* that were *pernicious*.

---

* Grandeur, &c. C. i. ii.[39]

38. Cf. Gibbon on the proximate cause of the decline of the Roman state: "The rise of a city, which swelled into an empire, may deserve, as a singular prodigy, the reflection of a philosophic mind. But the decline of Rome was the natural and inevitable effect of immoderate greatness. Prosperity ripened the principle of decay; the causes of destruction multiplied with the extent of conquest; and as soon as time or accident had removed the artificial supports, the stupendous fabric yielded to the pressure of its own weight. The story of its ruin is simple and obvious; and instead of inquiring *why* the Roman empire was destroyed, we should rather be surprised that it had subsisted so long" (Gibbon, *Decline and Fall*, vol. II, p. 509). It is however a *topos* with a long pedigree: cf. Lucan, *Pharsalia*, I.67–81; Filmer, *Patriarcha*, p. 26; and Harrington, *Oceana*, in Pocock, *Harrington*, p. 320.

39. A free translation of remarks at the beginning of chapter I and the end of chapter II of Montesquieu's *Considérations sur les causes de la grandeur des Romains, et de leur decadence* (1734): "on doit remarquer que ce qui a le plus contribué à rendre les Romains les maîtres du Monde, c'est qu'ayant combattu successivement contre tous les Peuples, ils ont toujours renoncé à leurs usages si-tôt qu'ils en ont trouvé de meilleurs"; "Si quelque Nation eut de la nature ou de son institution quelque avantage particulier, ils en firent d'abord usage" (Montesquieu, *Considérations*, pp. 90 and 104).

Thus the Admission of *Change*, which in the virtuous Ages led to the *Greatness*, in succeeding Times brought on the *Destruction* of the Republic.

The sagacious Romans soon found the Consequences of this Defect: They saw, that through a Want of original, *preventive*, and salutary Institutions, bad Manners were creeping insensibly on the State. Hence the Creation of the *Censors* had its Rise: An Office, which immediately took Cognizance of the Manners of the *Citizens*.

But this high Office was ineffectual in its End; because it had not Power universally to *prevent, but* only in Part to *remedy* the Evil. Hence, while *particular* and *detected Offences* only, could be punished by the *Censor,* the *Hearts* and *Manners* of the People were laid open to a *general Cor*[75]*ruption*, from the fatal Principle of *Novelty* and *Adoption*.

The Danger arising from this Principle manifestly increased with the increasing Empire: That *Identity* and *Integrity* of Manners and Principles, which is the Soul and Security of every free State, gave Way to Manners and Principles wholly *dissimilar*. New Maxims of Life, new Principles of Religion and Irreligion, of Honour and Dishonour, of Right and Wrong, picked up indiscriminately among the Nations which they conquered, by Degrees infused themselves into the Heads and Hearts of the *Roman* Citizens.

Here, then, we see the original Foundation of all the Misery and Ruin which ensued. On the Conquest of the *luxurious, immoral,* and *unprincipled* Tribes of Greece, the *Romans*, having no *preventive Remedy* in the Essence of their State, of Course *adopted* the *Luxury,* the *Immoralities,* the *Irreligion,* of the conquered People. [76]

"It seems to me (says the excellent Montesquieu) that the *Epicurean* Sect, which made its Way into Rome towards the Close of the Republic, contributed much to corrupt the Hearts of the *Romans*. The *Greeks* had been infatuated with it before them; accordingly, they were sooner corrupt. Polybius tells us, that in His Time, no *Greek* could be trusted, on the Security of his Oath; whereas, a *Roman* was inevitably bound by it."*—He adds, "Cyneas having discoursed on the *Epicurean* System

* Grandeur, &c. C. x.

at the Table of Pyrrhus, Fabricius wished that all the Enemies of Rome might hold the *Principles* of *such a Sect.*"*

Thus, as in the early Periods of the Commonwealth, they had adopted the *Virtues,* in the later Times they assumed the *Vices* of the conquered Nations. Thus, by unperceived Gradations, the same Prin[77]ciple, "The Admission of *Change,* first led to the *Greatness,* and then to the *Ruin* of the Republic."

All the particular Consequences that followed, were *occasional* and *inevitable.* The Rapacity, the Factions, the civil Wars; the enormous Profligacy of Individuals, the horrible Calamities of the State;—All these are finely pursued by Montesquieu; and were no more than the natural and incidental Effects of this general Cause, "The Loss of Manners and Principles."

Hence, the *Progress* and *Retreat* of the *Roman Power* resembled the *Flow* and the *Ebb* of a vast Ocean; which, rowzed from its Bed by central Concussions, *overwhelmed* and *forsook* the *Earth.*[41] [78]

SECT. X

How far these Facts can properly be apply'd to the political State of Great Britain

Though the Study of History be often instructive and useful, yet, in one Respect, it becomes the Source of frequent Error, even when it is written with Impartiality and Truth. This ariseth from a mistaken Application of historical Facts. Errors of this Kind are apt to creep into all Reasonings,

---

* Ib.[40]

40. A translation of the opening paragraph and note (a) of chapter X of Montesquieu's *Considérations sur les causes de la grandeur des Romains, et de leur decadence* (1734) (Montesquieu, *Considérations,* p. 160).

41. Perhaps informed by a memory of the image used by Montesquieu to evoke the collapse of the Roman empire: "Je n'ai pas le courage de parler des miseres qui suivirent, je dirai seulement que sous les derniers Empereurs, l'Empire réduit aux Fauxbourgs de Constantinople finit comme le Rhin qui n'est plus qu'un ruisseau lorsqu'il se perd dans l'Ocean"; "I have not the heart to speak of the miseries which ensued, I will say only that under the last Emperors the Empire, reduced to the suburbs of Constantinople, ended like the Rhine, which is no more than a stream when it loses itself in the ocean" (Montesquieu, *Considérations,* p. 285).

on every Subject, where Men and Manners are concerned: But they are liable to infect *political* Reasonings, above all others.

As the political Interests of Men form the principal Subject of History, the Reasoner on this Subject hath Recourse to Facts, as the best Support of his Argument. Yet, the Politician seems, of all others, most liable to be mistaken in the Application of History to his own [79] Purpose; because the political Connexions and Interests of Men are, above all others, *complicated* and *various*.

Hence, as no two political Constitutions were ever the *same* in *all* their Circumstances, though *similar* in *many*; so, all Arguments drawn from a *partial* Resemblance, must be inadequate and inconclusive; unless when it appears, that no other Circumstances took Place, by which That *partial* Resemblance might be *counteracted*, and its Effects destroyed.

Yet, it hath been a Practice too common among political Reasoners, from a *partial* Resemblance between two States, to infer a *total* one; and because they have been *like* in *some* Respects, to draw Conclusions, as if they had been *like* in *all*.

Much Caution, therefore, is necessary, in the Application of historical Facts: Without This, we shall run into perpetual Error. Let us, then, remark some of the most *essential* Circumstances, in which the Constitution of the *British* State [80] differs from those of SPARTA, ATHENS, and ROME; and then draw such Conclusions, as may be consistent with these Distinctions.

1. We may lay it down as a fundamental Truth generally acknowledged, that the *political* Constitution of GREAT BRITAIN, in its *main Outline*, is *better modeled* than those of SPARTA, ATHENS, or ROME. The legislative and executive Powers are more equally balanced, and more clearly distinguished. Now, if Laws could support themselves, it would follow, that this political State must *therefore* be of *longer Duration*. But as it hath been made appear, that the Duration of free States depends not so much on their mere *Form*, as on the *Manners* and *Principles* which support them; so, nothing can be decided concerning the *Duration* of the *British* State, from its mere *external Model*.

2. The *Christian* Religion, established in BRITAIN, is, in its own Nature, far [81] superior to that of these ancient Commonwealths. The absolute Perfection and glorious Attributes of the Deity; the great Principle of

universal Charity; the particular Duties of Man to Man, thence resulting; the Sanctions of future Reward and Punishment; all these tend to purify and exalt the Soul, far beyond the Rites of ancient Paganism: For This, even in its best Forms, was ever built on the History and Examples of deify'd Men, whose Lives had often been blotted with the most flagrant Crimes; and therefore, could never exalt the Heart of Man, beyond this weak Principle of Elevation.—But as the *Power* of a *Religion* depends, not only on its *excellent Genius*, but on its being *effectually impressed* on the Mind; so, no Consequence can be justly drawn, from the mere *un-apply'd* Excellence of its Nature.

3. That *Self-Consistence*, and perfect *Unity* of Parts which distinguished the Republic of SPARTA, cannot be expected nor [82] found in that of BRITAIN. For the first was the entire Work of a single Legislator, struck out at one Heat; all its Institutions conspiring to one End, and centering (like the Radii of a Circle) in one single Point: To This, the outward Form of Government, the internal State of Education, of Religion, Manners and Principles, were uniformly subordinate. But at the Time of the *Revolution,*[42] which was the first Aera of BRITAIN's Freedom, many prior Institutions and Establishments, both in Religion and Policy, Manners and Principles, had taken Place: These had been formed on the fortuitous Events of Time; and had resulted from a Variety of contending Parties; of *Power,* fluctuating at different Periods, between the *Kings,* the *Nobles,* the *Priesthood,* and the *People.* All these it was impossible for human Art to remove and new-model, without shaking the State to its Foundations: Hence, though the Form of the *British* Constitution, civil and religious, be of [83] unrivaled Excellence; yet in its very Birth it came attended with unalterable Weakness.—It wanted that general Self-Consistence, that entire Unity of Parts, as well as of established Habits, Manners and Principles, suited to the Genius of the State, which was the very Spirit and Support of the *Spartan* Commonwealth. In this Circumstance, it appears likewise inferior to the *Roman* Commonwealth; yet, perhaps, superior to that of *Athens.*

4. The *British* System of Polity and Religion, perfect in its leading Parts, but imperfectly united and supported, is not upheld in its native Power

42. I.e., 1688.

(like that of SPARTA) by correspondent and effectual Rules of Education. The Fundamental Laws of our Country, the Principles and Duties of Christianity, are indeed occasionally explained and taught, in a certain Manner and Degree: But it is in the Power of every Private Man to educate his Child, not only without a Reverence for These, but in an absolute Contempt [84] of them. It is much in every Parent's Option, whether he will impress his Childrens Hearts with such Habits and Principles as accord to the Genius of the State, or with Impunity suffer them to contract such Manners and Opinions as tend to its Dissolution. A Circumstance pregnant with Danger to this free State: For hence, Manners and Principles, its chief Support, are liable to be incurably perverted in the Heart, at that Time of Life, in which alone they can be effectually impressed.

5. In the important Circumstance of "the Admission of *Change*," or the "Principle of *Adoption*," the *British* Constitution is contrary to That of SPARTA; and nearly on a Level with Those of ATHENS and ROME.— Foreign Commerce, foreign Travel, new Manners, new Principles, new Modes of Dress, of Amusement, of Luxury, are here adopted with a Degree of Avidity almost unbounded.—Happy would the Writer esteem his [85] Labours; if this Principle, which *in some Respects* hath tended so much to the *Improvement* of his Country, could in any Degree be checked by his weak Admonitions, from *degenerating* into a *Cause* of its *Destruction*.

6. The last Circumstance of Note, here to be remarked, is "The Difference of Character among the several *Ranks* of the Community in these ancient free States, and That of *Britain*."

In Point of *Knowledge* and *Ability*, the Difference was great between the *Nobles* and the *People*, in these ancient States: In BRITAIN, the *Nobles* and the *People* (in their *legislative* Capacity) are fairly on a *Level*. When ALCIBIADES addressed the legislative Body of the *Athenian* People, he addressed *Coblers, Brasiers, Tanners, Tent-Makers*. When the People of ROME retired in Discontent to the sacred Mountain, they were appeased by the Fable of the *Belly, Head*, and *Hands*.[43] A *Lord* of Parliament would make but a sorry Fi[86]gure, who should come armed with *such* an *Apologue*, for the *Conviction* of a *British* House of *Commons*.

43. Cf. Livy, II.xxxii.8–12, and Plutarch, "Coriolanus," VI.2–4.

Again: In each of these ancient Republics, the collective Body of the *People* were much of one uniform Character; being Inhabitants of the same City, and nearly on a Level with Respect to Employment and Property. In ATHENS, they were all *Artisans* or *Tradesmen:* In SPARTA and ROME, they were all *Soldiers.* A low Degree of Knowledge was their general Lot: For much Knowledge can only be acquired by much Leisure; which their Occupations did not allow. The People of SPARTA were intentionally virtuous: Those of ATHENS were corrupt: Those of ROME were of a mixed Character. As these free States voted not by Representatives, the Presence of the People was necessary, in all Decisions of a public Nature: Hence, such a People from their Ignorance, Wants, collective Presence, and Pride of Power, must ever and suddenly be [87] swayed by the Eloquence of public Demagogues.

But the *collective* Body of the People of BRITAIN are of a Nature and Character less uniform, and essentially different. They may properly be divided into two Classes; "The *People* of the *Kingdom;*" and "the *Populace* of its *Cities.*"

The *Populace* of its *Cities* resemble Those of ATHENS in most Things; except only, that they are not possessed of the *legislative Power.* For the *People* of ATHENS were "a Body of *Labourers* and *Mechanics,* who earned their Bread with the Sweat of their Brows; too generally ignorant and ill-educated; too generally profligate in Manners, and void of Principle."

But the *People* of this *Kingdom,* in their *collective* Body, are upon the Whole, of a quite different Character. For under this Title are properly comprehended "all Those who send Representatives for the Counties to Parliament." This Catalogue [88] will include the landed *Gentry,* the beneficed Country *Clergy,* many of the more considerable *Merchants* and Men in *Trade,* the substantial and industrious *Freeholders* or *Yeomen:* A collective Body of Men, with all their incidental Failings, as *different* in Character from the *Populace* of any great *City,* as the *Air* of RICHMOND HILL from that of BILLINGSGATE or WAPPING.[44]

44. Respectively, a fashionable residential area in the west of London; an area in the east end of the city associated with the fish trade, and thence, by association, with coarse manners and language; and an impoverished area in the docklands to the east of the city.

SECT. XI

Of the general State of Manners and Principles, about the Time of the Revolution

At this famed Period, it is evident, that the Manners and Principles of the Nation did, upon the Whole, tend to the Establishment of *Liberty;* otherwise, Liberty had not been established. This Revolution was perhaps the noblest public *Reform* that ever was made in any State: And such a Reform, nothing but the *Pre*[89]*valence* of *upright Manners* and *Principles* could have *effected*.

The *religious* Principle of *Protestant Christianity* seems to have taken the Lead, even of the Love of civil Freedom. The Dread of *Popery* was, at least, equal to That of *arbitrary Power:* The national *Honour* and *Conscience* (on the whole) coincided with, and confirmed the *Christian* Principle: These three united Powers raised Liberty to the brightest Throne she ever sat on: A Throne which nothing but their *Contraries* can *shake*.

Yet notwithstanding the unrivaled Excellence of this civil and religious Establishment, there could be little Hope of its immediate and perfect Efficacy. Declaimers may express their Wonder, that a System so perfect should not at once attain its End: But they who take a nearer View of the Manners and Principles of those Times, will rather say, that the Tumults and Dissentions which instantly arose,[45] were in their own Nature *inevitable*. [90]

The Manners of the Times, tho' in the Main favourable to Liberty, were mixed with a gross Alloy of *private Licentiousness:* And hence, factious Measures of Course arose, from the Prospect of Power or Gain.* The preceding Age had caught a strong Tincture of *Vice,* from the prevalent Example of a debauched Court.[47] The *Education* of Children was

---

* See *Estimate,* V. i. Part 2.[46]

45. The parliaments of the 1690s, until at least the Treaty of Ryswick in 1697, were "peculiarly difficult" (J. P. Kenyon, *Stuart England* [Harmondsworth: Penguin Books, 1978], p. 270).

46. Cf. above, pp. 286–92.

47. That of the reign of Charles II (1660–85).

still left in an *imperfect* State: This great Revolution having confined itself
to the Reform of *public* Institutions; without ascending to the first great
Fountain of political Security, "the private and effectual Formation of the
infant Mind."

The *religious* Principle, though chiefly consonant with the new Constitution, and indeed its leading Support, was in *Part* at *Variance* with
it.—A numerous Body of *Papists* held a whole System of Principles diametrically opposite to its most essential Dictates.—Another Body of
Pro[91]testant *Jacobites* were at War with the Principles of the State: For
they held an hereditary and unalienable Right of Kings, founded on certain *mistaken* Passages of the sacred Scriptures.—A third Body of Men,[48]
though they allowed the Necessity and Justice of the Revolution, on the
Principle of an *Abdication,* yet still retained an Opinion at Variance with
the State: They asserted an *independent Hierarchy,* vindicated a religious
Intolerance, and on some misconstrued Passages of Scripture, affirmed
the Duty of a *passive Obedience* without Limitation.—A fourth Body was
That of some bigoted *Dissenters,* who not content with a religious Toleration which had been justly granted them, aimed, on a mistaken Principle
of Religion, to erect their own System upon the Ruins of the established
Church.—All these Parties held *religious Principles* at *Variance* with the
Laws of *Freedom.* [92]

The Principle of *Honour,* tho' in many, and great Instances, co-operating
with that of Religion; yet when not founded on it, was often at *Variance* with it. This Principle, as it hath appeared in modern Times, was in
its Origin chiefly *Military.* Hence it hath generally taken Cognizance of
Actions, not as they are *just* or *unjust,* but merely as they are *splendid* or
mean, brave or *cowardly:* Thus, it overlooks all Laws, both human and divine: Hence unbounded Contempt of Enemies, furious Party-Rage, unlimited Resentment and Revenge, *were* and still *are* its favourite Dictates.
Thus it hath come to pass, that Honour often forbids what Religion approves; and approves what Religion forbids. This uncontrouled and dangerous Principle mixed itself with the licentious Manners of the Times:

48. The non-jurors, so called because they refused to take the oath of allegiance
to William and Mary.

Hence, Attachments, Resentments, and Party-Rage, arose and were persisted in, essentially contradictory to the Principles of Freedom. [93]

Consonant with what hath been above delivered, the Principle of *Conscience* did not *correct*, but *followed* one or other of these various Principles, according to their Predominance and Power. And *These* being incurably discordant among themselves, the national Ideas of Right and Wrong, Just and Unjust, which were formed on *These*, could not but prove themselves of the like *motley* and *disagreeing* Complexion.

Here, then, we behold the natural and unavoidable Source of all the Dissentions that disgraced the Reigns of King WILLIAM and Queen ANNE.[49] And while some affect to wonder, how so generous a System of Religion and Polity, so noble a Constitution in Church and State, could fail to produce private Virtue and public Happiness; we now obtain an additional Proof of the irresistable Power of *pre-established Manners* and *Principles*, when at *Variance* with the *Laws* of *Freedom:* We may see, even to Demonstration, [94] that the *Animosities* of *Those Times* were *not incidental*, but *inevitable*.

SECT. XII

Of the Changes in Manners and Principles, through the succeeding Times

The Accession of GEORGE the First[50] seemed the Aera of perfect Freedom. And if an excellent King, at the Head of an unrivaled Constitution, could have secured Liberty; it had now been fixed on immoveable Foundations.

The Alloy of *licentious Manners* and *contradictory Principles* which had tarnished the preceding Reign, still maintained their Influence: But the declared and zealous Advocates for Liberty now assumed the Reins of Power, and began more effectually to combat those *false Principles* which were at *Enmity* with the *State*. [95]

Would to God, these intentional Friends of public Liberty had been as much the Friends of private Virtue and Religion! They would not, then,

49. I.e., the period 1688–1714.
50. 1714.

have undermined the Foundations, while they were building the Super-structure of civil Freedom.

The Seeds of Irreligion had for some Time been privately fermenting: But they did not break forth into open Growth till about this Period.— 'Tis remarkable, that BURNET,* enumerating the Dangers by which the State was threatened in the Year 1708, makes no Mention of *Irreligion,* as an Evil worth being obviated.[51] But soon after, this Pestilence came on, with a terrible Swiftness and Malignity.

The slavish Principle of absolute *Non-Resistance,* and an *independent Hierarchy,* were still prevalent in Part, especially among the *Clergy.* To combat *these,* and expose them to the public Contempt, certain Writers were encouraged by Those [96] in Power. A vigorous and effectual Attack was made on the Advocates for Despotism. But in their Zeal against Tyranny, these Writers supplanted Freedom.

They assailed *Superstition* with such Weapons as destroyed *Religion:* They opposed *Intolerance* by Arguments and Ridicule which tended to sweep away all public *Establishments:* While they only aimed (perhaps) to contend for *Freedom* of *Thought,* they unwarily sapped the Foundation of all salutary *Principles.*[†]

CATO's *Letters,* and the *Independent Whig,*[53] among other Tracts of less Note, seem palpable Instances of this Truth: The one was written in

---

* Conclusion of his History.

† See the Div. Leg. of Moses. Dedication Vol. ii. p. 6, &c.[52]

51. Gilbert Burnet (1643–1715); latitudinarian and Whig; adviser to William of Orange, later William III; bishop of Salisbury, 1689. His *History of My Own Times* was published posthumously in two volumes (1724, 1734). In the "Conclusion" to the History he states that his purpose in writing was "to give such a Discovery of Errors in Government, and of the Excesses and Follies of Parties, as may make the next Age wiser, by what I may tell them of the last" (Burnet, *History,* vol. II, p. 633). On the subject of religion, Burnet indeed sees danger arising, but from the direction of dogmatism and inflexible ecclesiastical discipline rather than from that of excessive free-thinking.

52. In the "Preface" to vol. II of *The Divine Legation of Moses* (1738) William Warburton relates a particular attack on vol. I in which the English clergy were "represented as so horribly corrupt, that *a great many of them were grown settled Infidels*" (p. vi).

53. Both early eighteenth-century periodicals.

Defence of *civil,* the other, of *religious* Liberty. Yet both tended, in their general Tenour, to relax those Principles by which alone Freedom, either civil or religious, can be sustained: By their intemperate Insults on religious Institutions; by their public and [97] avowed Contempt of all Opinions, Principles, (or, if you please) Prejudices, instilled into the infant Mind, as the necessary Regulators of human Conduct: By exalting unaided human Reason, far beyond the Rank she holds in Nature: By debasing all those Assistances which the Wisdom of Ages had prescribed and consecrated, as the necessary Means of correcting her vague and wandering Dictates.

While These Authors made this ill-judged, and perhaps undesigned Attack, on the Foundations of civil Liberty; others made a still bolder and more fatal Inroad; and opened a wider Door for *Licentiousness,* by an Attack on *Christianity* itself.

In this List of Enemies to their Country, it must be a Mortification to every Friend of Virtue and Liberty, to find the noble Author of the *Characteristics.*[54] His Morals were unblemished, his Love of Virtue and Freedom indisputable: But by confounding two Things, which he saw *accidently united,* though in their Nature [98] *essentially distinguished,* he polluted his *Arguments* against *Intolerance,* with the grossest *Buffoonries* on *Christianity.*

There is no Doubt, but that the current Reasonings of the Times had brought him to a Habit of Belief, that all This was harmless Pastime. To this Purpose he seems to speak himself. "'Tis certain, that in Matters of Learning and Philosophy, the Practice of *pulling down* is *pleasanter,* and affords more *Entertainment,* than that of *building* and *setting up.*—In the literate warring World, the *springing* of *Mines,* the *blowing up* of Towers, Bastions, and Ramparts of Philosophy, with *Systems, Hypotheses, Opinions,* and *Doctrines* into the Air, is a *Spectacle* of all other the most naturally *rejoicing.*"*

These intemperate Sallies of Gaiety may serve as a Comment on the Passage already cited from CATO's *Letters.*[56] They are a clear and

---

* Miscell. iii. Chap. 1.[55]

54. Anthony Ashley Cooper (1671–1713), 3rd earl of Shaftesbury; cf. above, p. 25, n. 3.

55. Shaftesbury, *Characteristicks,* vol. III, p. 83.

56. Cf. above, pp. 506–7.

concurrent Indication of the [99] ruling Principle of the Times; when *Opinions* and *Doctrines* began to be derided as Things *indifferent.* The noble Writer was naturally led to embrace this growing Error of the Times, by a too flattering Opinion which he had imbibed concerning unassisted human Nature; as being sufficient of itself to establish the unerring Practice of Virtue, unless beforehand sophisticated by servile Institutions.

The noble Writer, indeed, attempts a Vindication of this licentious Conduct, by an Appeal to the Practice of ancient GREECE and ROME. There, he tells us, "*Philosophy* had a free Course, and was permitted as a *Balance* against *Superstition.* And while some Sects, such as the *Pythagorean* and latter *Platonic,* joined in with the Superstition and Enthusiasm of the Times; the EPICUREAN, the *Academic,* and *others,* were allowed to use all the Force of *Wit* and *Raillery* against it."*—This hath a plau[100]sible Appearance: Yet I am perswaded, the noble Author would have looked grave, had he been put in Mind of the Remark which FABRICIUS made on the *Epicurean* Sect, "that he wished *such Principles* to all the *Enemies* of ROME."† Or had he recollected, that when the *irreligious* System of EPICURUS prevailed in GREECE and ROME, these *unprincipled* and *profligate* States were on the *Eve* of their *Destruction.*

Soon after the Author of the *Characteristics,* another more dissolute Writer appeared on the public Stage. I mean, the Author of "*The Fable of the Bees.*"⁵⁹ This Gentleman, as hath been observed above, leveled his Artillery on the whole Fabric of *Morals* and *Religion.* His System was diametrically opposite to that of Lord SHAFTESBURY: The one was founded on the *unaided Excellence,* the other on the *incurable Depravity* of *human Nature.* But now the vagrant Spirit of Irreligion [101] was Abroad; and the most inconsistent Productions were greedily swallowed, provided only they *disgraced* CHRISTIANITY.

The Avidity with which these Compositions were received, soon emboldened a succeeding Writer, to make a formal Attack on the Religion

---

* Letter on Enthusiasm.⁵⁷
† See above, p. 76.⁵⁸
57. Shaftesbury, *Characteristicks,* vol. I, p. 12.
58. Cf. above, p. 533 and n. 40.
59. Bernard Mandeville (1670–1733); cf. above, p. 122, n. 55.

of his Country: *Christianity as old as the Creation*[60] now appeared: In which the Gospel was grosly misrepresented, insulted, and disgraced; and in Compliance with the ruling Malady of the Times, that *poor* and *sickly* Creature, "unassisted *Human Reason*," was vainly exalted to the *Throne* of Eternal Truth!

Other inferior Workmen in this patriot Amusement of blowing up the Religion of their Country, such as Woolston, and Morgan,[61] I pass unnoticed.[62]

In a succeeding Period, and down to the present Time, the Evil hath increased, and been compleated. For now, not only *revealed* but *natural* Religion hath been publicly attacked, in the Writings [102] of Lord Bolingbroke: An Author who stands convicted of designed Profligacy, even on his own Confession. "Some Men there are, *the Pests of Society I think them,* who pretend a great Regard to Religion in general, but who take every Opportunity of declaiming publicly against that System of Religion, or at least that Church Establishment, which is received in Britain."*—You See, this patriot Writer proclaims his Abhorrence even of Those who assault the *Out-Works* of Religion: And then, with Modesty unparallel'd, proceeds to blow up the *Citadel.*

The last of these patriot Worthies, by which the present Age stands distinguished, is the Author of "Essays philosophical and moral:"[64] Who,

---

* Dissert. on Parties. Let. xii.[63]

60. A work published in 1730 by Matthew Tindal (1657–1733); cf. above, p. 184, n. 44.

61. Thomas Woolston (1668–1733); fellow of Sidney Sussex College, Cambridge; religious controversialist, mystic, and lunatic. Thomas Morgan, see above, p. 184, n. 44.

62. A dismissive gesture which anticipates Burke's more famous expression of contempt for the freethinkers of the late-seventeenth and early-eighteenth centuries: "Who, born within the last forty years, has read one word of Collins, and Toland, and Tindal, and Chubb, and Morgan, and that whole race who called themselves Freethinkers? Who now reads Bolingbroke? Who ever read him through? Ask the booksellers of London what is become of all these lights of the world" (Burke, *Reflections*, p. 140).

63. Bolingbroke, *A Dissertation upon Parties*, second edition (1735), p. 148.

64. David Hume (1711–76), whose *Essays, Moral and Political* had first been published in two volumes in 1741 and 1742.

disdaining the vulgar Practice of a particular Attack, *undermines* all the *Foundations* of *Religion, revealed* and *natural;* and with a Pen truly *Epicurean,*[65] dissolves at once all [103] the *Fears* of the *Guilty,* the *Comforts* of the *Afflicted,* and the *Hopes* of the *Virtuous.*

Such, then, hath been the Progress of this public Evil; which hath proceeded almost without *Cognizance* from the Magistrate: Instead of *That,* it is well known, that some of these public Enemies of their Country and Mankind were formerly pensioned, and others privately encouraged by Those in Power. How This came to pass, and aggravated the growing Evil, it is now necessary to point out.

We have seen above, that a Foundation was laid for this, in an ill-conducted Opposition to the Enemies of Freedom. They who were employed to sweep away *false Principles,* imprudently struck at *all Principles.*

But beyond This, a famous Minister[66] assumed, and long held the Reins of Power. There seems not the least Foundation for the Charge laid against him by his Enemies, "That his Design was to inslave his Country." Neither had he any [104] natural Inclination to corrupt Practices: Yet he rather chose to rule by These, than to resign his Power. Nay, perhaps he thought this corrupt System the only one, which, under the Circumstances of Those Times, could support that illustrious Family,[67] which was brought in, as the happy Support of Liberty. Farther, perhaps, he judged This the only possible Expedient for prolonging a *Peace,* which He thought *necessary,* till Time should wear out the false Principles, on which the expelled Family still held their Influence in the Minds of the

---

65. Although Hume includes an essay entitled "The Epicurean" among the four he devotes to the different schools of ancient philosophy, the consensus among scholars is that Hume's own philosophy lies closest to that of "The Sceptic" (Hume, *Essays,* pp. 138–80; cf. Harris, *Hume,* pp. 191–95). However, John Robertson has recently argued that Hume's thought, and indeed Enlightenment thought more generally in its commitment to the securing of human well-being in this world, rests upon moderate Epicurean foundations (Robertson, *Enlightenment,* pp. 316–24). See also James A. Harris, "The Epicurean in Hume," in Neven Leddy and Avi S. Lifschitz (eds.), *Epicurus in the Enlightenment* (Oxford: Voltaire Foundation, 2009), pp. 161–81.

66. Sir Robert Walpole; cf. above, p. 302, n. 25.

67. I.e., the House of Hanover.

People.—From *some* or *all* of these Motives, He not only *gave Way* to Corruption, but *encouraged* it. To this End, *Religion* was *discountenanced:* And *Christian Principle,* which would have been the firmest *Friend* of *Liberty,* was *discarded,* as the *Enemy* of *Corruption.*

In the mean Time, *Trade, Wealth,* and *Luxury* increased: These, in their *Extreme,* having an unalterable Tendency [105] to a Dissolution of Manners and Principles, went Hand in Hand with the Progress of Corruption; which, in its most improved State, this mistaken Minister left, as a lasting Legacy to his Country.*

The Effects of this established System of Corruption did not immediately appear: But about the Year fifty-seven, they came to their *Crisis;* advancing with the Appearances even of *public Ruin.*

That powerful Correctress, NECESSITY, gave a *temporary Union* to all Parties, and a *temporary Restoration* to the *State.*† But from the Deduction of Causes here given, it was natural to expect, that as soon as *Danger* ceased, *Faction* would arise.

It follows also, that it must arise on Foundations widely different from Those in the Reigns of WILLIAM and ANNE. For the Dissentions of these *past* Times were chiefly founded in *false Principles:* [106] Those of the *present* Age, on a *Want of Principle.*

For the false Principles which disgraced the Protestants of the last Age, are vanished. The mistaken Interpretations of Scripture, on which the *Jacobite,* the *Tory,* the *bigoted Dissenter,* founded their various Pretensions and Attempts, are *now* held in general Derision: A Preacher, of whatever religious Congregation, who should *now* advance these obsolete State-Heterodoxies, would be the Contempt of his wiser Audience.

Nay, what is more, these false Principles tending to Despotism, are generally banished, even from the Breasts of the Clergy; except only a very few of the most aged. For the Bishops being appointed by the Patrons of Liberty, have been such, as held Principles consistent with the

---

* See an Estimate, &c. Vol. ii. p. 204, &c.[68]
† See ib. Vol. i. p. the last.[69]
68. Cf. above, pp. 437–39.
69. Cf. above, pp. 343–44.

Freedom of the State: And much Caution having been required of them, and used by them, in the Appointments of their Clergy, the general Com[107]plexion of this Body hath changed from That of being the *Enemies,* to That of being the *Friends* of Freedom.

Much it were to be wished, that along with the *Tares,*[70] the *Wheat* had not also perished. But the general System of *Manners* being *relaxed* though *refined;** and *Education* still left more and more *imperfect;* the Principle of *Religion* being unhappily *destroyed* among certain Ranks, and *weakened* among *others;*†—That of *Honour* being thus left to its own *false* and *fantastic* Dictates;‡—and *Conscience* naturally following the *Whims* of its *untutored* Parent;—*Licentiousness* and *Faction,* founded on a *Want* of *Principle,* cannot but arise, and stand among the "*leading Characters* of the *present Times.*" [108]

SECT. XIII

Among what Ranks, Licentiousness and Faction may most probably be expected

Though this Want of Principle must naturally infect every Rank of Men, in a certain Degree; yet some Ranks stand more exposed to it than others.

And, that we may give as little Offence as possible, while we speak the Truth; let it be observed, that all Orders of Men being born with an equal Tendency to Virtue or Vice; their adopting the One, or falling into the Other, depends chiefly on the Temptations to which their *Rank* exposes them.

Let us consider the Temptations to Licentiousness and Faction, to which the *leading Ranks* stand exposed.

Wealth and Power give Opportunities of Indulgence; Indulgence naturally inflames Appetite.—Flattery awakens contempt; and Contempt

---

* See the Estimate, Part i.[71]

† Ib.[72]

‡ Ib.[73]

70. Matthew 13:24–30.

71. Cf. above, pp. 259–82.

72. Cf. above, pp. 259–82.

73. Cf. above, pp. 259–82.

weakens the Fear [109] of Offence or Shame.—Laws which bind little Men, are often too weak for Great ones.—Leisure, when not dignify'd by suitable Accomplishments, ends in Idleness; and Idleness is the Parent and the Nurse of licentious Folly. To such Temptations do the *Great* stand exposed, in the important Article of *Manners*.

With Respect to the *Principle* of *Religion,* their present Situation is no less unfavourable. Dissolute Opinions flatter their disordered Passions: Nor will they ever want Sycophants, to present this alluring Bait to their Desires.—The Maxims of Irreligion are now so generally established among Those with whom the young Men of Fashion converse, that they must be peculiarly fortunate, if they escape the *Infection.* Wherever This Taint is given, the Principles of *Honour* and *Conscience* become vague and ineffectual, if considered as the Supports of Liberty. Certain *Delicacies* of *personal* Conduct they may produce; but can never rise to an [110] unbiassed and steady Prosecution of the *public Welfare.*

Another Circumstance unfavourable to the *public* Virtue of the higher Ranks presents itself. Their Situation leads them to *expect,* and to *claim,* the great and *lucrative Offices* of the State. I need not *here* point out, how strongly This tends to betray them into the Extremes of selfish Views, Ambition, Party-Rage, Licentiousness, and Faction.*

Add to all these Considerations, their frequent and long-continued Meetings in the Capital: A Circumstance which, from the powerful Effects of *free Communication,* cannot but inflame all these Causes of political Dissention.

If we next examine the State of the *Populace* of the great Cities, we shall find that Their Situation naturally exposes them to such Temptations as lead to factious Conduct, when not early fortify'd by a virtuous Education. They [111] are often urged by *Want;* of which, *Discontent* and *Envy* are the inevitable Effects. They are let loose to every Impulse of Appetite, by frequent Opportunity and Secrecy of Action: They are tempted by wicked Examples; inflamed by evil Communication and intoxicating Liquors: And though the industrious Mechanic may sometimes escape the

* See the Estimate, &c. Vol. i. Part 2.[74]
74. Cf. above, pp. 285–313.

Infection; yet the Life of the *uninstructed Poor* in great Cities, is too commonly a horrid Compound of Riot and Distress, Rapacity and Thieving, Prostitution and Robbery, Wickedness and Despair.

Now if this Body of Men be indeed, what Candour itself cannot deny, "too generally ignorant and ill-educated; too generally profligate in Manners, and void of Principle"; it follows, that like the *Athenian Populace* of old, they must be liable to the *Seduction* of artful Men; the ready *Tools* of every unprincipled *Leader*, who may choose to misguide them, to the Ends of *Licentiousness* and *Faction*. [112]

But "*The* People *of* Great Britain, as above distinguished,* are of a Character essentially different from both These. The landed *Gentry*, the Country *Clergy*, the more considerable *Merchants* and Men in Trade, the substantial and industrious *Freeholders* and *Yeomen*," possess a *middle* State of Life, which guards them from many of those Temptations that surround the *higher* and the *lower* Ranks. Their *imaginary* Wants are *fewer* than those of the *Great:* Their *real* Wants are *fewer* than those of the *Poor:* Hence Their Appetites are less inflamed to Evil.—Their Education generally seconds this happy Situation, in a certain Degree: Though imperfect, it is commonly more consistent with the main Outlines of public Law, than that of the superior or inferior Ranks.—Their Principles of Religion confirm this Education: They stand not generally exposed to the Infection of dissolute Opinions. [113] Their Sentiments of *Honour* and *Conscience* are most commonly built on the *Doctrines* of *Christianity*.—Their *Numbers* and their *Station* conspire to *exclude* them from a *general Claim* to the lucrative Offices of the State. Their *collective Knowledge* is of sufficient Reach to prevent their *general Seduction* to the Purposes of *Licentiousness:* Their *Dispersion*, and rural Life, prevent those continued and unrestrained Communications, which are alike fatal to private and public Virtue.

Let not the Writer be misunderstood. There are Examples of Integrity and Dishonour, of Virtue and Vice, among all Degrees of Men. He only points out the Circumstances which naturally tend, upon the Whole, to form the several Ranks into these distinct Characters.

* See p. 87, 88.[75]
75. Cf. above, p. 537.

From this View of the several Ranks, it follows, that although "The *People* of this Kingdom" must inevitably partake of the various Manners and Principles of the *Great* and the *Populace*, with which [114] they at Times communicate; though they be subject to the common Failings of Men, and to the *incidental* Inroads of Licentiousness from *higher* and *lower* Life;—yet upon the Whole, and considered as one *collective Body*, they stand comparatively clear of many Temptations to Vice; and therefore must naturally be least exposed to the Influence of *Licentiousness* and *Faction*.

One Consequence, arising from their *Dispersion*, must not pass unnoticed. It not only prevents the general Depravation of their Manners and Principles, but likewise prevents their *uniting* in large *Bodies*, upon all *slight* Occasions. Hence, though they are apt to *doubt*, nay to be *alarmed*, on the *factious Clamours* of the *Capital*; yet they are not rowzed into *Action*, but on *singular* and *important* Emergencies.

To conclude: They are a *great*, but *quiescent* Power; on whose *collective Knowledge* and *Integrity*, the Freedom and Fate of this Nation must *finally* depend. In [115] the last Age, through the Influence of *false Principles*, pre-established or infused, they had well-nigh shaken the Foundations of Liberty:* In the present, *these* mistaken Principles being *no more*, They are now "the firmest *Bulwark* of BRITAIN's *Freedom*."

SECT. XIV

Of the most effectual Means of detecting Licentiousness and Faction

Where Faction is founded on false *Principles*, it is easily *detected*, because it is generally *avowed*. It implies no moral *Depravity*, but only an *Error* of the Mind: And he who holds this *Error*, is not naturally *ashamed* of it, because he holds it as a *Truth*.

But where Faction is founded on Licentiousness and Want of Principle, it [116] cannot be so easily detected: For as it implies a moral Depravity, it

---

* See above, p. 91.[76]

76. A reference to the instinctive Toryism of these fractions of English society; cf. above, p. 539.

will naturally attempt to *veil* itself; and to this End, will assume the *Garb* and *Appearance* of *Freedom.*

The favourite Subject of its Clamours will be the *Misconduct* of Those who *govern.* And in a Country where Liberty is justly ranked among the greatest national Blessings, the most plausible Pretence of Faction will be, "to load the executive Power with the Charge of Despotism."

In every free State there will frequently occur certain Subjects and Measures, "of *doubtful Expediency.*" These, in the wide Field of political Contention, may justly be stiled "the *debateable Grounds.*" On these doubtful Points, even the Friends of Liberty may sometimes differ: Therefore the Patrons of Faction will naturally lay hold on these, as the most successful and effectual Means of State Distraction: Because thus they may hope to mingle [117] with, and to pass for the Friends of Freedom.

When therefore such doubtful Measures become the Subject of political Contention; it may be difficult to determine, from the mere Circumstance of *Opinion, who* are the Friends of Liberty, and *who* the Abettors of Faction: Because, in these Points, there may be an incidental Difference of Opinion, even among the Friends of Liberty themselves.

A much surer Determination may be formed on the *Manner* and *Conduct* of the *dissenting Party:* For the Friend of Liberty, having no selfish Views, will be rational, honest, equitable, in the Prosecution of his Wishes. He who is actuated by the Spirit of Licentiousness and Faction, will be irrational, dishonest, iniquitous.

Let us, then, endeavour to particularize these distinctive *Marks* or *Characters:* Thus shall we best be able to determine, "*who* are the *Friends* of *Liberty,* and *who* the *Abettors* of *Licentiousness* and *Faction.*" [118]

SECT. XV

Of the Characteristic Marks of Liberty

These which follow, are perhaps some of the clearest *Characteristics* of the Spirit of *Liberty:* By which the Friends of public Freedom, though dissentient from any Measure of Government, will be evidently distinguished.—*Each* of these Marks may seem *decisive,* even when *separately* viewed: But to do Justice to this Argument, it will be necessary to consider and *weigh* them in *Union*; because as they in Part *depend* on *each other,* they will *illustrate each other,* and at once *receive* and *give* additional *Confirmation.*

1. "The Friend of Liberty will endeavour to preserve that just Balance of divided Power, established by Law, for the Security of Freedom."—Because the *public Welfare* is the leading Object of his Wishes; and can only be effectually [119] obtained by the Preservation of such a Balance.

This will be the general Aim and End of the true Friend of Liberty: This *End* will be prosecuted by *suitable Means;* and its *Reality* will be *confirmed* and *illustrated* by these which follow.

2. "He will be attached to Measures, without respecting Men."—Because the Passions and Interests of Individuals ought to yield to the public Weal.

3. "He will be generally self-consistent, both in Speech and Action."—Because, the public Welfare being the uniform Object of his Pursuits, This can only be steadily and effectually promoted, on clear and uniform Principles.

4. "He will not attempt to inflame an ignorant Populace against their legal Governors."—Because an ignorant Populace are, in all Cases, unqualify'd to decide on the Measures of Government.

5. "His Debates, either in the Senate, or from the Press, will be void of un[120]distinguishing and injurious Imputations on any whole Bodies of Men, who may differ from him in Opinion."—Because, Truth and the public Welfare being his desired End, he will clearly see, that *others* have the same Right of *approving,* as *Himself* hath of *disapproving,* the Measures of Government.

6. "He will not industriously and indiscriminately defame the private Characters of the Individuals who differ from him in Opinion."—Because Calumny thrown on Individuals is a still more aggravated Crime, than That which is promiscuously aimed at Bodies of Men.

SECT. XVI

Of the first characteristic Mark of Licentiousness and Faction

Though we have seen, that the Patrons of Faction will attempt to mix and confound themselves with the [121] Friends of Liberty; yet, in Spite of their Pretences, they will be detected by the following characteristic Marks, which will stand in *clear Opposition* to Those of *Freedom.*

These, like the former, may seem sufficiently decisive, even when *separately* viewed: But to do Justice to this Argument, it will in the same Manner be necessary to *consider* and *weigh* them in *Union:* Because, as they in Part *depend* on *each other,* they will *illustrate each other,* and at once *receive* and *give* additional *Confirmation.*

I. "The Leaders of Faction (being naturally of the higher Ranks)* would aim to establish an *aristocratic Power;* and *inslave* both *Prince* and *People* to their own Avarice and Ambition."

Thus, if any Set of Men[78] had in *former* Times been in Power; and while in Power, had oppressed embarrassed Ma[122]jesty; had threatened the Prince with a general Resignation; had thus intimidated him to their own Purposes; had by these Means usurped the *legal Prerogatives* of the *Crown;* and apply'd them rather to the Support of their own *Influence,* than to the *public Welfare:*—

If the *legal Privileges* of the *People* had fared no better in their Hands:— If These, too, had been swallowed up, in the great Gulph of aristocratic Power:—If the Members of the lower House, while they seemed to be the free Representatives of the People, had been in Truth, a great Part of them, no more than the *commissioned Deputies* of their *respective Chiefs,* whose Sentiments they declared, and whose Interests they pursued:—

If such a Set of Men, as soon as they had lost their Influence, should now rail at the Privileges of the Crown, as the Engines of Despotism, though they had been formerly allowed by the Wisdom of the State, as the occasional Securities of Freedom:—[123]

---

* See above, Sect. xiii.[77]

77. Cf. above, pp. 547–50.

78. A reference to William Pitt the Elder (1708–78) and his followers. During the Seven Years' War, Pitt had on several occasions confronted George II with ultimatums. Between 1761 and 1766 he had been in opposition (and Brown is composing this work during that period). In 1766, however, Pitt would go to the Lords as earl of Chatham, and would form an administration that would endure until 1768, when he would be forced to resign on grounds of ill-health. In the following pages Brown attacks Pitt and his followers as factious, while implicitly praising the policies of George III and his prime minister, the earl of Bute.

If they should now absurdly magnify and exalt the Privileges of the lower House, beyond the Limits prescribed by a free Constitution:—If their Pretence should be the Vindication of the People's Rights; while their real Motive was "the *Restoration* of their own *exorbitant Power*, founded on an *expected Majority* of their own *Dependents.*"—

If this Conduct was pursued by any Set of Men, they would stand convicted of a *clear Mark* of *Licentiousness* and *Faction*.

Such would be their main *End* or *Purpose:* And this *End* would be pursued by *suitable Means:* These Means, considered in *Union,* would still farther confirm and illustrate the End they aimed at: And these Means would be such as follow. [124]

SECT. XVII

A second Mark of Licentiousness and Faction

"The Patrons of Faction would be attached to Men, to the Neglect of Measures."

If the same Men, when formerly in Power, should have obstinately adhered to each other in every public Debate and Opinion; should have execrated every Man, as the Enemy of his Country, who dissented even in the slightest Article of political Belief:—

If on any sudden Change in the Fountain of Power, a more generous System of Government should have taken Place:—If the *Sovereign* had aimed to unite all *honest Men* of *all Parties,* and had invited them to co-operate for the Welfare of their Country:—

If these Men, determined still to engross all public Power, should threaten the Sovereign (as they had effectually [125] threatened his royal Predecessor) with a general Resignation:—

If their Leaders should be taken at their Word, and unexpectedly stripped of all Power and Influence:—

If on This, the Clamours of their attendant Populace should arise;* and for the Sake of the public Tranquillity, Overtures should be made by the Prince to the Discontented:—If the *same Principle* should still

---

* See Sect. xix.

predominate, and *Demands* in Favour of *Men* should be the *leading Object* of *Accommodation:*—

If these Demands should be not only irrational in their Kind, but exorbitant and oppressive in their Degree; requiring a *general Restoration* of All the Discontented, and a *general Dismission* of all who were in Power, tho' of known Fidelity to their King and Country:—

If such should be the Conduct of any Set of Men, they would stand evidently convicted of Licentiousness and Faction. [126]

SECT. XVIII

A third Mark of Licentiousness and Faction

"The Patrons of Faction would be *self-contradictory* and *inconsistent,* not only on *different,* but on *parallel* Occasions."

Thus, if the *Exercise* of a *Privilege* should be quietly *allowed* to *one* Officer of State, and by the *same Persons* should be *clamoured against* in his *Successor:* The Persons thus *acquiescing* and *clamouring* by *Turns,* would stand convicted of a *self-contradictory* and *inconsistent* Conduct: And without deciding on the Propriety or Impropriety of the Privilege in Question, would carry upon them a clear Mark of Licentiousness and Faction.

Again, if a certain Mode of political *Influence* on *Dependents* was generally exercised among all the Ranks of a free Country:—If the same Persons already [127] characterized, should *now condemn* This as a *despotic* Measure in the *Servants* of the *Crown,* which They themselves *formerly* exercised when in *Power,* and still *continue* to exercise towards their *private Dependents:*—These Gentlemen would betray a very notable Inconsistence in their Conduct: And therefore, without any Decision on the *Rectitude* of such a general *Practice,* would stand convicted of an undeniable Mark of Licentiousness and Faction.

SECT. XIX

A fourth Mark of Licentiousness and Faction

"The Patrons of Faction would endeavour to delude and inflame an ignorant and licentious Populace against their legal Governors."

A blind and unprincipled Populace have ever been the most effectual Engines of Sedition: And above all, Those of the [128] *Capital,* being near to the grand Scene of political Contention, must ever be a ready and dangerous Engine in the Hands of Licentiousness and Faction.

But in a Nation like this, to make the *Populace* of the *Capital* a more successful Instrument of Sedition, a Degree of Art would be necessary. For it appears above, that the *People* of this *Kingdom,* and the *Populace* of its *Cities,* are of a Character essentially *opposite* to each other: That the *one* is collectively *knowing* and *upright;* the *other,* collectively *ignorant* and *immoral.**—The first Step, therefore, that *Faction* would take, as the surest Method for Success, would be to *confound* the *one* with the *other;* and dignify "the *Clamour* of the *Populace,*" by stiling it "*the* VOICE *of the* PEOPLE."

The Fury of such a Populace, thus awakened by Vanity, Vice, and Ignorance, would arise in a Variety of Shapes. [129]

If an Order of the Senate should be given for the Burning of a *Paper* legally declared seditious; such a *Populace* would be incited to rescue it from the Fire: And they who had thus incited them would boast, that it was rescued by the Hands of "*the* PEOPLE."

Every talking Demagogue, who should oppose the Measures of Government, would be artfully and indiscriminately obtruded on such an ignorant *Populace,* as a *Patriot* or a *Heroe.* And They who had thus obtruded him would boast, that he was the *Favourite* of "*the* PEOPLE."

Every distinguished Friend to the Measures of Government would be artfully obtruded on such a Populace, as the Enemy of his Country: And They who had thus obtruded him would boast, that he was the *Detestation* of "*the* PEOPLE."

Every Act of the Legislature, which contradicted the Passions or partial Interests of such a *Populace* or their *Leaders,* would be branded by them, as arbitrary [130] and oppressive: And they would boast, that it was branded by the *Voice* of "*the* PEOPLE."

If daily or periodical Papers of Intelligence were circulated from the Capital through the Nation, and These were open to the Admission of every Thing which private Pique, Passion, or Interest, might suggest; they

* See above, Sect. xiii.[79]
79. Cf. above, pp. 547–50.

would of Course become the general Repositories of popular Slander: And as *Malice* is always more eager to *accuse,* than injured *Innocence* to *defend,* these Slanders would often seem to *preponderate* in the public Ear: And hence, would be boasted by Those who raised them, as the prevailing *Voice* of "*the* PEOPLE."

Thus, *hatched* by *Licentiousness,* FACTION would attain to its *enormous Growth:* The *unprincipled* among the *Great* would form the *Head,* the *unprincipled* among the *Populace* would form the *Body,* of this *rapacious Monster.* [131]

SECT. XX

A fifth Mark of Licentiousness and Faction

"The Abettors of Faction would throw injurious and undistinguishing Imputations on every Body of Men who differed from them in Opinion."

Having thus gained an ignorant and licentious Populace, as the Trumpets of Sedition; the Patrons of Faction would leave no Means untry'd to load their Adversaries with the most envenomed Calumny.

Thus if any mistaken Principle had formerly been maintained, but was now generally forsaken and derided; a Faction could not be detected by any clearer Mark, than by its Attempt to conjure up the Ghost of this *departed* Principle, in order to alarm and terrify not only the *Populace,* but the PEOPLE. [132]

If on This Pretence, any Men should attempt to revive Animosities which Time had bury'd;—should attempt to divide and distract the Subjects of an *united* Kingdom, whose *common Welfare* depended on their *Union;*—should revile all Men without Distinction, who were born in a *certain District;*[80] and indiscriminately endeavour to exclude them from

---

80. An allusion to the anti-Scottish prejudice which was provoked by the ascendancy of John Stuart (1713–92), third earl of Bute, in the years following the accession of George III in 1760. Following the signing of the Peace of Paris, which concluded the Seven Years' War in 1763, Bute was "Maligned, insulted, and manhandled wherever he went, . . . suffered threats of assassination, incurred the wrath of brilliant polemicists such as John Wilkes and Charles Churchill, and was lampooned in over 400 prints and broadsheets" (Karl Wolfgang Schweizer, *ODNB*).

a Participation of those public Trusts, Honours, and Emoluments, to which, with the rest of their Fellow-Subjects, they might stand intitled by their *Capacity* or *Virtue:*—Who would not discover, in this *unequal Conduct,* a clear and distinctive Mark of Licentiousness and Faction?

Again: If ever there had been a Time, when All who presumed to *dissent* in any Degree from those in Power, were indiscriminately and unjustly branded with the Name of *Jacobite* or *Tory;*—and if These very Men who had bestowed such Appellations should *now* deal them as freely round, on All who *assent* to Those [133] in Power:—This were surely a clear Indication, that the Spirit of Faction were abroad.

But if, in the Course of political Revolutions, some of these Men's *former Adherents* should *now* be their *Adversaries;* and some *former Adversaries* should *now* be their *Adherents;* another *characteristic* Circumstance would arise: For Those whom they had once *reviled,* they would now *applaud,* as being the *Friends* of *Liberty;* and Those whom they had formerly *applauded,* they would now *revile,* as having become *Jacobites* or *Tories.*—Such a Conduct, and such *Names* thus *arbitrarily imposed,* however speciously coloured over by the *Pretence* and *Cry* of *Liberty,* might seem to stand, with all impartial Judges, as a clear *Mark* of *Licentiousness* and *Faction.*

The Views of such Men would be still more apparent, should they insinuate,[81] that the *Prince* received Those very Men as his Ministers and Favourites, whose Principles [134] tended to the *Subversion* of his *Throne* and *Family.* This Insinuation, indeed, would not so much merit *Detestation,* as *Contempt* and *Ridicule.*

SECT. XXI

A sixth Mark of Licentiousness and Faction

"The Abettors and Instruments of Faction would promiscuously calumniate the private Characters of the principal Individuals of the opposing Party."

81. It was a frequent Pittite accusation that the policy of increasing the constitutional power and influence of the crown, toward which Bute was supposed to be encouraging George III, ran the risk of unsettling the constitution and might have the ultimate effect of undermining the position of the royal family.

It was the just Observation of an ancient Writer, that "the Wicked is an Abomination to the Righteous, and the Righteous an Abomination to the Wicked."[82]—Yet the Measures which these two Parties take, in their Treatment of each other, are essentially different.—The *good* Man never maliciously *stabs* the *Reputation* of his Neighbour: The *wicked* Man, [135] on the contrary, delights in this *most practicable,* but *most atrocious* of all *Mischiefs.*—Invenomed Hints, ambiguous Imputations, private Crimes darkly alledged, but void of all Foundation:—These are the deadly Weapons of the abandoned but cunning Defamer.

Here then is a secure and ample Field for every profligate Minister of Faction: Here "he tosseth about Arrows, Firebrands, and Death; and cries, am I not in Sport?"[83]

If a Prince, whose Words and Actions might justly be given, as an Example of Integrity to all his Subjects, should be ambiguously accused of such Things as his Honour would abhor:—

If such a Prince should be indirectly charged with Ignorance, for not distinguishing in a Point of Law, which even some of the ablest Lawyers in his Kingdom had not attended to:—

If neither the Virtues nor the Condescension of a Queen could protect her [136] from the Insults of Those whom she had never injured:—[84]

If any other Branch of a royal Family should be basely traduced, by the grossest and most audacious Calumnies,[85] studiously contrived to inflame an ignorant and unbridled Populace:—

If the Servants of the Crown, and Members of the Legislature, who had legally exerted themselves in Defence of their injured Sovereign, should in their private Character be impudently vilify'd, misrepresented,

---

82. Proverbs 29:27.

83. Proverbs 18:19.

84. On 8 September 1761, George III had married Charlotte of Mecklenberg–Strelitz (1744–1818), whom he had met for the first time only six hours before the ceremony. During the political uncertainties of the mid-1760s, Queen Charlotte was suspected of influencing George III's attitudes toward his politicians; according to George Grenville, she in particular nursed a strong aversion to Pitt.

85. A reference to the (apparently unfounded) allegations that George III's mother, the dowager Princess Augusta (1719–72), was Bute's mistress.

and abused; and even their unoffending Families traduced with study'd and unexampled Virulence:—

If neither Age nor Virtue should be a Security against the Arrows of public Calumny:—If a MAN of the most distinguished Worth in private Life, a known and zealous Friend of public Liberty, one of the Ornaments of his Age and Country, should be overwhelmed by a Load of the most unprovoked and malicious Slander; merely because he had dared to as[137]sert his own Right of private Judgment, in Opposition to the Opinion of another:—

If these Outrages should be publicly *committed* by *some*; and *winked* at, or *countenanced,* or *patronized* by *others*;—surely, all honest Men ought to join, in declaring their Abhorrence of such atrocious Acts of Licentiousness and Faction, perpetrated in Defiance of All *Laws,* both *human* and *divine.*

SECT. XXII

Some Objections obviated

Should it be objected to the Writer, that while he blames the Practice in others, he indiscriminately characterizeth whole Bodies of Men who dissent from public Measures; he would reply, that the Accusation is groundless. For he hath expressly distinguished Those who *dissent* on *Principles* of *Liberty,* from such as [138] *dissent* on *Motives* of *Licentiousness* and *Faction.*

Should it be objected, that he hath attacked even *private* Characters, in the Way of indirect Description: This Accusation would be equally ill-founded. For all personal Peculiarities arc avoided, save only the single Facts alluded to, as the Proofs of his Allegations: These were essentially necessary for the Support of the Argument; and relate not to *private* Life, but to *public* and *political* Conduct.

Should it be objected, that he hath indirectly censured Those, whose Conduct he had formerly applauded: He replies, that he never was attached to *Men,* but *Measures.*

Should it be objected, that some of these characteristic Marks may seem to involve Men of good Morals in private Life: He would reply, that the Affections of *good* Men in *private* Life may not *always* extend to the *Public.* [139]

Should it be objected, that some of these characteristic Marks may seem to involve Men, who have been eminently serviceable to their Country in public Stations: He would reply, that He ever hath been, and ever will be proud to do Justice to Merit, when exercised in any public Station.

Should it be objected, that he questions the Conduct of Those only who are now out of Power: He would reply, that he formerly questioned their Conduct with the same Freedom, when in the Fulness of their Power: And that his Reasons in both Instances were the same; because in both Instances he judged their general Conduct to be *essentially* ill-founded, narrow, selfish, reprehensible. [140]

SECT. XXIII

Of the Remedies against Licentiousness and Faction. The first Remedy.

Thus the Writer hath endeavoured to lay open the Foundations and Characters of Licentiousness and Faction: He now proceeds to consider the most effectual Means of checking them in their Progress; of restoring internal Unanimity; and securing public Freedom.

In every national Malady of this Nature, there are two Kinds of Remedies essentially distinct: The one is palliative, and temporary; the other is radical, and lasting.

The palliative Remedies ought to be first apply'd; because it will appear, that they are the only Means by which we can come at Those which are radical.

'Tis evident, then, that the first Advance towards a Cure of this national [141] Evil must arise from the steady Conduct of the Prince. For Faction, unopposed, and led on by the higher Ranks, will never cease in its Demands, till it terminates in the Possession of an unbounded aristocratic Power: This is a Power, which nothing but the Courage and Steadiness of the Prince can possibly contend with: Because the final Object of such a Faction will always be, "Those high and lucrative Offices of State, which are in *His* sole *Disposal*."

If a Sovereign once gives Way to the Storms in which such a Faction will involve him, his Peace and Freedom, together with Those of his

People, are inevitably destroyed. On the contrary, if amidst all the Tumults of Sedition, he discovers an unalterable Firmness and Fortitude, founded in upright Intentions and real Virtue; the Rage of hopeless Faction will by Degrees subside; and a Prospect of better Times will open upon *Him* and his *People*. This general Truth *might* [142] be *commented* on: But at present, the Writer can with Satisfaction leave it to the impartial *Public*, to find a *more instructive* and LIVING COMMENT.

SECT. XXIV

A second Remedy

The next Remedy, which can effectually aid the Firmness of the Prince, must be the Steadiness of the Minister, in discouraging, as far as in him lies, the Inroads of *Venality* and *Corruption*.

This is a large Topic, and fitter for a Book than a Section: However, what is most essential to the present Subject may be briefly touched on.

A plausible Objection, then, is here to be obviated: For a late Writer hath very calmly and systematically attempted to prove the universal and unconditional Necessity of political Corruption, in all free Governments.* [143]

What follows is the Foundation of his Argument. "All human Government is the Offspring of Violence and Corruption; and must inherit the Imperfection of both its Parents."† "All Governments must be administered by the same Violence and Corruption, to which they are indebted for their Origin."‡ "Corruption (*therefore*) must always increase in due Proportion to the Decrease of arbitrary Power; since where there is less Power to command Obedience, there must be more Bribery to purchase it; or there can be no Government carry'd on at all."§

---

* See a free Inquiry into the Nature and Origin of Evil, Let. v.[86]
† Origin of Evil, p. 128.[87]
‡ Ib. p. 129.[88]
§ Ib. p. 135.[89]
86. Jenyns, *Free Inquiry*, pp. 123–50.
87. Ibid., p. 128.
88. Ibid., p. 129.
89. Ibid., pp. 135–36.

Such is the Sum of this Gentleman's Argument: To which, the following Observations are offered, as a Reply.

There have been two different Pictures given of *Man,* by different Writers, diametrically opposite to each other. By some, the human Species hath been re[144]presented as a natural Society of Angels; by others, as a Crew of Devils. Both these Representations have arisen from a partial View of Mankind: One Party regarding his *social* Qualities only; the other overlooking These, and fixing on the Appetites which are commonly called the *selfish.*

Were Mankind of the first of these Characters, they would need no Law: Were they of the latter, no Law could unite or bind them. The Truth is, they are a Mixture of Both. As they have the several Modes of Self-Love, for the Preservation of the Individual; so, by *proper Culture,* they gain Habits of Benevolence, Religion, social Prudence, the Love of honest Reputation, and sometimes even a Regard for the general Welfare of the Society to which they belong. As these social Passions and Regards are strong or weak,[90] frequent or uncommon; the Character of a Nation is good or bad, honest or corrupt, upright or profligate. [145] A Variety of Proofs hath been given of these different Degrees of moral Character, in the preceding Parts of this Essay.*

But that we may not seem to build on a Principle which this Author admits not, we hear him virtually declaring all This himself in another Part of his Book. "Here *He (Man)* has an Opportunity given him of *improving* or *debasing* his Nature, in such a Manner as to render himself *fit* for a Rank of *higher Perfection* and Happiness; or to *degrade* himself to a State of *greater Imperfection* and Misery."† Again, he speaks of a *Reformation* of *Manners,* as a Thing *practicable:* And recommends it, as the only Remedy for political Evil.‡

---

* See above, Sect. vii, &c.[91]

† Origin of Evil, p. 93.[92]

‡ Ib. 149.[93]

90. Possibly a memory of, if probably not an allusion to, Andrew Marvell, "An Horatian Ode upon Cromwell's Return from Ireland," ll. 39–40. Such an echo would have pleased Thomas Hollis, who revered Marvell: cf. Blackburne, *Memoirs,* vol. I, pp. 104, 251, 361.

91. Cf. above, p. 516.

92. Jenyns, *Free Inquiry,* pp. 93–94.

93. Ibid., pp. 149–50.

But while he treats of the absolute *Necessity* of political Corruption, all the *better Part* of *Man* is *hid;* his *Imperfections* and *Vices* alone are *set in View*. During the Progress of this Argument, if it deserves that [146] Name, we hear of nothing but "such imperfect and *vicious* Creatures as *Men, tyrannizing* over *others* as imperfect and *vicious* as themselves":* We have nothing presented to us, but "Pride, Avarice, and Cruelty on one Side; Envy, Ignorance, and Obstinacy on the other; Injustice and Self-Interest on both."† In a Word, Mankind are represented as an *abandoned* and *incurable* Race, utterly *void* of all *good* Qualities; and such as "must be always bribed or beat into Obedience."‡

Here, then, this Maxim of the absolute and unconditional Necessity of Political Corruption appears in all its Nakedness and Deformity: For it is founded on "the supposed incurable Wickedness of Man": An Error too glaring to need a Confutation; and which there is still the less Occasion to confute, because this Author himself admits the contrary. [147]

It follows then, that his leading Proposition is as false in itself, as it is pernicious to Society, that "Corruption must always increase in due Proportion to the Decrease of arbitrary Power":[95] Because Virtue and Religion, upright Manners and Principles, properly instilled, may much better supply Corruption's Place.§

On this Foundation, therefore, it appears, that every upright Minister ought, as far as possible, to check the Progress of Corruption: And tho' at

---

* Origin of Evil, p. 126.

† Ib.

‡ Ib. p. 130.[94]

§ Were it necessary to pursue this Gentleman through all the Windings of his political Labyrinth, and trace him to the End of his Course, where he suddenly starts up in the Form of a severe Moralist; there could not, perhaps, be exhibited a more striking Instance of Self-Contradiction, in the whole Compass of literary Debate.—At present I shall only remark, that this Essay was published in the Year 1757, at a Time when the System of political Corruption much needed some Kind of Apology, because its fatal Effects began to glare too strongly upon the Nation to be longer doubted. Hence, though we should not inquire "*who* the Author is," we may give a *shrewd Guess,* "what *political School* he was *bred* in."

94. Ibid., pp. 126–27 and 130.

95. Ibid., p. 135.

Times he may be embarassed, and under a *po*[148]*litical Necessity* of yielding; 'tis clearly both his Duty and his Interest to oppose this dangerous and encroaching Spirit, in the leading Outlines of his public Conduct.

It is his Duty; both because Corruption can only flourish on the Ruins of Virtue and Religion, good Morals and Principles, without which public Liberty is essentially destroy'd; and because Corruption tends inevitably and invariably to weaken the public Administration of Government, by filling every high Department with the Venal, the Ignorant, the Selfish, the Dishonest.*

It is both his Duty and Interest; because *Licentiousness,* and its Attendants, *Venality* and *Faction,* are of an *insatiable* Appetite. The more the Venal are fed, they grow more importunate: If you gorge one of These to the full, and thus lay him to sleep; ten will rise in his Place, every one more clamourous than the first. [149]

The Minister, therefore, both in Consideration of his own Peace, and the public Welfare, ought as far as possible, to obviate this Evil in its *Beginnings;* fortify *Himself,* as well as the *State,* with the *Honest,* the *Firm,* and the *Capable;* resist, to the utmost, the exorbitant Demands of *Venality:* Thus *Faction* will either *bark* itself *asleep;* or *die despairing.*

SECT. XXV

Some concomitant Remedies

Let us now consider, what might be in the Power of the *Legislature* and the *Magistrate* immediately to effect.

1.'Tis generally acknowledged, that Power naturally follows Property.[97] Therefore exorbitant Property in Individuals must always be unfavourable

---

* See Estimate, Part ii.[96]

96. Cf. above, pp. 285–313.

97. A political commonplace in eighteenth-century England: e.g., Daniel Defoe, *The Original Power of the Collective Body of the People of England* (1702); *"there can be no Legal Power in* England, *but what has its Original in the Possessors; for Property is the Foundation of Power"* (p. 20). The idea is traceable in an English context to the political theory of James Harrington, who had explicitly linked political authority (or "empire") to the possession of property (or "dominion") (Harrington, *Oceana,* p. 11).

to civil Liberty; must always tend to produce Licentiousness and Faction; because it throws [150] exorbitant Power into the Hands of Individuals: And the greater the *Inequality* between the *Poor* and *Rich,* the more the *one* will ever be under the *Influence* of the *other*.

It should seem, then, to be the *particular* Interest even of the most *Wealthy,* if they be the real Friends of Liberty,—'tis certainly the *general* Interest of a *free Community;* that some legal Limitation of Property should take Place. I speak not of the Probability, but the Expediency of such a Measure.

2. It follows, that some *Regulation* in Respect to *Boroughs* would be of great Importance. For in Boroughs, contrary to all sound Policy, "Power is lodged without annexed Property."The natural Consequence is, that "this ill-placed Power will be seized by Those who are possessed of exorbitant Property." Thus Power settles on its natural Foundation: But a Foundation, in this Instance, most dangerous to Freedom; as it leads to the [151] Establishment of an Aristocracy. In This Instance, too, I speak not of the Probability, but the Expediency of the Measure.

3. The Limitation of extended Conquest and Empire might seem an Object worthy the Attention of the highest Powers.—ROME perished by its Avidity of unbounded Empire.[98] Colonies, when peopled beyond a certain Degree, become a Burthen to the Mother Country: They exhaust her Numbers; they distract her Attention; they divide her compacted Strength. Such Extent of Colonies, as may be necessary to maintain the Empire of the Seas, will always be a just Object of *British* Regard. More than this, sound Policy perhaps could hardly dictate.

4. This Limitation is of more Importance, as it would naturally set Bounds to another Excess: I mean, That of Trade and Wealth. This, the Writer knows, is of all other Topics the most unpopular: Notwith-

---

The linkage had however been challenged by John Locke, who in his *Two Treatises* (1690) had asked: "how will it appear, that *Property* in Land gives a Man Power over the Life of another? Or how will the Possession even of the whole Earth, give any one a Soveraign Arbitrary Authority over the Persons of Men?" (Locke, *Two Treatises,* "First Treatise," §41, p. 169).

98. Cf. above, p. 531, n. 38.

standing which, he presumes to persist in what appears to Him a demon[152]strative Truth, that "exorbitant Trade and Wealth are most dangerous to private Virtue and therefore to public Freedom." The Topic is too large, to be here insisted on. He therefore refers to what he hath already written on this Subject;* which hath been much clamoured against, indeed; but never confuted.† [153]

5. The immediate Care of upright Manners and Principles might seem an Object worthy the strictest Attention both of the Legislature and Magistrate.

To this End, if the growing Spirit of *Novelty* and *Adoption* could by any Means be checked, it would be a Work attended with the most salutary Consequences. The Writer would not willingly be thought chimerically to adopt all the Rigours of the *Spartan* State: But could wish to see a Law enacted, parallel to That of LACEDAEMON, by which their raw and unexperienced Youth were prohibited from bringing Home the new Follies and Vices of foreign Countries, picked up in a premature and too early Travel.‡

He would by no Means discourage the *Freedom* of the *Press:* Yet, sure, its *Licentiousness* might seem an Object of the Magistrate's Regard. The Search of Truth is good: But to search for This in the [154] Hoards of *Irreligion,* is

---

* See Estimate, Part iii. passim.[99]

† For the Conviction of Those who chuse rather to attend to *present* than *future* Consequences, the following Circumstance may deserve Notice. Much hath been said "on the Cause of the present exorbitant Price of Provisions, and general Distress of the Poor:" Every Cause hath been assigned except the true one, which seems to be "the sinking Value of Money, arising necessarily from the exorbitant Increase of Trade and Wealth." If this be so, it follows, that the Evil is incurable, excepting only by a general Augmentation of the Wages of the Poor.—Now This, which is the necessary Effect of the Exorbitancy of Commerce, naturally tends (by the increased Price of Manufactures) to the Destruction of Commerce. If the Exorbitancy of Trade should still run higher, this Evil will be aggravated in Proportion. The Consequences which must follow, are such as the Writer chuseth not to enlarge on; because he knows, the Spirit of the Times would not bear it.

‡ See Estimate, Vol. ii. Part i. Sect. 10.[100]

99. Cf. above, pp. 317–44.

100. Cf. above, pp. 380–81.

like searching for *Hope* in PANDORA's *Box;*[101] where the sole Reward of Industry can only be *Pestilence, Despair* and *Death.* National Virtue never was maintained, but by national Religion: He, therefore, who shakes the essential Principles of Religion, undermines the Virtue of his Fellow-Subjects; and therefore deserves to feel the Rigour of the Law, as a determined *Enemy* of his *Country.*—This may seem a practicable Remedy: But how to destroy those irreligious Writings, which already lie exposed on Stalls and Counters, or deposited in private Libraries, like so many Heaps of Poison, for the Gratification of Vice, and the Destruction of Virtue:—Or how to pluck from the Minds of Men those poisoned Arrows, which these Authors have already planted there!—That were a *Task indeed!*—The Shaft is already flown; and cannot be recalled: And this Nation, thro' succeeding Times will have Cause to say,—*"Haeret Lateri lethalis Arundo."*[102] [155]

Immoral Writings should seem no less the Object of the Magistrate's Attention. Tho' These may not shake the *Principles,* yet they inevitably corrupt the *Manners* of a Nation.

Personal Defamation, or Calumny thrown on *private* Characters, is another Evil, which seems rising at present with unheard-of Aggravations. Two *flagrant* Instances of This Enormity the Writer will pass unnoticed, lest he should seem to insult over the *Exiled* or the *Dead.** [156]

---

* In these two Kinds of modern Profligacy, *immoral Writings,* and *personal Calumny,* there is one professed Author,[103] now said to be living in this Kingdom with Impunity; who, in a better policed State would ere this have felt the full Weight of that public Punishment and Infamy which is due to an Enemy of Mankind. This Man, supposed to be one *C——,* first writ a Volume of execrable *Memoirs,* for the Corruption of Youth and Innocence: Since That, a *Reverie,* or *Dream,* which *Hunger* and *Malice* probably conspired to suggest; replete with the most impudent Falsehoods, and injurious Calumnies on Individuals, for the Entertainment of *base* and *envious* Minds.

101. In Greek mythology, Pandora was a woman fashioned out of clay by Hephaestus. She was created to be the instrument of Zeus's revenge on Prometheus for the transgression of stealing fire from heaven and giving it to men. Pandora was sent to Epithemeus, Prometheus's brother, with a box containing all the evils which have since afflicted mankind. Epithemeus opened the box, thereby releasing those evils. Only hope remained at the bottom of the box, to palliate man's condition.

102. "The lethal arrow clings to her side" (Virgil, *Aeneid,* IV.73).

103. John Cleland (1709–89), whose pornographic novel, *Memoirs of a Woman of Pleasure* (more commonly known as *Fanny Hill*), had been published in 1749.

SECT. XXVI

Of the chief and essential Remedy

All these may be regarded as temporary and concomitant Supports of Freedom: But the chief and essential Remedy to Licentiousness and Faction, the fundamental Means of the lasting and secure Establishment of civil Liberty, can only "lie in a general and prescribed improvement of the Laws of Education."

We have seen above, that upright Manners and Principles are the only Basis of true Liberty; that the infant Mind, if left to its own untutored Dictates, inevitably wanders into such Follies and Vices, as tend to the Destruction of itself and others. We have seen, that the early and continued Culture of the Heart can alone produce such upright Manners and Principles, as are necessary to check and subdue the selfish Passions of the Soul; and that Li[157]berty can only arise from a general Subordination of These, to the public Welfare. We have seen these Truths confirmed, by an Appeal to the State of three famed Republics, which by Turns *arose* and *fell,* on the very Principles here delivered. We have seen the Defects, as well as Excellencies, of our own public Constitution, both *civil* and *religious:* That its Form is excellent and unrivaled; but that the practical *Application* of this unrivaled Excellence is attended with Defects incurable: That it hath all along been inevitably counterworked[104] by Manners and Principles discordant with its Genius, and discordant with each other: That for Want of a prescribed Code of Education, to which all the Members of the Community should legally submit, the Manners and Principles on which alone the State can rest, are ineffectually instilled, are vague, fluctuating, and self-contradictory.

Nothing, then, is more evident, than that some Reform in this great Point, is [158] necessary, for the Security of public Freedom. Till this be effected, in Spite of all temporary Remedies, Licentiousness and Faction, tho' checked for a Time, will ever be gathering new Strength, and returning to the Charge with redoubled Fury.

104. Cf. above, p. 340, n. 21.

This Reform, to some, may appear easy to effect: By others it will be derided, as wholly impracticable. Perhaps the Truth may lie between these two Opinions: To throw the Manners and Principles of a Nation into any new Channel, is certainly a Work of no small Difficulty.—On the other Hand, we seem to have many Materials lying round us, ready to be converted into the Means of this great Work. A pure and rational Religion; a generous System of Policy, founded on that Religion; Manners, tho' apparently degenerating, yet by no Means generally profligate; much true Religion, Integrity, and Honour among the *middle* Ranks; many Instances of *domestic Worth* among the *higher*; and in Spite of the [159] Temptations that surround the *Great*, true *Piety*, and the *moral Virtues* adorning the *most exalted Station*.

Therefore, without dreaming of the perfect Republic of PLATO;—and fairly acknowledging the incurable Defect of our political State, in not having a correspondent and adequate Code of Education inwrought into its first Essence;—we may yet hope, that in a secondary and inferior Degree, something of this Kind may be still *inlaid:* It cannot have that perfect Efficacy, as if it had been originally *of the Piece:* Yet, if well conducted, it may strengthen the weak Parts; and *alleviate* Defects, though not compleatly *remove* them.

Among *what Ranks,* in the Writer's Opinion, these *Defects* in *Education* chiefly *lie,* may be sufficiently collected from some of the preceding Sections. But as to the most *effectual Methods* of *relieving* these *Defects,* he pretends not at present to attempt so great a Subject. [160]

This, however, he is well perswaded of; that till something of the Kind be attempted and performed; all the laboured Harangues that can be given from the *Bench,* the *Pulpit,* or the *Press,* will be of little Avail: They may tend *occasionally* to *obviate* some of the *Evils* of *Licentiousness;* but never can *radically cure them.*

SECT. XXVII

The Conclusion

These Remedies, however *just* in their *Nature,* can only be *effectual* through a proper Application: And this can only lie "in a zealous and unfeigned Union of the *Honest* among all *Ranks* and *Parties,* for the *Accomplishment* of *these Ends,* against the Patrons and Instruments of Licentiousness and Faction." [161]

This Union, at first View, seems of such a Nature as could hardly need to be inforced: Yet it is frequently retarded by several Circumstances.

Among the *Great,* this rational Union is often counteracted by the Ties of false Honour; a dangerous Principle, which we have already noted, as being productive of Party-Rage and Faction.* This Principle, even in honest Minds, will sometimes prevail over the Dictates of Religion and private Virtue. On this false Foundation, political Connexions are often maintained, in Defiance of a just Sense of public Utility: While the unhappy Man who acts on this mistaken Motive, is inwardly rent by two contrary and contending Powers. Severe Moralists may perhaps discard such a Character from the List of the *Honest:* But it should seem, that he is rather an Object of Clemency than Indignation. Remove but the unhappy Prejudice from his Breast; [162] And such a Character would press forward among the first, towards the *Goal* of *public Virtue.*

Again: This rational and salutary Union may be retarded by Connexions of *Friendship, Gratitude,* or *Blood.* This Cause tends to confirm and extend the Influence of the former. *Fathers, powerful Friends,* and *Patrons,* connect themselves with Parties, and cleave to them on a mistaken Principle: *Sons, obliged Friends,* and *Dependents,* are naturally inlisted in their Party; and are rivetted in it, not only by *false Honour,* but *Education, Gratitude, Affection.* How peculiarly unfortunate is this Circumstance; that the *generous Passions* should ever become the *Adversaries* of *public Virtue!*

The same false Attachment to Friends, Patrons, and Relations, naturally prevails, in a certain Proportion, among the middle Ranks of the Kingdom. Their Interests, Passions, and Prejudices, are not so immediately concerned as Those of the higher Ranks; and therefore 'tis natural [163] to

* See above, p. 92.[105]
105. Cf. above, p. 539–40.

suppose, that their mutual Attachments of mistaken Honour or private Affection, will upon the Whole be more moderate and less culpable. Yet still, while these false Attachments are prevalent among the *Great,* the *People* must in some Degree catch the Infection, from the various Relations which they bear to their Superiors. Hence untractable Prejudices arise, and are maintained: While *Measures* are less regarded, than the *Party* which *adopts* them.

But besides This, another Circumstance ariseth, which inevitably tends to *disunite,* and *distract* the *Honest* among the *People;* even when their personal Attachments are conquered by their Integrity. Their *Dispersion* in the Country hath already been remarked, as a Circumstance worthy of Attention. Here it meets us again, as a Cause of their frequent *Disunion.* We have seen how naturally (under the present State of Things) every factious Clamour that riseth in the Capital, is transmitted with aggravated Circumstances, through the [164] whole Kingdom.* And the People of the Villages being easy of Belief, because not suspecting the abandoned Profligacy of these *Town–Defamers,* are apt to receive every insinuated *personal Slander,* as a *Truth.* These Calumnies being seldom contradicted by the injured Party, take Root in the Minds of the less knowing. Hence Doubts arise; Surmises and Dislikes are spread; Facts, though void of all Foundation, are alledged and persisted in; the more credulous Part are misled: Thus an honest People are divided; and not only a *Province* or a *Village,* but even an *House* often set at Variance within itself.

These Contentions *sometimes* arise to a Degree which is ridiculous: And have formerly been so described *without Exception,* by the Tools of Faction. Notwithstanding This, every Friend of Liberty ought to grieve, if a *free,* an *honest,* and a *sensible* People should ever desist (were it possi[165]ble) to debate on Affairs of Government. Tho' they may be occasionally alarmed and misled on slight Occasions, yet their mature and collective Judgment on important Subjects, will *seldom* be *erroneous.* On

* See above, Sect. xix, p. 130.[106]
106. Cf. above, pp. 556–57.

this Foundation, MONTESQUIEU's Remark is solid: "Tell me not, that such a People will sometimes *reason ill.*" 'Tis sufficient, "that *they reason.*"*

The Guilt and ill Consequences, then, arise from the malevolent Clamours of the Capital, transmitted thence to the Provinces. These Clamours, though not of Power to seduce an *honest* PEOPLE into actual Sedition, are yet often sufficient to *alarm* and *divide* them.†

Much Caution, therefore, ought to be used by the Inhabitants of the *Country,* how they give Credit to the *political* Rumours of the *Town;* which are seldom spread without Design; and are in general spread most industriously by the Malevolent. They who act on good Prin[166]ciples, are apt to trust to the native Force of Truth: The Patrons of Falsehood are conscious of a Defect *here;* and therefore endeavour to supply it by a misapply'd Diligence and Cunning.

One Mark of Licentiousness and Faction is peculiarly applicable to these Clamours from the Metropolis: If they are fraught with *personal Calumny,* and attack private Characters, they assuredly come from the *Enemies* of *Virtue* and *Freedom.*

All These, therefore, a *sensible* and *honest* PEOPLE will learn to *suspect* and *deride.* This Foundation once laid, they will not be far from a *general Union* against the *hidden Designs* of *Licentiousness* and *Faction.*

In Conclusion, therefore, let the *Honest* among every *Rank* and *Party* recollect; that their first and highest Obligations are to God, their King,

---

* L'Esprit des Loix.[107]

† See above, Sect. xiii. p. 114.[108]

107. Brown compresses a passage from Book XIX, chapter 27 of Montesquieu's *Esprit des Loix* that draws a distinction between the effects of reasoning in free and despotic governments: "Dans une nation libre, il est très souvent indifférent que les particuliers raisonnent bien ou mal; il suffit qu'ils raisonnent: de là sort la liberté qui garantit des effets de ces mêmes raisonnements. De même, dans un gouvernement despotique, il est également pernicieux qu'on raisonne bien ou mal; il suffit qu'on raisonne pour que le principe du gouvernement soit choqué"; "In a free nation, it frequently doesn't matter whether individuals reason well or badly; it is enough that they engage in reasoning; from that springs the liberty which ensures that these very acts of reasoning will be effective. By the same token, in a despotic government it is equally harmful to reason well or badly; it is enough to engage in reasoning to offend against the principle of government."

108. Cf. above, p. 550.

and Country. That every *subordinate* Connexion ought to *yield* to *These*: That true *Honour* can never be at *Variance* with the Laws of *Religion* and [167] *Virtue:* That if any *Desertion* be *shameful,* it is the *Desertion* from *Truth* and the Welfare of their *Country:* If any *Attachment* be *honourable,* it is an impartial *Attachment* to the *public Weal,* unbiassed by private Affections and Regards. If any *Acknowledgment* be the certain Mark of a *great* and *ingenuous* Mind, it is the *Acknowledgment* of *its own Errors,* or those of a *Patron, Friend,* or *Ancestor.*

These Remarks the Writer submits to the Impartiality and Candor of his Countrymen; desiring that they may be regarded as his Mite, thrown in towards the Accomplishment of the Sovereign's Wish, on his Accession to the Throne; that of "founding the Liberty and Happiness of this Kingdom on the solid Basis of *Religion* and *Virtue,* and uniting ALL HONEST MEN in the steady Prosecution of this great Purpose."[109]

THE END

---

109. George III had ascended the throne on 25 October 1760, and had been crowned in Westminster Abbey on 22 September 1761.

Thomas Hollis's Character of John Brown

Character of the late Dr. Brown, Vicar of Newcastle.
[First published in the St. James's Chronicle.]
To the Printer of the Public Advertiser.

SIR,

There is a tribute of *candid Report* due to the memory of men of genius and learning, how unfortunate so ever they may have been in the application of their talents, or however they may have fallen short of that approbation, which the public has given to men of much inferior abilities, at the same time that it hath been denied to *them*. I would endeavour to apply this reflection to the case of the unhappy *Leucophaeus*,[1] who has just finished his mortal course, in a way which some people may think has fully justified the world in the unfavourable sentiments that were so generally entertained of his literary conduct. *Leucophaeus* is now out of the reach of every man's resentment, as well as of every man's envy; and I would willingly hope that a few dispassionate reflections upon his fortunes and his fate, from a person who knew something of him at different times of his life, may not be offensive to those who have candor enough to make the requisite allowances for errors and frailties, which, as they were not peculiar to him, so neither did they exceed in measure or malignity, errors and

---

The source for this text is Francis Blackburne, *Memoirs of Thomas Hollis, Esq.*, 2 vols (London, 1780), vol. II, pp. 714–17.

1. The Latin word for "dun-colored," or brown.

frailties, which have been excused in others who had but a small portion of his merit to qualify them. Merit he certainly had, and merit will be allowed him by the capable readers even of such of his writings as convey the most striking idea of the author's mental infirmities.

Few men have given earlier proofs of capacity and erudition than *Leucophaeus*. His rising genius was marked and distinguished by the *tendered* patronage of some who had gained,[2] and of others who thought they were gaining the summit of fame in the republic of letters. With certain of the latter *Leucophaeus* entered into the most intimate connection, upon the assurance of being conducted, in virtue of that alliance, to as much reputation, and as great a proportion of emolument as he had reason to look for. A fatal step! which he never afterwards could retrieve, when he most desired it. Had he preserved his independency, he had preserved his probity and honour; but he had parts, and he had ambition. The former might have eclipsed a jealous competition for same; the latter laid him open to practices proper to prevent it. No arts or allurements were omitted to attach him to a party, which easily found the means to consign him to contempt the moment it was suspected that he was uneasy in his bonds, and that he was meditating expedients to break them.

An intimate friend spent a long evening with him, when he was *literally* on the road to his ruin; that is to say, when he was going to confirm and cultivate the alliance abovementioned. *Leucophaeus's* prospects were then talked over. He was warned to be aware of consequences; but the connection was formed, and must be adhered to; and they who had heard *Leucophaeus* harangue on that occasion, concerning the world with which he was going to engage, and concerning what would become him in his commerce with it, would have sworn that nothing could surprize his prudence, nothing pervert his integrity.

Splendid and decorated *Guide Posts,* promising straight and easy roads, often stand at the head of dirty, crooked lanes. These were pointed out to

2. I.e., William Warburton. For Warburton's overture to Brown following the publication of *An Essay on Satire,* see his letter of Christmas Eve 1746 (Bodl. MS Eng. Misc. c. 390, fol. 398^r) and the "Introduction," above, pp. x–xii. On Brown's relationship to Warburton, see the interesting remarks of Andrew Kippis (Kippis, p. 660).

Leucophaeus at his first setting forwards. He soon found them fallacious indexes: He had the satisfaction, however, to have *one* example immediately before him, that shewed how well it might be worth the while of an *Aspirant* to *turn* and *wind* about, and even to be a little *bemired,* in order to come at a comfortable lodging, clean linen, and a complete change of raiment.

But these were blessings which were not intended for *Leucophaeus.* The *tempter*[3] could have given him the clue, which would have led his pupil through all difficulties; but that might have spoiled his own game. He contented himself therefore with escorting *Leucophaeus* to the thickest of the filth, and there he fairly left him to the scorn and derision of lookers on; calmly observing, with a shrug, "If the man *will* expose himself who can help it."

It happened, however, that out of this piteous condition *Leucophaeus* emerged, and with that vigor as in a great measure to recover his estimation. And here the *tempter saw* it necessary to strike in again. A little coaxing procured an act of oblivion for one of the cruelest insults that could be offered to an ingenuous mind; and to shew the sincerity of his reconciliation, the first thing *Leucophaeus* did was to disfigure one of his capital performances, by copying the ungracious manner of the *grand exemplar.*

At what period *Leucophaeus* lost himself with the public every one knows. At the same instant was he deserted by the *alliance,* and so apprehensive were they lest he should once more find such encouragement for his powers as might throw their importance into obscurity, that some pains were taken to have *one* door of preferment shut against him, even where the recommendation of the *alliance* would have been of no service to him, had it been kept open. But they succeeeded; and in that success added one more to the many instances upon record of the power and proclivity of many a man to do mischief, where he has neither the power nor inclination to do good. Certain fragments in the last thing *Leucophaeus* committed to the press, throw some faint light upon this part of his history.

3. Again presumably Warburton.

Leucophaeus now found himself in a wide world at enmity with him on every side. What was he to do? Should he return to the paths of truth and probity, to which he had been so long a stranger? Alas! his *credit,* his *weight* was gone. His *early* connections had left a stain upon his character, which the after-conduct of an angel could hardly have discharged from the minds of honest men. It appeared, by some very remarkable evidence, that he was suspected to be the scout of the *alliance,* even to the very last. It has since appeared, that his most zealous remonstrances against the imputation could not perfectly clear him of that suspicion. What remained then for him, but to do—what numbers (perhaps a majority) of his brethren had done before him—what his original patrons and conductors were then doing—what the dextrous part of mankind generally find their account in doing—In one word, he *temporized,* but with this difference from the calmer speculators of the ground before them—he made his evolutions too quick and visible. Unhappily for him, the changes in the upper regions were frequent, sudden, and unforeseen. To these he accommodated himself without hesitation, and it was impossible that so immediate and so nimble transitions in so conspicuous a character should not give the cue to the public to mark *him,* rather than an hundred others who really *temporized* no less than he, but who had the discretion not to notify it upon paper, or (if that was unavoidable in an occasional sermon or so) who had the art to balance so cleverly as to leave matters in that sort of see-saw way which affords the public no clear indications of their *present* attachments. Common fame says that the last effort of *Leucophaeus's* genius was a panegyric on the E—— of C———m.[4] This, probably, the sad catastrophe of the author broke off abruptly; otherwise the public had been favoured with it ere this. What the brotherhood in general think of the noble E——l, we shall hardly be informed in *print* before the end of January. Such is the difference between *Impetuosity* and *Discretion,* in committing the same sin.

The last province allotted to *Leucophaeus* was of a sort which implied a civil dismission from all his expectations at home. It is said to have

---

4. The Earl of Chatham; the title taken by William Pitt when he moved to the House of Lords.

been planned in a consultation of casuists, upon the same considerations which induce physicians to send their patients to Bath, when they chuse not to be longer troubled with their hypochondriacal complaints in town. *Leucophaeus* was *evidently, contemptuously, unaccountably* neglected; and the public was eternally asking, *Why?* He was a *temporizer.* What then? is not *temporizing* the *cardinal virtue* of the age? Is it not almost the *singular merit* of that class of men to which *Leucophaeus* belonged? To whomsoever his trimming character was obnoxious, it should not have been so to those who denounce utter exclusion against all who are inflexibly tenacious of unpolite truths. Is an obsequious blockhead a greater credit to the cause he espouses, or a greater ornament to the master who employs him, than an obsequious genius? No. But the former will be quiet, every way quiet; and geniuses are apt to speculate, and speculation is apt to run foul of system, and to do mischief, even where the meaning is good enough: aye, there was the rub. *Leucophaeus* speculated once upon a time on his *quiet* brethren, in the midst of their repose; and for this he has ever since been called an *impudent* writer. But has it been duly considered in what respectable school he learned his *impudence?* Did he bring any thing from that school but his *impudence?* And why should not *impudence* do as much for him as it has done for ———— others? So reasoned the public. And they who perhaps would not have employed *Leucophaeus* where an honester man was to be had, could suggest no reason to themselves why he should not be employed by those who were no honester than himself.

At length the dispute is ended. An office was contrived which would answer the highest demands of his ambition. He was to be the *Solomon* to a Queen of *Sheba.*[5] A little solemn grimace[6] in the quarter where it was first proposed drew him to act his part in this egregious farce. Of all the men upon earth *Leucophaeus* was the last to suspect design, when any thing was said to his advantage. Compliments on this occasion were not spared; and as they came from *the white-bearded* fellow no *gull* was suspected. Intoxicated with this prospect he became, what his insidious

---

5. An allusion to the proposal that Brown should guide the reformation of the education system of Russia; see the "Introduction," above, pp. xxii–xxiv.

6. I.e., pretense (*OED*, 3).

coaxers wanted to have him—perfectly ridiculous. After some time, the loudness of the laugh roused him from his reverie. The length of the nap had sobered him. He enquired seriously of those who knew the best where all this was to end, and—*behold! it was all a dream.*[7] The reflection was too much for the feeling indignant spirit of *Leucophaeus.* A speedy end was put to it by an act of desperation; for which, perhaps, at the final day of account, not *Leucophaeus* alone shall be answerable. I am,

SIR,

Your humble servant,

AEACUS.[8]

7. Genesis 41:7.
8. In Greek mythology the son of Zeus and the nymph Aegina, and the grand-father of Achilles. He was famed for his piety and justice, and became (with Minos and Rhadamanthus) a judge of the dead. Hence the appropriateness of Hollis's choice of pseudonym for this judicious verdict on a recently-deceased author.

Thomas Hollis's Annotations in His Copy of
Estimate of the Manners and Principles of the Times

Thomas Hollis's personal copy of Brown's *Estimate of the Manners and Principles of the Times* is in the Houghton Library, Harvard, press mark *EC75 H7267 Zz 7576. Twenty-one pages bear annotations, usually in the lower margin and linked to the text with a symbol. These annotations are transcribed below. The form of the reference is: page number in this edition; page number in Hollis's copy. Information about the reference symbol and its location is given in square brackets.

1. 263; 23 [reference symbol in the inner margin of l. 3]
   Lord Hrdwck undoubtedly was a most able & upright Chncllr; but as our Courts of Justice have been alike uncorrupt from the Revolution to this Time, this compliment must be understood not as of Truth, but convenience.
2. 266; 31 [reference symbol in l. 10, immediately after '*Things.*']
   Had those Countries, whilst they were free, committed the government of their Youth to philosophers not priests, they had in all probability preserved themselves from the Yoak of Bondage to this Day; whereas &c. &c. &c.
   Preface to Account of Denmark.
3. 270; 38 [reference symbol in l. 16, immediately after 'breeding.']
   Vive la Bagatelle.
4. 271; 43 [reference symbol in l. 7, immediately after 'there is']
   A forced compliment to Drawcansir Wrbrtn.
5. 274; 48 [reference symbol in l. 10, immediately after 'And *here*,']
   True, in the moral & most excellent plays of the Suspicious husband, the Charmer, & other such like favrite plays.

6. 274; 49 [reference symbol in l. 5, immediately after 'certain']
   Dissipation, & the love of baudry.

7. 287; 77 [reference symbol in l. 8, immediately after 'the *Few*,']
   It is apprehended this is a complement chiefly to Pitt; but be it to whom
   it may, every one knows, the public measures are determined not by the
   abilitys of the few, <u>but the voices of the many</u>, which are <u>solely</u> influenced
   by corruption: and he alludes to the inscription of a medal in which was
   the Bust of S^r. R. Wlpl with this Motto [*illegible*] is the Truth Regit
   NUMMIS animos.

8. 290; 83 [in the inner margin opposite l. 7]
   Hume . . :

9. 290; 83 [reference symbol in l. 10, immediately after 'he']
   It is apprehended, that does not <u>evidently</u> follow.

10. 290; 83 [reference symbol in l. 15, immediately after 'teach']
    2°. If he means the times of Sacheverel?

11. 291; 83 [reference symbol in the inner margin opposite l. 18]
    The contempt of the clergy arises not from a dislike to Religion, but to
    their System as in many respects <u>opposite</u> to it; & to the badness of their
    private Characters; ~~both~~ [*illegible insertion above the line*] of which see
    <u>faintly</u> traced out by the rev D^r. on the otherside.

12. 292; 87 [reference symbol in the inner margin opposite l. 2]
    And yet, as it dozes, the Church will be with him if he does.

13. 293; 91 [reference symbol in l. 2, immediately after 'Defence,']
    This Rebellion might even have been poked out by the Pitch forks of the
    Country men of the county of Rutland.

14. 293; 91 [reference symbol in inner margin opposite l. 11]
    That there was & is much effeminacy of spirit in england is readily
    admitted; but the grand occasioners of it were & are the ministry.

15. 294; 91 [reference symbol in l. 17, immediately after 'Season,']
    most true.

16. 294; 92 [reference symbol in l. 6, immediately after 'extinguished,']
    It has been said, that the voluntary boasted Subscription of the county of
    York did not amount to even six pence in the pound.

17. 300; 109 [reference symbol in inner margin, opposite l. 17]
    The remedy to this & all other our lesser evils, & THE ONLY, is a Par-
    liament [*inserted below the line:* Hs of Cmmns] <u>by Countys</u>.

18. 302; 114 [reference symbol in l. 15, immediately after 'Measures:']
    No one of them ever tyed the Nation.
19. 302; 114 [reference symbol in l. 18, immediately after 'was a']
    S^r. R. W.
20. 304; 119 [reference symbol in l. 10, immediately after 'circumstanced,']
    It is so, & has been so for many years; Why therefore <u>that</u> remark on
    the other [*inserted below the line:* p. 116.] side. "Yet for the sake of <u>truth</u>,
    it must be said, <u>the eternal clamours of a selfish & a factious people</u> &c.
    since those clamours & uneasinesses are founded in the highest Reason.
21. 304; 120
    If this be true, <u>as true it flagrantly is</u>, Why stigmatize abuse people groan-
    ing under these Evils, & making head against them, as Clamours, fac-
    tions &cet.
22. 304; 120 [reference symbol in outer margin, opposite l. 14]
    This is just but melancholy warning.
23. 307; 128 [reference symbol in l. 12, immediately after 'are rare;']
    This was the case remarkably in the Wlpln times & has been ever since.
24. 311; 139 [the phrase 'false honour' underlined in l. 6]
    It is false honour, as it opperates not in service to the Liberty of their
    country but to the maintenance of tyranny, nor can it be said even by the
    author to have generous ends beyond a certain sphere.
25. 311; 141 [reference symbol in l. 2, immediately after 'inconsistent,']
    How can the Character of that nation be respectable who, as a <u>point of
    Honour</u> rivets its own chains, & seeks by all ways to forge new ones for
    others. Nor can it be such from the after delineation of it by the author;
    witness "effeminate, insincere not benevolent, not virtuous, profligate, in
    manners weak, contemptible in private Life; though formidable in pub-
    lic," to what end TYRANY.
26. 332; 190 [reference symbol in l. 1, immediately before 'But the same']
    The discouragement <u>doth not appear</u>. In an excellent pamphlet on the
    enormous evils attending the use of spiritous Liquors, by that worthy, &
    even great man, & Love of his country, Dr. Stephen Hales.

    See the other side

27. 333; 191
    Had all the Bshps appeared at the passing of the Bill relating to spiritous
    liquors it had been lost in the Hse of Lds. Somany therefore staid away

under different pretences as prevented that event & the others who came then safely voted according to Decency & their Consciences.

28. 344; 221

A fashionable, fribble, prig young Gentleman being asked his opinion of this Book, replyed, "The man knows the Decalogue, & that this is a Sin, & that is a Sin; but he does not know the world."

APPENDIX C

Corrections to Copy Texts

printed edition *page.line*	*error*	*correct reading*
	Essays on the Characteristics (1751)	
16.23	others	other's
40.7	untroden	untrodden
65.7	emerge	immerge
80.14	firey	fiery
134.27	undoubtly	undoubtedly
218.3	amourous	amorous
246.19	Ethusiasm	Enthusiasm
248.25	goood	good
272.15	ann	and
278.11	Hrre	Here
301.22	umerated	numerated
336.21–22	do do	do
336.27	enjoying	enjoining
397.2	times	sometimes
	Estimate of the Manners and Principles of the Times (1757)	
90.12	quenceth	quencheth
138.15	Periods,	Periods.

printed edition		
page.line	*error*	*correct reading*
158.17	Brillancy	Brilliancy
160.14	Nation	Nations

Estimate of the Manners and Principles of the Times, vol. II (1758)

22.5	by upon others	upon by others
47.15	and as could	and such as could
54.21	stagitious	flagitious
116.18	despised	~.
124.18	rethailing	retailing
139.14	Bolingbrooke	Bolingbroke
175.17	bread	bred
190.18	Freedoom	Freedom
222.3	heretable	heritable

Explanatory Defence, &c. (1758)

51.15	prefering	preferring
62.19	orginal	original

Thoughts on Civil Liberty (1765)

63.11	imbibed	imbued
96.19	Tour	Tenour
116.25	Thus	thus

INDEX

Note: Works by John Brown are indexed at their title; works by all other authors are under the name of the author.

This book is set in Adobe Caslon Pro, a modern adaptation by Carol Twombly of faces cut by William Caslon, London, in the 1730's. Caslon's types were based on seventeenth-century Dutch old style designs and became very popular throughout Europe and the American colonies.

This book is printed on paper that is acid-free and meets the requirements of the American National Standard for Permanence of Paper for Printed Library Materials, z39.48-1992. ∞

Book design by Louise OFarrell
Gainesville, Florida

Typography by Apex CoVantage, Inc.
Madison, Wisconsin

Index by Indexing Partners, LLC
Rehoboth Beach, Delaware

Printed and bound by Worzalla Publishing Co.
Stevens Point, Wisconsin